The Cannon Reservoir
Human Ecology Project

*An Archaeological Study of Cultural Adaptations
in the Southern Prairie Peninsula*

This is a volume in

Studies in Archaeology

A complete list of titles in this series appears at the end of this volume.

The Cannon Reservoir
Human Ecology Project

An Archaeological Study of Cultural Adaptations in the Southern Prairie Peninsula

Edited by

Michael J. O'Brien
Robert E. Warren

Department of Anthropology
University of Missouri
Columbia, Missouri

Dennis E. Lewarch

Department of Anthropology
University of South Carolina
Columbia, South Carolina

1982

ACADEMIC PRESS

A Subsidiary of Harcourt Brace Jovanovich, Publishers

New York   London
Paris   San Diego   San Francisco   São Paulo   Sydney   Tokyo   Toronto

ACADEMIC PRESS, INC.
111 Fifth Avenue, New York, New York 10003

United Kingdom Edition published by
ACADEMIC PRESS, INC. (LONDON) LTD.
24/28 Oval Road, London NW1 7DX

Library of Congress Cataloging in Publication Data

Main entry under title:

The Cannon Reservoir Human Ecology Project.

    (Studies in archaeology)
    Bibliography: p.
    Includes index.
    1. Human ecology--Missouri--History. 2. Land
settlement patterns--Missouri--History. 3. Indians of
North America--Missouri--Antiquities. 4. Missouri--
Antiquities. 5. Clarence Cannon Reservoir (Mo.)
I. O'Brien, Michael J. II. Warren, Robert E.
III. Lewarch, Dennis E. IV. Series.
GF504.M8C36 1982   304.2'09778   82-11337
ISBN 0-12-523980-7

PRINTED IN THE UNITED STATES OF AMERICA

82 83 84 85   9 8 7 6 5 4 3 2 1

Contents

PART I   *Research Orientation*   *1*

1   Introduction   3

Michael J. O'Brien and Dale R. Henning

2   The Approach   13

Michael J. O'Brien and Robert E. Warren

Contributors

Numbers in parentheses indicate the pages on which the authors' contributions begin.

John R. Bozell (171)
Department of Anthropology
Division of Archaeological Research
University of Nebraska
Lincoln, Nebraska 68588

Theresa K. Donham* (117)
Division of Archaeological Research
University of Nebraska
Lincoln, Nebraska 68588

Dale R. Henning (3)
Department of Sociology, Anthropology,
   and Social Work
Luther College
Decorah, Iowa

Frances B. King (197)
Quaternary Studies Program
Illinois State Museum
Springfield, Illinois 62706

Dennis E. Lewarch (145)
Department of Anthropology
University of South Carolina
Columbia, South Carolina 29208

Roger D. Mason** (131, 301, 369)
Department of Sociology and Anthropology
Central Michigan University
Mt. Pleasant, Michigan 48859

Chad K. McDaniel (217)
Department of Anthropology
University of Missouri
Columbia, Missouri 65211

Michael J. O'Brien (3, 13, 71, 85, 103, 217, 255,
291, 301, 369, 391)
Department of Anthropology
University of Missouri
Columbia, Missouri 65211

Jacqueline E. Saunders (301)
Donham & Saunders
Cultural Resource Consultants
Monroe City, Missouri 63456

Robert E. Warren (13, 29, 71, 85, 103, 171, 255,
337, 369, 391)
Department of Anthropology
University of Missouri
Columbia, Missouri 65211

*Present address: Box 355, Perry, Missouri 63462.

**Present address: 1916 NE 73rd Street, Seattle, Washington 98115.

Figures

Tables

Preface

The Cannon Reservoir Human Ecology Project was formed in May 1977 as an interdisciplinary, regional archaeology program to investigate human adaptations on the southern fringes of the mid-continental Prairie Peninsula. The research centered on the area of northeastern Missouri in and around the site of the proposed Clarence Cannon Dam and Reservoir.

This volume is designed to provide an overview of the Cannon Project, demonstrating how objectives and goals have been integrated with various methods and techniques to generate and analyze a vast amount of data pertaining to man's presence in the southern Prairie Peninsula. The data have not yet been analyzed completely; and because of this, examples are sometimes used rather than completed synthetic overviews. This is not offered as an apology since it was quite clear from the beginning of the project that many years would be needed for complete analysis and data summation. Our aim is simply to present a timely example of an integration of a variety of archaeological–historical methods and techniques in a regional archaeological project. We also present a concise set of conclusions concerning cultural adaptation and change in one part of the midwestern United States.

We believe the work done on the Cannon Project will serve as a model both for cultural resource management studies and for basic archaeological research. This volume should be of interest not only to archaeologists, but to anthropologists in general, as well as to geographers, ecologists, and persons involved in Quaternary studies. Elements of each discipline's study are interwoven to produce the research design of the project and are reflected in the methods and techniques used to generate and analyze the data.

This volume is in seven parts. Part I, Research Orientation, is an introduction to the project. Chapters in this section define the objectives and goals of the project, describe the project area, present a brief history of archaeological work in the region, and discuss the research design.

Environment and Predictions (Part II) presents an assessment of the environment and implications for human settlement in the area. Chapters in this section describe the historical setting, note various physical and cultural changes that occurred during the Holocene, and present developmental models of prehistoric and historical settlement systems.

Part III, Regional Chronology, presents a chronology for the project area, from approximately

8000 B.C. to A.D. 1860. Chapters are divided into the preceramic, ceramic, and historical periods. Techniques used to order archaeological components from each period are discussed.

Functional and Economic Indicators (Part IV) assesses various artifact and ecofact classes, with chapters devoted to classification systems for lithic artifacts recovered from controlled surface collection and excavation and to analyses of floral and faunal materials from excavated sites.

Community Patterns (Part V) deals with spatial analysis of pattern at the community level. Three chapters treat aspects of prehistoric communities: first, the delineation of pattern analysis of surface artifact distribution; second, delineation of pattern from excavation; and third, delineation of pattern by comparing surface artifact distributions with subsurface remains. A fourth chapter analyzes the composition of historical communities at three successive levels: the community as a whole, the rural farmstead, and the rural household.

In Part VI, Patterns of Settlement, one chapter deals with the analysis of prehistoric settlement patterns and another with historical settlement patterns.

Based on data presented throughout the volume, Part VII, Concluding Remarks, presents a set of conclusions regarding cultural development in the project area during the Holocene.

Acknowledgments

The Cannon Reservoir Human Ecology Project was funded by the St. Louis District of the U.S. Army Corps of Engineers, under contract with the Board of Regents, University of Nebraska, Lincoln. Although it is usual in a publication to offer a perfunctory acknowledgment of the funding agency for its support, it is a pleasure in this instance to go beyond such a statement of fact. Simply put, the personnel in the St. Louis District have in many ways pioneered efforts to establish an extremely effective and pleasant working relationship between engineers and archaeologists. When the project was formed we were all more than a little unsure of the necessary steps involved in meeting the specifications of various federal laws and executive orders, from developing proposals to evaluating and completing determinations of eligibility of more than 1500 sites. Each time problems arose, patience and diligence showed that a solution was indeed possible.

At one time (circa 1977), the Cannon Project was the largest Corps of Engineers-sponsored project in the United States in terms of dollars allocated for cultural resource studies. The responsibilities attendant to managing and monitoring such a project are enormous, requiring constant communication between agency contract administrators and archaeologists.

A number of persons in the Corps of Engineers were instrumental in facilitating the project in numerous ways. A few of those who aided us include Richard Leverty, outdoor recreation planner, Washington, D.C.; Col. Leon E. McKinney and Col. Robert J. Dacey, and Jack R. Niemi, Jack F. Rasmussen, and John Clark of the St. Louis District. Our closest liaison was Owen D. Dutt, chief of the Environmental Studies Section, St. Louis District. His kind, adaptable, and, sometimes, firm hand provided a consistency we most sincerely appreciate. Mark Dunning, Ronald Pulcher, and especially Terry Norris, all in the Environmental Studies Section, worked with us closely on the project and continuously offered many kinds of assistance to us. All those already mentioned and many others, showed intense interest in all phases of the project, both fieldwork and analysis. Their explanation and clearing of multiple bureaucratic hurdles, development of logical budgets, and kind, considered advice in many and varied situations made our ignorance in many areas much easier to bear.

We also thank many individuals at the University of Nebraska. Among those who were particularly helpful are Dr. Max Larsen, then Dean of the College of Arts and Science, and Francis Schmehl and Carl Mueller of the Office of Grants and Contracts. Carl R. Falk, then director of the Division of Archaeological Research, provided administrative assistance and guided analysis of faunal material and integration of that analysis into the overall scope of the project. Laurie Soward, administrative assistant in the division, provided bookkeeping and offered advice on subjects ranging from personnel to equipment purchase. In many ways the success or failure of the project rested on her capable shoulders for several years.

Many other persons contributed to the success of the project. We acknowledge the assistance of Michael S. Weichman of the Missouri Historic Preservation Program in guiding us through several bureaucratic headaches, and James Denny, also of that office, for his advice on eligibility of historical structures in the project area. Kenneth Anderson, of the Historic American Buildings Survey (HABS), determined which eligible structures would be recorded by an architectural team. Clayton B. Fraser directed the HABS team, whose work added significantly to the historical part of our research.

We also thank Frank Koester, our heavy equipment operator, for his patience in working with us over a 2-year period. Through his efforts we were able to obtain a larger sample of subsurface features than ever imagined. His skill in removing topsoil from archaeological sites is second to none.

We gratefully acknowledge the assistance of several key people who worked on the project over the course of the fieldwork: Bruce E. Byland, field director of a portion of the site survey; David C. Teter, director of the excavation of Pigeon Roost Creek; Tom Miskell, director of the intensive surface collection program; Nellie Swift and Marianne Curry, co-directors of the field laboratory, and James M. Collins, who supervised many of the excavations.

The majority of cartography and illustration was done by Susan J. Vale, whose drawings have added significantly to the volume. She was assisted by Anne Price, who also proofread portions of the manuscript. Typing of the manuscript was done by Nancy Walker and Jean Sparks. We thank Eric E. Voigt for his critical review of a number of chapters and for his overall editorial assistance in various stages of manuscript production.

To our families—Nancy O'Brien; Pamela, Aaron, and Richard Warren; and Ruth Lewarch—we offer our sincere appreciation for the patience and encouragement shown during the many months of manuscript preparation and editing.

We also thank Stuart Struever of Northwestern University for inviting us to prepare this volume for Academic Press. Stuart's pioneering efforts in establishing the Foundation for Illinois Archaeology have demonstrated that with the right mix of professionals and local residents, a regional archaeological project can run smoothly and effectively. His program in many ways served as a model for the Cannon Project and provided training for several of our staff.

Finally, we sincerely thank the people of Perry, Missouri, for the kindness and generosity they extended to us during our stay. Although at times our work must have seemed a little mysterious, they made us feel that we were an important part of their community. The friendships we developed there will last a lifetime.

PART I

Research Orientation

The two chapters in this section serve as an introduction to the Cannon Reservoir Human Ecology Project. Chapter 1 states the objectives of the project, outlines its short- and long-term goals, presents a brief description of the project area (expanded in Part II), summarizes the history of archaeological work in the area since the 1940s to formation of the project in 1977, and outlines a series of special investigations accomplished since that date.

Chapter 2 summarizes the approach taken by the project. Aspects of ecological theory such as territoriality, patch ecology, grain response, and species diversity are discussed in terms of their applicability to human populations. The approach, modeled somewhat after Stuart Struever's original design for work in the lower Illinois River valley, is regional in scope and focuses on a broad range of archaeological problems connected with human adaptations in the Midwest during the Holocene. Important areas of interest are regional analyses of community (intrasite) and settlement (intersite) patterns.

As pointed out in Chapter 2, regional analysis does not focus on specific problems at specific points in time, such as the rise of Hopewell society, but follows individual problems within a region along cultural and temporal continuums. From a regional perspective, it is just as important to understand the reasons for the absence of Hopewell in a tributary valley, like that of the Salt, as it is to understand the nature of Hopewell in a main valley, like that of the Illinois River. Thus, a regional program such as the Cannon Project contributes significantly to research being done a short distance to the east by projects that are parallel in scope.

1

Introduction

MICHAEL J. O'BRIEN AND DALE R. HENNING

The Cannon Reservoir Human Ecology Project is a regional archaeological program designed to investigate processes of cultural adaptation and change in the central portion of the Salt River valley in northeastern Missouri. The Cannon Project is sponsored by the U.S. Army Corps of Engineers, and at its inception in May 1977 became one of the largest (in terms of money budgeted) federally funded archaeological projects in the United States. Attendant to its formation came the myriad details and problems usually associated with cultural resource management (CRM) projects, which were overcome only through considerable patience on the part of all parties.

The project has been, and continues to be, a very successful CRM program from a variety of standpoints. A number of the steps taken by the Corps of Engineers and project personnel to ensure coordination and integration of plans with various federal agencies were innovative and time-saving. Unfortunately, because of the quantity of archaeological data generated by the project, and the need to incorporate those data here, we have been forced to limit discussions, for the most part, to the archaeology. Nevertheless, we wish to emphasize at the outset the contract nature of the project for a number of reasons. First, we hope to show that with adequate time and funding (both of which the Corps of Engineers provided), contract archaeology can be approached much like noncontract archaeology. Although this may be quite evident to some archeologists, it is by no means a universally held notion. Second, the fact that the work was on contract dictated, to a degree, the scope of the project. Two limiting factors were (a) restriction of the study area to a predefined space and (b) in a few instances, the carrying out of field work at the Corps' request in locations slated for immediate impact because of construction connected with the reservoir. Both factors are expected in contract archaeology, and neither hampered implementation of the regional research design formulated for the project.

In summary, the Corps of Engineers gave us a free hand to explore new archaeological avenues when the opportunity arose. We never were denied permission to strike off in a new direction if we could demonstrate that it was in the best interest of the project.

Succeeding sections of this chapter present an overview of the Cannon Project and discuss research objectives and goals, the project area, previous archaeological work in the region, and studies carried out in conjunction with the project. Each of these topics is treated more extensively in subsequent chapters.

THE PROJECT OBJECTIVE

The objective of the Cannon Reservoir Human Ecology Project is to investigate processes of ecological adaptation and culture change in the central portion of the Salt River valley in northeastern Missouri (O'Brien and Warren 1980). More specifically, the project focuses on isolating "significant cultural patterns and processes in the region, as these are reflected in preserved material remains and documentary sources" (O'Brien and Warren 1979:1). Prehistoric and historic occupations of the region are of equal interest to us, and we deal with problems common to both spheres, using complementary data recovery techniques. Thus, research bears directly on the Holocene human ecology of the middle Salt River valley and, on a broader scale, to a balanced understanding of trends in cultural development in the greater Midwest. At an even higher level, we hope our conclusions are useful to the development and refinement of general anthropological theory regarding human response to a range of natural and cultural stimuli.

To meet our objectives, we formulated specific goals for the project to guide the subsequent 4 years of fieldwork and analysis.

GOALS OF THE PROJECT

Project goals were separated into immediate goals, which were achieved through fieldwork, and long-range goals, which were met only after detailed analysis.

Immediate Project Goals

The immediate goals of the project were

1. To locate, map, and date as accurately as possible all traces of prehistoric and historic (up to 1920) occupation within the project area
2. To identify the range of functional variability within and between these occupations
3. To select components for intensive surface collection and excavation of subsurface features
4. To select components for large-scale, more intensive excavation
5. For the historic period, to compile documentary data from sources such as land purchase records, population censuses, agricultural censuses, and tax records

Long-Range Project Goals

The long-range goals of the project were

1. To reconstruct the early nineteenth-century environment in the middle Salt River valley and contrast previous differences from this baseline
2. To delineate the outlines of changing spatial locations and settlement pattern complexity throughout 10,000 years of occupation of the region
3. To analyze the composition of prehistoric and historic communities in terms of content and context
4. To compare findings with previously defined patterns in the Midwest in order to clarify problems of (a) subsistence and exploitative patterns, (b) extraregional contacts and posited prehistoric "tradition lag" in the middle Salt River valley, and (c) for the historic period, the role of suprafamilial units in the organization of communities.

To meet these long-range goals, we employed analytical techniques that were sensitive to time, form, and function. These techniques, detailed in various sections of this volume, involved establishing technological and functional classification systems for various artifact classes and using stratigraphic and radiometric dating to order the classes temporally.

Analysis of the content of prehistoric and historic communities (long-range goals 3 and 4) was facilitated by the formation of technological and functional classes. Part II details a number of the sources we used to meet long-range goal 1—reconstructing the early historic environment in the middle Salt Valley. General Land Office (GLO) survey records aided our construction of maps of the locations of prairie and timber during 1816–1822. In some instances, we used land purchase records (Chapter 17) to augment this reconstruction. Analyses of floral (Chapter 11) and faunal (Chapter 10) remains from dated archaeological components and from interpolations of environmental data from other areas of the Midwest were used to refine the model.

Successful completion of long-range goal 2—delineation of changing settlement patterns throughout the last 10,000 years—was accomplished for the prehistoric period by intensive site survey (Chapter 16) and, for the historic period, by site survey and use of nineteenth-century maps, atlases, and documents (Chapter 17).

THE PROJECT AREA

The Clarence Cannon Dam and Reservoir[1] is located in the central Salt River drainage of northeastern Missouri (Figure 1.1). The axis of the main dam, located approximately 100 km upstream from the confluence of the Salt and Mississippi rivers, will impound water along the main stem of the Salt and its four major tributaries: the South, Middle, North, and Elk forks. Numerous smaller creeks and drainages also will be affected. Below the main dam site, a low-level re-regulation dam will impound a smaller pool to enhance continuous generation of hydroelectric power. The dam and reservoir complex were constructed by the U.S. Army Corps of Engineers to (a) generate hydroelectric power for surrounding municipalities, (b) control flooding along the Salt River and its tributaries, and (c) provide recreational services for an estimated 3 million visitors annually (Missouri Botanical Garden 1974).

The normal pool will impound water at or near the 606 ft. above mean sea level (AMSL) mark and will cover approximately 18,600 surface acres. The

Corps "take area"—which includes the pool area; a shoreline easement; and preserves designated as public access areas, recreation areas, and conservation areas—totals nearly 65,000 acres.

Archaeological site survey conducted in the region prior to 1977 was concentrated on this restricted acreage. Permission was granted by the Corps of Engineers in 1977 to provide logistical support for the University of Nebraska sponsored survey in selected portions of the uplands and prairie surrounding this acreage. This extension of the sample area was necessary to obtain an adequate regional assessment of the pattern of human settlement in the area. The previous study area had been restricted to bottomland and terraces, the heart of the oak–hickory biome, and had provided a limited sample of total human settlement because it had excluded coverage of the other major biome, the tall-grass prairie. The extended project boundary, which permitted an adequate assessment of human settlement patterns in the area, encompasses 1149 km[2], conforming to the area used by the Missouri Botanical Garden (1974) during their environmental impact study.

The Salt River basin is situated along the southern fringe of the Prairie Peninsula, a region characterized as a complex mosaic of prairie and forest biomes. The area is important because of its potential sensitivity to climatic change during the Holocene and its stability in the face of many cultural developments (such as Hopewell and Mississippian) a short distance to the south and east (Warren 1979:71).

Archaeological reconnaissance conducted in the area during the 1940s and 1950s by the Marion-Ralls Chapter of the Missouri Archaeological Society (Eichenberger 1944) documented a number of sites. This led to the conclusion that the area, situated along what might be considered a major ecotone, was especially rich in archaeological remains and perhaps held important chronological information regarding the development of ceremonial activities associated with moundbuilding and burial practices in the upper Mississippi Valley. These early investigations, although unable to answer many of the questions we posed, provided the basis for later, more in-depth studies of the complex rela-

[1]Due to be completed in 1983.

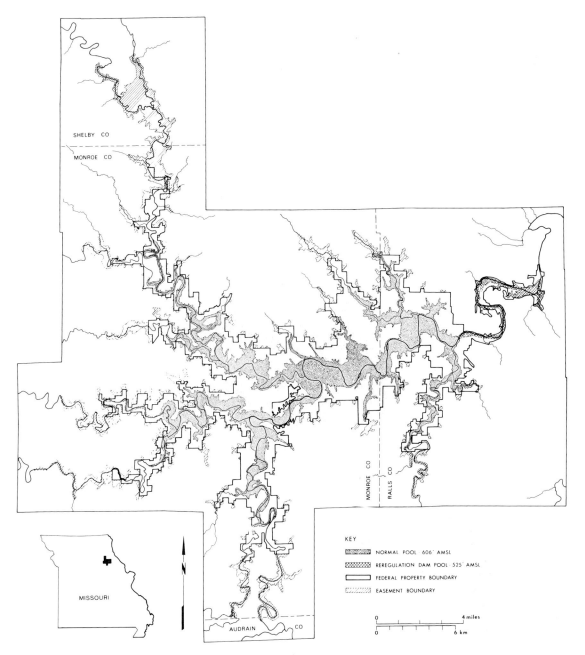

Figure 1.1. Map showing boundaries of the project area and Cannon Reservoir.

tionship between human populations and environment in the Cannon Reservoir area. Previous investigations are summarized in the following section.

HISTORY OF RESEARCH IN THE PROJECT AREA

We have divided our discussion into four sec-
tions, each corresponding to a major period of re-
search in the project area: (I) 1961–1964, when the
University of Missouri surveyed and tested sites
under contract from the National Park Service
(NPS); (II) 1967–1968, when the University of Mis-
souri excavated nine sites under contract from NPS;
(III) 1974–May, 1977, when the University of
Nebraska carried out further survey and testing
under contract from the Corps of Engineers; and
(IV) May, 1977–present, the period of the Cannon
Reservoir Human Ecology Project.

Period I

The rationale for the initial work appears in an
introduction to the University of Missouri report
submitted to the NPS for the period 1959–1961:

> The emphasis of the research was directed toward the
> recovery of a local cultural sequence within the Salt
> River Valley, expanding the knowledge of as many of
> the cultural periods as possible, and with special em-
> phasis placed upon the recovery of information con-
> cerning the ceremonies associated with the mound
> structures so prevalent within and adjacent to the pro-
> posed Joanna Reservoir[2] area [Chapman 1962:v].

Chapman felt that these objectives were at least
partially fulfilled after the initial three years' work:

> Although a full cultural sequence was not determined,
> and many questions were left unanswered concerning
> the ceremonial activities of those building the mounds
> in the area, it is felt that within the limits of the time and
> funds available that a fair insight into these problems
> was obtained. Another necessary step in progressing
> the overall goals of obtaining the full sequence of cul-

[2]The previous name of the reservoir.

tural development of the Joanna Reservoir area was
accomplished. Furthermore, many new insights into
ceremonial activities of both the Archaic and the
Woodland period were obtained [Chapman 1962:
v–vi].

Much of this initial testing phase consisted of the
excavation of burial mounds to gather data on interment practices. Although descriptive reports were
prepared on the findings, it was not until 1976 that
an intensive analysis of the osteological material
was presented (Klepinger and Henning 1976) and
not until 1979 that a comparison of osteological
material from several sites was made (Donham
1979b).

Several habitation sites were tested during this
period, yielding materials needed to create a regional artifact typology. However, a major problem
arose. There were isolated attempts, mainly by
Dale R. Henning, to develop a working typology
(Henning 1961), but there was never any concerted
effort to apply this system uniformly within the
reservoir area, as is exemplified in Heldman's 1962
report to NPS:

> Artifacts from sites surveyed and excavated were kept
> separate during laboratory analysis because even
> though much of the material appeared to be similar the
> quantity of material was considered to be too small to
> establish artifact types. Therefore, the material from
> each site has been placed into descriptive categories
> based on the similarity of traits for purposes of com-
> parison with artifacts and artifact types already estab-
> lished in areas geographically near the Joanna Reser-
> voir area [Heldman 1962:4].

Period II

Further excavation was carried out sporadically
over the next 10 years by several individuals,
chiefly Walter E. Klippel. Klippel's research interests were varied, but much of his work focused on a
hypothesis formulated in 1964 by Henning, who
suggested that tradition lag in terms of lithic artifact
types existed in the area, resulting in "the survival
and retention of Archaic stone tool technology with
the addition of pottery making in the Late Wood-

land" (D. R. Henning 1964:106). This possibility, linked with evidence from other preceramic sites in northeastern Missouri, was discussed by Klippel:

> The collation of these uncoordinated data has fostered interest, not only in the local Archaic manifestations themselves, but also in the potential the area might have for unraveling many general problems of cultural trends and development in the Midwest during the Archaic period [Klippel 1968:1].

Based on the results of the initial survey (Henning 1960), Klippel selected sites to excavate in hopes of obtaining data on local preceramic manifestations:

> Due to a series of regional problems related to prehistoric settlement patterns, depths of post-glacial deposits, and historic agricultural practices, considerable effort was spent locating nonceramic sites containing the kinds of data useful in making meaningful archeological interpretations [Klippel 1968:1].

Of seven sites tested only one "proved useful in fulfilling initial intentions to gain a fuller understanding of local nonceramic manifestations" (Klippel 1968:1).

An analysis of artifacts from that single site suggested that the assemblage was a "manifestation of a single phase" (Klippel 1968:84) and that the site had been occupied during a season when vegetal materials were being collected and prepared. Deposits, however, were shallow (preventing separation of culturally and/or temporally distinct strata) and produced no samples for radiometric dating.

Period III

In late 1974 a contract was signed between the University of Nebraska and the Corps of Engineers, initiating a new, more ambitious era in contract archaeology. A large-scale project was organized to study prehistoric remains threatened by the construction of the reservoir. In a statement of project goals and methods, Ruppert indicated that "the major research orientation of this project will be the definition and study of settlement–subsistence systems" (Ruppert 1975:2). Goals were to be met by

the inductive generation of descriptive and explanatory models based on the results of survey-and-testing operations and subsequent testing of hypotheses with data gathered from large-scale excavations.

Once a working taxonomy of sites and settlement types was formulated, certain sites of each type were to be chosen randomly for excavation; at least two sites of each settlement type were to be selected from a sample of sites in danger of destruction (Ruppert 1975:13): "The emphasis of major excavations should be toward recovery of data which will increase knowledge about settlement types and systems" (Ruppert 1975:14).

The rationale for excavation varied, ranging from imminent destruction of a site by reservoir-related activities to more traditional archaeological concerns, such as furthering the creation of lithic tool and ceramic typologies. Field procedures used during the 1975 and 1976 season of test excavation were fairly uniform: small, systematic surface collections were made at a few sites, plow zones were removed by mechanical stripping, and subsurface features were excavated by hand. These techniques often were augmented by backhoe trenches cut through sites to obtain stratigraphic data on cultural deposits.

In evaluating the design and results of these investigations, we have discovered a number of shortcomings. The rationale for the selection of sites to be tested, and the way sites were reported, did not follow the research design. Also, intrasite sampling procedures did not meet stated goals. In summary, there was no multistage strategy that permitted analysis at the testing level in order to structure larger excavations.

Material from these excavations, however, was later useful for various purposes: the pottery helped formulate a ceramic classification system; projectile points were used to date certain components and sites; and metric data on the shape and size of subsurface features were standardized and used to compile a classification system for these nonportable artifacts.

During 1976, the Corps of Engineers authorized the University of Nebraska to document and assess historic sites and structures in the region. This initial survey laid the groundwork for more in-depth investigation into historic-period settlement in the project area.

Period IV

Before a mitigation contract could be awarded to the University of Nebraska, the Corps of Engineers required completion of a comprehensive research design, a plan of action, and determinations of eligibility for the hundreds of sites found during survey. In May 1977 the Cannon Reservoir Human Ecology Project was formed, reflecting not simply a change in the name of the project but a complete reorientation (O'Brien 1977). Several persons involved in the formative stages of the program had been associated with large, interdisciplinary archaeological projects in Mesoamerica and had seen firsthand the mechanics involved in implementing such a program. These projects were successful in part because they integrated the work of specialists in other fields such as geomorphology, agronomy, and ethnobiology with archaeology, instead of treating the results of this work as ancillary data. Because of budgetary constraints on the Cannon Project, the decision to perform any given study was based on the assumption that the related, nonarchaeological work was required for successful completion of the project.

Nonarchaeological studies accomplished include the following:

1. Analysis of the geomorphology of the area, undertaken to provide information on the age of the river terraces and to establish a sequence of terrace formation. This study was vital to our understanding of the depositional and erosional history of the Salt River drainage and to the formulation of a predictive model for locating buried sites. Although the study succeeded in establishing a sequence of terrace formation throughout the project area, no chronologically sensitive artifacts or carbonized wood was recovered from backhoe cuts placed throughout the reservoir. Work was directed by Michael G. Foley of the University of Missouri–Columbia.

2. Analysis of snails from several sites in the area was designed to provide paleoclimatic data. Snails from Pigeon Roost Creek, a deep, stratified Wood-

land–Archaic–Dalton midden located on a small tributary of the Salt River, were of particular importance. This analysis was conducted under the direction of David Baerreis of the University of Wisconsin–Madison.

3. Analysis of paleoethnobotanical materials was undertaken to (*a*) provide a summary of recovered wood and seeds from each excavated site, (*b*) provide data on seasonal occupation of specific components, and (*c*) provide a summary statement of the proportional representation of various foodstuff in the paleodiet for specific time periods. Analysis of the prehistoric material was conducted by Frances B. King of the Illinois State Museum (Chapter 11); analysis of the historic material was done by Steven Millet of the University of Nebraska–Lincoln.

4. Analysis of the zooarchaeological material was initiated for the same reasons as those listed for ethnobotanical remains, plus the identification of specific butchering techniques. Analysis was directed by Carl R. Falk of the University of Nebraska–Lincoln (Chapter 10).

5. Documentation of certain historic structures located on Corps of Engineers' land was performed to provide information concerning house style and construction technique. This work, consisting of complete architectural plans and renderings plus drawings and photographs of interior and exterior trim, was performed by the Historic American Buildings Survey under the direction of Clayton B. Fraser.

6. Various other types of analysis were contracted for when necessary. Computer work was done at the University of Washington and the University of Missouri–Columbia; radiometric dating was done by the University of Texas at Austin Radiocarbon Laboratory, under the direction of Salvatore (Sam) Valastro, Jr.

The various types of analysis were subcontracted to individuals and institutions based upon knowledge of their previous work performance. Other specialized tasks were done by project personnel, who were picked for their expertise in such fields as archival research, use of soil and vegetation data, and artifact analysis. It must be stated, however, that due to the myriad types of data involved in such a large, regional project, much of the expertise

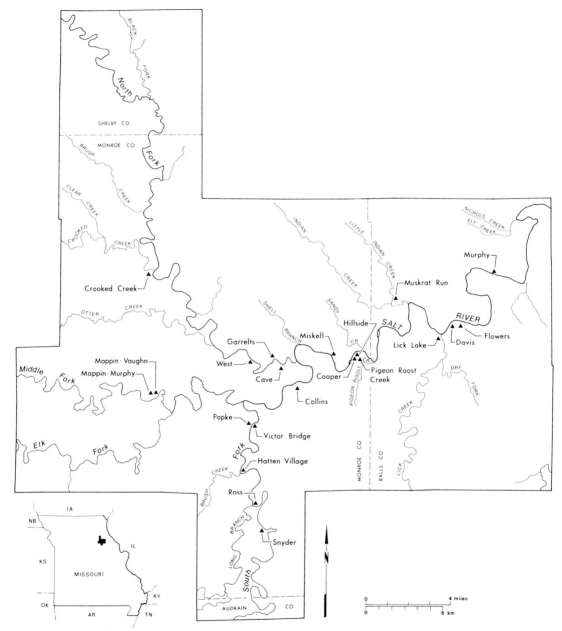

Figure 1.2. Locations of major archaeological sites mentioned in the text.

of the individuals involved was a result of on-the-job training.

THE DATA BASE

At the close of fieldwork in August 1980, over 1500 prehistoric and 350 historic sites had been located in the project area. Prior to May 1977, 33 sites had been excavated; since that time, 19 prehistoric sites and 7 historic sites have been excavated. Additionally, 37 sites were surface collected intensively. These activities have resulted in an enormous amount of material and data.

The majority of prehistoric sites in the region are shallow (<60 cm) deposits, many of which exist only in the plow zone. As explained in succeeding chapters, strategies used in dealing with these sites included surface collection and mechanical removal of the plow zone. In two instances deposits extended much deeper: Excavation of these two sites provided stratigraphic evidence of changes in tool form through time and also yielded radiometric samples to form the basis for a regional chronology.

Historic sites include standing residential and farm-related structures as well as the ruins of former farmsteads and sites of commercial and manufacturing facilities. Analysis of standing residential architecture provided a classification and typology of houses in the region; excavation in and around rural farmstead structures helped date the farmsteads and provided a detailed look at nineteenth-century household composition. Included in the historic data base are various archival materials, used to reconstruct settlement and community patterns and the economic base of the region during portions of the nineteenth century.

Due to the amount of data generated by the project, only a small portion can be reported here. Every effort has been made to synthesize information where possible and to provide examples of points made. Major sites from which data in this volume are used are shown in Figure 1.2. Together they represent a cross section of archaeological communities of the project area. When other sites are mentioned, their locations are shown in separate figures.

Because analysis is still on-going with respect to some aspects of the project, the results presented here often are not final statements. However, results to date are encouraging, and amply document trends and shifts in cultural adaptation throughout the Holocene in the southern Prairie Peninsula.

2

The Approach

MICHAEL J. O'BRIEN AND ROBERT E. WARREN

This chapter presents a brief overview of the approach taken by the Cannon Project to understand and explain various environmental and cultural changes in the middle Salt River valley throughout the Holocene. As detailed in the following, the scope of the project is a regional analysis that encompasses an ecological or systems approach that deals with the interplay of environmental and social relationships.

Since the terms *culture* and *cultural* are used throughout this volume, they should be defined. Despite the enormous variation in definitions of culture, we feel that the following statement summarizes the important elements of a culture:

> A culture is the total acquired lifeway or life-style of a group of people. It consists of the patterned, repetitive ways of thinking, feeling, and acting that are characteristic of the members of a particular society or segment of a society [Harris 1975:144].

Key words in this definition are *patterned* and *repetitive*. Throughout the course of this volume, a common concern is pattern recognition, that is,

identifying the range in cultural variability, isolating points or segments within this range, predicting temporally and spatially where these points or segments will recur, and testing these predictions. In summary, we are searching for patterns in the ways by which prehistoric and Euro-American peoples adapted to and modified their environment. Because archaeology is necessarily an inexact science due to the incompleteness of the archaeological record, there are many aspects of culture that cannot be examined (Rouse 1972b; Schiffer 1976). Also, given that the Cannon Project was founded to accomplish certain goals in an allotted time, several aspects of the existent archaeological record remain unexamined.

The underlying interest here is the evolution of culture from one state to another. If, as Binford (1962a:217) states, the goal of archaeology is to describe and explain the total range of cultural similarites and differences observable in space and through time, then an evolutionary perspective is "appropriate to the explanation of these similarities and differences" (Struever 1968:286). *Evolution* is used here to refer to a mechanism for explaining change, whether in terms of "differential persistence of variability" (Dunnell 1980b:38) or in terms of some other function. Hill (1977) and Dunnell (1978a), among others, have expressed the opinion that neither anthropology nor archaeology has made adequate use of evolutionary theory. Where such theory has been applied, it often has been done unsystematically. Given the depth of misunderstanding among archaeologists concerning the implications of cultural evolution and evolutionary theory, we limit our discussion to an examination of culture change.

In addition to using sets of universal processes or laws to account for sequences of entities, we offer functional explanations that refer to the roles played by entities in cultural systems (Dunnell 1980b:39). In other words, not all of our explanations deal with how systems came into being; we also investigate how, when systems are in place, they operate within the environment and how these man–environment interactions allow us to predict something about the cultural system. This approach is consistent with Struever's (1968:286) statement that culture is a "system of functionally interdependent parts in which change in one aspect is related in specifiable ways to change in others. Explanations for change in a cultural system require understanding of these linkages." Struever views cultural variations through space in terms of the differing adaptive requirements of specific environments or, more precisely, differing adaptive strategies to the requirements. Thus, varying ecological potentialities are tied to different exploitive economies. These in turn are linked to varying integrative requirements and, therefore, to different forms of social structure.

The discussion in the remainder of this chapter is divided into two major sections: human ecology and regional analysis. In the first we present some considerations of ecological concepts, later demonstrating in Chapter 5 how implications derived from these concepts apply to prehistoric hunter–gatherers. In the second part we present the basis for developing a regional approach to midwestern archaeology, summarize the benefits and limitations of the approach, and discuss the conceptual and methodological framework of implementing such an approach.

HUMAN ECOLOGY

Human ecology is a difficult concept to define and use productively since the term itself is, in some senses, redundant. If *ecology* is the study of interrelationships among organisms and their environment, and all components of ecosystems are interrelated systemically, one must avoid placing arbitrary and potentially undesirable limits on sets of factors considered during analysis. This problem is especially thorny in archaeological research, where assessment of natural variables often requires applications of distant ethnographic parallels, and the confounding effects of often nebulous cultural factors are to be expected. Adoption of the ecological approach has contributed to remarkably clear insights into interpreting the archaeological record and defining cultural processes (e.g., Simenstad *et al.* 1978). Benefits to our understanding of past human lifeways and cultural processes have far outweighed any drawbacks. Therefore, we have adopted an ecological framework for analyzing evidence of human behavior in the region, albeit with the necessary assumption that cultural forces may have had as important an effect as environmental variables on societies in the project area.

There are certain caveats that must be heeded when ecological principles are applied to archaeological explanation, or when ecological models are applied to human populations. Addressing the first point, Schiffer (1978; cited in Hardesty 1980:159), argues that the use of ecological principles in archaeological explanation is plagued with logical weaknesses, especially when ill-constructed analogs and trivial homologs are introduced. He argues that one proper role of general ecological principles in archaeological explanation is reduction, where "one discipline's principles can be deduced from the theoretical premises of another" (Schiffer 1978:15–16). Unfortunately, as Schiffer observes, neither general ecological principles nor agreed-upon principles of cultural process exist paradigmatically.

The second point, applying ecological models to human populations, also is rather inappropriate for many situations. Hardesty (1980:161) claims this is due to two characteristics of ecological theory. First, the theory that does exist has developed largely independently of human ecological data. In other words, hypotheses and underlying principles that compose the theory have been tested with data from nonhuman species. Second, ecological theory is in a state of flux, having many competing hypotheses and principles.

Hardesty (1980:161) points out that only the most foolhardy would use one ecological principle over another without showing why it has greater explanatory power. The transfer of general principles across disciplinary boundaries, then, is dependent upon the results of testing multiple hypotheses. He argues that the most productive relationship for ecology and archaeology "is one of *interaction* between general theory and a new data base" (Hardesty 1980:161) not one of donor and recipient of theories and models. This is certainly a better arrangement than now exists in archaeology, as many investigators set out on "search and seizure missions" (Hardesty 1980:161), intent on borrowing wholesale from ecology as much theory as they can carry back.

In light of these cautions, and in hope of applying certain principles of ecology to a new data base, we present a summary of the concepts that seem particularly relevant to our study. Our data base is composed largely of the material remains of prehistoric mobile-sedentary populations that lived in a river valley of the midwestern United States. These population aggregates developed subsistence strategies that required some amount of mobility for hunting and gathering activities but did not demand a nomadic way of life.

On a somewhat broader scale, we are concerned with environments within temperate deciduous forests, temperate grasslands, and the prairie–forest ecotone. It is suggested that river valleys under consideration have features in common that were exploited in similar ways by prehistoric populations within the region. These valleys contain very narrow, compact ecological zones running parallel to rivers; distance from the river to the bluff tops and uplands is usually less than 5 km. Rivers provide not only large quantities of potential food resources but also serve as means of transportation and communication. We are aware of variability in density of flora and fauna, climate, physiography, and other factors among the river valleys, but general characteristics allow for analogous adaptive patterns by different populations despite this variability.

Population and Territory

One factor considered is the use of space by human populations; it is reasonable to assume that there was a limit to the extent of space used. Sufficient ethnographic evidence exists for hunting and gathering populations to hypothesize that a population's distribution in space and time and its use of potential resources are nonrandom. It is suggested that prehistoric populations in the Midwest adapted to and exploited bounded areas, that is, territories. *Territory* is defined in terms of use and activities performed in a bounded area by that population.

The dimensions and considerations of territoriality are too vast to be dealt with adequately here. We have narrowed our focus to include the spacing of populations in relation to seasonal and long-term variability of the resource base. Seasonal variability is a crucial factor to understanding population behavior in terms of the extent of movement and regularity of movement in natural resource exploitation. Also important is an understanding of the net effects of seasonality on different economic structures, since many explanations of intersite variability in settlement patterning assume that seasonal exploitation of resources means that a population also moves its residential unit.

There are two dimensions to territoriality: (*a*) spacing of individuals (the manner in which individuals are identified with space) and (*b*) the nature of boundaries (the effective limits of individual and group activity). Important to both dimensions are degrees of, and specific mechanisms and processes involved in, intragroup and intergroup variability. Ecologists view territoriality as an adaptive response to selective pressures in particular environments. Animal ecologists have demonstrated close relationships between ecological forces that control animal populations and characteristics of their social systems, of which territoriality is but one part (Boughey 1973:112; Morse

1980:212). We similarly are interested in qualifying this relationship for human populations in a given environment. Unfortunately, most territorial behavior theory and its implications are derived from studies of nonhuman animals and may not be applicable to human populations. However, a few of the more general implications are presented here.

Ecologists consider territoriality among animals to have certain selective advantages; it allows for familiarity with a discrete area, efficient utilization of important or critical food resources, and evasion of predators (Klopfer 1969:83). The size of the territory will be partially regulated by the energy needs of the population but will not be so large as to excessively expose individuals to predators. Population size and density are regulated below the normal carrying capacity of the environment (cf. Boughey 1973:112); hence, territoriality is a regulatory mechanism. Under invariant environmental conditions, it discourages overpopulation and has a stabilizing effect.

Among animals, territorial behavior regulates space among individuals and groups. By definition, competing species limit each other's niche space and biomass (Odum 1959). This principle of interspecific competition seems applicable to human populations sharing the same geographic area and exploiting similar resources. It argues in favor of spacing mechanisms to avoid intergroup competition and confrontation.

Territory boundaries are not fixed geographically but are zones that fluctuate with shifts in subsistence strategies. This, at least, sets human niches apart from niches of other animals. One point of similarity between human and nonhuman territoriality is defense; both are likely to protect most strongly that portion for which the gains from defense exceed expenses (in energy) incurred (Morse 1980:212).

Variations also occur in the division of defended territory. In heterogeneous environments, not all loci of activity are included within the territory, and, therefore, defense may not have clear boundaries. Instead, concentric areas of inwardly increasing dominance may exist. Of importance is how space is divided within and between populations in terms of varying degrees of use.

Archaeologically, it is extremely difficult to define the spatial limits of a population, let alone

define its areas of dominance. If form and function of territoriality are adaptive responses to different selective pressures, one must attempt to pinpoint these pressures. Work must be structured to isolate the variables while simultaneously searching for regularities in the relationship between features of the environment (such as food availability) and human territorial behavior.

If territorial behavior is to be ascribed to mobile-sedentary populations, we need some understanding of the settlement system in terms of aggregation or dispersal of the population as well as of the variables that affect this behavior during an annual cycle. Seasonal exploitation of food and technological resources is characteristic of many hunting and gathering populations. Flannery (1968) has postulated that the seasonal availability of resources involves the scheduling of procurement activities to resolve conflicts of simultaneous availability of resources, optimal yields, and preference. There is an important corollary: An entire population or segments of a population may move either as an aggregate or become dispersed, according to necessary procurement strategies. In some cases, the spacing of resource zones requires that populations move their residential units for the sake of efficiency. It is possible that the environmental characteristics of midwestern river valleys structured the adaptive responses of mobile-sedentary populations. It was advantageous for such populations to select for scheduling of resource exploitations but *not* for shifts in residential locations.

One important aspect of human territoriality is the differential availability of resources (e.g., food, energy, and building material). All these resources vary in abundance in the Cannon Reservoir area, as in other regions. However, even if their availability were mapped by a particular group and this information were distributed among various sectors of the populations, the fact that abundance does vary would result in extractive strategies peculiar to specific resources and locations within the area.

Patch Ecology

Within any given area, one can define environmental zones that are characterized by the predominance of one or more elements, whether these are geomorphological, floral, or combinations of these and other elements. Zones may be conceptualized as mosaics of intersecting spatial subsets, or "patches," within areas that can vary in scale from biospheric to microscopic proportions. A series of recent publications deals with optimal utilization of these environments by various organisms. Wiens states:

> In the real world, environments are patchy. Factors influencing the proximate physiological or behavioral state or the ultimate fitness of individuals exhibit discontinuities on many scales in time and space. The patterns of these discontinuities produce an environmental patchwork which exerts powerful influences on the distribution of organisms, their interactions, and their adaptations [Wiens 1976:81].

> Patches are distinguished by discontinuities in environmental character states from their surrounding; implicit are the notions that the discontinuities have biological significance, and that they matter to the organism [Wiens 1976:83].

Regarding exploitative strategies within patchy environments, Wiens echos the often-cited work of Flannery (1968):

> The habitat patterns produced by these varied effects provide an environmental mosaic of patches. A variety of attributes or adaptive responses of populations develop within the selective regimes associated with this heterogeneity [Wiens 1976:90].

Grain Response

Grain response is viewed as different patterns of resource utilization with respect to interpatch and intrapatch variability. There are two forms of grain response: (*a*) fine-grained response, in which "an organism encounters and uses resources in the same proportions in which they actually occur" (Pianka 1974:206), and (*b*) coarse-grained response, in which "organisms . . . spend disproportionate amounts of time in different patches" (Pianka 1974:206). Thus, according to Wiens (1976), fine-grained responses to patchy environments are generalist strategies in which resources

are exploited randomly and in direct proportion to their relative abundance (cf. MacArthur and Pianka 1966). Coarse-grained responses, on the other hand, can be viewed as specialist strategies in which populations exploit patches nonrandomly and therefore show selective bias in their resource utilization strategies.

Osborn and Falk (1977:90) present a concise assessment of the temporal and spatial dimensions of patch variability and suggest that species diversity may be the most effective gradient along which variability can be measured. The spatial dimension reflects vertical and horizontal variation both within and among patches. Concerning the temporal dimension they, like Flannery (1968), note that resources, particularly food, vary in availability throughout an annual cycle, depending on the length of the growing season, the degree of simultaneous availability of other resources, and the degree of competition with other species. Variability along these dimensions influences the effectiveness, spacing, and scheduling of alternate resource strategies and must be taken into account when predicting human responses.

Osborn and Falk (1977:100–101) indicate that patch size affects grain responses, since effective numbers of distinctive patches are lower in areas with diverse patch sizes and are higher in areas with uniform patch sizes. Therefore, "greater between-patch heterogeneity and greater potential for development of a coarse-grained response (adaptive strategy)" (Osborn and Falk 1977:101) would be favored in regions characterized by varied patches that are similar in size. Conversely, there would be greater potential for fine-grained adaptive strategies "in a region characterized by greater homogeneity within and between patches in an environment composed of patches of widely varied size" (Osborn and Falk 1977:101).

Given increasing density of resource-extracting populations, Osborn and Falk predict strategy shifts from coarse-grained to fine-grained responses. Wiens (1976:92) notes that in small populations, only the optimal patch type should be occupied, but as population density increases, the quality of the habitat decreases. A point is reached where another habitat has equal potential quality. An opposite trend may be expected for resource-producing populations, depending on the degree to which intensification depletes limiting factors and the rate at which depleted areas can be rejuvenated or replaced.

Species Diversity

As indicated by Osborn and Falk (1977:91–98), species diversity is linked theoretically to a number of environmental variables important to considerations of human extractive strategies. Species diversity correlates inversely with amounts of excess energy and ratios of production-to-biomass and correlates directly with levels of successional maturity, levels of species dispersion (equitability), degrees of trophic complexity, demographic stability under internally and externally changing conditions, degrees of niche specialization, and faunal species diversity. Thus, individually aggregating plant and animal species are unlikely in ecological communities with high species diversity, and, as noted by Osborn and Falk (1977:104), such communities cannot be expected to yield substantial quantities of specific resources for human exploitation.

Analysis of the effects of these factors on patterns of human settlement indicates that species diversity conditions forms and degrees of group mobility among hunter–gatherers (Osborn and Falk 1977:104–105). Regions dominated by extensive areas with high species diversity favor "residential mobility," wherein groups exploit resources that are distributed evenly but limited quantitatively, and are forced to relocate when critical resources are exhausted. Logistical mobility, on the other hand, is favored in areas of low species diversity, where resources tend to aggregate in patches. In these cases, small subsets of residential groups detach settlements to exploit specific targeted resources. Social and demographic correlates also are implied by these associations. Intragroup economic specialization, likely expressed as sexual division of labor, is expected in areas with low species diversity; limits on fertility also are expected when absentee procurement groups are composed of males (Binford and Chasko 1976).

REGIONAL ANALYSIS

As Johnson (1977:479) notes, regional studies are of growing importance in anthropology; there is a continuing need for the expansion of spatial and temporal frameworks for the study of many aspects of human behavior. He notes also that the acceptance of archaeological settlement-pattern survey as a research strategy has created a demand for new theory and analytic methods that are appropriate to regional data. Based on Johnson's review of regional analysis, theories that do exist are limited mainly to situations involving market economies. The majority of analytical techniques he reviews are derived from spatial geography, and many techniques are not applicable to archaeological data in their present form.

Regional analysis is the analysis of a specific unit of geographic space in which study is focused on a specific population. In such an analysis the interactions of the population within a delimited geographic context are investigated. Instead of focusing broadly on a problem, such as the decline of Hopewell over the midwestern and eastern United States, regional analysis focuses on a particular area in which particular problems (e.g., how change in the environment leads to disintegration of the social order of Hopewellian peoples) can be studied.

The benefits of this approach are numerous. First, there is no presumption that one is looking at distinct ethnic entities, which alleviates the problem of trying to delineate spatial boundaries of certain cultural groups. In a strictly archaeological sense, there is no need to compose long trait lists from various areas or to search the literature exhaustively for references to the location of certain elements that occur over a wide geographic area. Second, regional analysis allows broadening one's scope to include other geographic areas as needed; one is not limited to the physical and cultural variables of the region under investigation. Third, regional analysis provides a framework for incorporating the results of more localized projects, such as small-area intensive surveys or single-site excavations.

The obvious limitation of regional analysis is that it can present a biased view of synchronous cultural developments. An example would be using data from the Cannon Reservoir area to study the rise and fall of Hopewell, even though there is almost no evidence of this manifestation in the area. Although an analysis of data from the project area would not lead us to an understanding of the entirety of Hopewell, it would allow us to better understand events that are synchronous with its development in the Illinois and Ohio river valleys and why cultures in the project area never participated in the Hopewell Interaction Sphere. In turn, results of analysis of these problems can be applied to the problem at large.

Ideally, archaeology would be composed of a series of geographically overlapping regional analyses, each employing similar field and analytical strategies, and all contributing toward construction of a general anthropological theory of prehistoric human behavior. It is too much to hope that long-term areal projects such as Cannon can be started on every river drainage in the Midwest, so we must be content to do what we can when such an opportunity arises. Fortunately, central and northeastern Missouri have had three regional archaeological projects that have added to our knowledge of prehistoric culture process: Longbranch Reservoir (Grantham 1977), Harry S. Truman Reservoir (Wood and McMillan 1976), and Cannon Reservoir. The Truman Project is of great importance, not only because of the size of the project area but because of its recovery of a wealth of data on late Pleistocene–early Holocene climate and culture.

To the east, in the lower Illinois River valley, Struever and his project's large-scale efforts to investigate myriad aspects of prehistory in the center of one of the United States' most fertile research areas are producing an enormous amount of data (Struever 1968,1971a,b). Most notable is the work being done on Middle Woodland settlement and community patterns (Asch 1976; Buikstra 1976) and Archaic and Woodland subsistence (Asch *et al.* 1972; Styles 1978; Asch and Asch 1980).

These regional projects, when coupled with sound, well-organized smaller efforts, for example, work at the Cherokee site in Iowa (Anderson and Semken 1980), are beginning to produce re-

sults useful in delineating environmental and cultural changes in the upper Midwest during the past 12,000 years. Such studies form the basis for new investigations of man–environment and man–man relationships.

Two aspects of regional analysis summarized in this chapter are settlement pattern analysis and community pattern analysis. As will be shown, there is considerable reason to divide research interests into these two spheres. Our approach has been to (*a*) analyze the data at each level separately and (*b*) combine the results to evaluate theories of cultural and environmental process in the project area.

Settlement Pattern Analysis

In the last 25 years settlement pattern analysis, as one approach to the recovery of archaeological data in a regional perspective, has gained wide acceptance in American archaeology. The general acceptance of this approach can be seen as tacit approval of the success of the method and techniques of archaeological site survey in gathering material and ordering data useful in solving problems of archaeological interest (see Schiffer *et al.* 1978). Site survey has gained in appeal because it offers the potential to collect quantifiable data that can be used to test implications of models of local, regional, and cross-cultural systemic interactions in a developmental perspective.

Willey, in his pioneering work in the Viru Valley (Peru), defines the term *settlement pattern* as "the way in which man disposed himself over the landscape on which he lived" (1953:1). Sanders (1971a) defines *settlement pattern studies* as those studies that deal with population distribution in a geographical region and analysis of the factors responsible for such distribution. He later refined the concept by defining the factors responsible for settlement distribution. Significant factors include natural resources and social institutions. He suggests the existence of subtle systemic interrelationships between these factors serves to pattern settlement and site configurations in an area (Sanders 1971b:545).

Settlement archaeology is defined by Trigger (1967:151) as "the study of social relationships using archaeological data." He elaborates on this definition by directing inquiry in settlement archaeology toward the study of both synchronic and diachronic aspects of the social relationships of past human populations; that is, toward both structural and developmental diversity within social relationships. The study of settlement patterns, then, is directed toward the explication and explanation of "functioning systems of economic, political and effective relationships" within social groupings of people (Trigger 1967:151).

Rouse (1972b:96) defines *settlement pattern* as the "manner in which a people's cultural activities and social institutions are distributed over the landscape." His definition is similar to Trigger's, since both focus upon the problem of determining how and why populations make the decisions they do with respect to settlement location.

Goals of Settlement Pattern Studies

Diversity in the goals of settlement pattern studies can be eliminated through the application of the concepts of intensive and extensive goals. The former are concerned with characterizing and analyzing diversity within sites, whereas the latter are concerned with diversity among sites. As Parsons (1972:130) notes, Sanders' (1956) work provides useful definitions in this regard. Sanders distinguished between community settlement patterns and zonal settlement patterns. The former contain as units of analysis single settlements (communities), whereas the latter "are concerned with the distribution of community sizes, distances between communities, density of population, and the symbiotic interrelationship between communities" (Sanders 1956:116).

In a similar vein, Trigger (1967, 1968) suggests that distinctions should be made between levels of organization and analysis within the concept of settlement pattern. The tripartite division he advocates yields analysis of (a) microstructure, consisting of the individual household structures; (b) macrostructure, consisting of the local structure (or community); and (c) distribution of settlements in a region. This division is related directly to an understanding of cultural processes involved in any group's yearly activities. The existence of a

system of mutual causal relationships between various aspects of culture is basic to anthropological archaeology.

What we summarized from Sanders and Trigger forms the basis of our distinction between community analysis and settlement pattern–system analysis. We will discuss the goals of the latter here and those of the former in the next section.

Based on our assessment of the stated objectives of numerous settlement pattern analyses, there are at least five basic goals: (a) assessment of ecological variability and relative productive potential of the study area, (b) location of sites in a survey area, (c) classification of sites into analytically meaningful taxa, (d) assignment of temporal affiliation to sites, and (e) evaluation of functional differences among sites.

Of these five goals, the second has received more attention in the literature than all others combined, although the debate still rages over the utility and nonutility of certain site-survey techniques. The fourth goal, temporal assessment, can be accomplished only if diagnostic cultural–temporal lithic or ceramic indicators are present. Another problem is that we often are dealing with temporal periods that extend over several hundred or thousand years.

The classification of sites into analytically meaningful taxa is an often mishandled problem. Important variables in any site taxonomy include size, the presence or absence of architecture, topographic location, and so on. Each of these, and any in combination, represent adequate criteria for classifying sites into groups that can be manipulated meaningfully (Byland 1975:19). When attempts to draw fine distinctions between sites in terms of the variety of functions that were undertaken at each one are based only on survey data, a limited degree of success is likely. Fortunately, progress has been made in other methods, such as intensive, controlled surface collection (Lewarch and O'Brien 1981a; O'Brien and Lewarch 1981), that augment archaeological survey data.

The assessment of the ecological variability and productive potential of a study area usually is accomplished prior to survey and should be an integral part of the research strategy during stratification of the area to be sampled. The previous discussion of ecological concepts and their implications for developing a predictive model of the settlement system and material manifestations of locational strategies as patterned over the landscape is reiterated here. The more fine-grained the environmental assessment is, the more viable the model will be.

An Assessment of Problems in Settlement Pattern Studies

Given the general definitions and goals of settlement pattern studies previously discussed, our attention is turned to conceptual and methodological problems that have existed in the past, and still exist. As Parsons (1972:132) notes, American archaeologists in the mid-1960s realized some of the methodological and analytical limitations of concepts and definitions used in settlement pattern analysis. He states that one of the more significant contributions of this reassessment was the development of the *settlement system* concept, a refinement of Chang's (1962) *annual subsistence region.* Parsons (1972:132) speculates that Winters (1967) may have been the first American archaeologist to use the term formally. In a later publication, Winters (1969) distinguished between settlement pattern and settlement system. He defines *settlement pattern* as "the geographic and physiographic relationships of a contemporaneous group of sites within a single culture" and *settlement system* as "the functional relationships among the sites contained within the settlement pattern . . . the functional relationship among a contemporaneous group of sites within a single culture" (Winters 1969:110). To Winters, the limits of culture were defined by the distribution of distinctive stylistic traits (Parsons 1972:132).

Another problem that has been addressed is the slighting of ideological and social factors affecting settlement location and patterning. In accordance with his conception of "secondary factors" contributing toward the general settlement pattern, Sanders (1967) states: "This does not mean that secondary factors do not operate throughout the cause and effect relationship. We shall here attempt to isolate the primary factor and only incidentally discuss other determinants of settlement

patterns in our test areas" (p. 53). As settlement pattern–system analysis has progressed, this bias is being considered, and alternative considerations are being offered (e.g., Plog and Hill 1971).

Another problem still current in settlement pattern studies is that most descriptions and models of settlement patterns tend to be unidimensional. That is, one variable or class of variables is used as a structuring principle for a particular settlement pattern (e.g., adaptation to resources, location in terms of critical resources, diffusion, and migration). Models based on some or all of these considerations may be appropriate, but they tend to ignore important questions such as, "To what kinds of selective pressures does a population respond in structuring settlement and subsistence strategies?" In other words, the models do not deal with the implications of site function in a systemic context.

In addition, insufficient attention has been given to the problem of contemporaneity of sites for a single population. It seems reasonable to consider settlement patterns and other aspects of human behavior as a *series* of adaptive responses to different selective pressures of the environment. Such an approach requires fairly complete and accurate environmental reconstruction for a region and a workable chronology based in part on diagnostic artifacts and radiometric dates.

On the methodological side, there still are many problems to be worked out in meeting the goals of settlement pattern survey and analysis. Often, problems occur in assessing survey results when little or no control exists in the collection of data from sites. The lack of rigor causes errors to be compounded throughout the course of analysis. Objective assessment of relative occupational density is difficulty, and many times impossible. The lack of objectivity in this measure leads to significant problems in accurately determining variations in demographic patterns and accurately estimating population levels through time. Lewarch (n.d.:4) terms this the "house of cards effect," where each higher level of inference is built on an increasingly shakier methodological or theoretical base.

Parsons (1972:142–143) enumerates several weaknesses inherent in the method, applicable to any regional settlement pattern study. First, there is a lack of systematic control over site function. Second, there is an element of subjectivity in the acquisition of demographic data. Third, there is a general lack of sampling rigor at the site level. Fourth, chronological control is limited at best to 200–300-year blocks. Fifth, the paleoenvironment and productivity of the modern environment are known poorly.

Parsons suggests that the first three weaknesses can be overcome through the application of more systematic artifact collection procedures. Rectifying the problems inherent in the fourth and fifth points, he feels, would require the coordination of extensive programs of excavation within the context of a regional survey (see Redman 1973), a procedure that would greatly increase costs. Our goal has been to design techniques that adequately meet the explanatory goals for settlement pattern analysis and that approach solution of the first three problems enumerated by Parsons. Our view is that although there are inherent weaknesses in any settlement pattern analysis, it is still an efficient means of gathering and ordering data applicable to a host of problems, the solutions of which are directly pertinent to understanding culture variability and change.

COMMUNITY PATTERN ANALYSIS

Here we reexamine briefly the relationship between community pattern and settlement pattern analyses and summarize the rationale for separating the two. We present a few examples to illustrate how such analyses have contributed to the overall definition of a settlement system. One can think of a community as a microcosm of the region; indeed, as Parsons (1972:145) notes, it often is necessary to analyze the structure of single or multiple communities to gain better understanding of the range of variability in site structure and function. The term *community* is used here to refer to the way remnants of a particular social unit are distributed within a single site. These remnants include, for prehistoric people: houses, pits, hearths, tools, burials, and so on. For peoples of the historic period, these would include: roads, residences and outbuildings, fences, farm imple-

ments, hardware, ceramic and crockery vessels, and so on.

The analysis of community patterning, unlike the classic settlement pattern survey method, is an intensive exercise. The techniques used in this type of study are those familiar to every archaeologist—mapping, surface collection, and excavation by hand or machine. Of these, the most noticeable improvement has been made in surface collection, not only in technique, but in conceptual orientation as well (Lewarch and O'Brien 1981a). Although surface collection long has been employed as a standard field procedure for locating dense subsurface materials and for assessing, in a general sense, the nature and function of sites (cf. Binford *et al.* 1970; Redman 1973), only recently have surface materials been regarded as distinct data sets in their own right. Archaeologists have come to the conclusion that one of the most economical ways to characterize a site is through intensive, controlled surface collection. There have been many recent advances in collection strategies and applicable analytical techniques. What we term *community studies* have been done in many parts of the world, in diverse environments, and in many areas with various densities of ground cover (Lewarch and O'Brien 1981a). As we note elsewhere in this volume, many of these advances are a direct result of work in cultural resource management.

We cannot overemphasize the role of community analysis in a regional approach to archaeology. An excellent example of this approach is provided by Whallon and Kantman (1969), who investigated sedentary settlement in the Keban Reservoir area in east-central Turkey. They systematically collected 26 sites: (*a*) to define the occupation periods represented at each site, (*b*) to determine community size during each period, and (*c*) to determine the condition of strata pertaining to the occupations. Analysis of the collections permitted formulation of a settlement pattern model characteristic of each period in the area.

Perhaps the most impressive example of community pattern analysis ever undertaken is the work by Millon and Cowgill at Teotihuacan. As a result of many years of archaeological survey in the Valley of Mexico, settlement patterns for the different periods of occupation were proposed. As Parsons (1972:142–143) notes, the problem inherent in these surveys precluded a detailed understanding of the individual communities and how they were interrelated to the settlement system and the environment. To initiate a better understanding of community development during the Late Formative and Classic periods, Millon began a detailed analysis of the internal structure of Teotihuacan, the largest community in the Valley of Mexico during these periods (Millon *et al.* 1973).

Controlled surface collections within a 36.5 km² area that encompassed the urban center provided data that served as the basis for explaining urban growth and defining site function through the location of specialized activity areas (Cowgill 1974). The result of preliminary analysis involving sherd distributions was the generation of sherd density maps for each occupational phase at the site. Cowgill (1974:) states:

> It is also fair to say that our work has given us a far better basis for making such estimates [of population] than is the case for most archeological projects. . . . Although a sizable range of uncertainty remains in our quantitative estimates, they rest on a far better basis than is usual for survey data [p. 370].

DEVELOPMENT OF A RESEARCH STRATEGY

Struever, in his classic article entitled "Problems, methods and organization: A disparity in the growth of archeology," states that as "anthropological theory has advanced, new and exciting problems have been conceptualized for archeology" (Struever 1971b:131). He feels that the introduction of cultural ecology, systems theory, and evolutionary concepts has made the elucidation of cultural processes an operational problem and not simply a slogan. Despite the introduction of these concepts, and even though archaeologists have turned to processual studies of subsistence–settlement systems, research strategies seldom are planned and carried out "explicitly to maximize recovery of data pertinent to defining these systems" (Struever 1971b:136).

As has been documented many times, a multistage research design offers the best chances for maximizing recovery of data and coordinating the articulation of research objectives with field and analytical method and technique. Redman (1973:62) states that four steps should be used in structuring a research project: (*a*) explicit use of deductive and inductive reasoning in the formulation of a research design and in the later stages of analysis, (*b*) programmatic and analytic feedback between different stages of research, (*c*) explicit utilization of probability sampling, and (*d*) formulation of analytic techniques appropriate to the hypotheses and subject matter under study.

We have presented in previous sections our interpretations of various ecological and anthropological concepts as well as a summary that relates to broad interests in (*a*) defining settlement and community patterns, (*b*) examining the interaction between human groups and their environment, and (*c*) delineating changes in these interactive systems through time. Models of the development of prehistoric and historic settlement and subsistence patterns, derived from the various concepts and an analysis of the Holocene environment, are presented in Chapter 5. The summarized strategies we employed to generate data useful for testing the implications of the models, taken from Struever's (1971b) "ideal" research program, follow.

In a series of interrelated articles, Struever (1968, 1971a, b) outlined his research strategy for describing and explaining culture change in the Illinois River valley from terminal Early Woodland to Middle Woodland times. Previous work indicated that a shift to higher levels of social complexity had taken place during this time, leading Struever to hypothesize that significant changes in subsistence and social organization were adaptive responses to selective pressures. To test this hypothesis, Struever's task was to describe the subsistence and organizational basis of the earlier and later systems and to demonstrate how changes in the earlier system were responses to those pressures. As in any regional archaeological analysis, the key to understanding these changes was the reconstruction of a cultural system, especially its settlement systems through time.

To accomplish his objective, Struever formulated the following procedures. First, the paleoenvironment would be reconstructed, with delineation of significant microenvironmental zones (cf. Flannery 1968). Second, each microenvironment would be sampled systematically by surface survey to locate a representative sample of sites in each zone, assuming that loci of activities related to extraction of different resources would correlate with the distribution of those resources. Third, surface collections (although he did not specify intensive, systematic collections) would be analyzed to aid in assigning sites to certain temporal units and in identifying functional variability among sites. Fourth, a series of randomly spaced test pits would be placed over the surface of a site to sample the population of artifacts, features, and so on. These test pits would yield data regarding the depositional history of the site based on soil and cultural remains. Fifth, large-scale excavations would be carried out in areas of the site where activity loci were defined by test excavations. Sixth, large sections of the site would be exposed to provide a sufficient sample of artifacts in association with features so that sampling error would be kept at a minimum.

As Parsons (1972:135) points out, completion of these stages would allow description of the settlement systems, but not necessarily an *explanation* of the changes from one system into another or the processes by which a single system changes as an adaptive response to extrasystemic input. To explain these adequately, it would be necessary to subject adjacent regions to similar analyses to understand the selective pressures impinging on the cultural system in the Illinois River valley.

As was noted earlier, it is not necessarily the goal of regional analysis to explain detailed change in each social system to the degree suggested by Struever (i.e., the shift in subsistence and social organization from the end of the Early Woodland period to the Middle Woodland period). Such an undertaking could be well beyond the limits of time and money available. It is within its scope, however, to describe and offer explanation for overall change in a region like the Cannon Reservoir area and to integrate the findings with the work of others to add to the corpus of knowledge on particular subjects. It also is within the scope of regional analysis to use Struever's findings from the Illinois River valley to structure a portion of our research goals and hypotheses.

THE CANNON PROJECT RESEARCH STRATEGY

Basically, our field and analytic strategy mirrored that proposed by Struever, with a few refinements in method and technique. These procedures are examined in detail in appropriate sections of this volume and are only summarized here. First, the Holocene environment for the project area was modeled through reference to palynological and other types of studies done in regions peripheral to the Cannon Reservoir area. Data derived from General Land Office survey records from the project area were used to construct a baseline from which to compare the earlier record. The project area was then subdivided by both geographic subarea and drainage class (Chapter 3), resulting in the formation of 25 sampling strata. These strata reflect diverse floral resources that can be controlled for quantitatively using techniques discussed in Chapter 3.

Second, based on these strata, a 10% stratified random sample of the project area was surveyed. The size of each sample unit was 160 acres (65 ha). Depending on vegetation cover, a variety of standard survey procedures was employed. In addition, a purposive survey of low-lying land to be impacted directly by reservoir impoundment was initiated.

Third, a sample of sites from different strata was targeted for intensive, controlled surface collection. Sample size at these sites ranged from 50–100%. The standard procedure was to collect artifacts by exact provenience or, on sites where artifact density was high, to use aggregate provenience (4 m² units). These collection strategies allowed: (a) formulation of preliminary notions regarding specific site function and the distribution through space of functionally distinct types of sites, (b) the span of occupation at these sites, and (c) the distribution of artifact classes and clusters of artifact classes across the sites.

Fourth, based on preliminary analysis of site

survey and intensive surface collection data, sites were selected for excavation. Previous testing documented that the majority of sites in the project area contain shallow deposits (20–50 cm deep), although one deep, stratified site contained materials from the Dalton–Early Archaic period through the Late Woodland period and provided the basis for a regional chronology. Excavation of other sites, both by hand and machinery, yielded a set of data necessary to define community patterns and to indicate functions that took place in various areas of the sites. Through the use of machinery, we were able to remove the plow zone from a large area of a number of sites, uncovering an array of pits, houses, and other subsurface features. Analysis of materials in intact portions of these features has allowed intrasite as well as intersite comparison of functional variability.

Research in the historic period (ca. 1820–1920) diverged somewhat from this strategy, given the nature of the data base. These divergences included: (*a*) analysis of documentary data (land entries, census schedules, genealogies, histories, and county records), (*b*) mapping of nineteenth-century farmsteads, and (*c*) architectural analysis of extant structures to define variability in the form and function of structures.

In summary, our research strategy was to use every means at our disposal, given monetary and temporal constraints, to describe the settlement system (i.e., settlement patterns, community patterns, and patterns of resource exploitation) and to test certain hypotheses and propositions concerning the kind and degree of cultural change in the area. Struever (1971b:150) notes that limitations to such analysis result not so much from methodological barriers but from our inability to use effectively the methods and body of knowledge that exist. Summarizing the state of regional analysis at the beginning of the 1970s, Parsons (1972:134) noted that "needless to say, a research program of the scope outlined by Struever has never been carried out. At the moment its major utility lies in reminding us what our present programs lack and cannot yet achieve." Possibly the major utility of the Cannon Project, and others like it, lies in reminding us that attaining the goals of regional analysis may yet be within reach.

PART II

Environment and Predictions

The three chapters in this section present environmental and cultural background data on a series of models to structure research in Holocene dynamics. Chapter 3 summarizes the historical setting of the Cannon Reservoir region and presents a comprehensive model of the physical environment of the area. Physical variables are not the only determinants of human behavior, but rather are important parts of the human environment. In the case of the southern Prairie Peninsula, these variables acted in concert to effect broad changes in the landscape and ecology of the region.

The environmental model constructed in Chapter 3 is based on Euro-American observations over the past 150 years, and whereas it provides a context useful for analyzing nineteenth-century settlement systems, it lacks the depth to provide a context for analyzing systems that existed in the region throughout the course of the Holocene. Chapter 4 provides this context, summarizing the changing physical and social conditions of the project area and providing a framework for evaluating the effects of those changing conditions on local groups.

Based on discussions in the physical and cultural contexts during the Holocene, Chapter 5 evaluates the significance of these sets of variables. This evaluation is in terms of (*a*) settlement and subsistence practices of local populations and (*b*) theoretical expectations in terms appropriate to analyzing traces of human behavior in the Cannon Reservoir region. For these purposes, models of prehistoric and historic cultural evolution in the area are developed, and sets of implications are derived from the models that are testable using data drawn from research.

3

The Historical Setting

ROBERT E. WARREN

The Prairie Peninsula is a complex mosaic of tall-grass prairie and deciduous forest that stretches eastward from the Great Plains to central Indiana (Figure 3.1). Formed during early postglacial times by a unique set of climatic factors, the Prairie Peninsula is notable for its long history of environmental variability, which has helped influence human adaptation in the Prairie Peninsula during the past 10,000 years.

The Cannon Reservoir area lies on the southern margin of the Prairie Peninsula in a region characterized by grassy upland flats and forested valleys. In light of the general goals of the Cannon Project noted earlier, one important objective was the development of a comprehensive model of the region's physical environment. Although we do not believe that physical variables are necessarily the only determinants of human behavior, we cannot accept the opposite view that cultural systems are shaped entirely by internal forces. Rather, we assume that physical variables are important interactive parts of any human environment and that understanding these "man–land" interactions is a

necessary step toward understanding "man–man" interactions as well.

In this chapter we present a model of the historic environment of the Cannon Reservoir region. This model, composed of observations made during the past 165 years, is useful in two respects. First, it provides an image that is pertinent to interpreting Euro-American settlement in the region during the nineteenth century. Second, it serves as a modern baseline that can be projected backward through time. This projection, in conjunction with paleoenvironmental observations from elsewhere in the Midwest, allows one to estimate the effects of Holocene climatic change on the regional environment and thereby provides a general picture of the changing physical contexts of prehistoric societies in the study area.

CLIMATE

Local climates respond to a worldwide, integrated system of climatic mechanisms. These

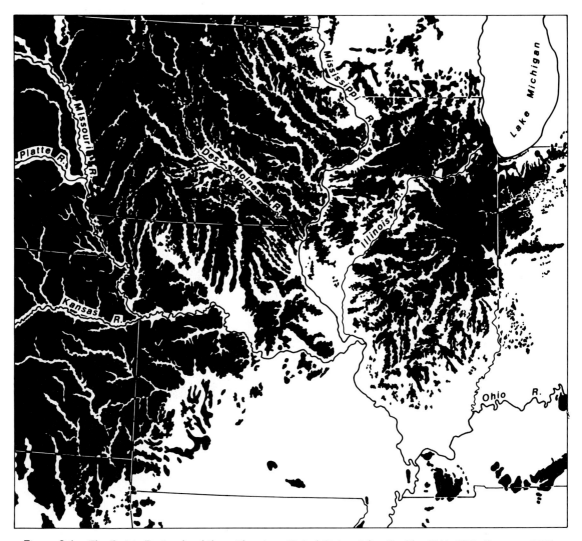

Figure 3.1. The Prairie Peninsula of the midwestern United States. (after Kuchler 1964, 1972; Transeau 1935).

mechanisms continuously adjust the earth's atmosphere to accommodate changes in the effects of solar energy and to account for the earth's complex distribution of oceans and landforms. Among the most important agents of climate and climatic change are differential patterns of air movement; these vary through time in distribution, temperature, moisture, direction, and strength.

Climates in the Prairie Peninsula are affected by four major streams of air (Borchert 1950; Bryson

1966): (*a*) cold, dry Canadian air that forms mean frontal zones along the northern edge of the Prairie Peninsula during winter; (*b*) cool dry Pacific westerlies from the northern Rocky Mountains that push across the Prairie Peninsula in winter due to a heightened equator-to-pole temperature gradient (Bryson and Murray 1977), but usually decrease in strength and abandon the Prairie Peninsula by midsummer; (*c*) a warm dry Pacific air mass, from the Great Basin and southern Rockies, that usually increases and decreases in strength in concordance with the cooler westerlies; and (*d*) relatively hot and moist air from the Gulf of Mexico that travels a year-round path across the southeastern United States. This air mass is weakest in winter, when its leading edge meets the strong Pacific air masses along the southern margin of the Prairie Peninsula. But as the westerlies subside, tropical air pushes farther west and north. By midsummer it flows over the eastern Plains and most of the eastern United States (including the Prairie Peninsula), meeting the Canadian air mass in a long frontal zone that stretches eastward from southern Manitoba to Newfoundland.

Borchert (1950) has shown how the varying seasonal effects of these airstreams give the Prairie Peninsula a distinctive climate. During winter, when strong westerlies drive a deep continental wedge between the Candian and Gulf air masses, the Midwest is relatively dry. To the northeast is a steep gradient of increasing snowfall, and to the southeast is a steep gradient of increasing winter rainfall. During summer, when tropical air pushes northward, mean precipitation is more uniform across the east. The prairies are again distinctive in that rainfall is more variable than in areas to the north and south. In contrast to the Great Lakes region, showers tend to come in shorter bursts, and there are longer dry intervals between rains.

The prairies also are distinguished by relatively frequent and severe droughts. When winter westerlies fail to subside in summer, the dryness typical of winter continues in the Midwest and often reaches critical proportions during July and August. Temperatures increase as well, and hot dry winds produce severe evaporative stress in a giant wedge coincident with the boundaries of the Prairie Peninsula.

The effects of these processes are reflected in weather records for northeastern Missouri. The area has a humid continental climate with warm summers and moisture throughout the year, but there is a great deal of seasonal variability, and each season has a distinct array of climatic features (Figure 3.2). Winters are usually cold and dry, with moderately strong westerly winds. Spring is progressively warmer and wetter, and winds peak in strength as the expanding Gulf air mass pushes

its interface with Pacific air across the region. Summers are normally hot, humid, and still. Mean rainfall peaks in May and June, prior to the temperature maxima for July and August, then drops off sharply before increasing again in September. This symmetric dip in late summer precipitation is common across the Prairie Peninsula, reflecting the frequency and timing of summer dry spells. Rainfall during a majority of years actually peaks in July (Borchert 1950:14), but late summer droughts are severe enough and occur often enough to deflate these monthly means. Autumn months are progressively cooler and drier, and increasing wind speeds reflect the resumption of dominant westerlies.

Variation above and below these seasonal means is an important characteristic of Prairie Peninsula climate; in fact, few years can be expected to approximate normal trends. Major drought years occur, on average, every 5 years (Borchert 1950), and major drought periods (i.e., sets of 3 or more consecutive years of below average precipitation) can be expected about every 20 years (Gribbin 1978). Effects of major droughts can be rapid and locally profound—influencing the cover, composition, and productivity of plants and the numbers or distributions of animals. By the end of the 1910–1914 dry period, thousands of oaks had perished along prairie–timber borders in Illinois (Transeau 1935) and were replaced by prairie grasses. During the 1930s, short-grass associations displaced tall grasses in Iowa and other prairie states, migrating downslope in hilly areas (Tomanek and Hulett 1970) and eastward among upland interfluves in the heart of the Prairie Peninsula (Borchert 1950). These shifts, controlled by local moisture regimes, begin to reverse themselves with the return of summer rains. Ground cover can be reestablished quickly, but several decades of moisture may be necessary to restore some grasses to their predrought proportions, and succession toward predrought compositions of plants can take much longer.

Several important points emerge from these observations. First, year-to-year variability in weather patterns must be viewed as an integral component of the modern Prairie Peninsula climate. Further, this variability has direct effects on local

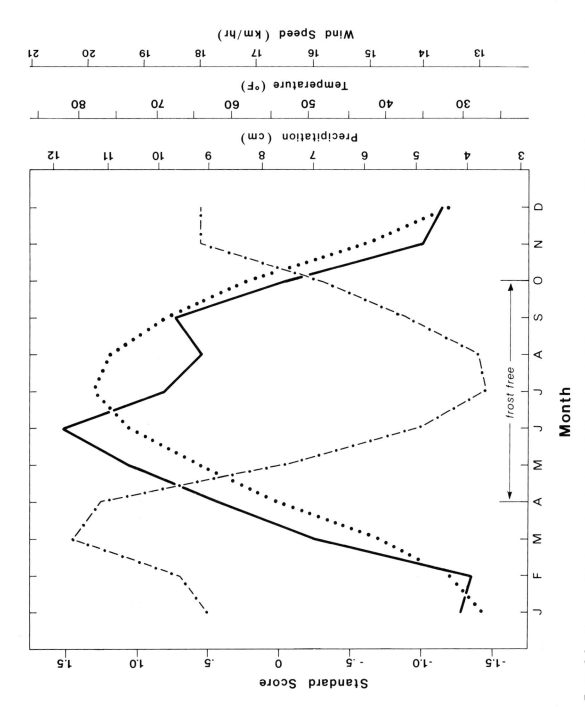

Figure 3.2. Mean monthly temperature (····) precipitation (—), and wind speeds (–·–) for northeastern Missouri; based on means of records for Quincy, IL (1941–1970), Kirksville, MO (1937–1966), and–or Columbia, MO (1931–1960). (Missouri Botanical Garden 1974.)

environments, usually keeping interfaces between floral communities in a constant state of flux. Second, this susceptibility to short-term change can be translated into long-term shifts, with even more profound environmental effects, when controlling air masses change position and stabilize in new configurations. Thus, the Prairie Peninsula climate, now delicately balanced between forest-like and steppe-like moisture conditions, can easily tilt one way or another with changing patterns of atmospheric circulation. These changes in turn can effect rapid transformations of plant and animal life—transformations of potentially great significance to human populations.

LANDFORMS

The bedrock surface of northeastern Missouri is composed of horizontally bedded limestones, sandstones, siltstones, and shales (Missouri Botanical Garden 1974). By late Tertiary times (about 1.8 million years ago) erosional processes had carved these deposits into a mature, hilly landscape drained by several major east-flowing and south-flowing streams. However, during the early Pleistocene, the first of a series of glaciers moved across the area, shearing off prominent hill tops, filling valleys with debris, and mantling the new ground surface with a level layer of drift. During the million years since glaciers last covered the area, erosion has incised many new valleys into the glacial plain. Several of these appear to follow the courses of older buried valleys, but large amounts of glacial drift remain, and the overall landscape is immature. Thus, broad upland flats are still a major feature of the area's physiography (Figure 3.3). Although most large streams follow meandering courses and are associated with well-developed terraces, bottomlands are generally flat or concave, and tributary valleys have youthful profiles with steep gradients. Signatures of Pleistocene glaciations are, then, quite evident on the modern landforms of northeastern Missouri.

Landforms in the Cannon Reservoir study area reflect these general trends. Flat uplands, which dip slightly toward the east at a rate of about 0.3 m/km, are preserved as level to gently sloping in-

terstream divides (Figure 3.4). Valley bottoms, also with level to gently sloping surfaces, vary greatly in width and orientation depending on the resistance and erosional history of underlying deposits. Between these two extremes are valley sides with moderate (3–10%) to steep (>10%) slopes. These slope classes are distributed widely across the project area; moderately sloping valley sides usually border upland flats, and steep valley sides often abut valley bottoms. However, steeper slopes are more common and more continuous in the northeastern portion of the region, whereas gentler valley sides are more extensive to the west and south.

These topographic patterns occur because local relief increases significantly as one moves downstream. Whereas extreme differences in local elevation range from 37–43 m where each of the four major tributaries of the Salt River enter the project area from the north, west, and south, relief is up to twice as great (73 m) in the northeastern corner of the region where the Salt makes its exit. Relatively steep valley sides not only occur more frequently along the lower Salt and its lateral tributaries, but they are quantitatively steeper there as well (Figure 3.3). Talus slopes greater than 45% are common, and vertical limestone cliffs often outcrop along the outer edge of modern stream meanders. These differences in terrain correlate with other environmental variables and have important implications for human land use. Rugged landscapes, for example, tend to buffer the evaporative effects of dry summer winds, offer better protection from winter storms, and issue forth greater numbers of freshwater and saline springs. They also tend to associate with shallow, rocky soils and place greater constraints on transportation networks and on appropriate locations for residential or other types of settlements.

Bottomland terraces in the project area have a complex and poorly understood history. They probably were formed during the last million years or so, after meltwaters from the retreating Kansan ice sheets scoured at least parts of the valley to bedrock and deposited large outwash boulders on floors of the incised channels (U.S. Army Corps of Engineers 1966). Following a rapid episode of alluvial deposition, it appears that several cycles of

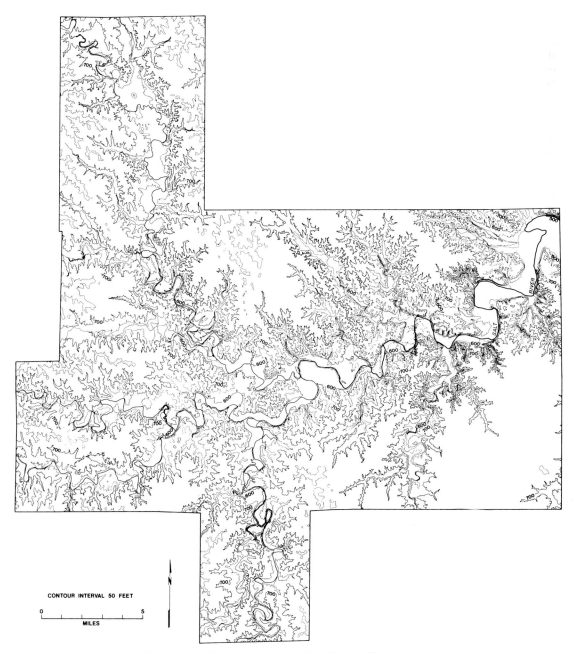

Figure 3.3. Topographic map of the Cannon Project area.

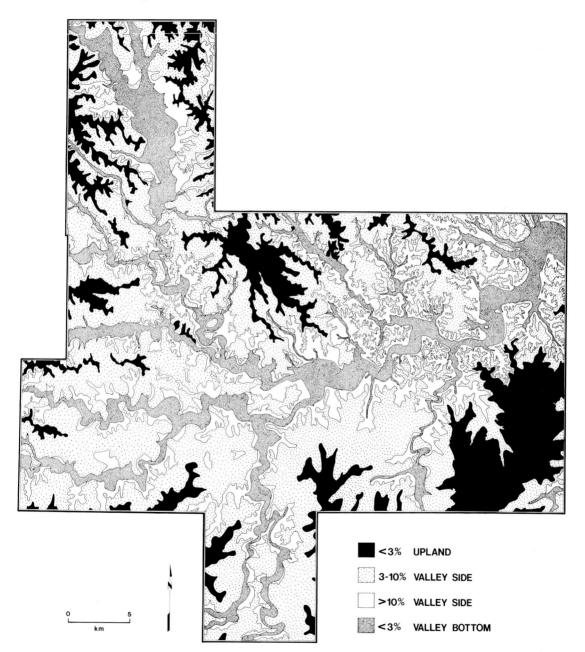

Figure 3.4. Slope map of the Cannon Project area (after Missouri Botanical Garden 1974).

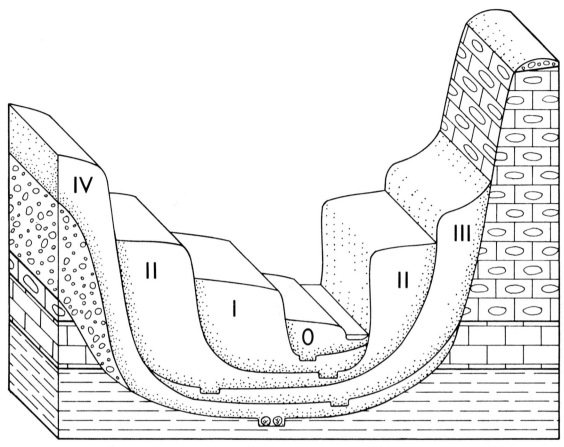

Figure 3.5. Idealized transverse section of bottomland terraces and modern flood plain deposits along the Salt River, showing hypothesized relationship between increasing terrace height (levels O–IV) and increasing terrace age.

stream incision and partial refilling occurred. An extensive program of geomorphological research, in which over 200 terraces were mapped, trenched, and/or cored, has led to recognition of four major Pleistocene cycles (Huxol 1980). Each cycle is represented by truncated remnants of former flood plains arranged in steplike fashion above modern streams (Figure 3.5).

Attempts to date these terraces have not succeeded yet, and stratigraphic and sedimentary analyses indicate that they are too homogeneous to allow meaningful ordering on the basis of internal structure. Terraces do sort into groups when their surface elevations are scaled against eleva-

tions of nearby major streams (Figure 3.6). Variability within these groups parallels that expressed by maximum elevations of active modern flood plains suggesting, in concert with sediment compositions, that the terraces are indeed remnants of extinct flood plains. Moreover, gaps between the elevation ranges of different groups tend to occur at consistent heights along streams, suggesting that each terrace group developed contemporaneously. Huxol (1980) proposed that the four major terrace levels observed along the Salt River and its larger tributaries represent synchronous periods of aggradation that were followed by episodes of down cutting and then partial refilling. If

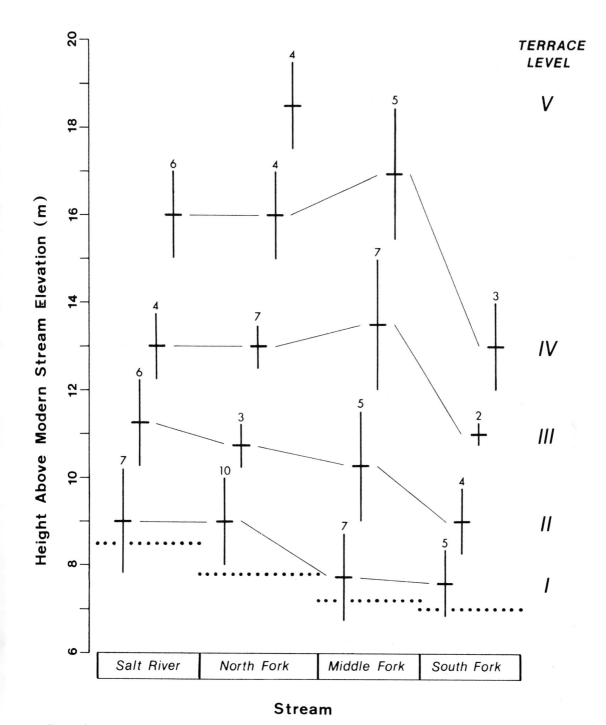

Figure 3.6. Mean heights (± 1 sd) above modern stream elevations of five terrace level classes (I–V), based on a sample of 89 terraces along four streams (see Huxol 1980:55–82). Arabic numbers denote sample size; dotted lines signify mean maximum heights of modern flood plain deposits.

so, heights of terrace groups should correlate monotonically with increasing age.

Without dates for the cycles of terrace formation and down cutting it is difficult to establish firm connections between geomorphic events in the Salt River valley and the Quaternary history of the Midwest. Reasoning, however, that: (a) the Mississippi River acts as a local base level for stream flow in the Salt Valley; (b) terrace levels in the basin probably reflect major fluctuations of discharge and sediment load in the Mississippi (cf. Brakenridge 1981); and (c) flow in the Mississippi was controlled by time-transgressive responses to periodic episodes of glacial outwash and changes in sea level (cf. Ruhe 1975:81), Huxol (1980) was able to narrow the range of possible associations. In light of work by Frye (1973) and others, he suggests that terrace level I may have developed during the later Woodfordian Stade (by about 13,000 B.P.), level II during the early Woodfordian or the late Farmdalian Interstade (about 23,000 B.P.), level III during the Altonian Stade (about 75,000 to 29,000 B.P.), and level IV during the early Sangamon Interglacial (about 300,000 B.P.). A fifth terrace level, recognized only along the North Fork (Figure 3.7), may date to the Illinoian Glacial (about 400,000 B.P.) or early Yarmouth Interglacial (about 1 million B.P.).

If correct, this model indicates that all terraces in the study area are middle to late Pleistocene in age. Other alluvial deposits, attributed by Huxol to the modern flood plain (i.e., periodically flooded surfaces less than 7–8.5 m above modern streams, which comprise about one-third the area of modern bottomlands), would date to the Twocreekan (12,800 to 11,500 B.P.) or Greatlakean (11,500 to 10,000 B.P.) substages of the terminal Pleistocene, or to the more recent Holocene period. The most rapid episode of alluviation may have occurred about 11,600 years ago when the Mississippi carried tremendous amounts of glacial meltwater to the Gulf (Emiliani 1980). Spring and summer floods along the Mississippi might have raised the local base level of the Salt, thereby decreasing its load capacity and increasing sedimentation. Holocene deposition rates probably fluctuated in response to changes in climate. A comparative study suggests that a period of widespread erosion began about 8000 B.P. in the Prairie Peninsula and was followed, about 3000 B.P., by a second episode of Holocene deposition (Bettis 1980). If these trends apply to the Cannon Reservoir region we should expect buried mid-Holocene flood plains along the Salt and its major tributaries. The higher terraces, situated above the reach of most modern floods, were probably relatively stable over the past 10,000 years.

Characteristic landform types in northeastern Missouri tend to cluster along an upland–lowland gradient of slope position. In any given locality these features can be grouped within a mutually exclusive series of land areas delimited precisely by contour elevation boundaries. Further, by establishing controls for interlocal variation of relief, slope position categories can be expanded to a regional scale with a comparable degree of precision. Five slope position categories, termed *drainage classes*, have been defined for the Cannon Project area (Warren 1976, 1979). Each drainage class correlates with a discrete set of landform types and with a number of other important environmental variables as well (Warren and O'Brien 1981). Together they partition the study area into a series of five ribbon-like zones that roughly parallel the courses of major streams or cap upland interstream divides (Figure 3.7).

Boundaries between drainage classes are composed of elevation contours that are redefined, from place to place, to account for changing river elevations and variation of maximum local relief (Figure 3.8). Drainage class 5, which includes all lands less than 20 feet (6.1 m) above mean elevations of major streams (MMStL), typically corresponds with flat to slightly sloping flood plains along major streams and lower tributaries. Its upper margin usually intersects risers of high bottomland terraces (Figure 3.9). Drainage class four occupies all areas above class 5 and less than 60 feet (18.3 m) above mean major stream level (i.e., 20–60 feet [6.1–18.3 m] AMMStL). It usually consists of level to moderately sloping bottomland terraces and sloping lower valley sides, rarely inundated by floods.

Drainage classes 3 through 1 occupy areas successively higher in elevation than the upper perimeter of class 4. But they differ from classes 5

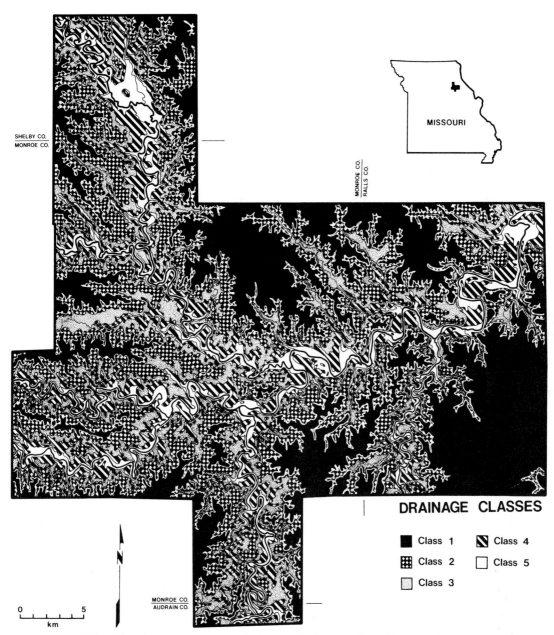

SHELBY CO.
MONROE CO.

MONROE CO.
RALLS CO.

MISSOURI

MONROE CO.
AUDRAIN CO.

0   5
km
N

DRAINAGE CLASSES

Class 1   Class 4
Class 2   Class 5
Class 3

Figure 3.7. Map of drainage classes in the Cannon Project area (from Warren and O'Brien 1981).

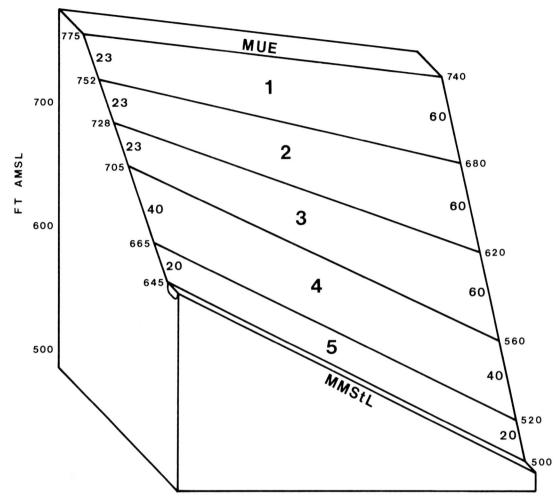

Figure 3.8. Idealized longitudinal section of the middle Salt River valley (looking northeast), showing relationships between drainage class intervals and downstream changes in river elevation (MMStL) and maximum local relief (MUE − MMStL). (From Warren and O'Brien 1981.)

and 4 in that their vertical intervals vary directly with downstream increases in maximum local relief (Figure 3.8). The two perimeters that separate the three classes divide the vertical relief above class 4, and below the maximum upland elevation (MUE), into three equal units. Thus, drainage class 3, which occupies middle valley sides with moderate to steep slopes, covers all areas above class 4 and below contours representing points one-third of the vertical distance between 60 feet

(18.3 m) AMMStL and the local MUE value. Class 2, lying above class 3 and below contours representing points ⅔ of the vertical distance between 60 feet (18.3 m) AMMStL and the local MUE, is generally composed of moderately sloping land along the upper margins of valley sides. Drainage class 1 includes all areas above class 2 and typically occupies level to slightly sloping upland flats.

In summary, the drainage class technique subdivides valleys into a series of precisely defined

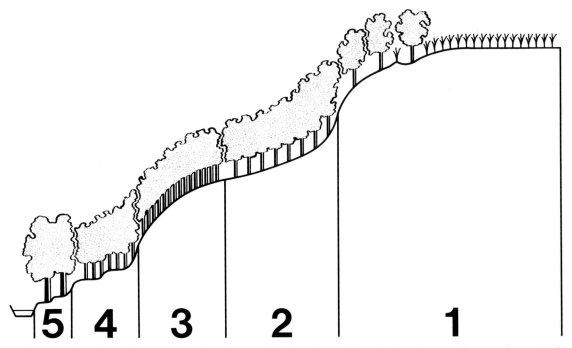

Figure 3.9. Idealized transverse section of the middle Salt River valley, showing drainage classes and associated floral and topographic characteristics (from Warren and O'Brien 1981).

slope position categories that form irregular linear bands running parallel to major streams. Classes generally contain distinct arrays of topographic features, and the technique is therefore a useful approach to landform classification in the Cannon Project study area. Furthermore, tests have shown that drainage classes significantly reflect patterned variation of dominant biome distributions, forest species compositions, tree diversities and densities, soil characteristics, and prehistoric and historic site locations (Warren and O'Brien 1981). Given this sensitivity to environmental and cultural variation, the technique has been used widely as a regional stratification device for a variety of studies in the Cannon Project area.

WATER

Water resources vary in location and magnitude across northeastern Missouri, reflecting local dif-

ferences in geomorphic structure and fluctuations of climatic patterns through time. Several kinds of water sources are important in the project area: surface drainage systems, surface impoundments, and subsurface aquifers. Quantities of water in all these sources are controlled directly by rainfall and evapotranspiration rates within the Salt River basin. Because moisture patterns in the Prairie Peninsula vary greatly between seasons and from one year to another, amounts of water in streams, lakes, and bedrock are also quite variable.

Surface drainages comprise the most extensive network of potential water sources in the area. Streams form a dendritic pattern in the central and eastern parts of the basin (Figure 3.10). Elsewhere they tend to flow north or south in trellis-like patterns, presumably due to erosion and stream capture along glacial incisions in the Kansan drift plain. Whatever the cause, the Salt River now has the largest catchment of any stream in northeastern Missouri. Furthermore, most of the Salt's

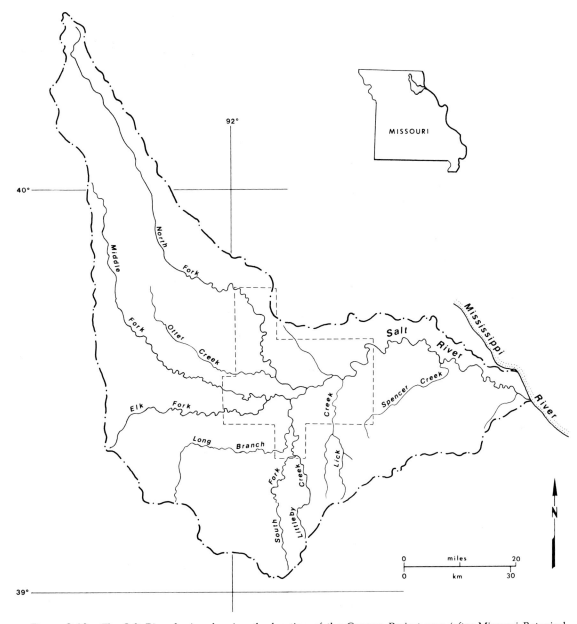

Figure 3.10. The Salt River basin, showing the location of the Cannon Project area (after Missouri Botanical Garden 1974).

major tributaries coalesce within the project area, and together they carry runoff from about 80% of the basin. Net stream discharge is relatively high within the project area, in comparison with the remainder of the drainage basin and with respect to northeastern Missouri as a whole.

Stream magnitudes also vary significantly within the project area, grading from small ephemeral tributaries in headwater ravines to perennial rivers associated with mature flood plains. In order to evaluate systematically this kind of variability, we have used the Strahler (1957) rank order technique, which assigns segments of streams to ordinal classes depending on the number of tributaries that enter them upstream (Weide and Weide 1973).

All headwater streams without tributaries are given a rank order of 1. When two first-order streams merge, a second-order stream is created, and so on. However, values change only at confluences of streams with identical ranks; juncture of a lower order stream with a higher order stream does not alter the rank of either stream.

The Salt River mainstream, originating at the confluence of Middle Fork and South Fork, is a seventh-order stream (Figure 3.11). Its five major tributaries (North Fork, Middle Fork, Elk Fork, Long Branch, and South Fork) are all rank orders 6 or 5. Progressively lower order streams increase in abundance at a geometric rate, but they are also of lesser magnitude. All fourth-order ($n = 11$) or larger streams flow all year long, as do most third-order streams (21/27), but very few second-order (13/127) or first-order (0/651) streams are perennial. Nonetheless, there are only a few places in the study area where water is more than 3 or 4 km away.

Stream flow variability exerts a strong influence on the local environment. High water can reshape land surfaces, restructure biotic interactions, and threaten man-made structures. Low water can cause stress among plants and animals dependent on streams for water or aquatic resources. As the climatic model presented earlier might lead us to expect, discharge of the Salt River varies significantly between seasons and from year to year. However, patterns of stream flow are not simple functions of rainfall or any other single climatic variable (compare Figures 3.2 and 3.12a). Peak stream flow occurs during April, when the Salt is on average about 1.8 m deeper than the annual mode. Rainfall is near the annual mean at this time, but rates of evaporation and transpiration are fairly low, ratios of runoff to infiltration are fairly high, and rates of ground water discharge are high due to warming spring temperatures. Thereafter, flow drops off abruptly toward an August low point, when rates of evapotranspiration and infiltration are both relatively high and there is a dip in late summer precipitation. Discharge is fairly constant through autumn and midwinter but rises during early spring, somewhat in anticipation of spring showers, due to snowmelt and surface thaw.

Times of abnormally high stream discharge generally parallel monthly means (Figure 3.12b). Major floods (30,000 cfs or 7.5 m above mean stream level) are most common during April, occurring about once every 10 years, and are quite rare during January. The probability of a major flood during any given year is about .42, but the effects of most are quite localized, and even record floods normally return to bank level in a matter of days.

Abnormally low discharge is common during late summer and autumn (Figure 3.12b). The relative smoothness of the low water curve indicates that the minor peaks that appear on the mean and high discharge curves for the months of July, September, and October are actually reflections of sporadic and infrequent flooding: Stream flow is more often low during these months. Stream flow is also low during periods of drought. During the dry 1930s the Salt River itself reportedly degenerated into a series of small pools, most of which were, as a local resident stated, "too shallow and hot to swim in."

Documented surface impoundments are uncommon in the project area. Several ponds were reported by early land surveyors and a few oxbows persist today along flood plains of major streams (Figure 3.13). Most are clustered in a few select localities, such as on wide bottomlands of the lower Salt and upper North Fork, and most are quite small. Certainly none approaches the size of large backwater lakes observed along the Mis-

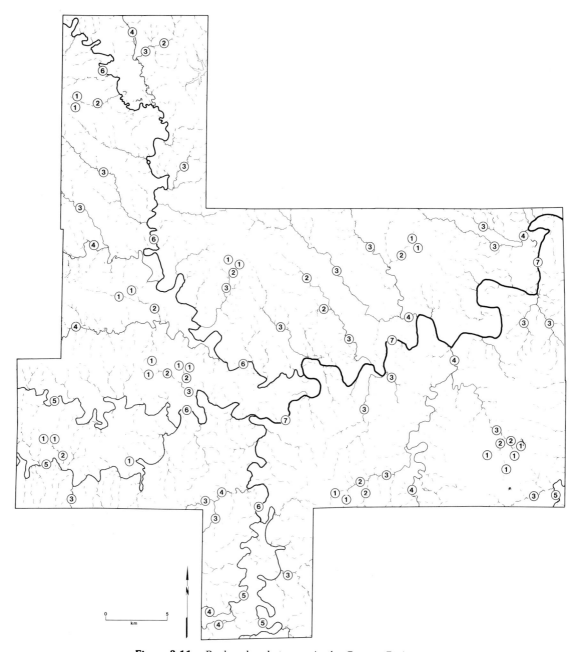

Figure 3.11. Rank-ordered streams in the Cannon Project area.

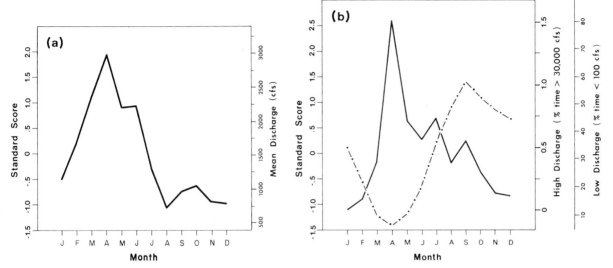

Figure 3.12. Stream-flow curves for the Salt River based on 49 years (1925–1973) of records 3.8 km upstream from dam site: (a) Mean monthly discharge; (b) monthly percentage of time river carries abnormally high discharge (—) (30,000 cfs) and low discharge (–·–·) (100 cfs). (Data from U.S. Army Corps of Engineers 1975.)

sissippi and Illinois rivers, and many probably shrank in size or dried up entirely during late summer dry spells or extended droughts. Nonetheless, even seasonal sloughs may have contained important subsistence resources in the Midwest (Limp and Reidhead 1979) and, despite the general concavity of the middle Salt River valley, they could have been locally important in the Cannon Project area.

Wetlands, documented in federal land survey and land sale records, occur in two distinct contexts: (a) low-lying bottomlands subject to annual flooding, and (b) level upland flats with poor surface drainage (Figure 3.13). Most of the former are composed of small and widely scattered segments of active flood plains, but one fairly broad area of wetlands is evident in the northeastern corner of the study area where the valley floor is notably wide and flat. Before the construction of artificial drainage networks, wet uplands were widespread in the Prairie Peninsula on flat, glaciated interstream divides (Winsor 1975). Here the combination of level terrain, impermeable claypan soils, and sparse networks of small streams often prevented rapid drainage of spring and early summer rains. Extensive but shallow and impermanent "lakes" commonly appeared on the upland prairies that often attracted large numbers of migrating waterfowl, established breeding grounds for noxious insects, and discouraged cultivation (Klippel and Maddox 1977). Several upland "swamps" are known from the project area, including rather large parts of the broad flat prairies east of North Fork and Lick Creek and smaller portions of the rolling prairies east and west of South Fork.

Freshwater springs occur widely in the project area. However, most perennial ones are concentrated in the northeastern part of the region along bluff bases of the Salt and its tributary streams (Figure 3.13). The terrain is relatively rough, and bedrock exposures below the water table are quite common. Spring discharge, ultimately regulated by rainfall patterns, normally fluctuates on a seasonal basis. Some springs flow more consistently than others, and a few were reportedly reliable and critically important water sources during the drought-stricken 1930s. Saltwater springs are relatively rare in the study area proper, but they attracted eighteenth-century French entrepreneurs just a few miles downstream.

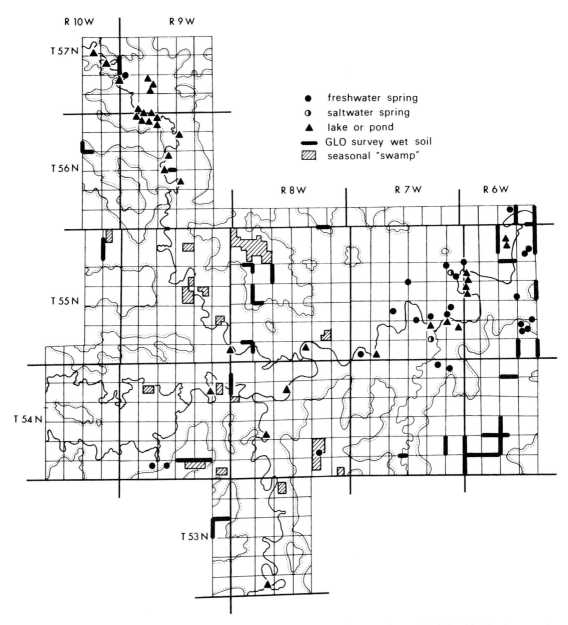

Figure 3.13. Historically known springs, lakes, and wetlands (data from GLO records, federal land-sales records, county atlases, and modern USGS topographic maps).

SOILS

Soils are formed, under the influence of topography, by long-term interactions of geological
substrates with climates and plant and animal life.
Soils are active components of functioning ecosystems that reflect the spatial variability of ecological processes and, at the same time, have varying degrees of suitability for different kinds of
human behavior. In this section we summarize
soil characteristics that were important to prehistoric and historic use of the Cannon Reservoir
region. We also discuss early historic perceptions
of soil quality as a framework for interpreting the
spatial patterning of frontier land purchases.

Five soil associations, defined as landscape
units containing discrete sets of similar soil types,
are recognized in the study area (Warren 1976; cf.
Watson 1979). These units tend to conform spatially to topographic slope positions, running in
bands parallel to streams or forming patches with
recurrent land form characteristics (Figure 3.14).
Similarities with distributions of drainage classes
are as real as they are apparent (Figure 3.7). Statistical tests show that soil associations covary significantly with drainage classes in Monroe and
Shelby counties (Warren and O'Brien 1981), the
only two counties for which modern soil surveys
were completed by 1979.

Soil associations I–III occur on valley sides and
interstream divides. The first, coincident with
drainage class 1, occupies level upland flats. Here
soils are deep silt loams with mature profiles. Developed in loess under a flora of prairie grasses,
they are naturally fertile and have moderately high
productivity ratings for modern row crops. However, they also are poorly drained; those on the
flattest landforms have dense claypan "B" horizons and are subject to seasonal ponding. Association II occurs downslope from I, usually along the
gently sloping margins of upland flats. These are
moderately well-drained loams and silt loams derived from loess and glacial till. They were formed
under prairie grasses or a transitional cover of
mixed grasses and trees, but are less suitable for
cultivation than soils in association I. The third
association occupies sloping valley sides. Soil tex-
tures here are quite variable, ranging from silty

clay loams to cherty silt loams. Most developed
under a forest cover in glacial till, and, although
they are well drained, agricultural productivity
generally is low.

Associations IV and V are formed of alluvial deposits in valley bottoms. Most soils in association
IV are loams or silt loams occurring on high level
terraces once covered by forests or prairies. Some
have surface drainage problems, but their productivity ratings are generally on a par with soils in
association I. Association V is composed of active
flood plain soils subject to seasonal inundation.
They follow the timbered courses of rivers and
some intermittent creeks and range in texture from
silty clays to fine sandy loams. Although often
poorly drained, soils in association V generally
have the highest agricultural productivities of any
in the region.

During the early nineteenth century, General
Land Office (GLO) surveyors laid out section corners and township and range lines across most of
northeastern Missouri. Following instructions by
the Surveyor General (see Dodds *et al.* 1943), field
notes contain a rich variety of information, including explicit references to soil qualities observed
along section boundaries. The project area was
surveyed between 1816 and 1822 by 10 different
survey teams, and soils were rated on all but a few
section lines. Most references are brief general descriptions, and not all surveyors phrased their ratings in the same terms. All seem to have had one
underlying variable in mind: the suitability of observed soils for frontier cultivation. Given this interpretation, all references can be classified within
a three-level ordinal ranking: (*a*) "rich" to "very
rich," "excellent" or "first rate" soils "fit for
cultivation," (*b*) "good" or "second rate" soils "fit
for cultivation," and (*c*) "poor" to "very poor,"
"thin" or "broken and rocky" or "third rate" soils
"not fit for cultivation."

A map of these soils evaluations (Figure 3.15)
shows a great deal of local continuity. Soils rated
"poor" are most common in the central and eastern portions of the study area where the terrain is
relatively rough. There are three general contexts
for poor soils: (*a*) sloping forested valley sides, (*b*)
poorly drained bottomlands, and (*c*) level or wet
upland prairies. Good and rich soils also occur in

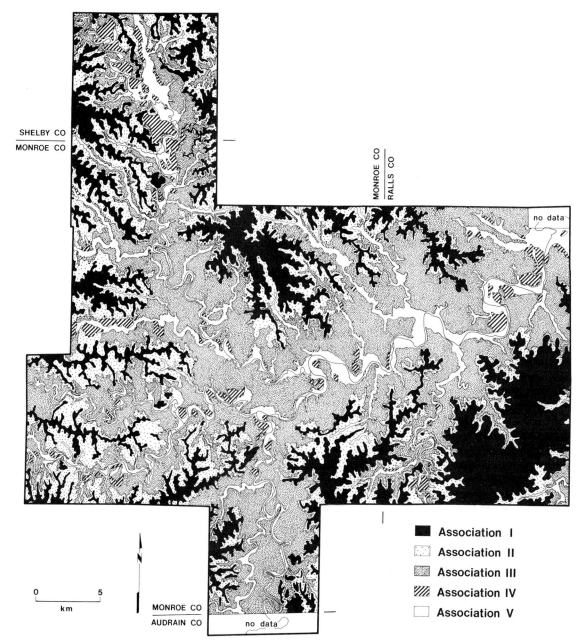

SHELBY CO
MONROE CO

MONROE CO
RALLS CO

no data

MONROE CO
AUDRAIN CO

no data

0   5
km

■ Association I
⠂ Association II
▦ Association III
▨ Association IV
□ Association V

Figure 3.14. Distribution of soil associations in the Cannon Project area.

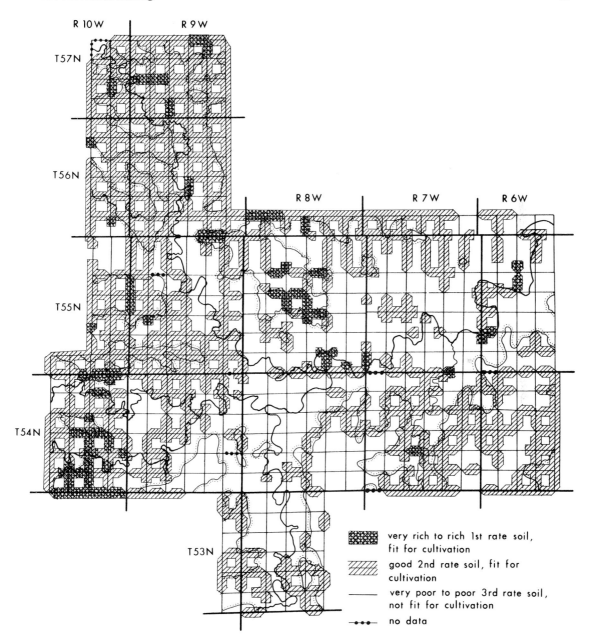

Figure 3.15. Map of soils evaluations by GLO surveyors (1816–1822).

central and eastern areas, but only on (*a*) high, well-drained bottomland terraces, (*b*) level upland forests, or (*c*) gently rolling uplands near the prairie–timber ecotone. To the west and north, where landscapes are much less rugged, high ratings are common in all but the steepest or wettest localities.

Several features of the GLO soils ratings are of interest here. First, we see only a rough correlation between their evaluations and modern ones based on soil fertility (see Chapter 15). Surveyors stressed readily observable characteristics, such as slope and wetness, and seem to have ignored the potential effects on productivity of artificial drainage or other landscape modification techniques. Second, there appears to have been no inherent devaluation of prairie soils by most surveyors unless they were level and wet. Although steel plows designed for efficient breaking of sod had not yet been invented, the potential agricultural value of rolling prairies was recognized. Third, there is a general correlation between soils rated "good" or "rich," and the distribution of hazelnut (*Corylus americana*) in forest undergrowth (see the following section). Thus, surveyors may well have used certain species of plants as indicators of soil quality.

FLORA

During the early nineteenth century and throughout much of the Holocene, the Prairie Peninsula was composed of a mosaic of deciduous forests and grasslands. Both communities were made up of distinct arrays of plants and animals, and each offered a different set of resources to prehistoric and historic human residents in the area. Attempts to understand the properties of the two communities are therefore of great interest to human ecologists.

Modern studies of Prairie Peninsula ecology are faced with many difficulties. The area is today most often referred to as an agricultural region, the "corn belt," rather than as a native floristic province. Consistent with this terminology, the original vegetation has been altered drastically by western economic pursuits. Most prairies have been replaced by extensive fields of corn, soybeans, and wheat. Many areas once forested also are now under cultivation, and most existing forests represent secondary regrowth on abandoned crop land or have been consistently logged, grazed, and protected from fires. Thus, the modern ecology of the Prairie Peninsula is of an entirely new order, and attempts to reconstruct native communities based solely on contemporary observations are hazardous at best (Bourdo 1956).

Fortunately, a wealth of pertinent information is contained in the preserved field notes of early GLO surveyors. These surveys, designed to systematically establish permanent section corners and to document resources of interest to western development, were conducted in the Cannon Reservoir region several years prior to colonial settlement (1816–1822). Included in the records are detailed plat maps that depict prairie–timber boundaries and descriptions of understory and overstory vegetation observed along section lines. Notes also document the common names, diameters, and distances and directions from corner posts of "bearing trees"—trees that were blazed to enable the relocation of section and quarter-section corners. These data enable the delimitation of prairie and forest communities and allow general studies of the compositions, diversities, densities, and resource potential of forests. Although biased in several ways (Warren 1976; Wood 1976), GLO records currently provide the best available information on presettlement vegetation patterns.

Prairie

Prairies orginally covered about 28% of the Cannon Project area (Figure 3.16). Most were restricted to upland contexts on broad, level interstream divides. A few occurred in bottomlands, most notably along the upper North Fork where upland ridges slope smoothly toward the valley floor, but bottomland prairies were nevertheless rare in comparison with larger river valleys elsewhere in the Prairie Peninsula (e.g., Zawacki and Hausfater 1969). Herbaceous species are not mentioned in GLO records, but prairies

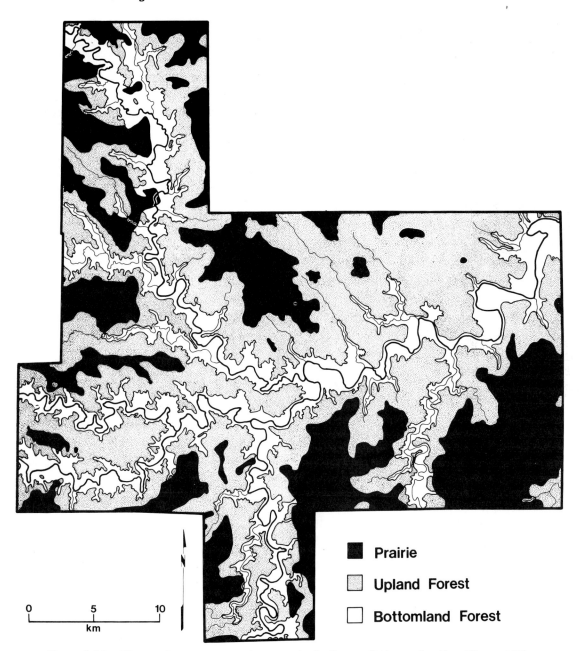

0   5   10
        km

■ Prairie

▨ Upland Forest

□ Bottomland Forest

Figure 3.16.   Nineteenth-century vegetation zones in the Cannon Project region (from Warren 1979).

probably were dominated by bluestem and other perennial grasses and a variety of sedges, legumes, and composites.

Three types of prairie can be distinguished in the study area. The first includes flat, seasonally ponded upland marshes underlain by impermeable subsoils. These areas, referred to as "wet prairies" by GLO surveyors and as "swamps" by later settlers, were ill-suited for agriculture prior to the adoption of drainage tiles to facilitate runoff and were avoided by Euro-Americans well into the nineteenth century (Bremer 1975). However, these "wet prairies" occasionally may have been important prehistorically by attracting waterfowl during spring migrations.

The second and most extensive type of prairie, occurring on rolling uplands and moderately sloping valley sides, was stereotypic of well-drained midwestern grasslands. Here edible floral resources probably were limited to the roots, shoots, and tubers of a small range of herbs, but a few species, such as the prairie turnip (Ockendon 1965), may have been abundant locally and considered valuable by hunter–gathers.

A third type of prairie, common on narrow strips of grassland in the northwestern part of the study area and near the prairie–timber ecotone elsewhere, contained a relatively diverse flora. Although dominated by herbaceous perennials, these areas also contained scattered trees and, in places, dense thickets of hazelnut, scrub oak, and grape vine. Most prairie trees were black oaks (*Quercus velutina*), a species comprising about 72% of the bearing tree sample ($n = 130$). Also represented were a few pin oaks (*Q. palustris*), white oaks (*Q. alba*), elms (*Ulmus* sp.), hickories (*Carya* sp.), and blackjack oaks (*Q. marilandica*). In open areas oaks usually develop broad crowns and may produce greater mast per individual than their forest-dwelling congenerics. However, prairie trees were extremely sparse in the project area. By applying the "closest individual" method of Cottam and Curtis (1956) to post-tree distances, we obtain a mean density of only 1.2 trees/ha. This is only about half the value ordinarily used to define the minimum density of oak barrens (Curtis 1959), suggesting that arboreal resources in Cannon Reservoir prairies were unproductive in comparison

with those documented in other sections of the Midwest (e.g., Zawacki and Hausfater 1969).

Forest

Prairie Peninsula forests are normally limited in distribution to the bottomlands and dissected valley walls of perennial streams. During the early nineteenth century, they covered about 72% of the Cannon Project region (Figure 3.16), dominating nearly all of drainage classes 3 through 5, ¾ of drainage class 2, and nearly one-third of class 1. They were most extensive in the northeastern portion of the project area, where relief is greatest, and tended to narrow upstream.

The sample of GLO bearing trees from forested parts of the region includes a total of 1955 trees located at 981 section and quarter-section corners, an average of about 2 trees per corner. Also available is a sample of 73 streamside witness trees used by surveyors to map positions of the right and left banks of the Salt River along a 22 km course in the northeastern part of the study area. Thirty distinct taxa are represented in the forest sample, including 26 distinguishable at the species level and 4 at the genus level.

A variety of approaches has been used to analyze vegetation data derived from GLO records. One inherent problem with the records is that datum points are widely spaced at half-mile intervals along section lines, and it is not possible to generate conventional tables that describe homogeneous *and* contiguous stands of trees. Thus, samples must be stratified for comparative analysis. Some botanists have used coarse-grained geographical strata, such as counties (Howell and Kucera 1956; Wuenscher and Valiunas 1967) or townships (Potzger *et al.* 1956). Others, more interested in fine-grained ecological relationships, have defined strata using landforms or soil variables (Delcourt and Delcourt 1974; Lindsey *et al.* 1965).

Our primary concern here is with intraregional variability of forests as a framework for understanding local resource differences within the Cannon Project area. Using a variant of direct gradient analysis (see Whittaker 1967), the Missouri Botanical Garden (1974) has shown that modern remnant

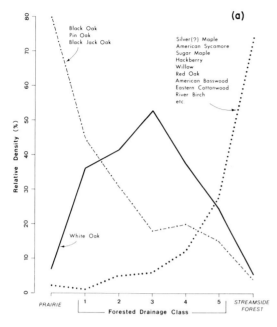

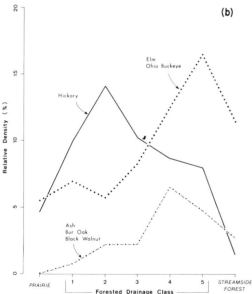

Figure 3.17. Relative densities of (a) three dominant modal groups and (b) three subdominant modal groups of important GLO taxa on a slope-position gradient.

forests in the region are sensitive to topographic variation along an upland–bottomland slope position gradient. Since drainage classes comprise a formalized sequence of slope positions that correlates strongly with available soils and landform data (see previous discussion), drainage classes were used to subdivide the sample of forest bearing trees into five units. Two additional samples, prairie bearing trees and trees reported from banks of the lower Salt River, were appended to opposite ends of the continuum.

Overall, presettlement forests in the study area were dominated by six major taxa: white oak, black oak, hickory, elm, pin oak, and sugar maple. Together, they comprise almost 90% of forest bearing trees (Table 3.1). Relative frequencies of these and other taxa are quite variable along the drainage class gradient. Summaries of these trends appear in Figure 3.17, which illustrates plots of relative densities of abundant GLO taxa (i.e., taxa with relative densities greater than 1% in at least one stratum) that have been consolidated into six *ecological groups* defined on the basis of shared modes (Whittaker 1975:127).

Group 1 accounts for most prairie trees and also dominates level to gently sloping upland forests (Figure 3.17). Included here are black oak—an early successional species tolerant of dry soils—and lesser numbers of pin oak and black jack oak. Hickory, the only taxon in group 2, is most abundant on moderately sloping margins of upland flats. Modern studies suggest that shagbark hickory (*C. ovata*) was probably the most locally important member of the genus (Missouri Botanical Garden 1974). White oak is the only species in group 3. It dominates in several drainage classes but favors steeply sloping land on middle valley sides. Group 4 is a relatively minor unit, subdominant on high bottomland terraces, which includes ash (*Fraxinus* sp.), bur oak (*Q. macrocarpa)*, and black walnut (*Juglans nigra*). Elm and Ohio buckeye (*Aesculus glabra*) peak on bottomland flood plains (group 5), whereas a great variety of taxa together dominate low, moist, streamside forests (group 6).

Close inspection of relative densities (Figure 3.17) implies that taxonomic richness tends to increase downslope along the drainage class gradient. To test this proposition, three measures of

TABLE 3.1.

Relative Densities of GLO Bearing Trees in the Cannon Project Region[a]

Taxon	Prairie (sample: 130)	Forested drainage class	
		1 (sample: 287)	2 (sample: 638)
Willow	-	-	-
Eastern cottonwood	.8	-	.2
Black walnut	-	-	1.1
Butternut	-	-	-
Walnut	-	-	.3
Black Hickory	-	-	-
Hickory	4.6	10.1	14.1
Eastern hop hornbeam	-	-	-
River birch	-	-	.6
White oak	6.9	36.2	41.7
Post oak	-	-	.5
Bur oak	-	-	-
Black jack oak	1.5	.7	-
Black oak	71.5	40.4	27.3
Pin oak	6.9	3.5	3.8
Northern red oak	1.5	-	1.3
Oak	-	-	-
Elm	5.4	7.0	5.8
Hackberry	-	-	.5
Red mulberry	-	-	.3
American sycamore	-	-	-
Serviceberry	-	-	-
Black cherry	.8	.7	-
Kentucky coffeetree	-	-	-
Honey locust	-	-	.2
Locust	-	.4	.3
Sugar maple	-	.4	.6
Silver (?) maple	-	-	-
Ohio buckeye	-	-	-
American basswood	-	-	.5
Black (?) gum	-	-	-
Blue ash	-	-	.2
Hoop ash	-	-	-
Ash	-	.7	.9

[a] Percentage of stratum.

species diversity were applied to GLO taxa. Results (Figure 3.18) show a monotonic increase of floral equitability (H is a measure of variance among relative densities) from prairies to streamside forests. Simple diversity d correlates directly with equitability ($r = .89$), despite moderate reversals at opposite ends of the continuum proba-

bly caused by sample size bias. A third variable, the Simpson index of dominance concentration (C is a measure of relative dominance among abundant species) correlates inversely with both diversity ($r = -.80$) and equitability ($r = -.95$), although a minor mode appears in drainage class 3 due to a predominance there of white oak. Over-

TABLE 3.1. (*continued*)

Forest drainage class			Streamside forest (sample: 73)
3 (sample: 488)	4 (sample: 329)	5 (sample: 213)	
–	–	.9	6.8
–	.6	3.8	4.1
.6	1.2	.9	–
.4	–	.9	–
.6	–	.5	1.4
–	.3	–	–
10.3	8.8	8.0	1.4
.2	–	–	–
.4	.9	1.4	2.7
53.1	38.6	24.4	5.5
.6	1.2	–	2.7
.2	1.5	1.4	–
.2	–	–	–
16.6	18.8	13.1	4.1
1.2	1.5	1.9	–
.8	.3	.5	5.5
–	–	.5	–
8.2	11.6	15.0	9.6
.4	1.2	5.6	9.6
.8	.3	.5	1.4
.2	.9	2.8	12.3
–	–	.5	–
.4	.3	–	–
–	–	.5	–
.4	.3	–	–
–	.3	–	1.4
1.6	3.7	6.1	9.6
–	.3	3.8	13.7
–	.9	1.4	1.4
1.0	2.4	2.4	4.1
.2	–	–	–
.2	.6	–	–
.4	.6	.5	–
.8	2.7	1.9	2.7

[a]Percentage of stratum.

all, the three measures indicate quite clearly that GLO taxa are progressively more diverse downslope from prairies and upland forests to timbered flood plains. Assuming that floral diversity correlates directly with levels of species dispersion and with levels of species diversity among faunal species (Margalef 1968; Whittaker 1972), we may conclude that terrestrial biota in the Cannon Reservoir region graded from aggregated and specialized forms in upland prairies to relatively dispersed and varied forms in flood plain forests. This does not necessarily mean that production of energy or biomass is greatest in bottomlands or that lowland forests, diverse as they are, contain relatively large

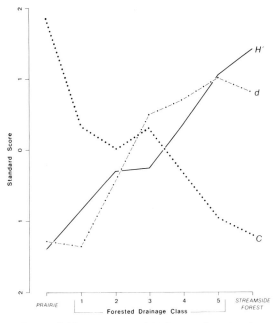

Figure 3.18. Variation of GLO taxon diversity along a slope-position gradient, plotted as standard scores of equitability (*H′*), simple diversity (*d*), and dominance concentration (*C*) (After Warren and Miskell 1981.)

decrease gradually into bottomland classes 4 and 5 (81% and 64% of maximum) and upland class 2 (71% of maximum) but drop off sharply into level upland forests and prairies (34% and 2% of maximum, respectively). Although resulting density estimates are probably only small fractions of actual values due to the bias of GLO surveyors against small trees (Bourdo 1956), results show clearly that forest densities varied a great deal in the study area and this variability was partially a function of landscape position and steepness of slope.

Application of stratum densities to individual taxa provides a more realistic image of species abundance than relative frequencies (Figure 3.19). Black oak, the proportional dominant of prairies and forested upland flats (Figure 3.17), is actually most dense in drainage class 2. Likewise, the mode for hickory shifts downslope and shows about equal densities for the genus in classes 2 and 3. White oak still peaks in drainage class 3, but its curve is more symmetrical. Incorporation of an admittedly small sample (*n* = 38) of trees-nearest-posts from the streamside forest data set indicates densities of most remaining major taxa increase toward riparian contexts at linear (elm) or expo-

amounts of resources useful to humans. Diversity of one kind may beget diversity of another, but diversity and productivity are not always directly correlated (Whittaker 1975), and humans are selective consumers of energy, nutrients, and technological resources. Thus, we must also consider absolute densities of forest taxa and translate those values into units of measurement relevant to human behavior.

Tree densities can be calculated from GLO records as an inverse function of distances between corner posts and bearing trees. Using the "closest individual" technique of Cottam and Curtis (1956) 1016 distances to trees-nearest-posts were (*a*) added to the radius of each nearest bearing tree, (*b*) stratified by biome and drainage class, (*c*) averaged, and (*d*) transformed into mean densities per stratum (see Warren 1976). Along the slope position gradient, these values form a unimodal bell-shaped curve peaking strongly on the steep valley sides of drainage class 3 (74 stems/ha). Densities

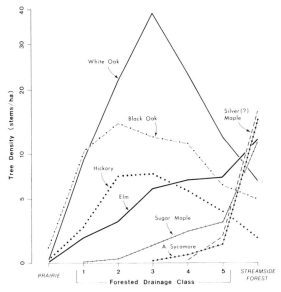

Figure 3.19. Absolute densities of selected GLO taxa along a slope-position gradient.

nential rates (silver maple, American sycamore, sugar maple).

Considered in geographic terms, the apparent correlation between forest density and ruggedness of terrain implies that: (*a*) forests were most dense in the northeastern portion of the project area and on sloping valley sides near major streams but (*b*) they were relatively sparse on dry upland interfluves and along the upper courses of small streams. Tests of these propositions should be illuminating since spatial variation of forest density has several interesting implications. First, since density is correlated inversely with the openness of the forest canopy and with the penetration of sunlight onto the forest floor, density variation across space should associate with distributions of understory flora adapted to varying degrees of shade tolerance (Whittaker 1975). Several species intolerant to shade, such as hazelnut and a variety of small native fruit trees, are known to have been important to prehistoric cultures in the Midwest (Ford 1977). Second, open woodlands generally contain proportionately greater amounts of biomass in the form of understory shrubs and herbs than do dense forests, thereby attracting important browsers, such as white-tailed deer and many other terrestrial or ground-nesting vertebrates seeking concealment in dense brush (King and Graham 1981). Third, sparsely timbered forests would be relatively easy to clear for cultivation. They may therefore have attracted early frontier settlers who required direct access to lumber and, at the same time, fields that could be rapidly prepared for planting (Warren *et al.* 1981). Fourth, high density forests are relatively mesic and insensitive to minor climatic change (Asch *et al.* 1972). Thus, predictable patches of sparse timber (i.e., patches that conform to dry physiographic contexts) may reflect areas sensitive to climate-induced fluctuations of the prairie–timber ecotone. On the other hand, anomalous patches of sparsely timbered forests (i.e., patches that transgress distinct zones of humidity) may signify local disturbance caused by fire.

In order to test the geographic implications of forest density variation and to evaluate any patterns that might occur in the Cannon Reservoir region, we generated a density map from GLO records using transformed distances between corner posts and trees-nearest-posts. One problem with this approach is that GLO records comprise an open lattice of datum points. Values for center points of sections ($n = 296$), a class of information not documented by GLO surveyors, therefore were interpolated using means of all available post-to-tree distances occurring along the four surrounding section lines. A second problem, less common in our GLO records, is missing data. Several corners occur in streams, and distances to bearing trees are either skewed or were not reported. A few others were simply not entered in surveyor logs. Missing values ($n = 12$) were estimated using means of all available "nearest distances" from the surrounding square-mile area. The resulting matrix, composed of 1147 distances, was then plotted and locally smoothed by substituting for each value the mean of its 9 or fewer nearest neighbors (i.e., those values occurring in the surrounding 1-mi^2 block). Smoothed distances were then transformed into densities ("closest individual" technique of Cottam and Curtis 1956), assigned Cartesian coordinates, and stored on tape at the Geographic Resources Center, University of Missouri–Columbia. Finally, prairie–timber boundaries and courses of major streams were digitized, and a spatial interpolation routine was used to project densities into between-point contexts.

A histogram of the results (Figure 3.20) shows a fairly smooth distribution, but one that is skewed strongly to the right due to the power function in the distance–density transformation. Values range from 3 to 521 stems/ha, signifying continuous variation from very sparse to very dense forests. The Cannon Project mean of 50.7 stems/ha, projected from a mean post-to-tree distance of 7.02 m, cannot be compared with results of most modern studies because of GLO surveyor bias toward large-stemmed bearing trees (Cannon Project minimum dbh [diameter at breast height] = 10.2 cm, modal dbh = 30.5 cm, mean dbh = 41.4 cm; see Warren 1976). However, estimates from other GLO samples indicate that the Cannon Project region as a whole was of moderately low density. Forests in the Black Belt region of western Alabama average 205 stems/ha (Jones and Patton

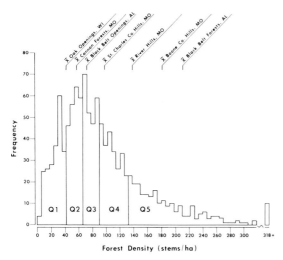

Figure 3.20. Histogram of GLO forest densities in the Cannon Reservoir region ($n = 1147$ interpolated and–or spatially smoothed data points), showing sample quintiles and comparative mean densities from Wisconsin (Cottam 1949), Missouri (Wuenscher and Valiunas 1967), and Alabama (Jones and Patton 1966).

1966). Mean densities range from 91 to 175 stems/ ha in a five-county area of dissected forests along the Missouri River in eastern Missouri, and average 132 stems/ha for the River Hills region as a whole (Wuenscher and Valiunas 1967). Closer to the Cannon Project mean are estimates of 35 stems/ha for disturbed oak openings in the prairie–forest border region of southwestern Wisconsin (Cottam 1949) and 65 stems/ha for oak–hickory openings on dry alkaline clay soils in Alabama's Black Belt (Jones and Patton 1966).

Despite these general trends, the histogram of locally smoothed values implies that up to 40% of Cannon Project forests were as dense as other more heavily timbered regions in the central and southeastern United States. This proposal is strongly supported by the Cannon Reservoir forest density map (Figure 3.21), which shows a notable degree of spatial aggregation among high-density datum points. Consistent with our expectations, the most extensive area of dense forest associates with heavily dissected terrain in the central and eastern sections of the region. Here, quintiles 4 and 5 form a nearly uninterrupted locus of dense

timber that spans the bottoms and steep valley sides of the Salt River and penetrates the lower reaches of its lateral tributaries. Upstream are smaller pockets of dense forest. Most of these also occur in dissected contexts, and they often are linked by strips of medium-density forest (quintile 3) that tend to parallel the courses of major streams.

In contrast, low-density forests (quintiles 1 and 2) occur consistently on gently sloping upland divides, often in association with small enclosed patches of upland prairie. They also are common along the upper reaches of small tributary streams and near the prairie–timber interface, where line descriptions by GLO surveyors often note areas of "thick brush" or "thin timber." In general, then, locations of high- and low-density forests are quite consistent with physiographic zonation in the Cannon Project region, and it is probably safe to conclude that major trends in nineteenth-century forest density variation are portrayed accurately in the density map.

Given this conclusion, attention should be focused on two rather anomalous patches of low-density forest that transect distinct physiographic zones. The first of these is a large ovoid area (6 km north–south by 5 km east–west) near the southwestern corner of the study area that projects northward from an upland prairie, crosses the lower Elk Fork, and terminates along north-facing slopes of the lower Middle Fork valley. The second, beginning about 3 miles east of the first, is a wedge-shaped area (5 km north–south by 6 km east–west) that extends eastward from a peninsula of upland prairie, crosses the South Fork, and intersects upland prairie on the east side of that river. Both areas are unique in that their datum points signify extensive quintile 1 forests, yet they cut across level uplands and steep valley sides in the same fashion. By way of contrast, valleys of the lower Middle Fork and Elk Fork are virtual mirror images of one another in terms of stream magnitude, topography, and soils, yet the band of medium- to high-density forest that parallels the former is not reflected along the Elk Fork. Consistent with the low-density definition are a number of GLO line description references to dense thickets in the forest understory. Many of these docu-

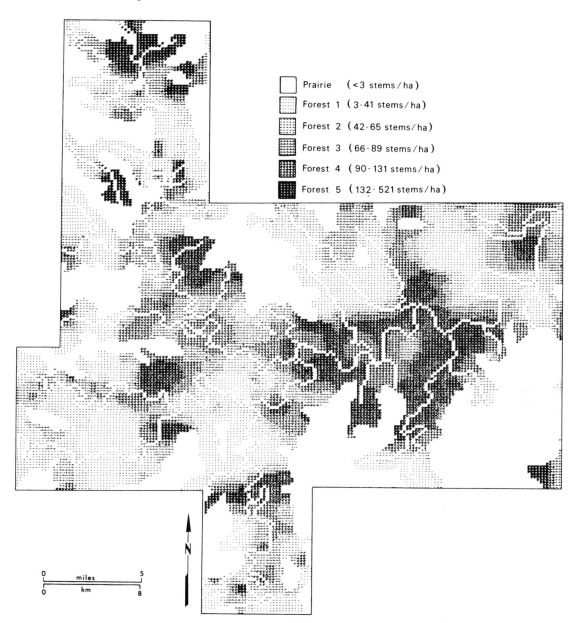

Figure 3.21. Early historic forest density, based on locally smoothed and transformed distance between corner posts and GLO bearing trees.

TABLE 3.2.

Potential Food Plants Reported in GLO Records[a]

Taxon	Resource	J	F	M	A	M	J	J	A	S	O	N	D	Yield per plant	Cyclicity (years)	Modal habitat (GLO records)
Sugar maple	Sap	X	X											10–15 gal	–	Bottomland forest
Silver(?) maple	Sap	X	X											5–7 gal	–	Bottomland forest
A. basswood	Sap, buds			X	X	X								–	–	Bottomland forest
Elm[b]	Cambium			X	X	X								–	–	Bottomland forest
Ash[c]	Cambium			X	X	X								–	–	Bottomland forest
Mulberry	Fruit						X	X						–	2–3	Valley side forest
Shadbush	Fruit						X	X						–	–	Bottomland forest
Greenbrier	Tuber						X	X	X					–	–	Forest understory
Plum	Fruit								X					–	annual	Ecotone
Cherry	Fruit								X	X				–	annual	Upland forest
Hazelnut	Nut								X	X				–	2–3	Ecotone, disturbed forest
Bur oak	Acorn								X	X				.25–1.5 bu	2–3	Bottomland forest
Black walnut	Nut									X	X			several bu	irregular	Bottomland forest
Butternut	Nut									X	X			.25–1.0 bu	2–3	Bottomland forest
Hickory[d]	Nut									X	X			1.5–2.0 bu	1–3	Upland forest
White oak	Acorn									X	X			.25–1.5 bu	4–10	Valley side forest
Black oak	Acorn									X	X			.25–1.5 bu	2–3	Prairie, upland forest
Red oak	Acorn									X	X			–	–	Bottomland forest
Paw paw	Fruit									X	X			–	–	Forest understory
Hawthorn	Fruit									X	X			–	–	Forest understory
Kentucky coffeetree	Seed									X	X			–	–	Bottomland forest
Honey locust	Seed									X	X			–	–	Valley side forest
Grape	Fruit									X	X			–	–	Ecotone, forest understory
Post oak	Acorn									X	X	X		–	–	Bottomland forest
Blackjack oak	Acorn									X	X	X		–	–	Ecotone, upland forest
Pin oak	Acorn									X	X	X		–	–	Prairie, upland forest
Hackberry	Fruit										X	X		–	most	Bottomland forest

[a] Data from Christenson et al. (1975), Geier (1975), Yarnell (1964), Zawacki and Hausfater (1969), Asch et al. (1972), Steyermark (1963).
[b] Data for American and slippery elm.
[c] Data for white and green ash.
[d] Data for shagbark, pignut, butternut, and mockernut hickory.

ment the presence of hazelnut, a shade-intolerant species normally found along the prairie–timber ecotone or in early successional phases of disturbed forests (Jones 1963; Mohlenbrock 1975). Together these data support an interpretation of open-canopy woodlands in both areas, perhaps caused by a runaway prairie fire not long before Euro-American settlement.

Of the 50 arboreal and herbaceous plant taxa recorded by GLO surveyors in the project area, 27 are known to have been used as food resources by American Indians, and several may also have been important to historic Euro-American settlers. These are listed in Table 3.2 by parts used, seasonal availability, cyclicity, yield per plant, and modal habitat. Nuts, fruits, and acorns comprise most of the documented plant resources, though the importance of maple sap should not be discounted. Sugar production played a major role in the settlement systems of several native groups (Yarnell 1964), and sugar maple groves near the damsite reportedly were tapped by local residents well into the present century. We emphasize that the list of food plants is far from complete. GLO records are biased heavily toward woody flora and do not record the great variety of herbaceous taxa important for their seeds, leaves, and roots.

Six taxa in Table 3.2 are suitable for estimating variability of floral resource productivity among environmental zones. Values were calculated by multiplying GLO taxon densities (stems/ha) by median yield over median cyclicity estimates, resulting in figures reflective of mean productivity across one average mast cycle. These estimates, scaled as resource volume/ha, are shown in Figure 3.22. Despite the dominance of white oak and black oak in most physiographic zones in the Cannon Reservoir region, the relatively low individual yields and wide mast intervals of these two species diminish their potential economic significance. In fact, these factors are of sufficient strength to cause hickory (a taxon that accounts for only 14% of this subsample of GLO bearing trees) to emerge as the greatest potential nut producer, accounting for 40% of nut yields in the region as a whole. Black oak comprises 34% of potential yields, white oak 21%, and the walnut–butternut complex (*Juglans* sp.) trails with only 4%. All four taxa

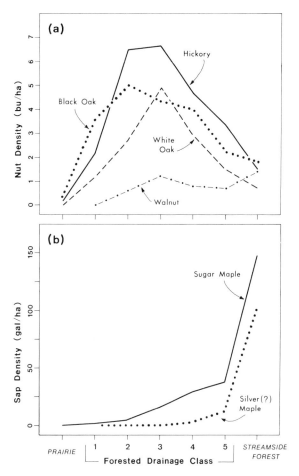

Figure 3.22. Yield estimates for selected (a) nut- and (b) sap-bearing trees along a slope-position gradient.

show modes on drainage classes 2 or 3, indicating that aggregate nut potential was much greater in sloping forested uplands and valley sides than in prairies, level upland forests, or forested bottomlands (Figure 3.22a). In contrast, estimates of maple sap productivity indicate far greater potential in bottomland contexts. Both species define J-shaped curves that peak strongly in riparian forests (Figure 3.22b).

These patterns show clearly that floral resources were not distributed evenly among physiographic zones and suggest that efficient collecting strategies would have focused on quite different con-

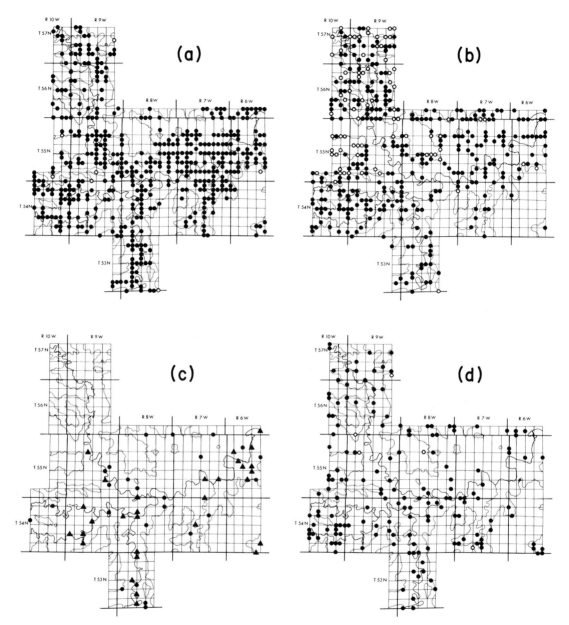

Figure 3.23. Geographic distributions of (a) white oak (*Quercus alba*), (b) black oak (*Quercus velutina*), (c) sugar maple (*Acer saccharum*) (denoted by ▲) and walnut (*Juglans* sp.) (denoted by ●), and (d) hickory (*Carya* sp.). In (a), (b), and (d), ● indicates forest bearing trees, and ○ signifies prairie bearing trees.

texts for extraction of nuts and sap. However, we have little reason to assume that floral compositions and resource densities were constant within drainage classes across the entire project area. As noted earlier, topographic relief and levels of effective moisture generally increase in the region from west to east. Since many plants are sensitive to moisture and slope gradients, we therefore might expect differential resource abundance from place to place. Maps of GLO bearing tree locations support this proposition (Figure 3.23). White oak, a relatively mesic species tolerant of steep slopes in the project area (Warren 1976), appears to be disproportionately abundant in the dense forests of the northeastern portion of the region and relatively sparse toward the west and north. Black oak, a more xeric species that is less tolerant of steep slopes, apparently increases in abundance from the southeast to the northwest. The hickory complex is dominated in the project area by species with intermediate moisture requirements and preferences for moderate slopes. This complex is distributed widely but seems to be most common in the south-central part of the area and least common toward the northeast. Walnut and sugar maple, both relatively mesic or hydric forms, apparently decrease in abundance toward the west and north. Contingency tables of frequency variation among sets of contiguous townships (not presented here) confirm these trends. There is a strong downstream progression of modes from black oak to hickory to white oak ($\chi^2 = 78.08$, df = 20, $p < .001$), and both walnut ($\chi^2 = 4.67$, df = 1, $p < .05$) and sugar maple ($\chi^2 = 6.67$, df = 1, $p < .01$) are, in comparison with aggregated frequencies for the white oak–hickory–black oak group, proportionately more abundant in the eastern half of the region (Ranges 6–8) than they are in the west (Ranges 9–10). Thus, it appears that arboreal resources generally were more abundant and more diverse downstream along the Salt River. Although all these taxa probably were available in most sections of the region, the differential quantities and nutritional qualities of their nuts and sap may well have made the central and eastern portions of the region more attractive to collectors of overstory resources.

Several recent paleoethnobotanical studies have shown that understory resources also were important to prehistoric hunter–gatherers in the Midwest (Ford 1977). One in particular, hazelnut, is of interest both because of its highly nutritious nuts (Asch *et al.* 1972) and its ecological implications. Precise information on the abundance and productivity of hazelnut is not available for the project area. The species was frequently mentioned in GLO understory line descriptions, and general trends in intraregional distribution can be inferred. As noted earlier, hazelnut is a shade-intolerant shrub generally believed to have been most common along the interface between prairie and forest. GLO data clearly support this idea (Figure 3.24a). Surveyor notations occur fairly consistently near the ecotone, and this is especially clear along northern and southern forest borders in the eastern half of the region. However, it is equally clear that mentions are more abundant toward the west and north than they are in the east, and this disparity is highlighted by an essentially complementary distribution of references to oak understory (Figure 3.24b). The narrowness of most western forests (1–4 km), and the correspondingly greater amount of forest edge, probably account for part of this trend. On the other hand, hazelnut also is common in several wide forests (7–10 km) along the North Fork and the lower Middle and Elk forks, but is quite rare in dissected terrain along the Salt River itself. Given (*a*) the species' intolerance of shade, (*b*) the fact that light penetration is low in dense closed-canopy forests, and (*c*) the predominance of dense forest in the central and eastern portions of the region (Figure 3.21), these anomalies probably reflect patches of sparse open-canopy woodlands, several of which may represent early successional stages of forests disturbed by fire.

Ecotone

Zones of transition between prairie and forest often were relatively narrow (3–10 m) in the central and southern Prairie Peninsula and were composed of slender contiguous bands of small trees (e.g., plum and hawthorn), shrubs (e.g., dogwood, hazelnut, and grape), and tall herbs (e.g., sunflower and goldenrod) (Shelford 1963). Plat

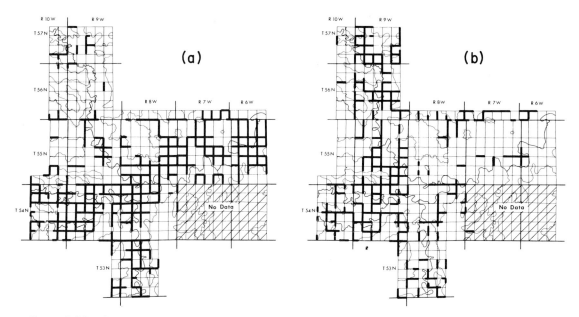

Figure 3.24. Geographic distributions of (a) oak (*Quercus* sp.) and (b) hazelnut (*Corylus americana*) in GLO line descriptions.

maps compiled by GLO surveyors imply that transitions in the Cannon Project region also were abrupt (Figure 4.2). This may well have been true in many localities, particularly where sharp topographic breaks occur along the margins of level uplands. However, several lines of evidence indicate that transitions in many other places were more gradual, perhaps reflecting forest invasion of prairie due to Neo-Boreal climatic changes (Chapter 4). First, trees in forested level uplands were less than half as dense as forests in general, and many upland forests enclosed isolated patches of prairie (Figure 3.21). Second, surveyor line descriptions indicate transitions themselves were sometimes diffuse and uncharacteristic of either prairie or timber. Several of these refer to intervening brushy zones dominated by hazelnut, plum (*Prunus* sp.), and black jack oak, and others note areas of mixed prairie and forest. Third, a number of gaps occur in mapped GLO prairie–timber boundaries (Figure 4.2). Although these gaps could merely represent incomplete portrayals of the ecotone, a striking number of them occur in localities containing soil series that are transitional

between soils developed under prairie and forest. Thus, it seems likely that many gaps signify areas in which zones of prairie–timber contact were fuzzy and difficult to map. Finally, as noted earlier, prairie trees were sufficiently common near forests that surveyors used them to mark section and quarter-section corners at nearly one-fifth of all prairie corners. In summary, these data suggest that characteristics of the prairie–timber ecotone were quite variable in the Cannon Project region. Transitions were apparently gradual in some areas, were composed of dense brush in others, and may have been relatively abrupt in the remainder.

FAUNA

Faunal resources were vital to prehistoric hunter–gathers in the Midwest and probably were of considerable importance to early Euro-American settlers as well. Evaluation of the diversity, abundance, distribution, and seasonal availability of these resources is therefore an important step in delineating the historic setting of the Cannon Project region. Animals are less tractable than plants, and there is no detailed nineteenth-century sample of faunal observations comparable to the floral information contained in GLO records. Furthermore, the habitats of many species have been altered or eliminated by western development, and the results of modern studies are at best hazardous guides to the past. Thus, our discussion of faunal resources is far less comprehensive than the topic deserves, and we must supplement data from the project area with information from a variety of sources.

Inventories of modern taxa, including one short-term study in the project area and many others in the greater Midwest, indicate that a variety of native forms still occur in the Cannon Reservoir region. These include about 30 species of freshwater mussels, 57 of fish, 15 of amphibians, 40 of reptiles, 170 of birds, and 47 of mammals (Missouri Botanical Garden 1974; R. D. Oesch, personal communication 1980). Of this total, only about one-third are common or abundant in the region today (Table 3.3). Many others, including a variety of secondary and tertiary producers that now are extirpated from the region or occur in limited numbers, formerly were more abundant and played important roles in the local ecosystem. In contrast, habitats of prairie–timber edge species, such as cottontail rabbit and white-tailed deer, have expanded due to land-clearing activities and the reduction of natural predators resulting in modern populations that are potentially larger than those of early historic times. Thus, modern census data are skewed strongly by modern environmental contexts, and estimates of primeval faunal composition and abundance must either be forgone or tempered with healthy margins of error.

Faced with these same problems in a study of the lower Illinois River valley, Styles (1978) used criteria developed by Jochim (1976) and others to estimate which species or sets of species would have been more or less useful and accessible to local prehistoric hunter–gathers. By synthesizing the results of floral reconstructions with studies of the niches, behavioral characteristics, and potential utilities of faunal resources, Styles ranked taxa along a scale of predicted economic value. Given the proximity of the Illinois River valley to the project region (ca. 100 km) and strong environmental parallels between the two area, Styles' rankings are of great interest to us.

Five highly productive taxa well suited for human exploitation emerge as "first line" resources in Styles' (1978) analysis. The first of these is white-tailed deer (*Odocoileus virginiana*), a large browser with high individual meat yields and a great deal of nonfood value as well (e.g., for hides, sinew, and workable bones). Early accounts indicate that deer were generally abundant in midwestern forests (Shelford 1963). Modern research suggests that groups were relatively large in comparison with other megafauna but had small home ranges and fairly low mobility (Schwartz and Schwartz 1981). Thus, deer comprised an attractive resource that was fairly predictable and available all year long. Accessibility probably was enhanced during autumn when herds aggregated to feed on upland acorn mast and also during winter when they often yarded during storms (Smith 1975). Wild turkeys (*Meleagris gallopavo*), characterized by fairly large body and clutch sizes, also were reportedly common in the Midwest (Shelford 1963). Groups of these large birds tend to aggregate in upland forests to feed on autumn acorn mast and would have been readily exploitable during winter flock formation. A third important species, raccoon (*Procyon lotor*), is relatively dense in bottomland forests. Meat yields and pelt values are both high, groups have relatively small home ranges, and the species is active and available all year long (Schwartz and Schwartz 1981). Accessibility may have been greatest during winter, when signs often facilitated tracking (Smith 1975).

The two remaining "first line" resource groups both are composed of multispecies taxonomic groups available only during certain seasons (Styles 1978). Because of its large sluggish channel and multitude of backwater lakes, the Illinois River was notable for its "unusually large and varied fish population" (Forbes and Richardson 1920) during the nineteenth and early twentieth centuries. In general terms, fish represented a massive, predictable, and highly renewable resource that was relatively easy to collect. This was especially true during spring spawning periods in

TABLE 3.3.

Selected Faunal Resources in the Cannon Project Region, Showing Primary Habitats and Hypothetical Seasons of Maximum Availability[a]

Taxon	Habitat[b]					Month[b]											
	Aquatic-riparian	Bottomland forest	Upland forest	Ecotone	Prairie	J	F	M	A	M	J	J	A	S	O	N	D
Freshwater mussels[c]	X					-	-	X	X	X	X	X	X	X	X	X	X
Fish[c]	X					X	X	X	X	X	X	X	X	X	X	X	X
Salamanders[c]	X	X				X	X	X	X	X	X	X	X	X	X	X	X
Frogs[c]	X	X	X			X	X	X	X	X	X	X	X	X	X	X	X
Aquatic turtles[c]	X					X	X	X	X	X	X	X	X	X	X	X	X
Three-toed box turtle		X	X	X		X	X	X	X	X	X	X	X	X	X	X	X
Ornate box turtle[c]				X	X	X	X	X	X	X	X	X	X	X	X	X	X
Lizards[c]		X	X			X	X	X	X	X	X	X	X	X	X	X	X
Snakes	X	X	X			X	X	X	X	X	X	X	X	X	X	X	X
Migratory waterfowl	X					X	X	X	-	-	-	-	-	X	X	X	X
Bobwhite[c]				X		X	X	X	-	-	-	-	X	X	X	X	X
Turkey[c]		X	X	X		X	X	X	-	-	-	-	X	X	X	X	X
Greater prairie chicken[d]					X	X	X	X	-	-	-	-	-	-	X	X	X
Passenger pigeon[d]		X	X	X		X	X	X	-	-	-	-	-	-	-	-	-
Opossum[c]		X	X	X		X	X	X	-	-	-	X	X	X	X	X	X
Shrews/moles[c]		X	X			X	X	X	X	X	X	X	X	X	X	X	X
Eastern cottontail[c]		X	X	X		X	X	-	-	-	-	-	-	-	X	X	X

Woodchuck[c]	X				X								–	–	X	X	X	X
Ground squirrels	X				X								–	–	X	X	X	X
Gray/Fox squirrels[c]	X		X		X								–	–	X	X	X	X
Plains pocket gopher	X			X	X					X	X	X	–	–	X	X	X	X
Beaver		X	X						X	X	X	X	X	X	–	X	X	X
Mice/rats[c]	X		X		X				X	X	X	X	X	X	X	X	X	X
Muskrat[c]	X				X			X	X	X	X	X	–	–	–	X	X	X
Coyote		X	X				X	X	X	X	X	X	–	–	–	X	X	X
Red/Gray foxes[c]	X		X		X		X	X	X	X	X	X	–	–	–	X	X	X
Wolves[d]	X		X		X		X	X	X	X	X	X	–	–	–	X	X	X
Raccoon[c]	X		X		X		X	X	X	X	X	X	–	–	–	X	X	X
Weasels	X	X	X		X		X	X	X	X	X	X	–	–	–	X	X	X
Badger	X				X		X	X	X	X	X	X	–	–	–	X	X	X
Striped skunk[c]	X	X	X	X	X		X	X	X	X	X	X	–	–	–	X	X	X
River otter		X	X				X	X	X	X	X	X	–	–	–	X	X	X
Bobcat[d]	X				X		X	X	X	–	–	–	–	–	–	X	X	X
Cougar[d]	X				X		X	X	X	–	–	–	–	–	–	X	X	X
Black bear[d]	X				X		X	X	X	–	–	–	–	–	–	X	X	X
White-tailed deer[c]	X		X		X		X	X	X	–	–	–	–	–	–	X	X	X
Wapiti[d]	X		X		X		X	X	X	–	–	–	–	–	–	–	–	–
Bison[d]		X	X				–	–	–	–	–	–	X	X	X	–	–	–

[a] Data from Missouri Botanical Garden (1974), Shelford (1963), Smith (1975), and Styles (1978).
[b] A blank space denotes habitat or month of inaccessibility; a dash denotes month of submaximal accessibility; an X denotes habitat or month of maximal accessibility.
[c] Taxon is common or abundant in region today.
[d] Taxon is extirpated or extinct.

flooded backwater lakes and also during summer and fall when lakes evaporated and trapped dense populations in small, shallow, readily harvestable locales (Limp and Reidhead 1979). Migratory waterfowl also were abundant seasonally and included a tremendous variety of ducks, geese, swans, and wading birds. Many of these are characterized by a relatively high meat yield and large clutch size, and huge flocks routinely made stopovers along the Mississippi and its major tributaries. A few species, including wood ducks and several large waders, ordinarily remained in many parts of the Midwest during summer, but peak densities occurred during spring and autumn.

In the lower Illinois River valley, then, five taxonomic groups stand out because of their potential returns of consistently high economic yields at relatively low costs of time and energy to hunters and gatherers. Given the proximity of the Cannon Project region, we might expect these same resources to have ranked as "first-line" foods in northeastern Missouri. With the possible exception of the three terrestrial species, however, this proposition probably is false. As noted earlier, the middle Salt River valley has a relatively narrow concave flood plain quite different from the wide convex flood plains of the Mississippi and Illinois rivers. As a result, backwater lakes in the Cannon Reservoir region are comparatively small and rare and could not have approached the productivity of backwaters to the east. Furthermore, distributional studies have shown that streams draining northern Missouri prairies generally support fewer species of fish than do other streams of comparable size (Pfleiger 1971), and abundance undoubtedly was lower in the Salt than in the Mississippi and Illinois rivers. Additionally, the Cannon Project region lies outside the main corridor of the Mississippi flyway, a major migration route for waterfowl, and stopovers are far less frequent or reliable on the Salt than along large north–south flowing rivers (Missouri Botanical Garden 1974). Thus, two potentially important taxonomic groups, fish and migratory waterfowl, probably could not have functioned as "first-line" foods in the middle Salt River valley. White-tailed deer, turkey, and raccoon, on the other hand, are much more likely to have provided yields comparable to unit areas of larger valleys. All are abundant today in the project area, and ample browse produced in relatively sparse nineteenth-century forests should have sustained fairly dense populations in the past. Nevertheless, absolute abundances of these and other forest-dwelling taxa, when measured as numbers of animals per unit length of river valley, probably were relatively low. The far greater breadths and diversities of habitats along major rivers undoubtedly could have supported larger and more closely packed populations of human hunter–gatherers than could have been supported along smaller, narrower tributary valleys such as that of the Salt River.

LITHIC RESOURCES

The erosion of Pleistocene drift has exposed a number of Paleozoic sedimentary formations in the project area (Figure 3.25). These include crystalline limestones of the Devonian series; siltstones, sandstones, shales, and fine limestones of the Kinderhookian series; crinoidal limestones of the Osagean series; cyclic deposits of sandstones, shales, limestones, and workable coal beds of the Marmaton and Cherokee groups; and siltstones and shales in channel fill deposits of the Pleasanton group (Branson 1944). Of interest here are the Burlington and Keokuk formations, members of the Osagean series that lie at or beneath the surface of most of the region. Both are massive limestone formations with a combined thickness of 45–60 m and contain abundant nodules of white to gray laminar chert. During prehistoric times, these cherts were used extensively in the region for the manufacture of stone tools, often after they had been intentionally heat-treated to improve flaking quality (Bleed and Meier 1980; Klippel 1970). Chert-bearing outcrops are common on steep bluff crests and upper talus slopes along major streams and the lower courses of smaller creeks. Residual nodules also are common in upland and bottomland creek beds, as are a variety of exotic pebbles eroded from glacial drifts that are suitable for controlled fracturing or grinding. Thus, lithic resources, although not ubiquitous in the region as a

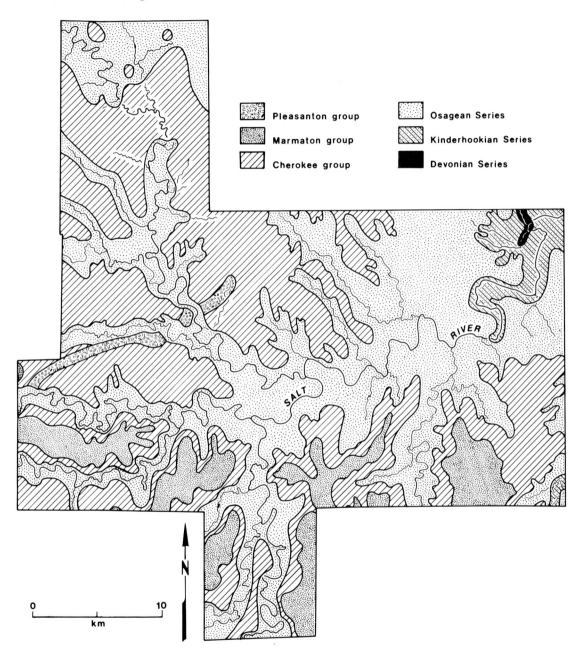

Figure 3.25. Distribution of major geologic groups and series (after McCracken 1961).

whole, are readily available in most dissected parts of the valley.

CONCLUSIONS

Information discussed in this chapter indicates quite clearly that the historic setting of the Cannon Project region was environmentally varied, both in time and from place to place. Three points deserve emphasis. First, climatic configurations in the southern Prairie Peninsula are susceptible to rapid and recurrent change, often causing short-term droughts that tend to check forest expansion and ensure the persistence of prairies. Second, the primary dimension of ecological variability within the region apparently is expressed along an upland–lowland gradient of slope position. This

model is supported strongly by distributions of landform types and major soil associations, by early historic and modern plant compositions, and by modern faunal distributions, hydrographic data, and outcrops of geologic formations. Thus, Cannon Reservoir microenvironments are viewed best as a series of narrow, parallel, contiguous bands that form concentric zones surrounding major streams and reflect increasing biotic diversity downslope. Third, variability also is expressed along an upstream gradient of decreasing topographic relief, increasing moisture stress, and decreasing proportions of mesophytic species. This trend probably is a general one that extends from the mouth of the Salt River to its headwaters, and it highlights the rather profound differences in resource abundance and diversity that serve to distinguish the Cannon Project region from the larger river valleys to the east.

4

Holocene Dynamics

ROBERT E. WARREN AND MICHAEL J. O'BRIEN

In the previous chapter a model of the historic environment of the project area was presented. Grounded in Euro-American observations over the past 150 years, the model provides an appropriate and useful context for the analysis of nineteenth-century settlement and subsistence practices in the region. However, human populations are known to have occupied the area for at least 10,000 years, and paleoenvironmental studies of the Prairie Peninsula document significant climatic change during that time. Moreover, archaeological research has revealed an equally impressive degree of prehistoric culture change in the Midwest. Thus, the historic model probably is not an accurate guide to the full spectrum of Holocene physical environments, and changing socioeconomic practices of nearby societies undoubtedly affected the behavior of prehistoric occupants of the Salt River valley. The objective of this chapter is to summarize the changing physical and social contexts of the project area and to thereby provide a framework for evaluating, in Chapter 5, the probable effects of those changes on local populations.

CLIMATIC CHANGE

Changes in regional climates are conditioned by a variety of factors, including topographic barriers to air flow and short-term screens from exposure to solar radiation. However, major causes of climatic change usually have worldwide effects since the atmosphere is an integrated system that reacts extensively to differential heat influx. In the Midwest we see an important expression of this principle on a seasonal basis. As the northern hemisphere cools during winter, equator-to-pole temperature differences increase and cause an expansion of mid-latitude westerlies. These air masses, dried by movement across the western Cordillera, deflate winter precipitation in the Prairie Peninsula, but they later yield to moist Gulf air as latitudinal temperature variation diminishes during spring and summer. Significantly, these same effects can occur over periods of hundreds or thousands of years with a year-round raising or lowering of north–south heat gradients.

Major climatic changes during the Pleistocene

THE CANNON RESERVOIR
HUMAN ECOLOGY PROJECT

also are attributable to variation of insolation, but over longer time periods and with more dramatic effects. As continents drifted poleward during the late Cenozoic, causing increased solar reflectivity in the northern hemisphere, cyclic changes in the earth's orbital geometry triggered fluctuations in the seasonal and latitudinal redistribution of solar energy (Hays *et al.* 1976; Imbrie and Imbrie 1979). During cold periods, winter snows failed to melt in summer, and massive ice sheets developed in northern latitudes. As noted in Chapter 3, several early Pleistocene glaciers expanded across the Cannon Project region, setting the stage for the predominant landforms seen in the area today.

During the last of the Pleistocene glaciations, when lobes of ice pushed southward into central Iowa and northeastern Illinois, a wide band of boreal forest stretched eastward from the Great Plains to the Atlantic coast (Wright 1971). In eastern Kansas and the Ozark Highland these forests were composed almost exclusively of spruce, while in southern Illinois they contained mixtures of spruce, oak, and herbaceous openings (Wright 1981). Spruce forests also dominated the upper half of northern Missouri, but they apparently were flanked on the south by mixed coniferous and deciduous communities containing spruce, birch, and maples (Frest and Fay 1980). The Cannon Reservoir region, which fell approximately on the interface between these two zones, probably supported a mixture of hardwoods and softwoods in which spruce was the major species.

When late Pleistocene temperatures rose and the long process of glacial melt accelerated, boreal plants and animals migrated northward, or became extinct, and were replaced by more diverse and temperate forms (Graham 1979). Early stages of this transition were nearly complete in western Missouri by 10,000 B.C. (King 1973), and change was well underway by this time in northwestern Iowa (Van Zant 1979) and central Illinois (J. King 1980). By 9000 B.C., when the earliest indisputable traces of human activity appear in the archaeological record of the Midwest, many sections of the midcontinent, including northeastern Missouri, probably were blanketed by a closed-canopy deciduous forest dominated by mesic species of oak, elm, ash, and hickory. Faunal communities included a vari-

ety of modern forms well within their historic ranges (e.g., deer, woodchuck, squirrels, pocket gopher), a few modern extralimital species (e.g., meadow vole), and several taxa facing imminent extinction (e.g., mastodon, ground sloth, peccary, moose) (Purdue and Styles 1980).

At about that same time, dry westerly winds began to flow across the Midwest with increasing strength and frequency (Webb and Bryson 1972). Remnant ice sheets still covered much of Canada (Bryson *et al.* 1970), heightening equator-to-pole temperature gradients, and Pacific air masses pushed prairie grasses eastward from the central Great Plains in a broad bisecting wedge (Wright 1976). The leading edge of this wedge passed through northeastern Missouri about 7000–8000 B.C. (Bernabo and Webb 1977). Grasses probably took control of drying upland flats in the region, while forests shrank toward relatively moist positions along stream courses and sloping valley sides.

During this prolonged dry period, usually referred to as the *Hypsithermal climatic episode* (Deevey and Flint 1957), westerlies apparently dominated midwestern weather patterns over progressively longer parts of the year. By 5000 B.C. moisture stress may have become quite severe. Prairies reached their maximum eastward extension at that time (Wright 1968), stretching significantly beyond their historic limits. In many localities they appear to have expanded downslope into contexts historically covered by forests, leading to increased rates of hillslope erosion and eolian deposition (Ahler 1973; Butzer 1977; Klippel 1971). Consistent with these interpretations are increased proportions of grassland mammals (bison, pronghorn, plains pocket mouse) in the western Ozark Highland (McMillan 1976) and higher incidences of prairie–timber-edge species (deer, cottontail) in historically forested localities of central Missouri (McMillan and Klippel 1981).

Furthermore, Purdue (1980) has demonstrated that body sizes of cottontails and gray squirrels from these same localities shifted significantly toward sizes that today occur farther west among their conspecifics. This suggests that climatic stress affected mammals that persisted in the Prairie Peninsula during the Hypsithermal as well as those whose ranges shifted eastward in response. Aquatic resources also were affected: Stream discharge decreased in Missouri and Illinois (Hill 1975; Klippel *et al.* 1978), lake levels dropped in Minnesota and Iowa (Brugman 1980; Van Zant 1979), and swamps became dessicated in bottomlands of the middle Mississippi Valley (King and Allen 1977). Together these data suggest that the middle Holocene was a period of severe and recurrent droughts in the Prairie Peninsula. Economically important components of early Holocene environments apparently persisted in many localities, particularly in major river valleys (Brown *et al.* 1977), but even there their quantities and proportions may have changed significantly (Butzer 1978).

Directions of these trends were reversed by about 3000 B.C. due to diminishing strengths of westerly winds and corresponding increases in effective moisture. Prairies began a slow westward retreat; forests reclaimed broken terrain; mammals shifted toward their pre-Hypsithermal sizes and distributions; upland soils tended to stabilize; and many streams, lakes, and springs were rejuvenated. However, moisture levels during the past 5000 years never matched those of early postglacial times (J. King 1980). Prairie grasses probably dominated the broad upland flats of northeastern Missouri throughout this later time period, while forests survived only along stream courses and on the sloping terrain of valley sides. Although relatively stable in comparison with earlier climatic regimes, fine-grained studies of the late Holocene document a series of climatic reversals that were of sufficient magnitude to affect some prehistoric economies in sensitive localities.

Following a relatively moist interval (3100–800 B.C.) during which forests expanded at the expense of prairie, a long period of somewhat drier conditions may have prevailed in the Prairie Peninsula (Figure 4.1). Precipitation "deteriorated" in the Great Plains during the Sub-Atlantic episode (Wendland 1978). However, summers were relatively cool and, after 250 B.C., moist in many parts of the Midwest (Baerreis *et al.* 1976). During the Scandic episode (A.D. 270–690), conditions are inferred as generally warmer and drier, a suggestion consistent with contemporary shifts in resource emphasis of prehistoric societies in central Illinois (King and Roper 1976). Warm temperatures proba-

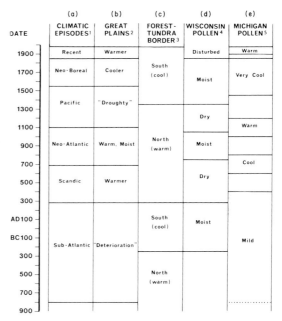

Figure 4.1. Late Holocene climatic patterns. Sources: (a) Wendland and Bryson 1974; (b) Wendland 1978; (c) Sorenson *et al.* 1971; (d) Swain 1978; (e) Bernabo 1981.

bly persisted during the Neo-Atlantic episode (A.D. 690–1100), but increased rainfall created a period of greater effective moisture. At the end of this episode a resurgence of westerlies created "droughty" conditions in the northern Plains and western Prairie Peninsula, which in some places effected a proportionate increase in the procurement of bison at the expense of deer (Bryson and Baerreis 1968). Warm temperatures in Michigan, comparable to those of the recent past, persisted until about A.D. 1300. Then, moister and much cooler conditions became widespread. Glaciers advanced in the Northwest (Denton and Karlen 1973) and in Europe (Lamb 1966), tree growth was affected in the Southwest (La Marche 1974), tundra displaced forest in Canada (Sorenson *et al.* 1971), and the Midwest was normally cool and wet (Fritts *et al.* 1979; Swain 1978). This episode, termed the Neo-Boreal or "Little Ice Age," persisted until the onset of warmer conditions during the late nineteenth century.

In summary, paleoenvironmental studies provide strong evidence that Holocene climatic change significantly affected regional environments in the Prairie Peninsula. Cool, moist episodes raised levels of effective precipitation, causing expansions of forests and increases in numbers of places capable of sustaining mesophytic species. Warm dry episodes reversed these effects. Moreover, it is possible to rank major segments of the Holocene on a gradient of effective moisture. The Hypsithermal (ca. 6500–3100 B.C.) was undoubtedly the driest and possibly the warmest of these periods; the early Holocene (ca. 8000–6500 B.C.) was relatively cool and moist; and the late Holocene (ca. 3100 B.C.–present) generally fell between these extremes. However, it is not yet possible to quantify Holocene climatic variation in northeastern Missouri or to outline in detail the effects of these changes on local plant and animal communities. Requisite to the former goal is a dynamic model of past weather patterns on a continental scale; the latter requires a comprehensive understanding of the effective niche requirements of a great variety of biological forms. Neither of these models is available. Nevertheless, we could significantly improve our understanding of Holocene dynamics by evaluating the local effects of climatic change during two different climatic regimes.

In 1976, Wood cautioned against the uncritical attachment of twentieth century weather records to floral data collected by General Land Office (GLO) surveyors during the early nineteenth century. Midwestern GLO surveys were conducted during the late Neo-Boreal episode, a well-documented period of cool and moist conditions much different from the relative warmth and dryness of the recent past (Figure 4.1). This constraint on the use of GLO records forces refinement of our projections into the past, but it also can provide insights into the magnitude of the effects of recent climatic change. By controlling for such variables as topography, soils, succession, and natural and artificial disturbance, comparisons of presettlement and modern flora from the same region should reveal differences arising from changes in climate. There are very few places in the Midwest suitable for such comparisons. Studies of this kind in northern Wisconsin document succesional differences caused by presettlement windthrows (Stearns

1949); nineteenth-century oak openings in southern Wisconsin reflect extensive encroachment of prairie into forest "niches" due to fire (Cottam 1949); changes in forest composition in central Missouri are attributable to selective cutting of marketable hardwoods (Wuenscher and Valiunas 1967); and most other studies of compositional change are (or would be) confounded by the historic effects of grazing, burning, or cutting of forests for agricultural purposes (Beilman and Brenner 1951; Auclair 1976).

Factors such as these also mitigate against floral comparisons in the Cannon Reservoir region (Missouri Botanical Garden 1974). However, edaphic traces of pre-Neo-Boreal biome distributions are sometimes contained in modern soil profiles. Analysis of soil development in Iowa shows that:

> The past 8000 yr of prairie environment has obliterated any imprint of pedogenesis under coniferous forest of late glacial time or under broadleaf forest of earlier Holocene time. . . . [However, a] climatic reversal during the past few thousand years has caused local expansion of forest on prairie resulting in formation of transitional or intergrade soils [Ruhe 1974:489–490].

Thus, if factors of disturbance can be assumed invariant through time, it is possible to contrast distributions of early nineteenth-century prairies and forests with soil traces of previous distributions. Results would provide a rough gauge of the relative impact of the Little Ice Age on vegetation cover, thereby establishing a minimal estimate of the magnitude of environmental change to be expected under similar degrees of climatic change at other times in the past.

Comparisons of GLO timber distributions with distributions of soils developed under forest or grassland often show significant discontinuities in the Midwest. In the northern Prairie Peninsula, where the prairie–timber interface is relatively diffuse and indeterminate (Davis 1977), presettlement prairie fires had pushed the ecotone well beyond the contacts between forest and grassland soils. Thus, modern studies document the reclamation of "well-developed forest soil" by timber, following the historic cessation of fires (Auclair and Cottam 1971; Cottam 1949:284). In the central and southern Prairie Peninsula, fires were apparently less fre-

Figure 4.2. Location of early-nineteenth-century prairie–forest ecotone in relation to distributions of soils developed under prairie, forest, and transitional flora.

quent or less effective (cf. King 1978). Overlays of GLO plat maps on modern soil maps show widespread encroachment of timber on prairie soils in Iowa (Loomis and McComb 1944; McComb and Riecken 1961), Illinois (Bailey *et al.* 1964), and Missouri (Howell and Kucera 1956). Significantly, transgressive forests "had not been present long enough or in thick enough stands to entirely change the soils to typical forest soils" (Fehrenbacher *et al.* 1968:169). This indicates that Neo-Boreal climates in the southern Prairie Peninsula were sufficiently cool and moist to expand the forest biome into former prairies, despite the possible counteracting effects of fire.

Trends in the Cannon Project region are consistent with other places in the southern Prairie Peninsula. Detailed soil maps are available for most of the project area, including all of Shelby and Monroe counties and most of Ralls County. All soil series are classified according to the predominant floral cover under which they developed (Watson 1979, and personal communication 1980). Prairie soils occupy about 38% of the region, covering extensive upland flats and smaller patches of high bottomland terraces (Figure 4.2). Forest soils (52% of the region) cover sloping valley sides and most bottomland terraces and flood plains. Sandwiched between these two zones are, in some places, transitional or intergrade soils (10% of region) that reflect diffuse ecotonal boundaries or unstable interfaces between prairie and timber (Ruhe 1974). Transitional soils generally form sinuous narrow bands that fringe the margins of level uplands, but they are relatively common and wide toward the west

where landforms are less rugged. Early historic timber covered 69% of that part of the region containing soils data; prairies (31% of the region) covered the remainder.

In comparison, the early historic prairie–timber boundary tends to parallel the line of contact between forest and grassland soils (Figure 4.2). A majority of transitional soils appears to be covered by timber. Trees also occupy grassland soils in several contexts, including three prominent but relatively narrow upland interfluves (i.e., east of Indian Creek, west of Lick Creek, and between Middle Fork and Elk Fork), most bottomland terraces, and the margins of upland flats. In order to quantify this apparent encroachment of forests, a series of 1742 systematically arranged points were crossclassified by GLO floral cover (prairie–timber) and biome of soil development (grassland–transitional–forest). Results show significant associations between timber flora and forest soils and between prairie flora and grassland soils (Table 4.1; $\chi^2 = 769.5$, df $= 2$, $p < .001$). Of greater interest here is the extent of early historic timber and prairie in relation to expected values predicted by proportions of soil types. If soils and floral cover are proportionately isomorphic, timber should cover 56.6% of the region (all forest soils and half of the transitional soils, or 986 of the 1742 classified points), and prairie should cover the remainder (43.4% of the region, or 756 points). In fact, timber comprises 69% of the region and is significantly overrepresented at an alpha of 0.001 ($\chi^2 = 116.2$, df $= 1$, $p < .001$). Three-fourths of all transitional soils and nearly one-third of all grassland soils are cov-

TABLE 4.1.

Crosstabulation of Presettlement Floral Cover on Biome of Soil Development

Biome of soil development	Presettlement flora		Total
	Timber	Prairie	
Forest soils	865	32	897
Transitional soils	135	42	177
Grassland soils	209	459	668
Total	1209	533	1742

ered by timber, whereas prairie occupies only 24% of the former and 4% of the latter.

In light of Ruhe's (1974) research and the late Holocene climatic sequence discussed earlier (Figure 4.1), we can postulate that biome distributions reflected in Cannon Project soils were probably more or less in place during the one or two millennia prior to the Neo-Boreal. If estimates of growing season temperature in Michigan (Bernabo 1981) and forest–tundra border movements in Canada (Sorenson *et al.* 1971) are reflective of long-term climatic variability in the central Midwest, conditions in the southern Prairie Peninsula probably were relatively stable in comparison with the Neo-Boreal and episodes preceding the Sub-Atlantic. During the interim, from 800 B.C. to A.D. 1500, temperature patterns cycle around means that are roughly comparable to those of the present century but may have been somewhat cooler or more moist. Had Euro-Americans not entered the region during the nineteenth century, we expect that the prairie–timber ecotone would today be retreating downslope toward zones of contact reflected in modern soil distributions.

During the Sub-Boreal climatic episode (3100–800 B.C.; Figure 6.1), when prairies shifted slowly westward after the Hypsithermal maximum, forests probably were rebounding and becoming more mesophytic in the Cannon Project region. The Hypsithermal itself appears to have been a period of maximum moisture stress. Prairies probably expanded well beyond the limits of 'grassland reflected in modern soil distributions, perhaps capturing most gently sloping valley sides and high bottomland terraces. Assuming early nineteenth-century forest densities (Figures 3.19, 3.20) are an accurate guide to relative densities in the past, timber during the Hypsithermal probably formed narrow galleries along the courses of tributary streams and was most extensive in the east-central portion of the region where terrain is relatively rugged. Mesophytic species could have persisted in streamside forests, and more xerophytic species of oak and hickory probably had suitable sites on protected hillslopes. Thus, resources from the full range of modern forest species would have been available, but the abundance and distribution of those resources were probably reduced and highly localized (King and Graham 1981; cf. Asch *et al.* 1972). Prior to the Hypsithermal, during the Boreal (7400–6500 B.C.) and Pre-Boreal (8100–7400 B.C.) episodes, prairies were expanding rapidly eastward across the Prairie Peninsula (Bernabo and Webb 1977). Forests may have blanketed the region during the early part of this sequence, but they probably began retreating toward their modern contexts by about 7500 B.C.

CULTURE CHANGE

Remains of prehistoric societies in the midwestern and eastern United States span a period of at least 12,000 years and range from small, simple hunting-and-gathering encampments to large, complex communities whose residents wielded influence over broad areas. To facilitate our understanding of this diverse array of cultural remains, archaeologists segregate information into generalized units that are distinguished on the basis of age, spatial distributions, and–or cultural content. Problems often arise when any two or three of these dimensions are synthesized because prehistoric culture change in the Eastern Woodlands was not always synchronous or panregional (Stoltman 1978). For this reason, our summary of prehistoric and historic sequences will focus on the central Mississippi River valley and will order cultural observations within a series of seven temporal periods. Although these periods are labeled with content-laden terms, it must be emphasized that trends in the central Midwest do not always reflect sequences elsewhere, and significant variation may also exist within our area of primary concern.

Late Pleistocene Hunters

The Paleo-Indian period in the Midwest dates from about 10,000 B.C. to 8000 B.C. Although most evidence of occupation during this period is limited to surface-collected artifacts, intact associations of diagnostic projectile points with extinct megafauna indicate that large game animals were a significant component of late Pleistocene subsistence economies. Excavated kill sites and butchering stations are scattered from the Plains to the Atlantic Seaboard and usually contain elements of bison or mammoth. Purported associations with mastodon were recently confirmed in the St. Louis area, where lanceolate fluted spear points, probably dating to the tenth millennium B.C., were found among the bones of slain animals (Graham *et al.* 1981). Although few habitation sites have been excavated and analyzed in detail, most observers believe that Paleo-Indian populations were composed of small familial bands that occupied temporary hunting and gathering encampments and roamed nomadically in pursuit of a limited range of resources.

Mobile Hunter–Gatherers

Early and middle Holocene hunter–gatherers focused on modern floral and faunal species. Two cultural periods are generally recognized in the Midwest. The Early Archaic period dates from 8000 B.C. to 6000 B.C. The beginning of the period correlates with stylistic changes in diagnostic artifacts, apparent increases in population density, environmental changes associated with glacial retreat, the disappearance of several species of large game animals, and changes in subsistence strategies. Interacting social groups apparently still were small and mobile and presumably still were linked by familial bonds. Most sites seem to represent temporary encampments situated in diverse contexts. Many appear in upland locales, often near small ephemeral streams in areas dominated historically by grassland flora (Klippel and Maddox 1977). Others are found in rock shelters (Klippel 1971) or on abandoned terraces of major streams (Joyer and Roper 1980). Whether these distinctive situations correspond to seasonal shifts in settlements (Fowler 1959) or to aseasonal activity centers with varied functions (Morse 1973) is still a matter of debate.

The Middle Archaic period, dating from about 6000 B.C. to 3000 B.C., brackets cultural complexes that seem to have shifted their economic orientation toward local forest and riverine resources. A broader spectrum of fauna was exploited, along with high-yield nut resources and some wild seeds (Ford 1977). Grinding stones constitute a significant component of artifact assemblages for the first time, perhaps reflecting a relatively greater reliance

on vegetal foods (Brown *et al.* 1977). Recent evidence suggests that exotic cultigens may have been introduced during this period. Maize pollen is reported from deposits at the Koster site (lower Illinois River valley) that date to 3500–3000 B.C. (Schoenwetter 1979), and carbonized maize fragments have been discovered in flotation samples from even earlier occupation levels at the site. However, both occurrences may be due to contamination from later occupations (Asch and Asch 1980), and the economic importance of domesticates to Middle Archaic peoples is far from clear. Consistent with the notion of more localized resource exploitation and increased sedentism are the remains of permanent habitation structures at Koster that may have been occupied through much of the year (Houart 1971). Outside the contexts of major river valleys, where the effects of the Hypsithermal may have been more severe, this apparent decrease in mobility may not have been possible.

Semisedentary Hunter–Gatherers

At the close of the mid-Holocene dry period, trends toward sedentism begin to appear more extensively across the Midwest. During an early phase of these developments, usually referred to as the Late Archaic period (3000–1000 B.C.), numbers of sites and frequencies of diagnostic artifacts suggest increasing population densities, and in some areas the increases appear to have been substantial. At the same time, artifact assemblages and associated remains began to take on distinctive characteristics in many areas, and regional traditions are clearly distinguishable for the first time. Interregional trade networks, presumably held together by reciprocal intergroup relationships, imported copper from the Great Lakes, marine shells from the Gulf Coast, and lithic raw materials from a variety of sources. Burials sometimes are covered with earthen mounds and frequently contain grave goods suggestive of social status differentiation (Klepinger and Henning 1976).

Sites are located in a variety of topographic contexts, including forested alluvial bottomlands and dissected uplands. Permanent houses, storage pits, and deep middens occur in eastern sections of

the Midwest (Winters 1969), and a two-part seasonal round composed of large upland warm-season
villages and small winter encampments is postulated for the lower Missouri River valley (Reeder
1980; Reid 1980). Remains of plants and animals
reflect an intensification of Middle Archaic subsistence practices. Deer and other mammals still were
significant staples, but nuts, wild seeds, and fish
increased in importance. Supplementary additions
to the Middle Archaic inventory include the seeds
of squash and gourd, tropical cultigens that appear
in southwestern Missouri by about 2200 B.C.
(Chomko and Crawford 1978; Kay *et al.* 1980).

Nearly coincident with the appearance of pottery
in the central Mississippi River valley is a postulated shift in settlement pattern. Documented Early
Woodland sites are relatively rare in upland contexts but are fairly common on levees and terrace
margins near some major streams (Asch *et al.* 1979).
Nevertheless, subsistence practices do not appear
to have changed much from the Late Archaic pattern; faunal remains are diverse, hickory nut shell is
abundant, and seeds of cultigens and native annuals are comparatively rare. Further, inferred
changes in technology and settlement may have
been localized processes. Early Woodland sites are
poorly documented along the lower Missouri River
(Griffin 1979; Johnson 1979), and although it is possible that population levels of aceramic groups declined markedly with the appearance of pottery, it
may instead be the case that a regional pluralism
developed in which societies of the Late Archaic
and Early Woodland traditions coexisted in separate areas or in different niches. In either case, it
appears that cultural complexes dating to the first
millennium B.C. did not differ radically from those
of antecedent groups. Subsistence systems were
structured around seasonal cycles, domesticates
still played a relatively small role in the diet, and
communities were small and perhaps loosely organized aggregates of economically semiautonomous
households.

Sedentary Hunter–Gatherers

After the widespread adoption of pottery in the
Midwest, nearly a millennium of population
growth and resource intensification followed. Although cultural complexes are clearly distinguishable along this continuum, both in social and technological terms, they share a common array of
subsistence resources and a common trajectory of
economic change.

The Middle Woodland period, dating from 200
B.C. to A.D. 400, ushered in a distinctive series of
cultural complexes with widespread contacts and
influence. Many societies in the central Mississippi
River valley were affected strongly by the Havana
tradition of west-central Illinois, a temporal and
cultural parallel of Ohio Hopewell. The Havana
tradition and related complexes in the Illinois River
valley maintained strong distribution centers in a
far-reaching trade network that was named by
Caldwell (1964) the *Hopewellian Interaction Sphere.*
Imports of obsidian, Knife River chalcedony, and
grizzly bear teeth were received from the Plains and
Rocky Mountains; copper, silver, and hematite
came from the upper Great Lakes; mineral resources, such as mica and steatite, came from the
Appalachians; and marine shells, shark teeth, and
barracuda mandibles came from the southern Atlantic and Gulf coasts (Struever and Houart 1972).
Exports included such exotic items as copper ear
spools and panpipes, as well as sociopolitical and
technological ideas that had varying impacts on
native groups participating in the system. Settlements in the Illinois River valley are of four types,
including large regional centers on the flood plain
with impressive earthworks, mounds, and dense
middens; villages or basecamps at bases of bluffs
near tributary streams that enter the valley; seasonal or special use sites on bottomlands; and burial
mounds on bluff tops bordering the valley
(Struever 1968). Analysis of burial goods and the
plans of regional centers indicates that some form
of personal status differentiation was practiced. It is
not yet clear whether prestige was conditioned by
age, sex, and personal ability (Braun 1979, 1981) or
by a rigid hierarchy of ascribed hereditary ranks
(Tainter 1977, 1981). Many researchers support the
latter interpretation, but Braun's demonstration of
the failure of status symbols to crosscut thoroughly
age and sex categories of burials argues strongly for
achieved status in the context of egalitarian social
organization.

Subsistence practices during the early half of the

Middle Woodland period are consistent with the egalitarian model. Stable resource catchments are implied by a regular spacing of sedentary floodplain villages along major streams and by skeletal studies that suggest local genetic continuity but interlocal isolation of populations (Buikstra 1976). Remains of tropical cultigens are relatively uncommon, and maize in particular was a minor dietary supplement (Bender *et al.* 1981). Instead, economies appear to reflect an intensification of earlier hunting-and-gathering lifeways (Ford 1979). Animals still provided the major protein intake, and hickory and other nuts were important sources of calories. However, seeds of mature annuals played roles of increasing significance. Starchy seeds—such as goosefoot, knotweed, and maygrass—are particularly abundant in flotation samples from recently excavated sites, and the oily seeds of sumpweed and sunflower show clear signs of domestication (Asch *et al.* 1979). In light of shrinking resource catchments due to population growth and local crowding, and the long-term unpredictability of nut masts and r-adapted animals such as deer, cultigens probably served as important buffers against local shortages. However, they did not constitute dietary staples and probably could not have supported large hereditarily ranked societies (Ford 1979).

Although Hopewellian influence on cultures of the central Mississippi River valley was distinctive, resident groups were not transformed uniformly into mirror images of the Havana tradition. Although some artifact styles and forms of burial ceremonialism in the Illinois and Mississippi river valleys often were homologous, traits such as these seem to have constituted only a thin veneer overlying traditional lifeways. However, by the end of the Middle Woodland period (A.D. 400) and during the early Late Woodland period (A.D. 400–700), intergroup contacts appear to have become more widespread and influential. Population pressure continued to increase in major river valleys, resulting in drastic constrictions of resource catchments and even greater susceptibility to local shortages (Styles 1978). Cultivation of native plant species may have assumed a major role during this period, but a stable maize agriculture was as yet undeveloped and risk-minimizing social needs favored the estab-

lishment of security linkages via intergroup marriage. Whereas degrees of intersocial status differentiation remained constant after the "decline" of Hopewell, interregional information flow and technological homogeneity appear to have increased (Braun 1977).

Sedentary Agriculturists

During the eighth century A.D., settlement and subsistence practices changed radically in many parts of the Midwest. Population growth and the constriction of hunting–gathering territories appear to have caused new heights of economic stress among Late Woodland villagers residing in major river valleys. Adoption of the bow and arrow increased the efficiency of large game hunting but also may have caused higher time investments for lower returns as local access to deer populations diminished. Fishing and collecting areas, perhaps controlled by individual villages, were limited in number and could only support finite numbers of people. Thus, as new residential groups budded from growing villages, they were forced increasingly to settle in upland contexts less suitable for a diffuse hunting–gathering lifeway. Even these new areas may have been saturated quite rapidly, and survival probably favored development of a more intensive subsistence regime. Due to weeding difficulties and the high moisture requirements of most native cultigens, seed cultivation may not have been susceptible to further intensification. Maize was, however, and it quickly assumed a major role in Late Woodland diets. Hunting and gathering still provided important protein and calorie sources, but as more and more upland forests fell into the subsistence territories of new upland villages, nut collecting declined (Asch *et al.* 1979).

Agricultural intensification had several important biological and cultural consequences. First, physiological health appears to have deteriorated. Maize is a valuable source of carbohydrates but a poor source of protein and other nutrients, and crops were liable to fail during droughts and infestations. Comparisons of Middle Woodland and terminal Late Woodland skeletal pathologies show, among later samples, decreasing signs of acute stress (e.g., Harris Lines), but more common signs of chronic stress (e.g., growth rate and cortical thickness of juvenile long bones), a higher incidence of weaning-age death, a 5–7-year drop in life expectancy of young adults, and an earlier onset of dental caries (Buikstra 1979; D. Cook 1976). Second, in the context of growing populations and a greater emphasis on the ownership of arable land, property disputes undoubtedly arose within communities, and territorial conflicts were more likely among villages. Supernatural intervention on behalf of crop yields may have also been requested more frequently, and together these factors could have favored greater permanence and authority for roles of political–religious leadership.

In the Midwest these trends culminated in the evolution of large, complex societies during the Mississippian period (A.D. 900–1700; Chapman 1980). As dependence on full-scale agriculture increased, various natural and cultural relationships were altered. Besides making the resource base extremely susceptible to natural disasters, this increased dependence probably forced agriculturists to become mutually dependent, both within and outside their own settlements. This could have led to the formation of alliances for mutual protection against poor harvests, manifested perhaps through such institutions as bride-exchange. Soon after A.D. 900 there could have been many multilineage villages present throughout the Mississippi and subsidiary valleys as a result of what began as village exogamy.

Instability of the resource base, as mentioned previously, would have been one result of a shift toward intensified food production. As Ford (1974:406) points out, raiding another's house or field was not a dependable means of coping with crop failure. Instead, he suggests that certain ritually controlled redistributions of food as part of community-wide ceremonies would occur, probably as part of the planting cycle. Such a system, once put into motion, could then develop under its own impetus. As Service (1962:148) notes, once centralization of authority begins, it can be so advantageous that it extends itself into new areas.

There has been considerable work done on delineating the patterns of sociopolitical organization of groups that existed in the central and southeastern United States during the Mississippian period

(Fowler 1975; M. O'Brien 1978; P. O'Brien 1972; Peebles 1971, 1974; Peebles and Kus 1977; Smith 1978a,b). Conclusions drawn from these studies fall into two groups: those viewing the climax of Mississippian society as a state and those viewing it as a chiefdom level of organization. Better supporting evidence exists for the latter position.

Recent work also indicates that cultures with markedly different levels of social complexity coexisted in different parts of the central and southeastern United States. At the upper end of this spectrum, in the central portion of the Mississippi River drainage, were a series of influential manifestations in the extensive American Bottom east of St. Louis. The area was dominated by Cahokia, a large community with a dense population and many impressive earthen structures. Over 100 mounds of various sizes rest within 11 residential areas that cover a total area of 15 km^2 (Fowler 1978). These areas are dominated by a single large public building foundation covering 6 ha and rising to a height of 30 m. Five plazas are postulated, and excavations indicate that the central portion of the community was fortified with a timber palisade. This chiefdom functioned as a major redistribution center for a far-flung trade network, and also appears to have housed elite sociopolitical leaders. Four other large centers (>50 ha) existed in the area, but it is not yet clear whether they constitute lesser elements of a complex settlement tier or temporally distinct communities. A series of smaller villages and hamlets also are present and probably supported the larger centers with some degree of economic input. The subsistence system appears to have relied heavily on maize agriculture, but beans constituted an important supplement. Hunting-and-gathering activities were still essential components of the subsistence system.

Cultural groups outside the American Bottom were influenced to varying degrees by the powerful Cahokia chiefdom. Although many groups seem to have increased their reliance on food production and population levels generally rose, complexes in areas not suited to the Cahokia lifeway maintained local orientations in a manner reminiscent of Late Woodland period manifestations. The nature of interactions among chiefdoms and tribes during the Mississippian period is poorly understood, but this avenue of research is vital to an understanding of culture change in areas peripheral to mainstream developments.

Protohistoric Agriculturists

After about A.D. 1500, the middle Salt River valley apparently was no longer used by Native Americans for permanent habitation. Hunters and gardeners of the Oneota archaeological complex occupied many parts of the Prairie Peninsula by A.D. 1350 (Henning 1970), but there is no evidence of contact with Oneota peoples in contemporary sites in the Cannon Reservoir area, and we have found no traces of Oneota occupation during or after the sixteenth century.

There is a similar lack of evidence for permanent occupation of the region by historic tribes. To the north were the Winnebago in southern and eastern Wisconsin (Lurie 1978) and the Ioway in a number of drainage systems in northern and eastern Iowa (Mott 1938; M. Wedel 1959). West of the Cannon Project region were the Missouri and Little Osage in northern central Missouri (Chapman 1959; Henning 1970) and the Kansa in northwest Missouri and northeast Kansas (W. Wedel 1959). The Osage occupied major drainages to the south and west (Chapman 1959), and to the east and northeast were the Sauk, Fox, and tribes of the Illinois Confederacy in western Illinois, eastern Iowa, and southwest Wisconsin (Bauxar 1978; Callender 1978 a,b,c). It seems likely that northeast Missouri occasionally was used by many of these groups for temporary hunting and gathering activities. However, even though the area was controlled by the Sauk and Fox during the late 1700s and early 1800s, none has been documented as permanent residents in historical or archaeological records.

Although neighboring tribes spoke different languages and could be distinguished culturally, these Indian groups displayed strong similarities in social organization, religious beliefs, subsistence systems, and technology. A summary of shared traits offers a profile against which patterns inferred from our prehistoric data can be compared.

Generally, these groups were patrilineal and patrilocal, and men often had more than one wife. Eight or more clans were maintained within each tribe. Clan members acquired specific socio-religious roles, and status differences among individuals were recognized by most groups. All believed in a far-off great spirit and, probably, in a number of intermediaries. Witchcraft was practiced and a variety of techniques were used to deal with its effects.

Subsistence practices were broad-based. Gardens produced corn, beans, squash, and other crops, and all groups hunted deer, bison, wapiti, bear, and smaller mammals. Bison were available in the Prairie Peninsula during the Neo-Boreal climatic episode, and many accounts suggest they often were taken in great numbers. Seasonal rounds generally included periods of time away from the permanent villages, when most able-bodied men and women hunted large mammals. Since group hunts required the participation of many people, they were scheduled to avoid interference with gardening activities. Fishing and gathering provided important supplements to the subsistence base.

Sex was an important criterion in the division of labor. The roles of hunter and warrior were reserved for adult males, whereas females were responsible for gardening, collecting, food processing, and early child rearing. Men worked periodically in the gardens, often performing such tasks as clearing trees and shrubs from plots prior to cultivation and planting.

Technologies of the six groups were quite similar. Before Euro-American contact brought the gun, the bow and arrow was the principal weapon for hunting and for warfare. Horses also were introduced historically; boat- and foot-power provided the modes of transportation during earlier times. All groups made pottery vessels, but the potter's art was hastily dropped in favor of metal containers when they could be obtained. Houses generally were long, ovoid wigwams covered with woven mats. These structures were warm, durable, and easy to build, and they ranged in size from very large multi-family dwellings (up to 30 m long) to small units suitable for one nuclear family. Salt was valued by all of the tribes, just as it was among early Euro-American settlers. In fact, the earliest French encounters with Sauk and Fox in the area occurred at salt licks along the lower Salt River.

Although not related necessarily to subsistence cycles, warfare played an important part in the seasonal round of activities. When listing their enemies, the members of a tribe often would enumerate most or all of their neighbors. Patterns of warfare may well have been responsible for the lack of permanent settlement in northeast Missouri at the time of Euro-American contact. Surrounded as it was by competing ethnic groups, the area appears to have served as a buffer zone between defended territories.

Rural Euro-American Agriculturists

Rural settlement of the Midwest can be viewed as a period of colonization by peoples from the East who were following a westward extension of the eastern forest environment with which they were familiar (Thomas 1909:213; Schroeder 1968:2). Many of the new settlers who went west of the Mississippi River during the late eighteenth and early nineteenth centuries were from the Upper South,[1] and many were from the Bluegrass region of Kentucky.

Upper South society at the time of westward extension was primarily rural, with subsistence based on corn and pork (Mason 1982). Socioeconomic goals of persons within this tradition were based on the desire to become members of the landed gentry, where wealth and social position were measured in slaves and land. Ownership of slaves allowed the production of cash crops such as hemp and tobacco, which augmented income from hog and corn production (Mason 1982). The basic socioeconomic unit within Upper South frontier society was the family, which functioned as a corporate group in terms of owning land and working it independently of outside interference.

One impetus for Midwest froner colonization was the ready availability of inexpensive land ($1.25/acre). However, without firsthand knowledge of an area, one's decisions on which parcels to purchase are tied to a certain amount of chance.

[1]Mitchell (1972:740) defines the pre-1860 Upper South as an agricultural region in the states of Maryland, Virginia, North Carolina, Kentucky, Tennessee, and Missouri.

Early settlers were cautious in these decisions, following closely the fertile river valleys west and north, and establishing staging areas, or jumping-off points, from which to make the next move. One important early community was the Boone's Lick area of central Missouri. Settled in 1807 by Daniel and Nathan Boone, this locale was the first area of deep loess soils to be encountered west of St. Charles, Missouri. A steady stream of settlers followed, mainly from Tennessee and Kentucky, attracted by the excellent soil.

Movement north and west of these population nodes progressed steadily between 1815 and 1825. By this time, the General Land Office had completed township surveys for much of northern Missouri and portions of Illinois, and land west of the Mississippi and north of the Missouri rivers was being sold out of the federal land office in St. Louis. By 1825, communities were being formed in various portions of the area. These communities were based on kinship, religious affiliations, and–or commonality of origin. Once these small communities were formed and the basis for economic expansion existed, waves of new settlers, often affines of persons already residing in the new communities, soon followed.

These new settlers, having access to information on the quality of soil, timber density, and so on, were able to make logical decisions regarding land purchases. Differential patterns of land purchase through time have been noted (Warren *et al.* 1981), which may be due in part to an increase in information gained by the settlers. In ecologically sensitive areas—such as the Prairie Peninsula, where prairie and timbered land were available—the number of locational choices facing the rural agriculturist would have been high.

In at least two areas of the Midwest, northeastern Missouri (Warren *et al.* 1981) and southern Iowa (Hudson 1969), this period of colonization was followed by a period of spread (Hudson 1969), or short-distance diffusion, in which new farmsteads were formed by the splitting off of younger families from their original locations. As these new settlements grew and land became increasingly scarce, intense competition often developed among the settlements for resources, and this resulted in a trend toward a regular spacing of farmsteads. These phases of rural settlement may not have existed in all portions of the Midwest since complex environmental and social characteristics, such as back-migration, may have caused serious distortions in the pattern (Mason 1982).

SUMMARY

Studies of environment and culture in the Midwest document a great deal of change during the past 10,000 years. Environmental change, which influences changes in cultural systems, is brought about mainly through climatic fluctuations, although it may be affected to some degree by the activities of man. By 7000 B.C., much of the Midwest was beginning to be affected by dry, westerly winds that dominated weather patterns during progressively longer parts of the year. By 5000 B.C., changes in vegetation were severe; the prairies reached their maximum eastward extent and stretched well beyond their historic limits. As forests shrank toward moist positions along stream courses and lower valley slopes, rates of hillslope erosion increased. These developments had profound effects on animal populations—changing the distributions, body sizes, and probably the densities of several species.

By 3000 B.C., these trends began to reverse themselves due to another series of climatic changes. Prairies retreated slowly westward, forests reclaimed hillsides and dissected uplands, and animal populations regained their pre-Hypsithermal sizes and distributions. Although the late Holocene climatic regime was relatively stable compared to earlier regimes, detailed analysis of this period has documented a series of climatic fluctuations suffi-

cient to affect some prehistoric economies in sensitive localities.

Cultural adaptations to these changes are well documented in some areas of the Midwest. By the middle Holocene, economic orientations in large river valleys seem to have shifted toward local forest and riverine resources with attendant increases in sedentism. Exotic cultigens may have been introduced during this period. At the close of the Hypsithermal, sedentism appears more extensively across the Midwest, with numbers of sites and frequencies of artifacts suggesting increases in population density. By about 200 B.C., population growth was causing local crowding and shrinking resource catchments, and because of the unpredictability of traditional resources, cultivated plants probably served as important buffers against local shortages.

By A.D. 800, continued population growth and further constriction of procurement territories caused economic stress among Late Woodland populations residing in major river valleys. Agricultural intensification may have been one way to alleviate this stress. This shift in subsistence strategy altered various cultural relationships, culminating in the evolution of large, complex societies.

Settlement of much of the Midwest after A.D. 1800 was a direct result of the availability of inexpensive land in a timbered environment similar to sections of the East. Strategies behind land purchases were conditioned by soil productivity, timber density, and proximity to kin. Communities, often composed of self-sufficient farmsteads linked by kinship ties, religious affiliation, or commonality of origin, became numerous throughout the Midwest.

5

Models of Adaptation and Change

ROBERT E. WARREN AND MICHAEL J. O'BRIEN

In the three preceding chapters we have discussed the theoretical orientation and research design of the Cannon Project, described the nineteenth-century environmental setting of the region, and outlined changes in the natural and cultural contexts of northeastern Missouri during the past 10,000 years. The objective here is to evaluate the significance of these contextual factors with respect to settlement and subsistence practices of past residents of the project area and to frame general theoretical expectations in more specific terms appropriate to the analysis of traces of human behavior in the Cannon Reservoir region. To this end, we have constructed models of prehistoric and historic cultural development in the area and derived implications from the models that are testable using data drawn from archaeological and documentary research.

The use of models as analytical tools has a long and productive history in anthropological research. Clarke (1972) argues that models play varied but integral roles in most empirical investigations and

suggests that these roles be recognized explicitly both in the writings and reasoning processes of researchers. The models presented here are abstracted from a variety of sources, including environmental studies of the Cannon Reservoir region, reconstructions of cultural development elsewhere in the Midwest, and our own theoretical perspectives on cultural adaptation and change. The models attempt to "codify what has gone before" (Haggett 1965:23) and provide a series of hypothetical constructs that can be contrasted with findings in the project area to determine how well results conform to model expectations.

We emphasize that the models themselves are not necessarily explanatory. They are merely sets of hypothetical generalizations that focus on select aspects of human behavior. To document that settlement and subsistence strategies change, and that these changes can be detected at certain points in time, is purely a descriptive effort that categorizes behavioral variation. However, formulation of the models and stages is an essential step toward un-

85

derstanding cultural change in the project area and represents a significant advance over the normative pattern approach.

A MODEL OF PREHISTORIC ADAPTATION AND CHANGE

Archaeological investigations in the Midwest have grappled with a host of interesting problems, and available models deal with such disparate topics as the origins of cultivation (Struever and Vickery 1973) and mechanisms of exotic goods exchange among distant societies (Struever and Houart 1972). These and many other issues are of interest, but in light of our primary research goals, the model presented here focuses on general modes of prehistoric adaptation to the Cannon Project region and changes in socioeconomic organization through time. Three sets of important contextual factors are emphasized: (*a*) the distributions and short-term fluctuations of economic resources in the region; (*b*) the changing environmental effects of major Holocene climatic shifts; and (*c*) the differential impacts on regional populations of such cultural factors as population growth, economic intensification, and intergroup transmission of materials and information.

Resource Variability

As noted earlier, archaeological research demonstrates that northeastern Missouri was occupied by native societies for at least 10,000 years. The lifeways of these groups were quite variable through time, ranging from that of mobile hunter–gatherers who extracted most of their resources from the natural environment to that of sedentary agriculturists who produced substantial proportions of their foodstuffs by growing domesticated plants in cultivated gardens and fields. However, paleoeconomic reconstructions also indicate that there were important parallels among the resource acquisition strategies of all these groups. Hunting, collection of fuel resources, and procurement of raw materials for tool manufacture and for the construction of residential structures were important

activities well into historic times. We therefore expect that the abundance and distribution of a number of natural resources had analogous effects on the settlement–subsistence practices of all prehistoric groups. Although the quantities and distributions of some resources undoubtedly changed in response to major climatic shifts, the relative abundance of many of them may not have varied greatly from place to place. Forest density, for instance, was probably greatest on steep slopes in mesic portions of the region during moist and dry episodes alike, and a few resources, such as lithic raw materials, were essentially invariant in distribution through time.

Four major characteristics of resource variability are emphasized here: (*a*) resource zonation and implications for the locations of residential sites, (*b*) geographic variation of resource composition and implications for the characteristics of short-term extractive sites, (*c*) effects of the prairie–timber ecotone on different forms of economic organization, and (*d*) seasonal variability of resource abundance and the cyclic patterning of extractive strategies. A useful model to keep in mind during the discussion of each of these topics is the concept of environmental patchiness mentioned in Chapter 2. *Patches* are defined as intersecting spatial subsets of ecosystems that are distinguishable by ecological criteria and are separated by selective discontinuities that influence the distributions, interactions, and adaptations of organisms (Wiens 1976). Paralleling this concept, ethological theories indicate that two forms of grain response—fine-grain and coarse-grain—can be expected among mobile organisms occupying different kinds of patches (MacArthur and Pianka 1966; Pianka 1974). The former is a generalist strategy in which resources are exploited in direct proportion to their relative abundance, whereas the coarse-grain response is a specialist strategy in which populations exploit patches selectively.

Incorporation of these concepts into models of prehistoric locational behavior requires adoption of a meaningful interactive link between patch composition and grain response. Floral species diversity, a readily quantifiable factor, is suitable for this role. It theoretically covaries in space and time with a variety of ecological variables pertinent to structures of human extractive strategies (Binford 1980; Binford and Chasko 1976). Important among these associations are direct correlations with levels of species dispersion and levels of diversity among faunal species (Margalef 1968; Whittaker 1972). Together these associations indicate that aggregating plant and animal species are unlikely in patches with high species diversity but are dominant components of homogeneous communities. As a result, human strategies of resource extraction can be expected to vary among patches with different diversities, and we can infer that this variation will in turn affect mobility requirements, site locations, and artifact assemblage compositions.

Two dimensions of ecological variability, patch composition and patch arrangement, are of critical importance to models of locational behavior in the Cannon Reservoir region. As was demonstrated in Chapter 3, the dimension of patch arrangement was quite variable in the region, both within and among the prairie and forest biomes. Significantly, this variability is modeled best as a series of narrow concentric bands that parallel courses of major streams, have V-shaped distributions in tributary valleys, and are aligned perpendicularly to downslope axes of surface strike. Of equal importance is the fact that in the project area the Salt River has a relatively narrow valley that rarely exceeds about 5 km in width (Figure 3.16). Thus, sedentary resources in all zones were well within reach of staging areas located anywhere in the region. Given minimal investments of travel time, most routine procurement tasks could probably have been completed within a single day. Therefore, it seems likely that residential sites of mobile–sedentary groups did not require direct access to immobile resources. Instead, villages or encampments could be located centrally with respect to subsistence needs and, at the same time, could occupy comfortable localities with convenient access to water, fuel, and avenues of intergroup contact. Artifact assemblages of residential sites should reflect diverse arrays of domestic activities. Expected to be common, for instance, are residues of manufacture and maintenance tasks, remains of food preparation and consumption, and traces of household structures and facilities. Intrasite patterning should be fairly complex and in many cases ought to show high material densities resulting from recurrent or relatively long-term occupations.

The dimension of patch composition, when reduced to the vector of floral diversity and examined in concert with the dimension of patch arrangement, allows us to derive a locational hypothesis for logistical extractive sites. First, it must be emphasized that in the Cannon Project region the patch concept is applied most appropriately at the biome level of abstraction. Variability at the species level is more accurately modeled as a series of independent Gaussian curves that peak in relative abundance at many points along environmental gradients. Accordingly, in the Cannon Project region arboreal species diversity increases continuously along a slope position gradient that ranges from level upland prairies to flood plain forests (Figure 3.18). Given the previously cited correlations of floral diversity with levels of population dispersion and faunal diversity, it can be concluded that terrestrial biota in the Cannon Project region generally graded from aggregated and specialized forms in upland prairie contexts to dispersed and varied forms in flood plain forest contexts. Important here is a hypothetical extension of this model: (a) upland resources suitable for human exploitation were relatively few in kind but quantitatively abundant, and (b) lowland resources were quantitatively diverse, but each specific resource was limited in quantity.

Because short-term extractive sites are expected to vary logistically with distributions and quantities of exploitable resources (Binford 1980), we predict that "coarse-grained responses predominated in uplands, fine-grained responses predominated in lowlands, and intermediate or mixed responses occurred in intervening areas" (O'Brien and Warren 1979:16). In uplands, where limited ranges of exploitable resources clustered locally in abundance, it is expected that logistical extractive sites are small (in comparison with most residential sites), are relatively uncommon, and are distributed nonrandomly with respect to resource locations. Because logistical extractive sites reflect narrow ranges of tasks, it is further expected that intrasite and intersite variability among upland components is fairly low. In lowlands, where diverse ranges of exploitable resources were scattered homogeneously, and in limited quantities, logistical extractive sites should be relatively abundant and spatially dispersed, with either random or uniform distributions. Because the potential range of lowland procurement tasks was relatively broad, it also is expected that levels of intersite variability are high while variability within sites is low. Specific occasions of site use probably were brief and left only a few highly localized remains (Binford 1979; Gould 1980). As Binford (1980) points out, however, it is likely that traces of recurrent local extraction build up gradually through time, resulting in sparse but visible patterns of specialized artifacts that comprise sites varying greatly in size (cf. Hayden 1978).

Effects of the prairie–timber ecotone on patterns of human settlement and resource extraction may have been significant in many parts of the Midwest during prehistoric and historic times (Hewes 1950; Hickerson 1970; Jordan 1964; King and Graham 1981; Peters 1970). As pointed out by Rhoades (1978), however, the related concepts of ecotone and edge effect are controversial among ecologists and often have been misused by others. The existence of tension zones between discrete ecological communities is questioned by supporters of Gleason's individualistic hypothesis (Curtis 1955; Curtis and McIntosh 1951; Gilbert and Curtis 1953), and postulates of floral and faunal abundance and diversity along edges (where species from adjacent communities supposedly intermingle with edge species) have not been demonstrated empirically (Whittaker 1975).

Thus, the notion that ecotones are "microcosmic Edens" that exhibit high resource potential, and thereby attract human settlement, probably is false. Nevertheless, settlements along narrow transitions may be expected in response to the varied resource needs of diffuse or mixed economies. Among frontier agriculturalists, for instance, edges may have attracted settlement because of ready access to fuel, building materials, natural pasture, and sparsely timbered soil that did not require heavy labor investment to clear for cultivation. Although ecotones themselves are not necessarily productive, or

are productive only on a seasonal basis, they can function as central staging areas from which critical resources of adjacent communities can be tapped efficiently (Warren *et al.* 1981).

Many species of plants and animals were available as potential subsistence resources in the Cannon Reservoir region only at specific times of the year. Other species could be hunted or collected all year long but were available maximally only during certain seasons. Because most species also occupied specific habitats or varied greatly in abundance across the landscape, natural resources must be evaluated on the dimensions of both time and place if we are to predict realistically the optimal scheduling, seasonality, and geographic focus of hunter–gatherer procurement systems in the region.

Our discussion of seasonal resource availability focuses on 18 major groups of plants and animals (Figure 5.1). These include each of the five taxa rated in Chapter 3 as possible "first-line" animal foods (white-tailed deer, turkey, raccoon, fish, and migratory waterfowl) plus an equal number of forms known to have been relied on prehistorically in the Midwest (cottontail rabbit, tree squirrels, semiaquatic mammals, freshwater mussels, and amphibians–reptiles). Also represented are eight plant resources. Five of these are well documented in archaeological contexts (hickory nuts, hazelnuts, acorns, fruits, and annual seeds) and three others, less likely to be preserved, are commonly referred to in ethnographic accounts (maple sap, cambium, and miscellaneous tubers and greens). This list, although certainly not exhaustive, probably includes the most accessible and productive native resources in the Cannon Project region.

We have used a simple dichotomy of bottomland versus upland resources to delineate the geographic variability of potential foods (Figure 5.1). Bottomlands, as defined here, include all aquatic, riparian, flood plain, and alluvial terrace habitats (drainage classes 4–5). Uplands are composed of forested valley side slopes and upland flats, the prairie–timber ecotone, and grassy open woodlands and prairies (drainage classes 1–3). Habitat designations, derived from GLO records and other sources (Tables 3.2 and 3.3), are generally clear-cut but in some

(a)   (b)

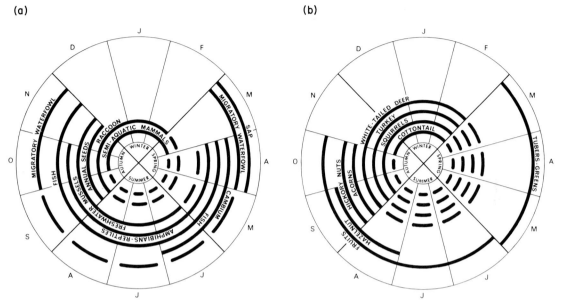

Figure 5.1. Seasonal availability of selected (*a*) bottomland and (*b*) upland resources (sources listed in Tables 3.2 and 3.3).

cases represent modal locales in which otherwise ubiquitous species, such as white-tailed deer, are seasonally most abundant or accessible.

Inspection of Figure 5.1 reveals that resources have year-round availability in upland and bottomland contexts. However, the diversities and quantities of potential resources tend to vary significantly within and among these habitats on a seasonal basis. Bottomland resources are relatively abundant during spring and summer. Maple sap, one of the earliest available plant resources in spring, runs in March and April. Also available are migrating waterfowl, fish, cambium, amphibians, and reptiles. Meanwhile, a variety of tubers and greens can be collected on upland hillsides and talus slopes (Struever 1969), but most other upland resources either are out of season or are relatively inaccessible at this time.

During summer a variety of fruits and berries ripen in upland contexts, particularly in sparsely timbered forests and along the prairie–timber ecotone. Once again bottomland resources are more abundant and varied. Fish, amphibians, reptiles,

and freshwater mussels are available in major streams and in shrinking flood plain ponds; nesting waterfowl, such as wood ducks, herons, rails, and shorebirds, occur in mesic forests and riparian contexts; and raccoons, opossums, and semiaquatic mammals can be hunted along streams and in bottomland forests. Moreover, many of the animals important in the uplands during autumn are equally accessible in the uplands and bottomlands during summer. Thus, resources of streams and bottomland forests probably were more attractive to hunter–gatherers in spring and summer than were resources of upland forests. Aggregating bison herds might have drawn hunters into upland prairies during late summer and early autumn, but recent syntheses of archaeological faunal remains suggest that bison either were scarce or rarely exploited along the southern Prairie Peninsula during prehistoric and early historic times (Purdue and Styles 1980; Shay 1978).

Resources increase significantly across much of the region during autumn when nuts, seeds, and a variety of animals would have attracted hunter–

gatherers both to upland and bottomland contexts. Upland resources reach an important annual mode at this time. Hazelnuts are available along the ecotone and in sparse forests during August and September, as are fruits of plum and cherry trees; fruits of the hawthorns, grapes, and pawpaw ripen in open woodlands and talus slope forests during September and October; hickory nuts and acorns can be collected during these same 2 months in upland forests; and such mammals as white-tailed deer, turkey, and tree squirrels, attracted by autumn mast and fruits, tend to aggregate and gain weight in upland forests and along the ecotone. Meanwhile, bottomland resources also are abundant during autumn. Fish and mussels are readily accessible in streams; raccoons, semiaquatic mammals, and amphibians–reptiles are active; seeds from a variety of native pioneer annuals mature in riparian and flood plain forests; and migrating waterfowl may return to local streams.

With the end of mast production in late November, native plant foods, unless stored, diminish in significance until spring. However, many mammals are active throughout winter and can be hunted or trapped in most forested parts of the region. Smith (1975) and Styles (1978) suggest that the accessibility of deer, turkey, raccoon, squirrels, and cottontail actually improves during winter due to contraction of their foraging territories, reduced vegetation cover, and increased tracking capabilities in snow. On the other hand, these and other species characteristically undergo marked weight loss during winter, and decreased returns per animal unit may have favored the storage of autumn plant resources.

Several important conclusions emerge from this discussion. First, potential native foods are most abundant and diverse during autumn, when many resources become available in upland and bottomland contexts. Efficient collection of resources would have required a careful scheduling of activities, but temporary surpluses were possible, and the virtual absence of winter plant foods would have favored storage of excess nuts, seeds, and acorns to supplement winter subsistence. Second, the availability of important bottomland resources during spring, summer, and autumn often would have favored the location of residential sites on

alluvial terraces. During climatic episodes similar to those of modern times, upland mast resources and mammals attracted to the forest edge were in most cases within 3 or 4 km of major streams. Under these conditions, seasonal relocation of villages probably would not have been necessary. However, during extended cool–moist periods, these distances could have increased significantly, and seasonal upland encampments may have enabled more efficient exploitation of autumn resources.

Environmental Change

Given the sensitivity of the southern Prairie Peninsula to Holocene climatic change, and the importance of hunting and gathering to subsistence economies of many prehistoric societies in the Midwest, we might expect significant long-term changes in settlement–subsistence practices in the Cannon Reservoir region. Implications of three major climatic periods are evaluated here: (a) the Pre-Boreal and Boreal episodes of the early Holocene, (b) the Hypsithermal, or Atlantic, episode of the middle Holocene, and (c) the Sub-Boreal and later episodes of more recent times.

During the early Holocene conditions were cooler and more moist than at present, and forests covered many areas occupied historically by prairie. An essentially modern array of arboreal genera was in place by about 8000 B.C., and although prairie grasses began to replace forests in drying upland contexts at about that same time, mast resources in the region probably were much more abundant and extensive than today. Proportions of species are difficult to estimate with available data, but habitat preferences of modern taxa are suggestive. Hickories, probably dominated by shagbark (*C. ovata*) and a few other species (Missouri Botanical Garden 1974; see also Rochow 1972), fall between black oak and white oak on the Cannon Reservoir moisture–drainage class gradient (Figure 3.17b) and prefer gentle slopes in the region (Warren 1976). They are prolific producers of calorie- and protein-rich nuts and should have been quite common in upland forests of the early Holocene. White and black oaks probably also were abundant. Moreover, mast-consuming vertebrates should have aggregated seasonally in upland forests, and edge species would have proliferated with the appearance and expansion of prairie. It seems probable, then, that during the early Holocene: (a) massive quantities of "first-line" foods were available seasonally in upland forests, and (b) zones of upland resources were much wider than they would be at any later time during the Holocene. Assuming a maximum radius of 7–10 km for daily collecting trips, it seems quite likely that many upland resources, particularly those along the prairie–timber ecotone, often were inaccessible from bottomland staging areas. Thus, efficiency in early Holocene foraging strategies may have favored the location of autumn residential encampments in upland contexts where access to resources could be maximized. At the same time, access to water also would have been desirable, and we might therefore expect many of these sites to occur along the margins of upland flats near the courses of tributary streams. Bottomland resources, perhaps as abundant and diverse as those of historic times, may have attracted procurement activities and settlement locations during the remainder of the year.

Environmental conditions during the Hypsithermal (6500–3000 B.C.) were radically different from those of the early Holocene and also may have been quite different from subsequent times. Due to the increasing persistence of dry westerly winds, prairies expanded eastward beyond their modern limits and probably captured many localities that were forested during the late Holocene. Streams and vertebrate resources also were affected, and we expect that settlement patterns changed as well. If forests contracted much beyond the limits shown in modern soils distributions (Figure 4.2), upland forests and mast-related resources would have been considerably reduced in area, and seasonal upland encampments would no longer have been productive or efficient. On the other hand, prairie expansion could have improved considerably the habitat of edge species. Many of these may have aggregated throughout the year along gallery forests and relatively mesic hillsides, and, although their numbers may have dropped in the region as a whole, they would have been readily accessible from bottomland encampments. However, aquatic and bottomland forest resources probably also

dwindled, and unless population pressure from competing societies forced a constriction of resource catchments and a shift toward "second-line" or "third-line" foods (i.e., those demanding greater time investment for procurement or processing), mid-Holocene residential sites in the Cannon Reservoir region are expected to represent small, short-term encampments of mobile hunter–gatherers who moved upstream or downstream into new catchments whenever local resources were depleted.

After about 5000 B.C., dry westerlies characteristic of the Hypsithermal began to subside in the Midwest. Effective moisture increased, causing an expansion of mesic forests, and climatic conditions tended to stabilize in configurations roughly intermediate between those of early historic and modern times. On average, prairie–timber boundaries probably coincided with zones of contact or transition between modern prairie and forest soils, and resource distributions in time and space were roughly similar to those described earlier (Chapter 3; Figure 5.1). Several cycles of increasing warmth and–or dryness are postulated (Chapter 4). Certainly none was as severe as the Hypsithermal itself, but it is quite possible that economic stress could have increased among groups already experiencing pressure on resources due to the onset of other droughty episodes.

Cultural Factors

Recent work in the Mississippi and Illinois river valleys suggests that three cultural factors played important roles in the evolution of prehistoric midwestern cultures: population growth, economic intensification, and varying forms of intergroup contact. In this section we discuss these variables and evaluate their potential evolutionary significance.

As noted in Chapter 4, sharp contrasts between the small temporary encampments of Paleo-Indian hunters and the large permanent towns of Mississippian agriculturists provide convincing evidence that midwestern populations grew significantly during the Holocene. Studies of mortuary mounds and cemeteries in major river valleys document this trend prehistorically (Buikstra 1979), and growth seems to have continued until Euro-American diseases decimated many indigenous populations during protohistoric and historic times. Although rates of growth may have changed through time, and densities probably differed from place to place, it is likely that numbers of people increased monotonically in the Midwest as a whole.

To simplify the complex relationship between population growth and economic intensification, and to integrate these factors with the model of environmental change, we approach the problem from a temporal perspective. In the preceding section we mentioned possible effects of climate on resource availability, noting the sensitivity of the southern Prairie Peninsula to Holocene climatic change. During the late Early Archaic and Middle Archaic periods (7000–3000 B.C.), climatic conditions were such that deer and other mast-related resources probably began to move downslope toward a more mesic habitat. As forests contracted, settlement locations and resource catchments also would have begun to shift toward lower slopes and bottomlands. However, human populations probably were quite small and sparse during the early Holocene, and changes were not necessarily severe enough to have forced major changes in subsistence practices. Populations in some regions may have diversified their procurement strategies, but there is little reason to suspect that population growth rates were high enough to cause crowding among neighboring bands. Without significant pressure on first-line resources, it would not have been necessary to rely on foods that either were less productive or were more difficult to obtain and prepare for consumption.

If we accept the notion that post-Hypsithermal climatic conditions were rebounding toward those of today at a fairly slow rate, then the curves for population growth and first-line resource availability could have crossed sometime during the early part of the Late Archaic period. To compensate for relative decreases in deer and other mast-related resources, hunter–gatherers would have (a) focused on smaller resource catchments, and (b) diversified their exploitive strategies by placing greater emphasis on less desirable resources.

Significantly, intensification of exploitive efforts within smaller resource areas would have led to decreased residential mobility. A completely sedentary lifeway may not have been necessary, but a shift toward semipermanent villages could have favored a relaxation of social controls on population growth and may have spurred higher growth rates. Thus, by the end of the Late Archaic period, economic stresses caused by slow rises in population density during earlier times may have been exacerbated by demographic effects of local intensification of resource exploitation.

During the Middle Woodland period, when sedentary villages appeared in major river valleys, population growth probably continued to increase. Resource catchments would have diminished further in size, often leading to periodic local shortages when mast-related resources failed to meet the needs of some villages. Subsistence strategies would have placed even greater emphasis on high-input resources, and the renowned Hopewell Interaction Sphere may have evolved as an economic security network that transferred resources from villages with temporary surpluses to those temporarily in need (Ford 1979).

The trajectories of growth and intensification apparently pointed upward throughout the Late Woodland period, possibly causing several related social and economic chages. First, the decline of Hopewell may have been due to a widespread failure of the interaction sphere as an economic security device. If populations grew out of pace with the capacities of local intensification, decreasing the chances that nearby villages could meet the needs of those suffering shortages, then the underlying benefits of the system would have diminished. Second, studies of subsistence remains dating to the first half of the Late Woodland period show differences in degree rather than in kind. In the lower Illinois River valley, Styles (1978:401) sees (a) an increase in localized resource exploitation; (b) a more intensive use of seeds and aquatic resources; and (c) a higher incidence of storage facilities. Third, this early Late Woodland adaptation apparently was successful for several hundred years, but by A.D. 800, growth and continued economic stress forced major changes in economic orientation. One result was a sudden expansion of permanent communities into upland contexts, areas that had previously been used only as procurement territories for bottomland villages. A second result, one that probably enabled upland expansion, was the rapid development of intensive food production based on a single major species.

As cultivation of native seed-producing plants approached the limits of intensification, continued population growth would have placed a severe burden on the resource base. This burden could have been alleviated by an economic shift in only one direction: Maize, a food source that had been in use in the Midwest for at least 600 years, was suitable for large-scale cultivation, could be grown successfully in a variety of contexts, and was easier to manage, harvest, and process. Maize agriculture would have allowed Late Woodland and early Mississippian communities to exist on smaller amounts of land in more diverse contexts but also would have required greater inputs of labor than the resource strategies of previous millennia. Thus, population growth rates may have increased dramatically, becoming an effect of culture change rather than simply an independent variable (Dumond 1965).

By A.D. 1000, the major river valleys presumably were densely settled by populations relying heavily on maize agriculture. Beans, squash, and sunflowers also were cultivated, and hunting still was important, but maize comprised the heart of the resource base. Intercommunal ties had become extremely important. As Ford (1974:406) suggests, ritually controlled redistribution of food as part of community-wide ceremonies could have helped ease tensions during food shortages. Despite these ties, it appears from the number of palisaded Mississippian centers that warfare, or the potential for warfare, was prevalent during that time period.

If prehistoric developments in major river valleys of the Midwest were as we have postulated—with consistent increases in population size, sedentism, and resource intensification—then these conditions could have instigated important cultural changes in marginal areas. Among these changes could have been the spread of main valley groups up tributaries such as the Salt River. A variety of resources were available along the Salt, but they were far less abundant or reliable than those in larger valleys. As daughter communities split off from established communities (Chapter 4), they may have had to move significant distances up these tributaries to establish new fields and hunting territories, and changes in social organization and resource strategies may have been necessary. Freedom of movement would have been limited after the advent of formal subsistence territories among tributary populations, and we expect that only under conditions of extreme economic stress would mainstream communities have engaged in conflict over tributary resources.

Whether or not these movements actually occurred, groups in major river valleys should have been in contact with those in marginal areas—if only indirectly through trade—and would have passed on to them a variety of materials and ideas. The degree to which these transmissions occurred can be measured partly through the analysis of artifact styles, human burials, and patterns of settlements and community organization. For instance, if the Middle Woodland period was a time of significant crowding and local resource intensification along the Salt, and if the Hopewell Interaction Sphere was a socioeconomic mechanism for alleviating local shortages, then in the Cannon Reservoir region we expect to see strong participation in the Hopewell Interaction Sphere evidenced by food remains, village complexity, and burial goods. If, on the other hand, crowding only was significant along major rivers, where abundant resources permitted sedentism and higher rates of population growth, then we expect to see only a thin veneer of Hopewellian artifact styles overlying more ancient patterns of settlement and subsistence.

Developmental Stages

The remainder of the model is composed of four developmental stages. Although the stages might be interpreted as discrete components, they in fact represent a series of points along a developmental continuum. From this perspective, the model serves as a heuristic guide to what is, in reality, a dynamic regional sequence. The stages are systemic in the sense that they interrelate strategies of resource acquisition, residence location, and social organization, but they do not go beyond the potential limits of the data and our interpretations.

Stage I

Stage I is characterized by small, mobile groups engaged in hunting and gathering activities. Populations dispersed during most of the year into what MacNeish (1972) terms seasonal microbands, but during part of the year they converged into macrobands for such cyclical activities as animal drives, mast harvests, and the observance of rituals. Microband camps contained semipermanent dwellings and were located in environmental zones with relatively high resource diversity. Seasonal macroband encampments, although larger, contained no permanent structures and were situated in zones supporting aggregate resources.

Stage I corresponds roughly to the Early and Middle Archaic periods (8000–3000 B.C.) and is characterized by emphasis on productive and renewable resources such as nuts and white-tailed deer. Microband residential groups probably consisted of fewer than 20 persons who exploited resources when and where they became available. Even with the onset of the Hypsithermal, the resource base probably was able to support these small, but growing, populations without the need for major changes in the exploitive strategies employed.

Stage II

Stage II is characterized by the presence of small communities with semipermanent structures located near perennial streams or lower stretches of their tributaries. No significant disparity among dwelling size or household goods existed, reflecting continued egalitarian social organization. Burials occurred near residences, either singly or in burial mounds used by residential or kinship groups. Because of population growth and the beginnings of resource intensification, communities were located on bottomland terraces to take advantage of a diverse range of foodstuffs. Deer and other first-line resources were important, as were a growing number of second-line resources, such as fish, nesting waterfowl, and plants with starchy seeds.

During this stage, the processing of vegetal foods became common, and there was a definite trend toward food storage. Pottery appears during Stage II, making it possible to transport, store, and cook food in permanent containers.

Stage II corresponds to the Late Archaic and Early Woodland periods (3000–200 B.C.) and reflects trends toward sedentary lifeways and increasingly diversified exploitive strategies. Resources were well known and predictable and could be extracted efficiently. Exotic cultigens such as cucurbits, and possibly maize, were adopted by the second millennium B.C., and this probably reinforced the value of bottomland settlements. As in the preceding stage, groups initially may have dispersed during various times of the year to harvest certain resources, but toward the close of Stage II we predict that they were living in fairly permanent communities and did not break into microbands.

Stage III

Stage III is characterized by increased dependence on horticulture and a sedentary way of life. Large communities were established along terraces of major waterways as populations experienced higher rates of growth. Inhabitants were able to maintain subsistence practices similar to those of the previous stage, but with increased emphasis on seed collection. Resource catchments were shrinking, but exploitive strategies evolved accordingly, and for a long time natural resources were able to support populations.

By the latter half of the stage, exploitive strategies were shifting to seed horticulture and other more "expensive" resources in response to severe crowding. Upland extractive sites were used to take advantage of certain resources, but as the dependence on bottomland resources increased, the relative number of these sites decreased from that present in Stage II. Horticulture also favored the recognition of household, family, and village rights to garden plots, and extra-kin group ties, such as bride exchange, probably were made with neighboring villages to reduce conflict.

Stage III corresponds to the Middle and early Late Woodland periods (200 B.C.–A.D. 700). These were critical periods for population groups living in midwestern river valleys during which important changes in subsistence practices and settlement patterns were necessitated by overcrowding and resource depletion.

Stage IV

The major distinctions between Stages III and IV were an increased dependence on maize agriculture and cultivation of other foods, such as squash and beans. Many communities increased in size (upwards of 5 ha), and contained 20 or more residences. Due to dependence on maize as a staple, extracommunity ties were strengthened to protect against local catastrophes, such as floods or crop failures. Stage IV settlements included large villages on river terraces and smaller (or new) villages located on subsidiary drainages. Population size increased considerably over that of Stage III due to the higher labor requirements of maize agriculture. If population densities were comparable to those of major valleys, we also expect to see an expansion of village sites into upland contexts.

Once dependence on maize agriculture had intensified and intergroup ties had grown stronger, formal networks for societywide redistribution of resources may have developed. This could have enabled control of the redistributive process by one or a few persons, leading in turn to incipient forms of social ranking.

Stage IV corresponds to the terminal Late Woodland and Mississippian periods (after A.D. 700) and is characterized by maize agriculture and intergroup alliances. Evidence of social ranking and fortified communities is common in many areas of the Midwest during the latter period, but few items associated with the Mississippian cultural tradition have been found in the project area. Although available radiometric dates from the project area indicate that it was inhabited during the period of Mississippian efflorescence (Chapter 7), apparently the inhabitants either were not participating in that tradition or were receiving nothing in return for their interactions. Even without participation in this panregional tradition, it is reasonable to postulate that some of the same cultural–evolutionary developments occurred in the Cannon Reservoir area as are typical of Mississippian.

A MODEL OF HISTORIC ADAPTATION AND CHANGE

The first stable intrusion of Euro-Americans into the Cannon Reservoir region began in 1818 when public lands were made available to buyers. Sales boomed during the 1830s, and by the end of the next decade over 90% of available lands had been purchased (Bremer 1975). Today, agriculture, which developed the region and sustained it economically for 160 years, is declining in occupational importance as industrialization and commerce enlarge their domination of the labor force.

These and many other salient characteristics of historic occupation in northeastern Missouri are well documented, particularly economic trends during the twentieth century (Missouri Botanical Garden 1974). However, comparatively little is known of early adaptations to the region, and the organization and dynamics of frontier land-use systems in the southern Prairie Peninsula are poorly understood. Because historic data are important to an understanding of sociocultural evolution in a frontier environment (i.e., in the context of pristine natural resources and changing cultural parameters), and because the Cannon Reservoir region comprises an interesting environmental context for frontier settlement (i.e., intermediate between narrow gallery forests to the north and west, and extensive deciduous forests to the south and east), the Cannon Project has incorporated historic materials and information into its sphere of inquiry. As is the case with prehistory, our primary interest is in patterns of settlement and community organization and associated economic and sociocultural trends.

The model of historic development presented here incorporates these areas of interest and serves both as a guide to research and as a source of testable hypotheses. It employs several important ecological concepts and focuses on changing locational behavior from the perspective of settlement geography. The structure of the model is adapted from Hudson's (1969) theory of rural settlement location, which explains changes in settlement configurations over time.

Hudson's theory, part of which he tested using

settlement data from the heart of the Prairie Peninsula in eastern Iowa, recognizes three processes of rural settlement (Hudson 1969). Although these processes overlap in time, their modes of importance appeared generally in sequence and therefore can be thought of as phases or stages of frontier occupation. The first process, *colonization,* involves expansion of a population into a new area. The second process, termed *spread,* is a spatial correlate of population growth wherein gaps between colonial settlements are filled in as established populations grow and density increases. The third process, *competition,* arises due to environmental limitations. As individuals compete for limited space and resources, weak competitors are forced out, population density decreases, and settlement locations stabilize.

Each stage of settlement should have a distinct, although not necessarily discrete, manifestation in space. As Hudson points out, two types of space are important here: *biotope space* and *niche space.* The former is defined as a unit of real geographic space that is composed of a nearly unlimited set of m environmental variables. Niche space, on the other hand, is a theoretical space viewed from the perspective of variables instead of land area. It is comprised of a set of n analytical vectors, upon which are aligned an equal number of linearly independent sets of interdependent environmental variables, reduced from the original set of m variables comprising biotope space. Niche space is conceptually similar to R-mode principal components space, in which a series of independent factors reduces variance (or dimensionality) among a larger array of m variables by aligning all interdependent variables on n dimensions.

The relationship between niche space and niche size also is important.

> The Hutchinsonian niche is a [Euclidean] hyperspace whose *dimensions* are defined as environmental variables and whose *size* is a function of the number of values that the environmental variables may assume for which an organism has *positive fitness* [Hardesty 1975:71, emphases in original].

The niche size of a population in a given biotope is defined by the operational limits of environmental variables that bracket the range of success of that population in niche space. This range of success (or fitness) is referred to here as a population's *realized niche* (see Hardesty 1975:73).

Given these definitions, biotope space is seen as a real world phenomenon upon which settlements can be mapped. Settlements also can be plotted on vectors or dimensions of niche space, which are defined on the basis of contextual characteristics of settlements. The realized niche cannot necessarily be mapped in biotope space since a complex function may be required to complete the transformation. Nevertheless, boundaries of realized niches can be defined in real space when: (*a*) only one or a few simple factors are sufficient to describe niche variability, and (*b*) interdependent variables tend to correlate spatially.

We should also point out that the realized niche may change radically across time or space as a function of shifts in cultural behavior. For instance, technological developments may enable exploitation of new parts of the environment and can thereby cause an expansion of the realized niche or a reordering of the economic importance of its vectors. Also, differential social linkages among immigrating frontier households, such as preexisting affinal kinship ties or cooperative economic arrangements, can select for spatial clustering of some frontier settlements. Thus, socioeconomic factors may be as important as variables of the physical environment in defining the realized niche, and these linkages, if expressed locally, could cause varied configurations of contemporary settlements within the region as a whole.

Stage I

During colonization, populations extend themselves into new areas. These new areas may be new environments, unexploited portions of old environments, or new territories. Because agricultural settlers entering the Cannon Reservoir region in 1818 were preceded historically by French salt producers and native hunter–gatherers, and because many environmental characteristics of the region differed from those of source areas, both of the latter criteria apply. Of greatest importance is the fact that the Cannon Reservoir region represented a new territory that had not been exploited heavily. Resources were virtually untapped, and we assume that immigrants attempted to maximize access to beneficial environmental characteristics when they settled. Locational decisions were conditioned by perceptions of economic potential formulated well behind the frontier, however, and we therefore suggest that the realized niche of colonizers in the Cannon Reservoir region was similar to those in regions from which they had emigrated.

Hudson (1969:370) suggests that the morphology of colonial settlement is regular in space (cf. Hodder 1977:240) and therefore does not correlate necessarily with subregional environmental zones. However, given the arguments that: (*a*) generalized niches can be expressed in biotope space, and (*b*) environmental zonation in the Cannon Reservoir region was expressed as bands that paralleled ma-

jor streams, we predict that the realized niche of colonists here can be mapped in real space as a linear configuration that correlates with a limited set of slope positions. Settlement morphology should therefore not be regular in the region as a whole (cf. Hudson 1969). Rather, settlements should associate with predictable sets of environmental parameters (both cultural and natural) as suggested in Figure 5.2. Population density is low, land holdings are small, and settlements correlate with specific niches in biotope space.

Settlement locations in Figure 5.2 also are dispersed in accordance with Hudson's expectations. However, Hudson's theory ignores the potential benefits acquired from settling near other settlements, whether existing or planned. Aside from facilitating neighborly sharing of labor for intensive tasks, proximal settlement can help maintain exist-

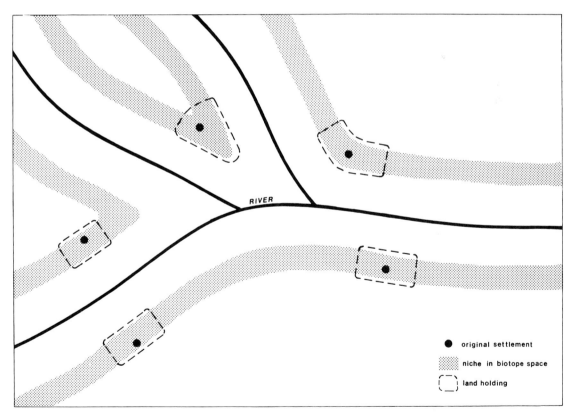

RIVER

● original settlement

▓ niche in biotope space

⌐⌐ land holding

Figure 5.2. Model of historic settlement pattern during Stage I (colonization (*n*=5) (from O'Brien and Warren 1979).

ing social ties between related nuclear families or between economically interdependent groups colonizing parts of a region contemporaneously. Also, fear of Indian reprisals may have persisted among some newcomers to northeastern Missouri (although native groups had largely evacuated the area by 1820), and these fears could have favored some clustering of settlements for purposes of mutual defense. Together, these factors suggest that early locational decisions took into account proximity to neighboring settlements and colonial settlements probably were clustered.

Stage II

During the spread process, population levels and numbers of settlements increase and fill up the realized niche. If technological advances occur at the same time, the niche itself may expand and allow settlement of new kinds of environments in a region. In either case, the spread process ends when populations approach carrying capacity and physical and cultural pressures cause a leveling off or a reversal of growth.

As stated earlier, spread is a spatial correlate of population growth wherein the magnitude function of population (i.e., density) shifts upwards, but not outwards, due to reproductive success. During colonization, in contrast, population levels of source and target areas together remain constant. The magnitude function shifts outward and downward, and density decreases as the occupied biotope expands. In reality, these two processes usually act together and represent components of the compound process of diffusion.

Assuming concurrence of these two processes in the Cannon Reservoir region, we expect two distinct, but overlapping, settlement patterns. First, population growth due to reproduction alone should be reflected in clustered settlements within the niche space. This process, referred to here as *budding* (Figure 5.3), results when offspring generally disperse short distances from parent settlements. The second expected result is a regular spacing of settlements within the realized niche (Figure 5.3). As in most frontier zones, immigration into the Cannon Project region continued long after

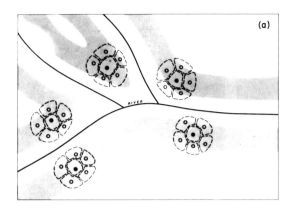

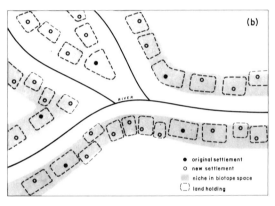

Figure 5.3. Model of historic settlement pattern during Stage II (spread) showing (*a*) budding process (*n*=30) and (*b*) immigration process (*n*=30) (from O'Brien and Warren 1979).

colonial settlements had been established. Given the nature of existing public land laws, wherein contiguous landholdings of approximately equal size were parceled out, locations of new settlements were "somewhat repelled" by those of earlier settlements (Hudson 1969:370), and the net result should be locational regularity within the realized niche.

Together, these two components of the spread phase should be expressed in space as a fairly regular distribution of settlements interrupted in several localities by settlement clusters. This general picture should have changed through time, however, since early clustered settlements probably gave

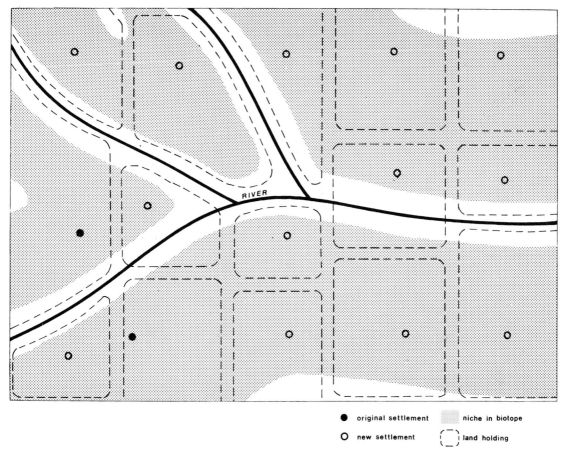

Figure 5.4. Model of historic settlement pattern during Stage III (competition ($n=15$) (from O'Brien and Warren 1979).

way to more regular spacing as the niche space filled up with immigrants. At the same time, the realized niche itself probably expanded as technological innovations (such as improved steel plows and artificial drainage techniques) allowed exploitation of new components of the regional biotope. In summary, these factors indicate Stage II was a dynamic period during which populations grew and dispersed along several trajectories. However, each trajectory had real limits imposed by carrying capacity constraints, and settlement pattern trends shifted when levels of stress increased.

Stage III

As a phase, Stage II ended when the upper limits of rural population were reached. At that point a third process, competition, became a dominant force affecting population levels, population density, and settlement patterns (Figure 5.4).

Competition among settlements is usually spurred by two major forces whose importance is most often confined to periods when population density is high. The first of these is related to the fact that there are lower limits on the size of an economically viable farm. When market prices drop, borderline operations can be forced out and are likely to be incorporated by larger operations. The second factor, evident during all phases of market fluctuation, is the desire of farmers to increase their net productivity and economic return. One of the most direct means of accomplishing this goal is to increase the size of one's landholdings. When the realized niche is completely occupied, there are no unexploited portions of the productive biotope, and farmers are forced to compete for each other's land. Competition, in effect, becomes a constant. As landholdings continue to change hands, due to the economic failure of small farms or disinterest among heirs, large farms tend to get larger, the total number of farms decreases, and rural population decreases.

Of further interest here is the fact that these trends have spatial correlates and should affect regional settlement patterns. First, as landholdings increase in size, the general stability of settlement locations increases. Second, mobility requirements among expanding farms will favor acquisitions of property as near as possible to farmstead locations. Third, as technological improvements continue to expand the effective limits of the realized niche, more and more of the biotope becomes suitable for settlement. Given these three factors, we expect patterns of rural settlement to become increasingly regular in the Cannon Reservoir region during Stage III, as farmstead locations approach a uniform network of "central places" due to constraints imposed by the boundaries of landholdings.

PART III

Regional Chronology

The three chapters in this section document the development of a regional chronology for the project area from the earliest occupation through the first half of the historic period. Chapter 6 deals with the preceramic period (ca. 6500–1150 B.C.). The data for this section comes from two stratified sites—Pigeon Roost Creek and Flowers—that produced over 90 complete, or relatively complete, projectile points from preceramic components. In addition, 16 radiometric dates were obtained from preceramic levels at the former site, and 3 from preceramic levels at the latter.

Chapter 7 summarizes efforts to establish and refine the ceramic period chronology. The project-area populations existed outside major spheres of influence to the east and southeast (i.e., Hopewellian and Mississippian manifestations) during the ceramic period, and many cultural and temporal markers highlighting these developments are missing from project area site inventories. This absence seriously confused the archaeological picture for many years, leading some investigators to suggest that the area had been abandoned during several periods. Through radiometric dating of several ceramic-bearing components and comparison with dated sequences elsewhere, a continuous sequence for the Middle Woodland through Mississippian periods has been formulated. Although Hopewell and Mississippian ceramic styles are absent, regional styles for the periods 200 B.C.–A.D. 400 and A.D. 800–1400 exist in the project area.

Chapter 8 summarizes the chronology for the early half of the historic period (the latter decades of the eighteenth century and up to the 1860s). This portion of the regional chronology is derived primarily from two sources: (a) primary and secondary historical accounts, including county and state histories, personal diaries, and unpublished overviews of economic and social development in various portions of the upper Midwest; and (b) a variety of records, such as plat maps of original land entries, land conveyance records, county court proceedings, and birth and death records. The chapter focuses on four aspects of the historic period: (a) periods of settlement; (b) formation of political units, such as counties and townships; (c) the founding of towns and villages; and (d) the evolution of communities into regional trade centers.

6

Chronology of the Preceramic Period

MICHAEL J. O'BRIEN AND ROBERT E. WARREN

The use of projectile point styles as "index fossils," reflecting the cultural and temporal ordering of archaeological components, has a long and proven history in archaeological research. However, efforts along these lines often are limited by the lack of projectile point sequences from dated, stratified deposits. This chapter presents the results of work geared toward creation of a stylistic sequence for the preceramic period in the middle Salt River valley. The term *projectile point* is used in the traditional sense, referring to lithic artifacts generally displaying symmetry of form, bifacial flaking, and usually some form of hafting modification. Emphasis is placed on visual assessment of gross morphological characteristics, which have been used to create unique classes or subclasses.

Data generated from material remains at two sites, Pigeon Roost Creek and Flowers, have been used. These sites represent the only stratified deposits excavated in the project area, and each contained ceramic and preceramic components. The former site is the more important of the two, having produced 86 complete or nearly complete points from preceramic levels. Flowers, due to limited ex-

cavation, produced only 6 points from preceramic levels. The vertical distribution of these points, however, complements data from Pigeon Roost Creek.

THE SITES

Pigeon Roost Creek

Pigeon Roost Creek, from which a sample of more than 150 relatively complete projectile points was drawn, is a stratified, multicomponent Dalton–Archaic–Woodland manifestation in the central portion of the project area. The results of analysis of stratigraphy and available radiometric determinations are summarized in Figure 6.1. Stratigraphic relationships are discussed later in this chapter in reference to major cultural units and, where appropriate, to arbitrary 10-cm units (the basic unit of excavation). This results in a somewhat simplified, although generally accurate, view of a complex depositional structure. Of interest here are (a) the lower portion of Zone I, corre-

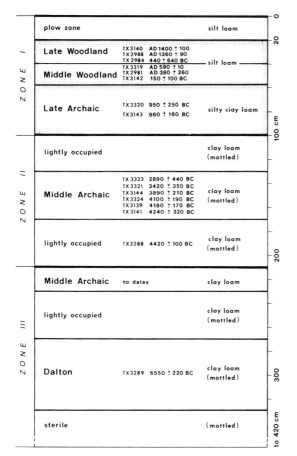

Figure 6.1. Generalized stratigraphic profile from a vertical section at Pigeon Roost Creek (after Teter and Warren 1979).

sponding to the Late Archaic period; (*b*) Zone II, corresponding to the Middle Archaic period; and (*c*) Zone III, corresponding to the Middle and Early Archaic–Dalton periods. These three depositional zones may be related to past climatic episodes. Geomorphological and floral analysis, when correlated with the radiocarbon sequence, should clarify stratigraphic relationships.

Stratigraphy

Based on our analysis, the internal subdivisions reflect a combination of natural and/or cultural breaks. Zone I is assigned tentatively to the Sub-

Boreal and more recent climatic episodes. The Late Archaic level (ca. 60–100 cm below ground surface) is defined by the distribution of diagnostic projectile point classes and by its stratigraphic position below a compact layer of limestone slabs (dating to the Late Woodland period) that extends across the site.

Zone II is assigned tentatively to the Boreal and Atlantic climatic episodes. Deposits from approximately 100–130 cm were utilized lightly. An upper Middle Archaic level (ca. 130–170 cm) is a sealed cultural deposit with clear stratigraphic limits. A relatively sterile layer (ca. 170–210 cm) appears to have been utilized only lightly.

Zone III is assigned tentatively to the Pre-Boreal episode. A hypothesized Middle Archaic level (ca. 210–230 cm) is a poorly documented occupation that was barely discernible in test units. Cultural assignment is based on stratigraphic position and the occurrence of a few characteristic projectile points. A second relatively sterile level (ca. 230–270 cm) is of variable thickness and separates the Middle Archaic and Early Archaic–Dalton levels everywhere but in the northwestern portion of the site. A deep Early Archaic–Dalton level (ca. 270–330 cm) is, in most areas, a sealed cultural deposit and contains characteristic Early Archaic and Dalton point forms.

Chronology

Ten radiocarbon dates are available from preceramic components at Pigeon Roost Creek. All assays were made on wood charcoal samples weighing at least 3 g. Results, ranked by mean sample depth, are presented in Table 6.1. The same ranking is followed in Figure 6.2, which depicts graphically the mean dates ± 1 standard deviation (S.D.).

Our interpretation of these dates was aided by the application of weighted averaging and statistical rejection techniques as recommended by Long and Rippeteau (1974:205–215). Together, these techniques can be used to evaluate the internal contemporaneity of archaeological components. The distribution of mean sample depths for all preceramic radiocarbon samples suggests that three clusters are present: (*a*) Late Archaic (83–85 cm); (*b*) upper Middle Archaic (135–152.5 cm); and inter-

TABLE 6.1.

Radiocarbon Dates from Pigeon Roost Creek[a]

Lab number	Date[b]	Date[c]	Corrected date (Damon et al. 1977)	Charcoal Sample[d]	Provenience	Depth range	Mean depth
Late Woodland							
TX-2984	2390 ± 640	449 ± 640 B.C.	520 ± 660 B.C.	Dispersed	66/35	20–25	22.5
TX-2988	590 ± 90	1369 ± 90 A.D.	1350 ± 150 A.D.	Dispersed	F. 14 68/37	20–30	25.0
TX-3140	550 ± 100	1400 ± 100 A.D.	1388 ± 160 A.D.	Consolidated	F. 14 67/37	20–35	27.5
Middle Woodland							
TX-3319	1360 ± 100	590 ± 100 A.D.	610 ± 160 A.D.	Dispersed	63/30 65/34 64/34 68/33	40–50	45.0
TX-2981	1570 ± 260	380 ± 260 A.D.	390 ± 290 A.D.	Dispersed	67/32	40–50	45.0
TX-3142	2100 ± 100	150 ± 100 B.C.	170 ± 180 B.C.	Dispersed	61/34	40–50	45.0
Late Archaic							
TX-3320	2900 ± 250	950 ± 250 B.C.	1150 ± 280 B.C.	Dispersed	67,68/30–33	60–100	83.0
TX-3143	2910 ± 160	960 ± 160 B.C.	1180 ± 200 B.C.	Consolidated	F. 1 53/39	80–90	85.0
Middle Archaic							
TX-3324	6050 ± 190	4100 ± 190 B.C.	4930 ± 230 B.C.	Dispersed	69/34	130–140	135.0
TX-3323	4840 ± 440	2890 ± 440 B.C.	3630 ± 460 B.C.	Dispersed	69/32,33	130–150	140.0
TX-3139	6130 ± 170	4180 ± 170 B.C.	5020 ± 220 B.C.	Dispersed	69/34	140–150	145.0
TX-3321	5370 ± 350	3420 ± 350 B.C.	4230 ± 390 B.C.	Dispersed	68,69/30	130–170	150.0
TX-3144	5840 ± 210	3890 ± 210 B.C.	4610 ± 260 B.C.	Dispersed	67,68/30,31	140–160	152.5
TX-3141	6190 ± 320	4240 ± 320 B.C.	5070 ± 350 B.C.	Dispersed	F. 11 67/33	170–180	175.0
TX-3288	6370 ± 100	4420 ± 100 B.C.	5240 ± 180 B.C.	Dispersed	66,67/32,33	180–190	185.0
Dalton							
TX-3289	8500 ± 220	6550 ± 220 B.C.	7390 ± 280 B.C.	Dispersed	68/30,31	300–310	305.0

[a] Source: Teter and Warren (1979).
[b] Libby half-life of 5568 years.
[c] Derived by subtracting 1950 from B.P. date.
[d] Dispersed samples are composite grouping of charcoal from one or more general levels combined to yield a sample size of 3 g.

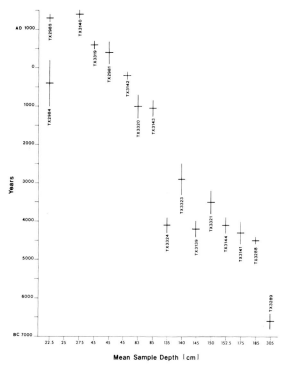

Figure 6.2. Uncorrected radiometric dates (± 1 S.D.) from ceramic and preceramic levels at Pigeon Roost Creek (from Teter and Warren 1979).

mediate Middle Archaic (175–185 cm). The single Early Archaic–Dalton date (305 cm) cannot be averaged.

Resulting cluster means of averaged dates are presented in Table 6.2. Evaluating individual dates against means using Chauvenet's criterion (accept if date falls within 0.5 sigma of cluster mean), we found support for the proposition that dates in the Late Archaic level refer to brief intervals of time (Teter and Warren 1979:235). Rejected dates occur in the upper and intermediate Middle Archaic clusters. Failure to meet Chauvenet's criterion does not imply necessarily that rejected dates are invalid; they may well be correct determinations that refer to a series of reoccupations over a long period of time. Since individual standard deviations do suggest that many of the dates are accurate, it seems reasonable to conclude that the Middle Archaic levels contain the remains of multiple occupations.

In summary, available radiometric and stratigraphic information suggest that all three preceramic periods are represented at Pigeon Roost Creek, although occupations were not continuous and several major gaps are evident. Dates from 83–85 cm may refer to a single Late Archaic period event (about 958 ± 131 B.C.), although the thickness of the corresponding cultural–stratigraphic unit implies that occupations occurred over an extended period of time. Two sets of dates are available from 100–170 cm: an upper cluster (135–153 cm) averages 3960 ± 168 B.C. and a lower cluster (175–185 cm) has a mean date of 4294 ± 92 B.C. Both sets fall within the Middle Archaic period, yet stratigraphic and radiometric dispersion once again imply that a series of occupations is represented (Teter and Warren 1979:237).

Flowers

Flowers, from which a sample of more than 50 relatively complete projectile points was drawn, is a stratified, multicomponent Archaic–Woodland manifestation in the central portion of the project area. The site was excavated in 1975, prior to our involvement with the project. Hence, we can only summarize briefly the stratigraphy of the site, relying on field notes and published vertical proveniences of artifacts (Ruppert 1976).

Stratigraphy

A simplified view of the stratigraphy shows a distinct band of dark soil, averaging 40 cm in width and overlying a lighter gray soil. The darker zone contained ceramic material that apparently was not subsequently encountered in the lighter soil beneath it. Since the site was not excavated extensively, the complete depositional history was never compiled. This fact makes assigning the excavators' 20–cm levels to a single cultural–temporal period tenuous, especially when the levels come from different areas of the site.

Chronology

Based on our reconstruction of excavated portions of the site, it is possible to "reverse-plot" ceramic material and projectile points to determine the depth of the ceramic–preceramic interface in

TABLE 6.2.

Weighted Mean Radiocarbon Dates for Five Depth Clusters and Individual Date Evaluations Using Chauvenet's Criterion[a]

Date	Label	Weighted mean	Evaluation
Late Woodland			
A.D. 1360 + 90	TX-2988	A.D. 1378 + 65	Accept
A.D. 1400 + 100	TX-3140		Accept
Middle Woodland			
A.D. 590 + 100	TX-3319		Reject
A.D. 380 + 260	TX-2981	A.D. 232 + 90	Accept
B.C. 150 + 100	TX-3142		Reject
Late Archaic			
B.C. 950 + 250	TX-3324	B.C. 958 + 131	Accept
B.C. 960 + 160	TX-3143		Accept
Upper Middle Archaic			
B.C. 4100 + 190	TX-3324		Accept
B.C. 2890 + 440	TX-3323		Reject
B.C. 4180 + 170	TX-3139	B.C. 3960 + 168	Reject
B.C. 3420 + 350	TX-3321		Reject
B.C. 3890 + 210	TX-3144		Accept
Intermediate Middle Archaic			
B.C. 4240 + 320	TX-3141	B.C. 4394 + 92	Reject
B.C. 4420 + 100	TX-3288		Accept

[a]Source: Teter and Warren (1979).

each excavation unit. As mentioned previously, the depth of this interface averages about 40 cm. The occurrence of ceramics with projectile point forms that are common to or restricted to the Woodland period is high, with close agreement between the lowest depths at which pottery occurs and the lowest depths at which diagnostic Woodland points occur. A single date from the preceramic period was obtained. The uncorrected determination is 2060 ± 85 B.C., and it dates a small, basin-shaped pit, the orifice of which was well down in the Archaic level.

THE PROJECTILE POINT CLASSIFICATION

The sample of 92 projectile points (86 from Pigeon Roost Creek and 6 from Flowers) utilized here contains nearly all complete or substantially complete specimens from preceramic levels at the two sites. Specimens lacking precise locational co-ordinates were excluded to maximize contextual accuracy.

Twenty-three major projectile point classes (incorporating 40 subclasses) from preceramic levels are represented in the sample. These were drawn from a classification of all projectile points recovered in the project area from 1959 to 1979. Classes were defined on the basis of shared morphological attributes; often, subclasses were employed to emphasize differences among certain variables, such as base shape, size of tangs, and degree of barbing (Curry and O'Brien 1981). A series of variables was established so that a simple code sequence could be used to identify each unique class or subclass. Variables considered to be of primary importance in separating one class from another are (a) primary hafting preparation; (b) shape of base; (c) shape of stem; (d) widest point of blade; (e) angle, degree, and shape of shoulders; (f) notch proportion and orientation; (g) shape of tangs; and (h) overall size. Definitions of projectile point classes occurring in preceramic levels are presented in the following sections.

Lanceolate Points

Class 1.0 includes large lanceolate forms with excurvate blades, contracting stems, and straight to convex bases (Figure 6.3). Subclasses are defined on the basis of the presence or absence of a hafting modification in the form of lateral grinding. Subclass 1.1 contains no modification; members of this subclass are similar to Sedalia points (Chapman 1975). Subclass 1.3 exhibits a modified haft element; specimens also are similar to Sedalia points.

Class 2.0 includes large, thin, finely chipped lanceolate blades with ground convex bases (Figure 6.3). These specimens may be Dalton point preforms, although Goodyear (1974) states that no Dalton preforms are ground.

Class 3.0 contains large, subtriangular, thin bifaces with slightly contracting proximal sections and straight bases. The hafting element is unmodified (Figure 6.3). The form and context of these specimens suggest that they represent Dalton point preforms.

Class 4.0 includes large lanceolate points with excurvate blades and contracting-to-straight bases. Three subclasses are present, two of which are important here. Subclass 4.2 contains hafting elements that are ground on lateral edges (Figure 6.3); points resemble the Agate Basin type (Chapman

1975). Subclass 4.3 contains specimens with lateral edge grinding and hafting elements that are longer than those on specimens in subclass 4.2 (Fig. 6.3). Points in subclass 4.3 are also larger than points in subclass 4.2, and they closely resemble Sedalia points.

Class 7.0 includes large points with incurvate–excurvate blades and hafting elements that have been well flaked along the edge. Two subclasses are defined on base shape. Subclass 7.1 contains specimens with slightly concave bases (Figure 6.3); points are similar to Sedalia and Wadlow (Perino 1968a) types.

Class 8.0 contains medium-sized lanceolate forms with excurvate blades and straight bases. The widest portion of the point is in the proximal third. Two subclasses are formed on the basis of hafting element modification, with subclass 8.1 exhibiting lateral edge grinding but no basal grinding (Figure 6.3). The overall shape is similar to Angostura points (Suhm and Jelks 1962).

Class 11.0 includes points with parallel-sided stems, slightly concave bases, and straight blades that contract from the top of the stem (Figure 6.3). Stems are well ground, and bases are thinned by the removal of long narrow flakes. These specimens may be completed Dalton preforms, although the reworking on all specimens suggests that they were well-used implements prior to loss–discard.

Class 12.0 includes medium-sized points with parallel to slightly incurvate ground stems and deeply concave ground bases from which one or more long, lamellar, flutelike flakes have been removed (Figure 6.3). All points recovered have been reworked in the classic "steeple-shaped" Dalton fashion. Points are identical or very similar to several Dalton varieties, such as Greenbrier (Cambron and Hulse 1965), Meserve (Suhm and Jelks 1962), and Serrated (Chapman 1975).

Side-notched Points

Class 14.0 includes points with excurvate blades, broad, shallow notches, and crude, somewhat rounded tangs. Subclass 14.1 is defined on the basis of a straight base (Figure 6.4). Specimens are similar to Big Sandy (Chapman 1975) and Brewerton side-

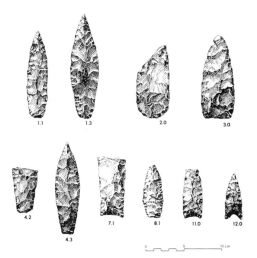

Figure 6.3. Archaic period lanceolate projectile point classes.

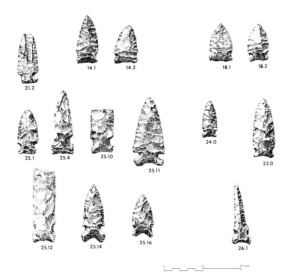

Figure 6.4. Archaic period side-notched projectile point classes.

notched (Ritchie 1971) points. Subclass 14.2 is defined on the basis of a concave base (Figure 6.4). Specimens are similar to the previously mentioned types.

Class 18.0 includes medium-sized points with excurvate blades, shallow notches, obtuse shoulders, and bases that often are as wide as the shoulders. Stems are broad with edges that expand moderately in incurvate arcs. Two subclasses are formed on the basis of base shape: subclass 18.1 specimens have straight bases, whereas subclass 18.2 specimens have slightly concave bases (Figure 6.4). Points in these subclasses are similar to Big Sandy and Brewerton side-notched types.

Class 21.0 contains points with straight to slightly excurvate blades, shoulders that are perpendicular to the long axis of the blade, stems that expand markedly in incurvate arcs, and straight bases that expand at least to the width of the blade. Subclasses are defined on the basis of the degree of shouldering and notch size. Subclass 21.2 specimens contain shoulders and notches that are pronounced (Figure 6.4). All bases are thinned and often are beveled. Points in this subclass resemble Edgewood (Bell 1958) and Ensor (Bell 1960) types.

Class 23.0 includes medium-sized, well-made points with excurvate blades, short and broad stems, moderately obtuse shoulders, and slightly concave bases that may be beveled and/or ground (Figure 6.4). Specimens resemble Osceola (Bell 1958), Hemphill (Perino 1971), and Big Sandy types.

Class 24.0 contains small points with straight to excurvate blades, moderate shoulders, equal-sized notches, short stems, and slightly concave bases that are as wide as the shoulders (Figure 6.4). Types that are similar include Big Sandy and Hanna (Perino 1971).

Class 25.0 contains a variety of medium-sized and large points with triangular to parallel blades, side notches, expanding stems, and concave to straight bases. There is considerable variability in this class, principally in the haft area. Subclass 25.1 members have triangular, excurvate blades, straight bases, rounded tangs, and a moderately expanding stem (Figure 6.4). Similar types include Big Sandy and Raddatz (Perino 1971). Subclass 25.4 specimens exhibit characteristics similar to the previous subclass except for markedly expanding stems and pronounced shoulders (Figure 6.4). Similar types include Osceola and Godar (Perino 1971). Subclass 25.10 specimens are medium-sized to large points with parallel blades, moderately expanding stems, pronounced shoulders, and slightly concave bases (Figure 6.4). Similar types include Osceola and Hemphill. Subclass 25.11 contains medium to large points with triangular to subtriangular blades, markedly expanding stems, rounded tangs, and slightly concave bases (Figure 6.4). Specimens are similar to Osceola and Hemphill points. Subclass 25.12 includes medium-sized points with parallel-sided blades; moderately expanding stems; broad, shallow notches; and slightly concave bases (Figure 6.4). Members are similar to Hemphill and Osceola points. Subclass 25.14 includes medium-sized points that exhibit markedly expanding stems, deep notches, squarish tangs, and deeply concave bases (Fig. 6.4). Similar types include Hemphill and Big Sandy. Subclass 25.16 contains medium-sized points with triangular, excurvate blades, moderately expanding stems, shallow notches, rounded and downturned tangs, and deeply concave bases (Figure 6.4). These specimens are similar to Big Sandy and Raddatz points.

Class 26 includes points with straight to incurvate triangular blades, stems that expand moderately in incurvate arcs, and basal concavities that are squarish, beveled, and ground (Figure 6.4). Subclass 26.1 specimens have a less pronounced concavity (under 3mm) than those in the other subclass. Specimens correlate with Graham Cave sidenotched points (Chapman 1975), which are common throughout northeastern and central Missouri.

Corner-notched Points

Class 31.0 includes large points with excurvate blades, markedly expanding stems, and slightly convex bases. Two subclasses are defined by the degree of barbing, with subclass 31.1 containing specimens with less pronounced barbs (Figure 6.5). Points in this subclass are similar to the Helton type (T. Cook 1976).

Class 36.0 includes points with incurvate–excurvate blades; broad, parallel-sided to moderately expanding stems; slight to pronounced barbs; and straight to slightly convex bases. Several subclasses are defined on the basis of base shape, degree of stem expansion, and degree of barbing. Subclass

36.1 specimens exhibit slightly convex bases, parallel-sided stems, and moderate barbing (Figure 6.5). These are similar to Etley and Stone square-stem types (Chapman 1975). Subclass 36.2 is similar to subclass 36.1, except examples exhibit moderately expanding stems (Figure 6.5). Points are similar to the Etley type. Subclass 36.4 specimens exhibit straight bases, moderately expanding stems, and slight barbs (Figure 6.5). Points are similar to the Etley type. Subclass 36.5 includes points with straight bases, parallel-sided stems, and pronounced barbs (Figure 6.5). Examples are similar to the Etley and Stone square-stem types. Subclass 36.6 includes points with straight bases, moderately expanding stems, and moderate barbing (Figure 6.5). Points are similar to the Etley type.

Class 38.0 includes large points with triangular excurvate blades, moderately expanding stems, lateral and basal edge grinding, and slightly concave to convex bases. Subclasses are defined on the shape of the base. Subclass 38.3 specimens exhibit slightly concave bases that have been ground heavily (Figure 6.5). Specimens are similar to Hardin barbed points (Bell 1960).

Class 40.0 includes a variety of medium-sized points with triangular blades, wide shoulders, and bifacially thinned bases. Subclasses are defined by base shape and degree of barbing. Subclass 40.5 specimens have slightly concave bases and are moderately barbed (Figure 6.5). Points are similar to Bulverde (Bell 1960) and Marshall (Bell 1958) types.

Class 45.0 contains a variety of medium-sized points with triangular, straight to excurvate blades, stems that expand moderately to markedly in incurvate arcs, and bifacially thinned bases. Subclasses are defined on the basis of the degree of barbing and base shape. Subclass 45.2 specimens contain convex bases, markedly expanding stems, and slight barbs (Figure 6.5). Points are similar to Big Creek (Perino 1971) and Williams (Bell 1960) types. Subclass 45.3 includes points with convex bases, moderately expanding stems, and pronounced barbs (Figure 6.5). Specimens are similar to Big Creek and Williams types. Subclass 45.4 specimens have straight bases, moderately expanding stems, and slight barbing. They are similar to the previously mentioned types.

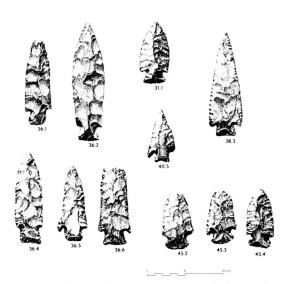

Figure 6.5.   Archaic period corner-notched projectile point classes.

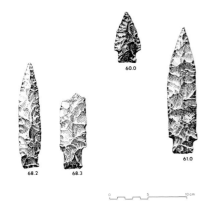

Figure 6.6. Archaic period stemmed projectile point classes.

Stemmed Points

Class 60.0 includes medium-sized points with triangular blades, parallel-sided stems, shoulders that are almost perpendicular to the long axis of the blade, and straight bases (Figure 6.6). Specimens are similar to the Kirk type (Bell 1960).

Class 61.0 includes points with incurvate–excurvate blades, broad parallel-sided stems, perpendicular shoulders, and straight bases (Figure 6.6). Specimens are similar to the Stone square-stem type.

Class 68.0 includes points with large, parallel-sided blades, parallel-sided bases, and obtuse shoulders. Subclasses are defined by base shape and the degree of shouldering. Subclass 68.2 specimens exhibit straight bases and moderately obtuse shoulders (Figure 6.6). Specimens are similar to Elk River (Cambron and Hulse 1965) and Stone square-stem types. Subclass 68.3 includes points with straight bases and fairly pronounced shoulders (Figure 6.6). Points are similar to Elk River and Stone square-stem.

PROJECTILE POINT CLASS DISTRIBUTIONS

Our analysis of projectile point class frequencies among stratigraphic units at the Pigeon Roost Creek and Flowers sites indicates that many of the temporal associations postulated on the basis of research conducted outside the Cannon Reservoir region are correct. Frequencies for the 35 subclasses at Pigeon Roost Creek are presented in Table 6.3. Relative projectile point frequencies by class (subclasses combined) at Pigeon Roost Creek are illustrated in Figure 6.7. The data from Flowers are summarized in Table 6.4. Our discussion will now focus on the stratigraphic variation within the 21 classes at Pigeon Roost Creek and the 5 classes at Flowers and also on important trends among subclasses.

Early Archaic–Dalton Period

The Early Archaic–Dalton component (ca. 270–330 cm) at Pigeon Roost Creek contains classes 2.0, 3.0, 4.0, 8.0, 11.0, 12.0, 25.0, 26.0, 38.0, and 60.0. Only two of these classes have members present in levels assigned to later cultural periods: classes 25.0 and 4.0. Based on morphological characteristics, we believe that the single examples of these two classes were classified correctly. Given that the majority of the representatives of classes 25.0 and 4.0 occur much higher in the sequence, these two specimens should be viewed as aberrances or as examples of projectile point classes that had an early development but never were popular until Middle and Late Archaic time.

Due to the small sample, it probably is not wise to place much emphasis on the frequencies of class occurrence by level except to note the disproportionately large number of class 3.0 specimens in the 300–310-cm level (Table 6.3). This class, similar to the Dalton preforms that are common in early period sites in Missouri and Arkansas, contains over 60% of points from that level. Classes 11.0 and 12.0, classic Dalton points, occur in the lowest four levels, one of class 11.0 in the 320–330-cm level and one of class 12.0 in the 310–320-, 300–310-, and 290–300-cm levels. Class 60.0, similar to the Kirk type, is another major constituent of the early occupation. Other classes present and similar types include Hardin barbed (38.3), Graham Cave side-notched (26.1), Angostura (8.1), Big Sandy (25.1), Agate Basin (4.2), and a form similar to Dalton preforms (except specimens exhibit heavy grinding [2.0]).

TABLE 6.3.

Frequencies of Projectile Points by Subclass in 19 Excavation Levels at Pigeon Roost Creek

Level (cm)	11.0	60.0	12.0	38.3	26.1	3.0	8.1	2.0	24.0	25.1	25.10	25.11	25.12	25.14	25.16	23.0	18.1
60–70																	
70–80																	
80–90																	
90–100																	
100–110													1				
110–120												1					
120–130														1			
130–140											1				2		
140–150												1					1
150–160															1	2	1
160–170														1	1		1
210–220									1								
220–230									1								
270–280						2		2		1							
280–290																	
290–300		2	1			2											
300–310			1	1	1	5	1										
310–320			1		1												
320–330	1	1															

Level (cm)	18.2	14.1	14.2	4.2	4.3	68.2	68.3	1.1	1.3	36.1	36.2	36.4	36.5	36.6	61.0	45.2	31.1	40.5
60–70				1	4		1	1	1	2	1			1	1	1	1	1
70–80						1			3		2	1	1	1			1	
80–90					2	3		1	2	1	1	1	1		1	1		
90–100							1											
100–110			1	1														
110–120																		
120–130																		
130–140	1		1															
140–150	1		3															
150–160	2		1															
160–170																		
210–220																		
220–230																		
270–280																		
280–290				1														
290–300																		
300–310																		
310–320																		
320–330																		

PROJECTILE POINT CLASS

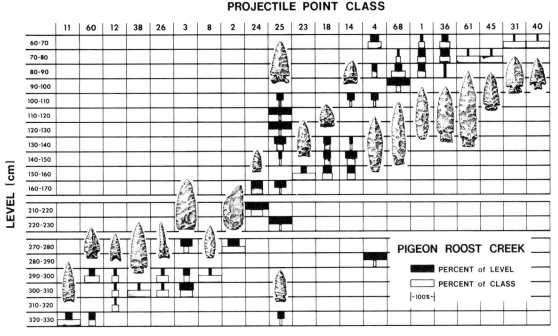

Figure 6.7. Relative projectile point class frequencies from preceramic levels at Pigeon Roost Creek, by percentage of level and percentage of class.

One conclusion to be drawn from the analysis of points from the lower 60 cm of Pigeon Roost Creek is that there is some amount of mixing in the deposit. This conclusion is suported by data from elsewhere in the Midwest where there is a documented shift from Dalton points to a variety of lanceolate and side-notched points, such as Graham Cave and Hardin barbed. However, an alternate interpreta-

tion can be offered. Because (*a*) the site was subjected to careful scrutiny during excavation of the lower levels to ensure that the excavation units were not cross-cutting natural strata, and (*b*) no such evidence was found, it is possible that the apparent mixing of Dalton points (including preforms) and other Early Archaic types is a result of tradition lag. Three-dimensional plots of artifact locations and stratigraphic sequences should resolve this issue.

Middle Archaic Period

The Middle Archaic period is represented at Pigeon Roost Creek by two components separated by a 40-cm-thick band of fill that contained few artifacts. These levels (ca. 130–170 cm and ca. 210–230 cm) are dominated by a variety of small to medium-sized side-notched points (classes 14.0, 18.0, 23.0, 24.0, and 25.0).

The lower component (Middle Archaic II) contains only two classes, each containing single speci-

TABLE 6.4.

Projectile Point Classes-Subclasses in Preceramic Levels at Flowers[a]

Level (cm)	Subclasses
40–60	61.0
60–80	7.1, 21.2, 25.4
80–100	45.3
100–120	--
120–140	45.4

[a]All frequencies are 1.

mens. The first, class 24.0, consists of small points similar to Big Sandy and Hanna types. The second, represented in the 220–230-cm level by subclass 25.1, is also similar to the Big Sandy type and to the Raddatz type as well.

The upper component (Middle Archaic I) contains specimens from all five classes represented in Middle Archaic levels. Classes 14.0, 18.0 and 25.0 dominate in the component, containing eight, seven, and eight members, respectively. There is a clear mode for class 25.0 in the 130–140-cm level, whereas classes 18.0 and 14.0 enter the sequence in the 150–160-cm level and lose their importance at 130 cm. Class 23.0 is present only in the 150–160-cm level, the level containing the highest frequency of Middle Archaic points.

To understand better the composition of this component, we now focus on the distribution of subclasses within it. Several subclasses of class 25.0 are represented in the 150–160-cm level. Subclass 25.12, which occurs only in the 100–110-cm level, is similar to Hemphill, Osceola, and Otter Creek types. Subclass 25.10, which occurs only in the 130–140-cm level, is also similar to the above-named types. Subclass 25.11, also similar to those types, occurs both in the 110–120-cm and 140–150-cm levels. Two specimens of subclass 25.16, similar to Big Sandy and Raddatz points, occur in the 130–140-cm level and one in the 160–170-cm level. Subclass 25.14, present in the 120–130-cm level, is similar to Big Sandy points. The distribution of this subclass is somewhat confusing since it occurs also in the 320–330-cm level, the deepest level of the site. As mentioned previously, this distribution may be due to the early occurrence of Big Sandy points, followed by several millennia of absence, or to the vagaries of point manufacture.

Class 18.0 consists of two subclasses, 18.1 and 18.2. The distributions of specimens in the subclasses remarkably mirror one another. One member of subclass 18.1, similar to Brewerton side-notched and Big Sandy types, is present in each of the middle levels of the component. One member of subclass 18.2, also similar to those two types, occurs in each of two of the middle levels and two occur in the third level.

Class 14.0 consists of two subclasses, 14.1 and 14.2. Subclass 14.1, also similar to Big Sandy and

Brewerton side-notched points, appears in the 150–160-cm level only. This small point with broad, shallow notches and a straight base seems to be an excellent temporal marker. Both specimens were excavated in close proximity to radiometric sample TX-3144 (3890 ± 210 B.C. [uncorrected]). Subclass 14.2, also similar to the above-named types, exhibits wide distribution throughout the component, from 100–160 cm, with a clear mode in the 140–150-cm level.

The single member of subclass 4.2 that falls in the level between the Middle Archaic I and Late Archaic components is identical in most respects to the specimen in that subclass that came from the 280–290-cm level. This may signal an early development of a style similar to the Agate Basin point, which eventually evolved into a style similar to the Sedalia point.

Late Archaic Period

Late Archaic components are present at both Pigeon Roost Creek and Flowers. The component at the former site contains examples from classes 1.0, 4.0, 31.0, 36.0, 40.0, 45.0, 61.0, and 68.0. Flowers contains points in classes 25.0, 45.0, and 61.0, but also present are two classes (7.0 and 21.0) not seen at Pigeon Roost Creek. Interestingly, there are, in addition to the two new classes, five subclasses present at Flowers that are not present at Pigeon Roost Creek.

In the Pigeon Roost Creek Late Archaic component, four of the eight classes contain five or more members–class 36.0 dominating with nine, followed by class 1.0 with eight, class 4.0 with seven, and class 68.0 with five. Point styles present include lanceolate (classes 1.0 and 4.0), corner-notched (classes 31.0, 36.0, 40.0, and 45.0), and stemmed (classes 61.0 and 68.0). Temporal trends among classes are informative: (*a*) class 1.0 is represented consistently throughout the component; (*b*) class 4.0 gains in frequency toward the top of the component; (*c*) class 36.0 gains strongly in the top half of the component; and (*d*) class 68.0 shows a clear mode in the 80–90-cm level. The remaining four classes are represented by single members, all of which occur in the upper half of the component.

Trends in subclass distributions are likewise informative. Subclass 4.2 is represented by single members in each of three levels: 60–70 cm, 100–110 cm (Late Archaic–Middle Archaic), and 280–290 cm (Early Archaic). As discussed previously, this subclass is not a good temporal marker because it occurs throughout the sequence. Subclass 4.3 gains in frequency, from two specimens in the 80–90-cm level to four in the 60–70-cm level. This frequency of points in the 60–70-cm level makes subclass 4.3 the dominant subclass in that level. Members of this subclass can be identified as Sedalia points, one hallmark of the Late Archaic period in northeastern Missouri.

Subclass 1.3 has two specimens in the 80–90-cm level, three in the 70–80-cm level, and one in the 60–70-cm level. Subclass 1.1 has single representatives in the 60–70-cm and 80–90-cm level. These specimens also are similar to Sedalia points.

Subclasses 36.1 and 36.2 are the only subclasses of class 36.0 to contain more than one member. Both examples of subclass 36.1 occur in the 60–70-cm level, whereas subclass 36.2 is found in the 60–70-cm, 70–80-cm (2), and 80–90 cm levels. Points in these subclasses are typical of the Etley type, another horizon marker for the Late Archaic period in portions of the Midwest.

Subclass 68.2 has its greatest representation in the 80–90-cm level, with three specimens, and then decreases to a single specimen in the succeeding level. These points are usually typed as Stone square-stem, another common Late Archaic point in much of Missouri.

Stratigraphic data from Flowers mirror fairly well the data from Pigeon Roost Creek. At Flowers, a single example of subclass 45.4, resembling Williams or Big Creek points, was the deepest point (120–140 cm). This was followed by a subclass 45.3 specimen (same types) at 80–100 cm. Three subclasses, each containing a single member, occurred in the 60–80 cm level: 21.2 (Edgewood, Ensor), 25.4 (Godar), and 7.1 (Sedalia, Wadlow). One specimen from class 61.0, similar to Stone square-stem, came from the 40–60-cm level. Like Pigeon Roost Creek, Flowers has lanceolate, corner-notched, and stemmed forms. An important difference is the presence of two side-notched subclasses (21.2 and 25.4) in the Late Archaic levels at Flowers. As noted previously, no side-notched points were found in the Late Archaic component at Pigeon Roost Creek. This scant bit of data could have important implications in ordering components from other sites. Future analysis may show that there is a Late Archaic horizon present at Flowers that is missing at Pigeon Roost Creek.

SUMMARY AND CONCLUSIONS

Pigeon Roost Creek contains a discontinuous series of four major preceramic occupation zones ranging in age from about 8500 to 2900 B.P. Analysis of projectile point classes in relation to stratigraphic units and radiometric determinations indicates that a number of important stylistic trends are present and implies the four major components actually contain many discrete occupations.

The lowermost occupation zone (270–330 cm) dates to the Early Archaic–Dalton periods (6550 ± 220 B.C.). Its point assemblage is dominated by Dalton preforms (class 3.0), Dalton points (classes 11.0 and 12.0), Kirk-like points (class 60.0) and Graham Cave side-notched points (subclass 26.1). Other types present include Angostura (class 8.0), Hardin barbed (subclass 38.3), and a type that is similar to Big Sandy (subclass 25.1). These artifact classes, and the associated radiocarbon date, correspond well with dated material elsewhere in Missouri (Chapman 1975). A 40-cm-thick relatively sterile zone, dated by interpolation from approximately 5900–5300 B.C., overlies the Early Archaic component (Teter and Warren 1979:246).

Above the sterile zone is a sparse component ranging in depth from 210–230 cm. We suggest that this zone may date to about 5000 B.C. The presence of two side-notched projectile points, both similar to the Big Sandy type (class 24.0 and subclass 25.1), is consistent with this interpretation and indicates that a stylistic shift took place in the Cannon Reservoir region sometime during the sixth millennium B.C.

Above a second, lightly occupied zone, which has an estimated time range of approximately 5000–4300 B.C., lies a relatively dense component ranging from around 130 to 170 cm in depth. All points in these levels are triangular to subtriangular side-notched forms with expanding stems. The sample is dominated by variants of the Big Sandy type (classes 14.0, 18.0, 23.0, 24.0, and 25.0). Associated radiometric dates and stratigraphic evidence indicate that a number of discrete occupations are represented. The most culturally dense levels (130–160 cm) fall toward the lower end of the component and probably date from about 4200–3300 B.C., but side-notched point classes continue up to the 100-cm level, or as recently as 2000–2500 B.C. Thus, point styles in the Cannon Reservoir region appear to have changed very little from the fifth through the third millennia B.C., lasting through at least the second half of Griffin's (1967) Middle Archaic period and into the Late Archaic period.

Because of the large gap in the stratigraphy between the Late Archaic and Middle Archaic components, possibly representing as much as 2000 years, we cannot firmly fix the end of the side-notched point form. Data from Modoc Rock Shelter in southwestern Illinois indicate that side-notched points were being replaced by corner-notched points by 3000 B.C. and, in turn, by straight-stemmed forms by approximately 2500 B.C. (Fowler 1959). This example could imply that a stylistic "tradition lag" is represented in the Cannon Reservoir region, but again, because of the lack of datable material in the intermediate zone, it is not easy to test this proposition.

A major stylistic shift does occur at Pigeon Roost Creek site above the relatively sterile layer, at about 100 cm. Here, lanceolate and stemmed forms replace side-notched forms. The three point types that dominate the component are Sedalia (classes 1.0 and 4.0), Etley (class 36.0), and Stone square-stem (class 68.0). All three types occur throughout much of the Late Archaic component. Radiocarbon dates from this component average around 955

B.C.; interpolation indicates its total range is 2040–500 B.C. Thus, lanceolate and stemmed points dominate the assemblage through most of the second and first millennia B.C., or during the final third of Griffin's (1967) Late Archaic period and most of his Early Woodland period. This contrasts again with developments in Illinois. There contemporary pottery-making peoples of the Red Ocher complex and Black Sand phase were making relatively small, contracting-stemmed points and small, rectangular-stemmed points. Thus, the argument for tradition lag in the Cannon Reservoir region is supported.

Flowers contains a 1-m-thick Late Archaic component from which a single date of 2060 ± 85 B.C. was obtained. The sequence at that site begins with corner-notched points (class 45.0), continues through side-notched (classes 21.0 and 25.0) and lanceolate (class 7.0) points, and ends with the appearance of a stemmed form (class 61.0). The Flowers site contains five subclasses (7.1, 21.2, 25.4, 45.3, and 45.4) not seen at Pigeon Roost Creek and also contains side-notched points in levels containing Late Archaic forms, a phenomenon missing in the excavated portion of the Late Archaic component at the Pigeon Roost Creek site.

The significance of the data presented here for understanding the dynamics of preceramic settlement-subsistence systems in the middle Salt River valley is clear. However, as has been noted elsewhere (Teter and Warren 1979: 249), the model developed here is based on evidence from only two sites and it still contains gaps. Future research on the Archaic in the Prairie Peninsula hopefully will fill in many of these gaps, especially that between the latest date of the upper Middle Archaic component and the earliest date of the Late Archaic component at the Pigeon Roost Creek site.

7

Chronology of the Ceramic Period

THERESA K. DONHAM

The ceramic-period chronology of the project area includes Middle and Late Woodland occupations ranging in time from approximately 200 B.C. to A.D. 1400. Changes in ceramic and projectile-point styles have allowed the definition of five ceramic period phases. The goal of this formulation is to provide a framework for additional between-site comparisons and analyses within the project area, and it is offered as an expansion of a two-phase chronology proposed by Hunt (1976, 1977a) for the Late Woodland period.

Analysis of the rimsherd inventory (1516 specimens from 42 sites) has indicated that most collections represent mixed, multiple components with little or no vertical segregation of ceramic materials. The approach employed here relies heavily on sherds recovered from dated contexts in the project area and comparisons with well-dated ceramic material from other parts of the Midwest. It should be noted that because of the introduction of ceramics into the project area by at least 200 B.C. (evidence of an earlier introduction is not well documented), and our ability to distinguish temporal variation in form and decorative style, we rely more heavily on

ceramics than projectile points in forming the chronology.

Woodland chronologies used for comparison have been developed for specific areas in Wisconsin, Iowa, Illinois, and Missouri (Figure 7.1). Stylistic and temporal parameters of ceramic manifestations differ among these research areas, but they hold in common the Havana ceramic tradition and some expression of Hopewell. Ceramics in the project area express this commonality and also exhibit what appear to be shifts in directions of interaction through time.

Thirty-eight radiometric sample means from 14 sites in the Cannon Reservoir area fall within the ceramic period. Rimsherds have been recovered in association with dated, carbonized materials that range in date from 150 ± 100 B.C. to A.D. 1400 ± 100 (Figure 7.2). These dates, and associated ceramics, are included in the discussions of each phase.

Before turning to a discussion of the phases, I focus on the ceramic-period levels at Pigeon Roost Creek, one of only two known sites in the project area with well stratified deposits. As I will discuss later, the ceramic period projectile-point sequence

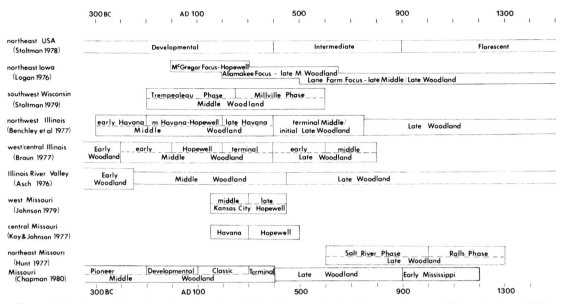

Figure 7.1. Comparison of midwestern chronological frameworks for the ceramic period (from Donham 1981).

from Pigeon Roost Creek is based on 94 complete, or relatively complete, specimens from Woodland and Mississippian levels. This enables us to document temporal change in point form and isolate important temporal markers. Despite the general utility of the sequence, there are major Woodland point classes that do not occur at Pigeon Roost Creek. Because of the compact nature of the Woodland levels at Pigeon Roost Creek (60 cm), projectile-point class modes often either are difficult to distinguish, or they cross-cut the Middle–Late Woodland boundary. Similarly, the ceramic assemblage from the site does not provide the necessary amount of information regarding temporal variability. Hence, the sequence at Pigeon Roost Creek provides only a framework for a ceramic-period chronology and is supplemented by data from dated contexts at unstratified sites.

CERAMIC-PERIOD CHRONOLOGY AT PIGEON ROOST CREEK

Levels at Pigeon Roost Creek that contain ceramic-period material are confined to the upper ⅔

of Zone I (Figure 6.1). The plow zone (0–20 cm) is a disturbed unit containing Late Woodland material. The Late Woodland level (20–40 cm) is defined on the basis of projectile-point styles and its position directly above a compact, culturally deposited layer of unmodified, broken limestone chunks. The Middle Woodland level (40–60 cm) is defined on the basis of projectile-point styles and its position within and below the limestone layer. The Late Archaic level (60–100 cm) is directly below this level (Chapter 6).

Six radiometric dates—three from Late Woodland and three from Middle Woodland levels—are available from ceramic-bearing components. Results, ranked by mean sample depth, are presented in Table 6.1. One date (TX-2984) is anomalous with respect to mean depth and assays of companion samples and is excluded from further consideration. Interpretation of the remaining dates is facilitated by the application of the weighted averaging and statistical rejection techniques mentioned in Chapter 6. Distribution of mean sample depths suggests the presence of two clusters: (*a*) Late Woodland (22.5–27.5 cm) and (*b*) Middle Woodland (45 cm).

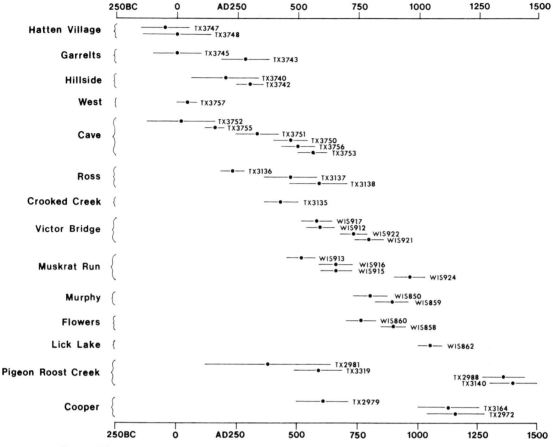

Figure 7.2. Radiometric dates (uncorrected) from ceramic components in the project area.

Evaluating individual dates against means using Chauvenet's criterion (Chapter 6), we find support for the proposition that dates in the Late Woodland level refer to discrete intervals of time. This conclusion is consistent with the contexts of the two Late Woodland dates; they were derived from the same feature and probably refer to a single point in time. Rejected dates occur in the Middle Woodland cluster (Table 6.2), suggesting that the levels contain the remains of multiple occupations. Given the 740-year range in mean dates for the two rejected dates from the Middle Woodland component, this seems a fair assessment.

Shifts in projectile-point form between pre-ceramic and ceramic levels at Pigeon Roost Creek

are noticeable: (*a*) lanceolate forms compose 7 of 21 classes in Archaic levels, but only 2 of 26 classes in Woodland levels; (*b*) side-notched classes drop from 6 of 21 to 4 of 26; (*c*) stemmed forms drop from 3 of 21 to 1 of 26; (*d*) corner-notched forms increase from 5 of 21 to 13 of 26; and (*e*) arrowpoints of various forms occur in 6 of 26 classes in the ceramic components, whereas they were absent in earlier levels.

Data on projectile-point classes from the ceramic-period components, both by the percentage of each class by level and the percentage of each level by class, at Pigeon Roost Creek are presented in Figure 7.3. Due to space limitations, only classes are discussed in this chapter. It should be noted,

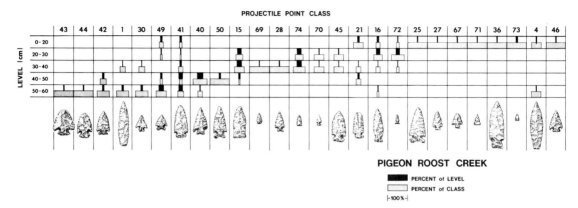

Figure 7.3. Relative projectile-point class frequencies from ceramic-bearing levels at Pigeon Roost Creek, by percentage of level and percentage of class.

however, that often a particular class contains subclasses, many of which vary temporally. Variables (dimensions) used in defining these classes are listed in Chapter 6. Instead of discussing here the stratigraphic position of each class at Pigeon Roost Creek, I discuss classes under the phase in which they appear or predominate.

MONROE PHASE 200 b.c.–a.d. 200

Monroe phase ceramics are representative of the Middle Woodland Havana tradition, a regional manifestation that has been identified throughout the Midwest. Middle Woodland Havana assemblages across the upper Mississippi Valley share technological and decorative features that permit relatively accurate identification of specimens (Benn 1978; Brown 1964; Chapman 1980; Kay and Johnson 1977; Loy 1968; Morse 1963; Stoltman 1979; Struever 1964). Havana ceramics predating a.d. 1 are distinguished by the overall thickness of vessel walls, the coarseness of the paste, and the size of nonplastic inclusions: Crushed-grit paste inclusions generally are numerous and range from 1–2 mm in diameter, and upper vessel wall thickness ranges from 8–12 mm. Interior beveling of the rim–lip juncture and lip flattening are common characteristics. Havana vessels tend to be unshouldered or to have constricted shoulders with direct rims; lips may be outflaring.

The most common Havana decoration identified in Missouri for this phase is interior rim–lip juncture impressions and exterior bosses. Decorations identified as characteristic of Illinois Valley Havana include thick-toothed, vertical, dentate stamping on the upper rim; zones filled with dentate stamping on the vessel body; and interior rim–lip juncture impressions with cord-wrapped or dentate-tool marks (Brown 1964). Other Middle Woodland Havana decorations include zoned incising or linear trailing with zoned dentate stamping, exterior cord-wrapped-tool impressions along the rim–lip juncture, and hollow reed or ovated punctures. Surface treatments include plain, cordmarked, and smoothed cordmarked (Benn 1978; Brown 1964; Logan 1976; Wray 1952). With the exception of vertical dentate stamping on the upper rim, each decoration is represented by at least one specimen from the project area.

Monroe phase Havana specimens occur at five of six sites with radiometric samples dating 200 b.c.–a.d. 200: Pigeon Roost Creek, Hatten Village, Garrelts, Cave, and Hillside. Monroe phase pottery also occurs in collections from Cooper, Crooked Creek, and Snyder.

Plain-embossed rimsherds (Figure 7.4) predominate Monroe phase assemblages at Pigeon Roost Creek and Garrelts. Some radiometric assays from these sites date to the early half of the Monroe phase but were not in direct association with ceramics. Havana cordmarked specimens (Figure 7.5)

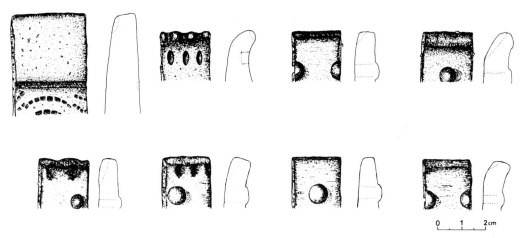

Figure 7.4.   Plain-surface Monroe phase rimsherds (from Donham 1981).

also occur at both sites. The earliest Havana specimens were surface finds at Snyder and Crooked Creek. One Havana plain sherd from a pit at Hillside was associated with a radiometric date of A.D. 200 ± 140 (TX-3740). This rimsherd is representative of late Monroe phase plain-embossed ceramics (i.e., vessels with plain surface treatment and exterior bosses) and postdates the more decorative Havana material.

Two more dates for the Monroe phase come from features at Hatten Village. A date of 50 ± 100 B.C.

(TX-3747) was obtained from carbonized wood lying directly beneath a burial in a large pit. Two small, cordmarked vessels were found broken beneath the skeleton and were associated directly with the carbon sample. These sherds are not characteristic of Havana ware and apparently represent a local manifestation of nonutilitarian or special use vessels that are relatively common at Pigeon Roost Creek, Hatten Village, Hillside, and Davis (Figure 7.6). Decorative modifications of these vessels vary and include conical punctates; cord-wrapped-tool

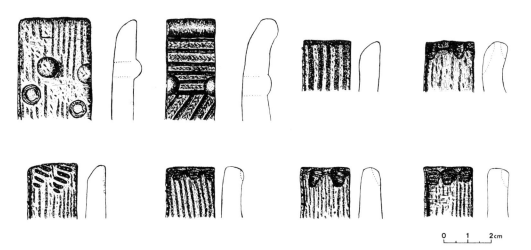

Figure 7.5.   Cordmarked Monroe phase rimsherds (from Donham 1981).

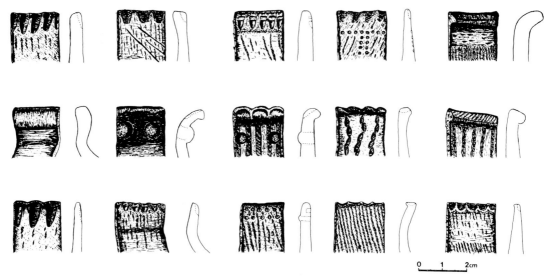

Figure 7.6. Monroe phase small vessel rimsherds (from Donham 1981).

impressions; small, hollow-reed impressions; smooth-tool impressions; incised lines; and interior and exterior bosses. If the Hatten Village date is accurate, then these vessels were manufactured throughout the Monroe phase, as is indicated by the younger specimen recovered from Hillside.

Miniature vessels also were being manufactured by the middle of the Monroe phase, as is suggested by the occurrence of miniature rimsherds in dated pits at the Hatten Village and Cave sites. A pit near the Hatten Village pit burial contained a miniature vessel rimsherd and dated to A.D. 0 ± 140 (TX-3748). A number of other pits in Strip Area (SA) 6 at Hatten Village also contained miniature vessel fragments. This area expressed the highest proportion of miniatures relative to total number of rimsherd specimens recovered (21%).

The final carbon sample dating to the Monroe phase presented here is from the Cave site, which has a series of dates extending through the Monroe and Central Valley phases. A sample dating to A.D. 160 ± 40 (TX-3755) came from a pit containing a miniature vessel rimsherd, platform-pipe bowl fragments, a clay dog or deer figurine, and a Middle Woodland projectile point (class 58).

A number of point classes continue from the Late Archaic into the Middle Woodland period. With the exception of class 31, all classes present in the upper level (60–70 cm) of the Late Archaic component at Pigeon Roost Creek (Figure 6.7) continue into at least the lower half of the Middle Woodland component. Based on stratigraphic data from that site (Figure 7.3), important holdover classes for the Monroe phase include classes 1 (Figure 6.3) and 40 (Figure 6.5). Class 21, absent in lower levels at Pigeon Roost Creek but present in the Archaic component at Flowers, also occurs.

New corner-notched classes include 30, 39, 41–44, and 49. Class 30 includes small points with straight to slightly incurvate or excurvate blades, expanding stems, and concave bases (Figure 7.7). Specimens are similar to the Frio type (Bell 1960). Class 39 (absent at Pigeon Roost Creek) contains large points with triangular, straight blades, broad stems that expand markedly in incurvate arcs, and slightly convex to straight bases that extend almost to the shoulders (Figure 7.7). Similar types include Castroville (Bell 1960). Class 41 contains medium-sized points with triangular, straight to excurvate blades, moderately expanding stems, and slightly convex to deeply concave bases (Figure 7.7). Specimens are similar to the Castroville type (Bell 1960). Class 42 includes well-made points with triangular, straight to excurvate blades; expanding stems; and straight to slightly concave bases (Figure 7.7). Points are similar to Brewerton corner-notched (Ritchie 1971) and Ensor (Cambron and Hulse 1965) types. Class 43 contains medium-sized points with excurvate blades, moderately to markedly expanding stems, and deeply concave bases (Figure 7.7). Specimens are similar to the Snyders type (Bell 1958). Class 44 includes medium-sized points with triangular, straight to excurvate blades; expanding stems; and convex bases (Figure 7.7). Points are similar to Gibson and Manker types (Montet-White 1968). Class 49 contains small to medium-sized points with straight, triangular blades; stems that expand in incurvate arcs; and concave bases that are thinned bifacially (Figure 7.7). Points are similar to Frio and Martindale types (Bell 1960).

The single, stemmed point class that is diagnostic of the Monroe phase is class 58. It consists of medium-sized points with straight to slightly excurvate or incurvate triangular blades, contracting stems, and straight to convex bases (Figure 7.7). Similar point types include Gary (Bell 1958), Waubesa (Perino 1971), and Dickson (Perino 1968a). The Dickson point often is referred to as a knife instead of a projectile point (Winters 1967), due to the abnormal wear that usually occurs along one or both edges of the blade. One specimen from class 58 came from a pit at the Cave site, in association with carbonized wood dating to A.D. 160 ± 40 (TX-3755).

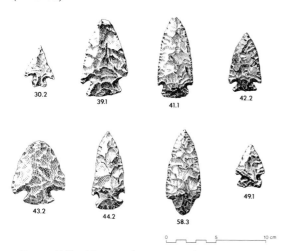

Figure 7.7. Monroe phase projectile point classes.

CENTRAL VALLEY PHASE A.D. 200–600

Ceramics in this phase express a definite continuity of Havana tradition stylistics with a marked increase in affinities with central Missouri styles. In the project area, sites dating to this phase contain primarily medium-sized, unshouldered, plain–embossed vessels and smoothed–cordmarked embossed vessels (the vessel surface was cordmarked first, then smoothed) (Figure 7.8). These decorative techniques are similar to, and contemporaneous with, those on Hopewell ceramics along the lower Missouri River (Chapman 1968). Chapman identifies Havana styles in central Missouri for this period and suggests, "In fact, the main thrust of the Havana tradition into the lower Missouri Valley area probably came during the latter part of the Hopewellian phase" (Chapman 1968:29). This suggestion is supported by recent radiocarbon dates from Hopewellian components at three sites in that area (Kay and Johnson 1977:214).

Additional ceramic styles occurring in later Central Valley components are similar to those from Boone phase, Stage I sites (Chapman 1980). This regional manifestation co-occurs with, but apparently does not affect changes in, the terminal Havana manifestation in the middle Salt River valley.

Although eight sites contain mean uncorrected radiometric dates that fall within the Central Valley phase, only three—Cave, Pigeon Roost Creek, and Crooked Creek—produced significant amounts of ceramics from well-dated contexts. The most complete series is from the Cave site, where four dates span a 250-year period. The two earliest dates, A.D. 330 ± 90 (TX-3751) and A.D. 470 ± 70 (TX-3750), express no significant difference of means and may date a single occupation (Donham 1981:37). Two embossed rims associated with the latter date were recovered from a pit containing three projectile points that are Middle to early Late Woodland classes (discussed later). Both ceramic specimens exhibit lip flattening, interior rim–lip juncture impressions, and exterior bosses. A third embossed rim was recovered from a possible hearth dating to A.D. 500 ± 70 (TX-3756). This date probably reflects the same occupation dated by the two previously discussed assays. The final date from Cave (A.D.

560 ± 60 [TX-3753]) came from a large pit that also contained a cordmarked, cordwrapped-tool-impressed rimsherd.

Two radiometric samples, which show no significant difference of means, were recovered from Pigeon Roost Creek. These samples, dating to A.D. 380 ± 260 (TX-2981) and A.D. 590 ± 100 (TX-3319), were recovered in close horizontal proximity at a depth of 40–50 cm. Although no ceramic material was associated directly with these samples, the level produced a high frequency of Central Valley phase embossed ceramic material.

The collection of ceramic material from the Cave site has a relatively high frequency of sherds with exterior bosses (30%); however, surface treatment is more varied at Cave than at Pigeon Roost Creek. The Cave collection contains undecorated specimens similar stylistically to Boone plain and Boone cordmarked types (Chapman 1980). Similar specimens occur in mortuary contexts at Starr mound and Hatten mound I (Figure 13.22) and in pits near burials at the Cave site. A number of the miniatures recovered from Hatten Village SA 6 are also of the Boone plain style.

The third Central Valley phase component that has an associated date is from Crooked Creek. A plain–embossed sherd (Figure 7.4) was recovered from a pit dating to A.D. 430 ± 70 (TX-3135).

The only reconstructable plain–embossed vessel of the Central Valley phase came from Collins. This vessel is thin-walled with a burnished exterior surface and is very similar to the numerous Pigeon Roost Creek specimens that date to the middle of the Central Valley phase. Additional, undated Central Valley ceramic components occur at Garrelts, Cooper, Hatten Village and Ross.

Projectile point classes associated with the Central Valley phase include a variety of corner-notched and shallow, side-notched forms. The former include classes 30 and 41, which continue from the preceding Monroe phase. One new class that probably dates to this phase, class 45, contains medium-sized points with triangular, straight to excurvate blades; stems that expand markedly in incurvate arcs; and straight to convex bases (Figure 7.9). Specimens are similar to Williams points (Bell 1960:96). This class occurs in the Late Archaic levels at Pigeon Roost Creek but is absent in the Middle Woodland levels.

Side-notched classes include 15, 16, and 20; class 1 continues from the preceding phase. Classes 15 and 16 are similar, containing medium-sized points with excurvate blades, moderately expanding stems, and broad, shallow notches (Figure 7.9). Class 15 contains points with broad stems, whereas class 16 point stems are more slender. Specimens are similar to Steuben-stemmed and Ansell points (Montet-White 1968). Class 20 points contain

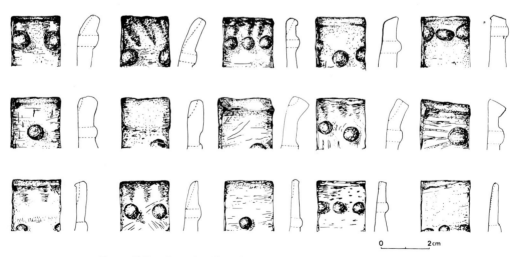

Figure 7.8. Central Valley phase rimsherds (from Donham 1981).

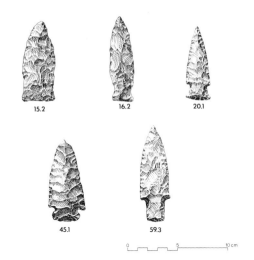

Figure 7.9. Central Valley phase projectile points.

straight to slightly excurvate blades, long and relatively broad stems, broad rectangular notches, and straight to slightly convex bases (Figure 7.9). Similar point types include Godley (Perino 1968a) and Baker's Creek (Perino 1971). There is a mode for class 15 in the 30–40-cm level at Pigeon Roost Creek, with 6 of 11 examples occurring in this level. Class 16 gains in frequency from Middle Woodland levels but does not reach its maximum frequency until the succeeding phase. At the Cave site, a class 15 point was recovered from a pit with Central Valley phase ceramics and carbonized wood dating to A.D. 470 ± 70 (TX-3750).

Only one stemmed point class, 59, can be assigned definitely to this phase. Points in this class are medium-sized and contain triangular, straight to slightly excurvate blades; parallel-sided stems; and convex to deeply concave bases (Figure 7.9). Similar types include Kramer (Perino 1968a) and Travis (Suhm and Jelks 1962). One specimen of this class was recovered from a pit at Cave, associated with a radiometric date of A.D. 500 ± 70 (TX-3756).

SALT RIVER PHASE A.D. 600–750

Salt River phase ceramics are representative of styles from the early and middle portions of the

Late Woodland period found throughout the Midwest. This phase first was defined by Hunt who characterized the ceramics as "having a fairly even representation of cordmarked and plain surfaced rims. The major decorative features include punch and bosses and rim-lip impressions. Undecorated sherds occur in large numbers" (1977a:8).

Hunt (1976) originally estimated dates for this phase as A.D. 500–650 and later altered them to A.D. 600–1000 (Hunt 1977a). These estimates were based on the seriation of a proportion matrix generated using six site collections and 15 decorative variables. Revision of the timespan was prompted by late dates from Murphy and Flowers (discussed below).

Identification of an early–middle Late Woodland phase for the central Salt River valley has been aided by the acquisition of additional ceramics and radiometric samples since Hunt's analysis. It appears that his original dates for the Salt River phase are more meaningful than the revised estimates. The Salt River phase demonstrates some continuation of the Central Valley phase, although expressing more definite connections with post-Hopewellian regional manifestations, such as the early part of the Boone phase and Weaver phase. In addition to the changes in vessel decoration summarized by Hunt (1976), there is increased variation in vessel size and shape, the number of unique decorations increases, and there is greater variation in rim form and lip alterations (Figure 7.10). The result of these trends is greater between-site differences in styles than occurred during the Central Valley phase as well as a higher degree of within-component heterogeneity.

Dated Salt River phase components occur at four sites: Victor Bridge, Muskrat Run, Cooper, and Ross. Undated components are common in the research area; well-represented components occur at Garrelts, Hatten Village, Hillside, Pigeon Roost Creek, and Davis.

The Victor Bridge component reflects continuities with the Central Valley phase as well as a distinctive connection with the central Missouri Boone phase. It contains two overlapping radiometric dates that average to the middle of the Salt River phase. Two plain–embossed specimens were recovered from a pit at Victor Bridge dating to A.D.

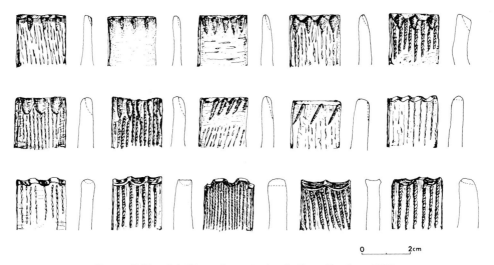

Figure 7.10.   Salt River phase rimsherds (from Donham 1981).

580 ± 65 (WIS-917). A second pit, containing a cordmarked, cordwrapped-tool-impressed rim-sherd dated to A.D. 595 ± 60 (WIS-912).

A reconstructed limestone-tempered vessel, characteristic of Boone phase pottery, was re-covered from Victor Bridge along with additional limestone-tempered sherds. Limestone tempering is quite common in Boone phase ceramics (Denny 1964) but occurs only sporadically in the middle Salt River valley and exclusively with Boone phase ce-ramic styles in Salt River phase components.

Two radiometric assays from Muskrat Run date to the Central Valley phase. Two pits contained carbonized material dating A.D. 660 ± 70 (WIS-916) and A.D. 660 ± 65 (WIS-915), respectively. The com-bined ceramic inventory from these two pits con-sists of 12 rimsherds reflecting eight surface-treat-ment–decorative combinations. Three specimens are cordmarked with exterior cordwrapped-tool impressions on the rim–lip juncture; two are plain–embossed and two are cordmarked with smooth-tool impressions. Three specimens are smoothed-cordmarked: One has interior smooth-tool impressions, one has exterior smooth-tool im-pressions, and one has exterior cordwrapped-tool impressions. A single specimen is cordmarked with no modifications. Lip thickness of the 12 rimsherds ranges from 2.8–5.3 mm with a mean

thickness of 4.15 mm. Variability in lip thickness is attributed to extreme differences in lip morphol-ogy; some vessel lips are thinned, whereas others are thickened gradually, flattened, or rolled over the exterior rim–lip juncture.

A single radiometric date for the Salt River phase came from Cooper. This sample, dating to A.D. 610 ± 110 (TX-2979), was recovered from a limestone hearth with no ceramics in direct association. Like the Muskrat Run and Victor Bridge components, the Cooper component expresses a relatively high incidence of undecorated specimens and speci-mens that exhibit rare combinations of decorative elements. Additional unique decorative modifica-tions have limited distribution in the project area. Although there are no lip-notched specimens asso-ciated with Salt River phase dates, their distribu-tion suggests that the period of highest popularity was during the Salt River phase. This modification occurs most frequently with cordmarked surface treatment. Smooth-tool impressions on the exterior of rim–lip junctures of cordmarked vessels also in-crease in popularity during the Salt River phase and continue into the Ralls phase.

Projectile-point classes that occur in the Salt River phase include continuations (classes 15, 16, 30, 40, and 45) from previous phrases and those that appear for the first time (classes 27, 63, and possibly 69 and 70). Class 27 includes small, corner-notched points with straight to slightly excurvate blades, stems that expand markedly in incurvate arcs, and straight to slightly convex bases (Figure 7.11). Similar point types include Pelican Lake (Perino 1971) and Ellis (Bell 1960).

The one stemmed point class, 63, contains medium-sized specimens with triangular, straight blades; moderately expanding, straight-edged stems; and straight bases that are thinned bifacially (Figure 7.11). Points are similar to the Baker's Creek type (Perino 1971), although Cannon Project specimens are somewhat larger.

Several arrowpoint classes (specimens under 38 mm long) occur on sites containing dated Salt River phase components, such as Hatten Village and Muskrat Run. These sites also contain later material, and it is impossible to determine the phase to which the arrowpoints belong. Class 69 contains corner-notched points with triangular blades and expanding stems (Figure 7.11). Similar types include Scallorn (Bell 1960) and Koster corner-notched (Perino 1971). Class 70 points exhibit side-notching, triangular blades, moderately expanding stems, and wide, slightly convex to concave bases (Figure 7.11). Points are similar to the Klunk side-notched type (Perino 1971), Koster corner-notched type (Perino 1971), and Scallorn type (Bell 1960).

At Pigeon Roost Creek, arrowpoints (classes 69, 70, 72, and 74) first occur in the 30–40-cm level, which dates to the Late Woodland period. Because the extensive plowing has disturbed the vertical distribution of material in the top 20–30 cm of the site, projectile point class percentages (Figure 7.3) probably do not reflect the original distribution of classes. For this reason, the assignment of point classes to the Salt River phase and the two succeed-ing phases is tentative. The assignments are based primarily on correlations with dated forms elsewhere in the Midwest.

RALLS PHASE A.D. 750–1000

The Ralls phase was defined by Chapman (1980), who dates the phase from A.D. 400–900. Chapman's trait list for the Ralls phase is taken primarily from traits described by Henning for sites excavated in Cannon Reservoir (Chapman 1980:126–127) and represents a mixture of the Central Valley, Salt River, and Ralls phases as defined here.

Ralls phase ceramics from Cannon Reservoir have, in the past, been described as expressing affinities with Illinois Valley Weaver ware (Cole 1964; Heldman 1962; A. Henning 1964; D. Henning 1962, 1964; Ruppert 1976). This comparability led D. Henning to conclude, "The similarity in ceramics is sufficient to indicate that a movement of peoples or some other form of direct influence comes out of Illinois" (1964:111).

Ceramics classified in Illinois as Weaver ware generally are associated with the time period between Hopewell and Maples Mills phases (Morse 1963; Wray and MacNeish 1961), dating to A.D. 400–900. It has been suggested that Havana and Weaver ceramics "form a continuum" (Roper 1977:252), but Struever (1964) marks the end of the Havana tradition in Illinois with the end of the Hopewell phase and considers Weaver ware too distinctive to be classified as a late variant of the Havana tradition. Primary Weaver surface modifications—cordwrapped-tool impressions and plain-tool impressions—are recognized by Struever (1964) as carryovers of Havana ceramic attributes (Figure 7.12). The primary criteria for separating Weaver and Havana ceramics is not based on decorations but on hardness and compactness of paste, size of temper inclusions, and vessel wall thickness (Morse 1963; Stoltman 1979; Wray and MacNeish 1961). These criteria are less relevant in the middle Salt River valley, where the Havana tradition was not transformed into a distinctive tradition following a Hopewell phase. It apparently disappeared gradually as the local variant took on features of more widespread regional ceramic manifestations.

Figure 7.11. Salt River phase projectile-point classes.

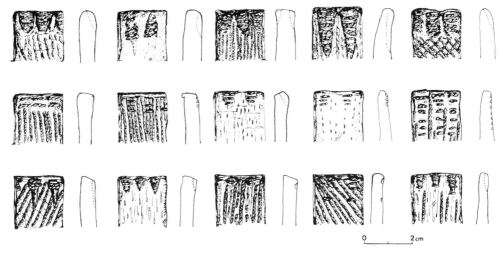

Figure 7.12.   Ralls phase rimsherds (from Donham 1981).

A number of Ralls phase components occur at sites that also contain Salt River phase components. Where there is no extensive mixing of components, the former are identified by the presence of ceramics with a uniformity of surface treatment and decorative schemes. This trend in decorative homogeneity is in contrast to the more varied decorations and morphologies present in the Salt River phase components.

Radiometric dates associated with the Ralls phase came from four sites, two of which also have dated Salt River phase components. Two samples from pits at Victor Bridge date to A.D. 730 ± 55 (WIS-922) and A.D. 795 ± 60 (WIS-921); the combined rimsherd inventory from these large pits numbers 13. These features represent the latest dated context in the project area for the plain-embossed specimens. Five rimsherds are plain-embossed, and one is cordmarked and decorated with exterior bosses. Additional specimens include three that are cordmarked with no modification, one plain specimen with no modification, one plain with punctates, one cordmarked with cord-wrapped-tool impressions, and one cordmarked with smooth-tool impressions.

Two overlapping dates came from Murphy: A.D. 800 ± 70 (WIS-850) and A.D. 890 ± 70 (WIS-859). A cordmarked, cordwrapped-tool-impressed rim-sherd was recovered in association with the earlier sample.

Two rimsherds were recovered from Flowers in association with Ralls phase dates. A thin-walled (2.3-mm), cordmarked, cordwrapped-tool-impressed rimsherd was recovered from pit fill containing carbonized material dated at A.D. 765 ± 60 (WIS-860). A second rimsherd, plain-surfaced with no modification other than lip rolling, came from a pit dating to A.D. 895 ± 50 (WIS-858). This rim style is not common in the project area but does occur occasionally at Cooper, Victor Bridge, Garrelts, Pigeon Roost Creek, and Flowers.

Projectile-point classes occurring in the Ralls phase possibly include a few side- and corner-notched forms that persist in popularity from earlier phases (Figure 7.13) and a host of arrowpoints. In addition to the classes discussed under the section on the Salt River phase, new classes include 72 and 73. Class 72 includes side-notched forms with straight, triangular blades, expanding stems, and convex or concave bases (Figure 7.13). Points are similar to the Schild spike-type (Perino 1971). Class 73 contains side-notched forms with triangular blades, slight notches, and slightly convex to concave bases (Figure 7.13). Points are similar to the Washington type (Cambron and Hulse 1965).

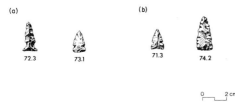

Figure 7.13. (a) Ralls phase and (b) Perry phase projectile point classes.

PERRY PHASE A.D. 1000–1400

The Perry phase is the latest ceramic phase represented in the project area and is affiliated with Mississippian-influenced Late Woodland manifestations identified for west-central Illinois and northeastern Missouri. The most representative component occurs at Cooper, from which two overlapping dates of A.D. 1130 ± 130 (TX-3164) and A.D. 1160 ± 120 (TX-2972) were derived. The only other dates associated with this phase came from nearby Pigeon Roost Creek. Two overlapping dates, A.D. 1360 ± 90 (TX-2988) and A.D. 1400 ± 100 (TX-3140), were assayed from material collected in the 20–30-cm level.

Perry phase ceramics consist primarily of thick-cord-impressed rimsherds similar to Maple Mills phase styles and plain, burnished Mississippian-like vessels with globular bodies and insloping, incurvate rims with very short necks (Figure 7.14). One rimsherd of this style was recovered from Cooper. Thick-cord-impressed specimens occur with greatest frequency at Cooper and occur also at Pigeon Roost Creek and Davis. One thick-cord-impressed specimen with a lug handle attached at the rim came from Cooper, and an effigy lug-handle that probably was attached to a vessel rim was recovered from Davis.

Projectile point classes assigned to this phase are arrowpoint classes 71 and 74. The former includes side-notched forms with straight, triangular blades (Figure 7.13) and are similar to Cahokia points (Perino 1968a). The latter contains triangular specimens with little or no modification (Figure 7.13) and are similar to the Fresno (Bell 1960) and Madison (Perino 1968a) types.

SUMMARY

Five ceramic phases have been proposed here in an attempt to synthesize changes in two aspects of Woodland material culture in the middle Salt River valley. The temporal parameters and stylistic traits of some phases are more easily separated from the overall Woodland pattern than are those of other phases. Not every excavated Woodland component in the project area has been placed definitely within the phase structure—additional research is required to complete this analysis. One definite statement can be made: Changes through time in middle Salt Valley ceramics reflect both regional trends that extend across the upper Mississippi River valley and local trends that apparently are unique to the middle Salt River valley.

The Monroe phase, a Middle Woodland man-

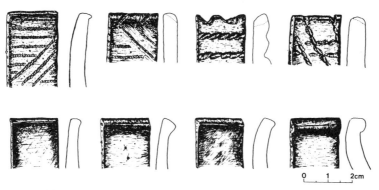

Figure 7.14. Perry phase rimsherds (from Donham 1981).

ifestation of the Havana tradition, expresses the beginnings of a local decorative tradition that continues throughout the Middle Woodland and early Late Woodland periods. The absence of a Hopewell-related phase in Middle Woodland assemblages is apparently offset by the presence of locally produced, well-made and finely decorated small vessels. From dated associations, these vessels occur contemporaneously with Illinois Hopewell phases.

The replacement of Havana tradition ceramics with Weaver ceramics in northwestern and west-central Illinois is not paralleled in the middle Salt River valley, due probably to the westward movement and continuation of the Havana tradition in Missouri during this time (Chapman 1968). The Central Valley phase is proposed to define better this period of incongruity with Illinois styles and continuity with Havana styles. As during the Illinois Hopewell phases, later central Missouri

Hopewell ceramics do not penetrate into the project area. The absence of Weaver ceramics between A.D. 200–500 in the project area suggests that the local manifestation was being influenced more by central Missouri than western Illinois.

Localization of ceramic styles tends to dissipate with the onset of the Salt River phase and reflects an increasingly larger area of diffusive post-Hopewellian regional systems. Interactivity with Illinois appears to increase through the Ralls phase as the upper Mississippi Valley region becomes more homogeneous in terms of material culture, particularly in ceramic styles.

Like most of northeastern Missouri, the project area does not exhibit wide-spread evidence of extended use by sedentary Mississippian groups. Occupation of the Salt Valley by post-A.D.-1000 groups is evidenced by Perry phase material, although this material is restricted to only a few sites.

8

A Regional Chronology
of the Early Historic Period

ROGER D. MASON

This chapter presents a brief overview of the chronology of the early historic occupation of the project area. It deals specifically with the organization of local government, the development of towns and regional centers, and pertinent historical events that affected the development of the middle Salt River valley. The time periods used to order the discussion chronologically are (*a*) 1817–1819, (*b*) 1820–1830, (*c*) 1831, (*d*) 1832–1839, and (*e*) 1840–Civil War. As will be shown, these periods mark the beginning and end of settlement influxes and the rise and decline of various towns and regional centers throughout the area.

Of necessity, many important as well as interesting features of this historic settlement era have not been included in the presentation. Some features, especially correlations between environmental and social dimensions with settlement location, are presented in Chapter 17. Others are treated in considerable detail in Mason (1982). Data for this chapter were extracted from both published and un-

published sources. Primary published sources include county histories (Holcombe 1884; Megown 1878; National Historical Company 1884) and several summaries of early Missouri history published in the *Missouri Historical Review* (Dorsey 1935; Thomas 1909; Viles 1920; Violette 1906). Unpublished sources consist of Monroe County records.

AN OVERVIEW OF SETTLEMENT IN THE SALT VALLEY

Except for sporadic settlement along the lower reaches of the Salt River during the eighteenth and early nineteenth centuries, permanent colonization of the Salt Valley did not begin until around 1818. This coincided with an influx of new settlers to, and population growth in, the Boone's Lick area to the south (Chapter 4). Settlement density there reached such a point that by late 1817, new arrivals found the land "considerable crowded, and all of the desirable location taken up" (Holcombe 1884:143).

Settlement of the middle Salt River valley was initiated following completion of the General Land Office survey in the summer of 1818 and the subsequent opening of land sales in the fall of that year at the land office in St. Louis. By the end of 1819, only a small amount of land in the project area had been sold. Because of proximity to the Mississippi River,

settlement was concentrated more to the east, along the lower reaches of the Salt River.

This early phase of colonization occurred during a period of economic expansion that culminated in the Panic of 1819. Economic expansion was facilitated by the easy credit policies of state and local banks that issued notes far in excess of the amount of specie available. This was accompanied by "exorbitant land speculation" promoted by the federal government's credit policy related to public land sales (Dorsey 1935:79). The economic collapse, the full force of which was not felt in Missouri until 1820, caused a marked decline in new settlement growth during the early 1820s. Another factor in this decline was the institution on July 1, 1820 of a cash-only policy for the purchase of federal public lands (Peters 1845:566–567). The effect of the depression during the early 1820s on public land sales in the project area can be seen in Figure 8.1.

Land entries began to increase rapidly during the late 1820s (Figure 8.1), reflecting ameliorating national economic conditions (Cole 1927). A total of 83.2% of public land in the project area was sold during the period 1828–1836, another period of easy credit and inflation. This era was followed in 1837 by another economic collapse. However, by this time 87.5% of all federal public land had been sold.

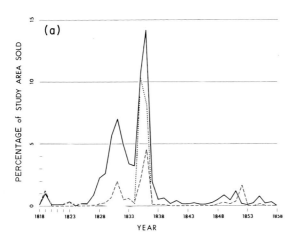

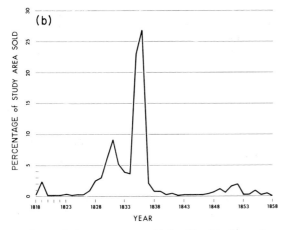

Figure 8.1. Percentage of federal land in the project area entered per year by (a) residents (—), nonresidents (---), and Eastern speculators (. . . .) and (b) total purchasers (from Mason 1982).

ORGANIZATION OF LOCAL GOVERNMENT AND SETTLEMENT PRIOR TO 1820

Pike County (Figure 8.2), which at the time of its formation in 1818 contained the entire middle and lower Salt River valley, was the first political unit established in northeastern Missouri. The town of Louisiana, located just south of the mouth of the Salt River, was founded as the county seat. Farther north and inland from the Mississippi River, the town of New London was founded in 1819. It soon became the seat of Ralls County, which was formed in December 1820 from a portion of Pike County (Figure 8.2).

Two small settlements in the project area were

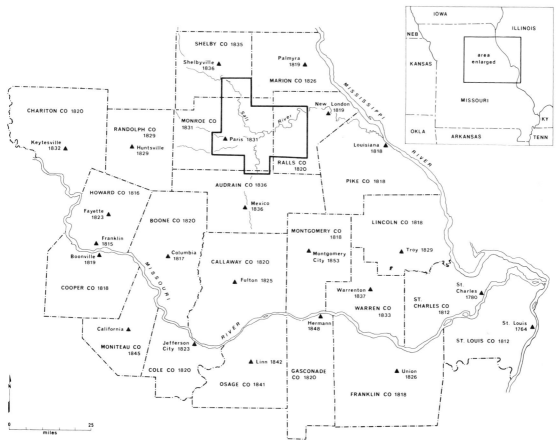

Figure 8.2.   Map of northeastern Missouri, showing locations of counties and county seats (▲) falling within the project area and dates of county formation (from Mason 1982).

formed in 1819. The Ely settlement, located in the eastern portion of the project area and south of the Salt River (Figure 15.1), was formed by three brothers and their brother-in-law who emigrated from Bath County, Kentucky (Chapter 15). The other early settlement was the Smith settlement, located along Middle Fork (Figure 15.1). This settlement consisted originally of Joseph Smith and his family, from Bath County, Kentucky, and James Adams and his brothers. These two settlements are typical of those in the Cannon Project area, in that they consisted of large family groups from the Bluegrass Region of Kentucky (Chapter 15).

ORGANIZATION OF LOCAL GOVERNMENT AND SETTLEMENT, 1820–1830

A strong, centralized county government with weak political townships as internal subdivisions apparently was characteristic of local political organization throughout the Upper South. Most political power in the county was held by the county court, which combined executive, legislative, and judicial functions. Members of the county court were usually members of the wealthy elite, or "planter" class (Elkins and McKitrick 1954:573).

This was the case in early Missouri during the 1820s, where members of the county court were appointed by the governor. County judges established county roads, organized political townships, set county tax rates, appropriated county funds, set polling places, issued business licenses, and acted as probate court. Counties were divided into political townships, each of which had several justices of the peace, a constable, and a polling place. The formation of new townships within a frontier

county was the result of population growth and the development of a more stable pioneer society.

During the organization of Ralls County in 1821, four townships were established. The majority of the project area was located in Salt River Township, with portions in Spencer Township on the east and Union Township (formed in 1822) on the west (Figure 8.3). Population growth in the western part of Ralls County led to the formation of Jackson Township in 1827, drawn from the western part of Salt

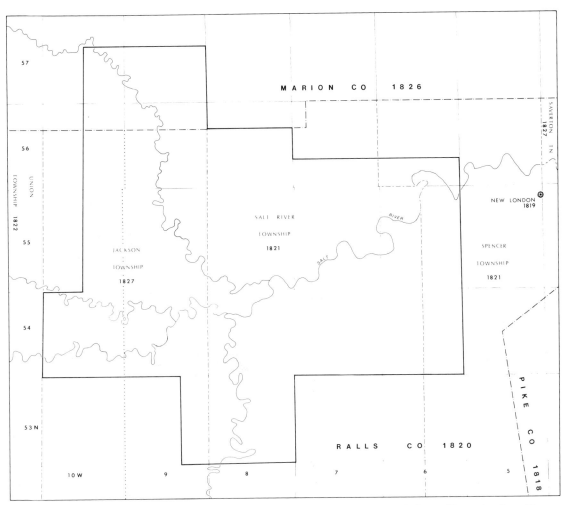

Figure 8.3. Map of local political boundaries (counties and townships) in 1830, with dates of formation (from Mason 1982).

River Township and the eastern part of Union Township (Figure 8.3).

An important function of the county court was establishing county roads. At the time of the formation of Ralls County, the only road (actually no more than a trail) through the project area led from Franklin (the county seat of Howard County before 1823 and center of the Boone's Lick settlement) to New London (Figure 8.2). This road crossed the southern part of the Cannon Reservoir area (Figure 8.4) and passed within a few kilometers of the Ely and Smith settlements. Roads connecting the Ely and Smith settlements with the road from New London to Franklin and Fayette (the new county seat of Howard County) were established during 1824–1825. The road through the Ely settlement led to Bouvet's Lick in the northeastern corner of the project area and then connected with roads to New London and Hannibal. The road through the Smith settlement went to Palmyra (Figures 8.2 and 8.4).

Most other settlements in the project area were formed during the 1820s and were located near the New London–Fayette road. One large, early settlement was located south of Elk Fork in the southwestern part of T54N, R9W and the southeastern part of T54N, R10W (Figure 15.1). Other early settlement areas were located along Pigeon Roost Creek (Mt. Prairie settlement) and upper Lick Creek (Figure 15.1). There also was early settlement on both sides of Salt River north of the Ely settlement in T55N, R6W. Two roads parallel to the original road through the Ely settlement were established to serve this area in 1828–1829.

Greater accessibility to eastern, rather than western, portions of the area is reflected in the higher population densities (not including slaves) of Salt River Township in the eastern part of the project area (Figure 8.3), which was about 1.04 persons/km^2 (2.7 persons/mile^2). Population density in Jackson Township to the west was 0.4/km^2 (1.7 persons/mile^2). More extreme, frontier conditions in 1830 in Jackson Township also were reflected in a lower proportion of slave owners. In Jackson Township 19% of the heads of households were slave owners, whereas in Salt River Township 31% of heads of households owned slaves. From analysis of land entry records it was noted that Salt River Township

slaveholders entered significantly more land than did nonslaveholders (Mason 1979). However, in Jackson Township there was no significant difference in the amount of land entered by slaveholders and nonslaveholders. It is probable that wealthier slaveholders there did not want to risk the financial loss that would have resulted from transporting goods a considerable distance to market.

ORGANIZATION OF LOCAL GOVERNMENT AND TOWN FORMATION IN 1831

Population increase in the western half of Ralls County during the late 1820s resulted in the formation of Monroe County by an act of the state General Assembly on January 6, 1831. The new county was subdivided into three townships (Union, Jackson, and Jefferson) running north–south, each comprising about one-third of the 52-km-wide county.

The first county court met at the house of Green V. Caldwell, located on the New London–Fayette road about 2 km west of its intersection with the Palmyra road. Caldwell had a store in his house and hoped that the county seat would be located near there. However, Caldwell died in the early part of 1831, and the commissioners appointed by the governor to choose the location of the county seat chose a site about 4 km to the northwest, on the south bank of Middle Fork. Most of the county seat site was located on land owned by James C. Fox, who donated 45 acres of this land to the county and later was named commissioner for the sale of town lots. The county seat was named Paris, after Paris, Kentucky.

The town of Florida, located at the confluence of North and South forks (Figure 8.4), actually was the first town platted in Monroe County, predating Paris by several months. The site of Florida was surveyed in March 1831, and the plat (containing 94 lots in 15 blocks) was recorded in May 1831. The "proprietors" of the town were six local residents who entered the 80-acre tract on February 10, 1831. Two were owners of nearby grist and saw mills.

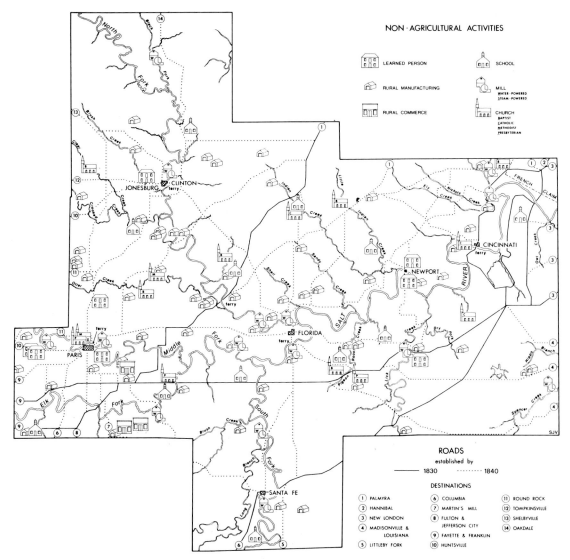

Figure 8.4. Map of roads, towns, mills, rural nonagricultural specialization, schools, and churches in the project area in 1840 (from Mason 1982).

Thus, Florida was located with respect to previously existing economic activities—unlike Paris, which was founded at a certain site for political reasons.

By 1838, at least 75% of the lots in Florida had passed out of the hands of the original proprietors, and commercial ventures began to appear. In 1834, the first merchant's licenses for Florida were issued (probably for dry goods), and by the latter half of the decade there were three or four groceries. Craft specializations found in Florida during the 1830s included blacksmith, tailor, shoemaker, saddler, furniture maker, tanner, and harness maker (Gregory 1965).

One reason for locating Florida at the confluence of North and Middle forks was that this point was thought to be the upper limit of navigation on the Salt River. However, the river actually was navigable only for a few months each year, during high water. Efforts to make it navigable for small steamboats began the year Florida was founded, when the General Assembly was persuaded to prohibit the construction of any dams on the Salt River below the forks (Gregory 1965). Further action was taken in 1834, when the Monroe County court appropriated $500 to clear the Salt River from the forks downstream to the Ralls County line.

The most ambitious attempt to make the upper reaches of the Salt River navigable was the incorporation of the Salt River Navigation Company by the General Assembly on January 25, 1837. This company was empowered to enter on any land along the river—for the purpose of making the river navigable for steamboats by dredging, changing its course, and erecting locks and dams—from the river's mouth to the forks at Florida. Commissioners of the company included John M. Clemens, the father of Samuel Clemens, who was born in Florida in 1835. Overland transportation from Florida to Paris was to have been provided by the Florida and Paris Rail Road Company, incorporated in February 1837.

These transporation companies were to be financed by subscription (the sale of stock at $50 per share). However, the companies never acquired the capital necessary to operate since little, if any, construction was ever carried out. It is probable that these ventures were proposed to the General Assembly in 1836, before the recession began, and were not acted on until early 1837. However, by this time contraction of the economy made capitalization of these ventures impossible.

TOWNSHIP AND TOWN FORMATION, 1832–1839

A period of economic expansion and easy credit encouraged migration to the Missouri frontier and stimulated a high volume of land entries in the early 1830s. This was reflected in the creation of new townships and the establishment of small towns that served as retail centers for the townships in which they were located and, occasionally, for parts of adjacent townships.

Settlement in the western part of the project area in 1830 was located primarily south of T55N, except for a small settlement cluster in T55N, R8W. Settlement moved north along North Fork and its tributaries in the early 1830s. The population increased to the point where a new township, Washington, was formed in 1833 (Figure 8.5). Settlement expanded also along the South Fork, resulting in the creation of South Fork Township in 1834 (Figure 8.5). In Ralls County, Salt River Township was divided so that the area north of the river became Saline Township (Figure 8.5). The southern part of Spencer Township along Spencer Creek became Jasper Township.

Three towns were platted in the eastern part of the Cannon Project area in 1834. All were located on the banks of the Salt River, but only one of them, Cincinnati, became a successful town. Newport, located between Florida and Cincinnati, and Bloomfield, located between New London and Cincinnati (Figure 8.5), may have been too close to already established towns to compete effectively as regional commercial centers.

Cincinnati was platted in June 1834 on the north bank of the Salt River, where a county road (established in 1828) forded the river (Figures 8.4 and 8.5). The original plat contained 40 lots; additions to the plat were made in May and August of 1836, bringing the total to 63. Although these additions to the plat could be taken as indications that Cincinnati was a successful, expanding town, only 28 lots had been sold by 1844. All original sales of lots took place during the period 1835–1838. Even though less than half the lots were sold, Cincinnati in 1837 had two stores, a tavern, a post office, and a Catholic chapel (Wetmore 1837:155).

Newport (more recently known as Joanna) was located on the north bank of the Salt River, 12 km (in a straight line) from Florida and 11 km from Cincinnati. It was platted in early 1834 by John J. Lyle, a physician and probably the only resident until 1835 or 1836, when two individuals—one of whom was a merchant—purchased lots. The merchant had a $4000 mortgage on his property, store, and stock and defaulted in 1838. There is no record

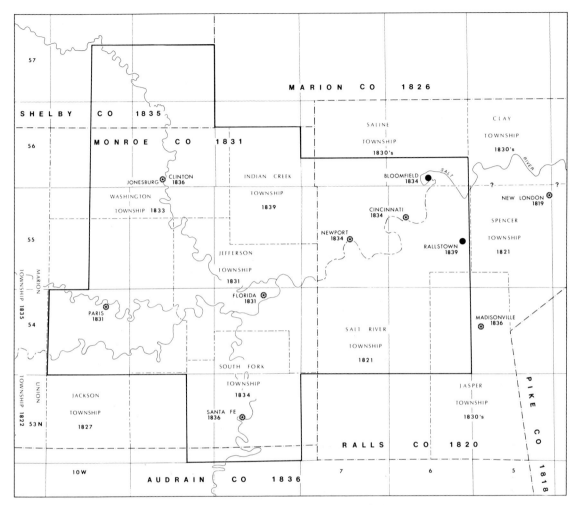

Figure 8.5.   Map of local political boundaries (counties and townships) in 1840, with dates of formation (from Mason 1982).

of any other lots in Newport being sold through 1878. It appears that Newport failed due to its proximity to Florida and Cincinnati, a relatively low population density in the surrounding area, and the effects of the 1837 recession.

Bloomfield, located in the northeastern part of the project area (Figure 8.5), was platted in 1834. The town site was not located on an existing road but was across the river from a steam mill that was owned by two wealthy land speculators from Marion County. These speculators bought the Bloom-

field plat and surrounding land and sold both as well as the mill in 1837. The buyer defaulted in 1840, and the town site eventually returned to one of the previous owners. There is no record through 1860 of any lots being sold in Bloomfield.

Towns were platted in the newly created Washington and South Fork townships in Monroe County in 1836, during the height of land speculation. However, these towns were founded by local residents, rather than absentee speculators. Two towns in Washington township, Clinton and

Jonesburg, were platted adjacent to each other.

These two towns were located on the west bank of North Fork (Figure 8.5) and were platted in August and September of that year. Clinton and Jonesburg were competing towns with only an alley separating them. Clinton was platted by two merchants and an operator of an adjacent saw-grist mill and ferry. The town consisted of 48 lots arranged along one long street that led to the ferry. By 1840, 27 lots had been sold.

Jonesburg was located directly south of Clinton and was platted by two local men, one of whom was a merchant. It appears from the date of his license that the merchant had an ongoing enterprise before the town was platted. The town consisted of 81 lots arranged around a central square. By 1840, 57 lots had been sold. Competition between the two towns was reflected in conflicts over proposed routes of county roads. Each group of town proprietors wanted county roads to run through their town and not the other.

Sante Fe was located on the South Fork (Figure 8.5) and was platted in October 1836 by a local doctor–farmer. The town consisted of 84 lots, with 2 lots being reserved for a meeting house. Few lots had been sold by 1840, when there were one store and several craftmen in town.

Two other towns were platted in or near the Cannon Reservoir area during the 1830s. Madisonville, located on Spencer Creek just outside the project area (Figure 8.5), became a fairly successful small town with several stores and services. Rallstown was the only platted town not located on a river or creek, being located instead on the prairie–timber boundary in the northeastern part of the project area (Figure 8.5). Rallstown was platted in September 1839 by four prosperous local farmers. There is no record of any lots being sold through 1860, probably due to the town's proximity to New London and the effects of an economic recession.

ECONOMIC EXPANSION, 1840 TO THE CIVIL WAR

By 1840 the period of initial settlement was over. Patterns of town location and rural settlement

(Chapter 17) already were well established. Subsequent changes were due largely to moderate increases in population density and the resulting competition among rural residents for land and among towns for primary service functions.

The pattern of towns and villages that was to endure for many years was formed almost simultaneously with initial settlement. All towns were functioning by 1836, only 8 years after the beginning of the major influx of settlers in 1828. By 1836, there was a regular spacing (of about 20 km) between most towns and villages. One exception to this spacing was Newport, which was located 10–15 km from Cincinnati and Florida. The failure of Newport as a commercial center is not surprising since it was competing with its larger neighbors. It is also possible that the lack of milling facilities, caused by the ban on damming the river below Florida, hindered the development of Newport and kept Cincinnati relatively small.

By 1840, Paris and Florida contained an almost equal number of residents (Table 8.1). By 1850, Paris began to expand at the expense of Florida, and by 1860, Florida had almost disappeared while Paris had almost doubled its 1850 population. Clinton–Jonesburg, Santa Fe, Cincinnati, and Newport remained villages (100 or less in population). Newport was the least successful of these villages, and it is doubtful that it had any economic functions after 1840.

The population history of these towns indicates that in the late 1830s and early 1840s Paris and Florida were competing for the status of primary rural service center. The success of Paris can be attributed to the fact that it was the county seat, combining administrative and economic functions, whereas the potential of Florida as a river transport center never was realized. By 1860, if not earlier, Florida was reduced to the status of a village serving primarily the residents of the local township.

Changes in population density (Table 8.2) in those portions of Ralls and Monroe counties falling within the project area show: (a) that the eastern part of the area had an initial higher population density due to its proximity to the Mississippi River and more settled areas; and (b) that during the 1830s the western half of the area, in newly formed Monroe County, developed much more rapidly

TABLE 8.1.

Population of Paris, Florida, Clinton-Jonesburg, Santa Fe, and Cincinnati in 1840–1860 and 1876

	1840[a]	1850[a]	1860[b]	1876[c]
Paris	289	572	1000	1400
Florida	281	316	160	100
Clinton-Jonesburg	88	99	–	–
Sante Fe	27	74	120	110
Cincinnati	60	50	–	–

[a] From manuscript census schedules.
[b] From Sutherland and McEvoy (1860).
[c] From Polk (1876).

than did the eastern half. This shift in development was due partly to the presence of Paris and Florida and partly to a greater abundance of upland prairie for cattle grazing, a zone avoided by earlier settlers (Chapter 17).

In the 1850s there were additions to the network of towns and villages in Monroe County. In 1852 the village of Elizabethtown was platted in Indian Creek Township (Figure 8.5), the only township in the west half of the project area that at that time was lacking a town or village. Indian Creek Township was settled largely by Catholics, and the town was platted around a Catholic church that had been organized in 1833.

Completion of the Hannibal and St. Joseph Railroad in 1857, across the southern part of Shelby County and through the extreme northeastern corner of Monroe County, caused several changes in town location. Clinton and Jonesburg were abandoned at this time, and businesses from these

towns moved north to the railroad. In the northeastern corner of Monroe County, the town of Monroe City was established on the rail line in 1857, and the county court created Monroe Township around the city. Monroe City served as a rail head for the area until 1870, when another rail line was completed connecting Hannibal and Paris.

Although Missouri was a slave state, the situation during the Civil War was confusing because Union and Confederate sympathizers lived in close proximity in many parts of the state, especially in the north and west. The major effect of the Civil War in the project area was to end the practice of slavery. Trexler (1914) and Viles (1920) note that this may have had more effect on the social system of the Upper South than on the economic system since there was no plantation system and slaves were kept more as house servants and status symbols than as a large field labor force. However, results of the abolition of slavery on the project area

TABLE 8.2.

Population Densities of Salt River and Jackson Townships in 1830 and of Parts of the Project Area in Ralls and Monroe Counties in 1840 and 1850[a]

	1830	1840	1850
Salt River Township/Ralls County	2.7	6.6	11.6
Jackson Township/Monroe County	1.7	12.9	15.5

[a] Per mi^2.

economy may have been more drastic due to the use of slaves as cowboys (Chapter 17).

SUMMARY

The pre-Civil War historic period in the project area can be summarized as one of extensive change, both economically as well as socially and politically. Five periods have been used here to order events chronologically. These periods represent times of continuous development in the area, ranging from the entrance of settlers in 1819 to the effects of the Civil War. In between are scattered multiple events and processes that shaped the geographic landscape. Some of these processes are discussed in Chapter 17.

One important aspect of the early historic period chronology is the shift in population density from east to west through time. Pre-1830 settlement was far greater in the eastern half of the project area, possibly due to perceived differences in quality and type of land and proximity to established trade centers. After 1830, the situation changed, and newly formed Monroe County grew at the expense of Ralls County, its eastern neighbor. This shift in development was caused by the establishment of Paris and Florida and the services they soon offered. A second contributing factor could have been the large expanses of prairie that were still available, on which cattle raisers could graze their herds.

Of additional interest is the emergence of towns during the 1830s and the efforts made in establishing their primacy as regional trade centers. The failures of many of these towns to develop as commercial centers can be attributed to their locations near established centers offering dependable service. Data regarding services offered by centers such as Florida and Paris exist and will be published in the future.

PART IV

Functional
and Economic Indicators

The three chapters in this section present the results of analysis of functional and economic indicators. Chapter 9 discusses the analysis of lithic artifacts, which bears directly on many aspects of research in the Cannon Reservoir region, from analyzing patterns of community structure to inferring site function within the settlement system. Technological as well as functional approaches are discussed, and the advantages and drawbacks of each are summarized. In Chapter 9, it is argued that in a regional analysis, where single provenience units at some sites may produce upwards of 200 lithic artifacts, detailed, microscopic analysis of use-wear patterns is too expensive and time-consuming to be carried out without some explicit sampling design. It also is argued that although form and function often are treated separately in lithic analysis, there are empirical reasons for assuming relationships between the two states.

In Chapter 10, the results of the analysis of vertebrate faunal remains from 11 components that span the Late Archaic to Mississippian periods are discussed. Two important lines of investigation form the basis for this work. First, are there differences in the composition of faunal assemblages from different periods and are these differences reflective of long-term change in resource procurement strategies through time? Second, what are the potential effects of seasonal resource availability on settlement–subsistence systems? Based on proportions of taxa represented in roughly contemporaneous assemblages, can it be determined whether certain sites were occupied all year long or only seasonally? Results of analysis along these lines of investigation bear directly on the model of prehistoric adaptation and change.

Chapter 11 summarizes the analysis of botanical remains from 10 sites in the project area. The lines of investigation guiding this work are identical to those listed for the analysis of the vertebrate fauna. Three questions, derived from the model, are posed: (a) Do sites reflect use of a broad spectrum of plant remains collected from various vegetation zones? (b) Are there long-term changes in the botanical record that indicate a shift from gathering to plant cultivation? (c) Do the remains reflect the apparent lack of interaction with nearby cultures as suggested by the lack of exchange goods?

9

Analysis of Lithic Artifacts

DENNIS E. LEWARCH

In this chapter I briefly review recent advances in lithic analysis to provide background information on decisions we made in creating the classification systems used by the project. I also will outline and evaluate the lithic analysis systems employed. Any discussion of lithic analysis systems must take into account rapid changes in lithic studies in recent years—changes in both the basic assumptions that serve to ground lithic analysis as well as changes in analytical techniques (Dunnell 1980a, 1981; Gould 1980; Hayden 1979; Odell and Odell-Vereecken 1980).

Expansion of lithic research and ethnoarchaeological studies have led to the revision of many previously held assumptions about technological and functional variability in stone artifact assemblages (Dunnell 1978b, c; Gould 1980; Hayden 1979; Jelinek 1976; Tringham *et al.* 1974; White and Thomas 1972). These changes, along with expanding contributions from lithic research in cultural resource management studies (see Schiffer 1979; Schiffer and House 1975), have resulted in the usu-

al kinds of problems inherent in any research undergoing development.

Some major problem areas include nonstandardized terminology, noncomparable classification systems, nonuniform measurement procedures, and generally dissimilar analysis techniques (Hayden 1979). In the absence of formal theory to guide increasingly diverse research programs, there are many fundamental contradictions among various approaches. As a result, even apparently simple tasks are difficult to standardize. These difficulties are mentioned to indicate that there is no single, uniform approach to lithic analysis within the discipline. Thus, any lithic classification system must be evaluated by pragmatic considerations weighed against research goals and, in CRM work, contract specifications.

In summary, a number of considerations must be taken into account when assessing the Cannon Project lithic analysis systems. Before reviewing the rationale behind classification paradigms, it is useful to briefly outline the current "state-of-the-art" in lithic analysis. This will place the Cannon Project classifications within a broader, discipline-wide perspective.

LITHIC ANALYSIS IN 1981: A BRIEF OVERVIEW

Technological analysis and use-wear, or functional, analysis are the most common approaches used in regional-scale lithic analysis studies of settlement–subsistence patterns. Technological studies characterize lithic assemblages in terms of the relative frequency and proportion of artifact classes that represent stages in chipped-stone artifact manufacture. A comparison of frequencies and proportions of classes represented at different sites in a region leads to inferences about kinds of activities carried out at each site. These inferences, in turn, are used to develop models of settlement function and functional patterning in the settlement–subsistence system. Functional analysis is based on direct observation of use-wear edge damage on artifact surfaces, at a number of different scales of analysis, using a variety of techniques (Hayden 1979).

Each type of analysis presents positive and negative aspects that must be weighed prior to implementation. The following sections outline the salient characteristics of the two kinds of analysis and conclude with a summary and evaluation of the relative research merits of each.

Technology-Based Systems for Settlement–Subsistence Analysis

Technology-based systems emphasize reduction strategies associated with chipped-stone manufacturing industries. The basic operating assumption is that studies of lithic reduction sequences can be useful sources of data for inferring the kinds of activities carried out within a settlement system. Comparison of the relative proportions of technological classes allows delineation of various functional kinds of settlements, such as base camps or extractive sites. Thus, "systemic, diachronic inter-relationships exist between settlement–subsistence patterns, population demography, and lithic technology" (Brose 1978:87).

Basic tenets of the technological analysis approach have been modified over the years in light of expanding archaeological research in site formation processes and the expansion of ethnoarchaeological studies. Both have provided increasing sophistication to the analysis of pattern in lithic systems—sophistication that has led to the deletion or revision of many of the more simplistic assumptions. Despite recognition of their limitations, technology-based studies continue to be fairly common in the archaeological literature (e.g. Brose 1978; Davis 1978; Goodyear 1974; House 1975; Schiffer and House 1975; Thomas 1973; Wilmsen 1970). Such research increasingly is being represented in terms of complex flow-charts that summarize the many stages, hence behavioral choices, in chipped-stone reduction sequences (see especially Brose 1978; House 1975; Sheets 1975).

Potential deficiencies of the technological approach include: (a) sampling problems, (b) false assumptions about the structure of lithic systems in human society, and (c) the lack of a relationship between technological variables and functional inferences. Bias can be introduced in a number of ways, especially during fieldwork. Perhaps the most elementary problem is the manner in which sites are selected for investigation, and, once such choices are made, how artifact classes are sampled within sites. Decisions made at both scales severely condition the range of variability that can be considered during analysis (Lewarch 1979a; Nance 1979).

One aspect of this problem is that formed artifacts (i.e., those receiving considerable modification to shape them into a particular form) often are the only artifacts that receive detailed attention during analysis. Amorphous "waste flakes" are usually accorded little consideration, even though they often represent the most numerous single lithic class in chipped-stone assemblages (Burton 1980; Dunnell 1978b; Lewarch 1979a).

Further difficulties arise via the counting units employed in the technological approach. Often a single formed artifact is equated with a single function, leading to a serious underrepresentation of the number of functional units. Most recent developments in use-wear analysis and ethnoarchaeology have demonstrated the use of portions of an artifact for a number of tasks (Dancey 1973; Dunnell and Lewarch 1974; Gould 1980; Hayden 1979; Jelinek 1976; Schiffer 1975).

The problem of counting units gradually blends into the problem of the types of assumptions archaeologists make about the structure of lithic artifact assemblages in human society. Various kinds of energy extraction systems require different approaches to technology that are based on a number of factors, such as lithic resource availability, mobility within the settlement system, and the role of lithic artifacts in the direct acquisition of energy (Binford 1979, 1980; Gould 1980; Gramly 1980; Hayden 1979).

These factors, along with a growing appreciation of site formation processes, have important implications for basic assumptions behind the technological approach. Foremost among these is the assumption that the co-occurrence of lithic classes and variation in class frequencies is a reflection of subsistence-related activities. Some archaeologists (e.g., Gould 1980; Schiffer 1976; Speth and Johnson 1976) have suggested that this assumption may not hold universally because of factors such as curation. Curation of artifacts significantly alters associational patterns, and items found in spatial association may have no direct functional interdependence, having arrived in adjacent space as a consequence of depositional patterns.

Another problem is determining the relationship of technology to artifact function. This topic has been treated fairly extensively (Ahler 1971; Dunnell 1978b, c; Gould 1980; Jelinek 1976; Schiffer 1975) and centers on the definition of functional classes. As Hayden and Kamminga note (1979:5): "While it is clear that there is no one-to-one relation between tool form and function, it is equally wrong to say there is no correlation."

One problem in making functional inferences from technological classes appears in the scale of analysis, where an artifact is treated as a single functional unit. A more appropriate system employs worn edges (Dancey 1973; Dunnell 1978b, c; Dunnell and Lewarch 1974; Knudson 1979; Odell 1979). However, as Schiffer (1975) notes, it is difficult to keep track of multiple use-wear edges on objects, especially when large numbers of artifacts are being considered.

Finally, there is the problem of defining the spatial pattern of lithic classes within sites. In most regional technological studies, assemblages are compared by treating sites as functional, analytical units. This approach presupposes that all lithic artifacts are characteristic of a cohesive, functional tool kit comprising all activities at a site. As archaeologists develop more expertise in spatial analysis techniques, they are constructing complex models detailing the spatial pattern of lithic classes within sites. While there clearly are difficulties involved in delineating *activity areas* (see Speth and Johnson 1976), these kinds of studies suggest that trait lists of lithic classes oversimplify the complex patterns that make up functional tool sets within sites.

To summarize, technological approaches that attempt to define variability in settlement–subsistence patterns clearly are essential to any sort of regional-scale understanding of human energy extraction systems. As Davis (1978:ii) notes: "Almost any analysis of lithic assemblages which is concerned with reconstruction of past subsistence patterns is in part an analysis of technological variability." Perhaps the key phrase here is "in part," since a more holistic approach would include both technologically and functionally based analyses. With this in mind, we turn now to a discussion of the functional approach.

Use-Wear Analysis for Delineation of Settlement–Subsistence Patterns

Use-wear analysis perhaps has been the most rapidly growing aspect of lithic studies, with basic assumptions and operating procedures being detailed in an expanding literature (Hayden 1979; Keeley 1980; Odell 1979; Odell and Odell–Vereecken 1980). The technique is based on measuring the physical evidence of tool use on the surface or edges of chipped-stone artifacts. Evidence includes damage, removal of flakes, striations, polish, or residues left by animal or plant material with which the tool has come into contact. A variety of examination techniques are employed, ranging from the unaided eye (Dancey 1973; Del Bene and Holley 1979; Dunnell and Lewarch 1974), to low-power magnification (Odell 1979; Odell and Odell–Vereecken 1980), high-power magnification (Keely 1980; Keely and Newcomer 1977; Newcomer and Keely 1979), and use of a scanning electron microscope (Hayden 1979).

However, as a number of lithic specialists have pointed out, there still are many problems to be worked out before these techniques can be applied on a wider scale. One problem is accuracy. As Dunnell (1981:5–6) notes, identification of use-wear patterns in many studies is far short of 100% accuracy. Another problem is that most recording systems (Ahler 1979; Keely 1980; Knudson 1979) do not seem applicable to recording tool-related attributes for large populations, certainly an important requisite for lithic assemblages generated by sophisticated sampling programs. Exceptions to this problem appear to be Odell's (1979) coding system as well as those of a few others (Dunnell and Campbell 1977; Dunnell and Lewarch 1974).

Generalizing the technique to large bodies of data can present considerable tactical difficulties. Intensive surface collection programs, such as that used by the Cannon Project, often generate approximately 3000 collection units for a single site, many units having several hundred lithic artifacts each. As Odell (1979) notes, for intensive use-wear analysis systems to become practical, they will have to be able to deal with data sets generated by regional-scale archaeology.

Standardization of descriptive terminology and criteria for distinguishing use-wear from other forms of damage are other requirements that must be met before microwear techniques can be employed extensively (Hayden 1979). At the present, it is difficult to compare results prepared by different researchers. This problem allows potentially serious interpersonal bias to enter the lithic analysis process. Given the time-consuming nature of such investigations, the only practical way to implement microwear analysis on a large scale is to employ multiple analysts to carry out the laboratory work. Without standardized criteria, this does not seem possible. Also pertinent to this problem is the fact that expertise in this sort of analysis appears to be developed only after a long period of practice and considerable experimentation. Developing an appreciation for subtle differences in use-wear patterns is a time-consuming art currently practiced by very few archaeologists.

Finally, a number of other problem areas have

been identified that require further resolution. Raw material appears to be an important factor conditioning wear traces. Various kinds of lithic material react differently with contact materials, thereby producing different kinds of use-wear patterns. This is related to the problem of sorting out use-wear traces from other sources of damage that affect chipped-stone artifacts.

All these basic difficulties combine to suggest that much more research must be done before microscopic use-wear analysis techniques will become viable research tools for dealing with regional chipped-stone assemblages. As Schiffer (1979) points out, the research potential of the microwear techniques is readily apparent but has yet to be fully realized in terms of practical application.

To summarize contemporary approaches to lithic analysis as ways of studying prehistoric settlement–subsistence patterns, both approaches suggest that multiple, corroborative measurements employing a number of variables appear to be the best means of tackling this difficult problem (Ahler 1979; Odell 1979; Tringham *et al.* 1974). This statement suggests that both technological and functional analysis systems should be applied to the same assemblage in sequential order. Patterns that result from such analyses should, in turn, be corroborated by plotting the classes in space to evaluate the spatial coherence of the technological and functional classes. Such an approach serves to test actual patterns of empirical variability against expectations suggested by formal archaeological theory dealing with function (Dunnell 1978b; Jelinek 1976). This type of approach, along with the pragmatic choices that accompany it, is examined in the next section, and the rationale for the Cannon Project analysis systems is outlined.

CONSIDERATIONS IN DEVELOPING THE CANNON PROJECT LITHIC ANALYSIS SYSTEMS

Several factors were considered prior to developing a series of lithic analysis systems. These include the following range of topics: (*a*) regional-scale research problems outlined in the 1977 research design; (*b*) assessment and assimilation of as much of the previous work carried out in the project area and adjacent region as was possible; (c) the expectation of large chipped-stone artifact assemblages from excavation and surface collection; (d) spatial control, both on a regional scale as well as on an intrasite scale; (e) differences in site formation processes; (f) potential problems in interpersonal variation during analysis; and (g) ways of minimizing coding errors during recording and keypunching.

The research design (O'Brien 1977) outlined a series of problems upon which data-gathering operations in the project area would be focused. Because of preservation factors, land-use patterns, and the geomorphology of the region, lithic analysis was an especially important element in defining settlement–subsistence patterns, documenting and measuring technological development and change, and facilitating temporal control of excavated and surface assemblages. Each task required different analytical systems.

Review of the literature indicated that delineation of prehistoric subsistence patterns required an optimal combination of technological and some sort of quantitative use-wear analysis. Studies appearing since we made that observation have tended to support our decision. As the literature review noted, archaeologists tend to infer functional differences between settlements on a regional scale based on interassemblage variability in class frequencies of formed lithics. These studies generally fail to examine "debitage" as a class that could be subdivided on the basis of utilized edges, thereby masking a considerable portion of the total functional variability of a system.

In order to more precisely compare subsistence patterns, use-wear analysis of some sort must be carried out on this important class of lithic material. In the Cannon Reservoir region, over 90% of most assemblages are composed of flakes. Many small, low density sites consist entirely of lithic material that might be described as debitage (Chapter 12). Ignoring this class would effectively write off much of the visible archaeological resource.

Evaluation of previous research in the project area focused on three topics. First, there was a need to coordinate and compile useful results that documented the range of technological variability in lithic assemblages and that outlined important

changes in chipped-stone assemblages through time (Eichenberger 1944; Klippel 1969, 1970, 1972; Osborn 1972). Previous work provided testable hypotheses and served to refine expectations about the range of empirical variability to be found in the lithic assemblages. Because of the long-term nature of the project and the rapid, discipline-wide changes in archaeology in the late 1960s and the early 1970s, many research problems current in 1977 had not been anticipated in the previous research in the Cannon Reservoir region. For example, most earlier work had concentrated on developing chronological models, which resulted in three biases: (a) analysis was carried out on formed artifacts to the virtual exclusion of unmodified lithics; (b) some excavations were designed to recover only artifacts larger than 2.5 cm (½ inch) in size, and (c) survey activities consisted of grab samples of selected, diagnostic classes of formed artifacts. Existing samples clearly were biased and inadequate to meet the data requirements of regional analysis.

Another important line of investigation that was undertaken prior to excavation was an evaluation of the thermal treatment of local chert resources (Bleed and Meier 1980; Klippel 1970). Concomitant with Bleed and Meier's (1980) work on heat treatment, experiments were undertaken in 1978 to identify fracture patterns that could be associated with various manufacturing techniques and stages in lithic reduction sequences. Considerable time was invested in calibrating types of use-wear patterns on heat-treated and naturally occurring chert. This experimental investigation served as the basis for establishing macroscopic use-wear patterns that could be discerned consistently in surface collection assemblages and that also could be distinguished from tillage-induced damage in plow zone contexts.

One of the most significant factors conditioning decisions about the lithic classification systems was the scale of research that was anticipated. A technologically based coding format had to accommodate hundreds of thousands of artifacts and be used by several researchers to sort consistently and accurately. Large assemblages produced by regional-scale research present unique, unfamiliar problems, as many archaeologists are only beginning to realize. Importantly, problems faced in collecting, processing, and analyzing these large assemblages are offset by considerable gains in the precision of research results. Especially important is the way in which patterns can be defined in data sets and tested via increased control of spatial information.

A major problem in classifying large assemblages, especially lithic assemblages dominated by "waste flakes," is that there is considerable variation across potential analytical attributes in the sample. It is difficult to know precisely what classes will be present, and in what frequencies, before analysis begins. Standard, simplified systems do not take into account a sufficient number of variables to differentiate between important classes. Taxonomic systems require control of all potentially occurring taxa before analysis begins.

One means of avoiding this problem is to implement paradigmatic or dimensional classification systems. These consist of a series of sequential choices that characterize some particular state (e.g., chipping) for a given dimension, such as type of wear. This sort of system employs a series of sequential number strings as class definitions and has the positive aspect of being capable of expansion during the classification process as unforeseen attributes arise. The technological classification system used on the Cannon Project employs a modified dimensional system consisting of technological class, presence of retouching, and presence of heat treatment. Technological classes were selected on frequency of occurrence in previously analyzed assemblages and in trial sorting experiments carried out in 1977. They represent fairly standard technological units employed in many lithic technology studies (Ahler 1975a,b; Binford and Quimby 1963; Crabtree 1972; Geier 1973; Montet-White 1963).

Use-wear coding was modeled after a system developed for CRM projects carried out on the lower Columbia River in Washington (Dunnell and Campbell 1977; Dunnell and Lewarch 1974). Counting units are utilized edges, corners, and points; recording units are individual artifacts with technological and provenience information.

Some types of analyses require standardized measurements, such as size of artifact. Instead of taking measurements on individual pieces, size-related information was obtained by sorting all artifacts through a series of graded wire-mesh screens and counting numbers of artifacts in each size class (cf. Ahler 1975a, b). The degree of precision of measurement that is lost is greatly outweighed by advantages such as consistency and speed with which the technique can be applied.

Any classification system must be able to control for differences in the formation-process history of artifacts. This is especially important when comparing subsurface and surface-collected assemblages. These differences proved to be important in formulating the use-wear analysis system. We determined that degrees of precision that conceivably might be gained through a microwear approach would likely be offset by formation process factors affecting surface materials in the project area.

Recent discussions of use-wear analysis have pointed out potential problems in distinguishing several kinds of use-wear patterns from post-depositional formation-process damage, such as abrasion of edges through contact with soil. These kinds of analytical problems are heightened for plow zone artifacts subjected repeatedly to mechanical tillage. We decided to exclude all patterns that unequivocably could not be assigned a human origin. This led to the development of the microwear system employed to analyze plow zone assemblages.

A series of flake scar criteria were developed that could be discriminated consistently using a $10\times$ hand lens. Such an approach follows suggestions made by Del Bene and Holley (1979), who outline the increase in sample size that can be analyzed through a macrowear approach.

Artifacts occurring in plow zone situations might be expected to suffer greater incidental edge damage (Baker 1975) than those from excavated contexts and to be of less use in functional analyses. Holley (1981) has shown that plow-induced edge damage can be sorted out from use-wear patterns using macroscopic chipping analyses. His study, using material from a site that had been subjected repeatedly to rotary tilling, suggests that use-wear analyses are feasible for plow zone-derived lithic assemblages. Potential biases caused by plowing can be evaluated further by the plotting of artifact class distributions in space. Recurring clusters of various kinds of non-plow-induced use-wear patterns in plow zone sites would argue against serious alteration of use-wear patterns through tillage.

With an appreciation of various factors that were considered in developing the various classification systems, we now review the basic assumptions that guided the Cannon Project lithic analysis.

Assumptions Made in Creating the Classification Systems

From analysis of previous work in the project area, basic assumptions were made about prehistoric human settlement and resource acquisition: (*a*) the research universe is characterized by a complex series of compact microenvironments; as a result (*b*) there is relatively easy access to all potential energy sources in the project area; and in addition, (*c*) cryptocrystalline lithic resources are universally available throughout the project area. These assumptions suggest that the most adaptive technological system would be a flake-based, "expedient artifact" system. To determine the implications of such a system, one must characterize the availability of raw material.

Chert is virtually ubiquitous in the project area as exposed tabular slabs or eroding nodules derived from the Burlington formation. These slabs and nodules can be obtained from rock outcrops, exposed cliffs, shallow soil exposures, and along river and stream banks and bottoms. Although availability essentially is uniform throughout the region, the quality of chert varies, depending on local impurities, inclusions, weathering histories, and type of exposure. Such variability possibly could offset the apparent uniformity in resource availability in that inclusion-free, finer grained outcrops might tend to be selected more frequently than less desirable sources. However, a "leveling" mechanism, thermal alteration, was available to produce more uniformity in the raw material.

Bleed and Meier (1980), using samples from the Cannon Reservoir region, reviewed and tested many assumptions concerning effects of heat treatment on the chipping properties of chert. They suggest some flaking properties, such as ease of flake detachment and length of flake, are improved

by thermal pretreatment, whereas others actually deteriorate. Nevertheless, this objective experiment tends to confirm observations made by Klippel (1970) that thermally altered cherts have superior chipping qualities. Control of such techniques serves to standardize the lithic assemblage by minimizing local variation in raw material quality.

Given the variety of available edges afforded by a flake-based industry, one would expect the presence of retouch to be a fairly poor predictor of the total number of available use edges in the assemblage. Since most functional needs are met by available flake edges, and since ubiquitous raw material sources mean that a dulled edge can be discarded, retouching would be used to create edges not easily available in debitage.

DESCRIPTION OF THE CANNON PROJECT LITHIC CLASSIFICATION SYSTEMS

Three kinds of lithic analysis systems were used during the project: technological, functional, and stylistic. General characteristics of the technological and functional classification systems are outlined below. The stylistic classification system is presented by Curry (1979); the system used for projectile point analysis is discussed briefly in Chapter 6.

Technological Analysis

Technological analysis utilizes commonly defined classes employed in general technological studies (Crabtree 1972) as well as studies in the Midwest (Ahler 1975a,b; Binford and Quimby 1963; Geier 1973; Montet-White 1968). The format (Table 9.1) is designed to categorize nonformed artifact classes as a means of generating "type-frequency" information. Columns are assigned to each major technological class, with divisions for retouching and/or heat treatment. Also included on the standard technological coding sheet are other kinds of information, including the frequencies of three formed artifact classes: ground stone, ceramics, and bifacially chipped pieces. The basic record is (*a*)

TABLE 9.1.

Coding Format for Technological Classes[a]

Column	Variable
1-2	Hectare designation
3-4	North coordinate
5-6	East coordinate
7	Size class
8	Cores
9	Retouched cores
10	Heat-treated cores
11	Heat-treated retouched cores
12-13	Core rejuvenation flakes
14-15	Retouched core rejuvenation flakes
16-17	Heat-treated core rejuvenation flakes
18-19	Heat-treated retouched core rejuvenation flakes
20-21	Core shatter
22	Retouched shatter
23-24	Heat-treated shatter
25	Heat-treated retouched shatter
26-27	Primary decortication
28	Retouched primary decortication
29-30	Heat-treated primary decortication
31	Heat-treated retouched primary decortication
32-33	Secondary decortication
34	Retouched secondary decortication
35-36	Heat-treated secondary decortication
37	Heat-treated retouched secondary decortication
38-39	Tertiary chunk
40-41	Retouched tertiary chunk
42-43	Heat-treated tertiary chunk
44-45	Heat-treated retouched tertiary chunk
46-48	Tertiary flake
49-50	Retouched tertiary flake
51-52	Heat-treated tertiary flake
53-54	Heat-treated retouched tertiary flake
55-56	Trimming flake
57	Retouched trimming flake
58-59	Heat-treated trimming flake
60	Heat-treated retouched trimming flake
61	Sharpening flake
62	Retouched sharpening flake
63	Heat-treated sharpening flake
64	Heat-treated retouched sharpening flake
65	Projectile point (including fragments)
66	Biface (including fragments)
67	Drills (including fragments)
68	Formed scrapers
69	Ceramics
70	Miscellaneous formed cryptocrystalline
71	Unformed ground stone
72	Miscellaneous unformed ground stone
73	Formed ground stone
74-75	Collector
76-78	Collection time (in seconds)
79	Lab analyst
80	Time of day

[a]From Miskell and Warren 1979.

a 2-m^2 unit within a hectare (aggregate data) or (*b*) the exact point on a site where the artifact occurred. For aggregate surface data, the record is subdivided into four artifact size grades. Information recorded in the technological coding format provides basic analytical data about internal site structure; based on preliminary analysis of this information, decisions concerning where to carry out more extensive work are made.

The technological analysis system consists basically of units that measure various stages of lithic reduction; definitions used in the following discussion are from Curry (1979). Columns 8–37 (Table 9.1) refer to the initial stages of reduction of a chert object. Various products and byproducts of this reduction include: (*a*) *cores*—pieces differentiated from unmodified chert by the presence of one or more flake scars and (in most cases) by the presence of a prepared striking edge; (*b*) *core rejuvenation flakes*—flakes removed in the process of cleaning the core face or striking platform to facilitate flake removal; (*c*) *core shatter*—angular, blocky pieces of chert with flake scars, a prepared striking platform, and no apparent inverse bulb of percussion; (*d*) *primary decortication flakes*—flakes with the cortex covering part of the dorsal surface. Columns 38–54 refer to the secondary stages of reduction, after the cortex has been removed from a core. Classes include: (*a*) *tertiary chunks*—small, angular, blocky pieces of chert exhibiting portions of flake scars, but no cortex; and (*b*) *tertiary flakes*—small to large flakes showing no sign of cortex (flakes may be byproducts, or end products, of manufacture).

Another group of items, columns 55–64, includes flakes removed during manufacture or maintenance of bifacially chipped forms: (*a*) *trimming flakes*—flakes removed during thinning and modification of a biface having a thin, sometimes barely discernible, striking platform with some step-fracturing along the striking platform edge of the dorsal surface where the edge of the biface was ground to facilitate removal of the flake (Sheets 1973:217); and (*b*) *(re)sharpening flakes*—flakes removed from the dull edges of bifacially flaked tools having faceted striking platforms that exhibit previous flake removal scars. The latter class exhibits faceting that is similar to that found on the striking platforms of flakes struck from prepared core edges (Schneider 1972:94). However, the striking plat-

form on a rejuvenation flake forms an acute angle to the rest of the flake, with an overhang or lip on the ventral face (Frison 1968:149).

Other classes included in the technological format—formed pieces—are for the most part self-explanatory. *Miscellaneous formed cryptocrystalline* refers to a piece of chert whose form is conditioned more by the physical properties of the parent material than by deliberate human action. Although it exhibits some modification, the condition of the chert is such that the resultant form is aberrant to the classification scheme. These pieces occur rarely in the assemblages. An additional note also is needed on *unformed ground stones*. These objects, although not truly falling in the classes of *formed objects*, exhibit some slight to fairly pronounced evidence of grinding on at least one surface. They are quite distinct from formed ground stone objects, which have been modified into roughly ovoid or circular shapes.

Use-Wear Analysis

As the review of use-wear studies indicated, there are a number of unresolved problems in functional analysis. After considerable experimentation with local chert, it was decided that a macrowear-based use-wear system would be most appropriate, given sample sizes and money available for laboratory analysis. The basic unit of analysis is the utilized edge, with the artifact used as the recording unit to maintain control of provenience.

As Schiffer (1975) notes, using individual worn edges as basic counting units during analysis presents major recording problems. In most lithic assemblages, individual artifacts exhibit more than one utilized edge. To account for this, a system was derived to code instances of edge damage on individual artifacts by using a number string for each tool or unique location of macrowear. Each record is an artifact with provenience, size, and technological class information. Following a block of identification information, a series of dimensions is coded for each individual tool. Each instance of use-wear has information about all dimensions arranged in sequence within a block of columns (see Table 9.2). The system is open-ended in two ways. First, an infinite number of tools can be accommodated in successive information blocks on cards.

TABLE 9.2.

Coding Format for Use-Wear Analysis

Columns	Variable
1-2	Hectare
3-4	North coordinate
5-6	East coordinate
7	Size class
8-9	Artifact sequence number
10-11	Technological class
	Tool 1
12-13	Kind of wear
14	Location of wear
15	Form of wear
16	Form of bifacial wear
17-18	Shape of worn area
19-20	Spine-plane angle of worn area
21-23	Length of worn area (in mm)
24	Maximum height of worn area
25-37	Tool 2 - if present, repeat coding string
38-50	Tool 3 - if present, repeat coding string
51-63	Tool 4 - if present, repeat coding string
64-76	Tool 5 - if present, repeat coding string
79-80	Sequence continuation code indicating more than five tools on an object

This allows for the coding of more than six tools on an individual artifact while still maintaining both artifact and tool counts for the purpose of assessing the number of tools per artifact. It was noted that most artifacts had less than six tools.

Second, various attribute states for each dimension had a number code that could be expanded as unforeseen attributes were encountered during analysis. For example, if three kinds of chipping wear were anticipated prior to analysis and a fourth type appeared in the course of laboratory work, we could assign a separate number code to be used in subsequent coding without totally reorganizing the classification system.

The Cannon Project use-wear classification is paradigmatic or dimensional, with each dimension containing a set of mutually exclusive states or modes. In actual application, some dimensions have modes that could be subdivided, but so doing would increase recording complexity. There are five qualitative dimensions and three quantitative

ones, each of which is presented in Table 9.3 and summarized in this section.

Dimension 1: Kind of Wear

This is a composite variable that notes various levels of use-wear intensity, the condition of the surface on which wear occurs, and relational properties of worn surfaces. Intensity of macrowear is graded from chipping to chipping–crushing to step-fracture crushing. It is obvious that a considerable amount of use-wear evidence that might be visible with a microscope is not accommodated under this system.

Wear was defined by the pattern of edge damage and location of edge damage, following suggestions by Tringham *et al.* (1974). *Chipping wear* was defined as small, overlapping flake scars forming a contiguous distribution along a potentially usable edge, with obliteration of lower portions of the arrises separating flake scars. Size of flake scars and the lack of well-defined arrises along the bottom of flake scars were criteria used to sort use-wear from retouching (Tringham *et al.* 1974). Based on experimental work with local materials, it was noted that retouching produced larger, discrete flake scars as a result of localized pressure applied with a punch. Pressure applied to an edge during use appeared to be distributed along a more diffuse area, producing fairly clear but small flake scars away from the edge but smoothing and obliterating separations between the flake scars at the working edge.

Chipping was defined as composed of small flake scars only. *Chipping–crushing* was defined as small flake scars on a flake with small step-fractures forming a band of more intensive damage at the working edge. *Crushing* represented "massive, macroscopic wear" (Ahler 1979:309) identified by severe step-fractures and edge modification. *Striations* were defined as small grooves cutting into a surface.

This relatively simple tripartite division parallels distinctions made in microscopic analyses but lacks the precision of microscopic systems (Hayden 1979). As a result, we are reasonably certain that all instances identified as use-wear actually *do* represent tool use, not the operation of site formation processes.

Intensity is measured by the amount of wear and the number of planes–edges on which it occurs. Ahler (1979:303) defines an *edge* as "a line formed by the intersection of the dorsal and ventral surfaces of an unmodified flake." Our definitions of wear on planes–edges follow those of Dunnell and Lewarch (1974): (*a*) *wear on an edge*—wear occurring only at a single edge formed by the intersection of two planes, (*b*) *wear on a unifacial plane*—wear extending from an edge formed by the intersection of two planes onto the surface of one of the planes, and (*c*) *wear on bifacial planes*—wear extending up both surfaces by the intersection of two planes. Each mode of dimension 1 (Table 9.2) represents a decision that assesses presence–absence of retouching, intensity of wear, and number of planes on which wear occurs.

Dimension 2: Location of Wear

This dimension addresses the problem of spatial location of wear from a kinematic perspective, as suggested by Ahler (1975a, 1979). Tasks such as

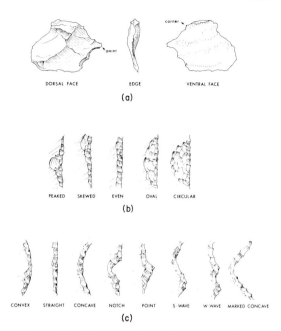

Figure 9.1. Diagram of three dimensions and associated modes used in the use-wear classification system; dimensions are (a) location of wear, (b) form of wear, and (c) shape of worn area.

cutting, scraping, or drilling ideally utilize different portions of available edges based on the properties of each task (Table 9.3). Location of wear is one means of sorting out this type of variability. Modes follow those employed by Dancey (1973) and Dunnell and Lewarch (1974). Figure 9.1 illustrates the various locational attributes.

Dimension 3: Form of Wear

Another dimension, form of wear, addresses the amount of working edge brought into contact with material being worked, direction of tool movement, and degree of penetration of the tool. Ahler's (1975b) observations on the kinematics of tool use and variation in wear patterns produced experimentally served as a guide in the definition of the modes. For unifacial tools (those with use-wear on a single surface), this dimension effectively characterizes movement of the tool against contact material. In bifacial tools (those with use-wear on opposite sides of the intersection of two planes and

TABLE 9.3.

Use-Wear Classification System

```
Dimension 1:  kind of wear
   Modes:
        1  Step-fracture crushing on natural plane
        2  Step-fracture crushing on retouched plane
        3  Bifacial step-fracture crushing on both planes
        4  Chipping on retouched plane
        5  Chipping on natural plane
        6  Bifacial chipping on both planes
        7  Striation on unifacial edge
        8  Striation on bifacial edges
        9  Retouch only, no wear
       10  Chipping and crushing on natural plane
       11  Chipping and crushing on retouched plane
       12  Bifacial chipping and crushing on retouched plane
       13  Bifacial crushing on retouched planes
       14  Bifacial chipping and crushing on natural planes
       15  Bifacial chipping on natural planes
Dimension 2:  location of wear
   Modes:
        1  Edge only
        2  Edge and face
        3  Corner and edge
        4  Corner and 2 edges
        5  Point only
        6  Point and edge
        7  Point and 2 edges
        9  Indeterminate
Dimension 3:  form of wear
   Modes:
        1  Peaked
        2  Skewed
        3  Even
        4  Oval (for projectile points)
        5  Circular (for projectile points)
        9  Indeterminate
```

that usually show use-wear on both surfaces), this dimension describes the dominant form of wear on the two surfaces. The shape of each mode (Table 9.3; Fig. 9.1) is roughly equivalent to Ahler's (1979:316) longitudinal asymmetry variables.

Dimension 4: Form of Bifacial Wear

This dimension quantifies symmetry in the wear of bifacial tools. Derived from Ahler's (1975b) work, it is designed to measure the amount of penetration

and direction of bifacial tool movement. Depending on the angle of use on contact material and intensity of use, one would expect different degrees of use-wear on both surfaces of a bifacial tool. The dimension approximates Ahler's (1979:316) facial asymmetry and bilateral asymmetry.

Dimension 5: Shape of Worn Area

Contact of a tool with worked material is affected by the shape of the edge. This dimension describes

TABLE 9.3. (*continued*)

```
Dimension 4:  form of bifacial wear
     Modes:
          1  Same wear form, equal wear on both faces
          2  Same wear form, one side worn heavier
          3  Different wear form on each side, equal wear on both sides
          4  Different wear form on each side, one side worn more heavily
          9  Indeterminate
Dimension 5:  shape of worn area
     Modes:
          1  Convex
          2  Straight
          3  Concave
          4  Notch
          5  Point
          6  S-Wave
          7  W-Wave
          8  Marked concave
          9  Indeterminate
Dimension 6:  spine-plane angle (in 5° increments)
      Modes:
          1  10°
          2  15°
        Etc.
Dimension 7:  length of worn area (in mm)
Dimension 8:  maximum height of worn area
```

the shape of the edge in plan view and serves to cross-check edge diminishment that would be expected to become more severe with intensified and/or prolonged use. Definitions are similar to those employed by Dancey (1973) and Dunnell and Lewarch (1974). The shape of each mode (Table 9.3; Fig. 9.1) is equivalent to Ahler's (1979:304) *edge outline*.

Dimension 6: Spine-Plane Angle

Numerous studies have demonstrated the importance of the working angle of an edge in the total functional configuration of a tool. There are two common measurements taken: (*a*) spine-plane angle and (*b*) edge angle. *Spine plane* refers to the angle formed by the two planes that intersect to form the entire edge of an object (Tringham *et al.* 1974). *Edge* refers only to the angle formed by the intersection of the used edge with another plane, which reflects

the edge shape after diminishment by use. Spine plane represents the angle available to the tool user before use and is likely to reflect the condition of the edge that was selected for use.

Lithic analysts have noted considerable variation in the edge angles employed for various tasks (Ahler 1975a; Hayden 1979; Tringham *et al.* 1974; Wilmsen 1970). In addition, there is the possibility that considerable interanalyst variability can enter into such measurements (Dibble and Bernard 1980). Increases in precision might not produce a concomitant increase in usable data because of "noise" introduced by measurement error.

After taking into account these factors, a technique was developed to measure spine-plane angles in 5° increments using cardboard wedges as templates. This technique provided sufficient precision, reduced the amount of interpersonal variation, and proved to be a rapid means of assessing the spine-plane angle.

Dimension 7: Length of Worn Area

Length of edge damage—a continuous, coherent pattern of use-wear along an edge—was measured to the nearest millimeter. This was done for each tool on an artifact and serves to corroborate qualitative dimensions dealing with the intensity of use and kinematic variables.

Dimension 8: Maximum Height of Worn Area

Maximum extent of damage extending up a plane was measured to the nearest millimeter. For bifacial tools, the plane having the most intensive wear was measured. This dimension is designed to measure intensity of use and degree of penetration into, and contact with, the worked material. Ahler's (1979:316) marginal asymmetry variable is analogous to this dimension.

Preliminary Evaluation of the Use-Wear Classification System

Given the complexity of the use-wear system and the fact that it represented a major investment of analysis time, the system was evaluated after a pilot study had been completed using surface-collected material from portions of Hatten Village (Chapter 12). Two factors were important in this evaluation.

First, we used observations on tool use derived from use-wear and ethnoarchaeological literature to determine if the empirical variability generated by the system actually met with predictions made by the functional model (Dunnell 1978b, c; Jelinek 1976). Basic questions included: Do the various use-wear modes occur as expected? Is tool use actually being measured, or are formation processes providing "noise"? What kinds of relationships appear to hold between use-wear variables and technological classes?

Second, after determining that the system was in fact doing what it was designed to do, we evaluated the structure of use-wear in the pilot study to generate a sampling design for the use-wear analysis of the remainder of the surface collections. This was accomplished by examining the relationship of use-wear classes to technological variables. By assigning probability factors to technological classes based on the likelihood of each one having use-wear evidence, a streamlined sampling program was developed to maximize analysis efficiency. Two complications developed that limited the success of this program.

The complexity of the relationships between use-wear structure and technological variables made generation of a simple probability equation impossible. Ideally, one can assign a likelihood of having use-wear to each technological class by comparing total objects in the technological class to total tools in that class. However, complications arise when factors such as artifact size, type of wear, and other variables are taken into account. A seemingly simple probability equation turns into a complex formula of questionable utilitarian value. A more serious problem was dwindling funds and time to implement the sampling program.

Nevertheless, results of this preliminary evaluation are important, not only in serving to demonstrate the utility of the use-wear classification system but also to provide important data on the structure of use-wear in a large sample of artifacts.

We can begin to assess the results by examining general patterns in the use-wear system. Data are drawn from six areas of Hatten Village that were surface collected and subsequently had the plow zone removed by mechanical stripping. The total artifact assemblage has 7485 cryptocrystalline unformed artifacts, with 2235 of these containing at least one tool.

All artifacts were first classified by a laboratory crew of 3–5 people. They noted technological variables and marked those edges that seemed to have evidence of use-wear damage. The entire assemblage was then reanalyzed by two laboratory analysts who coded use-wear.

Assessment of pattern in the tool system begins with examination of the relationship of artifact size and presence of retouching to use-wear variables. Artifact size classes are based on the United States system rather than the metric to coincide with the mesh size (e.g., 1-inch grid) used to sort artifacts. Retouching and size are important attributes in many traditional technologically oriented classification systems and often are used to infer artifact function. Growing use-wear and ethnoarchaeological evidence suggests such approaches tend to seriously underestimate the number of tools in an assemblage and overestimate tools used in tasks requiring large artifacts, steep edge angles, or intensity of pressure on working edges.

Table 9.4 summarizes the relationship of use-wear variables to artifact size and presence of retouching. A complex pattern can be noted. Larger artifacts (> 2.5 cm, or 1 inch) have a higher incidence of use-wear damage, represented as percentage of artifacts with use-wear out of total number of artifacts in that size class (84.2%). Larger artifacts also have higher incidences of wear on retouched surfaces (47.2%).

These results conform to expectations formulated from previous studies of use-wear. Larger items offer longer use-edges and have a wide variety of edges of varying angles. With a wide range of edge angles, one would expect frequent edge retouching to produce an edge angle suitable for a particular range of tasks. Large artifacts represent likely candidates for curation by virtue of having more available use edges and investment of labor in manufacturing suitable edges and angles through retouching.

Although there is a direct relationship between larger size and presence of retouching, large artifacts do not dominate the use-wear sample. Artifacts less than 1 inch in length account for a larger percentage of total number of tools. As expected, smaller artifacts with tools have a lower incidence of retouching than larger artifacts.

The relationship between artifact size and incidence of retouching is duplicated in the percentage of artifacts with use-wear versus the total number of artifacts in a size class. Over 80% of all >1-inch artifacts have tools, whereas only 10% of <½-inch (1.25 cm) artifacts have use-wear artifacts. Even though a low percentage of the smallest size class shows wear, this size class has so many members (4429) that it contributes an important percentage of tools to the total use-wear system.

These initial observations are clarified by reorganizing the data in Table 9.4 to assess the relative percentage of each size class in the total func-

tional system. Table 9.5 demonstrates two important patterns: (a) most tools do not occur on retouched planes (34% retouched versus 66% non-retouched) and (b) most tools (70%) occur on artifacts less than 1 inch in size. The majority of tools (53%) in the use-wear system are located on artifacts between ½ inch and 1 inch in size, with most of these (37% versus 16%) on unretouched surfaces.

Data in Tables 9.4 and 9.5 have important implications for lithic use-wear analysis. First, studies using only large, retouched artifacts appear to seriously underestimate the total number of tools in a flake-dominated assemblage. Most tools occur on relatively small (<1 inch) unretouched artifacts. Second, using two technological variables, size and presence of retouching, as a means of inferring function appears to be a difficult task. Complex relationships between size, retouching, total number of artifacts of a given size class in an assemblage, and number of artifacts with tools in each size class make it difficult to formulate a simple probability equation to predict use-wear from size and retouching alone.

One factor contributing to this problem is the presence of multiple tools on a single artifact. As more research is carried out in lithic use-wear analysis, multiple tools appear to play an important role in many use-wear systems (Hayden 1979; Schiffer 1975). Intuitively, more highly curated, large, retouched artifacts with greater linear area of usable working edge would be expected to have more tools per artifact. Table 9.6 confirms this expectation in the greater-than-1-inch size class. Artifacts do have higher percentages of members with more than one tool, with 39% having at least two tools per object. Artifacts between 1 inch and ½ inch in size approximate the pattern of multiple tools in the greater-than-1-inch size class but with a somewhat lower percentage of multiple tools.

Number of tools per artifact is considered in more detail in Table 9.7. Larger artifacts, as expected, have more tools per object when comparing total number of tools in a size class to total number of artifacts of the size class. Of more interest is the relationship of multiple tools when considering only artifacts with use-wear. There are

TABLE 9.4.

Relationship of Use-Wear to Artifact Size and Presence of Retouching in Sample from Hatten Village

Size Class (inch)	Number of All Artifacts	All artifacts with use-wear		Use-wear on natural plane			Use-wear on retouched plane		
	N	N	% of all artifacts	N	% of all artifacts	% of worn artifacts	N	% of all artifacts	% of worn artifacts
1	683	575	84.2	477	69.8	52.8	427	62.5	47.2
1/2	2373	1202	50.6	1094	46.1	69.5	480	20.2	30.5
1/4	4429	458	10.3	402	9.1	78.2	112	2.5	21.8
Totals	7485	2235		1973			1019		

TABLE 9.5.

Distribution of Use-Wear in Tool Assemblage from Hatten Village[a]

Size class (inch)	Use-wear on natural plane		Use-wear on retouched plane		Total use-wear	
	N	% of total tools in assemblage	N	% of total tools in assemblage	N	% of total tools in assemblage
1	477	15.9	427	14.3	904	30.2
1/2	1094	36.6	480	16.0	1574	52.6
1/4	402	13.4	112	3.7	514	17.2
Totals	1973	65.9	1019	34.0	2992	100.0

[a] Data from Table 9.4.

TABLE 9.6.

Number of Tools per Artifact by Size Class in Sample from Hatten Village

Size class (inch)	1 TOOL		2 TOOLS		3 TOOLS		4 TOOLS		5 TOOLS	
	N	% of artifacts with tools	N	% of artifacts with tools	N	% of artifacts with tools	N	% of artifacts with tools	N	% of artifacts with tools
1	575	100.00	226	39.3	93	16.1	38	6.6	11	1.9
1/2	1202	100.00	318	26.4	78	6.4	19	1.5	6	.5
1/4	458	100.00	59	12.8	10	2.1	2	.4	0	.0

TABLE 9.7.

Ratio of Tools to Artifacts by Size Class in Sample from Hatten Village

Size class (inch)	Total Artifacts	Total artifacts with use-wear	Total tools	Number of tools per object in total artifacts	Number of tools per worn artifact
1	683	575	904	1.32	1.57
1/2	2373	1202	1574	0.66	1.30
1/4	4429	458	514	0.11	1.12

TABLE 9.8.

Relationship of Retouching to Use-Wear by Size Class in Sample from Hatten Village

Size class (inch)	Total artifacts with use-wear	Tool 1 with retouch	% Tool 1 retouch of total use-wear artifacts
1	575	286	49.7
1/2	1202	345	28.7
1/4	458	94	20.5

fairly equal ratios of tools per artifact, with larger artifacts having the largest ratio.

The most important result of this analysis is confirmation of the hypothesis that object-based analysis systems are inappropriate for use-wear studies. Functional patterns in flake-dominated lithic assemblages represent choices made for potentially useful edges, not individual objects. Nearly one-third of all tools in the use-wear sample occur on artifacts with at least one other tool.

Artifact size and variability in range of available edge angles condition intensity of artifact use. Table 9.8 summarizes the relationship between retouching and size. *Tool 1* is defined as the first tool coded by the lab analyst and is used here to include artifacts having only a single tool as well as those with multiple tools. Assessing the amount of retouch associated with Tool 1 gives an approximate indication of the relative importance of edge modification and intensity of tool use. As expected, larger artifacts have a higher incidence of retouching. This may represent initial modification of an edge to obtain a suitable edge angle or resharpening following use.

Intensity of use is examined in more detail in Table 9.9. The relationship of size to general use-wear variables can be seen if one reorganizes data appearing in previous tables and adds information about unifacial and bifacial wear patterns. Over 95% of all use-wear patterns are unifacial. Larger artifacts have a slightly higher incidence of bifacial tools, but bifacial wear comprises only a small portion of total use-wear patterns. Data in Table 9.9 illustrate that retouching occurs more frequently on

larger artifacts yet comprises a small portion of total use-wear attributes.

Intensity of use-wear is also summarized in Table 9.10, which presents type of wear ranked by intensity, from chipping to bifacial crushing on retouched surfaces. Greater-than-1-inch artifacts have a higher relative percentage of more intensive edge damage types. The next smallest size class has a fairly even division of wear throughout all ranges of intensity, whereas the <½-inch size class has a higher incidence of less intense wear classes.

Comparing the relative percentage of wear types by size classes based on the percentage of all tools results in similar patterns. The "% of All Wear" columns in Table 9.10 indicates that chipping–crushing wear is most common, followed by crushing only and chipping only, although the latter two wear types have relatively similar percentages of total wear.

Table 9.11 presents information on the distribution of the six most common wear types across technological classes. Most wear occurs on tertiary flakes and secondary decortication flakes. This pattern is consistent within each use-wear class.

Table 9.12 reorganizes data from Table 9.11 to calculate the relative importance of use-wear classes within each technological class. Technological artifacts that tend to be larger, such as cores and primary decortication flakes, have higher relative percentages of more intensive wear types. This is expected and conforms to previously noted patterns relating size to intensity of use. Other technological classes show almost equal percentages divided among the major wear types. This reflects

TABLE 9.9.

Relationship of Size to General Use-Wear in Sample from Hatten Village

	Size class					
	1 inch		1/2 inch		1/4 inch	
Use-wear	N	% of Use-wear	N	% of Use-wear	N	% of Use-wear
Unifacial wear	861	95.1	1546	98.2	505	98.6
Bifacial wear	36	4.0	28	1.8	7	1.4
Use-wear natural plane	477	52.7	1094	69.5	402	78.5
Use-wear retouch plane	428	47.3	480	30.5	110	21.5

TABLE 9.10.

Type of Wear by Size Class in Sample from Hatten Village

	Size class								
	1 inch			1/2 inch			1/4 inch		
Type of wear	N	% of size class	% of all wear	N	% of size class	% of all wear	N	% of size class	% of all wear
Chipping	96	10.61	3.21	359	22.81	12.00	184	35.94	6.15
Chipping on retouch	24	2.76	.84	28	1.78	.94	8	1.57	.27
Bifacial chipping	4	.44	.13	5	.32	.17	1	.19	.03
Bifacial chipping on retouch	2	.22	.08	3	.19	.01	0	.00	.00
Chipping/crushing	271	29.94	9.06	603	38.31	20.16	172	33.59	5.75
Chipping/crushing on retouch	50	5.52	1.67	51	3.24	1.70	18	3.52	.60
Bifacial chipping/ crushing	4	.44	.13	5	.32	.17	4	.78	.13
Bifacial chipping/ crushing on retouch	11	1.22	.37	8	.51	.27	0	.00	.00
Crushing	96	10.61	3.20	117	7.43	3.91	41	8.01	1.37
Crushing on retouch	331	36.57	11.07	388	24.65	12.97	82	16.01	2.74
Bifacial crushing	4	.44	.13	2	.12	.06	0	.00	.00
Bifacial crushing on retouch	11	1.22	.37	5	.32	.17	2	.39	.06
Totals	904	99.99	30.24	1574	96.76	52.53	512	100.00	17.10

TABLE 9.11.

Most Common Use-Wear Classes by Technological Class in Sample from Hatten Village

Technological class	Number of Artifacts With Wear	Chip		Chip on retouch	
		N	% of use-wear class	N	% of use-wear class
Core	49	2	.3	0	0
Heat treated core	1	0	0	0	0
Core rejuvenation	67	10	1.7	6	10.0
Heat-treated core rejuvenation	7	3	.5	0	0
Core shatter	4	0	0	0	0
Primary decortication	3	0	0	1	1.7
Secondary decortication	383	76	12.9	14	23.3
Heat-treated secondary decortication	96	33	5.6	5	8.3
Tertiary chunk	217	27	4.6	3	5.0
Heat-treated tertiary chunk	56	11	1.9	2	3.3
Tertiary flake	1045	340	57.6	18	30.0
Heat-treated tertiary flake	286	82	13.9	9	15.0
Trimming flake	3	0	0	1	1.7
Sharpening flake	11	3	.5	1	1.7
Heat-treated sharpening flake	6	3	.5	0	0
Totals	2234	590	100	60	100

the fact that some technological classes, such as tertiary flakes, occur in all size classes. By only considering technological classes, considerable variation in use-wear differences between size classes is minimized. This is demonstrated in Table 9.12, where the number of tools per worn artifact is nearly the same across all technological classes.

A better view of the relationship between size, use-wear, and technological variables is obtained by comparing artifact counts from technological coding of the assemblage and subsequent use-wear coding of the same material. Table 9.13 presents the relationship between technological classes and number of tools. There are some obvious discrep-

ancies in identification between the technological coding and the use-wear assessment of core rejuvenation flake classes. For the other classes there is a wide range of values for the percentage of artifacts with wear and number of tools per artifact. These values do not have a simple relationship to average size of objects in a given technological class, although technological classes with larger artifacts tend to exhibit greater percentages of artifacts with wear and more tools per artifact.

Table 9.14 clarifies the role of artifact size in the probability that a given technological class has evidence of use-wear. Every technological class exhibits a higher percentage of worn artifacts in the two

TABLE 9.11. (*continued*)

	Use-wear class						
	Chip/ crush		Chip/ crush retouch		Crush		Crush retouch	
N	% of use-wear class	N	% of use-wear class	N	% of use-wear class	N	% of use-wear class
20	2.2	4	3.4	8	3.4	27	3.9
0	0	0	0	0	0	1	.1
23	2.5	10	8.5	7	3.0	34	4.9
3	.3	2	1.7	2	.9	3	.4
1	.1	0	0	0	0	3	.4
0	0	0	0	0	0	2	.3
142	15.6	25	21.4	49	20.9	135	19.6
33	3.6	4	3.4	10	4.3	22	3.2
90	9.9	15	12.8	26	11.1	84	12.2
23	2.5	3	2.6	10	4.3	23	3.3
439	48.3	42	35.9	103	43.8	265	38.4
122	13.4	11	9.4	19	8.1	82	11.9
2	.2	0	0	0	0	1	.1
7	.8	1	.9	1	.4	2	.3
3	.3	0	0	0	0	2	.3
908	99.7	117	100	235	100.2	686	99.3

largest size classes. This relationship follows a consistent pattern previously noted for other attributes in the use-wear classification. But again, although smaller artifacts have lower percentages of worn artifacts, small artifacts are numerically more frequent. Thus, small objects contribute about the same number of worn objects as large artifacts to the total use-wear assemblage.

This preliminary evaluation of the use-wear analysis system has employed only a few variables and made assessments using simple inspection of pattern in counts and percentages. Even at that gross level of analysis, consistent patterns have emerged, suggesting that the classification system worked correctly in delineating use-wear patterns in an assemblage consisting primarily of unformed flakes.

CONCLUSIONS

Three kinds of lithic analysis systems were developed for the unique problems of the Cannon Project; two have been presented here: technological and functional analysis. Two important factors conditioning lithic analysis need reiteration.

First, virtually all lithic assemblages recovered

TABLE 9.12.

Importance of Use-Wear Classes by Technological Class in Sample from Hatten Village

		Use-wear class	
Technological class	Number of artifacts with wear	Chip % of tech. class	Chip on retouch % of tech. class
Core	49	3.3	0.0
Heat-treated core	1	0.0	0.0
Core rejuvenation flake	67	11.1	6.7
Heat-treated core rejuvenation flake	7	23.1	0.0
Core shatter	4	0.0	0.0
Primary decortication	3	0.0	0.0
Secondary decortication	383	17.2	3.2
Heat-treated secondary decortication	96	30.8	4.7
Tertiary chunk	217	11.0	1.2
Heat-treated tertiary chunk	56	15.3	2.8
Tertiary flake	1045	28.2	1.5
Heat-treated tertiary flake	286	25.2	2.8
Trimming flake	3	0.0	25.0
Sharpening flake	11	20.0	6.7
Heat-treated sharpening flake	6	37.5	0.0
Totals	2234		

TABLE 9.13.

Relationship of Technological Classes to Tool in Sample from Hatten Village

Technological class	Number of artifacts coded during technological analysis	Number of artifacts with wear	Technological artifacts with wear	Tool per technologic artifact
Core	52	49	94.2	1.1
Heat-treated core	9	1	11.1	0.1
Core rejuvenation flakes	3	67	–	–
Heat-treated core rejuvenation flakes	1	7	–	–
Core shatter	5	4	80.0	0.8
Primary decortication	55	3	5.5	0.0
Secondary decortication	690	383	55.5	0.6
Heat-treated secondary decortication	155	96	61.9	0.6
Tertiary chunk	736	217	29.5	0.3
Heat-treated tertiary chunk	136	56	41.2	0.5
Tertiary flake	4489	1045	23.3	0.2
Heat-treated tertiary flake	824	286	34.7	0.3
Trimming flake	26	3	11.5	0.1
Sharpening flake	27	11	40.7	0.5
Heat-treated sharpening flake	12	6	50.0	0.6
Totals	7220	2234		

TABLE 9.12. (*continued*)

		Use-wear class			
Chip/crush % of tech. class	Chip/crush retouch % of tech. class	Crush % of tech. class	Crush retouch % of tech. class	Number of total tools	Tool per worn artifact
32.8	6.6	13.1	44.3	61	1.24
0.0	0.0	0.0	100.0	1	1.00
25.6	11.1	7.8	37.8	90	1.34
23.1	15.4	15.4	23.1	13	1.86
25.0	0.0	0.0	75.0	4	1.00
33.0	0.0	0.0	66.0	3	1.00
32.2	5.7	11.1	30.6	441	1.15
30.8	3.7	9.3	20.6	107	1.11
36.7	6.1	10.6	34.3	245	1.13
31.9	4.2	13.9	31.9	72	1.29
36.4	3.5	8.5	22.0	1207	1.16
37.5	3.4	5.8	25.2	325	1.14
50.0	0.0	0.0	25.0	4	1.33
46.7	6.7	6.7	13.3	15	1.36
37.5	0.0	0.0	25.0	8	1.33
				2596	

during surface collection and excavation of sites in the project area are composed mainly of flakes. This phenomenon is a result of the ubiquitous distribution of available lithic resources in the project area. Flake-based industries have important consequences for the archaeologist in terms of field and laboratory techniques. Flake assemblages usually contain many thousands of elements, a fact that results in large sample sizes that must be processed in the laboratory. Large populations represent a difficult problem for use-wear analysis since the appropriate counting unit is the utilized edge, not an individual artifact. Sampling for variation in use-wear patterns is a task that must be taken into account during both field and laboratory work. This leads to the second major factor: volume of material and number of provenience units.

There are well over 50,000 individual provenience units in the Cannon Project data set, most of which are from intensive surface collection. Some sites have over 3000 collection units, with artifacts sorted into four size classes, producing approximately 11,000 lines of data for a single site. It is an understatement to suggest that controlling provenience and analytical data on samples of this magnitude is an overwhelming job. As a result, not all goals of the lithic analysis systems have been met as of this date, but results obtained thus far can be summarized and evaluated with the experience that hindsight provides.

The technological classification system is the most completely tested of the lithic classification systems. Technological classes for chipped-stone artifacts have been plotted in space to delineate patterns in tool manufacture and possible use. Recurring clusters of various technological classes have demonstrated the utility of the system for regional analysis. There are some potential problems in terms of subtle differences in class definitions between laboratory analysts, despite

TABLE 9.14.

Worn Artifacts by Technological Class and Size in Sample from Hatten Village

	Size class		
	1 inch		
Technological class	Artifacts with tools	Total technological artifacts	% worn
Core	49	52	94
Heat-treated core	1	9	11
Core rejuvenation flake	65	4	-
Heat-teated core rejuvenation flake	7	2	-
Core shatter	3	5	60
Primary decortication	2	15	13
Secondary decortication	183	223	82
Heat-treated secondary decortication	28	37	76
Tertiary chunk	82	130	63
Heat-treated tertiary chunk	10	17	59
Tertiary flake	116	152	76
Heat-treated tertiary flake	22	29	76
Trimming flake	1	2	50
Sharpening flake	2	0	-
Heat-treated sharpening flake	1	0	-

monitoring programs designed to minimize such potential problems. Preliminary statistics on differences between laboratory workers suggest that this problem can be eliminated during more detailed analysis.

Perhaps most important are the contributions made to the general field of lithic analysis from preliminary results generated by the use-wear classification system. One deficiency is that many relationships between use-wear modes, such as edge angles and kinematic variables, have yet to be explored in detail. Another task that remains is plotting use-wear classes across space, by site and by microenvironment, to fully assess the role of various classes in energy extraction.

One important result is the demonstration of complex relationships between variables such as artifact size, multiple tools, and kind of technological artifact. Such complexity precludes assignment of simple probability values for likelihood of

use-wear based only on size and presence of retouching and conforms to expectations drawn from ethnoarchaeology.

A number of points made in the growing use wear literature have been confirmed. The utilized edge and not an individual artifact is clearly the appropriate unit of analysis. Multiple tools, even on small artifacts, make up an important component of the total use-wear system. The contribution of small, unformed flakes to the total use-wear system was not anticipated and represents an important contribution to use-wear studies. This has broader implications for archaeological research as well. For example, amateur collecting of larger, formed lithic artifacts (e.g., projectile points) has been extensively documented (cf. Schiffer and House 1975). Often, such activities are assumed to destroy the research potential of sites collected by amateurs. Although temporally diagnostic artifacts are seriously depleted in such cases, small, un-

TABLE 9.14. (*continued*)

Size class					
1/2 inch			1/4 inch		
Artifacts with tools	Total technological class	% worn	Artifacts with tools	Total technological class	% worn
0	0	0	0	0	0
0	0	0	0	0	0
2	1	–	0	0	0
0	0	0	0	0	0
1	1	100	0	0	0
1	23	4	0	17	0
164	264	62	36	203	18
54	67	81	14	15	27
114	289	39	20	317	6
32	56	57	14	63	22
649	1361	48	279	3181	9
173	260	67	91	535	17
1	8	13	1	16	6
7	10	70	2	17	12
4	8	50	1	4	25

formed flakes are not; material that may contain *most* of the functional evidence in the sample of chipped-stone objects in the lithic assemblage of that site.

One contribution of the Cannon Project analytical systems is that they worked. Hundreds of thousands of artifacts were processed and analyzed by six full-time laboratory personnel in less than two years. Many detailed analyses remain to be completed, but all lithic materials have been analyzed using the technological system—certainly no small feat.

10

Analysis of Vertebrate Remains

JOHN R. BOZELL AND ROBERT E. WARREN

Vertebrate remains can provide important insights into prehistoric systems of settlement and subsistence. A variety of factors affect observable characteristics of faunal assemblages, and in many cases these factors can be isolated and used to reconstruct past lifeways. Interpretations then can be compared with predictions drawn from models to determine how well results conform to expectations. When discrepancies are found, there is reason to question the models and to revise them to account for new observations. The objective of this chapter is to evaluate vertebrate remains from 11 archaeological components in the Cannon Reservoir region. Samples date from the Late Archaic–Late Woodland periods and provide an opportunity to (a) document possible long-term changes in patterns of vertebrate exploitation and (b) evaluate the potential effects of seasonal resource availability on settlement–subsistence systems. Results bear directly on the model presented in Chapter 5 and aid in the development of an integrated picture of Archaic and Woodland cultural adaptations in the Cannon Reservoir region.

METHODS OF RECONSTRUCTION

To identify qualitative or quantitative change within a subsistence system, one must detect shifts in the economic significance of particular species among well-dated archaeological contexts. This task is not a simple one since any number of variables can bias observations and create an erroneous image of long-term change. Perhaps most important among these factors is seasonal variation of resource availability. For instance, in comparing an older assemblage from an autumn butchering encampment with a younger one from a summer fishing village, one might infer a basic shift in the subsistence system from terrestrial to aquatic resources. In fact, the assemblages may reflect seasonal differences in a subsistence system that did not change through time, and any hypothesis of long-term system change would be false due to a lack of control over seasonality as a systemic variable. To control for systemic seasonality, discussion centers on (a) the seasonal availability of important vertebrate taxa, (b) determination of the

TABLE 10.1.

Summary of Identified Vertebrate Remains from the Cannon Reservoir Region, Organized by Class and Site

	Late Archaic			Early Woodland
Class	Miskell	Cooper	Pigeon Roost Creek	Collins
Fish				
Number	77[a]	36	7	1
Percentage of total	19.4	19.7	3.9	.9
Amphibian and Reptile				
Number	145	30	20	–
Percentage of total	36.6	16.4	11.2	–
Bird				
Number	2	3	17	1
Percentage of total	.5	1.6	9.5	.9
Mammal				
Number	172	114	134	104
Percentage of total	43.4	62.3	75.3	98.1
Total number of identified elements	396	183	178	106

[a]Number of identified elements.

season of death for several individuals of white-tailed deer, and (c) evaluation of the implications of other seasonal indicators from each site.

Four factors contribute to the processes involved in seasonal exploitation of faunal resources. First, potential energy or nutritional yields may vary seasonally in a given environment. Second, the entire resource procurement process—including the selection, location, pursuit, capture, processing, and storage of resources—involves consideration of the seasonal availability of desirable taxa (Styles 1978). Third, since resource availability varies seasonally in different environmental zones, the number, size, and function of sites in settlement–subsistence systems are influenced by resource distributions within environmental zones and the operational concerns of procurement scheduling. Finally, variability in the use of zones may reflect shifts in the nature of the seasonal round in the settlement–subsistence system for a particular culture.

THE VERTEBRATE ASSEMBLAGES

Eleven vertebrate assemblages representing four cultural traditions are used in the analysis. These include three Late Archaic (LA) assemblages (Cooper, Miskell, and Pigeon Roost Creek), one Early Woodland (EW) assemblage (Collins), three Middle Woodland (MW) assemblages (Hatten Village, Pigeon Roost Creek, and Hillside), and four Late Woodland (LW) assemblages (Muskrat Run, Victor Bridge, Cooper, and Pigeon Roost Creek). Site descriptions for Cooper, Hatten Village, Hillside, and Collins are presented in Chapter 13; Pigeon Roost Creek is described in Chapter 6; Muskrat Run, Victor Bridge, and Miskell are described briefly here, as are vertebrate assemblages from all of the sample components.

All vertebrate remains used in this chapter have been described in detail elsewhere (citations follow). Only identifiable elements are discussed here. Specimens were considered identifiable if

TABLE 10.1. (*continued*)

Middle Woodland			Late Woodland			
Hatten Village (SA 6)	Pigeon Roost Creek	Hillside	Muskrat Run	Victor Bridge	Cooper	Pigeon Roost Creek
30	18	7	422	238	10	12
23.8	2.3	6.0	57.6	42.4	9.3	1.7
38	72	1	150	78	7	68
30.1	9.3	.9	20.5	13.9	6.5	9.6
1	82	-	4	18	2	74
.8	10.6	-	.5	3.2	1.9	10.5
57	599	109	156	227	89	551
45.2	77.7	93.1	21.3	40.5	82.4	78.2
126	771	117	732	561	108	705

they were recognizable elements or element fragments that could be classified at or below the family level. Table 10.1 summarizes identifiable vertebrate remains by class for each component.

Cooper

Cooper contains major Late Archaic and Late Woodland components and, based on the presence of a few sherds similar to those of the Monroe phase, may contain a Middle Woodland component as well. Due to an inability to define precisely the limits of this Middle Woodland component, faunal remains from this time period cannot be separated from those of the Late Woodland component. The Archaic component (located in the large strip area shown in Figure 13.19) was quite localized and was identified by a concentration of aceramic pits containing diagnostic Late Archaic projectile points.

From the Late Archaic component there are 183 elements representing 22 taxa (Bozell 1980a). Mam-

mals dominate the assemblage (62% of elements), although remains of fish and reptiles also are abundant (26% of elements). White-tailed deer (*Odocoileus virginianus*) is the predominant taxon. Other important taxa include eastern cottontail (*Sylvilagus floridanus*) and tree squirrels (*Sciurus* spp.).

The vertebrate assemblage from the Woodland component, consisting of 108 specimens and 19 taxa, is the smallest Late Woodland faunal assemblage described here. Mammals dominate the sample (82%), whereas fish (9%), reptiles (6%), and birds (2%) are comparatively rare. White-tailed deer (66%) is the most abundant species.

Pigeon Roost Creek

There are three faunal assemblages from Pigeon Roost Creek. The Late Archaic assemblage consists of 178 identifiable elements representing 23 taxa (Bozell 1981a). Mammals constitute over 75% of the elements (Table 10.1), followed by reptiles (11%), birds (10%), and fish (4%). Species diversity is greatest among mammals and reptiles. In addition to white-tailed deer, soft-shelled turtle (*Trionyx* spp.), turkey (*Meleagris gallopavo*), and eastern cottontail are common.

The Middle Woodland assemblage is the largest sample analyzed. It includes 771 elements representing 38 taxa. The sample is dominated by mammals (78%), but also includes birds (11%), reptiles (9%), and fish (2%). A number of species are represented, including white-tailed deer, turkey, box–water turtle (Emydinae), tree squirrel, eastern cottontail, beaver (*Castor canadensis*), and raccoon (*Procyon lotor*).

The Late Woodland assemblage contains 705 elements representing 36 taxa. It also is dominated by mammalian remains (78%), and proportions of other classes are quite similar to those from other components of the site (Table 10.1). Key taxa include white-tailed deer, box–water turtle, turkey, and tree squirrel.

Miskell

Miskell is located on a high terrace adjacent to a steep cutoff bank of the Salt River. Thirty-six subsurface pits were excavated in one portion of the site, producing a number of Archaic projectile points. Radiometric dates are not available, but on the basis of projectile point styles the component has been assigned to the Late Archaic period (Angus and Ruppert 1977). The vertebrate assemblage from Miskell is twice as large as that from any other Late Archaic component. A total of 396 elements representing 25 taxa was identified. Mammalian remains are common (43%), but reptiles and fish together outnumber mammals (Table 10.1). White-tailed deer is the dominant taxon, followed by soft-shelled turtle, coyote (*Canis latrans*), and taxa from three families of fish (sucker, gar, and bass).

Collins

The Early Woodland faunal assemblage from Collins (106 identifiable elements) contains only six taxa (Klippel 1972). The sample is predominantly mammalian (98%), with fish and bird remains contributing less than 2%. Dominant taxa include white-tailed deer (83%) and fox (*Vulpes* spp.) (9%).

Hatten Village

Excavations at Hatten Village revealed three spatially distinct clusters of features (Chapter 12), each of which is interpreted as a discrete Woodland community. Only strip area (SA) 6 yielded enough information to classify and date an occupation. Radiometric dates, ceramics, and projectile point classes indicate that the area was inhabited during the middle part of the Middle Woodland period. Vertebrates from SA 6 are represented by 126 elements and 10 taxa (Bozell 1979). Mammals are common (45%), but reptiles and fish together dominate the assemblage (53%). Key taxa are white-tailed deer (44%), box–water turtle (30%), sucker (13%), and sunfish–bass (10%).

Hillside

The Middle Woodland assemblage from Hillside contains 117 identifiable elements and eight taxa (Bozell 1980b). The sample is primarily mammalian (93%), although remains of fish and reptiles also occur. White-tailed deer is the only abundant taxon (87%).

Muskrat Run

Muskrat Run is a fairly large Late Woodland village located on a high, gently sloping terrace near the mouth of Indian Creek. Mechanical stripping and trenching activities exposed 20 pits at the site, many of which contained vertebrate remains. The faunal assemblage from Muskrat Run is the second largest of the samples. It contains 732 elements and 33 taxa (Hunt 1977b) and is the only sample dominated by fish (58%). Mammals (21%) and amphibian–reptiles (20%) also are common, but birds are not (Table 10.1). Dominant taxa include several forms of sunfish–bass and suckers. Catfish (*Ictalurus* spp.), box–water turtle, and white-tailed deer also are well represented.

Victor Bridge

Victor Bridge is located on a high terrace near an ephemeral tributary of South Fork. A small portion of the site was stripped by machinery, exposing 15 pits (Hunt 1977c). Ceramic material and radiometric dates indicate a Late Woodland occupation. A total of 561 elements representing 29 taxa was identified. The assemblage is similar in character to that from Muskrat Run in that it is dominated by fish remains (42%). Mammalian remains also constitute a substantial portion of the sample (40%), whereas amphibian–reptile elements compose 14%, and birds 2%. Dominant taxa include sucker (primarily redhorse—*Moxostoma* spp.), sunfish–bass, and white-tailed deer.

VERTEBRATE TAXA ENCOUNTERED

The following discussion focuses on taxa from the components in order to isolate variability in patterns of vertebrate resource use in the Cannon Reservoir region.

Fish

Fish remains occur in all assemblages (Table 10.2). Proportions and diversity of species vary greatly from site to site, although species of three families dominate the assemblages: Catostomidae (sucker), Ictaluridae (catfish), and Centrarchidae (sunfish–bass). Modern creel census data for game fish in the Salt River indicate channel catfish (*Ictalurus punctatus*) and bullheads (*I. melas* and *I. natalis*) are the three most commonly caught taxa, followed by freshwater drum (*Aplodinotus grunniens*) (Missouri Botanical Garden 1974:168). Although drum are caught frequently today, they are rare in prehistoric assemblages. In comparison, suckers and sunfish–bass are relatively rare in modern catches (5–10% of the annual census). Discrepancies between modern and prehistoric data may be a function of change in environmental conditions over the past 5000 years. However, studies using different sampling methods often yield distinctive results, and discrepancies may instead be due to differing procurement techniques. Samples from extensive seining operations in the Salt Basin were dominated by shiners (*Notropis lutrensis, N. umbratilis*) and minnows (*Pimephales notatus*), whereas intensive shocking experiments produced large quantities of gizzard shad (*Dorosoma cepedianum*), river carpsucker (*Carpoides carpio*), northern redhorse (*M. macrolepidotum*), and longnose gar (*Lepisosteus osseus*) (Missouri Botanical Garden 1974:164–167).

A wide variety of fishing techniques were used by native groups, including spears, bows and arrows, dip nets, wiers, seines, and hooks and lines (Rostlund 1952). The actual techniques employed by prehistoric groups in the Cannon Reservoir region are difficult to ascertain. The abundance of suckers in assemblages may indicate the use of seines or various netting techniques since a majority of these species are bottom feeders (Pflieger 1975:178). Although measurements were not taken on fish remains, it is evident from visual inspection that a majority of elements in the samples are from small or medium-sized fish. Styles (1978) notes that small individuals could have been captured with nets. Large quantities of elements from individuals of the sunfish–bass family in several assemblages may reflect expanded use of spearing and hooking during some periods (Smith 1975:62).

Amphibians and Reptiles

With the exception of Collins, remains of reptiles occur in all assemblages (Table 10.3). The two most common taxa are box–water turtles (Emydinae) and soft-shell turtles (*Trionyx* spp.). Ornate box turtle (*Terrapene ornata*) and common snapping turtle (*Chelydra serpentina*) are abundant in the region today (Missouri Botanical Garden 1974:118–119). Although turtle elements are fairly common in prehistoric contexts, the amount of usable meat is relatively low when compared to larger mammals. Capture of turtles may not have been a major focus of collecting activities; rather, they probably were collected when encountered (Parmalee *et al.* 1972). Aquatic and semiaquatic species (e.g., snapping turtle and soft-shelled turtle) may occur in archae-

TABLE 10.2.

Summary of Identified Fish Remains from the Cannon Reservoir Region, Organized by Taxa and Site

| Taxa | Late Archaic | | | Early Woodland |
	Miskell	Cooper	Pigeon Roost Creek	Collins
Lepisosteus sp. (gar)	17[a]	6	1	–
Esocidae (pike)	–	–	–	–
Cyprinidae (minnow)	3	17	–	1
Catostomidae (sucker)	5	2	1	–
Moxostoma spp. (redhorse)	–	–	2	–
Moxostoma erythrurum (golden redhorse)	–	–	–	–
Moxostoma carinatum (river redhorse)	–	–	–	–
Ictaluridae (catfishes)	25	–	–	–
Ictalurus spp. (catfish)	–	4	–	–
Ictalurus melas (black bullhead)	–	–	–	–
Ictalurus punctatus (channel catfish)	–	–	–	–
Noturus sp. (madtom/stonecat)	–	–	–	–
Pylodictus olivaris (flathead catfish)	–	–	–	–
Centrarchidae (sunfish/bass)	24	5	–	–
Micropterus sp. (bass)	2	–	3	–
Micropterus salmoides (largemouth bass)	–	–	–	–
Lepomis sp. (sunfish/bluegill)	–	–	–	–
Pomoxis sp. (crappie)	–	–	–	–
Percidae (perch)	–	–	–	–
Aplodinotus grunniens (freshwater drum)	1	2	–	–
Total number of identified elements	77	36	7	1

[a]Number of identified elements.

ological contexts as a result of capture during fishing activities.

Overall, amphibians and reptiles are subdominant in the Cannon Project assemblages. The highest percentages of occurrence are at Miskell (Late Archaic), Hatten Village (Middle Woodland), and Muskrat Run (Late Woodland). Fluctuations in proportions of turtle remains show a slight correlation with proportions of fish ($r = 0.3$), and this trend may indicate that turtle resources were, for the most part, a by-product of fish procurement.

Birds

Turkey (*Meleagris gallopavo*) is by far the most well-represented bird taxon in Cannon Project as-

TABLE 10.2. (*continued*)

| | Middle Woodland | | | Late Woodland | | |
Hatten Village (SA 6)	Pigeon Roost Creek	Hillside	Muskrat Run	Victor Bridge	Cooper	Pigeon Roost Creek
–	–	–	9	–	4	1
–	1	–	1	3	–	–
–	1	–	33	35	3	–
13	4	4	61	71	1	1
4	3	–	50	62	–	3
–	–	–	–	–	–	1
–	2	–	–	–	–	–
–	2	–	41	–	–	–
–	–	1	–	16	1	–
–	–	–	–	–	–	1
–	1	–	–	–	–	–
–	–	–	7	–	–	–
–	–	–	–	–	–	1
11	–	2	166	39	1	1
1	4	–	–	2	–	2
–	–	–	12	–	–	–
1	–	–	34	4	–	1
–	–	–	4	2	–	–
–	–	–	–	3	–	–
–	–	–	4	1	–	–
30	18	7	422	238	10	12

semblages (Table 10.4). However, avian remains are notably rare in the samples, representing only 5% of elements in all assemblages combined. The dominance of turkey elements (90%) among bird remains probably is a function of several factors. First, although migratory waterfowl are abundant in many other assemblages from sites in riverine environments in the Midwest (cf. Parmalee *et al.* 1972; Smith 1975; Styles 1978), suitable habitats are uncommon in the project area. Second, turkeys probably were a valued food resource because of their size and year-round availability. Third, in the fall, turkeys aggregate in upland deciduous forests and the prairie–forest ecotone to feed on nut and acorn mast, making procurement relatively easy and more cost-efficient.

TABLE 10.3.

Summary of Identified Amphibian and Reptile Remains from the Cannon Reservoir Region, Organized by Taxa and Site

| Taxa | Late Archaic | | | Early Woodland |
	Miskell	Cooper	Pigeon Roost Creek	Collins
Anurans (frog/toad)	-	-	-	-
Bufo sp. (toad)	-	-	-	-
Rana sp. (frog)	1[a]			
Chelydra serpentina (common snapping turtle)	-	-	-	-
Emydinae (box/water turtle)	14	1	2	-
Terrapene sp. (box turtle)	8	3	3	-
Graptemys sp. (map turtle)	-	-	-	-
Chrysemys picta (western painted turtle)	-	-	-	-
Pseudemys sp. (slider)	3	-	-	-
Trionyx sp. (soft shelled turtle)	82	1	13	-
Serpentes (snake)	11	-	-	-
Colubridae (nonvenomous snake)	17	15	1	-
Thamnophis sp. (garter snake)	6	-	-	-
Crotalidae (venomous snake)	3	10	1	-
Total number of identified elements	145	30	20	-

[a]Number of identified elements.

TABLE 10.4.

Summary of Identified Bird Remains from the Cannon Reservoir Region, Organized by Taxa and Site

| Taxa | Late Archaic | | | Early Woodland |
	Miskell	Cooper	Pigeon Roost Creek	Collins
Accipitridae (hawks and allies)	-	-	-	-
Buteo sp. (hawk)	-	-	1[a]	-
Buteo jamaicensis (red-tailed hawk)	-	-	-	-
Tetraonidae (prairie chicken/ grouse)	-	-	-	-
Colinus virginianus (bob-white)	-	-	-	-
Meleagris gallopavo (turkey)	-	3	16	1
Columbidae (pigeon/dove)	-	-	-	-
Caprimulgidae (goatsuckers)	2	-	-	-
Pircidae (woodpecker)	-	-	-	-
Total number of identified elements	2	3	17	1

[a]Number of identified elements.

TABLE 10.3. (*continued*)

| | Middle Woodland | | | Late Woodland | | |
Hatten Village (SA 6)	Pigeon Roost Creek	Hillside	Muskrat Run	Victor Bridge	Cooper	Pigeon Roost Creek
-	-	-	-	6	-	-
-	-	-	43	4	-	-
-	-	-	-	3	-	-
-	4	-	-	-	-	6
37	36	1	-	-	1	20
-	3	-	42	26	2	6
-	4	-	-	-	-	-
1	5	-	30	6	1	11
-	1	-	-	-	-	-
-	-	-	23	-	3	4
-	-	-	5	-	-	-
-	13	-	5	33	-	15
-	-	-	2	-	-	-
-	6	-	-	-	-	6
38	72	1	150	78	7	68

TABLE 10.4. (*continued*)

| | Middle Woodland | | | Late Woodland | | |
Hatten Village (SA 6)	Pigeon Roost Creek	Hillside	Muskrat Run	Victor Bridge	Cooper	Pigeon Roost Creek
-	1	-	-	-	-	-
-	-	±	-	-	-	-
-	-	-	-	-	-	1
-	1	-	-	-	-	-
-	-	-	-	7	-	-
1	80	-	3	6	2	72
-	-	-	-	-	-	1
-	-	-	-	-	-	-
-	-	-	1	5	-	-
1	82	-	4	18	2	74

TABLE 10.5.

Summary of Identified Mammal Remains from the Cannon Reservoir Region, Organized by Taxa and Site

	Late Archaic			Early Woodland
Taxa	Miskell	Cooper	Pigeon Roost Creek	Collins
Soricidae (shrew)	2 [a]	2	–	–
Scalopus aquaticus (eastern mole)	3	–	1	–
Sylvilagus floridanus (eastern cottontail)	–	15	9	–
Marmota monax (woodchuck)	–	–	–	–
Spermophilus sp. (ground squirrel)	–	9	–	–
Sciurus spp. (squirrel)	2	11	4	2
Sciurus carolinensis (gray squirrel)	–	–	–	–
Sciurus niger (fox squirrel)	–	–	–	–
Geomys bursarius (plains pocket gopher)	1	1	2	–
Castor canadensis (beaver)	6	–	6	–
Peromyscus sp. (white-footed mouse)	–	–	–	–
Microtus sp. (vole)	–	4	–	4
Ondatra zibethicus (muskrat)	–	1	1	–
Canidae (canids)	–	–	2	–
Canis spp. (domestic dog/coyote)	–	–	–	–
Canis latrans (coyote)	62	–	–	–
Vulpes sp. (fox)	3	3	2	10
Procyon lotor (raccoon)	–	1	7	–
Mephitis mephitis (striped skunk)	–	–	1	–
Lynx rufus (bobcat)	–	–	–	–
Cervus canadensis (wapiti)	–	–	–	–
Odocoileus virginianus (white-tailed deer)	93	67	98	88
Bovidae (bison/cow)	–	–	1	–
Total number of identified elements	172	114	134	104

[a] Number of identified elements.

Mammals

Vertebrate remains from prehistoric midwestern faunal assemblages often are dominated by the bones and teeth of mammals, and the Cannon Project samples generally are no exception. Only at Muskrat Run and Victor Bridge are mammal elements less common than elements of another class (Table 10.1).

Mammalian samples are consistently dominated by white-tailed deer (Table 10.5). Several other taxa commonly occur in the assemblages but usually in small proportions. These include eastern cottontail, tree squirrels, muskrat (*Ondatra zibethicus*), beaver, canids (Canidae), raccoon, striped skunk (*Mephitis mephitis*), bobcat (*Lynx rufus*), and wapiti (*Cervus canadensis*). With the exception of bobcat and wapiti, all are common in the project area today (Missouri Botanical Garden 1974:134).

A number of small rodents and insectivores occur in the assemblages, but their importance as prehistoric food sources is questionable. Eastern mole (*Scalopus aquaticus*), ground squirrels (*Spermophilus* spp.), plains pocket gopher (*Geomys bur-*

TABLE 10.5. (*continued*)

Middle Woodland			Late Woodland			
Hatten Village (SA 6)	Pigeon Roost Creek	Hillside	Muskrat Run	Victor Bridge	Cooper	Pigeon Roost Creek
-	-	-	2	-	-	-
-	1	-	1	7	-	8
-	20	4	11	23	1	23
-	-	-	9	-	4	-
-	1	-	-	-	-	-
-	34	2	11	34	5	35
-	3	-	-	-	-	-
-	-	-	5	-	-	-
-	46	-	2	5	-	21
2	19	-	-	-	-	4
-	1	-	1	-	-	1
-	3	-	-	12	-	2
-	5	-	1	-	-	7
-	2	-	-	-	-	1
-	4	-	-	6	1	8
-	2	1	-	-	1	-
-	2	-	-	1	-	2
-	16	-	9	9	2	19
-	7	-	1	-	1	3
-	2	-	-	-	-	1
-	5	-	-	-	3	1
55	426	102	103	130	71	413
-	-	-	-	-	-	2
57	599	109	156	227	89	551

sarius), mice (*Peromyscus* spp.), and voles (*Microtus* spp.) could have been important during times of famine, or as occasional dietary supplements, but this is unlikely considering the availability of more productive faunal resources (Parmalee *et al.* 1972). Rather, most of these remains may have entered the archaeological record via natural processes (e.g., burrowing and/or excretion by carnivores).

The importance of white-tailed deer to prehistoric economies in the Cannon Project region cannot be overemphasized. This large mammal undoubtedly functioned as an important source of food and clothing and also provided raw material for tool manufacture. Ethnographic research among the Menomini (Hoffman 1970), Winnebago (Radin 1970), Chippewa (Densmore 1929), and various southeastern tribes (Swanton 1946), indicates that deer frequently were hunted by stalking with spears or bows and arrows. Communal techniques (e.g., surrounds, drives, and firing of forests and prairie) also have been reported.

A variety of smaller mammals also made significant dietary contributions in the project area (Table 10.5). Many of these probably were hunted with traps and snares and, after around A.D. 800, with bow and arrow.

INTERASSEMBLAGE VARIABILITY

As documented in Tables 10.1–10.5, within-taxon proportions of vertebrate elements show a great deal of interassemblage variability. In this section we: (*a*) identify dimensions of proportional variation of taxa among assemblages, (*b*) define groups of components in which proportions of major vertebrate taxa are similar, and (*c*) evaluate several possible causes of the observed variation.

In comparing assemblages an important assumption is made: Interassemblage variation of relative frequencies of elements associates directly with variation in the relative economic importance of different vertebrate taxa. In making this assumption it is not implied that relative frequencies of vertebrate elements are accurate guides to either: (*a*) the proportionate numbers of individuals, (*b*) the relative masses of edible tissue, or (*c*) the relative nutritional inputs of taxa represented in an assemblage. Indeed, an important body of zooarchaeological research has emphasized the common weakness of these correlations. The assumption here simply maintains that comparative *differences* among assemblages, in terms of relative proportions of element frequencies, correlate directly with differences in the relative economic importance of vertebrate taxa. Thus, in a hypothetical faunal assemblage (A) dominated by elements of a species of minnow, we would not necessarily infer that minnows were the most important vertebrate resource. However, if minnow elements were relatively rare in a second assemblage (B), we would assume that minnows were *more* important in occupation A than in occupation B.

Dimensions

The first step in evaluating interassemblage variability is to define units of analysis. Although a variety of approaches to variable definition are possible with faunal remains, basic taxonomic groups were selected as initial variables since these units are unambiguous and also tend to reflect environmental and short-term temporal variation. Given the small size of most Cannon Project vertebrate samples, taxa were lumped into units that (*a*) con-

tained no fewer than 50 total elements, and (*b*) comprised 5% of elements in at least one assemblage. The 11 resulting units include three classes (fish, amphibians, birds), three orders or families (turtles, snakes, canids), four genera or species (eastern cottontail, tree squirrels, raccoon, white-tailed deer), and one unit containing a variety of uncommon forms (other mammals). Element frequencies then were transformed into relative frequencies to control for variation of sample size.

A number of statistical techniques are available for detecting trends or patterns in large and/or complex sets of numerical data. The vertebrate data set, comprised of 11 cases (i.e., assemblages) and 11 variables (i.e., taxa) is fairly small and has a simple enough underlying structure that formal techniques were not necessary for detecting major dimensions of variability. Instead, broken-line graphs of relative frequencies (not presented here) were compiled for each assemblage. The graphs were sorted into groups characterized by similar patterns and were then ordered in two dimensions on the basis of relative pattern similarity among cases. The resulting configuration clearly showed that (*a*) two taxa, fish and white-tailed deer, account for much of the variation among cases and that (*b*) these same two taxa are inversely correlated ($r = -.81$) and together they comprise the major dimension of variability within the sample of cases. A scattergram of assemblages plotted on the fish and deer variables show these trends quite well (Figure 10.1). The configuration also indicates that three distinct groups of cases represented in the sample (groups A–C) can be identified in sequence by decreasing proportions of deer elements and increasing proportions of fish.

An intervariable correlation matrix (not presented here) indicates that only one other variable associates strongly with the fish–deer dimension. Amphibian elements, which occur at only three sites (Muskrat Run, Victor Bridge, and Miskell) and contribute relatively little to interassemblage variability, correlate directly with relative frequencies of fish elements ($r = .88$) and inversely with proportions of deer ($r = -.63$). Thus, the three groups shown in Figure 10.1 are ordered along a deer–fish/amphibian dimension (dimension I) and can be defined as follows:

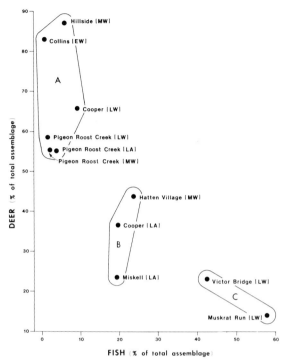

Figure 10.1. Scattergram of relative frequencies of fish elements (*X* axis) and deer elements (*Y* axis) in 11 Cannon Project faunal assemblages; solid lines enclose groups of similar cases (groups A–C).

1. *Group A* has high proportions of deer elements ($\bar{x} = 67.5\% \pm$ S.D. $= 14.2$) and low proportions of both fish ($4.0\% \pm 3.2$) and amphibians ($0\% \pm 0$).

2. *Group B* has intermediate proportions of both deer ($34.6\% \pm 10.2$) and fish ($21.0\% \pm 2.5$) and low proportions of amphibians ($0.1\% \pm 0.2$).

3. *Group C* has low proportions of deer elements ($18.6\% \pm 6.4$) and high proportions of both fish ($50.1\% \pm 10.8$) and amphibians ($4.1\% \pm 2.5$).

Graphs summarizing proportions of all 11 taxa in groups A–C (Figure 10.2) reiterate the patterns just described and illustrate the failure of other taxa to correlate with dimension I. They also suggest that proportions of several additional taxa are quite variable (e.g., turtles, canids, and birds). The correlation matrix mentioned earlier indicates this variation is patterned in several instances, and the

patterns suggest that two relatively weak dimensions can be defined that vary independently of dimension I and each other.

Three associated taxa comprise dimension II. Turtles, the third most proportionately variable taxa in the sample, correlate inversely with tree squirrels ($r = -.62$) and cottontail ($r = -.49$), whereas tree squirrels and cottontail are directly associated with each other ($r = .63$). Thus, dimension II orders assemblages along a continuum of increasing proportions of turtles, and decreasing proportions of squirrels–cottontail. The net effects of this dimension on case coordinates shown in Figure 10.1 are to: (*a*) decrease the distances between assemblages in group A since none of these cases scores high or low on the dimension II continuum; (*b*) shift the Hatten Village and Miskell assemblages away from the Cooper (Late Archaic) assemblage since Hatten Village and Miskell have relatively high proportions of squirrels–cottontail; and (*c*) shift the position of Muskrat Run in the direction of Hatten Village and Miskell since Muskrat Run has a slight overrepresentation of turtles.

The third dimension, signaled by a direct correlation between proportions of birds and raccoon ($r = .84$), reflects a relatively high rate of occurrence of these taxa in the three assemblages from Pigeon Roost Creek. The only effect of dimension III on coordinates in Figure 10.1 is to highlight the remarkable similarity of vertebrate assemblages from these three components.

In summary, proportionate variability of major taxa in Cannon Project vertebrate samples is expressed best along a dimension (I) of increasing numbers of deer remains and decreasing numbers of fish and amphibians. Gaps occur on this continuum between sets of similar assemblages, and three groups or clusters of samples can be isolated. Moreover, incorporation of two additional dimensions (II and III), both unrelated to the first, tends to increase the similarity of cases within groups and thus reinforces the integrity of the groups. Group A is composed of six cases. All have high proportions of deer elements, low proportions of fish–amphibians, and intermediate proportions of turtles and tree squirrels–cottontail. Three cases (all from Pigeon Roost Creek) have very similar proportions of all taxa, including abnormally high frequencies

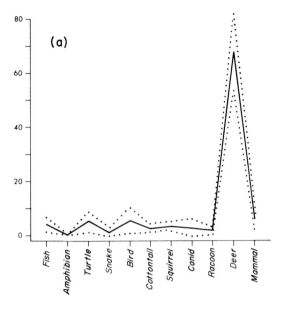

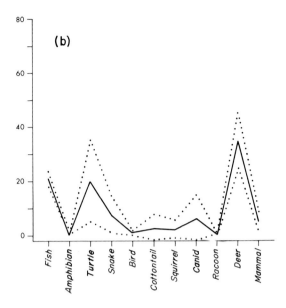

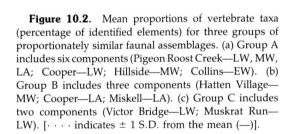

Figure 10.2. Mean proportions of vertebrate taxa (percentage of identified elements) for three groups of proportionately similar faunal assemblages. (a) Group A includes six components (Pigeon Roost Creek—LW, MW, LA; Cooper—LW; Hillside—MW; Collins—EW). (b) Group B includes three components (Hatten Village—MW; Cooper—LA; Miskell—LA). (c) Group C includes two components (Victor Bridge—LW; Muskrat Run—LW). [· · · · indicates ± 1 S.D. from the mean (—)].

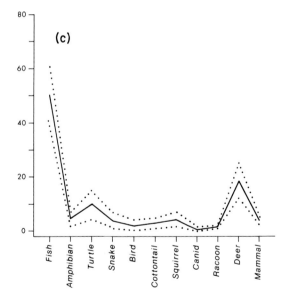

of birds and raccoon. Group B is comprised of three cases. All have intermediate proportions of deer and fish elements, low proportions of amphibians and birds–raccoon, and relatively high proportions of either turtles (Miskell, Hatten Village) or squirrels–cottontail (Cooper—Late Archaic). Group C includes two cases, both of which are high in fish–amphibians, low in deer, and relatively high in either turtles (Muskrat Run) or squirrels–cottontail and birds–raccoon (Victor Bridge).

Recovery Bias

A fundamental assumption of comparative research in archaeology is that varied techniques of artifact recovery have not created artificial patterns in the data one wishes to order and explain. Few archaeologists care to expend the time to discover that differences among samples are due solely to recovery bias. Even more frightening is the prospect of attributing patterns induced by recovery bias to behavioral variation within or among the culture(s) under study. Unfortunately, techniques used to recover the faunal assemblages reported here have varied a great deal. Soil from all components was sifted through metal screens, but at no two sites were procedures identical in terms of mesh size and/or in the proportions of excavation units sifted through screens with different sizes of mesh. Since bones of inland fish and amphibians tend to be smaller than bones of white-tailed deer, it is conceivable that most of the interassemblage variability described previously is attributable to excavation techniques alone. Given this possibility, the recovery bias hypothesis is the first one tested.

Given the general correlation between (a) element sizes of fish–amphibians and deer, and (b) the ordering of assemblages along a dimension of varying proportions of fish–amphibians and deer, perhaps the best means of testing for recovery bias is to compare the relative fineness of recovery procedures used at each component with the positions of components along the continuum from fish–amphibians to deer. The implication is that fine-grained recovery will correlate consistently with high proportions of fish–amphibian elements, and coarse-grained recovery will correlate with high proportions of deer.

Four levels of recovery were used. On a gradient of increasing coarseness, these include: (a) hydraulic screening of features and 20–25% of general levels with 1/16-inch mesh and 75–80% of general levels with 1/4-inch mesh (Pigeon Roost Creek— LW, MW, LA; Victor Bridge; Muskrat Run; Miskell); (b) hydraulic screening of features with 1/16-inch mesh and dry screening of general levels with 1/4-inch mesh (Collins); (c) hydraulic screening of all deposits with 1/4-inch mesh (Cooper—LW, LA), and (d) dry screening of some features with 1/4-inch mesh and others with 1/2-inch mesh (Hillside; Hatten Village).

Comparison indicates that coarseness of recovery does not correlate directly with proportions of deer elements. Groups A–C, ordered along dimension I from low to high proportions of fish–amphibians, consistently crosscut recovery levels. Three of six level-one components (fine-grained recovery) belong to Group A assemblages (high deer), and one group A assemblage occurs in each of the remaining coarseness levels. Similarly, group B assemblages occur in fine-grained, medium coarsegrained, and coarse-grained levels. Only the two assemblages in group C occur in a single-grain level (fine-grained) and are consistent with the hypothesis of recovery bias. Thus, it is concluded that although recovery bias may affect details of assemblage configuration and proportions of variables, it could not have caused the basic patterning expressed along dimension I.

Temporal Variation

The model of settlement–subsistence practices presented in Chapter 5 predicts that economic systems changed in the Cannon Reservoir region in response to population growth and environmental and social contexts of local inhabitants. As human population densities increased and crowding became a problem for hunter–gatherers, sizes of resource catchments decreased, and groups were forced to intensify their procurement strategies in smaller extractive territories. One predicted effect of this local intensification is a net shift toward the procurement of second-line resources. First-line resources, such as white-tailed deer, turkey, and raccoon, would have been important throughout this sequence of change. However, their proportional contributions to prehistoric diets would have diminished as fish and other relatively labor intensive or less productive taxa were relied on more heavily.

According to the model, resource intensification began during the Late Archaic period. Group mobility decreased, and permanent settlements were established, although residence may have shifted seasonally to take advantage of undepleted food and fuel resources and to maximize residential comfort. Groups became sedentary during the Middle Woodland period. Several exotic and native cultigens provided important supplements to the diet, but hunting and gathering still were central to subsistence activities. If the model is correct, Middle Woodland settlements were occupied all year long, and vertebrate remains should reflect a shift toward second-line taxa. These same trends continued throughout the Late Woodland period, although after about A.D. 800 maize agriculture assumed a predominant role in subsistence economies.

Radiometric dates for the vertebrate assemblages span a 4000-year period ranging from 2600 B.C. to A.D. 1300 (Chapters 6, 7, and 13). Miskell, the only undated component, contains projectile point classes that indicate it is the oldest of the assemblages. Thus, the assemblages bracket the Late Archaic through early Mississippian periods, and they offer an excellent opportunity to test the settlement–subsistence model (Chapter 5).

Temporal variation in proportions of major vertebrate taxa is shown in Figure 10.3. Perhaps the most striking implication of the figure is the apparent lack of systematic shifts through time. Fish and amphibians are relatively abundant toward the upper end of the sequence (early Late Woodland period), but their proportions decline in the two most recent assemblages. Deer show a steady rise among Late Archaic and Early Woodland components, but their proportions fluctuate widely in the Middle and Late Woodland periods. Other taxa rise and fall sporadically throughout the sequence.

Despite the apparent absence of long-term shifts in proportion of taxa, one notable trend emerges when Figure 10.3 is compared with the three groups of proportionately similar vertebrate assemblages depicted in Figure 10.1. With the exception of the Early Woodland period, which contains only one component, all time periods are represented by one or more group A assemblages *and* at least one group B or C assemblage. The Late Archaic and Middle Woodland periods are identical in this respect. Both periods contain assemblages characterized by (a) high proportions of deer and low proportions of fish–amphibians (group A) and (b) intermediate proportions of deer and fish and low proportions of amphibians (group B). The Late Woodland period contains two group A assemblages and two with relatively high proportions of fish–amphibians and low proportions of deer (group C). Thus, each of the three periods has a complementary association of high-deer–low-fish assemblages with either intermediate-deer–fish or low-deer–high-fish assemblages.

Two conclusions can be derived from these observations. First, there are no discernible differences between Late Archaic and Middle Woodland faunal assemblages. Both contain complementary examples of group A and group B patterns. Thus, temporal results are inconsistent with the expectation that growing populations and constricting resource catchments caused more intensive reliance on second-line vertebrate resources during the Middle Woodland period. Second, with the possible exception of two early Late Woodland assemblages dating the the eighth century A.D. (Victor Bridge and Muskrat Run), fluctuations in proportions of vertebrate taxa seem to occur sporadically through time and apparently do not reflect consistent long-term change. This implies that much of the proportional variation seen among vertebrate assemblages may be attributable to short-term synchronic factors, such as systemic differences in the scheduling of resource procurement activities and associated differences in the seasons of site occupations.

Seasonal Variation

Given the possibility that synchronic factors account for some variability among vertebrate assemblages, seasonal shifts in settlement locations and resource scheduling should be considered most likely among possible causes. As noted in

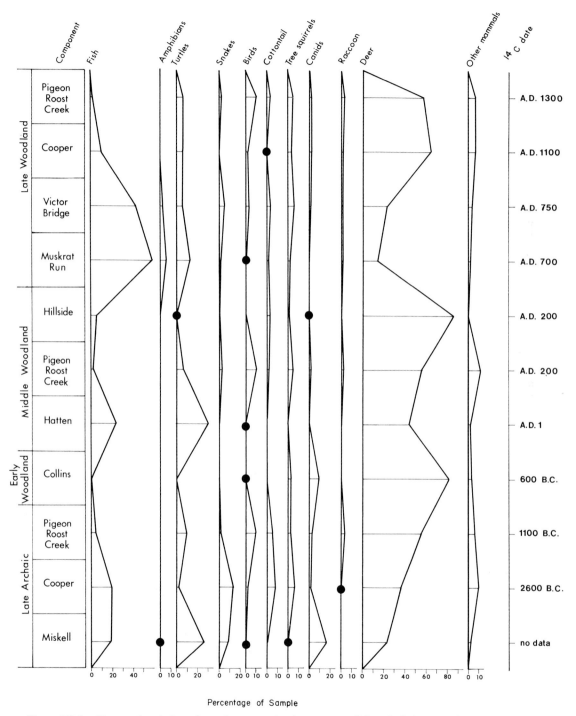

Figure 10.3. Temporal variation of vertebrate remains (percentage of identified elements) from 11 components in the Cannon Reservoir region (● = <1%).

Chapter 3, seasonal changes in the availability of plant and animal resources are strongly patterned in the Cannon Reservoir region, and groups undoubtedly took advantage of resource cyclicity. Although it is argued in Chapter 5 that the relative narrowness of resource zones in the region could have enabled semisedentary or sedentary occupations of bottomland villages by Late Archaic and Woodland period hunter–gatherers, it is also possible that sedentism would have caused local depletions of key vertebrate populations as well as timber resources needed for fuel and construction materials (Griffin 1977). An effective means of circumventing these problems could have been seasonal movements of communities upstream or downstream into relatively pristine localities with more readily accessible food and fuel resources. Thus, an alternative prediction would be a semisedentary lifeway among resident hunter–gatherers comprised of a two-part seasonal round. Narrow resource zonation would still have affected this system by enabling settlement in bottomlands. However, other factors considered in selecting specific site locations (e.g., access to water and protected contexts) would have influenced locational strategies regardless of season. As a result, both warm season and cool season sites would occur in bottomlands, and because of commonalities in factors of site selection, they might well occur in virtually identical physical contexts. Nevertheless, it is unlikely that this settlement system could have survived in the face of rising population pressure and constriction of resource catchments. Packing of groups along stream courses would have placed constraints on seasonal community mobility, and under these conditions, year-round sedentism may have been necessary.

In order to evaluate these propositions, seasonal indicators are used to determine whether components were occupied during warm seasons, cool seasons, or all year long. First, the occurrences and proportions of taxa whose accessibilities varied seasonally are examined in each assemblage in order to systematically generate hypotheses of season of occupation. These hypotheses then are tested using data from aged deer mandibles and/or indications of the seasonal availability of plant species

included in samples of charred plant remains from each component.

Resource Availability

As noted in Chapter 3, vertebrate resources in the Cannon Reservoir region tend to fluctuate in availability across seasons. In general, there are three discernible forms of modality among these patterns: (a) some taxa, including several species of migratory waterfowl, normally occur in the region only during one or two months of the year; (b) a number of taxa, including many species of fish and reptiles, remain in the region all year long but are readily accessible only 6 or 7 months per year; and (c) a variety of forms, including white-tailed deer and many other terrestrial species, are available all year long but are more accessible in some seasons than in others. If it is assumed that hunter–gatherers took advantage of these cycles, either inadvertently or consciously, then estimates of season of occupation can be made based on occurrences of season-sensitive taxa in assemblages.

To derive estimates of season of occupation from the 11 Cannon Project vertebrate assemblages, taxa and seasonal data presented in Table 3.3 were used to scale each taxon by its monthly level of availability. Three levels of availability are recognized: (a) maximal, denoted by an "X" in the table (full score); (b) submaximal, denoted by a dash (half score); and (c) minimal, denoted by a blank space (no score). Use of this scheme to rank each taxon occurring in an assemblage enables summation for the total number of scaled taxa represented in each month over the course of a year. Moreover, these values can be standardized for interassemblage comparison by: (a) dividing each monthly sum of taxa by the total number of taxa in the assemblage to determine proportions of available taxa represented for each month (unweighted proportions); (b) replacing simple occurrence scores for each taxon with relative element frequencies and summing by month to determine proportions of available taxa represented for each month (weighted proportions); and (c) subtracting weighted proportions from unweighted proportions to determine the percentage of deviation of expected from observed proportions

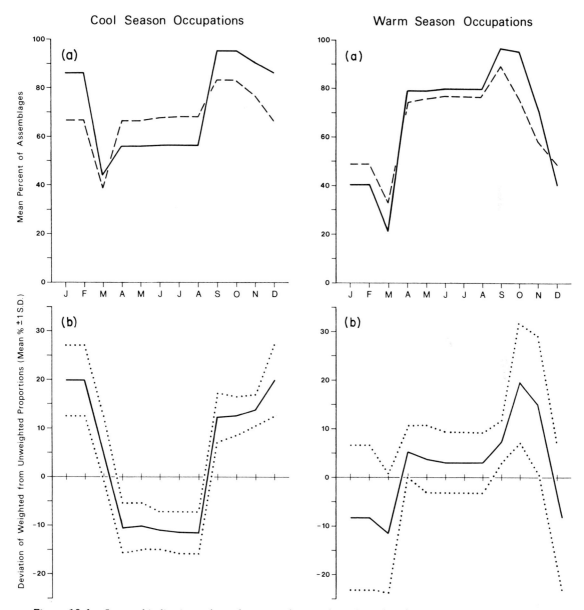

Figure 10.4. Seasonal indications of vertebrate taxa from six hypothetical cool season components (Pigeon Roost Creek—LW, MW, LA; Cooper—LW; Hillside—MW; Collins—EW) and five hypothetical warm season components (Victor Bridge—LW; Muskrat Run—LW; Hatten Village—MW; Cooper—LA; Miskell—LA) showing (a) mean weighted (—) and unweighted (--) proportions of available taxa, and (b) mean deviations of weight proportions from unweighted proportions.

(i.e., the monthly over- and underrepresentations of element frequencies in comparison with proportions of occurring taxa).

Application of these procedures indicates that two distinct patterns occur in the Cannon Project vertebrate assemblages (Figure 10.4). Hypothetical cool season occupations (Pigeon Roost Creek—LW, MW, LA; Cooper—LW; Hillside—MW; Collins—EW) are characterized by: (a) uniform proportions of winter and summer taxa and relatively high proportions of autumn taxa (unweighted proportions); (b) high proportions of autumn and winter elements and low proportions of spring and summer elements (weighted proportions); and (c) disproportionate overrepresentations of autumn and winter elements and underrepresentations of late spring and summer elements. In contrast, hypothetical warm season occupations (Victor Bridge—LW; Muskrat Run—LW; Hatten Village—MW; Cooper—LA; Miskell—LA) are distinguished by: (a) high proportions of late spring, summer, and early autumn taxa and low proportions of late autumn, winter, and early spring taxa (unweighted proportions); (b) high proportions of late spring, summer, and autumn elements and low proportions of winter and early spring elements (weighted proportions); and (c) relatively high overrepresentations of late autumn elements, slight overrepresentations of late spring, summer, and early autumn elements, and underrepresentations of winter and early spring elements.

These results conform quite closely to the three groups (A–C) of assemblages defined on the basis of proportions of major vertebrate taxa (Figure 10.1). Hypothetical cool season occupations are composed exclusively of group A assemblages, whereas group B and C assemblages are together isomorphic with hypothetical warm season occupations. Thus, patterns derived from seasonal differences in resource availability associate closely with patterns derived from simple proportions of taxa. This suggests that many of the sporadic long-term fluctuations shown in Figure 10.3 are attributable to seasonal variation of site occupations. However, it should be emphasized that these two sets of results, although scaled in different ways, are ultimately derived from the same basic data,

and independent seasonal indicators are needed to test the seasonality proposition.

Deer Mandibles

Assuming that fawns are born most often during late May and early June (Schwartz and Schwartz 1981:346), age at death can be estimated by examining tooth eruption and dental wear. With relatively young individuals, these same techniques can yield results precise enough to determine the approximate season of death. Although differences in browsing conditions and variation in times of birth are potential sources of error, and results are not always as reliable as tooth section data, eruption–wear studies are important in providing an independent means of evaluating seasonal hypotheses.

Thirty-one mandibles from 9 of the 11 vertebrate assemblages were analyzed, using standard procedures outlined by Ryel et al. (1961) and Severinghaus (1949), to establish age and season of death. Of this total, 28 mandibles provided seasonal estimates ranging in level of precision from 2 to 6 months. Results are summarized in Table 10.6, along with seasonal indications provided by calculations of resource availability.

Four seasonal ranges were identified among mandibles from hypothesized cool season occupations. These include: (a) five specimens killed sometime between early December and late March (two each from Pigeon Roost Creek—LW, LA; one from Pigeon Roost Creek—MW); (b) four specimens killed sometime between early June and late November (three from Pigeon Roost Creek—LW; one from Hillside—MW); (c) two specimens killed during November and December (both from Pigeon Roost Creek—MW); and (d) one specimen killed between December and February (Cooper—LW). In summary, all specimens are consistent with the cool season hypothesis. The 6-month range represented by nine of the specimens (December–May and June–November) overlaps the ranges estimated by resource availability (September–February or March), and the three specimens with 2- and 3-month ranges (November–December and December–February) fall squarely within the predicted range. Thus, deer mandibles fail to provide information that calls the hypothesis into question, and three specimens offer direct support for late fall–winter occupations at two of the five sites containing specimens suitable for analysis.

Six seasonal ranges are represented by mandibles from hypothesized warm season occupations. These include: (a) six specimens killed between early December and late May (one from Victor Bridge—LW; five from Muskrat Run—LW); (b) three specimens killed between early September and late December (all from Muskrat Run—LW); (c) two specimens killed between early September and late December (both from Hatten Village—MW); (d) two specimens killed during December, January, or February (both from Victor Bridge—LW); (e) two specimens killed between early July and late November (both from Muskrat Run—LW); and (f) one specimen killed during October or November (Cooper—LA). In summary, all specimens from Hatten Village and Cooper (LA) are consistent with the warm season hypothesis, but several specimens from Victor Bridge and Muskrat Run are not. The consistent specimens overlap, or fall squarely within, the predicted April–November range. However, two specimens from Victor Bridge fall entirely *outside* the prediction, and the two most common patterns at Muskrat Run (five December–May and three November–December) overlap the predicted range only in April–May and November. Histograms of monthly indications (not presented here) show strong modes for both sites during winter (December–February at Victor Bridge and December at Muskrat Run), yet at Muskrat Run there also are two mandibles that fall entirely within the April–November prediction. In the light of the seasonal availability results, which show predominant occurrences and proportions of warm season taxa for all four sites with mandibles, Hatten Village and Cooper (LA) were warm season occupations, but Victor Bridge and Muskrat Run were occupied all year long.

Plant Remains

Seasonal indications of charred plant remains are available for 10 of the vertebrate assemblages (Table 10.6). Hickory nut shells occur in all of these, and fragments of walnut and hazelnut occur in most (Chapter 11). Acorns, a probable second-line floral resource, occur only at Victor Bridge. Seasonal implications of these remains are minimal since their months of availability (August–October) overlap the hypothesized ranges of both warm season and cool season occupations. However, at Victor Bridge they represent a significant complement to the three deer mandibles and offer additional support for the hypothesis of year-round occupation.

Implications of other plant taxa are more informative, although they have been identified at only eight components. Two ranges are represented among hypothesized cool season occupations. One tuber fragment (possibly groundnut) recovered from the Late Woodland component at Pigeon Roost Creek may represent a fall, winter, or spring collection. August through November ranges are indicated at Collins and Pigeon Roost Creek (LA, MW), where samples include remains of sumpweed, giant ragweed, chenopod, knotweed, and pepo squash (Chapter 11). Thus, seasonal indications of plant taxa are consistent with those derived from vertebrate remains.

Plant remains from hypothesized warm season occupations are dominated by late spring, summer, and early fall taxa. Maygrass, chenopod, knotweed, and persimmon suggest a May–September range for Hatten Village; late spring–summer taxa (bedstraw and chenopod) occur at Miskell; and sumpweed provide a late summer indication for Cooper (LA).

Knotweed seeds from Victor Bridge (early LW) provide another late summer indication. This one is of particular interest since it increases further the range of independent seasonal indicators from that site, and together these data are strongly indicative of year-round occupation.

Overview

A series of seasonal indications—including occurrences and proportions of seasonally available taxa, aged deer mandibles, and remains of seasonally available plants—indicate that much of the interassemblage variability documented among Cannon Project vertebrate samples is an expression of

TABLE 10.6.

Summary of Seasonal Indications for Eleven Components in the Cannon Reservoir Region[a]

	Cool season occupations[b]											
	J	F	M	A	M	J	J	A	S	O	N	D

Pigeon Roost Creek (Late Woodland)
- a. unweighted proportion
- b. weighted proportion
- c. % deviation
- d. deer mandibles 1.
-                     2.
-                     3.
-                     4.
-                     5.
- e. nuts
- f. other plants

Cooper (Late Woodland)
- a. unweighted proportion
- b. weighted proportion
- c. % deviation
- d. deer mandible
- e. nuts

Hillside (Middle Woodland)
- a. unweighted proportion
- b. weighted proportion
- c. % deviation
- d. deer mandible
- e. nuts

Pigeon Roost Creek (Middle Woodland)
- a. unweighted proportion
- b. weighted proportion
- c. % deviation
- d. deer mandibles 1.
-                     2.
-                     3.
- e. nuts
- f. other plants

Collins (Early Woodland)
- a. unweighted proportion
- b. weighted proportion
- c. % deviation
- e. nuts
- f. other plants

Pigeon Roost Creek (Late Archaic)
- a. unweighted proportion
- b. weighted proportion
- c. % deviation
- d. deer mandibles 1.
-                     2.
- e. nuts
- f. other plants

[a]Projected months of occupation are indicated by: (a) unweighted proportion of available vertebrate taxa, (b) proportion of vertebrate taxa weighted by percent of elements in sample, (c) percent deviation of weighted proportion from unweighted proportion, (d) tooth eruption in deer mandibles, (e) charred

TABLE 10.6. (*continued*)

	Warm season occupations[b]											
	J	F	M	A	M	J	J	A	S	O	N	D
Victor Bridge (Late Woodland)												
a. unweighted proportion				▬	▬	▬	▬	▬	▬	▬		
b. weighted proportion				▬	▬	▬	▬	▬	▬	▬		
c. % deviation				–	–	–	–	–	–	▬		
d. deer mandibles 1.	▬											▬
2.	▬											▬
3.	▬	▬	▬									▬
e. nuts										▬		
f. other plants							▬					
Muskrat Run (Late Woodland)												
a. unweighted proportion				▬	▬	▬	▬	▬	▬			
b. weighted proportion				▬	▬	▬	▬	▬	▬	▬		
c. % deviation				▬	▬	▬	▬	▬	▬	▬		
d. deer mandibles 1.	▬	▬	▬	▬								▬
2.	▬	▬	▬	▬								▬
3.	▬	▬	▬	▬								▬
4.	▬	▬	▬	▬								▬
5.	▬	▬	▬	▬								▬
6.										▬	▬	
7.										▬	▬	
8.										▬	▬	
9.									▬	▬	▬	
10.									▬	▬	▬	
Hatten Village (Middle Woodland)												
a. unweighted proportion										▬	▬	
b. weighted proportion					▬	▬	▬	▬	▬	▬		
c. % deviation					▬	▬	▬	▬	▬	▬	▬	
d. deer mandibles 1.										▬	▬	
2.										▬	▬	
e. nuts							–	–				
f. other plants					▬	▬	▬	▬	▬	▬		
Cooper (Late Archaic)												
a. unweighted proportion					▬	▬	▬	▬	▬	▬		
b. weighted proportion					▬	▬	▬	▬	▬	▬		
c. % deviation										▬	▬	
d. deer mandible										▬		
e. nuts							▬					
Miskell (Archaic)												
a. unweighted proportion					▬	▬	▬	▬	▬	▬		
b. weighted proportion					▬	▬	▬	▬	▬	▬		
c. % deviation										▬	▬	
e. nuts							–	▬				
f. other plants					▬	▬	▬	▬	▬	▬		

nuts, and (f) other charred plants. Six sites lack one or more seasonal indicators.

[b] Solid bars denote ranges of projected months of procurement; dashes denote ambiguous or questionable months of procurement; blank spaces denote unlikely months of procurement.

two related factors—(a) seasonal differences in site occupation and (b) relative seasonal specialization in the procurement of faunal and floral resources that fluctuate in availability from month to month. Group A assemblages are dominated by taxa that are most accessible during autumn, winter, and early spring. Independent seasonal indicators are consistent with the proposition that all six group A components represent cool season occupations.[1] Group B assemblages have relatively high proportions of late spring, summer, and autumn taxa. Seasonal indicators, including remains of a variety of plants that become available during late spring or summer, strongly support the proposition that group B components were occupied during warm seasons. Proportions of seasonally available taxa in group C assemblages are similar to those of group B. Floral remains from one of these sites (Victor Bridge) are consistent with a warm season identification, as are several aged deer mandibles from the other site (Muskrat Run). However, mandibles indicate that Victor Bridge, and probably Muskrat Run, also were occupied during winter and early spring. It is therefore concluded that group C components were occupied all year long.

---

[1]After writing this chapter we received additional seasonal indications for three of the hypothesized cool season occupations (Bozell 1981a). Microscopic analysis of growth increments in thin-sectioned teeth can sometimes reveal an animal's age and season of death. Analysis of dental annuli in two specimens from the Late Woodland component at Cooper indicate an early winter death for a squirrel premolar and a winter death for a woodchuck molar. Three specimens from the Middle Woodland component at Pigeon Roost Creek died in late fall (one raccoon molar and one white-tailed deer incisor) or late winter (one raccoon premolar). Five specimens from the Late Woodland component at Pigeon Roost Creek indicate deaths during winter (one squirrel incisor), early spring (one raccoon premolar), late winter (one raccoon molar and one white-tailed deer incisor), and late summer (one white-tailed deer incisor). All but one of these specimens overlap the proposed October to March occupation span and are consistent with the cool season hypothesis. The exception (i.e., the late summer deer incisor from the Late Woodland component at Pigeon Roost Creek) may require a revision of our model if its seasonal indication can be supported by independent evidence.

CONCLUSIONS

Vertebrate remains from the Cannon Project faunal assemblages vary in several interesting ways. In this chapter, one major and two relatively minor dimensions of variability were identified within the proportions of major taxa, and three groups of similar assemblages were defined. Three hypotheses that might account for these differences were tested. Results indicate that: (a) recovery bias shows little or no association with recognized trends and could not have created the most significant dimension of variability; (b) sporadic fluctuations in proportions of major taxa characterize most of the 4000-year time span represented in the sample, and long-term temporal variation seems to associate only with two early Late Woodland assemblages; and (c) seasonal variation correlates closely with the three defined groups of similar assemblages, indicating that variation among all but the early Late Woodland assemblages (both of which apparently were occupied all year long) can be explained by seasonal scheduling of resource procurement and seasonal movement of communities.

In contrast to the model of prehistoric development presented in Chapter 5, these results show no evidence of changing patterns of settlement or vertebrate exploitation in the Cannon Project region from Late Archaic through Middle Woodland times. Late Archaic groups appear to have followed a semisedentary lifeway in which warm season occupations (e.g., Cooper and Miskell) were abandoned about mid-autumn, and cool season sites (e.g., Pigeon Roost Creek) were occupied until early spring. At the same time, plant and animal species varied from season to season, either in abundance or in degree of accessibility. These changes are reflected in differing proportions of taxa within the warm and cool season vertebrate assemblages and suggest that procurement strategies took advantage of seasonal peaks in resource availability. White-tailed deer probably were an important resource all year long, but fish and other warm season resources increased in importance during summer and early fall.

Only one Early Woodland component (Collins) is represented in the vertebrate sample, and it is not possible to establish whether the hypothesized sedentary settlement pattern persisted during the first millennium B.C. However, seasonal indicators suggest that Collins was a cool season occupation, and it seems likely that unsampled warm season components also occur in the region.

Assemblages dating to the Middle Woodland period include one warm season occupation (Hatten Village) and two cool season occupations (Pigeon Roost Creek and Hillside). Proportions of vertebrate taxa in these sets of components are virtually identical to their conseasonal counterparts from the Late Archaic period, and the seasonal differences between them suggest that Middle Woodland groups in the Cannon Reservoir region shared a semisedentary lifeway with their Late Archaic predecessors. Both of these conclusions are inconsistent with predictions of the settlement–subsistence model. In Chapter 5 it is proposed that due to population growth and constricted resource catchments, Middle Woodland groups were forced to occupy sedentary villages and to rely on increasing proportions of second-line resources in the diet. Instead, there is no evidence of change in vertebrate resources, and settlements appear to have been abandoned and reoccupied from season to season. Significantly, this implied that Middle Woodland population densities in the middle Salt River valley were not high enough to cause serious economic stress among local groups. First-line floral and faunal resources, supplemented by periodic collections of less productive taxa, apparently were sufficient to maintain populations in the region, and the extra time and energy requirements of resource intensification do not appear to have been necessary. Furthermore, reliance on economic security networks would have been superfluous under these conditions, and relatively low population densities may therefore explain why exotic trade items diagnostic of the Hopewell Interaction Sphere fail to occur in the Cannon Reservoir region.

Not until the eighth century A.D. do settlement–subsistence systems appear to have changed greatly from those of Late Archaic–Middle Woodland times. Vertebrate assemblages and seasonal indications from early Late Woodland period components (Victor Bridge and probably Muskrat Run) represent the earliest known year-round occupations of permanent villages in the Cannon Project region. Remains of fish, probably second-line resources in the middle Salt River valley, are remarkably abundant in these two assemblages (even more abundant than in warm season assemblages of the Late Archaic and Middle Woodland periods), suggesting that population densities may finally have surpassed the upper threshold allowed by first-line procurement strategies. Thus, it is not until Late Woodland times in the Cannon Reservoir region that we see evidence of the levels of economic stress that seem to have appeared nearly 1000 years earlier in nearby major river valleys.

Subsistence systems appear to have changed again by A.D. 1100. Assemblages from Cooper and Pigeon Roost Creek, both Late Woodland tradition components dating to the Mississippian period (Perry phase), apparently represent temporary, cool season occupations similar to those from the Middle Woodland period and earlier times. Unfortunately, data from contemporary warm season occupations are not available, and it is not clear whether these components represent cool season occupations of semisedentary groups residing within the region or seasonal encampments of groups residing outside the region during other parts of the year. Either way, the region must have experienced a significant population decline during early Mississippian times, a decline that was not reversed until Euro-American settlers immigrated during the early nineteenth century.

11

Analysis of Archaeobotanical Remains

FRANCES B. KING

The spatial distribution of prehistoric food resources within the Cannon Project region varied widely, with significant differences in the diversity of arboreal and herbaceous plant species in different drainage classes (Chapter 3). Along a gradient from driest to wettest, these drainage classes include level uplands (covered by tall-grass prairie or xerophytic forest dominated by oak and hickory); upper, middle, and lower valley slopes; and flood plains. Coinciding with the increase in moisture is an increase in the diversity of arboreal plant species that served as food resources for prehistoric human populations. Although there are locations in which the transition from upland prairie to forest is abrupt, indicating possible edaphic changes or recent disturbances (e.g., fire), the change between the two major vegetation types is often more gradual and incorporates an open forest with a grassy understory (i.e., "barrens"). This open forest is probably either a result of (a) periodic fires burning into the forest and killing young trees and less fire-resistant species (King 1978; Wuenscher and Valiunas 1967) or (b) the gradual encroachment of for-est into prairie as a result of late Holocene climatic cooling and conditions more favorable for tree growth in marginal upland environments (Wood 1976).

The primary factor responsible for differences in soil development and natural potential vegetation (itself the result of soils, slope, and amount of solar insolation) in the area is topographic relief produced by dendritic stream dissection of the till plain by the Salt River and its tributaries. The flat interfluves most often were covered with prairie or dry oak–hickory forest at the time of Euro-American settlement, whereas lower slopes and protected ravines had increasing amounts of mesic species, such as basswood (*Tilia americana*), sugar maple, sycamore, bur oak, black walnut, hackberry, and cottonwood. For this reason, it has been suggested that resources from every zone would be within easy reach of residential sites located anywhere in the region, and as a result, settlement patterns might be more environmentally localized than is typical in other parts of the Midwest (Chapter 5).

Because from any point within the study area

one is within reach of all vegetation types, movement of encampments for collecting food resources should have been minimal. Other criteria would become more important in site selection (e.g., proximity to water, ease of protection, and comfort). At the same time, broken topography in some parts of the region would buffer the effects of climatic change.

Against this environmental background, four cultural stages have been postulated that potentially could be reflected in the archaeobotanical remains (Chapter 5). These include: Stage 1, characterized by small, mobile groups engaged in hunting and gathering activities (Early and Middle Archaic); Stage 2, characterized by the presence of small, discrete communities with semipermanent or permanent structures and some plant cultivation, located near major rivers or lower stretches of tributaries (Late Archaic and Early Woodland); Stage 3, characterized by increased dependence on horticulture as a more permanent subsistence base and a more sedentary way of life resulting in larger communities along lower terraces of large waterways (Middle and early Late Woodland); and Stage 4, characterized by an increased dependence on maize agriculture that is reflected in still larger community size (Late Woodland–Mississippian). Based on the lack of artifactual evidence, it is felt that very little interaction occurred between the inhabitants of the Cannon Reservoir region and Mississippian communities to the southeast and certain social features characteristic of Stage 4 may not have been developed or adopted in the middle Salt River valley.

Analysis of plant remains from project area sites can also serve to answer several questions arising from this model:

1. Do individual sites reflect use of a broad spectrum of plant resources collected in various vegetation zones?
2. Do changes occur through time, indicating a gradual shift from gathering to considerable emphasis on plant cultivation?
3. Do plant remains reflect the apparent lack of interaction with nearby Mississippian cultures as suggested by the lack of exchange goods?

Plant remains from several sites are discussed in the next section, followed by a discussion of plants and implications for reconstructing settlement–subsistence activities in the Cannon Project region.

SITE COLLECTIONS

Plant remains were identified from more than 1200 samples from 12 sites in the Cannon Project region. These samples include material from Dalton, Archaic, and Woodland components and indicate something of the subsistence changes that took place in the area through time. The plant remains from these sites are summarized in Table 11.1 and are displayed in Figure 11.1.

Pigeon Roost Creek

Pigeon Roost Creek has yielded the most subsistence data from the Cannon Project region.[1] Three deposition zones have been described for the site. The youngest of these, Zone I, is composed of (*a*) a disturbed plow zone (0–20 cm); (*b*) Middle and Late Woodland levels (20–60 cm) within and below a compact, culturally deposited layer of unmodified broken limestone; and (*c*) a Late Archaic level beneath the limestone layer. A lightly occupied zone separates Zone I from a Middle Archaic level (130–170 cm), which is separated from a deep Dalton–Early Archaic level (270–330 cm) by a lightly occupied layer. Although the three depositional zones contain six major occupation levels ranging in age from ca. 8900–570 years B.P., projectile-point class trends and radiometric dates suggest a greater number of discrete occupations (Chapter 6, Figure 6.1).

In Table 11.1 samples have been combined on the basis of depth since cultural deposits at the site are relatively flat and frequently are separated by sterile or lightly occupied levels. Samples from the Dalton–Early Archaic levels contain few plant remains. Taxa represented include hickory (*Carya* spp.), black walnut (*Juglans nigra*), hazelnut (*Corylus americana*), one fragment of a tuber (possibly

---

[1]Site-specific data for Pigeon Roost Creek appear in Chapter 6; data for other sites appear in Chapters 10 and 13.

TABLE 11.1.

Summary of Plant Remains from Various Archaeological Components in the Project Area

Site	Percentage (Weight Basis)					Average weight per sample (G)	Seeds and other remains
	Charcoal	Hickory	Black Walnut	Hazelnut	Acorns		
LATE WOODLAND							
Pigeon Roost Creek	15.2	79.7	4.2	.8	–	.7	–
Cooper (features)	14.5	78.2	6.7	.7	–	3.8	maize, sumpweed
Cooper (1m²)	7.9	82.4	9.1	.4	.3	.7	maize, sumpweed, butternut
Ross	99.7	.3	–	–	–	8.9	chenopod, grape, greenbrier, persimmon
Hatten Village SA 2	26.2	71.2	2.1	.1	.4	2.5	–
Hatten Village SA 3	90.7	6.7	1.3	–	1.3	.3	buffalo bur
Garrelts I (Feature 23)	21.6	77.9	.5	–	–	4.8	maygrass
Flowers (Level 1)	70.6	26.0	1.2	1.2	.9	.9	butternut, grass, blackberry
Flowers (Level 2)	74.6	22.5	2.2	.3	.5	3.1	maygrass, knotweed, grape, grass
Flowers (Level 3)	56.3	39.5	2.7	1.1	.3	1.7	–
Flowers (Level 4)	9.1	80.8	9.5	.4	.1	2.2	maygrass, hawthorn
West	53.1	47.2	–	–	–	2.3	chenopod

(continued)

TABLE 11.1. (continued)

Percentage (Weight Basis)

Site	Charcoal	Hickory	Black Walnut	Hazelnut	Acorns	Average weight per sample (G)	Seeds and other remains
MIDDLE WOODLAND							
Hillside	97.1	2.0	.6	.3	–	1.5	–
Pigeon Roost Creek	9.1	84.9	5.3	.7	–	8.1	sumpweed, pepo squash
Hatten Village SA 6	94.8	4.8	.2	.2	–	.7	chenopod, maygrass, knotweed
LATE ARCHAIC/EARLY WOODLAND							
Collins	93.2	6.8	–	–	–	4.9	–
Pigeon Roost Creek	3.4	90.8	5.7	.1	–	2.6	sumpweed, ragweed, bottle gourd
Cooper (features)	4.8	59.6	35.4	.2	–	5.6	cf. sumpweed
Cooper (1m²)	–	73.4	26.6	–	–	4.4	–
Miskell	8.7	86.6	4.6	.1	–	7.1	bedstraw
Flowers (Level 5)	6.3	92.0	1.7	.1	–	6.1	blackberry or raspberry
Flowers (Level 6)	13.8	84.5	1.7	–	–	2.7	–
MIDDLE ARCHAIC							
Pigeon Roost Creek	5.1	88.8	6.1	–	–	.4	–
DALTON							
Pigeon Roost Creek	9.1	86.4	4.5	–	–	.2	cf. ragweed

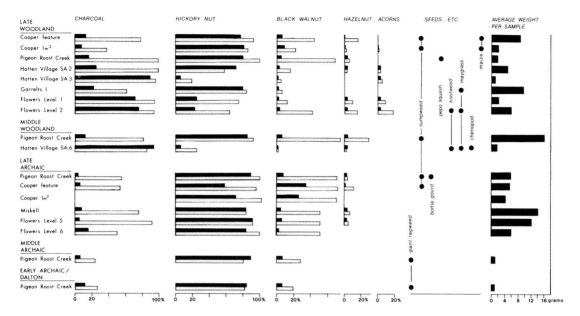

Figure 11.1.   Comparison of relative abundance and frequency of occurrence of plant remains recovered from various archaeological components [■ percentage (weight basis); ☐ percentage of total sample of occurrences; ● = <1%].

groundnut, *Apios americana*), and one giant ragweed (*Ambrosia trifida*) seed.

The deep Middle Archaic occupation levels (210–230 cm) contain no carbonized plant remains. Fresh and uncarbonized seeds are abundant in many samples, suggesting possible insect activity. This proposition is supported by the presence of insect borings in many seeds.

The majority of plant remains come from Zone II, a Middle Archaic occupation that produced 90% of the carbonized charcoal and nutshell from the site. The most abundant type of plant remains is carbonized hickory nutshell, generally shagbark hickory (*C. ovata*), that comprises 80–90% of the material, whereas black walnut (*J. nigra*) ranges between 4–6%, and hazelnut from 0–4%. The upper 30 cm of Zone II (100–130 cm) contains sparse material; most notable are a fragment of groundnut and a rind fragment of bottle gourd (*Lagenaria* sp.), measuring 6.4 mm in thickness. On the basis of what is known about the history of bottle gourd in the Midwest, it is likely that this fragment is associ-

ated with the overlying Late Archaic material, rather than with the Middle Archaic component.

Zone I contains a variety of plant remains. Along with the suite of carbonized nutshell found in the other zones, the Late Archaic component contains 3 sumpweed (*Iva annua*) seeds (1 measurable seed = 4.5 × 3.5 mm; reconstructed size = 4.9 × 3.8 mm), 35 possible giant ragweed seeds, and a possible persimmon (*Diospyros virginiana*) seed. Cucurbit seeds and rind (*Cucurbita pepo*) occur in the Middle Woodland component, as does a single carbonized sumpweed seed measuring 3.0 by 3.0 mm (reconstructed size = 3.3 × 3.3 mm). The Late Woodland component contains 1 squash seed as well as 2 fragments of maize kernels.

Variation in charcoal and nutshell weights by zone within the site shows few differences between samples. However, a comparison of relative weights of occurrence of various types of remains (the number of samples of occurrence rather than relative weight) is interesting. Figure 11.2 shows both relative occurrence and relative abundance for

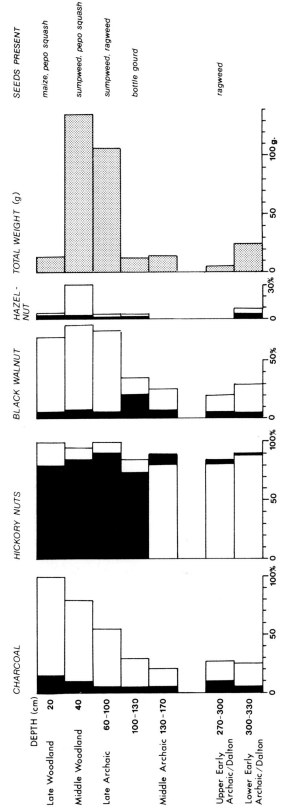

Figure 11.2. Summary of carbonized plant remains from Pigeon Roost Creek [■ percentage (weight basis); □ percentage of total sample of occurrences].

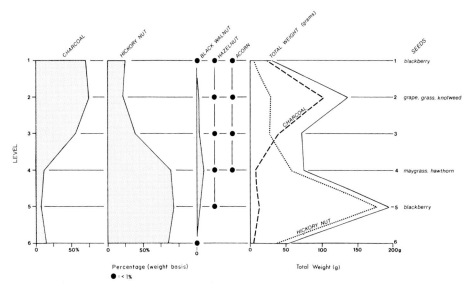

Figure 11.3. Summary of carbonized plant remains from Flowers.

the occupation levels. As can be seen, relative abundance remains very similar through time, with the percentage of each type of plant remains fluctuating very little. However, the distribution of plant remains across the site changes substantially through time. Charcoal occurs in approximately 30% of the Middle Archaic and Dalton samples and in 55–100% of the Late Archaic and more recent samples. Likewise, black walnut, which accounts for only 5% of the weight throughout the sequence, occurs in 18–30% of samples from older components and in 80–90% of younger samples, despite its continued low abundance.

Hazelnut, with an abundance of .7% of total weight, occurs in 29% of all samples in the Middle Woodland component. This pattern of more uniform distribution of various types of carbonized remains (decreased intrasite variability) may indicate (*a*) a change in activity areas or site function through time, (*b*) an increase in the volume of plant remains present (i.e., the more material of a certain type there is present, the more likely it is to be sampled), or (*c*) a greater number of occupants and therefore more disturbance and mixing of materials.

It should be evident from the previous discus-

sion that Pigeon Roost Creek not only yields the most plant remains of any site in the project area, it offers the opportunity to examine subtle changes in plant utilization through time. Data from the site are of great assistance in testing certain implications of the settlement system model.

Flowers

Significant data on plant use also were recovered from Flowers, a Late Archaic–Late Woodland site lying 50–250 m south of the Salt River mainstem. The site is stratified, with fairly clear breaks between Archaic and Woodland components (Chapter 6). The 10-cm-deep excavation levels (Figure 11.3) show distinct and intriguing changes through time. Although the number of samples remains fairly constant among levels, the total amount of carbonized plant material fluctuates considerably. Peaks occur in levels 2 and 5 and probably coincide with Late Archaic and Late Woodland occupations. Late Archaic levels (4–6) contain primarily hickory (greater than 80%), whereas Late Woodland levels (1–3) contain 68–80% wood charcoal.

The amount of black walnut—generally considered a slightly less desirable nut because of its flavor, the convoluted nut cavity and thick husk—increases from .4% of the total in level 6 to 9.5% in level 4. Increased use of black walnut, coupled with the general increase in nutshell debris at the site, suggests the possibility of a population heavily dependent on nuts for food, and possibly for fuel as well. The season of occupation may have been fall, although nuts are stored easily and could have been consumed anytime during the year. In addition, food available in seasons other than fall usually are poorly preserved and thus are poorly represented in archaeological sites. There are three seed types in levels 4–6: raspberry or blackberry (*Rubus* spp.), hawthorn (*Crataegus* spp.), and maygrass (*Phalaris caroliniana*).

Although Late Woodland levels continue to have some hickory as well as black walnut, hazelnut, and acorn, there is a predominance of wood charcoal, suggesting a slight shift in the season of occupation or less reliance on nuts. The presence of maygrass and knotweed (*Polygonum* spp.) seeds (as well as grape and blackberry–raspberry) suggests a summer occupation and possibly increased reliance on the harvesting of wild plant seeds.

Hatten Village

Originally considered a single extensive site, Hatten Village actually contains three separate and spatially distinct residential areas. Preliminary evidence suggests the possibility that each area represents a seasonally distinct occupation. The three areas are distinguished by their strip area designations: SA 2, 3, and 6 (Figure 12.2). The southernmost area (SA 6) dates to the Middle Woodland period, whereas the others (SA 2 and 3) probably are Late Woodland occupations.

The predominant plant material is charcoal, which occurs in 100% of the samples from SA 2, 96% of those from SA 3, and 87% of those from SA 6. Charcoal comprises 80–100% of the total weight of material from all feature clusters, with the exception of SA 2, House Cluster (HC) 2 (Figure 13.11), where there is a large quantity (63.1g out of a total of 76.4g) of carbonized hickory nutshell. The charcoal taxa include oak, hickory, poplar or willow,

ash, elm, maple, mulberry, honey locust, cherry, and walnut. Thus, a wide range of slope and bottomland forest species is represented by the charcoal at the site.

Although much less common than charcoal, hickory nutshell fragments are the second most abundant plant remains, occurring in 57.1%, 17.9%, and 24.4% of the samples from SA 2, 3, and 6, respectively. Virtually all carbonized hickory is from the thick-walled, large-fruited shagbark and shellbark (*Carya laciniosa*) hickories. Hickory comprises between 1.7–14.5% of the total weight of plant remains, except in SA 2, HC 2, where it is 91.8% of the total. In general, hickory percentages are greater for SA 2 features than for features in SA 3 or 6. Likewise, black walnut, hazelnut, and acorn all occur more frequently in SA 2. On a weight basis, charcoal is more abundant in SA 6 and 3, and hickory and other nutshell debris is more abundant in SA 2.

In addition to charcoal and nutshell, a number of carbonized seeds also was recovered from Hatten Village. Besides the few carbonized seeds of buffalo bur (*Solanum rostratum*), a weedy pioneer, that occur in SA 3, the sample includes 12 maygrass, 44 chenopod, 14 knotweed, and 1 persimmon seed and 22 fragments and/or seeds too distorted to be identified. Although discussed later, it should be noted that seeds from SA 6 include three potential native cultigens (maygrass, chenopod, and knotweed) that may have been used for food by Middle Woodland occupants of the site, along with persimmons.

In summary, there are three types of features at Hatten Village: those relatively high in hickory and other nutshell debris, those relatively high in charcoal, and those high in charcoal and seeds. In SA 2 features probably represent either different seasons of occupation or locales of different activities. The large amount of hickory nutshell in one feature suggests that at least one activity was processing this nut for food. Because of the paucity of nutshell debris from SA 6, we conclude that this area may have been occupied during a different season than was SA 2. The presence of carbonized seeds with the burial suggests a mid- to late-summer occupation.

Collins

Initial excavations at the Late Archaic–Early Woodland Collins site uncovered 17 circular to ovoid, basin-shaped pits dating to 2600–2500 years B.P. (Klippel 1972:38). Carbonized plant remains are abundant in a number of features and include not only charcoal and nutshell but also seeds .of several probable native cultigens (chenopod, giant ragweed, sumpweed, and knotweed). These seeds represent some of the first finds of such antiquity and supported the then-recent hypothesis that agriculture had its roots in the Archaic stage in eastern North America (Fowler 1971) and that the earliest of the cultivated plants were probably indigenous to the Midwest (Klippel 1972:54). Although it has been shown that the first domesticated plants of eastern North America were squash and bottle gourd introduced from Mexico (Kay *et al.* 1980), the material from Collins did much to stimulate later archaeological research in the Cannon Reservoir area.

Carbonized sumpweed seeds from Collins are of particular interest because of the quantity ($n = 219$) and their reconstructed achene size ($\bar{x} = 4.9$ by 3.4 mm) is somewhat larger than that of modern wild specimens, indicating that they may have been in an early stage of domestication (Klippel 1972:54, Yarnell 1977:865).

Of the 18 samples of plant remains recovered from the 1979 excavations at Collins, 10 (55.6%) contain charcoal and 3 (16.7%) contain hickory. Unfortunately, no other types of carbonized nutshell or seeds were present, and the plant remains do not add appreciably to our knowledge of the use of native plants at the site.

Ross

Ross, a Late Woodland community, contains few botanical remains; the most abundant is wood charcoal, which occurs in 67 of 70 samples (95.7%). Carbonized taxa include sycamore, walnut, the red oak group, oak, ash, elm or hackberry, and maple. A number of samples contain charcoal from very slow growing, probably upland, oak.

Hickory nutshells occur in 16 samples. Ten are from a possible house (Chapter 13) where 76.1% of the 13 samples contain hickory, compared with 10.5% of the samples from the rest of the site (6 of 57 samples). Although hickory nutshell debris occurs in low quantities, its presence indicates that the hickory nut probably was used either as food or fuel. Carbonized seeds from the site included one each of grape, grass, chenopod, and greenbrier (*Smilax* spp.) and are too few in number to indicate either usage or season.

Garrelts

Garrelts is a large site containing Late Archaic and Late Woodland components. Although plant remains from 175 samples from Garrelts were examined, many samples contain only modern seed contaminants or small spherical manganese nodules. However, 78 samples (44.6%) contain charcoal, 25 (14.3%) contain hickory, 2 (1.1%) contain black walnut, and 3 (1.7%) contain hazelnut.

Feature 23, a Late Woodland pit, is distinctly different from the rest of the site. It contains 14.9% of the charcoal and 71.7% of the hickory nut from the site as well as a small amount of butternut (*Juglans cinerea*) shell fragments. Feature 23 also contains the majority of seeds (approximately 575 carbonized maygrass seeds).

West

Fourteen samples from West were examined; of these, three contain charcoal (one held 17.0 g; the others, much less) and two contain hickory nutshell debris (one of which held 151.0 g). Also present are two carbonized chenopod seeds and a single carbonized ash seed.

Cooper

One hundred seventy-eight samples from middens and features at the main Cooper excavation were examined for plant remains. About one-fifth of these samples are from 10 features and 5 midden excavation units (each 1 m²) that date to the Late Archaic period. The remainder (146 samples) are from Late Woodland features (12) and middens (92

1-m² units), most of which were located in and around a linear configuration of 6 hearth areas (Figure 13.19).

The most abundant type of plant remains in the Late Archaic features is hickory nutshell (59.6% of total weight), followed by black walnut (35.4%), charcoal (4.8%), and hazelnut (.2%). Hickory nut is relatively more abundant in the 1-m² excavations, where it accounts for 73.4% of the total; black walnut (26.6%) is less abundant, and charcoal and hazelnut are absent. Rates of occurrence are higher than relative abundances. Hickory occurs in 96.0% of features, black walnut in 76.0%, charcoal in 56.0%, and hazelnut in 12.0%. One feature contains a charred fragment of sumpweed seed.

Samples from Late Woodland features and middens are relatively small but are more diverse than the Late Archaic samples and contain different proportions of taxa. Hickory nutshell (78.2%), charcoal (14.5%), and hazelnut (.7%) are more abundant in features, and black walnut (6.7%) is less abundant. These same trends are reflected in percentages for 1-m² excavations. Rates of occurrence also tend to shift in these directions. Hickory occurs in 91.2% of features, charcoal in 79.4%, black walnut in 44.1%, and hazelnut in 17.6%. Although the magnitudes of these changes are not great, they may reflect seasonal differences in occupation (Chapter 10). Features from the component also contain a fragment of a maize kernel and two sumpweed seeds. The 1-m² excavations produced 10 other maize fragments that were distributed extensively, but in low numbers, among the hearth areas.

Hillside

Sixty-seven samples from Hillside were examined. Of these, 60 (89.6%) contain charcoal, 11 (16.4%) contain hickory, 2 (3.0%) contain black walnut, and 3 (4.5%) contain hazelnut. On a weight basis, charcoal is 97.3% of the carbonized plant remains, hickory is 1.8%, black walnut is .6%, and hazelnut is .2%. The average weight of charcoal is 1.65 g/sample. Significantly higher amounts of charcoal occur in F 55, 56, and 57, with a total of 73.2g. All charcoal belongs to a species in the red oak group. No carbonized seeds were recovered.

Miskell

Thirty-six pit features and a midden deposit (Angus and Ruppert 1977) were excavated at Miskell; 33 samples were examined for carbonized plant remains. Of these, 25 (75.7%) contain charcoal, 28 (84.8%) contain hickory nutshell, 17 (51.5%) contain walnut shell, and 1 (3.0%) contains hazelnut shell fragments. Likewise, on the basis of weight, hickory nut is again the most abundant, comprising 86.6% of the total carbonized remains. Wood charcoal accounts for 8.7%, black walnut for 4.6%, and hazelnut for .04% of the total carbonized plant remains for the site. The abundance of hickory and walnut at the site indicates their obvious importance to the Late Archaic inhabitants. Carbonized seeds include a single seed each of chenopod and bedstraw (*Galium* sp.).

PLANT TAXA ENCOUNTERED

The various plant taxa encountered in archaeological sites in the Cannon Reservoir region are shown in Table 11.2 and are discussed briefly in the following section.

Cultigens and Possible Cultigens

Bottle gourd (*Lagenaria* sp.) and pepo squash (*Cucurbita pepo*) both occur at Pigeon Roost Creek. The earliest occurrence of both cucurbits in archaeological contexts in Missouri is at Phillips Spring, in Hickory County, on the western edge of the Ozarks. There, these exotic cultigens occur in contexts dated to 4300 B.P. (Kay *et al.* 1980; F. King 1980). There are numerous other sites in the Midwest and Southwest with material of comparable age.

The Pigeon Roost Creek material is in the form of two small, squash rind fragments and possible seed fragments from Late and Middle Woodland levels and a bottle gourd rind fragment from Late Archaic levels. The fragment of bottle gourd rind is approximately 10 mm² and 6.4 mm thick and is reddish-brown in color. It is near the maximum thickness of gourds recovered from Salts Cave, Kentucky, described by Cutler as including many that were "thicker and woodier than usual for specimens north of Mexico" (Yarnell 1969:51).

Maygrass (*Phalaris caroliniana*) has been found in numerous Midwestern archaeological sites and is very likely a native cultigen. Maygrass is an annual, spring-flowering grass with a dense terminal inflorescence. Maturation of seeds extends from early May until late June, and although the grains are small (1.8–2.3 mm in length), their nutritional content is probably comparable with that of cultivated cereal grains such as wheat (Cowan 1978). Analysis of paleofeces from Newt Kash Hollow (Kentucky) demonstrates that maygrass, along with sumpweed and chenopod, was a common dietary component (Cowan 1978). Maygrass grains have also been found in paleofecal samples from Salts and Mammoth caves (Kentucky), sites along the Little Tennessee and Duck rivers in Tennessee, the White River region of the Arkansas Ozarks, and sites in the lower Illinois River valley.

Maygrass presently does not occur in Illinois or Kentucky, and there is a record of occurrence for only one county in Tennessee. Therefore, archaeological evidence of maygrass from these states comes from outside its modern range, leading to speculation that it may have been cultivated during Late Archaic through Mississippian times. Steyermark (1963) shows an extreme western and southeastern distribution in Missouri. Cowan (1978) shows additional occurrences in western, south-central, and eastern (St. Louis County) Missouri. Thus, maygrass appears to be distributed widely and sparsely over the southern half of the state.

Maygrass occurs in samples excavated from Hatten Village (SA 6), Garrelts (F 23), and Flowers (levels 2 and 4). If prehistoric inhabitants of the project area were using it as a food, it must have been fairly abundant. Given its modern distribution, it may have been cultivated in this area as well.

Sumpweed (*Iva annua* and var. *macrocarpa*) is unique among native cultigens in eastern North America in that it became extinct during late Protohistoric or early Historic times. Between its first occurrence in the archaeological record and its disappearance, the average size of archaeological specimens increased from a size of approximately 3 mm in length to as large as 9 mm (Mississippian-age achenes from southern Missouri and northern Arkansas) and even 13 mm (Ozark Bluff Dwellers) (Yarnell 1976, 1977; Jones 1960), an increase in length of almost 1 mm per millennium. Large specimens have been recovered in northwestern Arkansas and from Kansas City to eastern Kentucky (Yarnell 1972:355). Ample paleofecal evidence exists from sites such as Salts and Mammoth caves and Newt Kash Hollow to demonstrate that sumpweed was an important food plant in Kentucky 2000–3000 years ago.

Sumpweed achenes are similar in appearance and structure to those of another composite, sunflower (*Helianthus* spp.); both are comparable in nutritional value. The seed is covered with a thin dry coat or *pericarp* that also is similar to the sunflower's, except that it possesses an objectionable odor and taste. Sumpweed grows presently in habitats that are disturbed, open, or flooded seasonally. It appears to be an edge species, occurring between permanently wet and better drained soils (Asch and Asch 1978), the width of its distribution depending on competition from other plants. Within this zone, sumpweed often occurs in dense stands, although these are generally of small size (Asch and Asch 1978:309).

During the 1968 excavations at Collins, 219 carbonized sumpweed achenes with an average reconstructed length and width of 4.9 by 3.4 mm (range = 3.3–6.5 × 2.3–5.0 mm) were recovered (Yarnell 1977; Klippel 1972). During more recent excavations, sumpweed achenes were recovered from Late Archaic (Pigeon Roost Creek and Cooper) and Late Woodland (Cooper) samples, although no additional seeds were recovered from the 1979 Collins excavations. The Late Archaic seed from Pigeon Roost Creek has a reconstructed length and width of 4.9 by 3.7 mm and is very close to the average of the Collins achenes. Two of the 4 seeds from Cooper were measurable and have reconstructed lengths and widths of 5.2 by 3.5 and 3.5 by 2.6 mm, well within the range of the Collins achenes.

Maize (*Zea mays*) is represented in several Late Woodland samples from Cooper by a few kernel or

TABLE 11.2.

Plant Taxa Recovered from Archaeological Components in the Project Area[a]

Common name	Scientific name	Part recovered
Ash	*Fraxinus* spp.	wood
Bedstraw	*Galium* spp.	leaves (potherb)
		seeds (beverage)
Blackberry, rasp-berry, dewberry	*Rubus* spp.	fruit
Black walnut	*Juglans nigra*	nuts, wood
Buffalo bur	*Solanum rostratum*	-
Bottle gourd	*Lagenaria siceraria*	fruit
Butternut	*Juglans cinerea*	nuts
Chenopod	*Chenopodium* spp.	seeds
Cherry or plum	*Prunus* spp.	wood
Elm or hackberry	*Ulmus* spp. or *Celtis* spp.	wood
Grape	*Vitis* spp.	fruit
Greenbrier	*Smilax* spp.	shoots (potherb)
Grass	Gramineae	-
Ground nut	*Apios americana*	tubers
Hawthorn	*Crataegus* spp.	fruit
Hazelnut	*Corylus americana*	nuts
Hickory	*Carya* spp.	nuts, wood
Honey locust	*Gleditsia triacanthos*	wood
Knotweed	*Polygonum* spp.	seeds
Maize (corn)	*Zea mays*	seeds
Maple	*Acer* spp.	wood
Maygrass	*Phalaris caroliniana*	seeds
Mulberry	*Morus rubra*	wood
Oak (white oak, red oak)	*Quercus* spp.	acorns, wood
Pepo squash	*Cucurbita pepo*	fruit
Persimmon	*Diospyros virginiana*	fruit, wood
Poplar or willow	*Populus* spp., *Salix* spp.	wood
Ragweed	*Ambrosia trifida*	seeds
Red cedar	*Juniperus virginiana*	-
Sycamore	*Platanus occidentalis*	-
Sumpweed	*Iva annua* and var. *macrocarpa*	seeds

[a]Based on King (1976) except where noted; taxonomy follows Steyermark (1963).
[b]Based on data listed in Zawacki and Hausfater (1969). C.H.V. = comparative

cupule fragments. Maize probably was introduced into the Midwest by about 2200 B.P. (Yarnell 1976), although it does not appear to have become common or widespread until much later. Maize from the site comes from various levels in the midden but probably dates to the twelfth century A.D.

Chenopod (*Chenopodium* spp.) seeds occur in several samples from Collins, Garrelts, Hatten Village SA 6, Miskell, and West and are common in archaeological sites in the Midwest. Although there are many native species, the one most often encountered in archaeological sites, *Chenopodium bushianum* (Asch and Asch 1977), is related closely to a species domesticated in Mexico (Wilson 1981). The carbonized chenopod seeds from the Cannon Project cannot be identified to species.

Knotweed (*Polygonum* spp., especially *P. erectum*) also occurs in archaeological sites and has

TABLE 11.2. (*continued*)

C.H.V.[b] (%)	Season of availability	Habitat
79	–	open woods, bottoms, slopes
–	late spring, early summer	oak-hickory forest, bottomlands
–	summer	widespread
80	fall	widespread, lower slopes, bottomlands
–	–	disturbed, common
–	–	cultivated
55	fall	moist woods
–	late summer	disturbed, floodplain
71	–	moist woods, bottomlands
73	–	oak-hickory forest, bottomlands
–	fall	widespread
–	spring	oak-hickory forest, bottomlands
–	–	widespread
–	spring, fall, winter	thickets, bottomlands
–	summer	moist woods
–	late summer	thickets, bottomlands
98	fall	widespread
94	–	bottomlands
–	late summer	bottomlands, disturbed
–	summer	cultivated
69–84	–	bottomlands, moist woods
–	early summer	moist ground, disturbed not present in reservoir area today
–	–	bottomlands, lower slopes
83–92	fall	widespread
–	late summer, fall	cultivated
96	fall	bottomlands, open woods
–	–	bottomlands, river banks
–	late summer, fall	disturbed, floodplain
–	–	dry, rocky, steep slopes
–	–	bottomlands, lower slopes
–	late summer	disturbed, floodplain

heat value (amount of heat produced by wood as compared to an equal amount of bituminous coal).

been considered a possible cultigen, particularly in the lower Illinois River valley. Likewise, giant ragweed (*Ambrosia trifida*) is a common pioneer plant that produces a relatively large seed that can, under the right circumstances, be removed easily from the thick pericarp.

Taken individually, the small number of carbonized seeds of *Phalaris, Chenopodium, Polygonum,* and *Ambrosia* found in sites in the Cannon Project area do not necessarily demonstrate their use by aboriginal inhabitants for food. These plants all might have grown readily in disturbed environments, such as around an aboriginal camp, and many archaeological occurrences of chenopod and knotweed are certain to represent the fortuitous inclusion of such weed seeds. However, the presence of several species together (knotweed, chenopod, and maygrass from Hatten Village SA 6) appears to be more than coincidental and suggests that these plants were being gathered and used as food.

Nuts

Oak (*Quercus* spp.) are by far the most important nut-producing tree species in the project area. They account for 69% of forest bearing trees in the GLO survey, in comparison to 11.0% for hickory, and 1.3% for black walnut and butternut combined (Warren 1976). The dominant oak species is white oak (*Q. alba*), the acorns of which are low in bitter tannic acids. Wuenscher and Valiunas (1967) found white oak to be the most important species in the River Hills region of Missouri, with black oak, elm, hickory, ash, and sugar maple also significant.

The dominant hickory apparently is the mesophytic shagbark (*C. ovata*) species (Missouri Botanical Garden 1974). Subdominant species include pignut (*C. glabra*), black (*C. texana*), mockernut (*C. tomentosa*), and bitternut (*C. cordiformis*); shellbark (*C. laciniosa*) probably occurs also (Steyermark 1963). As its name implies, bitternut hickory is extremely bitter and unpalatable, whereas shagbark hickory has relatively large, sweet nuts. It is not surprising, then, that virtually all hickory nutshell from the Cannon Project area is of the thick-shelled shagbark–shellbark type.

Black walnut (*Juglans nigra*) is common throughout Missouri, occurring in rich soils at the base of slopes or bluffs, in valleys along streams, and in open upland woods. It is a subdominant species in the Cannon Reservoir region and accounts for only about 1% of forest bearing trees.

Butternut (*Juglans cinerea*) is related closely to black walnut and also has nuts with sweet, edible kernels. Butternut occurs in rich soils along the base of slopes or bluffs and along streams. It is common in the Ozarks and the eastern half of Missouri. However, butternut is more mesophytic than black walnut and is limited somewhat in distribution.

Hazelnut (*Corylus americana*) occurs in dry or moist thickets, in woodlands, along borders of forests, in valleys, and in uplands (Steyermark 1963:524). It is common throughout Missouri. In the GLO surveys of the Cannon Reservoir area, it is

one of the three most abundant taxa mentioned in understory line descriptions. Nuts of this species ripen in late summer and are sweet, easily collected, and easily shelled. Because hazelnut is a shrub rather than a tree, and because the nuts are relatively small, human collectors must compete with birds and small mammals.

Wild Fruits, Seeds, and Tubers

Bedstraw (*Galium* spp.) is a common plant that frequently forms dense tangles, especially on moist ground, during the spring. Some species have a sweet-scented foliage and have been used historically for stuffing mattresses (thus the name). The ripened fruits (spring–summer) are bristly and adhere to clothing and skin. If the mature fruits are dried and roasted, they can be used to make a coffee-like drink. Although the young plants can be used as "greens," the stems are covered with hooked hairs that make them rather unpalatable. Because of the bristles and hairs, both seeds and plants might be picked up on clothing and firewood and ultimately end up in a campfire. One carbonized bedstraw seed was recovered from Miskell.

Buffalo bur (*Solanum rostratum*) is a weedy plant found on disturbed ground, rocky open exposures, and alluvial soils. The plant is not edible, and under certain circumstances has been reported to cause poisoning of livestock. Buffalo bur produces many seeds, making it fairly common in seed assemblages from archaeological sites. Carbonized seeds of this species occur in SA 6 at Hatten Village.

Blackberry, raspberry, and dewberry (*Rubus* spp.) are from a large genus with many species. The plants are difficult to distinguish, and the seeds (with few exceptions) are almost impossible to distinguish one from another. Of the 16 species listed by Steyermark (1963:834–843) for Missouri, only 2 (*Rubus occidentalis*, black raspberry, and *R. pensilvanicus*, high-bush blackberry) are shown for Monroe County, whereas another species (*R. flagellaris*, dewberry) is widespread throughout the state and is probably present in the county. Black raspberry occurs in open woods, along bluffs, and in thickets; high-bush blackberry and dewberry occur in these habitats as well as on prairie. As a group, the 3 species bear fruit from June into August. Carbonized *Rubus* seeds occur in levels 1 and 5 at Flowers.

Hawthorn (*Crataegus* spp.) is another large genus and includes 50 species in Missouri, 10 of which occur in the Cannon Reservoir area. At least 2 species have relatively large, edible fruits that mature during the late summer and fall. *Crataegus mollis,* a common species with edible fruit, occurs in open woods and on fertile soil along small streams. Part of a carbonized hawthorn seed was recovered from level 4 at Flowers.

Persimmon (*Diospyros virginiana*) is a small tree commonly found throughout southern and central Missouri. It occurs in open woods, glades, prairies, thickets, alluvial woods, and valleys along streams. The edible fruits ripen in the fall and often are said to be better after frost. Part of a carbonized persimmon seed was recovered from SA 6 at Hatten Village.

Grape (*Vitis* spp.) is a common vine and eight species are listed by Steyermark (1963) as occurring in Missouri; five are found in the Cannon Reservoir area. As a group, these species grow in open woods, thickets, glades, on rocky slopes, bluffs, alluvial soils, and sand bars. At least two species have permanently sweet fruits, the others become sweet after frost. Carbonized grape seeds were recovered from Ross and level 2 of Flowers.

Greenbrier (*Smilax* spp.) is a herbaceous vine occurring in woods, thickets, and along streams. Several species are listed by Steyermark (1963: 450–452) for the Cannon Reservoir area. These include species with edible young shoots and species whose roots can be used in drinks (e.g., sarsaparilla). The seed is large and covered only with a thin flesh and is eaten by birds and animals. One seed was recovered from Ross.

Groundnut (*Apios americana*) is a small herbaceous vine in the legume family. It is common throughout Missouri and is found in wet meadows and low thickets, on stream banks, and around ponds and sloughs. The plant, also known as *Pomme de Terre* because of its edible, starchy tubers, was held in high esteem by early historic American Indians as well as by early Euro-American settlers (Steyermark 1963:947–948). Several small tubers,

tentatively identified as groundnut, were recovered from Pigeon Roost Creek.

DISCUSSION OF PLANT REMAINS

Because of the better preservation provided by the accumulation of sediments on the lower slopes and in river valleys, the majority of Cannon Reservoir area sites having significant plant remains occur in the flood plain and on terraces. The remains of 31 plant taxa were recovered from sites in the project area, although the archaeobotanical flora is dominated by nutshell debris from a few taxa. Both intersite and intrasite variability in plant remains are low, undoubtedly because fragile remains are lacking.

Patterns seen in the distribution of plant remains in the Cannon Reservoir area sites seem typical of those from other midwestern sites: (*a*) an early dominance by hickory; (*b*) the appearance of cucurbits during the Middle–Late Archaic period and the presence of seeds of native plant species shortly thereafter; (*c*) a subsequent increase in the abundance of seeds of native plant species; and (*d*) the first appearance of maize during the Late Woodland period, long after the introduction of other exotic cultigens and the initial utilization of native plant species.

However, the amount of maize recovered from the project area is small. Likewise, sumpweed seeds are relatively small in size, and sunflower seeds are absent. Taken together, these characteristics of the archaeobotanical flora probably reflect the lack of interaction with nearby Mississippian cultures, as suggested by the paucity of artifactual evidence.

The dominant plant remain recovered from Dalton–Early Archaic through Middle Woodland components is hickory, which occurs in more than 80% of the samples and also comprises more than 80% of the total weight of all carbonized remains. In Dalton and Middle Archaic samples from Pigeon Roost Creek, charcoal and black walnut also occur in approximately 25% of the samples, although each represents less than 10% of the total weight of plant remains.

Although relative percentages of charcoal and black walnut do not change during the Late Archaic, they become more abundant, reflecting the increase in the total amount of carbonized plant remains. Charcoal occurs in 50–94% of the samples from Pigeon Roost Creek, and black walnut, in 50–70%. If the site was occupied more intensely through time, as indicated by the increase in amounts of carbonized material, increased human activity also may have acted to distribute and mix the remains as well, decreasing intrasite variability. Sumpweed occurs for the first time at Pigeon Roost Creek during the Late Archaic period, and one uncarbonized fragment of bottle gourd dates to this period as well.

The Middle Woodland assemblage, Hillside, SA 6 at Hatten Village, and a level from Pigeon Roost Creek, is more varied than that of the Late Archaic period. At Pigeon Roost Creek hickory nut is dominant, whereas charcoal and black walnut are of widespread, but minor, importance. Charcoal dominates the other two samples, where remains of mast resources are relatively uncommon. Seeds and other plant remains include sumpweed, pepo squash, chenopod, maygrass, and knotweed.

Archaeobotanical remains from the Late Woodland period are represented by material from seven sites (eight, if Hatten Village is subdivided). The Late Woodland data also are variable, suggesting there may have been distinct seasonal or site use differences during the Woodland periods. Although some sites are dominated by hickory nutshell (Cooper, Pigeon Roost Creek, Hatten Village SA 2, and Garrelts), others show a dominance of wood charcoal (Hatten Village SA 3, and Flowers), perhaps indicating either increased usage during seasons when nuts were not available or decreased nut usage. Either or both possibilities are supported by the presence of seeds of native plants and potential cultigens available during the summer (maygrass) or late summer–fall (sumpweed, chenopod, knotweed, and maize). The average weight of carbonized remains per sample is lower for the Late Woodland and Middle Woodland periods and may reflect seasonal occupation, specialized activities, and/or a smaller or more dispersed population.

Comparisons with Other Areas

Perhaps the best studied archaeological sites in close proximity to the Cannon Reservoir are those in the lower Illinois River valley (Asch et al. 1972; Asch and Asch 1978). The Salt and Illinois rivers flow into the Mississippi River within a 100 kilometers of one another, and the study areas are separated by approximately 125 km. However, whereas the Salt River cuts through an Illinoian age till plain, the Illinois River is an older and larger system carved into Mississippian limestone. Because the Illinois River is also an underfit stream, occupying a considerably broader stream valley than it currently needs, it meanders across its flood plain producing a much greater number and diversity of flood plain features (e.g., natural levees, sloughs, and backwater lakes) than occur on the Salt River. The mudflats that form annually as the backwater lakes evaporate provide habitats for large populations of annual herbaceous seed-producing species, including sumpweed, chenopod, and knotweed. In addition to the copious plant resources, the lower Illinois River valley contains abundant aquatic faunal resources and annually attracts immense numbers of migratory waterfowl. It has been suggested that these extremely productive flood plain environments may have prompted the intensive use of wild seeds, which led to the domestication of plants native to eastern North America (Asch and Asch 1978; Struever and Vickery 1973).

In comparison, the Salt River has a much narrower flood plain that lacks backwater and oxbow lakes and habitats where stands of wild seed-producing plants might have become established during prehistoric times. Flood plain faunal resources also are more limited than those of the Illinois River valley. At the same time, the close proximity of slope and upland nut-producing trees would make the scattered seed-producing plants that did occur of less value. The intensive use of wild seeds could be expected to have occurred along the Illinois River some time before it became desirable or necessary along the Salt River.

Comparing the archaeobotanical record of the two areas, one notices a low level of nut and seed usage at Koster in the lower Illinois River valley prior to 7500 B.P. This has no parallel in the Cannon Reservoir area, where the dominant type of carbonized plant remain is hickory nutshell. Perhaps this contrast reflects some of the differences in the relative abundance of various floral and faunal resources in the two river valleys, or it could be due to different site functions.

However, by about 7500 B.P., nuts apparently began to play an important part in the diet of prehistoric populations at Koster, and the first wild-size *Iva* occurs. This is the earliest documented occurrence of sumpweed in an archaeological context (Asch and Asch 1978).

During the Late Archaic period, the quantity of *Iva* increases considerably in comparison to other seeds in the lower Illinois River valley, although seed size continues to fall within the range of wild populations (Asch and Asch 1978). In the Cannon Project area, *Iva* occurs first in the Late Archaic levels. However, the increase in abundance during this period in the lower Illinois River valley is reflected in the relatively large number of sumpweed seeds in the Late Archaic–Early Woodland levels at Collins.

In the lower Illinois River valley, Middle Woodland sites show a significant increase in seed abundance, suggestive of "intensive harvesting," as well as a representation of three possible cultigens: *Chenopodium bushianum* (chenopod), *Polygonum erectum* (knotweed), and *Phalaris caroliniana* (maygrass) (Asch and Asch 1978). Wilson (1981) notes that *C. bushianum* shows many morphological similarities to the Mexican weed-crop complex of chenopods, possibly indicating prehistoric genetic interaction between species indigenous to Mexico and those of eastern North America. Evidence of such interaction increases the probability that *Chenopodium* was cultivated in eastern North America and possibly domesticated, rather than just harvested.

Only one Middle Woodland site, Hatten Village SA 6, contains all three possible cultigens (chenopod, knotweed, and maygrass). The site also contains little nutshell debris, which might be interpreted as reflecting a subsistence shift to reliance on small seeds, such as occurred in the lower Illinois River valley. An equally likely explanation, however, is that it reflects a short, late-summer, rather than a summer-through-fall, occupation.

Late Woodland sites in the lower Illinois River valley have yielded large seed masses that contain chenopod, knotweed, and maygrass seeds. At this same time, maize became common (although not abundant), and various types of nuts underwent a sharp decline in usage. In the Cannon Project area, the apparent importance of wild and/or domesticated seeds is not as great, and only occasionally are seeds of possible cultigens recovered from Late Woodland samples. Instead, hickory nut remains abundant, and other nuts—including black walnut, hazelnut, and acorns—also occur frequently. Small seeds probably were used to the extent that they were available.

SUMMARY

Plant remains from the Cannon Project area are typical of those from other, similarly situated, sites in the Midwest. Comparison of the archaeobotanical record of the Cannon Project area with that of other river valleys, exemplified by the lower Illinois River valley, suggests several things. Although the linear arrangement of vegetation types in the Cannon Reservoir area may have fostered localized settlement, a prerequisite for plant cultivation, the environment of the Salt River valley was not conducive to the adoption of intensive harvesting of small seeds or to the domestication of native plants. Throughout the archaeological record in the Cannon Reservoir area, nuts remain a primary vegetal food resource. At the same time, the presence of exotic cultigens and native plant domesticates demonstrates knowledge of these plants.

The Cannon Reservoir area was not potentially as productive in food resources as the Illinois River valley. However, the high diversity of vegetation types and plant food resources undoubtedly enabled the inhabitants to survive fluctuations in the availability of various food resources with less, if any, stress than that faced by groups dependent on a more limited number of plant resources or tied to cultivation.

PART V

Community Patterns

The four chapters in this section discuss our efforts to define the structure and content of prehistoric and historic communities in the Cannon Reservoir region. Three chapters deal with prehistoric communities. Chapter 12 presents the results of analysis of general site surface structure and intrasite surface distributions of artifact classes. Surface data are treated as information sets in their own right, independent of subsurface remains. Analysis of these data can be done quickly and relatively inexpensively and can be used to structure further fieldwork. Several important patterns in the distributions of surface materials at five sites are noted, patterns that are used to test implications of the settlement–subsistence model.

Chapter 13 discusses the structure and organization of prehistoric communities as revealed through excavated data. The archaeological community is composed of individual elements that co-occur spatially to form household clusters. Analysis begins with examination of these elements, both their form and function, and proceeds toward analysis of sets of elements and the spatial distribution of sets. The spatial organizations of various archaeological communities are discussed, and similarities and differences among them are highlighted. The final section of the chapter discusses the social organization of two communities based

on analysis of burial data.

Chapter 14 compares surface and subsurface artifact assemblages from three sites to construct a model of isomorphism between the two types of assemblages. The data used in this analysis are presented in Chapters 12 and 13. Two lines of investigation are important here: (a) the degree to which variable surface artifact density predicts the presence and location of subsurface archaeological features, and (b) the degree to which surface distributions of artifact classes reflect the subsurface distributions of those classes.

Chapter 15 details the analysis of the structure of historic communities from three perspectives: (a) the community as a whole, (b) the farmstead, and (c) the household. The chapter is tied intricately to Chapter 17, which discusses the patterns of historic period settlement in the Cannon Reservoir region. Data presented in Chapter 15 are used in part to examine the validity of implications of human settlement presented in Chapter 5, especially settlement during the colonization stage of the model. At the household level of analysis, data from two excavated residences belonging to a single extended family are used to examine (a) the material classes associated with nineteenth-century settlers in the region and (b) the patterns of discard of these classes.

12

Prehistoric Community Patterns:
Surface Definition

MICHAEL J. O'BRIEN AND CHAD K. MCDANIEL

Intensive, systematic surface collection is a field technique that is relatively new to archaeology, but one that is being applied with increasing frequency (Kohler and Schlanger 1980; Lewarch 1979a; Lewarch and O'Brien 1981a; Miskell and Warren 1979; O'Brien and Lewarch 1979; O'Brien and Lewarch 1981; Raab 1979). Surface artifacts have long been used by archaeologists to find sites and to aid in determining excavation strategies, but it is only in recent years that surface data have been examined in their own right as sources of primary data with which substantive research questions can be meaningfully answered. This theme is expanded throughout this discussion.

A major portion of this chapter reports the results of preliminary analyses of 5 surface collected sites in the project area. These sites were selected from among 37 sites (Figure 12.1) where either total or sampled intensive surface collections were made. These 37 sites were selected for intensive surface collection on the basis of (a) initial indications of period of occupation and (b) location within the project area, in an attempt to gather data for all periods, from all drainage classes, in all geographic subareas of the region (Table 12.1).

The analyses reported are of two types. First, we discuss the general site structure of each of the five sites as revealed by surface data. Then, we move on to an analysis of intrasite patterning at four sites. *General site structure* refers to the density distribution of all artifacts, taken together without regard for artifact class, across the surface of a site. By examining this data, one can determine such things as: (a) the spatial extent of activity and occupational areas; (b) general intensities of artifact deposition; (c) topographic associations of these areas and activities; and (d) degrees and manners in which agricultural and other site formation processes might have contributed to these patterns. *Intrasite patterning* is revealed by examination of the distributions of specific artifact classes. These distributions are examined for correlations (or the absence of correlation) with topography and other artifact classes. Examinations of these patterns of association and

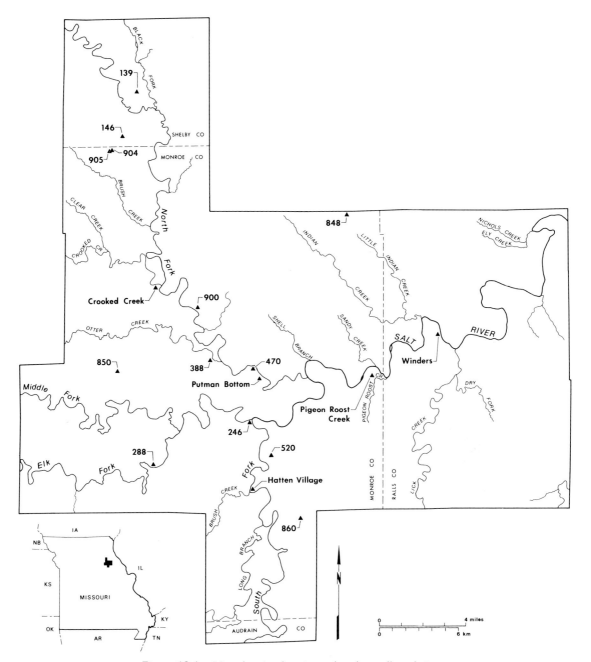

Figure 12.1. Map showing locations of surface-collected sites.

TABLE 12.1.

Environmental Characteristics of Surface-Collected Sites

Site	Subarea	Drainage Class	Elevation (m)
23MN246[a]	C	5	175
23MN288	B	4	189
23MN388	A	5	177
23MN470	C	4	175
23MN520	D	2	201
23MN848	C	1	213
23MN850	B	2	219
23MN860	D	1	226
23MN900	A	4	184
23MN904	A	4	206
23MN905	A	3	207
23SY139	A	5	197
23SY146	A	2	226
Hatten Village	D	5	189
Crooked Creek	C	4	184
Pigeon Roost Creek	C	4	169
Winders	C	4	166
Putman Bottom A	C	4	175
B	C	4	175
C	C	4	174
D	C	4	175
E	C	4	175
F	C	4	174
G	C	4	177
H	C	4	177
I	C	4	180
J	C	4	183
K	C	4	183
L	C	3	189
M	C	3	186
N (West)	C	3	186
O	C	4	186
P	C	4	187
Q	C	4	186
R	C	3	187
S	C	3	186
T	C	3	184

[a] See Figure 12.1 for site locations.

dissociation, occurrence and co-ocurrence, suggest activity-specific, localized assemblages and thus, functionally distinct activity areas. Again at this level, questions of spatial extent, activity intensity, and site formation biases are examined.

Before the presentation of these substantive findings, however, some additional observations on the general nature of surface collection and its implementation and role in the Cannon Project are required. These include (*a*) the role of intensive surface collection in the regional framework of the project; (*b*) a brief review of factors contributing to surface formation; and (*c*) the specific collection techniques used in this study.

SURFACE COLLECTION IN THE REGIONAL ANALYTIC FRAMEWORK

As mentioned in Chapter 2, intensive, controlled surface collection is an integral part of a regional archaeological program. Adequate tests of settlement system hypotheses that provide the general theoretical framework for the Cannon Project require detailed site content data that archaeologists have tended to regard as available only via excavation. Although excavation is essential for solving many archaeological problems, it is expensive and time consuming. Because the Cannon Project was faced with (*a*) limited funding relative to the area encompassed by the project and (*b*) limited time vis-à-vis both funding and the size of the area, intensive systematic surface collection came to play a major role in the overall research design. It served as an alternative to excavation in most of the study area and also increased the efficiency of several of the excavations undertaken.

The surface data thus collected are being used in the analysis of both local (community) and regional (settlement) patterns. In this chapter, as noted, surface data are used to examine the "local" patterning presented by the intrasite distributions of artifact classes and their spatial co-occurence. Chapter 14 extends this examination of local pattern by discussing the relationship between surface artifact density and the subsurface distributions of archaeological features, such as pits, hearths, middens, and houses. In Chapter 16, surface data indications of site content become important in examining relationships among sites in the settlement system through time. Taken together, these various types and levels of analysis indicate the general robustness of surface data and their ability to help solve archaeological problems at the local and regional level.

Despite the general utility of the method in generating data useful in regional research, there are a number of biases both natural and cultural that affect one's ability to detect some levels of patterning in the data. Biases that act upon surface artifact assemblages often can be controlled for in analysis if some understanding of them is gained. The more important processes are discussed in this chapter, along with methods for determining the effects of biasing.

A REVIEW OF SURFACE FORMATION PROCESSES

As has been pointed out elsewhere (Lewarch and O'Brien 1981a), recent work on formation processes that create artifact assemblages on modern surfaces are important for three reasons. First, knowledge of potential biases must be taken into account if one is to use surface-derived data for quantitative research. Second, contemporary recovery contexts contribute toward documenting postdepositional processes that operate on modern surfaces and that created past surfaces. Third, these studies demonstrate the complexity of all formation processes and illustrate problems inherent in understanding archaeological contexts. Given these complexities, a priori assumptions about the research potential of *any* archaeological material are precluded until (*a*) preliminary evaluation demonstrates which processes affect archaeological materials most seriously and (*b*) the degree to which potential biases limit the research potential of archaeological deposits are documented (Dunnell and Dancey n.d.; Lewarch and O'Brien 1981a; Schiffer 1976).

Space does not permit in-depth coverage here of the multitude of natural and cultural processes that together act to form surfaces and affect artifact distributions on those surfaces. We can, however, isolate and evaluate those believed to be the most serious in temperate environments, such as the Cannon Reservoir region (see Lewarch and O'Brien 1981a for an extensive discussion of these processes). Natural processes include (*a*) erosion; (*b*) colluvial and alluvial deposition; (*c*) duration of exposure; and (*d*) degree of slope. Cultural processes include a variety of prehistoric disturbances and modern agriculturally related disturbance.

Natural Processes

Natural processes, which act cyclically and often are difficult to separate analytically, are partitioned here into subtractive versus additive regimes. Subtractive or erosional processes are conditioned by factors such as slope gradient, duration of surface exposure, climate, and vegetation. The most severe factor is slope gradient, the effects of which are self-evident (see Rick 1976).

Vegetation acts for and against the use of intensive surface collection as a data generating strategy. Although it protects and stabilizes surfaces, it also obscures visibility of the ground surface. Natural vegetation in the Cannon Project area consists of broadleaf deciduous trees, low plants, and short grass. The effects of the latter two on visibility can be countered by cutting and plowing, whereas the effect of dense stands of trees on visibility poses problems not tackled by the project. The high frequency of sites in the region allowed exclusion of sites in forested areas from further consideration, without biasing the sample.

Rainfall in the region often is quite heavy and does contribute to surface erosion. The project area is typical of most temperate environments, which are characterized by Strakhov (1967) as having an annual rainfall of 50–150 cm and an erosion rate of 100–240 tons of sediment/km² per year. In some parts of the project area severe sheet erosion and gully formation were noted. Headward advance of gullies into archaeological sites was documented in a few instances and precluded any efforts at surface collection.

Duration of surface exposure can be shortened by the rapid regrowth of grass and bushes over disturbed areas and by the planting of agricultural crops. The most severe problems during exposure occur in moderately steep plowed fields where, due to abnormally heavy rains or drought, newly planted seeds do not germinate to help stabilize the soil. During 1980, Cannon Project crews documented the fact that some archaeological site surfaces in plowed fields were obliterated by torrential rains that followed months of drought.

Additive or depositional processes can result from several forces—most notable in the project area are colluvial and alluvial forces—that can be either long- or short-term. Excellent studies on the effects of alluvial deposition on recovery of surface artifacts include those by Kirkby and Kirkby (1976) and Anderson (n.d.). In the project area the situation is not difficult to generalize. Based on shovel testing in many bottomland and terrace locales, the depth to subsoil rarely exceeds 60 cm; extensive backhoe trenching confirms this generalized model. There are two instances, however, of archaeological deposits extending down several meters. One site, Flowers, is located below Cannon

Dam, where the valley begins to widen out and the natural river flow would have slowed considerably. The other site, Pigeon Roost Creek, is located near the junction of a tributary creek and the Salt River. Alluvial sediments deep within the site probably were deposited during long-term stages of high water in the Salt Valley, when the flow of the tributary was reduced and its sediments were deposited. Thus, the generalized model of little alluvial buildup in the valley must be altered to account for individual deviations.

A more serious process is colluvial deposition, which must be evaluated when one recovers materials from sites at the base of steep slopes. This problem was noted during analysis of material from Winders, a small site located on an alluvial lobe extending from the base of a bluff near the Salt River mainstem. Many items recovered from intensive surface collection of the site were angular pieces of chert derived from glacial till deposits further upslope. Without careful separation of material during analysis, slope wash could have biased the collection severely. Other problems of colluvial deposition connected with Winders are detailed in Chapter 14.

In summary, natural forces that act in concert or in cycles to form and modify surfaces can be quite severe and are cause for concern when one is trying to assess potential biases affecting surface artifact distributions. If, however, one notes in detail the microenvironment of a site, taking into account as many factors as possible, it often is possible at a later date to correlate the biases with uncommon or unexpected anomalies in the artifact pattern. When there is a large enough sample of sites from which to choose, certain sites that potentially contain considerable biasing can be avoided.

Cultural Processes

The most common type of cultural process affecting contemporary surfaces is agricultural tillage. There is a growing literature on this subject (Dancey 1974; Lewarch 1979b; Lewarch and O'Brien 1981a, b; Redman and Watson 1970; Roper 1976; Talmage and Chesler 1977; Trubowitz 1978), and only a brief summary will be presented here. Lewarch and O'Brien (1981a) state that "mechanical tillage can be viewed as a large-scale formation process that is unique to modern surfaces but which is related by laws of physics to occupational disturbance" (p. 308).

Given that large portions of the archaeological record have been subjected to tillage, it becomes necessary to understand the effects of the process on various-sized objects. Five factors that must be considered when using plow zone archaeological materials include (*a*) horizontal displacement; (*b*) vertical displacement; (*c*) changes in class frequency after tillage; (*d*) alteration of form and content of features; and (*e*) changes in condition and preservation of artifact assemblages (Lewarch and O'Brien 1981a, b). Points *a–c* are discussed in this chapter; points *d* and *e* are discussed in Chapter 14.

Displacement within aggregate artifact patterns was tested by Cannon personnel in a controlled experiment where all variables except duration and direction of tillage were held constant (Lewarch 1979b; Lewarch and O'Brien 1981b). Results (summarized in Lewarch and O'Brien 1981a:309) "indicated little transverse displacement and variable amounts of longitudinal displacement, influences by size of artifact, duration of tillage, and population size of pattern." Thus, magnitude of lateral displacement appears to be less of a problem than has been assumed by many archaeologists. Studies by other investigators (e.g., Roper 1976; Trubowitz 1978), have led to similar conclusions. Longitudinal displacement appears to be object-size related: The larger the object the more chance there is that it will be dragged a significant distance from its pretillage spot.

Unlike lateral and longitudinal displacement, vertical movement and resulting segregation of artifacts by size is a cumulative directional process (Lewarch and O'Brien 1981a:310). There is an asymptotic relationship between number of cultivations and change in class frequencies: the greater the number of machine passes, the smaller the change. However, large artifacts *are* overrepresented in surface assemblages relative to total plow zone populations. Based on various statistical models for predicting plow zone artifact frequencies (Ammerman and Feldman 1978; Lewarch and O'Brien 1981b; Trubowitz 1978), one can take this and other factors into account when analyzing surface artifact class frequencies. This should not,

however, replace more experimentation to refine the models.

Another cultural factor that conditions surface assemblages is density of occupation, and concurrently, reoccupation. Many sites in midwestern river valleys were occupied, either seasonally or continually, for thousands of years. In areas where soil deposition occurs rapidly, discrete sealed surfaces may date to very short temporal periods. Where reoccupation of the same area occurs, the layers become superimposed through time. However, in the Cannon Project region, the majority of sites occur in areas where deposition rates are slow, and as a result, there is considerable mixing of temporally distinct deposits. Because these reoccupations do not occur directly over spots of previous occupations, there is a tendency for archaeological sites to accrete through time, with portions of more recent occupations covering portions of previous ones.

Kirkby and Kirkby (1976) developed a model of upward mixing of cultural material and noted that many early sites will be located by surface survey only if they were reoccupied. This mixing is attributed to the building and rebuilding of structures, the excavating of pits, and other types of human disturbance of earlier deposits. These same types of disturbances can affect contemporary debris scatters, as can areal cleaning (trash removal) and trampling.

The final cultural factor considered here is amateur surface collecting. Collectors generally favor projectile points and point parts, items used by archaeologists to assign sites to temporal periods. As Lewarch and O'Brien (1981a:317) point out, this "problem is one of uncontrolled, relatively unknown systematic bias." Several archaeologists (e.g. House and Schiffer 1975; Morse 1973) suggest that one can mitigate these effects to some degree by talking to local collectors to identify classes of artifacts that came from certain sites.

In summary, cultural processes contribute at least as much bias to archaeological surface exposures as do natural processes. Some of these biases, especially those caused by agriculturally related activities, can be controlled to a certain extent by reference to preliminary models and through experimentation within various types of particulate media. Problems like those caused by multiple, overlapping components can be alleviated through locational information on diagnostic artifacts (i.e., where on a site particular diagnostic pieces occur) and through careful analysis of variability in the spatial distribution of other artifact classes.

The intent of this section is not to paint a bleak picture of the utility of surface collection as a regional data-generating method. On the contrary, intensive surface collection has proven to be an effective, cost-efficient means of sampling sites across a region. However, it is important to point out biases that affect interpretation and to note that even after every analytical tool has been exhausted, one could still fail to demonstrate unbiased pattern at some scale of analysis. As Lewarch and O'Brien (1981a:318) note, these failures are as instructive as other kinds of results since they point out the limitations of surface assemblages for solving certain kinds of archaeological problems. This leads to a more informed decision about how best to deal with the resource base.

The following section outlines the collection techniques we employed to maximize material recovery. Strategies were based on consideration of factors mentioned previously, including local topography, percentage of ground visibility, and artifact density.

COLLECTION TECHNIQUES

Two general strategies organized surface collecting procedures: One treated a preconceived notion of a site as the sampling unit; the other utilized unbounded space as the sampling unit. The latter method, variously termed *siteless survey* (Dunnell and Dancey n.d.), *nonsite survey* (Thomas 1975), or *zonal survey*, aids in defining distributions of artifacts between high density clusters (sites) that normally would go unrecorded (Lewarch and O'Brien 1981a). This approach was used to survey a 43.1-ha portion of a large river bottom on the North Fork (discussed in the following section). On the basis of spatial contiguity of artifacts shown on large-scale distribution maps, artifact concentrations were consolidated into 20 cases.

The former strategy, which uses a previously defined cluster of artifacts as the collection area, was the basis for the collection at all other sites. Specific recovery techniques were tailored to fit the size and density of the site in question. In some cases, the total surface of a site was collected, whereas in others, the site surface was sampled at a 50% rate. Two basic collection techniques were used: *block provenience* and *point provenience*.

The former entails establishing a series of systematically arranged 2 by 2-m squares in which all materials are collected. This technique is best suited to large sites with dense scatters of surface artifacts (Miskell and Warren 1979:54). Two-by-two-meter blocks are located within hectare designations, which blanket the site to be collected. The first hectare usually is placed in the extreme southwestern portion of the site, and others are placed as needed. Datum points lie in the southwestern corner of each hectare, and all collection-square proveniences are labeled by distances north and east of these points. Where sites are sampled at a 50% rate, sample squares are arranged in a systematic, checkerboard pattern.

The point provenience technique plots artifacts individually and is most suitable on small sites with sparse surface debris. Collectors move across a site searching 1-m-wide corridors for cultural material, which they flag with surveyor pins. A transit is used to plot the distance and bearing of each item from datum, and specimens are bagged and labeled accordingly.

Most surface collections were made in cultivated fields with uniform surface visibility. Other sites were plowed prior to collection to ensure a high degree of intersite comparability.

ANALYSIS OF SURFACE DATA

As noted in the introduction to this chapter, the results of analysis of surface data from five sites in the project area are divided into: (*a*) discussion of general site structure and (*b*) intrasite analysis. By focusing on a few sites, attention can be directed toward differences and similarities among patterns of artifact distribution as these relate to the overall structure of the sites and proposed functional areas within them.

Sites included here are restricted to bottomland and lower terrace locales. Also, only sites dating to the Middle and Late Woodland periods are discussed, although in the case of Pigeon Roost Creek, there are sealed, older deposits present. This results in a limited assessment of differences in site structure for different periods but facilitates in a restricted space the observation of variability in size and complexity of sites in the Cannon Reservoir region.

Analysis of General Site Structure

Analysis of the general site structure of five sites is discussed here; selection was made partly on completeness of analysis and partly on level of internal complexity. It will be demonstrated that the surface collection method, employing a variety of field and analytical techniques, is applicable to large, structurally complex sites as well as to small, low-density ones. The size of the sites in the sample ranges from approximately 10 ha to less than 1 ha. Functional interpretation of sites in the sample indicates that both residential and procurement–processing (logistical) sites are represented.

Interpretation of general site structure is based on visual assessment of total artifact density by means of density gradient maps. Except for the map of Hatten Village, all surface artifact density maps were produced by the same technique. We derived density gradients (levels) by taking the collection unit with the highest artifact density at each site and scaling the frequencies between 1 and that highest value into quarters. Along with the four density classes, each map shows noncollected squares as well as collected squares that contained no material. For example, if the highest frequency in a collection unit at site A is 80, then density levels would be 1–20, 21–40, 41–60, and 61–80. All units at that site containing frequencies within each range would be identified similarly. In the discussion, numbers in parentheses following a density level—for example, level 4 (16–20)—refer to the range in artifact frequency per 2-m^2 unit that falls within that particular density level.

Density gradients for each site are different, so levels for each site are marked on each general artifact density map. Because of the vast differences

in artifact density from site to site, a single schema masks important intrasite variation. The map for Hatten Village has density levels of 1–5, 6–25, 26–50, and 51+ artifacts per unit. These intervals were chosen because of the tremendous variation in density from area to area on the site. It also should be noted that for visual clarity, artifacts from sites G and T in Putman Bottom, which were collected by point provenience, have been given aggregate proveniences.

Hatten Village

Hatten Village was selected for intensive surface collection because its large size (98,000 m^2 of surface material scatter) and position on the first terrace above South Fork indicated a residential site. Temporally diagnostic projectile points collected during survey (1959) and resurvey (1978) indicated that the site dated to the Middle and Late Woodland periods. Therefore, it could be integrated with the chronology for the region and was seen as a likely source of data to test one segment of the settlement–system model: Late Woodland residential sites are located on bottomland terraces (Chapter 5).

Site size precluded a 100% collection strategy, so total collections were planned in areas that initially were believed to contain the densest concentrations of lithic material (Ha 1–4, the eastern half of Ha 7, and the east-central portion of Ha 8 [Figure 12.2]). Areas between concentrations were collected in a 50% "checkerboard" fashion.[1] During analysis, three distinct areas of concentration were noted (Figure 12.3). The first is located in the northern portion of Ha 1 and extends west into Ha 2. The second concentration occurs in Ha 10, on the west-facing slope of a high terrace. Squares surrounding this cluster show low densities of artifacts and gradually turn sterile to the northeast and southeast. The largest concentration is in the southern portion of the site (Ha 8 and 9), where artifact frequencies up to 201 per unit occur. Quantities of pottery and other temporally diagnostic artifacts were recovered in this area.

---

[1]In Figure 12.3 density values for noncollected units were interpolated by averaging the values of adjacent squares within the bounds of each hectare.

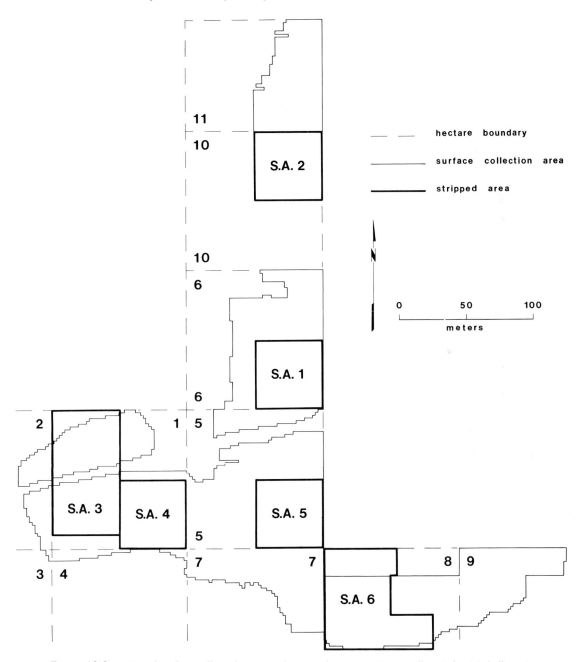

Figure 12.2. Map of surface-collected areas and stripped areas at Hatten Village (after Miskell 1979).

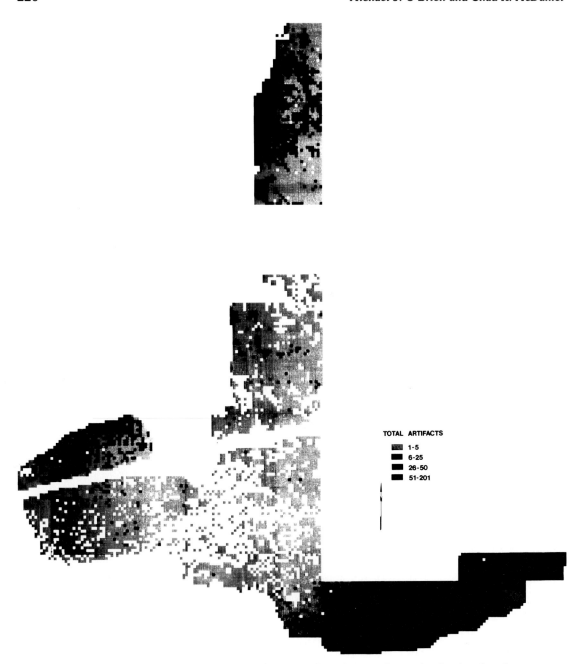

Figure 12.3. General site structure map of Hatten Village showing density levels of total artifacts.

The densest units are in the southeastern corner of the collection area (Ha 9), where densities of 51+ artifacts per unit (density level 4) occur in a large contiguous area. Density level 3 (26–50) units outline this area, grading into units at density level 2 (6–25), which continue westward throughout Ha 8. Units at density level 3 are common in Ha 8, usually occurring in contiguous blocks of 2–20+ units. As discussed in Chapters 13 and 14, this area (SA 6 in Figure 12.2) contained 36 subsurface features. Analysis indicates Ha 8 and 9 reflect one or more residential complexes, with the largest number of subsurface features probably still to be located in Ha 9, the unexcavated portion of the high density concentration.

The concentration in the western portion of the site is similar in structure to the one just described, but artifact density is lower. Density level 3 units occur sporadically throughout the area, usually surrounded by density level 2 units. Mechanical removal of topsoil in the northern half of SA 3 (Figure 12.2) revealed numerous pits, suggesting that the area had served as a residential site during some portion of the Woodland period. The subsurface data from this area are not yet analyzed.

The highest density level area in the northern portion of the collected area is confined to several units along the western edge of Ha 11, although density level 3 units occur sporadically in the northern quarter of Ha 10. Connecting these units is an area with widespread occurrence of density level 2 (6–25) units. Mechanical removal of topsoil in the collected portion of Ha 10 (SA 2 in Figure 12.2) revealed a series of pits clustered in the northwestern corner. Based on preliminary analysis of the pottery, the pits date to the latter portion of the Middle Woodland and early portion of the Late Woodland periods.

Density level 2 units occur in Ha 6, possibly as a result of a localized activity area. Plow zone removal in the southeastern corner of the hectare (SA 1 in Figure 12.2) revealed no pits or other subsurface features.

In summary, the density gradient map reveals the presence of at least three spatially discrete areas of high artifact density, each containing clusters of subsurface pits. Stripped low density areas (SA 1, 4, 5 and the southern half of SA 3) revealed no

subsurface features. From this it is inferred that the density distribution reflects cultural patterning that has been somewhat blurred by agricultural activity but mainly undisturbed by natural processes. Analysis shows that Hatten Village should not be viewed as a single site but rather as a large, bottomland-terrace locale over which prehistoric activities occurred and the density distributions of related artifacts can be surveyed. This notion of "nonsite" survey will be explored later in this section.

Pigeon Roost Creek

Pigeon Roost Creek is located on a bottomland terrace at the base of a high bluff, near the confluence of a small tributary with the Salt River. The site was selected for intensive surface collection because of its proximity to a perennial spring and marsh, the presence of Late Woodland artifacts on the surface, and the occurrence of fire-cracked rock

TOTAL ARTIFACTS

▦ 1–12
▥ 13–24
▪ 25–37
■ 38–50

Figure 12.4.   General site structure map of Pigeon Roost Creek showing density levels of total artifacts.

and pottery in shovel tests placed in the site. Due to the diversity of artifact classes noted during initial survey, it was assumed that the site served a residential function. Subsequent excavation revealed cultural material-bearing strata extending down to 3.5 m and dating from the Dalton–Early Archaic through Late Woodland periods.

Areas of highest artifact density occur on a line paralleling the bluff and then running eastward over a low rise just south of the marsh. Artifact frequencies within this linear concentration run as high as 50 per unit (Figure 12.4). Units at density levels 3 (25–37) and 2 (13–24) surround level 4 (38–50) units, gradually grading into level 1 units to the south and east.

Based on present knowledge of the site, including its considerable depth and complexity, it is rea-

sonable to assume that the general patterning suggested by the surface artifact distribution reflects only later occupations of the site, where numerous Late Woodland pits and an extensive limestone block "platform" were found within 40–50 cm of the surface. It is unknown whether or not extensive subsurface remains occur in the southern portion of the site.

The formation process that perhaps contributed the greatest bias to the surface collection is deposition of colluvial material. The slope above the site is covered with chert chunks that, although offering an unlimited lithic resource to prehistoric inhabitants, created problems during the collection and analysis. Unless a piece of lithic material definitely could be described as the result of human modification, or unless it showed signs of prepared flake

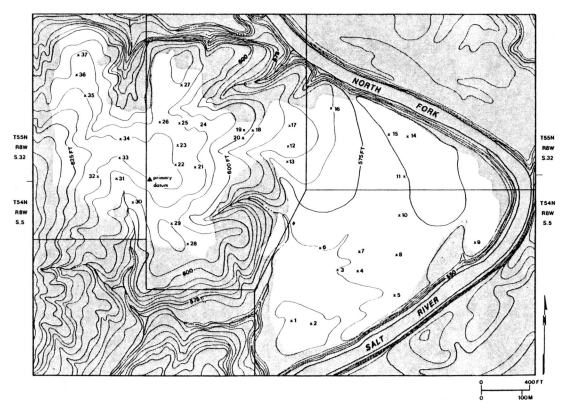

Figure 12.5. Map of the Putman Bottom locality, showing collection stations (1–37) and extent of collection area (unshaded area) (from Warren and Miskell 1981).

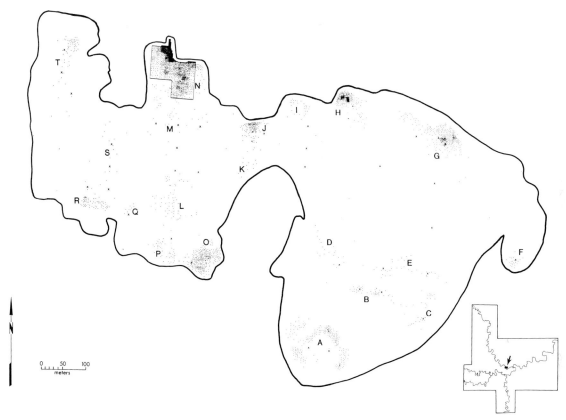

Figure 12.6.   Map of artifact scatter in Putman Bottom. Each dot represents four artifacts, letters denote sites, and x signifies transit station (after Warren and Miskell 1981).

removal, it was not considered cultural material during analysis. This may have resulted in an underrepresentation of cores.

The Putman Bottom Locality

Surface collection of a 43.1-ha area known locally as "Putman Bottom" was the most ambitious such endeavor undertaken by the Cannon Project. The area is a level to moderately sloping bottomland terrace and flood plain bench located along North Fork, in the central portion of the project area (Figure 12.5). The following discussion is adapted from Warren and Miskell (1981).

The locality occupies a large slipoff slope inside a river meander and was heavily forested during the early nineteenth century. The area had been plowed during 1978, and a sparse cover of young weedy regrowth had sprouted just prior to collection in the spring of 1979. Microerosion, the process of greatest concern, seemed minimal and appeared to have had a uniform influence on the area sampled. Sheet erosion was evident in three areas [sloping terrace face near Stations 16–19; ravines near Stations 13 and 27 (Figure 12.5)] and probably caused some downslope movement of artifacts.

The primary objective of the surface collection was to generate data to test one aspect of the settlement–subsistence model. The implication is that lowland settings, which contain varied and dispersed natural resources, are characterized by functionally diverse archaeological assemblages. The ecological dimensions of patch composition

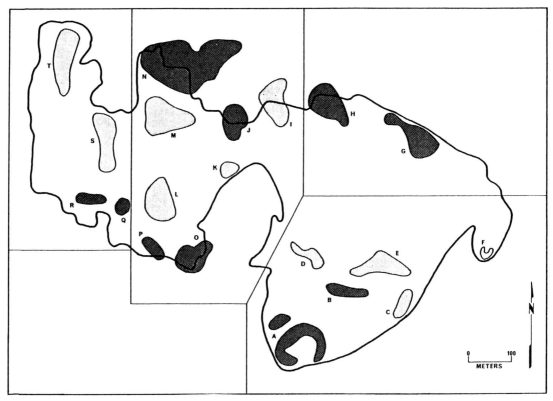

Figure 12.7.   Locations of sites in Putman Bottom, dichotomized on the basis of artifact class patterning, size grade patterning, and mean surface artifact density (from Warren and Miskell 1981). (Dense sites dominated by small unretouched tertiary flakes, sharpening flakes, and trimming flakes, indicated by ▨. Sparse sites dominated by large retouched chunks, cores, and secondary and tertiary flakes indicated by ▧.)

and arrangement imply that residential and logistical sites both occur in bottomlands: The former in situations that maximize domestic consideration and the latter in a variety of contexts conditioned by the distribution of targeted resources (Chapters 2 and 5).

To test this hypothesis, the technological variability in lithic assemblages from sites in Putman Bottom was examined. The data base consists of a series of artifact samples collected from the surface of 20 sites using the *siteless survey* or *nonsite* approach, which utilizes space rather than a single cluster of artifacts as the sampling unit. As stated previously, this method aids in defining distributions of artifacts between high density clusters (i.e.,

between sites) that normally would go unrecorded (Lewarch and O'Brien 1981a,b).

Surface collection of a 43.1-ha area yielded 15,969 artifacts. Distributions of these objects indicate that concentrations vary widely in size, density, and location (Figure 12.6). For the purposes of comparative analysis, artifact concentrations were consolidated into 20 cases on the basis of the spatial contiguity of artifacts as shown on large-scale distribution maps.

In the course of the project, different kinds of technological patterns were recognized among sites and were evaluated in terms of temporal, spatial, and surface magnitude variables to derive an empirical hypothesis that explained observed associations. Results indicate that two kinds of sites are represented in Putman Bottom: (*a*) *residential sites,* which have high artifact densities indicative of intensive and/or recurrent occupations and artifact assemblages that represent light domestic activities; and (*b*) *procurement–processing sites,* which have low artifact densities indicative of infrequent and/or temporary utilization and artifact assemblages that represent resource extraction and/ or heavy processing activities (Figure 12.7; Chapter 16). These findings are consistent with the expectations of the settlement model: That functional diversity is high among sites in Prairie Peninsula bottomlands containing varied and dispersed resources and that settlement locations in narrow, banded environments are conditioned as much by domestic requirements as by strategic resource needs (Warren and Miskell 1981).

In the following analysis, sites G, N, and T are examined in terms of general site structure. The first two are hypothesized residential sites, and the latter is an hypothesized procurement–processing site. Sites N and T are located on upland terraces in the northwestern corner of the collected area (Figure 12.7); site G is located on a bottomland terrace in the northeastern corner of the area. Sites G and T were collected by point provenience, but for our discussion the point data have been converted into aggregate provenience. Site N (referred to hereafter as the *West site*) was collected by aggregate provenience, although a few artifacts that fell outside the grid were collected by point provenience (Figure 12.6). These few points are disregarded in this analysis. Also excluded from this discussion is the southern projection of the gridded area (Figure 12.6). Previous analysis has shown that exclusion of this area does not seriously affect the overall distribution.

Site G

Site G is represented by a fairly dense scatter of lithic material over a slight rise in the bottomland. A total of 1567 pieces of lithic debris was collected, including one Late Woodland and one possible Middle Archaic projectile point. The area of highest artifact density is on the east end; artifact frequency and density decreases to the west and northwest (Figure 12.8). Six units in the eastern half of the site

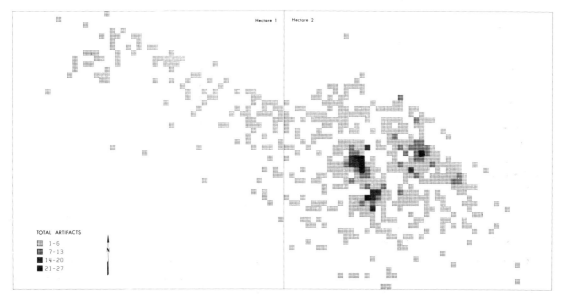

Figure 12.8. General site structure map of Putman Bottom site G showing density levels of total artifacts (point provenience data grouped spatially into aggregate provenience data in 2 ha).

are at level 4 density (21–27), with adjacent units at level 3 density (14–20). All units in the western half are at level 1 density (1–6). It is apparent that plowing contributed to some of the pattern; the direction of plowing was noted as being northwest–southeast over the scatter.

Site T

Site T is represented by a sparse surface scatter of 247 artifacts spread over approximately 4000 m² of an upland terrace. A single Late Woodland projectile point was the only diagnostic artifact recovered. The area of the site with the highest artifact density is in the northern half, with density and frequency trailing off to the south (Figure 12.9). Only four units on the site contain more than four artifacts (density level 4), and the vast majority contain only one artifact. The direction of plowing was north–south in this corner of the collection area, and it undoubtedly contributed to the artifact pattern.

West

West consists of a dense concentration of lithic material located on a high terrace above Putman Bottom. Only the western portion of the site was collected because of dense tree cover to the east. The areas of high artifact density border the western edge of the wooded area and continue into it (Figure 12.10). Three contiguous squares at the southwestern edge of the concentration are at density level 4 (57–76) and are surrounded by units at density level 3 (38–56). This high density area contained half the subsurface features identified at the site (Chapter 14). Isolated density level 2 units occur sporadically throughout the collected area, and form one small cluster in the extreme northeastern corner. The site was plowed north–south, which probably pulled some material from the high density area.

Intrasite Analysis: The Spatial Distribution of Technological Classes

In this section we will examine the spatial distributions of technological artifact classes and groups of classes from Pigeon Roost Creek and the three sites in Putman Bottom. Omitted from discussion is Hatten Village since its size and complexity preclude its inclusion in this analysis.

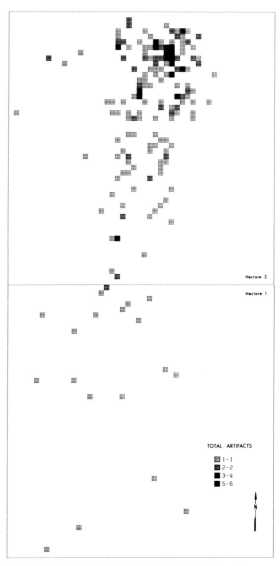

Figure 12.9. General site structure map of Putman Bottom site T showing density levels of total artifacts (point provenience data grouped spatially into aggregate provenience data in 2 ha).

One hypothesis guiding this analysis is that concentrations of artifact classes on a site result from specific functions that were carried out in spatially discrete areas. Functions include storage, cooking, food processing, tool manufacture, tool maintenance, and various cutting–scraping tasks. Classes

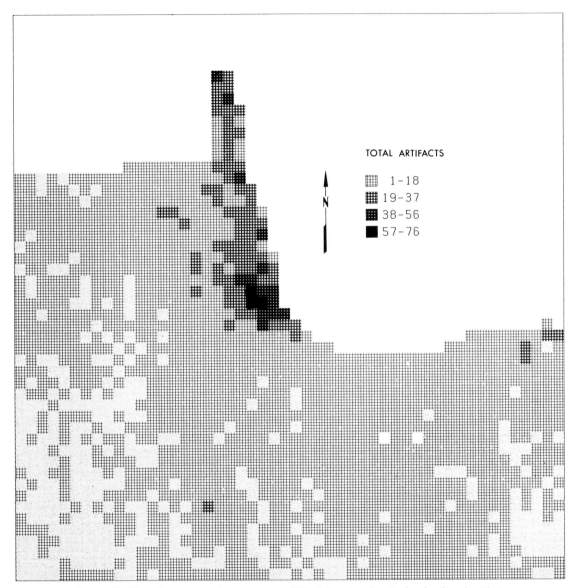

Figure 12.10.   General site structure map of West showing density levels of total artifacts.

associated with the activities are listed in the following discussion.

Because of space limitations, many technological classes have been combined into major class groups. Flake-based class groups include (*a*) cores, core rejuvenation flakes, core shatter, and primary and secondary decortication flakes; (*b*) tertiary flakes–chunks; and (*c*) trimming–sharpening flakes.

The first class group is composed of byproducts of initial lithic reduction; distribution of elements in this group should indicate areas of tool manufacture. The second class group is composed of by-products of secondary lithic reduction and final products of manufacture. The distribution of these elements may add to the patterning suggested by the distribution of initial reduction elements and/or indicate separate areas for final flake production. The third class group contains trimming–sharpening flakes, indicative of tool-maintenance activities.

To separate material associated solely with lithic reduction and tool maintenance from that used for various functional purposes, all retouched pieces, regardless of technological class, are plotted together; thus, for the flake classes just discussed, only unretouched artifacts are included.

Other class groups discussed include chipped formed artifacts (projectile points, bifaces, drills, and unifacial scrapers); ceramics; and ground stone.

Chipped formed artifacts can indicate a variety of functions, including hide preparation, cambium stripping, and butchering. Because use-wear analysis of artifacts in this general class has not been completed, all chipped formed artifacts have been aggregated. Ceramics are related to several functions, the major two being cooking and storage. Ground stone items also can be used for a variety of tasks, including the preparation of plant for consumption.

Plots of various class groups and all retouched flakes are presented in this section to facilitate the observation of distributions and the identification of concentrations of class material. Totals of artifact frequencies by technological and size class are presented in tables. The distribution maps follow the format used for the general structure maps: Four density levels are shown that are each one-fourth of the maximum frequency per unit of a class group. The exceptions are instances where the maximum frequency of a class is less than four, and the number of density levels drops accordingly (i.e., where the maximum frequency is two, the number of density levels is two). As before, numbers in parentheses following a density level des-

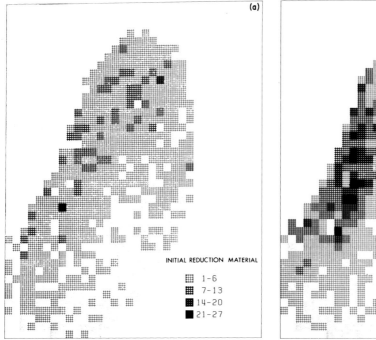

INITIAL REDUCTION MATERIAL

▦ 1-6
▦ 7-13
▦ 14-20
■ 21-27

TERTIARY FLAKES–CHUNKS

▦ 1-8
▦ 9-16
▦ 17-24
■ 25-33

Figure 12.11. Density gradient maps for class groups at Pigeon Roost Creek: (a) initial reduction material, (b) tertiary flakes–chunks.

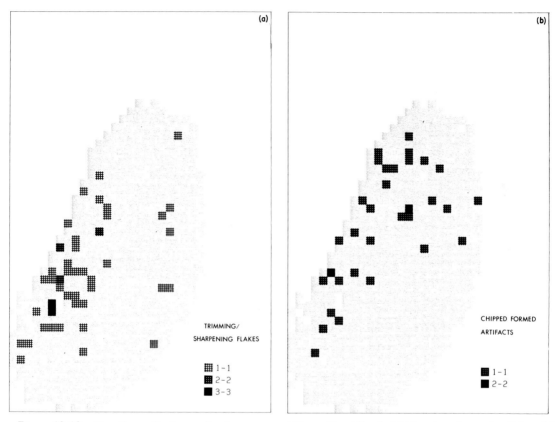

Figure 12.12. Density gradient maps for class groups at Pigeon Roost Creek: (a) trimming–sharpening flakes, (b) chipped formed artifacts.

ignation refer to the range in frequency of artifacts per 2-m² unit that falls in that particular density level. With these considerations in mind, attention can be focused on the distributions of classes at the four sites.

Pigeon Roost Creek

The distributions of most class groups at Pigeon Roost Creek generally reflect the pattern suggested by the total surface artifact distribution map (Figure 12.4). Material occurs most frequently along the western edge of the site (along the bluff base) and extends eastward across the northernmost third of the site.

Units with high frequencies of cores and reduction flakes are scattered in fairly random fashion along this line and gradually decrease in number to the south and east (Figure 12.11). A single density level 4 unit (21–27) occurs in the west-central portion of the site; level 2 (7–13) units occur along the bluff base, with a large cluster of units located in the northern quarter of the site. This distribution suggests that core preparation and initial-stage lithic reduction work were done over large portions of the site.

The distribution of tertiary flakes and chunks (Figure 12.11) is similar to the distribution of initial reduction material. Again, the densest units occur along the bluff base, with a concentration of level 4 (25–33) squares being located in the northern portion of the site and another concentration in the west-central part of the site.

Trimming–sharpening flakes show a definite shift in distribution from that of the previously mentioned class groups (Figure 12.12). Although the general trend is similar, the area in the northern part of the site that contains dense concentrations of lithic reduction-related material contains almost no tool-resharpening material. The densest units occur in the southern third of the site (level 3 = 3 artifacts/unit), with scattered occurrences to the north and east.

Projectile points, bifaces, and scrapers (shown as a composite in Figure 12.12) occur sporadically over the northern and western parts of the site but never in any clear concentrations. However, ceramics (Figure 12.13) show a remarkably restricted distribution, being confined mainly to the northern third of the site. A distinct concentration of sherds occurs in the same high density area defined by one concentration of tertiary

flakes–chunks. Ground stone also exhibits a fairly restricted distribution, occurring only in the northern half of the site (Figure 12.13). Four of six ground stone artifacts came from a 100-m^2 area in the northwestern corner of the collection area.

Artifacts exhibiting retouch occur over much of the site (Figure 12.14). Although the highest frequencies are along the bluff base, the distribution within this area is more or less continuous. Three of the four density level 4 units (12–15) occur in and around the proposed food-processing–cooking area and are surrounded by density level 3 (8–11) and density level 2 (4–7) squares. This suggests (*a*) that many retouched pieces were used in food preparation and/or (*b*) that other household tasks were done in the same area as food preparation.

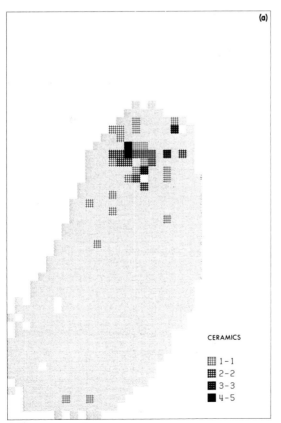

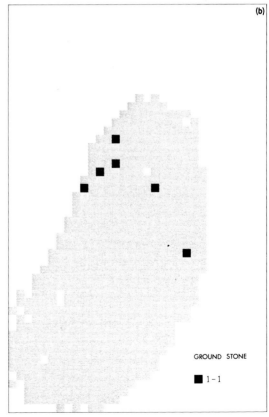

Figure 12.13. Density gradient maps for class groups at Pigeon Roost Creek: (a) ceramics, (b) ground stone.

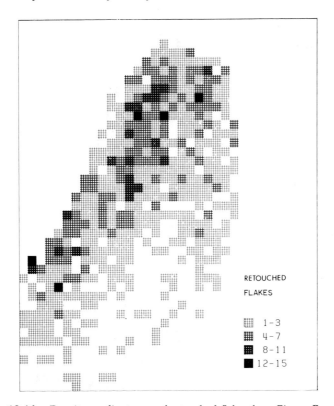

Figure 12.14.   Density gradient map of retouched flakes from Pigeon Roost Creek.

Examination of class frequencies (Table 12.2) and density distributions allows certain intrasite functional inferences to be drawn. First, the occurrence of ceramics and ground stone, usually assumed to be female-related activities, in the northern portion of the site suggests that food processing and storage were conducted in that area during the latest occupation of the site [Late Woodland Perry phase (Chapter 7)]. Inspection of the distribution indicates there may have been discrete areas in which each activity was conducted: Ground stone artifacts occur on the periphery of, but not within, the ceramic concentration. Food processing possibly was carried out in these peripheral areas, and the food was then cooked or stored in the area of high ceramic density.

Trimming–sharpening flakes, by-products of tool edge rejuvenation, occur mainly to the south of the ceramic and ground stone material. These

artifacts, usually associated with male-related activities, do not occur in dense concentrations but instead are dispersed along the base of the bluff. The nonoverlapping distributions of these flakes and ceramics–ground stone argues for sexual division of labor at Pigeon Roost Creek.

The distribution of retouched artifacts indicates that these items were used for a wide variety of functions, many of which appear to have taken place over the northern and western portions of the site. It is reasonable to assume that when retouched members of individual technological and functional classes are plotted, the patterning will become more clear.

In summary, the surface of Pigeon Roost Creek contains high frequencies of items associated with a habitation site: retouched pieces of various classes, ceramics, ground stone, bifaces, projectile points, and unifacial scrapers (Table 12.2). The

TABLE 12.2.

Frequencies of Artifacts by Technological Class and Size Class at Pigeon Roost Creek

Technological class	Size class			Total per class
	1	2	3	
Cores	6	0	0	6
Retouched cores	8	0	0	8
Heat-treated retouched cores	1	0	0	1
Core rejuvenation flakes	2	2	0	4
Retouched core rejuvenation flakes	12	1	0	13
Heat-treated retouched core rejuvenation flakes	1	0	0	1
Heat-treated retouched shatter	0	1	0	1
Primary decortication flakes	1	1	2	4
Heat-treated primary decortication flakes	1	1	0	2
Secondary decortication flakes	148	699	356	1203
Retouched secondary decortication flakes	80	123	11	214
Heat-treated secondary decortication flakes	19	99	74	192
Heat-treated retouched secondary decortication flakes	13	44	5	62
Tertiary chunks	77	472	425	974
Retouched tertiary chunks	49	87	21	157
Heat-treated tertiary chunks	11	69	60	140
Heat-treated retouched tertiary chunks	9	47	7	63
Tertiary flakes	25	670	1365	2060
Retouched tertiary flakes	43	329	140	512
Heat-treated tertiary flakes	5	203	465	673
Heat-treated retouched tertiary flakes	4	179	70	253
Trimming flakes	1	2	7	10
Heat-treated trimming flakes	0	7	9	16
Heat-treated retouched trimming flakes	0	1	1	2
Sharpening flakes	0	8	13	21
Retouched sharpening flakes	0	4	3	7
Heat-treated sharpening flakes	0	1	3	4
Heat-treated retouched sharpening flakes	0	1	1	2
Projectile points (including fragments)	5	4	0	9
Bifaces (including fragments)	12	9	0	21
Drills	1	1	0	2
Formed scrapers	2	0	0	2
Ceramics	42	18	2	62
Unformed ground stone	1	0	0	1
Miscellaneous unformed ground stone	1	1	0	2
Formed ground stone	3	0	0	3
Total number of artifacts	583	3084	3040	6707

composite and individual class distributions indicate occupation was concentrated along the western and northern end of the collected area. Cooking and food preparation were carried out in the area just south of the spring, tool maintenance was restricted to an area south of the food preparation area, and tool production occurred in several areas of the site.

West

The distribution of class groups in Ha 1 at West reflects the pattern seen in the total surface artifact map (Figure 12.10): The majority of highest density level units occurs in the upper central portion of the site, just west of the wooded, uncollected area. One problem in interpreting class distributions at

West is the tremendous weighting of frequencies toward the high density area of the site, which creates large low density areas to the west and south and masks low density concentrations in parts of the high density area that were not used intensively or recurrently. We will correct for these

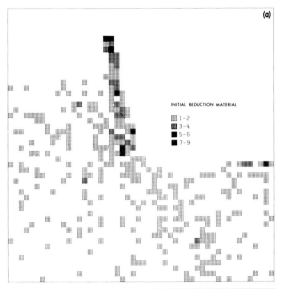

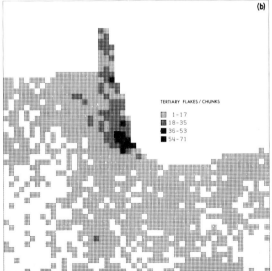

Figure 12.15. Density gradient maps for class groups at West: (a) initial lithic reduction material, (b) tertiary flakes–chunks.

problems in future analysis by splitting the site and treating the high and low density areas separately.

Initial lithic reduction classes occur rather uniformly across the hectare (Figure 12.15), suggesting that the distribution of this class group is not biased greatly by the disproportional representation of material within and outside the high density area. This representation indicates that initial stages of lithic reduction were carried out in several areas of the site, although most intensively in the north and south ends of the dense area. The concentration of density level 4 (7–9) and 3 (5–6) units in the south end of the high density area is directly over four features containing large quantities of lithic material (Chapter 14).

The distribution of tertiary flakes–chunks (Figure 12.15) shows a dense concentration of pieces occurring in a nine-unit area at the south end of the central dense area of the site. Units within this concentration contain between 36 and 71 pieces. A few density level 2 (18–35) units occur just west of the mean concentration, and one unit occurs well south of the main site area. These isolated concentrations may be chance occurrences or they may indicate subsidiary activity areas.

Trimming–sharpening flakes exhibit a ubiquitous distribution (Figure 12.16), occurring over many portions of the site in clusters of units containing one–three pieces. A single density level 4 unit (10–13) is at the southern end of the main site area, along with an adjacent density level 2 unit (4–6). As discussed in Chapter 14, subsurface features directly under this concentration contained high frequencies of bifaces and trimming–sharpening flakes.

Chipped formed artifacts, ceramics, and ground stone occur sporadically over most areas of the collected zone but in no particular concentrations (distributions of chipped formed artifacts and ground stone are shown in Figures 12.16 and 12.17, respectively). The most important information imparted by these distributions is that they are not restricted to the densest area of the site; for each class group, frequencies are higher outside than inside the main site area.

Retouched flakes occur with considerable frequency over most of the collected area (Figure 12.17). Importantly, concentrations occur away

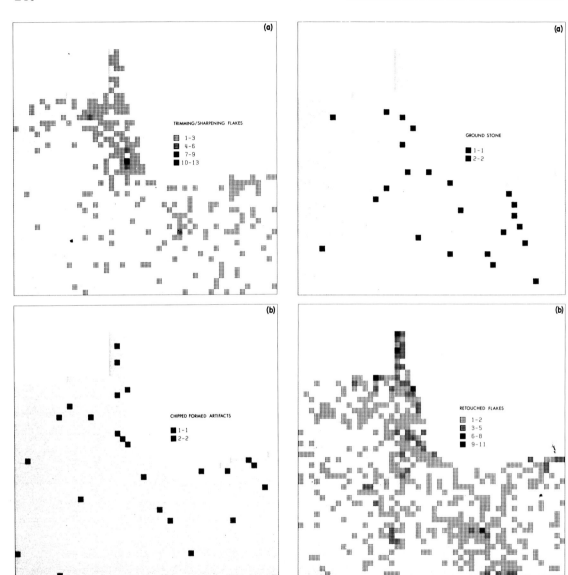

Figure 12.16. Density gradient maps for class groups at West: (a) trimming–sharpening flakes, (b) chipped formed artifacts.

Figure 12.17. Density gradient maps for class groups at West: (a) ground stone, (b) retouched flakes.

from the dense part of the site, with several sets of contiguous units falling in density levels 3 (6–8) and 2 (3–5). Within the central portion of the site, the densest concentration of retouched flakes is located in the northern area, as opposed to the heaviest concentrations of lithic reduction and

maintenance material, which occur in the southern part.

In summary, the collective frequencies (Table 12.3) and density distributions of lithic and ceramic classes at West are not as patterned as those at Pigeon Roost Creek. The one class group that

TABLE 12.3.

Frequencies of Artifacts by Technological Class and Size Class at West

Technological class	Size Class				Total per class
	1	2	3	4	
Cores	25	0	0	0	25
Retouched cores	5	0	0	0	5
Heat-treated cores	8	0	0	0	8
Core rejuvenation flakes	3	1	0	0	4
Retouched core rejuvenation flakes	5	0	0	0	5
Heat-treated core rejuvenation flakes	1	0	0	0	1
Core shatter	2	0	0	0	2
Retouched shatter	1	0	0	0	1
Heat-treated shatter	1	0	0	0	1
Primary decortication flakes	4	5	5	0	14
Retouched primary decortication flakes	1	0	0	0	1
Heat-treated primary decortication flakes	0	0	2	0	2
Secondary decortication flakes	68	104	123	44	339
Retouched secondary decortication flakes	32	15	2	1	50
Heat-treated secondary decortication flakes	10	29	36	10	85
Heat-treated retouched secondary decortication flakes	12	7	0	0	19
Tertiary chunks	29	98	244	199	570
Retouched tertiary chunks	25	22	6	0	53
Heat-treated tertiary chunks	10	45	133	104	292
Heat-treated retouched tertiary chunks	7	13	6	0	26
Tertiary flakes	29	385	1248	986	2648
Retouched tertiary flakes	56	200	82	5	343
Heat-treated tertiary flakes	7	243	805	451	1506
Heat-treated retouched tertiary flakes	16	142	56	2	216
Trimming flakes	0	12	70	44	126
Retouched trimming flakes	0	3	0	1	4
Heat-treated trimming flakes	0	5	45	24	74
Heat-treated retouched trimming flakes	0	1	2	2	5
Sharpening flakes	1	21	45	19	86
Retouched sharpening flakes	0	5	1	0	6
Heat-treated sharpening flakes	0	12	37	11	60
Heat-treated retouched sharpening flakes	0	6	0	0	6
Projectile points (including fragments)	0	3	2	0	5
Bifaces (including fragments)	4	7	3	0	14
Drills	0	2	1	0	3
Formed scrapers	3	0	0	0	3
Ceramics	1	9	11	0	21
Unformed ground stone	10	1	0	0	11
Miscellaneous unformed ground stone	1	0	0	0	1
Formed ground stone	11	1	0	0	12
Total number of artifacts	388	1397	2965	1903	6653

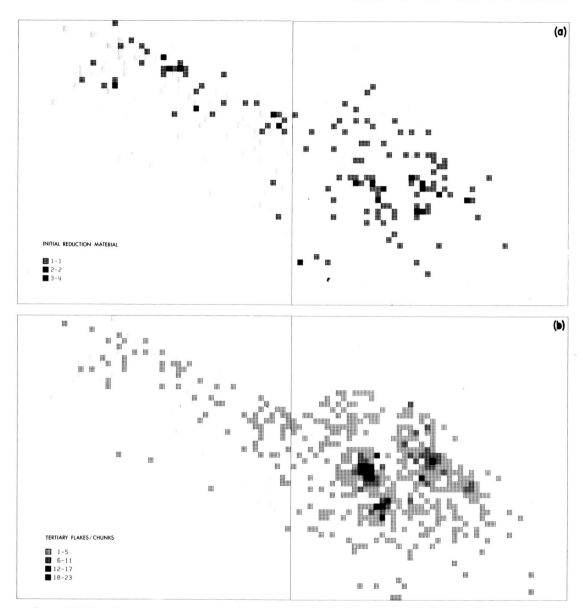

Figure 12.18. Density gradient maps for class groups at Putman Bottom site G: (a) initial reduction material, (b) tertiary flakes–chunks.

shows the most clustered distribution, tertiary flakes–chunks, contains such high frequencies of specimens that the distribution is somewhat misleading. The distribution of lithic reduction pieces indicates that lithic manufacturing was not restricted to a single area; small concentrations containing relatively high frequencies occur over many portions of the site. However, tool maintenance was restricted mainly to the southern end of the high density area.

The distributions of chipped formed pieces, ceramics, and ground stone are of little help in identifying intrasite specialized areas since they are fairly ubiquitous in the collected area. Retouched pieces also occur over much of the site surface, with a high proportion of elements being located in the high density area. Within this area there are more retouched pieces in the northern part than in the southern part, possibly because of differences in area function. Based on the disproportionate amounts of tertiary flakes–chunks and trimming–sharpening flakes in the southern end of the high density area, we have assumed that this was a lithic work area for flake manufacture and tool maintenance. Retouched pieces occur either in low frequencies or not at all in this area, supporting an interpretation that lithic production perhaps was the only activity done in that specific locale. This area is discussed further in Chapter 14.

Based on analysis of the surface material, the proposition that West is a residential site is supported. The site is dense, with a surface assemblage dominated by small artifacts that reflect processes of tool manufacture and maintenance (Table 12.3). It also contains high frequencies of other artifacts commonly associated with residential site activities, such as food preparation and cooking.

Putman Bottom Site G

The distribution of initial reduction classes at site G in Putman Bottom (Figure 12.18) reflects the distribution shown on the general structure map (Figure 12.8). The highest frequencies occur in the eastern half of the site (Ha 2) and tail off into Ha 1. Four concentrations of material, two in each hectare, are evident. Each of the two in Ha 2 contains single density level 3 (3–4) units, with at least three density level 2 units in close proximity. The two concentrations are separated by a sterile northwest–southeast-trending area. The larger of the two concentrations in Ha 1 contains a single density level 3 unit and two density level 2 units; the smaller contains two density level 2 units.

The distribution of tertiary flakes–chunks (Figure 12.18) is highly patterned, with three dense concentrations located in Ha 2. These occur in the same area as the concentrations of initial reduction classes, and each contains at least 1 density level 4 (18–23) unit, accompanied by 7–15 density level 3 (12–17) and/or density level 2 (6–11) units. A fourth concentration, consisting of 3 density level 2 squares, occurs in the extreme eastern part of the site.

Trimming–sharpening flakes occur in various parts of Ha 2 and along the eastern edge of Ha 1 (Figure 12.19). The densest concentration occurs in the same location defined by dense concentrations of tertiary pieces and initial reduction pieces. This indicates that the location functioned as an area for complete flake tool manufacture and tool maintenance. The cluster of level 1 units along the eastern border of Ha 1 was not noticed initially during inspection of other class group distributions because densities of units in the cluster were suppressed by higher densities elsewhere. Reinspection of the distribution of both previously discussed class groups shows that units within the concentration defined by trimming–sharpening flakes do contain medium-range artifact densities for those class groups. Thus, the area appears to be another localized center for lithic tool manufacture and maintenance.

Six bifacially chipped artifacts were recovered from the site, five from the central portion of Ha 2 and one from the extreme western edge of Ha 1. All five in Ha 2 occur outside the concentrations of lithic manufacture–maintenance debris. Eleven ground stone artifacts were found in Ha 2, and none in Ha 1 (Figure 12.19). Some pieces occur in previously identified clusters, whereas others are on the periphery of the site.

Retouched flakes occur in every area of the site, with the heaviest concentration in the central portion of Ha 2 (Figure 12.20). Less dense concentrations can be discerned along the border between

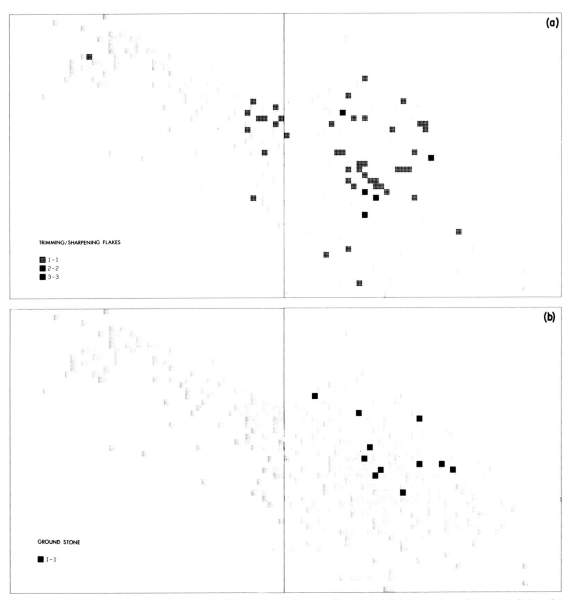

Figure 12.19. Density gradient maps for class groups at Putman Bottom site G: (a) trimming–sharpening flakes, (b) ground stone.

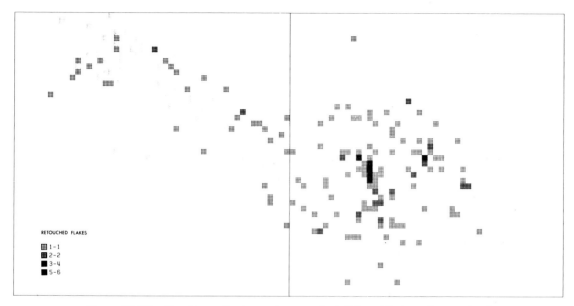

Figure 12.20. Density gradient map for retouched flakes at Putman Bottom site G.

the two hectares and in the extreme western portion of the site.

In summary, the class group distributions suggest there are at least two, and possibly three, areas in Ha 2 where all identified activities were carried out. These include initial lithic reduction, production of flake tools, tool maintenance, food preparation, and a number of unidentified functions requiring retouched flakes. Although large, relatively dense concentrations of class groups are identified easily, less dense concentrations also are present, suggesting that some functions, especially initial reduction of stone, were done on many areas of the site. Given the light artifact density at the site, and the fact that the site has been plowed repeatedly, it is probable that some less dense concentrations have been obliterated.

The presence of high frequencies of initial lithic reduction material, retouched flakes, tool maintenance debris, and ground stone supports the proposition that site G is residential.

Putman Bottom Site T

The distribution of most, if not all, class groups at site T in Putman Bottom is dependent on general artifact density (i.e., most concentrations occur in areas of highest overall artifact density). Addi-

tionally, intrasite variability is difficult to detect because of overall low artifact density. Due to the nature of procurement–processing sites, a frequency of two artifacts in any unit, or a cluster of low frequencies of a particular class group in adjacent units, may be highly significant and may define small functional areas. There are several areas of interest regarding procurement–processing sites that can be explored. First, are there spatially discrete areas within the defined boundaries of the site where certain tasks in the procurement–processing efforts were carried out, or were all steps carried out without regard to location? Second, were multiple tools used in carrying out steps of the process? Third, if multiple tools were used, do the intersections of their locations form identifiable clusters? These questions are explored later.

Initial reduction debris occurs sporadically over the site in densities of one or two pieces per unit (Figure 12.21). Approximately 13% of the assemblage is initial reduction material (Table 12.5), a percentage that is higher than that for West and site G. This is a little surprising, but as discussed later, it is not a significant feature of the assemblage.

The high percentage of unretouched tertiary

TABLE 12.4.

Frequencies of Artifacts by Technological Class and Size Class at Putman Bottom Site G

	Size Class				Total per class
Technological class	1	2	3	4	
Cores	3	0	0	0	3
Retouched cores	1	0	0	0	1
Heat-treated cores	1	0	0	0	1
Core rejuvenation flakes	3	1	0	0	4
Retouched core rejuvenation flakes	2	0	0	0	2
Heat-treated retouched core rejuvenation flakes	1	0	0	0	1
Retouched shatter	1	0	0	0	1
Heat-treated shatter	1	0	0	0	1
Primary decortication flakes	0	1	0	0	1
Secondary decortication flakes	17	55	24	1	97
Retouched secondary decortication flakes	8	10	4	0	22
Heat-treated secondary decortication flakes	1	24	21	0	46
Heat-treated retouched secondary decortication flakes	4	2	3	0	9
Tertiary chunks	15	45	77	19	156
Retouched tertiary chunks	4	7	4	0	15
Heat-treated tertiary chunks	5	15	17	4	41
Heat-treated retouched tertiary chunks	1	8	1	0	10
Tertiary flakes	6	154	442	151	753
Retouched tertiary flakes	6	32	17	0	55
Heat-treated tertiary flakes	4	68	150	22	244
Heat-treated retouched tertiary flakes	5	34	13	0	52
Trimming flakes	0	0	11	1	12
Heat-treated trimming flakes	0	2	1	3	6
Sharpening flakes	0	10	10	0	20
Retouched sharpening flakes	0	2	0	0	2
Heat-treated sharpening flakes	0	7	10	1	18
Heat-treated retouched sharpening flakes	0	2	2	0	4
Projectile points (including fragments)	1	0	1	0	2
Bifaces (including fragments)	0	1	0	0	1
Drills	0	0	1	0	1
Formed scrapers	2	0	0	0	2
Unformed ground stone	1	0	0	0	1
Formed ground stone	10	0	0	0	10
Total number of artifacts	103	480	809	202	1594

flakes–chunks (55%) also was not anticipated. These pieces occur throughout the site, with a heavy concentration in the high density area (Figure 12.21). One hypothesis to be tested with further analysis is that many of these artifacts contain use-wear on unretouched edges and faces.

Only three trimming–sharpening flakes are present, and all occur in various portions of Ha 2. Three chipped formed artifacts also are present— two along the western edge of the high density area in Ha 2 and one in Ha 1 (Figure 12.22). Three pieces of ground stone occur in the northern half of Ha 2 (Figure 12.22). These frequencies indicate that tool maintenance was not an important func-

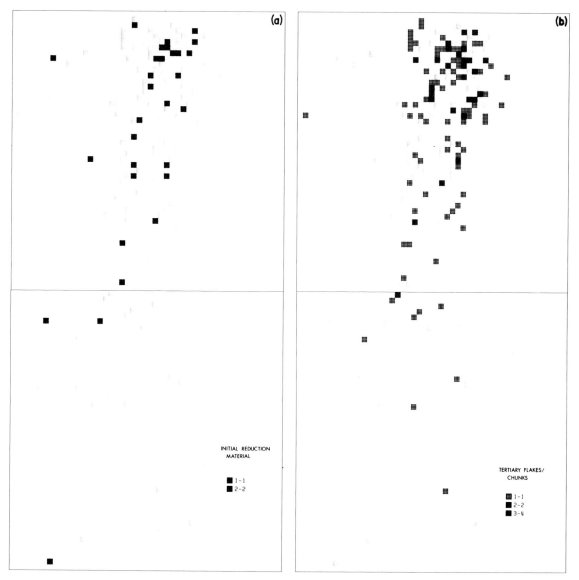

Figure 12.21. Density gradient maps for class groups at Putman Bottom site T: (a) initial lithic reduction material, (b) tertiary flakes–chunks.

tion at the site but that cutting and grinding functions were. Four chipped or ground artifacts occur in and around the high density area, identifying it as the possible center of the processing activity. The three pieces of ground stone exhibit heavy smoothing on at least one surface, but none shows

pitting or evidence of battering, which would occur if the pieces had been used as hammerstones.

Retouched pieces, accounting for 30% of the assemblage, have been found throughout the site, with the densest concentration in the northern end of Ha 2 (Figure 12.22). Although this con-

TABLE 12.5.

Frequencies of Artifacts by Technological Class and Size Class at Putman Bottom Site T

| | Size class | | | | Total per |
Technological class	1	2	3	4	class
Cores	9	0	0	0	9
Retouched cores	1	0	0	0	1
Heat-treated cores	1	0	0	0	1
Core rejuvenation flakes	1	0	0	0	1
Heat-treated retouched shatter	1	0	0	0	1
Primary decortication flakes	1	0	0	0	1
Secondary decortication flakes	7	7	2	0	16
Retouched secondary decortication flakes	12	0	1	0	13
Heat-treated secondary decortication flakes	0	1	2	0	3
Tertiary chunks	13	11	9	2	35
Retouched tertiary chunks	6	1	0	0	7
Heat-treated tertiary chunks	2	4	5	0	11
Heat-treated retouched tertiary chunks	0	1	0	0	1
Tertiary flakes	5	25	26	6	62
Retouched tertiary flakes	13	18	4	0	35
Heat-treated tertiary flakes	3	7	14	1	25
Heat-treated retouched tertiary flakes	4	9	1	0	14
Heat-treated trimming flakes	0	0	1	0	1
Retouched sharpening falkes	0	0	1	0	1
Heat-treated sharpening flakes	0	1	1	0	2
Heat-treated retouched sharpening flakes	0	1	0	0	1
Projectile points (including fragments)	1	0	0	0	1
Bifaces (including fragments)	0	0	1	0	1
Formed scrapers	1	0	0	0	1
Unformed ground stone	1	0	0	0	1
Formed ground stone	2	0	0	0	2
Total number of artifacts	84	86	68	9	247

centration is to some degree conditioned by over-all artifact density distribution, five contiguous density level 2 and 3 units form a definite cluster in the central portion of the area. This is the same area that contains high frequencies of initial reduction classes and unretouched tertiary flakes.

In summary, site T exhibits the proposed characteristics of procurement–processing sites. The high percentage of retouched artifacts (30%) is consistent with expectations, as is the low percentage of trimming–sharpening flakes. The presence of bifacially flaked and ground stone tools neither supports nor refutes the hypothesis since both classes of material can occur at either residential or procurement–processing sites. The percentage of initial reduction material (13%) is slightly higher than expected, possibly a result of the need for flakes used during procurement–processing. Non-retouched secondary decortication flakes were included in the proposed criteria for procurement–processing site assemblages due to the fact that if rough, heavy tools were used during an activity, secondary decortication flakes would be removed by repeated blows to the artifact. As will be proposed in the following section, activities at site T appear to have been light-duty, resulting in less removal of cortex flakes.

The distribution of class groups at site T sug-

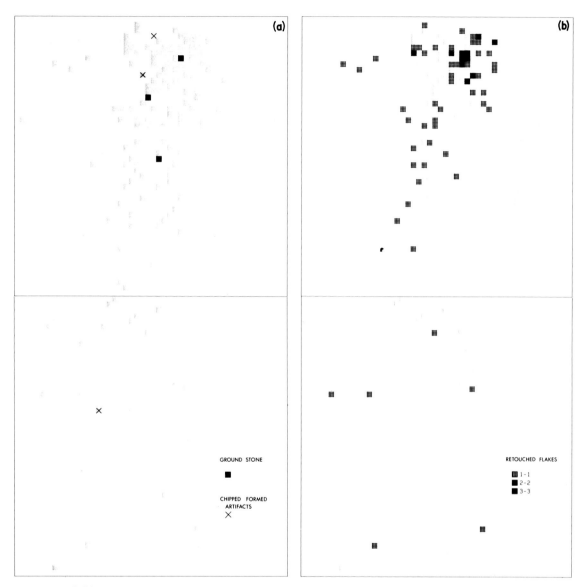

Figure 12.22. Density gradient maps for class groups at Putman Bottom site T: (a) chipped formed artifacts and ground stone, (b) retouched flakes.

gests that the major center of activity is at the northern end of Ha 2. Concentrated in this area are initial reduction elements, tertiary flakes, retouched pieces, and ground stone. No other obvious clusters exist.

Based on analysis of the site, the three questions posed earlier can be answered. First, there is a single area within the site in which all identified functions were carried out, including initial lithic reduction, tool production, and tool use. Second, there are multiple classes of tools present within the activity area, including retouched and unretouched flakes, bifacially chipped tools, and ground stone implements. Third, within the activity area there is a fairly well-defined concentration of retouched flakes, whereas other classes occur throughout the activity area in no particular concentration.

SUMMARY AND CONCLUSIONS

Two major topics have been addressed in this chapter through reference to the spatial distribution of surface collected artifacts. The first is analysis of the general structure of archaeological sites as defined by levels of total artifact density across site surfaces. The second is analysis of intrasite structure as defined by the distribution of densities of technological artifact classes and class groups across site surfaces. If various cultural and natural biases summarized earlier can be eliminated, each type of analysis can contribute important data, at succeeding levels of investigation, regarding the composition of prehistoric communities. Through the use of examples from the project area—including a large, structurally complex residential locale (Hatten Village), a small residential site (Pigeon Roost Creek), and a large residential and procurement–processing bottomland terrace (Putman Bottom)—the utility of surface collection has been shown to be an effective mechanism for generating data useful in answering regional archaeological questions.

Analysis of general site structure is a quick, efficient means of surveying total artifact density across a surface and can be used to plan future work at a site. As discussed, this analysis helped us determine where we would mechanically remove the plow zone at Hatten Village to permit the location of subsurface features. This preliminary work also is useful in generating site-specific and regional-scale hypotheses to be tested with other data. Based on preliminary assessment of sites discussed in this chapter, several site-specific propositions were developed to guide excavation, including: (a) high-density areas at Hatten Village represent residential sites containing multiple subsurface features; (b) habitation at Pigeon Roost Creek occurred along the west edge and northern

end of the site; and (c) the most likely area at West in which to find subsurface features was along the west edge of the wooded area. Regional-scale hypotheses included the dichotomy in structure and composition of residential versus procurement–processing sites, based on initial results of work in Putman Bottom.

At the second level of analysis—intrasite structure—two lines of investigation are important: (a) frequencies of artifact classes at a site and (b) distributions of those frequencies across a site. Artifact class frequencies allow one to make predictions regarding the function of a site, but they impart no information about where those functions might have occurred. This information is gained only through analysis of both the density distribution of individual artifact classes or class groups and the overlapping density distributions of multiple classes or class groups. Based on these observations, propositions regarding the use of space within an archaeological community can be generated and tested through further work. Conclusions drawn from the intrasite structural analysis of the four sites discussed are presented in the following pages.

We identified two types of sites, residential and procurement–processing, by evaluating the content of surface assemblages. Residential sites contain high artifact densities indicative of intensive and/or recurrent occupations and assemblages that repersent household activities. Procurement–processing sites have low artifact densities, which are indicative of infrequent and/or temporary utilization, and assemblages that represent resource extraction and/or processing activities.

Based on this dichotomy, we propose that residential site assemblages are characterized by artifacts that reflect processes of tool manufacture and maintenance; food processing, cooking, and storage; and skinning and butchering. Artifacts include initial lithic reduction classes, tertiary flakes–chunks, trimming–sharpening flakes, small bifacially chipped tools, ceramics, and ground stone. Procurement–processing site assemblages are characterized by artifacts that reflect processes of tool use, including retouched cores and flakes, and nonretouched secondary flakes.

To determine the accuracy of the model, data

TABLE 12.6.

Frequencies and Percentages of Technological Class Groups at Pigeon Roost Creek, West, and Putman Bottom Sites G and T

	Pigeon Roost Creek		West		G		T	
	N	%	N	%	N	%	N	%
Initial reduction flakes	1411	21.0	481	7.2	153	9.6	31	12.5
Tertiary flakes/chunks	3847	57.3	5016	75.4	1194	74.9	133	53.8
Trimming/sharpening flakes	51	0.7	346	5.2	56	3.5	3	1.2
Chipped formed artifacts	34	0.5	25	0.4	6	0.4	3	1.2
Ceramics	62	0.9	21	0.3	–	–	–	–
Ground stone	6	0.1	24	0.4	11	0.7	3	1.2
Retouched flakes	1296	19.3	740	11.1	174	10.9	74	29.9
Total	6707	99.8	6653	100.0	1594	100.0	247	99.8

TABLE 12.7.

Contingency Table of Observed (O) and Expected (E) Values for Retouched Artifacts by Size Class at Pigeon Roost Creek, West, and Putman Bottom Sites G and T[a]

	Size class					
	1 inch		1/2 inch		1/4 inch	
	O	E	O	E	O	E
Pigeon Roost Creek	220	256.58	817	774.29	259	265.13
West	160	144.32	414	435.54	155	149.14
Site G	33	34.45	97	103.96	44	35.60
Site T	37	14.65	30	44.21	7	4.37

[a] Less than ¼-inch objects from Putman Bottom sites not included.

from the four sites can be evaluated by comparing the percentages of technological class groups from each site (Table 12.6). The proposition derived from the site dichotomy model states that procurement–processing sites have assemblages dominated by large artifacts (≥ 1 inch) that reflect processes of tool use. These artifacts include various classes of retouched chunks and flakes and non-retouched secondary decortication flakes.

To test the relationship between artifact size and site type, chi-square values were calculated for retouched artifacts by size class (1 inch, ½ inch, ¼ inch) at each site. Inspection of Table 12.7 shows that site T, a presumed procurement–processing site, contains a much higher proportion of large objects and considerably fewer small objects than expected. Deviations from expected values at other sites are much less pronounced, as shown in Figure 12.23, which graphs standard-score values for retouched artifacts by size class at Pigeon Roost Creek, West, and Putman Bottom sites G and T. Based on this analysis, site T clearly is in a class of its own.

One portion of the model—that procurement–processing sites contain more secondary decortication flakes than do residential sites—is not supported by data from site T. The site contains the second lowest percentage of secondary decortication flakes of the four sites analyzed. This was

noted during earlier analysis (Warren and Miskell 1981) and might be explained by the performance of primarily light-duty tasks at the site. At other procurement–processing sites in Putman Bottom heavier, more crudely made tools used for heavy-duty tasks, such as chopping and pounding (hence, removal of cortex flakes during use), appear with much higher frequency.

The distribution of artifact class groups across the surface of site T shows that activities at the site occurred within a limited area. Activities include lithic reduction, for the manufacture of flake tools, and tool use. Within the general activity area there is a fairly well-defined concentration of retouched artifacts suggesting that the main function at the site occurred in that small area.

Based on the intrasite analysis of three residential sites, it is difficult to model the internal structure of a Woodland community. Intrasite distributions of class groups at residential sites indicate that some activities were restricted to specific areas, whereas others were carried out randomly. At Pigeon Roost Creek, areas for food processing and cooking were located north of tool maintenance areas. At West, tool maintenance appears to have been restricted to the southern end of the main high density area, whereas functions involving retouched tools were concentrated to the north. At site G, the overlapping distributions of

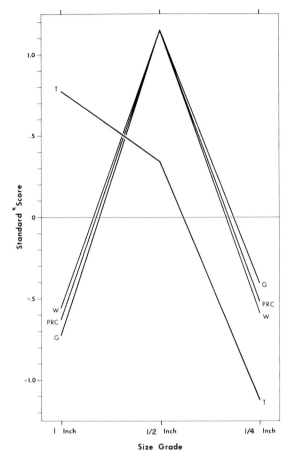

Figure 12.23. Standard-score values for retouched artifacts by size class at Pigeon Roost Creek (PRC), West (W), and Putman Bottom sites G (G) and T (T).

some of the functions carried out at these sites are as yet undefined. As discussed in Chapter 9, frequencies of different types of use-wear at each site and distributional plots of these frequencies across each site are needed. Plotting different use-wear patterns, which are indicative of various functions, should further define activity areas isolated at each site and allow identification of functions that are now only implied.

In summary, it should be noted that sites in the project area still are highly structured despite many years of agricultural and other types of disturbance. Biases resulting from these disturbances more likely than not can be eliminated during fieldwork and subsequent analysis. The emphasis within the Cannon Project on using surface data in a regional framework came from a realization that the types of data just discussed can be generated quickly and relatively inexpensively. As more projects employ surface material in their research, both the limitations and potential of the method will be better defined.

The analysis presented in this chapter is a first step in explaining community patterning in the Cannon Reservoir region. It by no means is an explanation of adaptation and change through time. As Hodder and Orton (1976:31) note, "The identification of a structured pattern does not mean that anything has been explained. The identification is simply an aid in the interpretation of the spatial process which produced the pattern." However, identification of structured patterns in surface-derived data, taken *in conjunction* with site context variables (Chapter 16), site content variables identified through excavation (Chapters 13 and 14), and analysis of floral and faunal remains (Chapters 10 and 11), adds significantly to our testing of the implications derived from the model of prehistoric adaptation and change (Chapter 5). It is in this systemic sense that surface data can be best viewed.

various class groups form small high density areas in which many activities were carried out.

Artifact class group frequencies and density distributions have allowed us to partition the data set into residential versus light procurement–processing versus heavy procurement–processing, but

13

Prehistoric Community Patterns: Subsurface Definition

MICHAEL J. O'BRIEN AND ROBERT E. WARREN

In this chapter we examine the structure and organization of prehistoric communities derived from excavated data. The basic tenet, an outgrowth of the model of prehistoric cultural development in the Cannon Project area, is that pre-Mississippian societies were egalitarian in nature. Based on findings to date, no archaeological evidence indicating a level beyond this type of organization has been found. Therefore, we assume that household clusters (defined later) will show complementary form and function (i.e., they will not differ significantly within or between contemporaneous sites).

The chapter is divided into three parts. The first addresses the composition of a community, presenting examples of various archaeological features that together comprise a "typical" egalitarian residential community. Analysis moves from individual elements to groups of co-occurring elements to spatially discrete aggregates of these groups that comprise an archaeological site. The second part of the chapter addresses the spatial configuration of a number of communities, highlighting similarities and differences among them. The third part discusses the social organization of two communities as it has been inferred from burial data.

Prior to these discussions, we mention problems involved in interpreting subsurface site structure in the project area. As we have noted previously, the majority of sites consist of shallow deposits, primarily of lithic material, that have been subjected to agricultural disturbances for many years. In addition, most sites appear to be multicomponent, having been occupied for many thousands of years. The shallow nature of the sites and the length of occupation often have led to some mixing of culturally distinct deposits (Donham 1979a), forcing us to: (a) exercise extreme caution in defining community patterns for specific temporal periods and (b) conclude that certain sites are too complex to understand except in the most elementary fashion.

The problem of contemporaneity can be alleviated through radiometric dating, cross-dating diagnostic projectile points, and seriating ceramic material. Although these techniques are applicable in many situations, sub-plow zone features some-times occur for which there is no temporal control. In discussing the spatial configuration of some communities, what actually may be represented is a composite picture of long-term development. With these caveats noted, the "typical" egalitarian community can be discussed.

COMMUNITY COMPOSITION

The term *typical* refers to sites that are composed of many similar structural elements, often occur-ring in the same proportion. Instead of using a single site to develop a model of the prehistoric community, we have employed several sites to ob-serve the range in variability among their structural elements. In some instances an entire site, or at least a large portion of it, was excavated; therefore, the sample of structural elements is quite large. The following discussion is divided into analyses of: (*a*) house form, (*b*) facilities, and (*c*) the household cluster.

House Form

A minimum of four houses has been found after 20 years' work in the project area, despite careful excavation that resulted in the removal of thou-sands of cubic meters of overburden. Numerous isolated postmolds and portions of what might be the remains of residential structures have been found, raising the number of possible house re-mains to 10 to 12. Based on the presence at many sites of multiple subsurface pits that have yielded large quantities of artifactual evidence of intensive occupation, we believe that some form of residen-tial structures must have been present. Why the evidence for these structures is so scant is open to speculation, but with our present understanding, we feel that the following factors undoubtedly have contributed to the situation: (*a*) many structures were ephemeral (i.e., not occupied all year long) and, hence, were not made to last more than a few seasons (cf. Yellen 1977); (*b*) erosion has been se-vere in some areas, obliterating any evidence of postmolds; and (*c*) plowing has obliterated some traces.

Three of the four houses were found at the Ross site. They were located on a gently sloping hillside, and their remains probably were protected by soil deposition from the upper slope. The houses were found in 1960 after a heavy rain, when the house stains contrasted sharply with the lighter sur-rounding soil. Two were excavated in 1960, the third in 1978; the following descriptions are from Heldman (1962) and Collins (1979).

The plow zone stain over House 1 was 30–35 cm deep, 6–7 m on a side, and contained numerous fragments of burned limestone, charcoal, burned clay, animal bone, and shell, along with 45 lithic artifacts. Once this layer was removed, postmolds showed up in the subsoil. The pattern of the postmolds was essentially trapezoidal, with three large center posts (Figure 13.1). The east and west walls arched inward toward the south wall, in con-trast to the sharply defined northeastern and north-western corners. Thirty-one postmolds, ranging in diameter from 7 to 13 cm, represented remnants of wall posts. When cross-sectioned, all postmolds came to a point at their deepest penetration into the subsoil. Evidence of a prepared floor or fireplace was present in an area between the three center support posts. This area contained a concentration of what appeared to be soil that had been baked, as if below a hearth. A doorway was indicated in the

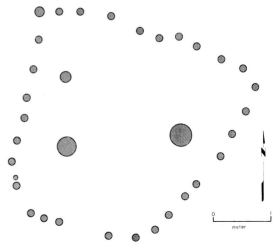

Figure 13.1. Plan of House 1 at Ross (from Collins 1979).

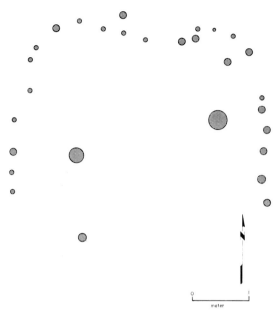

Figure 13.2. Plan of House 2 at Ross (from Collins 1979).

south wall by a lack of postmolds in the line of the wall.

House 2 was represented by a dark stain of approximately the same size and depth as that of House 1. The composition of the overlying deposit was also similar, containing 69 lithic artifacts. Unlike House 1, this structure had only three walls; it was open on the south end (Figure 13.2). Twenty-six wall posts and two interior posts provided support for the structure. Postmolds ranged in diameter from 6.5 to 13 cm, and all exhibited pointed bottoms. Unlike House 1, the postmolds in this structure contained varying amounts of river gravel and chert that had served to support the posts. No evidence of a floor was found.

House 3 was not as well defined as the two previously described houses. The wall was composed of 21 wall posts (6–13 cm in diameter) with at least 1 large interior support (Figure 13.3). Numerous small postmolds were scattered about the interior, indicative of some type of household activity yet to be defined. Several small postmolds also were scattered around the exterior of the house. As in Houses 1 and 2, the doorway opened south.

The fourth house was found at Collins. Remains consisted of nine widely spaced postmolds arranged in an oblong pattern (Figure 13.4). Postmolds ranged from 5 to 14 cm in diameter. An additional postmold to the north possibly indicates a post, from which sticks and branches could have been lashed to the house to form a windbreak. The house was open to the southeast. Within the house were four large pits that had been excavated 40–60 cm into subsoil. These contained large quantities of burned earth, deer bone, and limestone. Based on the context of these features, they probably were contemporaneous with the house.

A fifth structure, from the Cooper site, could be considered a house due to its semicircular arrangement of postmolds and central hearth area. Unlike the other four houses, it was open to the north. Due to this orientation and the amount of openness, the structure is considered as a possible screen and is discussed later in the chapter.

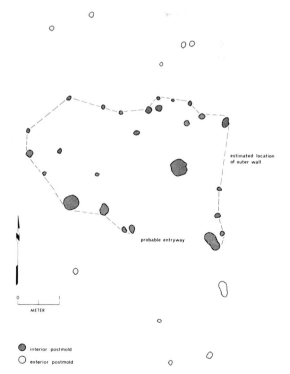

Figure 13.3. Plan of House 3 at Ross (from Collins 1979).

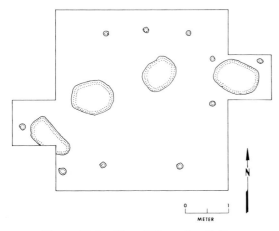

Figure 13.4.   Plan of House 1 at Collins.

four houses probably were of the "arbor roof type" construction discussed by Binford (1962b:50). Anchored in the ground, the wall posts would have been bent toward the center of the house, secured, and then covered with thatch, bark, or mats. Unlike the Mississippian-period houses in the Carlyle Reservoir (Binford *et al.* 1970), at least three houses at Cannon Reservoir contained what we believe are interior support posts.

Given the size of these structures, we assume that they housed nuclear families. If Naroll's (1962) estimate of an average of 10 m² of roofed area per person is used, the houses in the Cannon Project area seem woefully small. Yellen (1977:86) reports average diameters of 2 m for huts that house !Kung nuclear families. The applicability of Naroll's figure to hunting–gathering populations has been called into question (Jochim 1976:175) because Naroll's data were derived from structures at sites of sedentary agriculturists. The sizes of the Cannon Project houses are fairly consistent with those reported elsewhere in the Midwest (cf. Kuttruff 1972; Williams 1974). Possible considerations for variations in house size include: (*a*) roofed space versus heat loss during cool periods; (*b*) lack of engineering skills to exceed certain limits of roof span; (*c*) desired degree of performance; and (*d*) available building materials (cf. Jochim 1976; Yellen 1977).

As Flannery (1976:23) points out in his discussion of early Mesoamerican house types, "It is difficult to summarize a subject about which so little is known." The matter is equally difficult here, given the paucity of house remains from the project area and a general lack of knowledge regarding house styles in the Midwest. Table 13.1 summarizes data from the four houses discussed previously. Certainly no repetitive pattern of house structure exists, although Houses 1 and 2 at Ross are fairly similar in general shape. Three houses (Houses 2 and 3 at Ross, House 1 at Collins) either had no south wall or had a large opening to the south; three houses (Houses 1–3 at Ross) had large interior support posts located within 1 m of the north wall. These posts could have served as supports for windbreaks or as suspension posts.

Although they display differences in detail, all

Facilities

Included under the term *facilities* is a variety of structures that usually are classified by archaeologists as features. We limit discussion mainly to pits, by far the most numerous archaeological feature at sites in the Cannon Project. These facilities were

TABLE 13.1.

Number of Wall Posts, Diameter of Wall Posts, and Size of Enclosed Area for Prehistoric Houses in the Project Area

House number	Number of wall posts	Diameter of wall posts (cm)	Enclosed area (m²)
Ross 1	31	7–13	11
Ross 2	26	6.5–13	14
Ross 3	21	6–13	13
Collins 1	9	5–14	11

Figure 13.5. Subsurface features at Collins at the topsoil–subsoil interface (from Klippel 1972).

excavated for, and may have served, a wide range of purposes. As Binford *et al.* (1970:16) point out, analysis of these features is essential to understanding the structure of a community:

> Cultural features are types of *facilities* representing a major investment of a social unit and as such are extremely important indicators of the nature of the activities conducted at a given location. Our efforts in this regard have included analysis of feature form and content. As we will show, classes of features can be defined on the basis of this dual analysis.

In almost all cases, the first point at which a pit feature could be recognized was at the top of the subsoil, where there was a contrast in color between the dark feature fill and the lighter soil matrix (Figure 13.5). Thus, discussion of feature form is biased in part because a portion of some features was lost after decades of plowing. However, the reconstructions presented here are fairly accurate since, in many cases, topsoil apparently was deep enough that the plow did not reach the subsoil, preventing removal of the upper part of a feature.

The Nature of Household Facilities

Before turning to the classification of household facilities, we will consider the depositional processes through which cultural material came to be

part of the feature matrix. Feature fill is divided into two categories—primary and secondary—(i.e., material that was deliberately placed into a pit versus materials that were included in the fill by erosional processes). Although this division is sound in theory, the categories often are difficult to distinguish. This problem occurs not only in the Midwest but at many types of sites elsewhere. Shackley (1976:17) notes that for pits at an Iron Age site at Danebury, England, it was possible to model the secondary fill process through observation. One of her observations was that the quantity and variety of cultural material was much greater in cylindrical pits than in bell-shaped pits due to the nature of pit shape. Bell-shaped pit walls quickly eroded or collapsed, filling in the pit, whereas there was much less erosion of cylindrical pit walls. The latter type also exhibited a greater degree of evenness in stratification of deposits due to a lesser degree of edge erosion.

In some cases, pits in the Cannon Project area contained materials from both the Archaic and Woodland periods. When pits showed obvious stratigraphy, assigning levels within features to particular cultural episodes posed little problem. Many pits were not stratified, and we were faced with deciding whether each matrix contained primary fill from different cultural periods or whether some fill was a result of secondary depositional processes.

Another problem is controlling for rates of deposition, both cultural and natural. Over a 3-year period (1977–1979), it was noted that pits left open from one season to the next often would be completely silted in upon return. Fieldwork lasted through one extremely dry summer (1979), during which we noted that after a few torrential downpours in midsummer, pits silted in at higher rates than when the ground maintained a constant rate of moisture. Sedimentation rates varied from 2–6 cm of buildup after a 1-inch rain. Despite the ability to distinguish lenses of fine-grained sediments in feature profiles, we were unable to estimate sedimentation rates during the prehistoric period.

Classification of Household Facilities: Form

Household facilities, or features, can be classified in general by shape and by a series of metric variables. Shape can be described by the co-occur-

TABLE 13.2.

Dimensions and Attributes of Feature Shape

	Dimensions		
Outline	Profile	Base	
(1) Circular	(1) Bell	(1) Flat	
(2) Elliptical	(2) Hourglass	(2) Shallow concave	
(3) Ovoid	(3) Cylinder	(3) Moderate concave	
(4) Amorphous	(4) Basin	(4) Extremely concave	
	(5) Compound	(5) Compound	

rence of n number of analytical dimensions having x number of attributes. Dimensions included in the analysis presented here are outline shape, profile shape, and base shape; attributes under each dimension are listed in Table 13.2. The most common feature profile shape of facilities in the project area is a basin, occurring in 362 of 408 features excavated since 1976. The most commonly occurring feature shape classes are ovoid basins with flat or slightly concave bottoms. In the discussion, various characteristics of features based on profile shape are described (Figure 13.6). This single dimension appears to be tied intricately to function and is the best overall delimiter of feature morphology.

Bell-Shaped Pits These features are distinguishable in profile by a relatively constricted orifice from which the walls expand outward toward a flat or slightly concave base that has a diameter greater than that of the orifice. Examples in the project area are quite unlike those reported from elsewhere, in that their orifices and base outlines are ovoid rather than circular. The depth of complete examples ranges from 24 to 48 cm, and the maximum width ranges from 38 to 121 cm (most are around 90 cm). Maximum orifice length varies from 14 cm on the smallest pit to 112 cm on the largest. Volume ranges from .07 to .41 m^3.

Hourglass-Shaped Pits These features are distinguishable in profile by an hourglass shape—the walls contract from the orifice to a point about midway between orifice and base, then expand

outward to a flat or slightly concave base. In most examples, the midpoint aperture is roughly half the orifice and basal lengths. Feature depth in this class ranges from 31 to 68 cm, width from 44 to 136 cm, length from 97 to 170 cm, and volume from .14 to .73 m^3.

Cylindrical Pits Cylindrical features have parallel, vertical walls and flat to slightly concave bases. Depth ranges from 15 to 33 cm, diameter from 17 to 50 cm, and volume from .02 to .24 m^3.

Basin-Shaped Pits Basins have walls that curve inward from the orifice to a flat or concave base. The size of these features varies greatly from small, shallow depressions, to massive pits up to 2.5 m in diameter and 80 cm in depth.

Compound Pits Compound pits result from a pit being cut into a wall or floor of an earlier feature, creating a dual-level pit. This variation seems restricted to basin-shaped pits.

Summary The range in variation of pit shape is great, extending from small basins with diameters of 15–30 cm and depths of 10 cm to large depressions with volumes of almost 1 m^3. The most common pit form is the basin (362 examples from a sample of 408), followed by compound (16), bell-shaped (15), hourglass-shaped (10), and cylindrical (5).

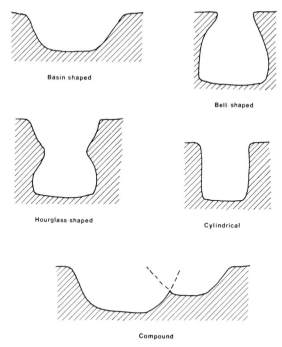

Basin-shaped

Bell-shaped

Hourglass-shaped

Cylindrical

Compound

Figure 13.6. Profile shapes of features in the project area.

Classification of Household Facilities: Function

Based on the analysis of cultural material from archaeological features in the project area, a number of apparent functions are implied. Two types of function are recognized: primary and secondary. The former designates the original function for which the pit was excavated (if this can be determined), and the second, the function a pit served at a later time. The term *trash pit* is seen quite frequently in the archaeological literature because it is a convenient catchall term for pits that contain cultural material. Most archaeologists would agree that the cultural refuse (pottery, lithic debitage, and animal bone) that accumulates in these features may or may not have been thrown in purposely. Even if placement was intentional, the refuse may have been deposited in a pit that had been excavated for another purpose and had simply outlived its usefulness for its original task.

During fieldwork and subsequent analysis, ex-treme care was taken to note subtle changes in deposition within pits. The same care was exercised in noting apparent clusters of cultural material within features to aid in determining primary versus secondary function. Practically all pits contained some cultural material, from a few flakes or pieces of pottery to caches of tools or complete ceramic vessels. In many cases, it was possible to determine that a least a portion of the fill was derived from the surrounding area. Due to the amount of agricultural disturbance of many sites, some amount of pit fill and nonpit material was mixed. In light of these problems, the following facility functions are proposed. Facilities under consideration are not limited exclusively to pits, although, as mentioned, these compose the majority of the archaeological feature assemblage at Cannon Project sites.

Burial Pits Human burial pits are rare in the project area; the majority of interments occur in mounds. Three sites—Cave, Hatten Village, and Muskrat Run—however, did contain burial pits. The number of burial pits per number of individuals from each site is 14/21, 2/2, and 1/1, respectively. At Cave the 14 pits were grouped into a 25-m² area (Figure 13.7), whereas at Hatten Village the 2 pits were some distance apart. The usual context was a shallow grave with no visible marker. Adult individuals of both sexes as well as children were

Figure 13.7. Burial pits in the cemetery area at Cave.

found in these pits. Inclusions of artifacts as funerary items are discussed later in this chapter.

Storage Pits   Pits to which a storage (cache) function can be assigned are rare. At the Garrelts site, 3 of 145 pits contained lithic implements in high enough frequencies to suggest that they had been cached. Feature 9 contained eight bifacially chipped pieces of approximately the same size arranged in the bottom of the pit, and F 45 contained nine large, ground-stone pieces (manos) in association with charred walnut shell. No definite food storage pits were found in the project area, although many pits that contained food stuff remains might have served this purpose.

Processing Pits   Apparent processing facilities occur at quite a few sites in the project area. These pits can be distinguished by the remains, or by by-products, of single or multiple activities (e.g., tool manufacture and maintenance, butchering, nut processing, and pigment processing). As with other features, the problem is in distinguishing primary from secondary use (i.e., Are the remains and by-products a result of an activity that took place in the pit or were they deposited there afterwards?). In some instances, it is evident that the processing took place near the pit, especially where the by-products or remains are dense or numerous and when other evidence is present. Many features at Garrelts contained walnut hulls and from one to four manos, or nutting stones, indicating that considerable nut processing was done at the site.

Hearths   Features inferred to be hearths appear in two forms: (*a*) scatters of fire-cracked limestone blocks on the ground surface or in shallow, basin-shaped pits and (*b*) shallow pits with carbonized wood and burned earth, but little or no limestone. The presence of fire-cracked rock does not indicate necessarily that a hearth existed, although evidence exists for this interpretation (e.g., burned earth under rock scatters). It is assumed that rocks were used for heat retention. Rock-scatter hearths range in diameter from 30 cm to over 1 m; pit hearths range in diameter from 30 to 60 cm. The clearest evidence of an *in situ* hearth was F 6 at Ross. The cross-section of this basin-shaped pit showed

four distinct levels: (*a*) a 10-cm-thick band of charcoal lining the bottom of the pit; (*b*) a 10-cm-thick lens of burned earth that extended up the side of the pit; (*c*) an 8-cm-thick layer of dark soil containing charcoal and burned earth; and (*d*) a layer of slightly stained silt that contained few artifacts. Specific functions of hearths include heat-treatment of chert, nut-roasting, roasting of game, and other activities that require maintenance and regulation of intense heat or fire within defined spatial limits.

Burial Platforms   One burial platform was found in the project area during work at the Garrelts site in 1959. The platform measured approximately 5.5 by 6 m and was composed of a single layer of flat limestone slabs (Henning 1962). Three individuals—two adults and a juvenile—were found lying on the slabs in the center of the platform, possibly having been placed there in one or more bundles. Mounds in the project area often contain limestone slab platforms over which the mound was then constructed, and the possibility exists that the platform at Garrelts was prepared but that the mound was never constructed.

Classification of Household Facilities: Form and Function

Having established general form and functional classes of facilities, we now investigate whether or not there is a significant relationship between the two. In other words, are there certain functions that are always carried out in a single form class or do functions vary across a range of form classes? In an attempt to distinguish possible relationships, 35 features from Strip Area 6 (SA 6) at Hatten Village were selected for intensive analysis.[1] These features form a fairly tight spatial cluster and are separated by considerable distances from other feature-bearing areas of the site (Chapter 12). The features are distributed nonrandomly in SA 6, forming three small loci of 5–12 features each and a linear configuration of 5 features along the southern margin of the terrace on which the site is located (Figure 13.11). If this part of the site represents a single residential community composed of nuclear fami-

[1]Thirty-six features were present in the cluster, but some data from F 8 are missing.

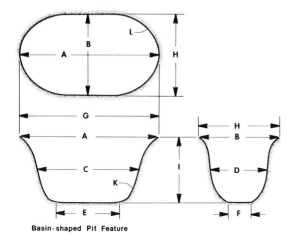

Basin-shaped Pit Feature

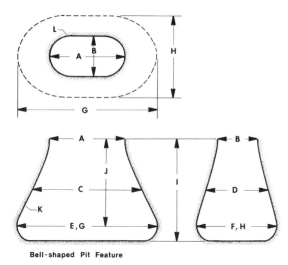

Bell-shaped Pit Feature

Figure 13.8.   Location of size measurements taken on pit features. Measurements: (A) orifice length; (B) orifice width; (C) middepth length; (D) middepth width; (E) basal length; (F) basal width; (G) maximum length; (H) maximum width; (I) maximum depth; (J) depth of maximum length; (K) profile length; (L) orifice circumference; and volume.

lies, there should be evidence that recurrent functions took place within each locus of facilities. These recurrent functions should be reflected in complementary occurrences of different form classes within each locus.

We began the analysis by taking a series of 13

shape and size measurements of each feature (Figure 13.8). Variables were transformed as follows: (*a*) linear measurements (variables A–J in Figure 13.8) were standardized by case (i.e., within feature) to represent pattern variation; (*b*) curvilinear measurements (variables K–L in Figure 13.8) were normalized (square root) and standardized by variable (i.e., across features) to retain magnitude and pattern variation; and (*c*) volume was normalized (cube root) and standardized by variable (i.e., across features) to represent magnitude variation. Next, a Q-mode principal components analysis (programs FACTOR and SCORE in Statistical Analysis System 1979 [Helwig and Council 1979]) was done to align the 35 cases along a series of independent axes, each of which accounts for decreasing amounts of shape–size variance among features.

Four principal components (eigenvalues greater than 1) were extracted and rotated using varimax criteria (Table 13.3). A plot of feature loadings on the first 2 factors, which together account for 87% of total variance, is shown in Figure 13.9. Groups of similar features (Ia, Ib; IIa, IIb; III; IV) were defined by ranking the loadings of features on each factor and adjusting these scores to account for obvious spatial clustering of features on cross-plots of factors 1–4. Factor scores (Table 13.4) indicate that features loading highly on factor 1 (group Ia) are small, shallow, basin-shaped pits with relatively long orifices and maximum lengths, low volumes, short profile lengths, and short depth measurements. Features loading highly on factor 2 (group IIa) are large, relatively shallow pits with high volumes, long profile lengths and orifice circumferences, and low depth measurements. Between these extremes are two groups (Ib, IIb) that share formal properties with groups Ia and IIa but that are intermediate in size. Group III also is defined by intermediate size, but such characteristics as high middepth length, relatively high basal dimensions, low orifice circumferences, and moderately low depth measurements signify shallow pits with relatively narrow mouths and expanding bases. Finally, group IV is composed of large, oblong, moderately deep, narrow-based pits with high profile lengths.

Cross-correlation of these metric groupings with qualitative classes of profile form indicates that

TABLE 13.3.

Q-mode Principal Components Analysis of Shape and Size Variation among 35 Features from Hatten Village SA 6

	Sorted varimax rotated loadings				
Feature	Factor 1	Factor 2	Factor 3	Factor 4	Communality
31	.96	.10	.12	.23	.99
32	.90	.36	.19	-.11	.99
36	.90	.04	.41	.06	.99
3	.90	-.01	.34	.24	.98
35	.90	.09	-.00	.38	.96
30	.86	.35	.27	.18	.98
29	.79	.42	.36	.19	.96
22	.77	.41	.48	.02	.99
23	.75	.26	.59	-.14	1.00
28	.73	.30	.61	-.04	.99
17	.67	-.07	.66	.30	.99
25	.66	.65	.37	-.01	.99
4	-.06	.96	.07	.22	.98
27	.20	.95	.12	.18	.99
1	.18	.95	.06	.07	.95
21	.18	.94	.21	.16	.99
13	.06	.77	.54	.28	.97
33	.61	.76	.09	.02	.95
14	.05	.75	.46	.41	.95
26	.56	.75	.30	.17	.99
6	.25	.75	.54	.18	.94
34	.52	.72	.46	.04	1.00
12	.14	.71	.62	.26	.99
5	.61	.68	.40	-.04	1.00
2	.54	.67	.50	-.05	.99
24	.60	.64	.44	-.13	.99
10	.26	.63	.54	.47	.98
18	.48	.16	.84	.01	.97
11	.35	.47	.79	.15	1.00
19	.35	.50	.72	.26	.97
20	.51	.32	.70	.36	.99
16	.46	.44	.65	.34	.95
7	.59	.29	.60	.38	.94
9	.20	.47	.18	.76	.87
15	.32	.52	.41	.65	.97
Eigenvalue	25.6	5.0	2.1	1.4	
Cumulative Proportion of Variance	.73	.87	.93	.98	

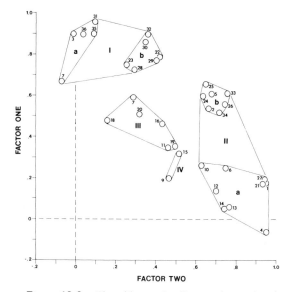

Figure 13.9. Plot of feature loadings on factors 1 and 2 from principal components analysis of 35 features at Hatten Village SA 6. Roman numerals (I–IV) denote major groups; letters (a, b) denote subgroups; arabic numerals (1–36) denote features.

groups Ia, Ib, and IIb are composed exclusively of basin-shaped features that differ little except in size. Group IIa includes four large basins, three hourglass-shaped pits, and two compound forms. The feature form that correlates most highly with factor 3 is the bell-shaped pit, but others in group III are basin and compound forms. Group IV includes two deep pits, one a basin and the other a compound form.

Encouraged by these results in defining feature classes based on metric determination, but still not satisfied because of the mixing of larger basins with complex hourglass-shaped features (groups IIa, III, and IV), we decided to choose 2 of the 13 measurement variables for a bivariate plot. Previous attempts at choosing meaningful variables ended with mixed results (Collins 1979). After the principal components analysis, it was determined that profile length and volume contributed the most variance to factors 1 and 2 and would aid in separating distinct groups. For the plot (Figure 13.10), the cube root of volume is graphed against the square root of profile length to maintain a linear relationship between the two variables.

TABLE 13.4.

Factor Scores of 13 Shape/Size Variables Obtained by a Q-mode Principal Components Analysis of 35 Features from Hatten Village SA 6

Variables	Factor scores			
	Factor 1	Factor 2	Factor 3	Factor 4
Orifice length	1.26	.15	.17	.83
Orifice width	.42	.18	.83	-.37
Middepth length	-.49	.41	1.28	-1.98
Middepth width	.97	-.43	.11	.58
Basal length	.20	-.36	.70	-.44
Basal width	-.58	-.13	.84	-1.02
Maximum length	1.20	.18	.30	.79
Maximum width	.92	-.41	.21	.54
Maximum depth	-.69	-1.40	-.80	.50
Depth of maximum length	-.79	-2.02	-1.33	-.56
Profile length	-1.52	1.05	-.00	1.23
Orifice circumference	.69	1.73	-2.43	-1.22
Volume	-1.58	1.05	.12	1.11

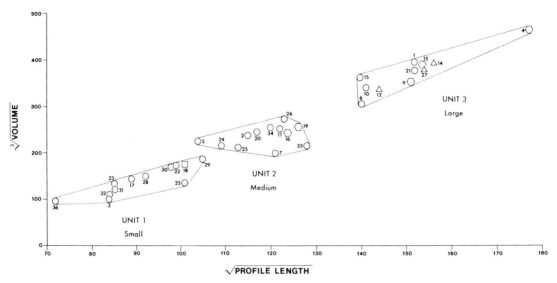

Figure 13.10. Bivariate plot of cube of volume against square root of profile length for 35 features from Hatten Village SA 6; basin-shaped (○); hourglass-shaped (△); bell-shaped (□); compound (◯).

To segregate groups, the bivariate plot was compared to the plot of factors 1 and 2. Groups Ia and Ib were joined into unit 1 and the rest into units 2 and 3, with the midpoint between F33 and F 6 on the bivariate plot used to divide the latter two units. The linear–volumetric parameters for the newly formed groups are as follows: (*a*) unit 1 (50–110 cm/.07–.08 m³); (*b*) unit 2 (110–180 cm/.08–.27 m³); and (*c*) unit 3 (180 cm/.27 m³). If F 4 is dropped from unit 3, the new parameters of that group become (180–256 cm/.27–.64 m³).

This analysis was especially helpful in separating basin-shaped pits, a feature form class that contains considerable variation in size and volume. By cross-cutting the bivariate plot with feature profile shape, a new classification of feature form at Hatten Village can be constructed, as shown in Table 13.5. This classification ignores shape dimensions mentioned earlier, such as orifice and base shape, to keep the classes relatively simple. If variability exists in feature content from one class to another, these other dimensions can be considered later.

Frequencies and/or weight of artifacts by class from features at Hatten Village SA 6 are presented in Table 13.5. The distribution of the raw data is not particularly helpful in understanding feature func-

tion. Despite a tendency for frequencies and weights of items to increase relative to feature volume, anomalies exist. In interpreting the distribution of lithic class frequencies (cores and chipping debris, flakes, bifaces, and ground stone) we believe that distribution is, in great part, related to erosional processes and the resultant deposition of secondary fill derived from outside the feature. These secondary materials may have come from areas adjacent to the pit or from some distance away.

There are some artifact classes that contribute to the inference of feature function (e.g., burned limestone, sandstone, burned earth, and human bone). The correlation between weights of artifacts within classes and particular feature form and functional classes is discussed in the following section. In addition, the function of a single feature is inferred on the basis of frequencies of chert artifacts.

Hearths Burned limestone, burned sandstone, burned earth, and carbonized wood are used as evidence of hearths. The artifact class with the greatest variability between features is burned limestone, weights of which range from 0 to 11,380 g. Although most large and medium-sized features

TABLE 13.5.

Frequencies or Weights of Artifacts by Class from Features at Hatten Village SA 6

	Hematite (g)	Limestone (g)	Burned earth (g)	Sandstone (g)	Ceramics	Burial	Cores
Basin							
Small							
3	–	–	1	–	–	–	–
17	–	–	–	–	–	–	–
22	–	1631	–	40	7	–	3
23	–	50	–	–	–	–	–·
28	–	–	–	–	–	–	–
29	2	–	–	–	3	–	–
30	–	5	–	–·	–	–	–
31	–	3218	–	–	–	–	–
32	–	–	–	–	–	–	1
35	–	–	–	–	–	–	–
36	–	–	–	–	2	–	–
Medium							
2	–	91	32	–	16	–	–
5	–	600	–	–	12	–	–
7	163	360	–	–	3	–	–
11	–	6890	38	4	40	–	1
20	–	892	–	–	6	–	–
24	–	1440	21	290	39	–	2
25	–	250	–	8	14	–	–
26	–	2162	380	465	25	–	5
33	–	318	–	–	18	–	–
34	–	8	5	–	1	–	–
Large							
1	–	250	25	–	66	–	–
6	–	850	19	–	26	–	2
10	72	4612	6	–	24	–	5
15	2	948	10	–	21	–	2
21	–	11380	101	210	105	–	6
Hourglass							
Large							
12	–	1	4	–	14	–	–
14	6	512	46	5	58	–	1
27	–	509	–	–	73	–	3
Compound							
Medium							
16	17	1112	–	–	9	–	–
19	–	1088	14	–	39	X	–
Large							
4	–	8854	127	246	309	X	7
9	28	3114	103	495	371	–	45
13	–	6102	25	19	143	–	7
Bell							
Small							
18	–	19	–	–	–	–	–

(continued)

TABLE 13.5. (*continued*)

	Rejuvenation flakes/shatter	Primary flakes	Secondary flakes	Tertiary chunks	Tertiary flakes	Trimming/ Sharpening flakes
Basin						
Small						
3	–	–	–	–	1	–
17	–	–	–	–	–	2
22	–	–	–	–	7	1
23	–	–	2	–	2	–
28	–	–	2	1	3	–
29	–	–	1	–	4	–
30	–	–	1	–	8	–
31	–	–	1	1	2	1
32	–	–	4	–	5	–
35	–	–	–	–	–	–
36	–	–	–	–	–	–
Medium						
2	–	–	1	–	14	–
5	–	–	6	–	14	–
7	–	–	7	–	5	2
11	1	1	9	7	27	10
20	–	–	7	–	19	3
24	–	1	2	–	6	–
25	–	1	5	–	10	1
26	–	1	14	2	114	4
33	–	1	1	3	8	1
34	–	–	1	1	8	1
Large						
1	–	–	2	1	39	–
6	1	1	4	–	26	2
10	6	–	37	12	118	94
15	1	–	23	6	52	10
21	–	–	20	1	39	–
Hourglass						
Large						
12	1	–	20	7	40	8
14	–	–	27	7	50	8
27	1	–	16	1	73	4
Compound						
Medium						
16	–	–	10	3	20	7
19	–	–	19	4	37	6
Large						
4	2	–	26	5	90	8
9	39	–	122	26	227	54
13	10	–	29	2	48	10
Bell						
Small						
18	–	–	1	–	13	5

TABLE 13.5. (*continued*)

	Projectile points	Bifaces	Drills	Formed ground stone	Unformed ground stone	Totals
Basin						
Small						
3	–	1	–	–	–	2
17	–	–	–	–	–	2
22	1	–	–	–	–	12
23	–	–	–	–	–	4
28	–	–	–	–	–	6
29	–	1	–	–	–	6
30	–	–	–	–	–	9
31	–	–	–	–	–	5
32	1	–	–	–	–	11
35	–	–	–	–	–	–
36	–	–	–	–	–	–
Medium						
2	–	–	–	–	–	15
5	1	–	–	–	–	21
7	–	–	–	–	–	14
11	–	2	–	–	–	58
20	–	1	–	–	–	30
24	–	–	–	–	2	13
25	–	–	–	–	–	17
26	–	2	–	–	–	142
33	–	–	–	–	–	14
34	–	–	–	–	–	11
Large						
1	3	–	–	–	1	45
6	1	–	–	–	–	38
10	–	–	–	–	–	272
15	–	–	–	–	–	94
21	–	–	–	–	2	68
Hourglass						
Large						
12	–	1	–	–	1	78
14	2	2	–	–	–	97
27	1	2	–	–	–	101
Compound						
Medium						
16	–	–	–	–	–	40
19	2	–	–	–	–	68
Large						
4	1	2	–	–	1	142
9	1	8	1	–	–	523
13	–	–	–	–	–	106
Bell						
Small						
18	–	–	–	–	–	19

TABLE 13.6.

**Weight and Density of Burned Limestone, Burned Earth, and Sandstone, and Presence/
Absence of Large Chunks of Carbonized Wood from Seven Features at Hatten Village SA 6**

Feature	Limestone (g)	Density[a]	Burned Earth (g)	Density[a]	Sandstone (g)	Density[a]	Charcoal chunks
4	8,854	9.03	127	.13	246	.25	P
9	3,114	7.12	103	.24	495	1.13	P
10	4,612	12.04	6	.01	0	0	P
11	6,890	42.26	38	.23	4	.02	P
13	6,102	11.00	25	.04	19	.03	P
21	11,380	20.92	101	.18	210	.39	P
26	2,162	.11	380	1.91	465	2.35	P

[a]Density = grams/decimeter^3.

contain at least 500 g of limestone, there are two small, basin-shaped features that contain at least 1600 g. To obtain a density value for burned limestone present in each feature, the weight of burned limestone was divided by feature volume. This procedure was repeated for sandstone and burned earth. When results were rank-ordered by feature for each class, six features ranked in the upper quartile in at least two of three volumetric categories (Table 13.6). Field descriptions indicated that these six features were among seven that contained large quantities of carbonized wood. The seventh feature (F 10) was added to the sample in light of this fact.

For the seven features, the average weight of burned limestone is 6159 g, with a mean density of 14.64 g/dm^3; the average weight of burned earth is 111 g and the mean density is 0.39 g/dm^3; and the average weight of sandstone is 206 g with a mean density of .59 g/dm^3. Three hearths are represented in large compound pits, two in medium-sized basin-shaped pits, and two in large, basin-shaped pits.

It must be reiterated that the four artifact classes used to define hearths may actually represent deposition of hearth components, rather than intact hearths. Only in F 4 was the hearth intact before it was covered by a human burial.

Burial Pits Features 4 and 19 contained human burials, although this function was of a secondary nature in F 4. Feature 4 was a compound pit, the largest facility excavated at the site (volume = .98 m^3). A layer of burned limestone with an overlying layer of charcoal and burned earth was positioned directly under the burial, indicating an earlier hearth. The body was flexed tightly and was resting on its right side. A few apparent grave inclusions—a pipe stem, a baked clay object, and a small pot—were present. Recovered from flotation samples were 112 carbonized seeds, including chenopodium, maygrass, and knotweed. These may be remnants from an activity connected with the hearth.

Feature 19 also was a compound feature, with a volume of .18 m^3. The burial was poorly preserved—only the skull, a few ribs, and a few leg bones survived. The burial position could not be determined, and no funerary items were associated with the burial.

Based on these features, burial facilities at Hatten Village SA 6 are compound in shape, although it is unclear why the main pits contained two distinct depressions. In both cases it is possible that an existing pit was expanded to incorporate the burial. Considerable variation in volume between F 4 and F 19 (a factor of 5×) may indicate that the smaller volume was about the minimum required for burial.

Processing Pits The only clear example of a processing pit at Hatten Village was F 9, a large compound facility. The pit contained 45 cores, 22 of which were heat-treated. This frequency of cores was over six times greater than that in any other pit at the site. In addition, there were 39 core rejuvenation flakes (four times the number found in any other feature) and 227 tertiary flakes, the majority of which were heat-treated. Besides the high frequencies of cores and flakes, there were 8 bifaces and 54 trimming–resharpening flakes. Feature 9 was listed previously as a hearth, based on the presence of a large quantity of burned limestone, burned earth, sandstone, and charcoal. With the added information from lithic analysis, the indication is that the facility was an area for heat-treating chert and manufacturing bifacially chipped implements.

Having investigated the form and function of archaeological features in general, and subsequently having applied the resultant classes to features at Hatten Village, attention is focused on the spatial distribution of features at sites that were excavated extensively. Examination will be at two levels—the household and the community—in an attempt to understand both the composition of the individual units that form the community and the spatial configuration of the sum total of units.

The Archaeological Household

It is important to note the difference between ethnographic and archaeological households. As Winter (1974) states, an *ethnographic household* can be defined loosely as a group of people who cooperate in performing a wide range of domestic activities (e.g., from obtaining and preparing food to "maintaining a house and other facilities that serve as the spatial focus for the group" (p. 981). An *archaeological household* is one that is inferred through analysis of the archaeological record. Things that can be studied are "household composition, activities, the relation between household and family, and interaction between households" (Winter 1974:981). As with other aspects of the archaeological record, we are again dealing with remnant activity patterns (Rouse 1972a).

The importance of the distinction between the two types of households is heightened with regard to the Cannon Project. As noted earlier in this chapter, house remains are scarce; definite traces of

houses have been found only at two sites—Ross and Collins. Areas at other sites are inferred to be remains of houses or activity areas connected with houses, but the evidence often is tenuous; it is impossible to reconstruct many of the activities associated with prehistoric households.

An important concept introduced by Winter (1972, 1974, 1976) is the *household cluster,* composed of cultural features frequently found in spatial association (Winter 1974:981). These features include evidence of: (*a*) house structures (floors and pits); (*b*) burials; (*c*) large subsurface storage pits; (*d*) hearths; and sometimes (*e*) miscellaneous features (small pits). Winter (1976:25) notes that the concept proved useful for organizing and comparing data from the Formative period in the Valley of Oaxaca, where three kinds of facilities—houses, bell-shaped pits, and graves—occurred consistently in spatial concentrations, separated by open areas. These three main facilities sometimes were accompanied by ancillary facilities, such as pit ovens, other types of pits, or midden deposits (Winter 1976). He also states that "it was not always possible in the Tierras Largas excavations to find *all* the elements just listed in any one household cluster" (p. 25). This situation is paralleled in the Cannon Project region. Due to the probable seasonal nature of many occupations (Chapters 10 and 11), postdepositional disturbances, lack of functional indicators in many pits, the inability to recognize function, or any combination of these factors, functional elements of the household cluster can be overlooked (or unrecoverable) in the archaeological record.

Hatten Village: SA 6

As discussed in Chapter 12, Hatten Village originally was estimated to be a single site covering approximately 98,000 m². After controlled surface collection and mechanical removal of the plow zone from a large portion of the site, the area was found to contain three discrete clusters of features. Each was separated from the other by 150–300 m. Based on analysis of feature content, the areas are presumed to be residential. Thirty-one of the 36 features in SA 6 were arranged in three clusters, possibly representing the remains of work areas related to three distinct households. Five features were not grouped; they extended east from HC III and were spaced 12–15 m apart except for two small, closely spaced features at the eastern end of the alignment.

The line of pits at the southern end of the strip area may have been used by all three households or, as is discussed later, may date to an earlier occupation. The absence of house patterns in the excavated area may be due to their destruction, to differential preservation due to soil characteristics, to their ephemeral nature, or to their being located off the stripped portion of the site. Impermanence

of structures also is likely since it appears that the SA 6 Middle Woodland community was occupied only from spring through early fall (Chapters 10 and 11). If the community existed only during the warm seasons, light, temporary shelters would have sufficed, and evidence for these structures might be virtually nonexistent.

The distribution of household facilities can be viewed by form class and by functional class (Figure 13.11). The distribution of form classes shows

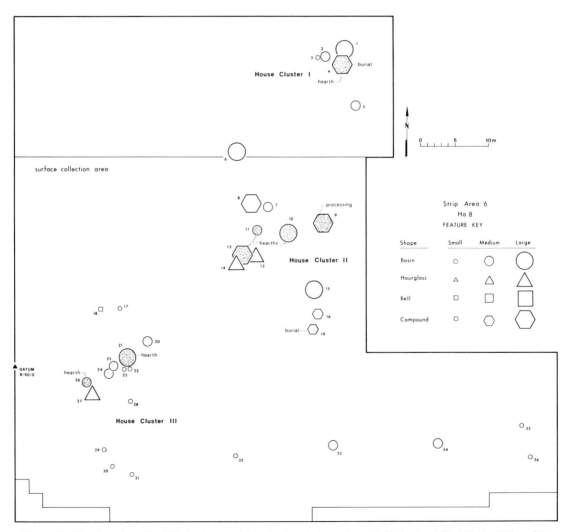

Figure 13.11. Location of facilities by form and function in relation to household clusters I–III at Hatten Village SA 6.

that basins occur in all three household clusters and along the southern edge of SA 6. One noticeable feature in the distribution of form classes is the high frequency of large pits of all shapes (except bell) in HC II, whereas the remainder are medium-sized. This compares with the presence of two large features in HC I and 2 in HC III.

The distribution of functional classes shows that each household cluster contains at least one hearth. The three hearths in HC II may not have been contemporaneous or may reflect a different set of household activities (e.g., intensive food preparation) than those carried out in HC I and III. In each household cluster, hearths are located centrally within the cluster, surrounded by various other facilities. The single chert heat-treating–biface manufacturing area (F 9) occurs in HC II. Burials occur in HC I and II.

Contemporaneity among household clusters in SA 6 is difficult to document except on the most general level. Radiometric assays from F 4 and F 6 date to 50 ± 100 B.C. (TX-3747) and A.D. 0 ± 140 (TX-3748), respectively.[2] Some facilities in each cluster contain ceramics, although frequencies vary considerably from pit to pit. One line of evidence, consisting of differing frequencies of ceramic material between small, basin-shaped pits and all other pits, suggests that an aceramic occupation may be represented at the site. All but one non-ceramic-bearing pit (F 3) are located either in HC III or along the southern border of SA 6. Fisher's Exact Test was used to test the null hypothesis (H_0) that there was no significant difference in frequencies of occurrence of pottery in small, basin-shaped pits versus all other pits (Donham 1981). From the results of this test we can reject the H_0 and conclude that the presence of ceramics in the small, basin-shaped pits occurs less often than would be expected by chance alone ($p = .0017$; $p_{.01} = .005$), in comparison with frequencies of occurrence in medium and large basin-shaped pits.

Removal of the aceramic sample of pits from the household clusters reduces the number of pits in HC I to four and the number in HC III to seven. If aceramic pits are contemporaneous with ceramic-bearing (Middle Woodland) pits in SA 6, that is, do

not date to an earlier period, then a possible explanation for the absence of pottery in these features is that pottery was not connected with the function the pits served. Specific functions cannot be assigned on the basis of feature contents.

In summary, data from Hatten Village SA 6 suggest the presence of three Middle Woodland household clusters characterized by: (a) limestone hearths located in medium to large, basin-shaped and compound pits; (b) burial in compound pits; and (c) at least one lithic processing pit. These household clusters form discrete spatial units that are 15–17 m apart. Botanical and faunal data suggest a spring through early fall occupation, which might be the reason that house remains were not recognized at the site. Due to the considerable number of functionally uninterpretable facilities within the three clusters, we are left with a tantalizing, yet fragmentary, view of a small Middle Woodland community. To build on this basic outline of household structure and associated activities, we focus attention on another small community, the Ross site.

Ross

Ross is located on a low bench near the right bank of the South Fork. The site is represented by a scatter of materials that conforms to the margins of the silt bench on which the site is situated. The Ross site covers an area 230 by 60 m in size. The three houses described earlier in this chapter are located along the southern edge of the bench; a possible fourth house is located just west of the cluster of houses (Figure 13.12). Fifteen pits (all basin-shaped) have been found at the site, the majority of which are situated along the upper edge of the bench above the houses. There do not appear to be tight clusters of facilities such as those at Hatten Village: The only possible cluster consists of Features 2, 4, 5, 6, and 10.

Since all 15 features are basin-shaped, excavations at Ross increased significantly our knowledge of the range in size of this form class. Following the form classification scheme used for pits at Hatten Village, the square root of profile length was plotted against the cube root of volume for Ross features. The upper limits of units 1 and 3 were the same as at Hatten Village; the upper limits of unit 2

---

[2]All radiometric dates in this chapter are uncorrected.

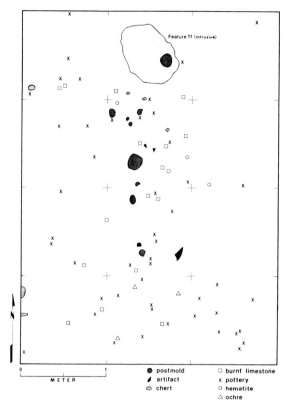

Figure 13.12. Plan of House 4 at Ross (from Collins 1979).

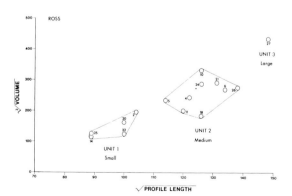

Figure 13.13. Bivariate plot of cube root of volume against square root of profile length for 15 features from Ross.

were raised slightly (Figure 13.13). Raising the upper limits of unit 2 did not affect the parameters of units 2 and 3 defined at Hatten Village but simply clarified the relationship between the units. Unit 1 contains five features, unit 2 contains nine, and unit 3 contains one. The distribution of features is shown in Figure 13.14.

The same problems encountered in assessing facility function at Hatten Village exist with Ross facilities. Three features (6, 10, and 27) contain at least 2500 g of burned limestone, but only one (F 6) contains at least 50 g of burned earth. By standards applied to features at Hatten Village—high densities of limestone, sandstone, burned earth, and charcoal—only F 6 qualifies as a hearth. However, inspection of several features during excavation allows revision of these standards. Feature 27 contained layers of large chunks of charcoal and burned limestone; F 10 contained quantities of both charcoal and limestone throughout the pit fill, indicating that the remains of a hearth had been dumped into the pit. Feature 24, the third largest pit by volume (.23 m³), contained only 111 g of burned limestone but had numerous intact charred logs at the bottom. Below this level were five postholes (4–6 cm in diameter) arranged pentagonally and extending an average of 20 cm below the bottom of the pit. One possible function of these posts was as supports for a rack used to suspend meat or vessels over an open fire. This is the only example of this type of structure found in the project area.

One important result of excavation at Ross is the fact that features are located some distance from the houses (Figure 13.14). The distance from any house to its nearest feature (H 4 and F 20) is 10 m. If H 4, a possible windscreen, is removed from the sample, the distance is a little over 20 m. If the pits and houses are contemporaneous, then there was considerable spatial segregation of living versus working space.

Faunal and floral remains were scarce in all pits and do not contribute much to an assessment of the seasonal occupation of the site (Chapter 11). Carbonized hickory nut occurred in sufficient frequencies in 10 excavation squares around H 4 to indicate a fall occupation for that structure. The three radiometric assays from F 6 date to A.D. 230 ± 50

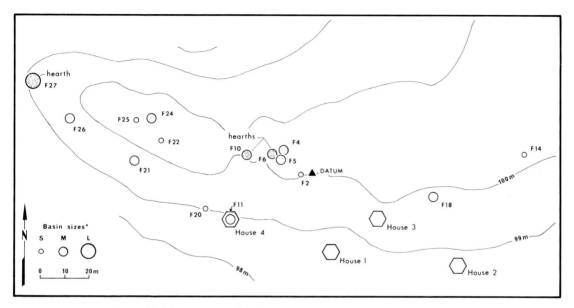

Figure 13.14. Location of facilities and houses at Ross (after Collins 1979).

(TX-3136), A.D. 470 ± 110 (TX-3137), and A.D. 590 ± 120 (TX-3138), indicating a late Middle Woodland–early Late Woodland occupation.

In summary, excavations at the Ross site added substantially to the feature classification and aided in readjusting profile length–volumetric ratios of basin-shaped pits. Based on the absence of facilities near the houses, it seems plausible that at least a portion of the pits were contemporaneous with some or all of the structures.

Other Excavated Sites

Presented in this section are data derived from excavation of other prehistoric archaeological sites in the Cannon Reservoir region. Relevant data concerning the spatial configuration of the sites, periods of occupation, and other important features of community patterning have been abstracted from more detailed analyses.

Garrelts

Garrelts covers approximately 4.5 ha of a linear erosional remnant along the North Fork. A small portion of the site was excavated in 1961, mainly in

areas of dark soil staining. Efforts in 1978 were directed toward opening large areas of the site, and, to this end, the area shown in Figure 13.15 was stripped of plow zone. After plow zone removal, 145 features were excavated, and seven blocks of varying size were excavated over remnants of

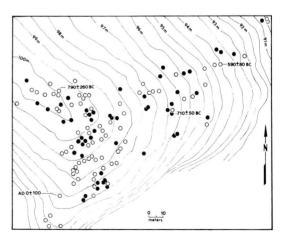

Figure 13.15. Location of features with two or more sherds (●) or less than two sherds (○) at Garrelts (after Donham 1981).

larger stains that were interpreted as potential houses. Postmolds were found in a few of these areas, but none occurred in a definable pattern.

The spatial distribution of features at Garrelts does not suggest the presence of distinct household clusters. Features occurred on the southeastern corner of the narrow ridge and spread downslope for over 100 m. If pits of different temporal periods could be separated, some patterning might be evident.

Radiometric determinations from carbonized wood in four features date to 790 ± 260 B.C. (TX-3746), 710 ± 50 B.C. (TX-3744), 590 ± 80 B.C. (TX-3743) and A.D. 0 ± 100 (TX-3745), or Early–Middle Woodland for all four. Based on the presence of temporally diagnostic projectile points, the site also was occupied during the Late Archaic period.

In Figure 13.15, pits containing less than two sherds are plotted against those containing two or more sherds. The plot shows that the distributions of the two groups are similar. To test the H_0 that there is no significant difference in distance either from pits with <2 sherds to like pits or from pits with ≥2 sherds to like pits, Donham (1981:153) computed distances from the center point of each feature to the center point of its nearest like-neighbor and calculated chi-square values based on observed and expected mean distance between neighbors. The resultant values are not significant ($p = .50–.70$), and the null hypothesis cannot be rejected.

Cave

The Cave site is defined by a scatter of cultural material over a 5.65-ha area along middle and lower slopes and lobe extensions of the North Fork valley. It is located in an area of many archaeological sites, including three mortuary mounds located upslope to the south. Topsoil was removed from a major portion of the site in 1979, exposing 63 pits (Figure 13.16). Of these, 60 were basin-shaped, and there was one each of the bell, hourglass, and compound forms. Fourteen pits, containing 21 primary and secondary burials (Donham 1981:148), were located in a 25 m² cemetery area at the south end of the site (Figure 13.7). Radiometric assays were made on carbonized wood from four of the pits. One sample dates to the Early Woodland period, one to the

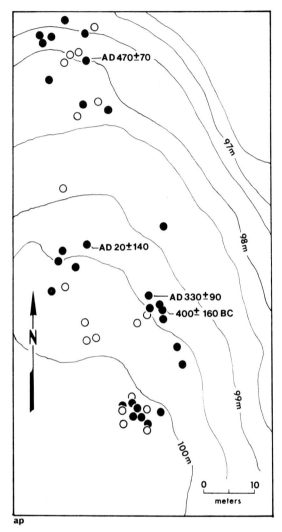

Figure 13.16. Location of features with two or more sherds (●) or less than two sherds (○) at Cave (after Donham 1981).

Middle Woodland period, and two to the early half of the Late Woodland period (discussed later).

Facilities at the Cave site exhibit more pronounced clustering that those at the nearby Garrelts site, although one cluster contained two pits (A.D. 330 ± 90 [TX-3751] and 400 ± 160 B.C. [TX-3754]) that obviously are not contemporaneous. Based on the number of aceramic pits, it is probable that occupation of the site spanned several thousand years. Two other radiocarbon samples date to A.D. 20 ± 140 (TX-3752) and A.D. 470 ± 70 (TX-3750). Analysis of projectile points from pit fill in the cemetery area indicates that the temporal span of the burials is at least several hundred years.

Hillside

The Hillside site is located on a narrow blufftop projection above the mainstem of the Salt River. Surface scatter covered approximately 9500 m². To the south of Hillside, at the crest of the bluff knoll, are two low, eroded mounds (Donham 1981:143). Topsoil was removed from the eastern portion of the site in 1977 and 1979, exposing 58 pits (Figure 13.17). Three radiometric dates—570 ± 90 B.C. (TX-3741), A.D. 200 ± 140 (TX-3740), and A.D. 300 ± 60 (TX-3742)—indicate that the site was occupied during the late half of the Early Woodland period and also during the Middle Woodland period.

The distribution of features is similar to that at the Cave site (i.e., a linear configuration of ceramic-bearing and aceramic pits along the slope of a ridge or lobe extending down toward the river). At Hillside, pits with <2 sherds occurred in two clusters, separated by pits with two or more sherds (Figure 13.17). Form classes are bell-shaped (4), hourglass-shaped (1), compound (5), and basin-shaped (48).

Collins

Collins is located on a low terrace on the right bank of Salt River. The site was excavated in 1968 by Walter E. Klippel, who was interested in delimiting the transition between the Late Archaic and Early Woodland periods in the region. Based on two radiocarbon dates (660 ± 200 B.C. [M-2142] and 570 ± 150 B.C. [M-2143], Collins was designated an Early Woodland site (Klippel 1972). Although the two dates fall within the Early Woodland period, many of the horizon markers of contemporaneous sites in Illinois and Missouri are missing. To clarify the nature of Collins, and with the hope of uncovering an Early Woodland community, the site was reexcavated in 1979. According to preliminary analysis of cultural material from features, the site appears to have been occupied most heavily during the Late Archaic and Early Woodland periods, with

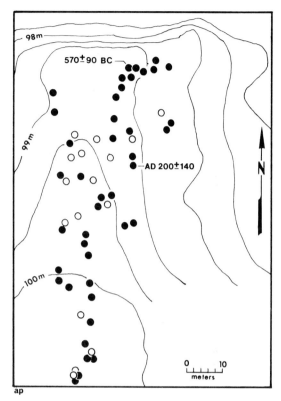

Figure 13.17. Location of features with two or more sherds (●) or less than two sherds (○) at Hillside (after Donham 1981).

a small occupation during the Late Woodland period.

The distribution of features is shown in Figure 13.18. There are three tightly grouped clusters of three or more pits and two occurrences of pits within a few centimeters of one another. The site area containing the pits and house is small in comparison to the amount of area stripped by machinery; the maximum distance from any one feature to another is less than 30 m. The most interesting aspect of the feature distribution is the occurrence of four features within the single residential structure (Figure 13.18). As discussed earlier, these pits probably are contemporaneous with the house. Based on feature content, F 12 was a hearth and was situated in a central area of food preparation (presence of burned bone, bifacially chipped imple-

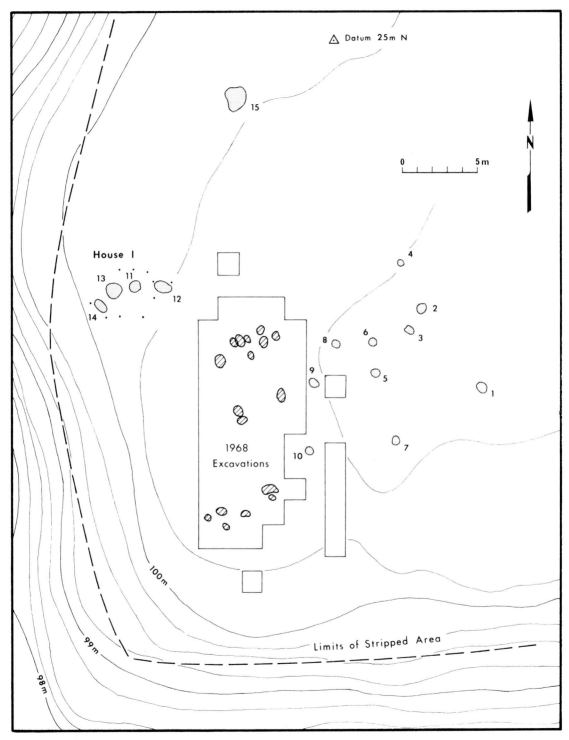

Figure 13.18. Location of features, House 1, and 1968 excavations at Collins.

ments, and worked flakes). The primary function of the other pits is unknown.

Detailed analysis of material from Collins will add considerably to knowledge of the nature of Early Woodland period occupation in the project area. The preliminary results indicate that an argument for the persistence of Late Archaic projectile points into later periods (i.e., tradition lag) is tenable (Chapter 6). The lack of diagnostic Early Woodland pottery at the site is not surprising when viewed in terms of this process.

Analysis of the faunal and floral material suggests that Collins was a cool season occupation. Both fall (deer and walnut–hickory nuts) and late summer (seeds from herbaceous plants) foodstuffs were recovered in some abundance from the pits (Chapters 10 and 11). Possible native cultigens recovered in 1968 include giant ragweed, chenopodium, sumpweed, and knotweed (Klippel 1972). If Collins was a community that was occupied by a small group during the cool season, this may explain the presence of a fairly substantial residential structure on the site.

Cooper

Cooper is located on the right bank of the mainstem of the Salt River in the east-central portion of the project area. Surface scatter of varying density covered approximately 6.5 ha of a narrow, dissected terrace (Donham 1979a; 1981:145). A large portion of topsoil was removed in 1977, uncovering 16 large and medium-sized pits (Figure 13.19). When the western edge of the cut was profiled, a band of artifacts running the length of the profile was noticed. Of this intact deposit, 200 m² subsequently were excavated. Additionally, a small cemetery on an adjacent ridge top to the south was investigated (Donham 1979a).

The site proved to be one of the most complex archaeological situations dealt with during the course of the project. In the southern portion of the site, artifacts appeared to be in situ, laying on a fairly horizontal plane (Figure 13.20). To the north, this upper artifact layer was underlain by other layers that often were difficult to separate. The site never had been plowed, but the growth of large trees had caused severe displacement of artifacts in some areas. Six hearths and seven pits were located

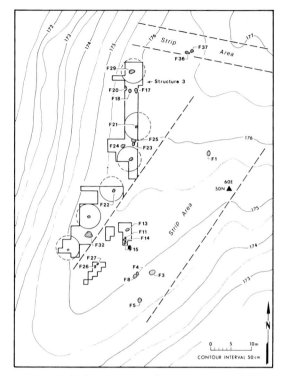

Figure 13.19. Location of hearth areas and features at Cooper (after Bozell 1980a).

Figure 13.20. Distribution of artifacts in units 56–61N, 33–38E at Cooper (looking west).

within the excavated area (Figure 13.19). It was assumed that the hearths were focal points for a number of activities; therefore, hearth areas were treated as larger units of analysis.

Analysis of one hearth area follows. Five radiocarbon dates were derived from carbonized wood samples. One sample located in the stripped area and beneath the *in situ* component in the southern part of the site dated to 2600 ± 120 B.C. (TX-2978). Three samples from the central portion of the site, within midden fill, dated to the Late Woodland and early Mississippian periods (A.D. 610 ± 110 [TX-2979], A.D. 1130 ± 130 [TX3164], and A.D. 1160 ± 120 [TX-2972]). A fourth sample (TX-2976) from the same general area dated to the Middle Woodland period but had a very large standard deviation (A.D. 140 ± 690 years). The midden and hearth areas have been assigned to the Late Woodland period on the basis of the radiocarbon dates. The subsurface features in the stripped portion of the site (beneath the midden) are assigned to the Late Archaic period. Based on faunal analysis, that is, the dichotomy in seasons represented in the two samples (Chapter 10), this segmentation seems appropriate.

Despite its complex nature, Cooper did present an opportunity to examine a prehistoric community that had not been subjected to the many types of disturbance that drastically affected other sites. Observation of the spatial configuration of the lower midden in the northern half of the site suggested the presence of three house floors. This was based primarily on the arrangement of lithic artifacts in three spatially discrete clusters. After removal of the materials and further excavation, a well-defined pattern of postmolds was observed in one floor, although sporadic postmolds were associated with the other floors (Donham 1979a:101). The pattern outlined by the postmolds, a partially enclosed structure that opened on the north (Figure 13.21), suggests that (*a*) it served as a sunscreen rather than as a windbreak or (*b*), given that the season of occupation was fall–winter, postmolds enclosing the structure must have been missed during excavation. Six postmolds with diameters of 8.5–9 cm were present; the maximum diameter of the shelter is 3.8 m, similar to houses at Ross and Collins. The central hearth area consisted of a dispersed concentration of burned limestone ringed by small quantities of burned and unburned bone. Along the exterior wall of the structure was a series of pits containing small amounts of refuse.

Tool distributions within the structure were less dense and more homogeneous than those occurring outside. Twenty-two bifacially flaked tools occurred within and around the structure; five of the seven bifaces located inside occurred in the southeastern corner. Two concentrations of cobble tools associated with broken limestone slabs were present in the southern half of the structure. Outside the structure there was a markedly higher frequency of pitted cobbles, cores, and flake tools (Donham 1979a:107).

Given the long temporal span of the site, it is possible that as procurement strategies changed, so did the role played by the site in different settlement–subsistence systems. Based on floral and faunal remains (Chapters 10 and 11), the Late Archaic component was occupied from spring through early autumn. The Late Woodland component probably was occupied from late fall through early spring. The few corn kernels recovered from this component probably represent holdovers from a warm season occupation elsewhere.

Overview

Discussion thus far has centered on two topics: (*a*) the composition of a prehistoric community and (*b*) the spatial configuration of a sample of communities excavated in the Cannon Project region. Analysis of community composition included examination of archaeological features, termed *household facilities,* to define formal and functional classifications. Classes of features based on form and function then were plotted spatially to observe their distribution within two communities—Hatten Village SA 6 and Ross.

The concept of a household cluster—cultural features frequently found in spatial association—was found to be a useful level of analysis for organizing and comparing data from Archaic and Woodland sites. Types of facilities occurring in household clusters include hearths, burial pits, storage pits, and house structures. At Hatten Village SA 6, three household clusters occur in close proximity, separated by vacant areas. Each contains at least one hearth in a medium to large basin-shaped or com-

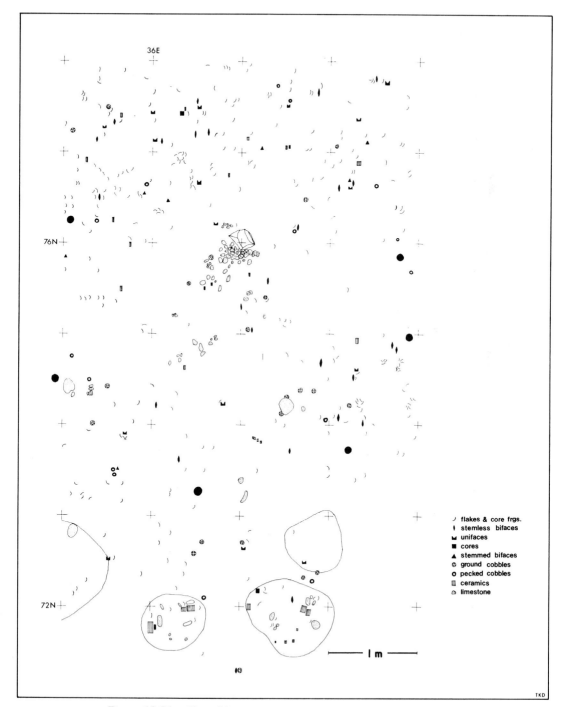

Figure 13.21.   Plan of Structure 3 area at Cooper (from Donham 1979a).

pound pit, two contain a burial in a compound pit, one contains a lithic processing pit, and all contain miscellaneous basin-shaped pits.

Analysis of the spatial configuration of communities revealed that long duration of occupation resulted in the formation of complex archaeological sites. Subsurface pits containing both Archaic and Woodland materials are not unusual, and pits often contain no diagnostic material. These factors make discussion of changes in community patterning tenuous at best. Future analysis of feature content, especially lithic items, should aid in delimiting functional areas within sites. By using temporally diagnostic markers where possible, to tie together different features containing like assemblages, it should be easier to detect site-space utilization.

Based on analysis of floral and vertebrate remains, seasons of occupation can be assigned to some assemblages. One interesting observation emerges from this assignment—all sites containing confirmed or possible house structures also contained evidence of fall–winter occupations. These include (a) the Late Woodland component at Cooper (structures may be houses), (b) Ross, and (c) Collins. No definite warm season components (Hatten Village—Middle Woodland, Cooper—Late Archaic, and Miskell—Late Archaic) have yielded evidence of house structures. It seems reasonable that during the warm seasons, shelters, if they existed at all, were extremely light-duty shades or screens that would leave few archaeologically recoverable traces.

Having reviewed the data on the composition and spatial configuration of prehistoric communities, focus is shifted to the third major topic of this chapter, the ways in which communities were organized socially.

THE ORGANIZATION OF COMMUNITIES

The discussion of community organization centers on data derived from excavation and analysis of burials since the composition of mortuary units, and items included with burials, can yield information useful in determining the social status of individuals and inferring levels of social organization.

As noted earlier in this chapter, the model of sociopolitical development in the Cannon Project area states that pre-Mississippian groups never progressed beyond an egalitarian level. Using models proposed by Service (1962), Fried (1967), Binford (1971), and others, Buikstra (1976) summarized those elements of egalitarian society that are relevant to the analysis of mortuary behavior: Age and sex are major determinants of status, followed by those related to subsistence activity. Status is not ascribed but rather is achieved during an individual's ontogeny within certain limits defined by age, sex, and personal attributes. Given these conditions, one might expect differentiation within a burial program to be associated clearly with biologically defined characters. Although age and sex would be the most obvious elements of differentiation, other "unusual" characteristics, such as extreme stature or deformity, might have qualified a person for differential treatment.

Differential treatment in burial practices may be manifest in any of several areas, including: (a) preburial treatment; (b) location of a grave relative to other graves; and (c) placement of objects in the grave. In summary, these variables are parts of the total energy expenditure directed toward interment of an individual. If it is assumed that social position is proportional to the sum of energy expended on an individual, then a means to measure such energy is required. To this end, we will examine mortuary areas in the Cannon Reservoir region—for which there exist fairly good temporal control, an understanding of burial sequences (in the case of multiple episodes), and skeletal data—to obtain some estimate of the variance in mortuary practices and to determine if intra- and intersite patterns exist.

Due to the paucity of human osteological materials from the area, severe limitations are placed on our ability to achieve our goal. There are only three sites in the project area that have yielded 16 or more individuals each and only a handful that have yielded osteological material for which age and sex could be determined (Figure 13.22). A comprehensive mortuary study never was undertaken for a variety of reasons, the foremost being that most mortuary mounds are located out of the direct impact zone of the reservoir. The Lick Spring site,

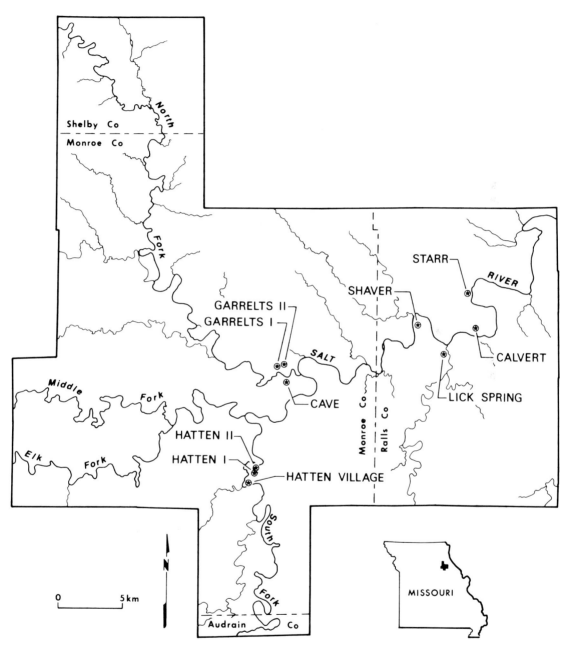

Figure 13.22.   Map of sites in the project area yielding human osteological material for which age and sex could be determined.

threatened by construction of a marina, was excavated in 1977; a second mortuary area was discovered during removal of topsoil at the Cave site. Excavation of these two areas represents the majority of work done in the project area on mortuary sites since 1977. Seven of the nine remaining sites (Garrelts I and II, Hatten I and II, Starr, Shaver, and Calvert) were excavated in the late 1950s–early 1960s. Of these, Hatten I is the most important, containing over 100 Late Archaic burials.

Table 13.7 summarizes data from excavated mortuary mounds and areas. As can be seen from the table, the most common burial facility was a mound, although one platform (possibly an unfinished mound) and two pits were used also. Mound burials occurred during both the Archaic and Woodland periods; based on the small sample, pit and platform burials occurred only during the Woodland period. Due to erosion, the original dimensions of most mounds are impossible to determine. The diameters of the few mounds for which measurements exist range from 10 to 16 m; Hatten mound I was oblong, measuring approximately 15 × 8 m.

The following discussion concerns the structure and content of Lick Spring Mound D and Hatten Mound I; comparisons between the Late Woodland components of each are made. The large skeletal sample from the Archaic component at Hatten has not been duplicated in the project area but offers data useful for formulating hypotheses about Archaic society in the Salt River valley.

Hatten Mound I

Hatten mound I consisted of three separately prepared areas: (*a*) a 2.5-x-2-m central chamber constructed of limestone slabs; (*b*) a 3-m-diameter chamber of limestone slabs; and (*c*) a mound of layers of limestone slabs containing large and small chert cobbles. The 3-m-diameter chamber contained alternating layers of dirt and limestone slabs. At the interface between mound fill and subsoil were found four skulls (three infants and one adult) and one extended adult female. Fifteen *Anculosa* shell beads and a clay elbow pipe were associated with the extended individual. Two isolated skulls and a fragmentary vessel were found in the

chamber fill above the extended skeleton (Klepinger and Henning 1976:101). Based on the artifacts within and around the chamber, this upper portion of the mound dated to the Late Woodland period.

The central chamber contained the skulls of two young adults and two infants plus an articulated arm (Klepinger and Henning 1976:100). No grave inclusions were found. Twenty sherds from chamber fill date to the Late Woodland period.

The third portion of the mound contained alternating layers of human bone—much of it cremated—and limestone. The upper layer of bone was capped with chert cobbles. In the fourth and lowermost layer bone was placed in a more orderly fashion, either being arranged in neat piles in small, scooped out depressions in the submound floor or as flexed, articulated burials. Cremated bone in this level was less frequent than in the upper three levels. Of the 109 individuals, 19 relatively complete single burials were recovered; at least 5 were bundle burials, and 9 were flexed (Klepinger and Henning 1976:106). The combination of single, multiple, and cremated individuals within the same layer suggests that periodic burial ceremonies were held months or years apart, during which time remains were kept for final disposition. Apparently, many of the bones were lost during that time, but the skull was the most important item deposited (Klepinger and Henning 1976:107).

Artifacts were found with 15 single burials; 2 of these 15 had definite artifact caches associated with them. Approximately 10 multiple burials had some associated artifacts, including hematite, galena, chert tools, ochre, and mussel shell. Cache 1, associated with the skulls of three infants, was divided into a small concentration of material against one of the skulls and other material around the entire group. Objects in the small concentration included one bone awl, one galena disk, 26 pieces of worked hematite, one polished bird bone, one piece of limonite, one chert flake, one antler fragment, and 32 small pieces of galena. Artifacts outside the cache included one projectile point, one stemmed biface, one broken gorget, one perforator, one raccoon mandible, one granite hammer, one bone awl, and three antler flaking tools (Klepinger and Henning 1976:126, Figure 3).

TABLE 13.7.

Summary of Data from Excavated Mortuary Mounds, Platforms, and Areas

						Female				
	Mound	Platform	Pit	Archaic	Woodland	Infant	Juvenile	Subadult	Adult	Mature adult
Hatten II	X	–	–	X	–	–	–	–	–	–
Garrelts I	–	X	–	–	?	–	–	–	–	–
Garrelts II	X	–	–	–	?	–	–	–	–	–
Hatten Village	–	–	X	X	X	–	–	–	1	–
Cave	X	–	X	X	X	–	–	–	–	–
Starr	X	–	–	–	X	–	–	–	–	–
Shaver	X	–	–	–	X	–	–	–	–	–
Calvert	X	–	–	–	X	–	–	–	–	–
Lick Spring	X	–	–	X	X	–	–	–	–	–
Hatten I	X	–	–	X	–	–	–	–	–	–
Cobble									29	
Hatten I	X	–	–	–	X	–	–	–	1	–
Circular										
Hatten I	X	–	–	–	X	–	–	–	–	–
Rectangular										

	Male					Indeterminate					
	Infant	Juvenile	Subadult	Adult	Mature Adult	Infant	Juvenile	Subadult	Adult	Mature adult	Total
Hatten II	–	–	–	–	–	–	–	–	2	–	2
Garrelts I	–	–	–	–	–	–	1	–	2	–	3
Garrelts II	–	–	–	–	–	–	–	4	–	–	4
Hatten Village	–	–	–	–	–	–	–	1	–	–	2
Cave	–	–	–	–	–	–	–	1	3	–	21
Starr	–	–	–	–	–	–	2	–	3	–	–
Shaver	–	–	–	–	–	–	–	–	–	–	–
Calvert	–	–	–	–	–	–	2	3	2	–	7
Lick Spring	–	–	1	–	–	3	1	–	8	–	12+[a]
Hatten I	–	–	–	26	4	5	27	7	10	–	109
Cobble											
Hatten I	–	–	–	–	–	–	–	–	1	–	5
Circular											
Hatten I	–	–	–	–	–	2	–	–	2	–	4
Rectangular											

[a]Plus pieces of 4–6 others.

Cache 2 was located adjacent to an adolescent skull, although several other skulls were nearby. Associated artifacts consisted of chunks of hematite and galena, one small mano, two split and incised beaver incisors, two drills, one projectile point and a fragment of another, and four tools made from deer bone–antler (Klepinger and Henning 1976:127).

Undoubtedly, this portion of Hatten mound dates to the Archaic period. Projectile points found throughout the mound are similar in style to dated points encountered elsewhere in the Midwest. Three radiometric dates—one from level 3 and two from level 4—date to the Late Archaic period. However, the dates from these levels, derived from uncarbonized bone, are inverted. The sample from level 3 (WIS-923) dates to 2210 ± 65 B.C., whereas the two samples from level 4 (WIS-929 and

WIS-963) date to 500 ± 55 B.C. and 650 ± 80 B.C., respectively. There are two possible causes of this inversion: (*a*) The sample from level 3 actually dates a portion of level 4, having been intruded from below, or (*b*) uncarbonized bone from the site failed to provide accurate radiometric dates.

Lick Spring Mound D

The Lick Spring mound group consists of four earth and limestone mounds arranged in pairs on a low bluff extension above Lick Creek. Mound D, excavated during 1977, produced 12 fairly complete individuals and portions of at least 6 others (Donham 1979b). The mound represents a minimum of three construction stages: (*a*) a layer of small limestone cobbles was placed over a prepared surface, forming a rough circle; (*b*) a chamber was excavated

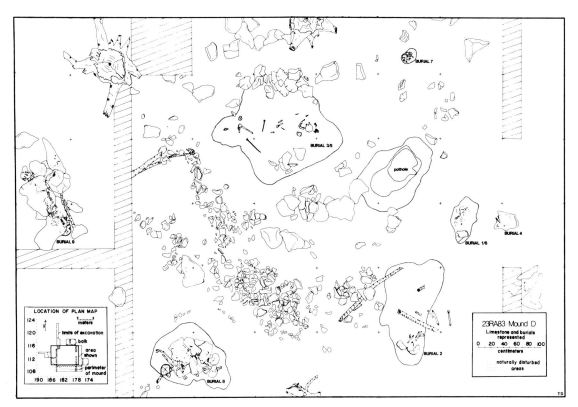

Figure 13.23. Excavation plan of Mound D, Lick Spring mound group, showing location of burials and mapped features (from Donham 1979b).

into the prepared surface; and (*c*) limestone slabs were placed around the chamber to define its outline (Figure 13.23). Artifacts recovered from mound fill date to the Late Woodland period. Pieces of other skeletons, interpreted as postdating the main burials, were found scattered over various portions of the mounds.

Remains from three individuals were present in the central chamber. These included a 25–40-year-old male (burial 5), an adult of indeterminable age and sex (burial 3), and an infant. Both adults appeared to be positioned, disarticulated partial skeletons (i.e., secondary interments). Infant teeth and cranial fragments were scattered throughout the chamber fill. A fragmentary ceramic vessel, pieces of which were found in the fill, may have been a grave inclusion (Donham 1979b:282).

Extrachamber interments were both primary and secondary. A secondary cache of skull fragments (burial 7), a partial skeleton (burial 4), and superimposed infants (burials 1 and 6) with partial skeletons were deposited on the slopes surrounding the central chamber (Figure 13.23). Burials 8, 9, and possibly 2, contained articulated primary inhumations placed in shallow depressions around the southern perimeter of the mound. All three graves were marked on the surface of the mound with limestone slabs (Donham 1979b:284).

Interment in Mound D apparently was not determined on the basis of age or sex; young and old occur, and both sexes are represented among individuals in two of the three adult age groups (Figure 13.24). Most burials were articulated, and, among articulated burials, the flexed position is most frequent. Other variables (Figure 13.24) seem to be patterned randomly. Few apparent grave goods were found with the burials; two broken projectile points were associated with burial 9, and isolated chert flakes or sherds were associated with a few other individuals.

Comparison of Hatten and Lick Spring Late Woodland Components

The Woodland component at Hatten and Mound D at Lick Spring can be compared to document similarities and differences between two roughly contemporaneous mortuary areas. The structures

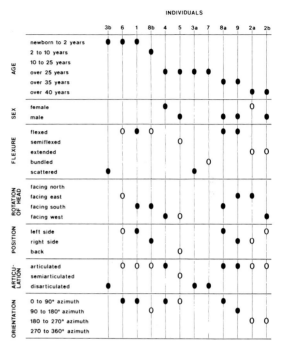

Figure 13.24. Summary of selected attributes (trait present [●]; trait probably present [O]) of the Mound D skeletal series (from Donham 1979b).

of the mounds are similar, both containing at least one interior chamber. Vessel designs present in interchamber and extrachamber contexts at both sites also are similar. The number of individuals from the sites to which a rough estimate of age can be given is comparable—16 for Lick Spring and 18 for Hatten. Both series lack sufficient preservation for reliable sexing, and several individuals can only be aged within the 25–45-year-old range (Figure 13.25). Hatten contained no adults over 45 years of age (Klepinger and Henning 1976:134).

One aspect of mortuary practices that is of interest is the differentiation—by age, sex, and processing of the body—between individuals located in central chambers and those located on mound peripheries. Chambered individuals, when present in mounds with peripheral burials, have been inferred to be more prominent than peripheral individuals (Perino 1968b) and to have elicited a higher level of energy expenditure than individual lime-

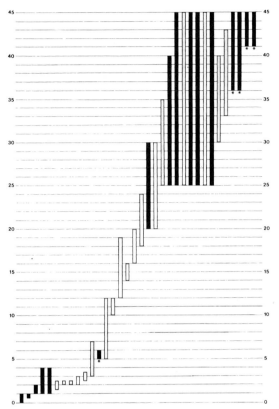

Figure 13.25. Comparison of ranges of estimated age at death of Mound D (■; *n* = 16) and Hatten Mound (□; *n* = 18) Woodland component skeletal series. Asterisk indicates skeletons that post-date Late Woodland components. Adults of indeterminable age are shown in the 25–45 age range (from Donham 1979b).

stone-covered interments (Tainter 1977). However, as Donham (1979b) notes, structural and biological relationships between primary interments and chambered groups within and among mortuary sites are poorly defined in the Salt valley due to incomplete mound excavation (excavation of central areas only) and poor preservation of osteological material. One periphery primary interment similar to those found in Mound D was observed at Starr mound (A. Henning 1964); age and sex were not reported.

In Mound D, only one individual was definitely accompanied by grave inclusions (burial 9—two

point fragments). This individual also was located the farthest distance from the mound apex and was covered with more limestone slabs than other individuals. A large boulder was placed over the limestone grave markers. In terms of relative energy expended on individuals, burial 9 represents the highest level (Donham 1979b:286). If it is inferred that higher social position is represented by the greatest sum of energy expended on an individual, then at Mound D, persons of higher social position were buried in peripheral areas. Donham (1979b) suggests that such locational preference is understandable if mortuary mounds are composed of village refuse (as in the case of Mound D) and central chambers were areas of human cremation or gradual decomposition.

Comparison of Hatten Mound I Archaic and Late Woodland Components

As Klepinger and Henning (1976) demonstrate, there are similarities as well as differences in interment programs between the two components at Hatten. Both primary and secondary inhumations were practiced by Archaic and Late Woodland peoples. In both components male and females of all ages, from infant to adult, were buried similarly in a communal cemetery. If differential treatment of the corpse and inclusion of grave offerings indicate that an individual held an especially high status during life, then the extended female burial in the Late Woodland component "would indicate that women could achieve an important social position in that culture" (Klepinger and Henning 1976:161). Regarding the Archaic component, Klepinger and Henning (1976) postulate that the recovery of grave inclusions with infants (Cache 1) implies that "a certain ascribed status was available to those too young to have earned it" (p. 161).

Three artificially deformed female crania were found in the Archaic component. Klepinger and Henning (1976) offer as an explanation for this phenomenon the selection of women as mates from groups outside the natal territory. These women could have come from the lower Illinois River valley, where nearly all people interred in the Archaic component of the Klunk mounds practiced frontal–occipital cranial deformation (K. B. Hunter, personal communication, in Klepinger and Henning 1976:142). Given the presence of these anomalies in female crania, one can propose that the Hatten mound population had a patrilocal residence pattern. This proposition was tested further by Klepinger and Henning, who compared the homogeneity of males and females with regard to certain metric traits. After removal of the three artificially deformed female crania from the sample, *F*-tests on each of six cranial metric variables with the largest sample size (maximum length, maximum breadth, minimum frontal breadth, head circumference, biorbital breadth, and cephalic index) revealed significant variances ($p < .05$) among females on two variables (maximum length and cephalic index). These same tests on male skulls showed no significant variance. As Lane and Sublett (1972) point out, in a patrilocal society one should find greater heterogeneity among females than males.

There was a striking increase in dental caries from the Archaic (34 of 1000 permanent teeth, or 3.4%) to the Late Woodland period (13 of 87 permanent teeth, or 14.9%). This probably reflects a change in dietary pattern, with a higher percentage of carbohydrate-rich plants (not necessarily corn) in the Late Woodland diet (data from Klepinger and Henning 1976).

Conclusions

One of Buikstra's (1976) elements of an egalitarian society is that status is not ascribed but achieved. We would add the preamble, "if status differences do exist" to her statement. Based on our interpretations of the mortuary populations at Hatten and Lick Spring, we believe status differences did exist within Late Archaic and Late Woodland societies. We also believe that these status differences were based on achievement and not ascription. On this point, we disagree with Klepinger and Henning (1976:161) who postulate that recovery of grave inclusions with infants and juveniles implies that a "certain ascribed status was available to those too young to have earned it." Although we agree that infants were too young to achieve status, there is no reason to believe that infants were not afforded the same *achieved* status as their parents. Given such an arrangement, the visible signs of achievement of a parent or parents could be interred with a dead infant.

Another point must be made—that one of two Archaic caches (Cache 2) at Hatten was found near an adolescent skull. The age range given by Klepinger and Henning (1976:134) for adolescents is 13–18 years. This range makes it possible for the individual to have achieved some degree of status after acceptance into the "adult" society. Klepinger and Henning do not correlate associations of other grave inclusions with age–sex of individuals. If it were the case that grave goods were *not* associated with adolescents in the 12–14 year range, the period which we could speculate directly postdated entrance rites into "adult" society, then this would indicate that status was not ascribed. A male in this age category would very likely not have been able to achieve any measure of status above that afforded everyone. Based on the age estimates of Hatten skeletons supplied by Klepinger and Henning (1976: Tables 1 and 2), the adolescent category often can be subdivided into 2–3-year ranges, but sex rarely can be assessed. Future correlation of Hatten individuals with grave inclusions should aid in answering the question of achieved versus ascribed status.

14

Prehistoric Community Patterns:
Surface to Subsurface Comparison

MICHAEL J. O'BRIEN

The purpose of this chapter is to compare surface and subsurface artifact assemblages from three sites to determine: (a) how well variable densities of surface artifacts predict the presence and location of subsurface features and (b) how well the distributions of artifact classes on the surface reflect the distributions of those same classes below the surface. These are important considerations in the study of prehistoric communities, especially in a regional analysis. A model of surface–subsurface relationships across a region could contribute significantly to development of an excavation strategy that would result in tremendous savings of time and money and that would maximize data recovery.

As pointed out, basic models can be constructed from site-specific data, and their implications can be tested on other sites before applying the model to an entire region. It is not assumed that such models are applicable to the archaeology of other regions, where the archaeological record could be affected by different erosional and depositional regimes.

Beginning, perhaps, with the work of Binford *et al.* (1970) in Carlyle Reservoir, Illinois and continuing through the work of Redman and Watson (1970) and Tolstoy and Fish (1975), among others, surface remains have been used to predict the existence and location of subsurface features, such as houses, trash pits, and other nonportable artifacts. The proposition guiding these inferences is that dense surface remains indicate dense subsurface deposits and light surface remains indicate light subsurface deposits. As has been pointed out, this is not an incommutable rule. As noted elsewhere (Lewarch and O'Brien 1981a), the success of such predictions is conditioned by several factors including artifact classes used for comparison, depth of deposit, and degree of specificity of the prediction.

Most of the polemic in the surface–subsurface isomorphism debate is a reaction to a statement by Redman and Watson (1970:280), framed as an hy-

THE CANNON RESERVOIR
HUMAN ECOLOGY PROJECT

pothesis, that "surface and subsurface artifact distributions are related so that a description of the first will allow prediction of the second." This hypothesis has been subject to considerable misinterpretation because many archaeologists fail to take into account a number of the qualifying observations that appear in the article (Lewarch and O'Brien 1981a:314).

There do appear to be general erosional–depositional regimes where one can expect high correspondence between surface and subsurface classes (Hesse 1971; Redman and Watson 1970; Synenki 1977), but such studies *can* produce the opposite effects. One axiom does seem to hold true: The degree of isomorphism between surface and subsurface can be expected to diminish with increasing depth of deposit. Since the majority of sites in the Cannon Project area are shallow (less than 50–60 cm), this condition is not considered a major problem.

In this discussion three specific questions are addressed with reference to several sites in the Cannon Project area: (*a*) do dense concentrations of surface material indicate the presence of subsurface features; (*b*) what kind of spatial correlation exists between the two, that is, are features located directly beneath areas of high artifact densities; and (*c*) to what degree of certainty can one predict whether or not features will occur? To answer these questions, data collected from portions of 2 ha at Hatten Village, 1 ha at West, and 1 ha at Crooked Creek are used. At each site the plow zone was removed after the surface was intensively and systematically surface collected. At Hatten Village, selected high and low areas of surface artifact density were stripped by machine; at West, ⅔ of the collected area was stripped; and at Crooked Creek, a small portion of the area collected was stripped by hand.

Based on preliminary analysis of surface artifact density distributions at Hatten Village (Chapter 12), it was predicted, prior to stripping, that there were at least three spatially discrete groups of subsurface features. After removal of the plow zone subsurface, features were found within the limits of their predicted locations. At Crooked Creek, these results were duplicated. At West, predicted locations of features were not nearly as accurate.

SURFACE ARTIFACT DENSITY AND LOCATION OF SUBSURFACE FEATURES

Hatten Village

To test the predicted location of three concentrations of subsurface features at Hatten Village, the plow zone was removed from a 50-by-50-m block encompassing each concentration by a bulldozer–belly scraper combination. A larger area subsequently was opened in Ha 8 (SA 6). Only strip areas (SA) 2 and 6 are discussed here.

Strip area 6 revealed 36 features, 31 of which were arranged in three fairly tight clusters. An additional 5 features ran from east to west along the southern edge of the open area (Figure 13.11). The cluster in the northern quarter of Ha 8 was in an area that was not surface collected; field observations of artifact density in this area led to the belief that features would be found here, so the area was subsequently stripped. Figure 14.1 illustrates that the southern and central feature clusters occur in areas dominated by density levels 3 (6–17 artifacts/unit), 4 (18–28), and 5 (29–71).[1] The majority of features occur in units of density levels 3 or 4, although four features in the southern cluster occur in a density level 2 unit. For the most part, density level 5 units are south and east of the southern and central clusters, and they continue into Ha 9 (Figure 12.3). All 5 features outside these clusters are within 2–3 m of a level 5 unit (because of a 50% collection rate, every other unit in the lower right-hand extension of Ha 8 [Figure 14.1] contains an interpolated value).

For this single strip area, units with density values of up to 6 artifacts/unit (density level 3) contain subsurface features, although all units containing features are adjacent to density level 4 units. To provide another view of this relationship, intervals between density levels were changed to the same levels used in Figure 12.3 (Figure 14.2). The result is similar to that depicted in Fig. 14.1, but there is some loss in resolution. Features in the southern

[1]Compare Figure 14.1 with Figure 12.3; density level values have been changed in Figure 14.1 to accentuate patterning within SA 6.

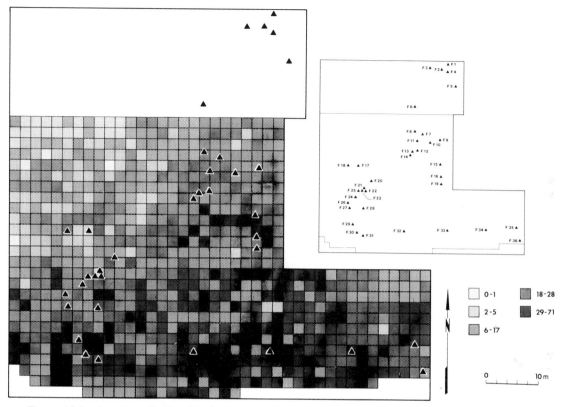

Figure 14.1.   Location of subsurface features (▲) relative to surface artifact density at Hatten Village SA 6.

portion of the strip area are located in areas of high artifact density, whereas features in the central and northern portions are located in, or adjacent to, units at density levels 3 (26–50) and 2 (6–25). Based on comparisons of these distributions with actual unit artifact frequencies (not presented here), it appears that a mean density of 20 artifacts per unit indicates a subsurface feature may occur in the immediate vicinity of the unit. *However*, a few features in SA 6 are located in units with frequencies as low as 2/unit.

Strip Area 2 in Ha 10 contains 11 features, 9 of which are located in the northwestern quadrant (Figure 14.3). Artifact density is an excellent predictor of subsurface features in this area, as illustrated by the patterned distribution of surface artifacts: a tightly clustered set of units with fairly high frequencies relative to adjacent squares to the east and

south. Nine features occur in units with surface artifact frequencies greater than 8; all 9 are adjacent to units containing at least 18 artifacts. The 2 features to the east are in units with 4–5 artifacts. Since the area to the west was not surface collected or stripped, it is not known whether features extend in that direction. The area to the north of SA 2 was collected, and relatively high frequencies continued in that direction (Figure 12.3), including one area of extremely high artifact density (10 contiguous units, each containing 58–104 artifacts). It appears that only the southeastern corner of a dense occupation area was investigated.

West

Plotting total artifact distributions from the surface collection of West revealed a high density area

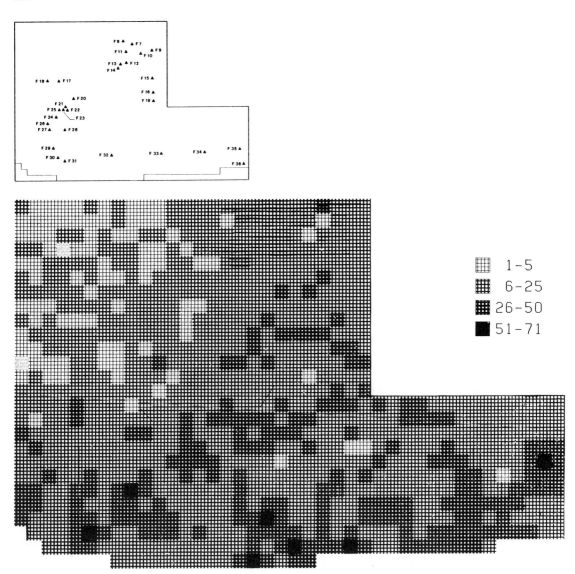

Figure 14.2. Location of subsurface features relative to surface artifact density at Hatten Village SA 6, with levels reset to density gradients shown in Figure 12.3.

in the northern portion of the collection area, surrounded by zones of decreasing frequencies. This is represented in Figure 14.4 by the distribution of standard-score values. The density of surface artifacts decreases rapidly to the west and southwest, but artifact frequencies remain relatively high to the south, where isolated high frequency areas are surrounded by areas of lower artifact density. It was

obvious during collection that the area of greatest artifact density was to the northeast, in a dense grove of trees, and, therefore, could not be collected. Based on the observed artifact density distributions, it was predicted that features would be found in the northern part of the site, in and around the high surface density area.

The plow zone of the entire surface-collected

area in Ha 1 was stripped by machinery; nine sub-surface features were found. Unexpectedly, only four features were located in the high density area; the other five were found in an area southwest of this cluster. Surface artifact frequencies in units containing these five features range from zero to five. The six units that contain portions of F 10, the largest pit excavated at the site, totalled only 11 surface artifacts. Thus, the degree of isomorphism present at West is dissimilar to that at Hatten Village. At West, features were found in the highest density area, but they were also present in areas of extremely low density.

Crooked Creek

When the Crooked Creek site was plowed and surface collected, the densest area of the site was noted as being on the western third of the small terrace on which the site is situated (Figure 14.5). At this point there was interest in determining the

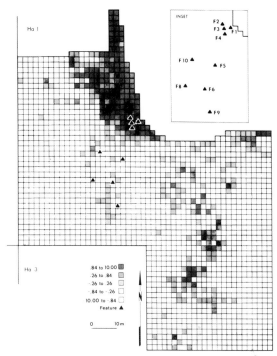

Figure 14.4.   Location of subsurface features relative to surface artifact density at West, with levels determined by standard scores.

time required to hand-strip the plow zone and whether or not the results were much improved over removal by heavy machinery. Due to time limitations, only a small area (242 m²) was opened in the zone of greatest surface artifact density (Figure 14.6). Even in this small area, nine pits and one concentration of hematite were uncovered (one pit and the hematite concentration occurred in the north to south trench and are not shown in Figure 14.6). Since areas with low surface artifact density were not opened, a lower limit on artifact frequency versus presence of subsurface features cannot be placed. In the main excavation, block units that contained features had surface artifact frequencies of 19–32. Feature 8, a small, shallow, basin-shaped pit that was uncovered in the north–south excavation trench, was in a unit that contained only seven surface artifacts. Undoubtedly, further plow zone removal would have resulted in the discovery of more features; however, land-lease problems with the local tenant precluded further work.

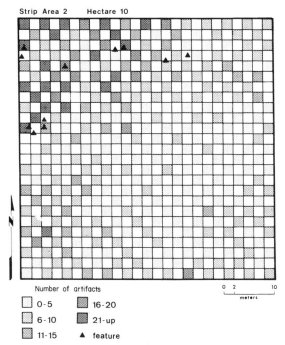

Figure 14.3.   Location of subsurface features relative to surface artifact density at Hatten Village SA 2, HA 10 (from Collins and Griffin 1979).

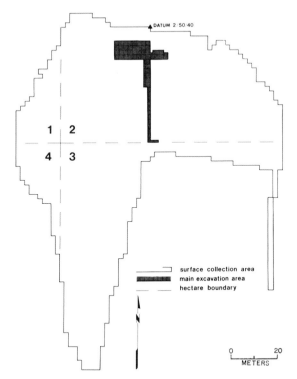

Figure 14.5. Map of surface-collected area at Crooked Creek (after Teter and O'Brien 1979).

Considerations for Predictability

Based on the examples presented here, it is difficult to model the relationship between density of surface artifacts and the presence of subsurface features. Whereas at some sites it appears that high density areas indicate the presence of subsurface features, other sites contain features in areas of extremely light density. It seems more appropriate to state that on sites where surface artifact density varies greatly from area to area, there is a high degree of probability of finding features in high density areas. Factors worth considering when attempting to predict the location of subsurface features from surface artifact distributions include:

Depth of Plow Zone

Sites in the Cannon Project area have plow zones of less than 30 cm, most averaging 25 cm. Therefore, artifacts dragged to the surface through plow-

ing are from a buried surface that is not far removed vertically from the modern surface. Isomorphism is more likely to exist over a shorter vertical distance between horizontal surfaces than over longer distances.

Depth of Deposit

As mentioned previously, isomorphism is partly a function of depth; deep, multicomponent sites will not reflect surface–subsurface isomorphism, except possibly in the upper levels.

Subsurface Conditions

Before removing the plow zone from a site, or even prior to surface-collecting a site, one should shovel-test it to determine not only the depth of the plow zone but also subsurface conditions. One site, Winders, in the project area was surface collected in 1977 and was found to contain dense concentrations of material (up to 80 artifacts/unit). Based on analysis, the most likely areas for feature occurrence were delimited. During surface collection, shovel tests were placed at random intervals over the site to determine the composition of the substrate. The site lies on a wide alluvial fan at the mouth of a deep ravine above the mainstem of the Salt River. The fan is composed of angular pieces of glacial till that have been carried down by an intermittent stream and deposited onto the floodplain; shovel-testing revealed the presence of cultural material to a depth of 40 cm, intermixed with outwash. Because we hoped to find pockets of subsoil in and around the outwash deposits that would contain

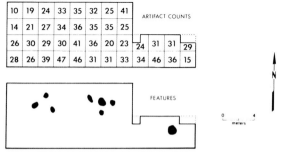

Figure 14.6. Location of subsurface features relative to surface artifact frequencies in the main excavated portion of Crooked Creek.

subsurface features, the decision was made to mechanically remove the plow zone. It turned out that the fan extends over the entire site, a situation that is not conducive to mechanical stripping. In retrospect, more shovel-testing would have revealed this and saved considerable time and expense.

The Impreciseness of the Isomorphic Structure

Based on what has been presented so far, one can see that the relationship between surface and subsurface remains is complex and varies considerably from site to site. The imprecision in the ability of one to predict the other necessitates elaborate planning of the steps in the fieldwork process. One thing has been noted for all sites in the project area where surface collection has preceded plow zone removal: To ensure that one does not miss subsurface features, large areas adjacent to high density surface areas should be opened. This is evident at Hatten Village and especially evident at West. At the former, the majority of features found were just outside the highest density areas, whereas at the latter, five of nine features were found in areas of extremely light surface artifact density.

In summary, the results of work on isomorphism between surface artifact density and the location of subsurface features is encouraging and should provide the basis for future work by other investigators analyzing similar sites. It is clear from this research that no single model of isomorphism between surface and subsurface now exists that describes the norm, variance from the norm, and factors that condition the variance. Numerous factors—such as depth of deposit, depth of plow zone, erosion, type of substrate, length of occupation, and so on—contribute to site structure and must be taken into account.

THE DISTRIBUTION OF SURFACE VERSUS SUBSURFACE ARTIFACT CLASSES

Having investigated the complicated relationships between surface density and the presence–location of subsurface archaeological features at three sites, we now turn our attention to the

degree of isomorphism between the distribution of artifact classes on and beneath the surface. This line of investigation seems particularly important to cultural resource management. For example, one may want to preserve unexposed portions of a site from excavation and yet be able to predict something about the subsurface artifact assemblage.

The stripped portion of West is used to examine the possibility of accurately inferring subsurface structure based on the distribution of surface artifacts derived from features or midden deposits through plowing and other disturbances. Data from West are used because of (*a*) the different degrees of isomorphism between the location of features and surface artifact density and (*b*) the presence of nonpit features inferred to be lithic work areas. As will be shown, select classes of artifacts recovered from the site surface reveal this type of subsurface structure better than others.

Nine subsurface features were excavated at West; their locations are shown in Figure 14.4. Five features (4–6, 8, and 10) contained definite pit outlines at the base of the plow zone, whereas Features 1–3 were defined by dense concentrations of lithic material at the plow zone–subsoil interface. Feature 9, a small concentration of burned limestone, probably represents the contents of a plowed-out pit. Pit feature orifices ranged in size from 40 by 50 cm to 2 by 4 m; feature depth varied between 6 and 30 cm. The lithic scatters covered areas of 4–8 m². Frequencies or weights of artifact classes present in each feature are shown in Table 14.1.

The largest pit excavated, F 10 (.80 m³), contained over 30,000 g of limestone, whereas the smallest pit, F 4 (.09 m³), contained no limestone but the greatest number of flakes (257). Based on the jumbled nature of pit fill, it is assumed that pit material (heat-treated chert debitage and burned limestone) was of secondary nature, possibly derived from lithic reduction areas. The three lithic scatters were composed of material from all stages of lithic tool manufacture. The contents of F 10— animal bone, shell, and 226 pieces of pottery— support a previous conclusion (Warren and Miskell 1981) that West functioned as a residential site (Chapter 12).

Numerous artifact class distributions were used in the surface–subsurface comparison, including

TABLE 14.1.

Contents of Subsurface Features at West

	Feature								
	Pits					Lithic concentrations			
Artifact class	4	5	6	8	10	1	2	3	9
Cores	1	2	–	–	7	13	10	12	–
Core rejuvenation flakes	19	–	–	–	1	16	7	13	–
Core shatter	–	–	–	–	–	1	–	–	–
Primary flakes	–	–	–	–	2	8	2	8	–
Secondary flakes	6	1	–	–	23	31	27	48	1
Tertiary chunks	9	–	–	2	23	35	20	46	–
Tertiary flakes	212	8	3	4	110	607	–	1260	1
Trimming/sharpening flakes	10	–	–	–	–	10	29	58	–
Bifaces	–	–	–	–	1	5	2	2	–
Hammerstones	–	–	–	–	–	–	1	1	–
Projectile points	–	–	–	–	–	–	2	–	1
Burned limestone (g)	–	292	975	6963	30,163	–	–	–	83
Hematite (g)	–	–	–	–	22	–	–	–	–
Sandstone (g)	–	–	–	–	238	–	–	–	–
Pottery (n)	–	–	–	–	226	–	–	–	–

cores, core fragments, core rejuvenation flakes, primary and secondary decortication flakes, tertiary flakes, trimming–sharpening flakes, and ceramics. In addition, spatial intersections of several artifact classes were plotted to assess any overlap with feature location and function. Only two classes— tertiary flakes and trimming–sharpening flakes— proved useful in obtaining overlapping patterning. As illustrated in Figure 12.15, nine units with the highest frequencies of tertiary flakes occur around Features 1–4, three of which contain the most tertiary flakes of any features (Table 14.1). Figure 12.16 illustrates a similar pattern for trimming–sharpening flakes: Three of the five highest frequency units are located directly over, or adjacent to, Features 1–4, the only features that contain artifacts of this class.

Distribution of initial reduction material (Figure 12.15) correlates to a certain degree with the location of features that contain these classes, but the distribution of this class is quite widespread. Although sandstone and burned limestone were not surface collected, their presence in a unit was noted in the field, and a visual assessment of density was made. The assessment for one 2-by-2-m unit over F 10 was "a few pieces noted"; no other unit received a mention of limestone. Thus, although over 30,000 g of limestone were recovered from F 10, only a few pieces were noted on the surface. It appears that for this particular case, large artifacts—such as cores, pieces of sandstone, and limestone chunks—were not reliable predictors of the location, function, or structure of buried deposits. This is not in keeping with other published results (Lewarch and O'Brien 1981a,b), where in controlled tillage–related experiments, large objects are consistently overrepresented in subsequent collection. Smaller objects, such as flakes, consistently are represented by lower percentages of recovery (Lewarch 1979b).

Based solely on the analysis of the spatial distribution of densities of artifact classes at West, one would propose that the majority of pits and work areas occur in the northeastern part of the site. Based on the distribution of cores and core fragments, there are no apparent non-density-dependent patterns (see Chapter 12) to the location of lithic work areas. When one adds to this the distribution of tertiary flakes, a definite pattern emerges, with a concentration of surface flakes in the southern end of the general high density area. Finally, based on the distribution of trimming–sharpening flakes, the southern end of the high density area also is seen as an area for lithic tool maintenance. Nine of the 10 bifacially flaked tools excavated at the site occurred in Features 1–3, directly within units that contained high frequencies of trimming–sharpening flakes. These three features also contained both hammerstones and two of the three projectile points recovered.

SUMMARY

Two lines of investigation were followed in this chapter: (*a*) the relationship between surface artifact density and the location of subsurface archaeological features and (*b*) the spatial relationship between distributions of surface and subsurface artifact classes. Both issues have an important bearing on CRM archaeology and deserve detailed consideration.

To develop a preliminary model of the degree of isomorphism between surface artifact density and subsurface features, or, in practical terms—does an analysis of the first allow predictions about the second?—three sites were used as examples. At Hatten Village a density of 20 artifacts/unit proved to be a fairly good indicator of subsurface features. Although single unit densities do not mean necessarily that subsurface features are located within these units, concentrations of high density units indicate *general* locations of subsurface features. In other words, because of natural and cultural processes that have affected surface distributions, topsoil from areas in and around high-density clusters must be removed to define feature locations.

Because of the small area opened at Crooked Creek, and then only in one of the densest portions of the site, little information can be added to the model derived from work at Hatten Village. Subsurface features occur in units with frequencies of 21–36 artifacts, reflecting the situation at Hatten Village.

Data from West add considerably to the model since five subsurface features occur well outside the high density zone at the site in areas of extremely low surface artifact density. Based on this finding, which may or may not be a localized phenomenon, it is clear that no simple model of isomorphism between subsurface and surface remains is applicable to the entire project area. Various considerations must be taken into account, including depth of plowing, amount of erosion, and rate of soil deposition (Chapter 12). We have found that the use of extensive test pits across a site surface prior to plow zone removal will aid in determining the effects of these processes.

To investigate the spatial relationship between surface and subsurface distributions of individual artifact classes, data from West were used. Two artifact classes, tertiary flakes and trimming–sharpening flakes, showed significant overlap between surface and subsurface distributions. Nine units with high frequencies of surface-collected tertiary flakes occurred around three of the four features containing the most tertiary flakes, and three of the five units containing the highest frequencies of surface-collected trimming–sharpening flakes were located over or adjacent to the only four subsurface features containing artifacts of that class. One significant discovery was that larger artifacts—such as cores, limestone chunks, and pieces of sandstone—did not reflect subsurface concentrations of these materials. Based on previous research, this finding was not anticipated.

One important result of work at West was our demonstration that small artifacts, such as trimming–sharpening flakes, are important segments of the total artifact assemblage and can be used successfully in surface collection analysis. Small artifacts not only impart considerable information about the context of subsurface deposits but also identify functions implied by the deposits. This result should have important implications for work at other shallow, plowed archaeological sites in the Midwest and elsewhere.

15

The Structure of Historic Communities

MICHAEL J. O'BRIEN, ROGER D. MASON,
AND JACQUELINE E. SAUNDERS

Analysis of the structure of rural Euro-American communities was conducted on three levels: the community, the farmstead, and the household. This tripartite analysis allows an ever-narrowing focus from general community structure down to the basic spatial unit of analysis—the *household*—which is defined as a group of related people living in the same residence who coöperate in performing a wide range of domestic activities (Winter 1974:981). The results of these analyses cannot be understood fully if they are separated from the Euro-American settlement pattern analysis (Chapter 17), which forms the framework for all work on historic period occupation of the project area.

South (1977a,b) and others have shown recently that historical archaeology has come of age and has developed methods and theory grounded in anthropology. It also has been demonstrated (e.g., Lewis 1977) that historical archaeology can be used to examine sociocultural change in an historical situation. In 1977 the project began to examine historic period sociocultural change in the project area as it was reflected on the three levels mentioned

previously. Given that there were over 350 nineteenth-century sites in the project area and numerous historical records to document some of these sites, there was an excellent opportunity to understand cultural change during the early nineteenth century.

Understanding the composition of a rural community at any level requires a data set over which there is chronological and spatial control. This criterion governed selection of a sample of sites for detailed study. If a particular site could be tied to a number of documentary sources—such as land purchase records, census data, genealogies, tax records, etc.—it was considered as a possibility for more intensive study. Other factors influencing selection of the final sample of sites included (*a*) amount of postdepositional disturbance (either from farming or reservoir-clearing activities); (*b*) whether or not the plan of a farmstead was known (derived from ground inspection or interviews with local residents); and (*c*) the presence of standing architecture to guide excavation.

It must be noted that the sample of sites for

excavation was dictated by the scope of work provided by the Corps of Engineers. They, in consultation with various project personnel, composed a list of 21 sites at which work could be conducted. These were drawn from the 34 sites determined eligible for inclusion on the National Register of Historic Places. The 21 sites were those whose integrity was most complete, as measured against the three criteria just mentioned. A fourth criterion also was assessed—the degree of completeness of the archival record for a particular site [i.e., land acquisition and conveyance data, census data, etc. (Chapter 17)].

It also must be noted that the Corps of Engineers was quite specific as to what portions of sites could be excavated: Excavation was limited to areas within or immediately adjacent to previously identified significant structures. This contract specification precluded, in most cases, the sampling of areas of the farmstead away from the main residential structure. In a few instances, permission was obtained to sample peripheral areas, but, for the most part, residences were outlined, and the intervening areas were excavated completely. This restriction obviously presents a bias when one tries to assess the functional implications of refuse disposal patterns away from residential structures, but this bias is overcome partially through the intensive mapping of farmsteads.

As is noted later in this chapter, because of dwindling time and money, only 7 of the 21 farmsteads were excavated extensively. The other 14 sites were mapped, surface collected when possible, and photographed. Importantly, 5 of the 7 excavated sites were located in a section of the project area known historically as the "Smith settlement." In this case, the decision was made to bypass a "regional sample" and to concentrate resources in an area over which there existed good control of both chronology and archival data. Given the time and budget limitations, it was believed that understanding the archaeology of a single community in greater detail was better than knowing a little about several unrelated sites. In retrospect, this decision is viewed as a valid research strategy and will be discussed later in this chapter.

Our efforts were enhanced by the assistance of the Historic American Buildings Survey (HABS), whose architects produced architectural plans and drawings for 15 structures located in the impact area of the reservoir. Their documentation of construction technique and efforts in dating different phases of construction of the buildings made our analysis much easier.

THE ORGANIZATION OF RURAL COMMUNITIES

The term *community* is difficult to define, not only in archaeological terms, but in anthropological ones as well. Gjerde's (1979:405) definition of community as "a social unit occupying a space in which its members interact" can be expanded to incorporate common goals and institutions that enable the members to identify with the sense of community. Sussman (1959:1) follows this notion of community: "A community is said to exist when interaction between individuals has the purpose of meeting individual needs and obtaining group goals."

Reconstruction of historic communities, a goal common to much recent work in settlement geography, can be accomplished, as Gjerde (1979:406) notes "by observing the spatial patterns of interaction of human groups and by determining the probable affinitive and institutional ties among the selected inhabitants."

Communities in the Study Area

Communities established during the early colonization phase of settlement are of particular interest because: (a) They represent initial settlement of a relatively unknown area and can be examined in a "pristine state"; (b) excellent documentary data of their formation exist; and (c) relatively little is known of early-nineteenth-century Euro-American archaeological assemblages in the Midwest. Two early communities identified from historical documents are detailed here. They were chosen on the basis of (a) differences in locational strategies on the part of their founders and (b) the existence of fairly detailed records on land ownership and kin affinity. Due to incomplete analysis of other early communities in the project area, it is unclear how representative these communities are. They do, however, offer pertinent data for testing the model of nineteenth-century settlement as discussed in Chapter 17. The two communities are the Smith

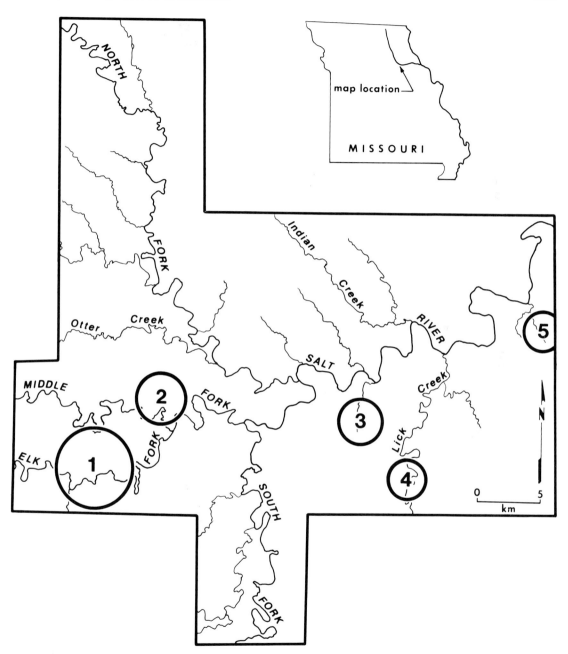

Figure 15.1.   Locations of early historic settlements in the project area. (1) Elk Fork settlement; (2) Smith settlement; (3) Mt. Prairie settlement; (4) Lick Creek settlement; (5) Ely settlement (from Warren *et al.*, 1981).

settlement, located in the west third of the project area, and the Mt. Prairie settlement, located in the east-central portion of the project area (Figure 15.1).

The Mt. Prairie Settlement

Field survey of the Mt. Prairie settlement located the sites of seven farmsteads, all represented by standing structures or foundations (Figure 15.2). The earliest documented farmstead was established in 1821 by Stephen Scobee, Sr., and all others of that decade have been tied to individuals appearing in the 1830 census. Distribution of farmsteads is consistent, with all situated on upland margins overlooking Pigeon Roost Creek or tributary streams and most near the 1820s prairie–timber boundary. The farmsteads form a U-shaped settle-

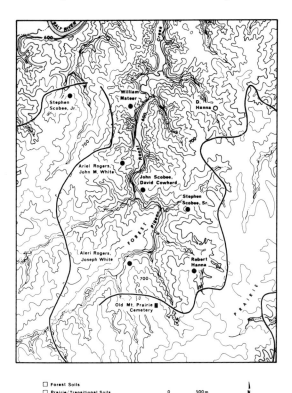

Figure 15.2. Map of Mt. Prairie community showing known and probable locations of early nineteenth-century farmsteads (from Warren *et al.*, 1981).

ment pattern that surrounds the upper reaches of Pigeon Roost Creek and generally parallels the ecotone (Figure 15.2).

Although data on social and kin relationships are incomplete, it is possible in some instances to correlate ownership with data from original land purchase records to derive state and county of origin for original land entrants. Coincidence of surnames among early residents implies that kin-based social interactions were common within the area. Furthermore, the community maintained a post office that served colonists in distant loci until at least 1831 (Powers 1931). Two churches—Presbyterian and Baptist—were established early in the colonization phase and served members as far away as Florida, Missouri. These data tentatively suggest that the Mt. Prairie settlement functioned as a distinct, socially interdependent community, composed of economically independent individuals.

Economic independence of the community was not reflected in early commercial development within the settlement. Prior to 1840, there are no indications that stores, taverns, or mills were constructed in the community. The earliest evidence of commercial ventures appears in Florida, some 8 km to the northwest, where mills were constructed on the North and South fork of the Salt River to process agricultural products of the region. Stores and taverns were constructed shortly thereafter to accommodate a growing population in the central Salt River area.

The Smith Settlement

The Smith settlement (Figure 15.3) was founded in approximately 1820, when Joseph Smith, Sr., and his family immigrated to the lower Middle Fork locality from Bath County, Kentucky. The earliest record of land entry for Joseph Smith is in Section 34, T55N, R9W (Figure 15.3), where, sometime during 1819–1820, land entered by Randolph Biggs was assigned to Smith. Records indicate that Smith had at least six children,[1] one of which (Alexander W.)

---

[1]It is possible that "James H. Smith, Sr." (the Sr.–Jr. designations were never given in land transactions; they were assigned by us for clarity) was a son of Joseph, Sr. We doubt this, however, since he is never mentioned in Joseph's will, as all other children are. Although he also may be no kin, we treat him as a brother to Joseph and treat "James H. Smith, Jr." as his son.

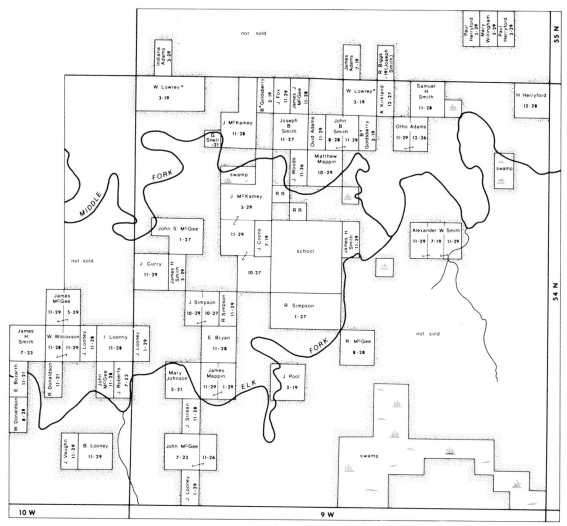

Figure 15.3. Land entry map for the Smith settlement, 1819–1829. Asterisk indicates a speculator land entry.

entered land in 1819, about 3 km south of the land assigned to his father.

Other families, many of which were friends or relatives of the Smiths, settled in this area during the next decade. The Mappin and Johnson families, for example, were related by marriage to the Smiths; marriages occurred both in Kentucky and later in the Smith settlement. Joseph Smith's (proposed) brother, James H. (Sr.), entered land in Section 23, T54N, R10W in July, 1823, placing him some 5 km southwest of his brother's holdings.

Social and kinship interactions among the Smiths and other families clearly influenced the resulting aggregations of farmsteads. It appears that two distinct processes were involved: (a) budding and proximal settlement of new family units and (b) mass colonial immigration of interacting social units that maintained social linkages established prior to migration (Chapter 5; Warren et al. 1981). The budding process is commonly recognized as an aspect of the spread phase, conforming to Hudson's (1969) theory of cluster development.

However, this process alone cannot account for the early establishment of the Smith settlement. The second process, termed *interdependent migration* (Warren *et al.* 1981), constituted the relocation of an interacting social network that profoundly affected the configuration of colonial settlement in the area.

The following section outlines a model of land-purchasing strategies through time, using data on the Smith settlement. Environmental variables are weighed against social variables, such as kinship and marriage ties, and these in turn are weighed against other variables, such as logistics and mobility. Data consist of land purchases by the Smith siblings, the Mappins, and the McKameys, all of whom immigrated to the middle Salt River area during the 1820s.

Before turning attention to the formation of the community, one should note that the Smith settlement, paralleling the Mt. Prairie settlement, never contained a commercial center. During the 1820s, the nearest distribution points for goods and services were New London and Palmyra, well to the east and northeast of the project area. In the 1830s, after the founding of Paris (to the west) and Florida (to the east), it became much easier to get needed supplies.

The Formation of a Community

During preliminary analysis, environmental factors were treated separately from other factors that contributed to the settlement pattern represented in Figure 15.3. By 1829, all Smiths, Mappins, McKameys, and many other families had entered land in T54N, R9W, the eastern portion of T54N, R10W, and the southern portion of T55N, R9W. This marked the end of the colonization period for these families. Many of them made additional purchases of land during the next decade (the spread phase), but these additions did not represent an entrance into an unknown environment.

During the early stages of analysis of settlement in this area, it was posited that the location of farmsteads dating to 1819–1829 would reflect the distribution noted in the Mt. Prairie settlement (i.e., near or on the prairie–timber boundary). Location near the ecotone, coupled with a desire to locate near kin, should be represented by a linear settle-

ment pattern: Farmsteads located along the prairie border with close kin groups holding adjoining land. Location along the ecotone could have been due to the presence of sufficient trees for use in erecting structures but not so many trees as to make cultivation difficult. The richer prairie soils, although usually incapable of being broken until the advent of the steel plow, were encroached upon in places by stands of timber. This kept the soil fairly loose, and once the timber was burned and stumps removed, the soil was broken easily by non-steel-tipped plows.

Environmental Conditions

Three variables relating to land purchases between 1819 and 1829 are investigated in this section: tree density, soil fertility, and crop productivity. These are three key determinants to the chronological development of land-purchase strategies.

Tree Density   Figure 15.4 illustrates five levels of tree density (by quintiles) for the Smith settlement area. The figure is an enlargement of a section of Figure 3.21. Patches of prairie (<3 stems/ha) occur along the northern boundary of the area and encroach quite heavily into the area along its southern border. An isolated patch occurs in the western quarter of the area. Level 1 (3–41 stems/ha) density occurs sporadically throughout the area, the largest segment being in the center of the settlement. This large zone of sparsely timbered land extends across all topographic features: from upland prairie, through the Elk Fork bottoms, across the upland divide between Elk and Middle forks, and into the Middle Fork bottoms. This anomaly surely must be a result of fire, possibly one that occurred just prior to the GLO survey.

Level 2 density (42–65 stems/ha) occurs on upland divides but also extends into bottomlands. Level 3 (66–89 stems/ha) occurs on gentle to steep slopes and extends into a few broader bottomlands. Levels 4 (90–131 stems/ha) and 5 (132–521 stems/ha) are restricted to lower slopes and bottomlands. As we will show, this complex mosaic of dense and sparse vegetation was deciphered by nineteenth-century settlers, and the information was used to plan land purchases.

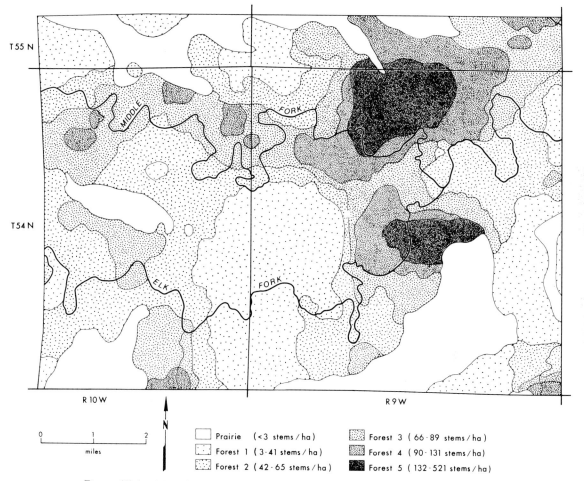

Figure 15.4. Map showing tree density for land in and around the Smith settlement.

Soil Fertility A soil fertility ranking was derived for T54N, R9W by analyzing the GLO surveyor's (Byrd Lockhart) line description of the soil along each section line and by ranking his comments from "rich" to "poor" (Figure 15.5). This is a somewhat subjective procedure since his comments tended to vary in places from "a little broken but good soil" to "might do for farming" (Chapter 3). Where we were unsure of the rank, both were shown. The analysis was limited to the single township because other surveyors who laid out lines to the west and north did not provide comparable soil descriptions.

The spatial trend for the first- and second-rate land is an X shape that crosses in Section 15. Based strictly on this written assessment of early-nineteenth-century soil, we might expect the earliest occupants to have settled along the top tier of sections of the township and then in a southwesterly trend through the middle of the section.

Crop Productivity A crop productivity index was calculated for each 40-acre quarter–quarter section by measuring the acreage of each soil type as represented on Soil Conservation Service (SCS) field sheets, converting the resultant values to per-

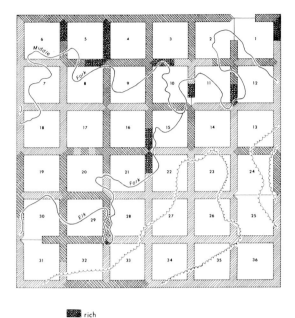

rich
good
poor

Figure 15.5. Map showing soil fertility rankings for land in and around the Smith settlement (T54N, R9W) based on General Land Office descriptions, August 4–26, 1816, Byrd Lockhart, Jr., surveyor.

centages, multiplying these percentages by productivity indices for each soil type as furnished by the SCS, adding these values, and dividing the final figure by 100 (Figure 15.6). This index was compiled to determine if high value areas, representing good crop land, were being bought earlier than units of low value. Obviously, this index was not available to early-nineteenth-century settlers, but there may have been some soil types with high productivity indices being selected over lesser quality soils that had lower productivity indices.

Generally, the higher values parallel the river in units through which the river flows or in units containing large, fertile bottoms. Certain areas near the prairie–timber boundary also show significantly higher productivity indices.

Land Settlement

Patterns of land entry in the Smith settlement can be discerned by dividing entries into separate

periods. This is illustrated in Figure 15.7, which shows land purchases by period for the years 1819–1829. Once the pattern of general land entry has been defined and explained, attention can turn to patterns of land entry by selected individuals and to subsequent patterns of expansion of those individuals' land-holdings.

If our assumptions are correct, the patterns in land entry and settlement location noted for the Mt. Prairie community also should hold for the Smith settlement. Thus, one would expect location on or near the prairie–timber boundary.

A trend appears when one maps the land entries on timber and soil maps. The three earliest purchases (1819), in zones of relatively high timber density, are all adjacent to or within a kilometer of prairie, in areas that do not have particularly high soil productivity indices.

The next purchases occurred between 1821 and 1825, when seven entrants bought land in the southwestern corner of T54N, R9W and the south-

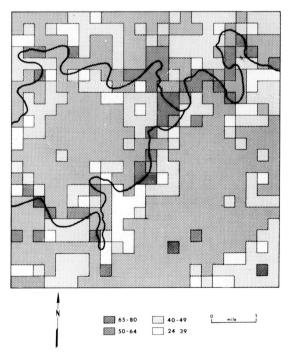

N

65-80   40-49
50-64   24 39

0   mile   1

Figure 15.6. Crop productivity index for land in and around the Smith settlement (T54N, R9W) based on United States Soil Conservation Service figures.

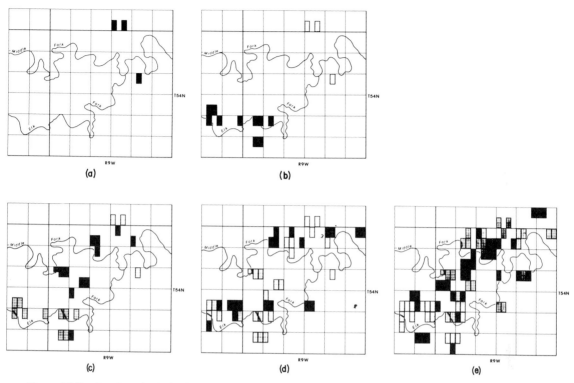

Figure 15.7.   Land entries in the Smith settlement by period. Black squares indicate purchases in the following years: (a) 1819, (b) 1820–1825, (c) 1826–1827, (d) 1828, (e) 1829.

eastern corner of T54N, R10W, an area of low timber density. Among these entrants were James H. Smith and Mary Johnson, daughter of Joseph Smith. These seven entries still are near the prairie–timber boundary, but unlike the 1819 purchases, they are near a permanent source of water, the Elk Fork. It is evident that the inhabitants of this early Elk Fork community were selecting land that was not timbered heavily and that was adjacent to or near the river. Not known is the degree of kin ties among the settlers that could account for their entering land in such close proximity to one another.

The next period of land entry studied is 1826–1827. Some of Joseph Smith's sons are included among entrants during this period. Landholders in the Elk Fork area began buying land to the northeast as Smith's sons expanded their holdings to the southwest. By the end of 1827, only a small gap existed between the two. During this period a shift in land-purchasing strategy occurred:

Instead of buying land in sparsely timbered areas, the entrants bought land according to soil productivity, regardless of how much timber was on it. This is not reflected so much in the soil productivity map (Figure 15.6) but in the map showing the ranking of soil as reported by the GLO surveyor (Figure 15.5). As mentioned earlier, the trend for better soil is in a diagonal from the northeast to the southwest and across the upper tier and part of the second tier of sections in the township (Figure 15.5). This trend in soil productivity is reflected in the pattern of settlement during the period 1826–1827.

We suggest two hypotheses for this development: (*a*) by 1826, the GLO surveyor's records were obtainable from the government (or were in the land purchase office) and were used by entrants to gauge their purchases, and/or (*b*) the new entrants were in communication with persons already living in the area and were told where the most productive land was located. Certainly new purchases by persons already living in the study area were based on experience with the environment and knowledge of which land was most productive.

The next period, 1828, shows a polarity in settlement between the southwestern and northern central portions of the study area. This is due mainly to expansion of landholdings by existing settlers and an attempt on the part of some of them to keep their new purchases as close as possible to their original holdings. All Smith brothers had made their initial purchases by the end of this period.

The last period dealt with here, 1829, saw considerable expansion in landholdings by existing settlers, plus some influx of new settlers. Expansion and new purchases still were in areas of good soil, regardless of tree density. By the end of this period, John McKamey had become the largest landholder in the area, having bought a corridor of land from the top to the middle of T54N, R9W.

In summary, decisions about land purchases in and around the Smith settlement involved five considerations: (*a*) tree density; (*b*) proximity to the prairie–timber boundary; (*c*) soil fertility; (*d*) distance to kin; and (*e*) compactness of landholdings. Of note is the importance of factors *a* and *b* during the first half of the third decade of the nineteenth century, the early colonization period, and the rise in importance of factor *c* during the second half of the decade.[2] Discussed below is the relationship of

factors *d* and *e* to the spatial distribution of landholdings of several persons in the Smith settlement to determine if existing patterns might be explained by these factors.

Individual Patterns of Land Entry

In simplified terms, two basic patterns of land entry by an individual were identified: *consolidated* (nucleated) and *dispersed*. For present purposes, if a person bought land more than a mile away from his residence, and there are no contiguous boundaries between the two parcels of land, then that pattern is designated as dispersed. Conversely, if parcels are within a mile of each other, the pattern is designated as consolidated. This rough breakdown allows inspection of the question of logistics (i.e., how much effort is needed to maintain one's holdings).

Consolidated Pattern   Certainly the most consolidated landholding in the settlement was that of John McKamey (Figure 15.8), who, by 1829, had contiguous landholdings throughout the upper half of the township. By 1833 he owned 1160 acres, all but 80 of which had contiguous borders. Based on ranking by wealth[3] for the entire known population of the Cannon Project area, derived from the 1830 census, he ranked fifth of 271 heads of household.

His land was along the western edge of the band of good soil identified by the GLO surveyor. In fact, his holdings in Section 5 were in a locale almost unparalleled in the study area for soil fertility. His decision in 1831 to expand his holdings to the western edge of Section 17, an area of poorer soils, appears to have been based on his decision to keep his holdings consolidated.

Another example of consolidated landholdings is illustrated in the distribution of land entered by Alexander Smith, son of Joseph Smith (Figure 15.8). All purchases were joined by common bor-

---

[2]Recent research, conducted after this chapter was written, indicates that certain cultural factors were as important as physical ones in land purchase decisions (Warren *et al.* 1982; see also Footnote 3 to Chapter 17). A discriminant function analysis of dated first land entries in the Smith settlement correctly classified (using jackknife posterior classification procedures) 66% of 633 40–acre quadrats into four purchase periods. Consistent with the interpretations presented in this chapter, soil evaluations of GLO surveyors compose the most powerful of 36 discriminating variables. Good soil ratings are overrepresented in the first (1819–1825), second (1826–1829), and third (1830–1833) periods, and are underrepresented in the fourth (1834–1855). However, the variable that associates most strongly with purchases of the second period is distance to nearest road. Over 80% of purchases during this period are in the two nearest road distance quintiles, and a county road constructed in 1825 bisects remarkably well the diagonal configuration of settlement shown in Figure 15.7. GLO soil evaluations also form a northeast–southwest diagonal, but it is displaced

somewhat to the southeast. Soil quality undoubtedly was an important consideration in land purchase decisions, but access to routes of transportation apparently was a more important factor during the second period of land purchases in the Smith settlement.

[3]Wealth is based on amount of land and number of slaves owned (Mason 1982).

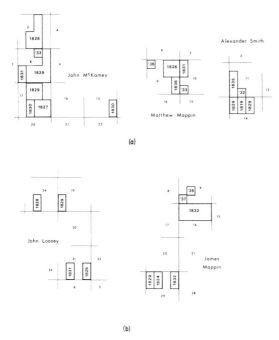

Figure 15.8. (a) Nucleated versus (b) dispersed patterns of land purchase.

ders, creating a compact holding. The land he entered, lying south of Middle Fork, was sparsely timbered and was located in an area of lesser soil fertility. Purchase of this 360 acres, much of it not the best land in the area, suggests a decision on Smith's part to amalgamate his holdings, sacrificing higher productivity for logistical reasons.

The third example is illustrated in the distribution of land entered in Sections 9 and 10 by Matthew Mappin (Figure 15.8). From 1829 to 1836 Mappin successfully bought land adjacent to or within a quarter-mile of his original 160-acre entry. It is clear that Mappin was selective in his choice of land; in 1833 he passed up adjacent land to the south of his original holding in favor of a tract to the southeast. It was not until 1836 that he purchased the 80 acres passed over previously.

Dispersed Pattern   Two examples of dispersed patterns of land acquisition for the early period are those of John Looney and James Mappin (Figure 15.8). Looney's entrance of land in Section 24 in 1828 mirrored the pattern for that year of buying land in sparsely timbered areas. In 1829 he

bought additional land, just to the east of this original holding, in a sparsely timbered area but also purchased 80 acres well to the south (Section 31). This purchase included approximately 40 acres of moderately timbered land and 40 acres of prairie. Given that there was considerable distance between the two purchases of 1829, this appears to be a deliberate move to gain access to the prairie–timber boundary. This access was broadened in 1831 when Looney bought 80 acres to the west of the 1829 purchase (Figure 15.8).

James Mappin's landholdings show an early tendency for consolidation, followed by an orientation toward dispersed holdings (Figure 15.8). His early purchases (1824–1832) are in the southwestern corner of T65N, R9W, whereas his later purchases spread out to the north. In 1832 he purchased the northern half of Section 16 and in 1834 sold a portion of his original holdings (including his house) and moved to the new location. This movement must have been considered so advantageous that it outweighed the factor of distance to the holdings that he still maintained to the south. Based on soil classification (Figure 15.5), this move from good soil to soil of the same quality was not drastic. However, the move from a relatively sparsely timbered area to one of moderate tree density was more marked.

In summary, two patterns of land acquisition—consolidated and dispersed—were in operation throughout the 1820s and 1830s. Some settlers preferred to consolidate their holdings, often at the expense of maximum productivity, whereas others made the decision to buy a certain tract of land at the expense of decentralizing their operation. Although there is a slight tendency in the data for purchases to start out as consolidated and change over time to dispersed, the number of analyzed cases is too small to confirm this as a general trend.

THE ORGANIZATION OF RURAL FARMSTEADS

Rural farmsteads are numerous in the project area, and many were in operation until the early 1970s, when they were purchased by the Corps of Engineers. Sale of the land resulted in the destruction of many farm structures through vandalism or salvage operations. By the time site survey was carried out (late 1977), few standing outbuildings existed. The few that did remain consisted mainly of heavy timber barns that could not be dismantled easily or buildings that were in such poor condition that reusable materials could not be salvaged. It was often the case that piles of rubble and foundations allowed at least tentative reconstruction of a number of structures.

Spatial Configuration

The typical farmstead in the project area consists of a residence (discussed later in this chapter), house service structures, and dependency structures. Location for the residence and dependency structures is usually determined by topography, vegetation, or aesthetics. The residence most often is placed with the long axis (facade) parallel to the main access through the property, whether this is a public road or lane. Farmsteads established during the colonization phase were located in areas not served by many public roads; hence, lanes were cut through property (or possibly through several properties) to provide access to a county road.

House Service Structures

House service structures include privies, cellars, smokehouses, laundry houses, well houses, and tool–storage sheds. These structures for the most part are located within the house yard or just outside it. The most intraclass variety in these classes of structures exists in root cellars, which range in size from 2 by 2 m and 1.5 m deep to over 3.5 by 4 m and 2.5 m deep. They may be attachments to residences or separate structures and may have fairly elaborate superstructures erected over them. The location of the cellar is almost always to the rear of the house, although it occasionally may be off to one side.

Dependency Structures

Dependency structures—including barns, hen houses, hog houses, corn cribs, and granaries—are usually sited to take advantage of sun exposure, prevailing winds, and natural drainage. Buildings often are clustered in a compact square to accommodate the needs of the farmer or landowner. Typical of small nineteenth-century farms is the sub-

stitution of smaller, specialized, multipurpose structures that could be constructed and maintained by a minimal work force for large multipurpose structures.

The most variety in dependency structures is in barns, which take on any number of shapes and sizes and range from small, single-aisle, frame structures to two-story, multiaisle buildings constructed of heavy timber with mortice-and-tenon joints. The norm is a structure measuring approximately 8 by 10 m, containing a loft and two aisles, and capped by a steeply gabled roof. Barns usually are located well to the rear of the residence, often separated from it by one or two fenced barnyards. In a few instances the barn and barnyard are in front of the house, usually as a result of sloping terrain to the rear of the residence.

Economic Development and Change in Organization

Change in the economic status of a person or family often led to changes in everyday life, including the replacement of a residence with one more elaborate or modification and upgrading of a farmstead. If we relate the configuration of farmsteads to particular modes of production, then shifts in one should be reflected in the other. The difference in composition of a farmstead belonging to a subsistence farmer compared to that of a farmer producing for a market economy is dramatic, the former consisting of possibly a barn and shed, and the latter of a variety of specialized structures.

Without mechanization, which forces the twentieth-century farmer to house various types of machinery used in planting, plowing, disking, cultivating, spraying, and combining, a midnineteenth-century farmer could have applied his extra capital toward elaboration of the few structures he had. Gauging by some modifications to structures in the project area, this certainly was practiced.

The Samuel H. Smith Farmstead: A Model of Farmstead Development

The one example of change in farmstead layout that is well documented is the Samuel H. Smith house and farmstead, located in the northern portion of the Smith settlement. The farm, which was in operation for over 140 years, exhibits a life history that is common in rural areas: The farmstead grows in number of structures until a peak is reached, probably around the period 1900–1930; the number of structures then declines as modern farming practices replace older ones and electricity negates the need for spring houses, icehouses, and smokehouses.

Figure 15.9 shows the maximum extent of the farmstead and date of erection of various outbuildings. The farmstead was begun around 1830 when Samuel H. Smith erected a two-story double-pen log house on a 160-acre tract of land he entered in 1828. It is presumed that the original barn sat on or near the site. Over the years, Smith (and eventually his son-in-law) added structures for hogs, sheep, and chickens; grain storage sheds; a milkhouse; an icehouse; a smokehouse, and a root cellar. By 1960, most structures had been razed and were a sign of the changing times: from diversified farm interests to agricultural specialization.

Smith's ability to expand his farmstead and to extend his interests into sheep raising was made possible by wealth that was greater than that of his neighbors. This wealth was symbolized by the construction of a large, timber addition to his already massive log home, around 1850. This created what must have been one of the grandest pre-Civil War residences in the area, adding to Smith's prominence in the community.

THE ORGANIZATION OF RURAL HOUSEHOLDS: THE RESIDENTIAL STRUCTURE

One result of archaeological survey and archival research was identification of over 350 pre-1920 residences, consisting of standing structures, foundations, and known locations. Tree- and structure-clearing operations in the proposed reservoir area began prior to 1977 and hindered attempts to document many of the structures.

Goals for this part of the project included: (*a*) locating discernible traces of nineteenth- and early-twentieth-century occupation; (*b*) determining which sites were eligible for inclusion on the National Register of Historic Places; (*c*) dating main blocks and additions of eligible residential structures; (*d*) mapping those residences and related

farmsteads; (*e*) preparing architectural renderings of houses determined eligible; (*f*) creating a classification system for houses; and (*g*) analyzing functional inferences derived from the classification system. All but step (*g*) have been completed.

Creation of a classification system is necessary to categorize objectively stylistic and formal elements of house construction. Such a classification also ensures objective comparison of different structures. As pointed out elsewhere (O'Brien *et al.* 1980), this system can be used as an initial sorting procedure for determining the eligibility of a structure for inclusion on the National Register. Used in such a role, it can answer questions concerning duplication of style: Are there similar or identical structures present in a particular area, some of which may not need mitigation?

The Need for a Classification System

The need for classification of historic residences is not new to historical geography. Kniffen saw a need to construct a typology that would deal with the myriad forms he observed in the eastern and southeastern United States:

> it was deemed necessary to set up concurrently a typology quantified as to numerical importance and qualified as to areal and temporal positions, and to seek out origins, routes of diffusion, adaptations, and other processes affecting change or stability [Kniffen 1965:550].

Kniffen's success in assessing the geographic movement of certain architectural trends is due to his careful treatment of variability within certain large-scale types, such as the I-house.

Jakle's (1976) study of rural houses in a two-county area of Illinois is one example of classification in which house characteristics were combined to identify structure types and, with inclusion of architectural style, house types. He notes that although geographers have long been interested in identifying house types and tracing their origin and diffusion, they have not used an objective classification scheme to meet their objectives: "They have yet to agree as to which house characteristics are really significant and how these characteristics should be scaled" (Jakle 1976:31).

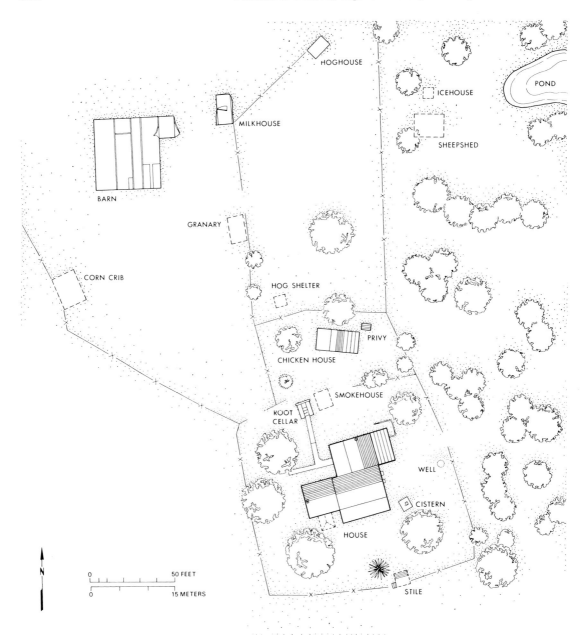

Figure 15.9. Spatial configuration of the Samuel Smith farmstead.

A Classification System for Nineteenth-Century Houses

The classification system developed for houses in the project area employs a set of *n* attributes arranged under 31 dimensions. These dimensions range from type of construction material to house shape, number and placement of chimneys, number and location of entrances, lower- and upper-story facade arrangement, and so on. The number of individual attributes under each dimension varies according to the number of different examples observed in the sample of houses [*n* = 65] used in analysis. The system is described fully in O'Brien *et al.* (1980).

The sample used in this classification forms the basis for a typology of residential structures (O'Brien *et al.* 1980), derived from the co-occurrence of certain attributes on a structure. The major criteria for type formation are facade arrangement and basic floor plan. Whereas other dimensions, such as chimney placement, are important in defining a certain class, these dimensions are not weighted as heavily as whether the floor plan consists of one, two, or three rooms or whether the facade is characterized by a door–window versus window–door arrangement.

Types were not developed as temporal markers. Although many types are time sensitive, others existed over a long temporal span. It is well documented that log construction generally was re-

placed by light frame construction, but construction material is not viewed as significant to a type definition because several types are represented by frame as well as log examples. In addition, our sample is too small to segregate house types by material. Given a larger sample, it would be interesting to plot the temporal and geographic distribution of the various types. There are, however, few dates of construction available for examples in the project area, rendering inadequate any attempts to plot the distribution of types by time.

Based on our combination of the key dimensions identified in the classification, 35 basic types of residential structures are proposed, ranging from simple, single-block log cabins to more complex, 2-story structures. Most structures exhibit numerous additions to the original block, compounding the problem of identifying the exact nature of the original residence. Also, structures of one type evolve into another; the clearest example of this is the addition of mirror-image one-room blocks (usually frame) to the end of an original log block (Figure 15.10). This reflects one of the simplest means of adding an extra room onto a one-room block.

Although exact ages of the additions cannot always be assessed, we judge that most first additions to early single-pen log houses were constructed within 10 to 20 years of erection of the original structure. Had time permitted, family genealogies would have been compiled, and these data compared against tax and probate records to deter-

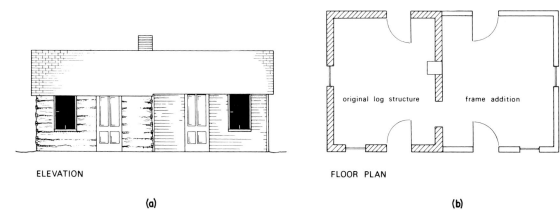

ELEVATION   FLOOR PLAN

(a)   (b)

Figure 15.10. (a) Facade and (b) floor plan of mirror-image log–frame structure and addition.

mine the relationship between family size and dates of additions to various houses. There should be a critical point where an addition becomes necessary due to increased family size. It is known that the average household size in the project area increased from 5.6 in 1830 to 6.6 in 1850 (Mason 1982).

Analysis of rural residential structures in the project area is by no means complete, especially in the areas of the functional aspects of architectural elements and use of space within houses. To these ends, data generated from the historic house project will be coupled with archaeological data to attempt to isolate and explain observed patterns of rural architectural development. In summary, we believe that rural architecture has not been appreciated either for its aesthetic value or, more importantly, for its value in analyzing the function of a basic, social unit: the rural farmstead. To do this objectively, we need a systematic set of operations to guide analysis of standing structures. Such a set of operations has been outlined here.

THE ORGANIZATION OF RURAL HOUSEHOLDS: DISTRIBUTIONS OF PORTABLE ARTIFACTS

Intrasite analysis of the distribution of Euro-American material classes was aimed toward defining a pattern of artifact use and discard, similar to South's (1977a) historic patterns for the Southeast and the Atlantic Seaboard.

Five of the seven sites excavated were located within the Smith settlement and, as stated previously, were chosen from the sample primarily on the basis of completeness of documentary research, slight amount of postdepositional disturbance, and the chance to study in depth contemporary farmsteads in the same community. The sites include the Matthew Mappin–John Murphy house and the Mary Mappin–Fielding Vaughn house, selected because of the opportunity to study two generations of a family at different locales: the house belonging to Matthew Mappin and that of his daughter, Mary Thomas Mappin Vaughn.

As mentioned previously, excavation for the most part was confined to the area in and adjacent to the residence. At Mappin–Vaughn the entire house foundation and an area extending several meters out from the house in all directions were

excavated. At Mappin–Murphy the original 1820s log house was outlined and excavated, along with the immediately adjacent area. Although these samples represent biased views of the two farmsteads, they do allow formulation of empirical statements concerning patterns of refuse disposal as well as observations concerning the architecture of the structures.

Analysis is still being carried out on some material, including: (*a*) faunal remains, to determine percentages of species represented, butchering techniques, patterns of disposal, elements of animals present in the archaeological record, etc.; (*b*) ceramics, to provide more precise dating of deposits and to create a paradigmatic classification of ceramic material; and (*c*) crockery, to distinguish patterns of flow of locally produced goods. Examples of analysis of the two sites are presented in the following sections to demonstrate the range in variability in what is termed here the *Upper South pattern*. There are a few assumptions that must be made regarding this pattern and these are presented first.

As South (1977a:86) states, a household in any particular society represents a system within a system, with the latter imposing on each household some degree of uniformity in the relationships among its parts. This uniformity may be revealed in various classes of portable and nonportable artifacts. According to South (1977a:86):

> [The quantity of remains resulting from any activity] would not necessarily parallel the importance placed on the activity within the cultural system but would have a definite relationship to the remains of other activities. It is these relationships among the by-products of human behavior that might be expected to reveal regularity when compared on an intersite basis.

In the next section variation within material classes will be observed when compared on an intersite basis. Our basic postulate follows that made by South (1977a:87), that there was a pattern to discarding by-products of human behavior around an occupation site that "might be viewed as a per capita, per year contribution to the archeological record."

This study examines the assemblage from excavated portions of each site, combining morphological classes of artifacts into two functional classes:

kitchen and architecture. Kitchen-related classes include ceramics, nonwindow glass, crockery, bone, and shell. Architectural classes include limestone, brick, plaster–chinking, machine-cut and wire nails, and window glass. It is important to note that artifacts are dealt with by provenience only in a few instances. As South (1977a:88) points out, after a site has been occupied for decades or a century, the archaeological record may become quite muddled. To demonstrate that a particular activity with attendant by-products took place in a particular area is difficult.

One should note that the following discussion is a bit particularistic since it deals with only two excavated sites and assemblages. However, from these particularistic site analyses are drawn several inferences regarding several aspects of Euro-American behavior.

Mappin–Vaughn

Mappin–Vaughn was excavated in 1978 to determine the accuracy of reports that the site contained the remains of a nineteenth-century slave cabin, possibly connected with the farmstead of Matthew Mappin. Subsequent documentary investigation revealed that the land on which the site was located belonged to Fielding Vaughn, who married Mary Thomas Mappin around the time of the Civil War.

No standing structure was present; only a few fireplace stones were visible on the surface. Excavation exposed the foundation of a three-room structure: The main two-room block was oriented east–west, with the later, single-room addition located centrally on the south wall (Figure 15.11). Local informants stated that the house was of frame construction resting on log sills and that entry was from the east gable end of the house, a rare occurrence in residential structures in the area. Excavation indicated that the main block was divided centrally into two rooms, supported by stone and rubble piers at each corner and along the central dividing wall. The addition also was supported by piers. The fact that the structure rested on piers as opposed to a solid perimeter explains the presence of material classes under the house (Figure 15.12). The site was excavated, leaving as many artifacts in place as possible (Figure 15.13) to facilitate our understanding of the artifact distribution.

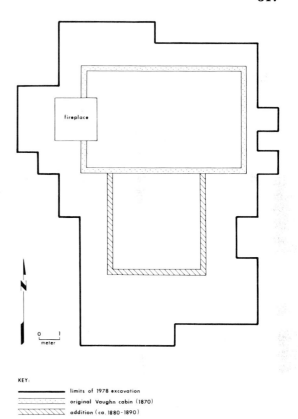

KEY:

————— limits of 1978 excavation

⌁⌁⌁⌁⌁⌁ original Vaughn cabin (1870)

▨▨▨▨▨▨ addition (ca. 1880-1890)

Figure 15.11.   Excavation outline and construction phases at Mappin–Vaughn.

An informant stated that the house had been abandoned for some years prior to its demolition around 1915, when it was dismantled partially by hand and the remaining elements were pulled down with mules. The techniques used to raze a house contribute directly to the distribution of material, especially building elements such as nails, roofing pieces, plaster, and interior hardware, such as doorknobs.

Distribution of Various Artifact Classes

The first stage of analysis was directed toward counting and weighing the classes of recovered material. These classes were as follows: brick, limestone, gravel, plaster, chinking, modern building materials, botanical, bone, shell, charcoal, cinder, prehistoric pottery, cultural lithics, gunflints, glass, ceramics, crockery, coins, marbles, buttons, beads,

Figure 15.12. Photograph of the Mappin–Vaughn excavation, looking west.

Figure 15.13.   Plan of the Mappin–Vaughn excavation showing construction elements and artifacts left in place.

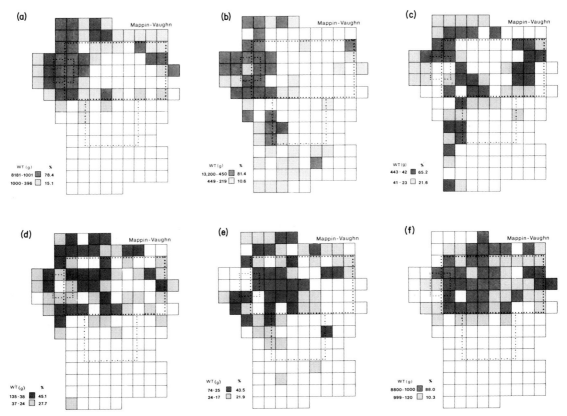

Figure 15.14. Distribution of architectural classes at Mappin–Vaughn: (a) limestone, (b) brick, (c) pane glass, (d) machine-cut nails, (e) wire nails, (f) plaster.

metals, and plastic, rubber, and leather. Once these totals were tabulated for each provenience, ceramic, crockery, and glass objects were reconstructed when possible. Each reconstructed vessel then was cataloged by both form and function. For example, glass was cataloged by forms—such as jars, bottles, and tumblers—and by function—such as consumable liquid container and canning container. Specific subcategories of those broad functional types also were used; for instance, consumable liquid containers included vessels for patent medicine, prescriptions, bitters, alcoholic beverages, etc. The distributions of individual vessel pieces then were mapped (Saunders and Mason 1979:337–338).

Architectural Classes   The distribution of architecturally related materials was analyzed to un-

derstand how the residence was constructed and how it was razed. The latter was necessary to assess what degree of postdepositional disturbance the site had sustained.

Limestone   Figure 15.14 shows the distribution of weights of limestone by quintiles, with the two highest quintiles plotted. The distribution highlights the hearth area and support piers. It is possible that at a later date some stone was added between piers, possibly as a windbreak, but that the entire perimeter was not enclosed. Other archaeological evidence supports the notion that the perimeter of the structure was not enclosed completely: (*a*) a concentration of bottles was found under the house, just to the south of the pier at the northwestern corner of the structure, and (*b*) the distribution of crockery, bone, shell, glass, and ceramic material within the perimeter of the original structure suggests that trash was being discarded beneath it.

The paucity of limestone around the addition suggests that the perimeter of the later room also was never enclosed. Stones used in piers for the addition were larger than those used to support the original structure. They also were less friable than the others, and fewer pieces were found during water-screening.[4]

Brick The distribution of brick fragments recovered from water-screening is plotted by the upper two quintiles in Figure 15.14. It shows the same distribution of brick as is shown in Figure 15.13: The heaviest concentration is adjacent to the hearth area and at the southwestern corner of the addition, where bricks were incorporated into the piers. It is assumed that the upper portion of the chimney was made of brick and that the scarcity of complete bricks indicates they were salvaged for use elsewhere.

Nails Nails were separated into square, machine-cut nails and wire nails. These were further subdivided by pennyweight. The distributions of these two subclasses are interesting in that they impart considerable information regarding the nature of demolition. Figure 15.14 illustrates the distribution of the upper two quintiles for each subclass. These distributions suggest that when the structure was torn down, materials were piled in what had been the west room of the structure. In corroboration, a local informant stated that the materials were piled and left, but not burned.

Analysis of the distribution of machine-cut versus wire nails by pennyweight yielded results complementary to the distribution of each subclass as a whole. It appears that very little effort was expended to salvage such things as ornamental trim (if present) or even possibly built-in cabinets (both requiring smaller pennyweight nails). This observation is based on the assumption that if these had been salvaged there should be a somewhat more

even distribution of smaller nails. Analysis showed that a greater percentage of these nails occurred where we presume the materials to have been dumped.

Plaster The distribution of plaster in the upper two quintiles is presented in Figure 15.14. Based on the distribution, which is similar to that for nails, we presume that plaster and lath walls were piled along with the other lumber in the area of the west room. However, we have inferred that walls in the south addition were never plastered. When walls are demolished (dragged down), certainly much of the plaster falls in place; it is unlikely that the ground would then be picked clean of plaster fragments. Since almost no plaster was recovered from squares within or adjacent to the outside walls of the addition, one may assume that the room was not plastered.

Pane Glass Large pieces of windowpane were recovered in four squares just north of the chimney and in three squares along the southern wall of the original block. The distribution of weights of pane glass in the upper two quintiles is illustrated in Figure 15.14. Based on locations of concentrations it is assumed the original block had opposing windows, probably one each on the north and south walls of the house, located near the chimney end of the structure. It is likely that there also was a small window on the west side of the addition. It is difficult to determine from the distribution, but it is possible that small windows flanked the entranceway into the east-facing facade (Note: four units in the two upper score ranges, two on each side of the door).

Kitchen-Related Classes The second set of classes analyzed consisted of kitchen-related classes, including ceramic, crockery, glass, bone, and shell. The distribution of these classes are summarized in the following discussion in a very brief fashion since analysis is not complete. The distributions do provide data about the manner in which refuse was discarded.

Ceramics Counts of ceramics by excavation unit are presented in Figure 15.15. The densest concentrations are around the southwestern corner of

---

[4]The weights shown for limestone and brick are derived only from material recovered during water–screening. Large pieces (usually averaging 10 cm or more in size) were left *in situ* and were mapped, but not weighed.

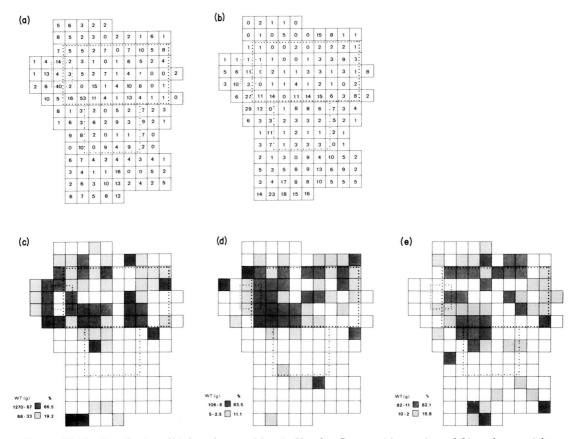

Figure 15.15. Distribution of kitchen classes at Mappin–Vaughn: Counts—(a) ceramics and (b) crockery; weight—(c) glass, (d) bone, and (e) shell.

the main block and directly south of the addition. With few exceptions, squares directly under or just inside the sills of the original structure contain higher frequencies of ceramics than squares outside the perimeter of the house, indicating that trash was deliberately swept or thrown under the structure. In the addition, squares under or inside the sill perimeter often contain lower sherd frequencies than squares outside the perimeter, possibly indicating a change in waste disposal through time. Further analysis of temporally sensitive ceramic markers will aid in this identification.

The distribution of sherds from single vessels suggests that objects were not broken in place upon demolition of the house but that they had been discarded previously, with pieces being tossed indiscriminately.

Crockery The similarity in pattern between the distribution of crockery and ceramics is quite noticeable. Figure 15.15 illustrates the raw counts per square. The two densest areas are around the southwestern corner of the main block and the area south of the addition. Units under the sills and within the perimeter of the original house contain higher counts than those outside; units beneath the addition usually contain less than those outside.

The distribution of sherds from single crockery vessels suggests that the disposal pattern illustrated by the distribution of ceramic sherds from single vessels holds constant: Containers were broken prior to discard and pieces were thrown or tossed randomly.

Glass   For present purposes glass has not been broken down into subclasses, such as tableware, canning jars, and bottles. The distribution of 86% of glassware weight by square is shown in Figure 15.15. The majority of glass was recovered from units under and around the original structure; high-frequency squares in the extreme southern portion of the excavation may indicate the presence of a dump to the side of the addition. A cache of seven bitters and medicine bottles was found just beneath the northwestern corner of the original block. These bottles apparently had been hidden behind a pier and subsequently were broken during demolition of the house.

Bone   As mentioned previously, analysis of the faunal material is currently in progress. However, we can make a few tentative statements concerning the assemblage and its distribution. Due to the unprotected nature of the site, it is possible that some faunal material has disintegrated. Based on the intact portion of the assemblage, we can state that a wide range of small mammals was being consumed as well as deer, turkey, chicken, and other fowl. One key element is pig (*Sus scrofa*). Further analysis may reveal that pigs were turned out into the forest and then harvested as needed.

The distribution of 95% of bone by weight is shown in Figure 15.15, the largest percentage occurring under the west half of the original structure. This may be due to food having been tossed out the windows near the fireplace and then either swept or kicked under the structure. Intrastructure activities involved in food preparation and consumption may have been restricted to the main block since little bone ended up under the addition, even though indications are that the addition also was on piers. To determine whether or not the presence of limestone may have contributed to the preservation of the bone, distributions of the two classes were inspected with inconclusive results. There is a correlation between bone and limestone in the west half of the original house, but there are units in other excavated areas that have concentra-

tions of limestone but that do not have bone present in any quantity. Mode of discard and not differential preservation probably best explains the pattern of distribution.

Shell   Distribution of freshwater mussel shells by weight is presented in Figure 15.15. There are three fairly distinct concentrations: (*a*) along the northern wall of the main block, (*b*) under the southeastern corner of the main block, and (*c*) under the northwestern corner of the addition. This latter distribution is different than that for bone, since almost none was found under the addition. Shells may have been pitched from the kitchen window or thrown out a door that may have existed in the south side of the original house. If the shells predate the addition, then it is evident that there was no concern for getting mussel shell out of sight; rather, the occupants were content to let it rest where it was discarded.

Mappin—Murphy

The Mappin–Murphy house site was excavated to gather information on an upper-middle-class landowner in the Smith settlement, Matthew Mappin, who entered land containing the house site in 1829. It was known from the work of the Historic American Buildings Survey that the impressive heavy-timber Georgian house postdated that entry by at least 10 years. Assuming Mappin and his family lived in the area prior to building the large house, it was feasible that one might find the foundation of a log house. One logical place to search for this cabin was under a large Victorian addition placed to the rear of the Georgian block around 1893. After removal of floorboards and joists from the addition, the base of the chimney and several pier supports of the earlier log structure were found. The cabin served as a kitchen area to the 1840 block, and was tied to it by a common wall, but had no direct access to the 1840 block until later in the nineteenth century.

The original log house, which lasted until 1893–1894 when the structure was razed for the larger Victorian addition, was two-rooms wide with a fireplace in the west end (Figure 15.16). The house probably sat on piers; the locations of most

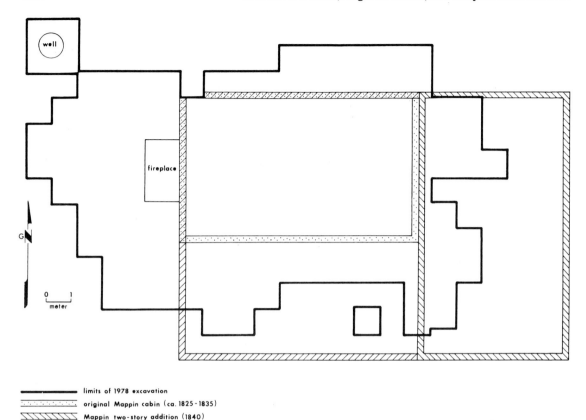

limits of 1978 excavation
original Mappin cabin (ca. 1825-1835)
Mappin two-story addition (1840)
Murphy addition (1894)

Figure 15.16. Excavation outline and construction phases at Mappin–Murphy.

are unknown since stones from the piers were re-used for the north perimeter wall of the 1893 addition. This wall was placed directly over the location of the earlier cabin wall.

Because of the different construction phases of the house and demolition of the original structure, it is probable that the archaeological deposit was disturbed to varying degrees at different periods. The only units felt to be relatively undisturbed are those 14 m² under the 1840 block, which should date from the first occupation of the log house until construction of the main block. Material in this area could have been deposited only during an 11–12-year period.

Distribution of Various Artifact Classes

The stages of analysis of Mappin–Murphy were identical to those of Mappin–Vaughn: Material was sorted into classes, reconstruction of vessels was completed, and distributions of classes were mapped. In the field, architectural elements and many artifacts were drawn in place (Figure 15.17).

Architectural Classes As with Mappin–Vaughn, distributions of architectural classes are reflective of the mode of destruction of portions of the house.

Limestone Distribution of weight of limestone in the upper two quintiles is shown in Figure 15.18. As expected, the majority of squares in the upper quintile are grouped to the west of the original structure, around the area containing the chimney base (Figure 15.19). The limestone chimney (visible at the far right in Figure 15.20) was torn down in 1893, along with the original log structure, scatter-

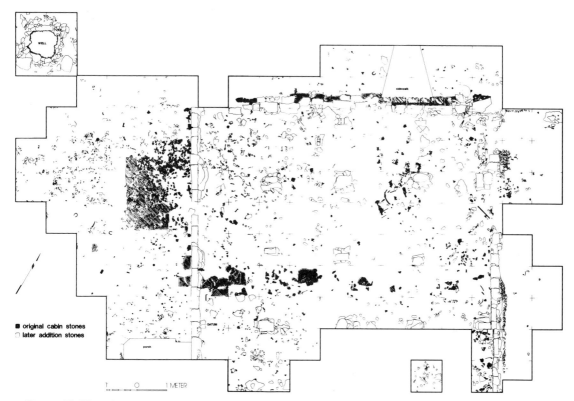

Figure 15.17. Plan of the Mappin–Murphy excavation showing construction elements and artifacts left in place.

ing the limestone slabs. Some of these dressed slabs were then used as piers for the addition, resulting in high weights in excavation units along load-bearing walls of the addition.

Brick Figure 15.18 illustrates the distribution of brick by weight in the upper quintile (73%). It is known that a brick chimney and flue were constructed along the interior dividing wall of the log structure, probably around the midnineteenth century (visible in Figure 15.20). The chimney and flue were torn down when the log structure was razed, accounting for brick fragments within the perimeter of the original cabin but not for those under the 1840 block. Excavation under the floor of the 1840 block yielded quantities of brick fragments along the solid foundation, leading us to believe that the original log house had a brick, or stone and brick, fireplace and chimney on the east end that was torn down in 1840 so that the heavy-timber block could

abut the earlier structure. If this were the case, the hearth area inside the earlier structure would have been removed, yielding a distribution of brick fragments like that shown. The complete bricks saved from this demolition could have been used to construct the new flue and chimney on the interior dividing wall of the log structure.

Nails Distributions of wire and machine-cut nails (Figure 15.18) are difficult to interpret. For both subclasses there are many more nails located outside the perimeter of the log structure than within it. For machine-cut nails, there are only five squares located totally within the perimeter that fall within the two highest quintiles; for wire nails, there are 11 units. For wire nails, just over half the units in the upper two quintiles fall to the west of the house; for machine-cut nails, the occurrence is slightly lower.

Under the 1840 block, 26 wire nails were re-

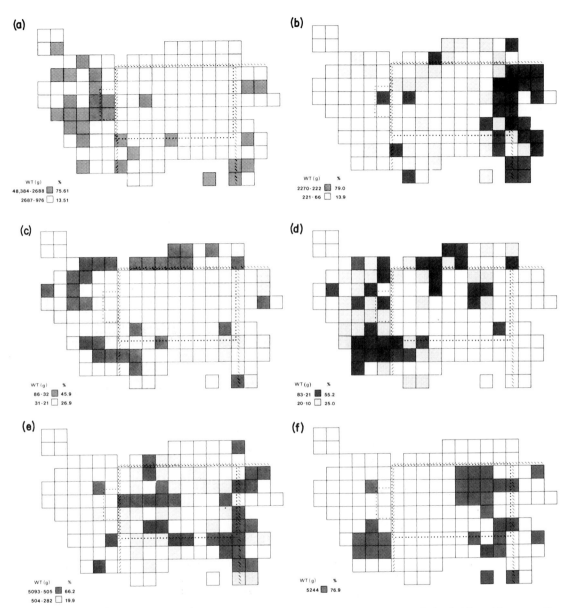

Figure 15.18. Distribution of architectural classes at Mappin–Murphy: (a) limestone; (b) brick; (c) machine-cut nails; (d) wire nails; (e) plaster; (f) pane glass.

Figure 15.19.   View (looking north) of a portion of the excavated area of Mappin–Murphy showing the chimney base, scattered construction rubble, and artifacts.

covered as opposed to 251 machine-cut nails. This trend is repeated in the rest of the site, an exception being the few squares in the northwestern portion of the original log structure. For the 152 excavation units, there are 1000 more machine-cut nails than wire nails.

The majority of machine-cut nails would have been used to fasten weatherboarding over logs in the original structure (see Figure 15.20). Wire nails would have been used later in replacing weather-boarding or in making other repairs. What is surprising is the small number of nails found within the perimeter of the log structure. This indicates that there was little woodwork inside the structure or woodwork inside was removed carefully. The disproportionately higher counts of nails to the west and north of the structure may be explained if we consider the area as a dump site for materials

derived from razing the structure or as the site of major construction activity.

Plaster–Chinking   The distribution of plaster–chinking (upper two quintiles by weight) is shown in Figure 15.18. No attempt was made to sort plaster from chinking[5] due to time and because materials from both classes found beneath the floor of the 1893 addition should date to the original structure. The same is true of material under the 1840 block, which probably was removed when the east-end fireplace and chimney were razed. Distribution within the perimeter of the original structure is not patterned at a level that is easily discernible. It is possible that some plaster fell during our removal

[5]Plaster is much more friable than lime–based chinking, although each often contains animal hair as a binder.

of floor boards and joists in preparing for excavation, but we were careful to remove all surface debris prior to excavating a unit. An interesting phenomenon is the low frequency of plaster–chinking occurring at the site relative to Mappin–Vaughn and other excavated sites in the project area. The reason is that small limestone slabs and–or pieces of wood were used for the major part of the chinking effort, with plaster and lime-based chinking used to fill in smaller gaps.

Pane Glass   Pane glass is concentrated in three distinct areas: (*a*) at the southwestern exterior corner of the original structure, (*b*) in the northeastern corner of the original structure, and (*c*) in the southeastern corner of the structure. Distribution of pane glass by weight (upper quintile only) is presented in Figure 15.18. The concentration in the southeastern corner is directly under an upper window in the 1840 block that was removed during the 1893 renovation. Pieces from the seven squares in the area almost equal the weight of the lower half of a 6-over-6 double-hung sash, indicating they may have been from a similar type window. The other two concentrations contain the remains of more than one sash, possibly representing trash piles of broken glass from when the original structure was razed.

Kitchen-Related Classes   As with kitchen-related classes from Mappin–Vaughn, classes from Mappin–Murphy are still under analysis. Distribution of selected classes help illustrate discard patterns and postdepositional processes.

Figure 15.20.   Photograph of the Mappin–Murphy house (ca. 1893), looking southwest. The original cabin, with siding and a second chimney, abuts the main structure on the right.

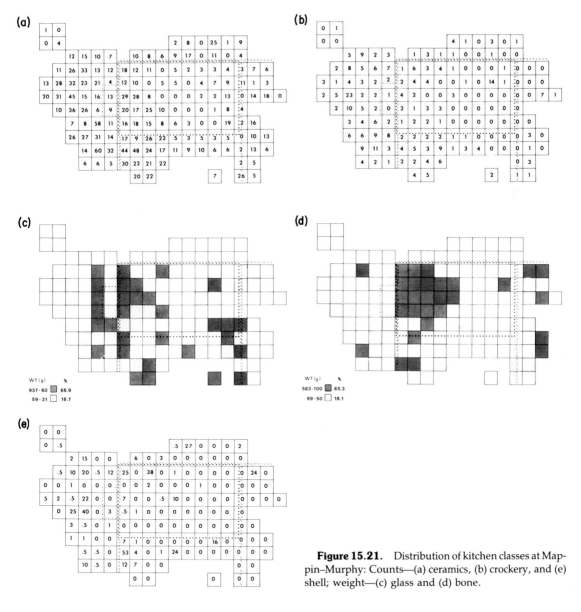

Figure 15.21. Distribution of kitchen classes at Mappin–Murphy: Counts—(a) ceramics, (b) crockery, and (e) shell; weight—(c) glass and (d) bone.

Ceramics   Counts of ceramic fragments by excavation unit are presented in Figure 15.21. Distribution is similar to that from Mappin–Vaughn: There is a line of debris just under the perimeter of the log structure, with decreasing frequencies toward the center of the house. The area surrounding the structure, especially to the west and south, contains units with high frequencies. Further anal-

ysis of the ceramic material, especially the identification of temporally sensitive markers, may aid in distinguishing different disposal patterns through time.

Crockery   Distribution of crockery pieces, presented in Figure 15.21, is skewed to one-half of the excavation—under the west half of the log house

TABLE 15.1.

Frequencies and Weights of Architectural and Kitchen-Related Artifacts from Mappin–Vaughn and Mappin–Murphy

| | Mappin/Vaughn | | | | | | |
| | Main block | | Addition | | Perimeter | | Total |
	n	%	n	%	n	%	
Architectural classes:							
Limestone (g)	50334	39.8	1571	1.2	746335	58.5	798240
Brick (g)	30729	34.0	1819	2.0	57712	63.9	90260
Plaster (g)	70938	67.5	854	0.8	33260	31.6	105052
Wire nails (n)	1073	44.3	159	6.6	1190	49.1	2422
Machine-cut nails (n)	1586	47.5	185	5.5	1568	47.0	3339
Pane glass (g)	2045	46.5	189	4.3	2164	49.1	4399
Kitchen-related classes:							
Ceramics (n)	239	34.3	55	7.9	401	57.6	695
Ceramics (g)	1075	46.1	69	2.9	1186	50.9	2331
Crockery (n)	141	21.5	47	7.1	468	71.4	656
Glass (g)	4540	58.9	376	4.9	2780	36.1	7697
Bone (g)	769	83.3	13	1.4	140	15.2	923
Shell (g)	491	56.0	157	17.9	227	25.9	876

and adjacent yard area. This distribution, taken in conjunction with the ceramic distribution, indicates that the area to the west served as an immediate refuse zone for discarded vessels.

Glassware   The largest concentration of glassware is inside the west wall of the log structure (Figure 15.21). Within this concentration are the remains of at least a dozen bottles (bitters and patent medicine) of varying sizes. As at Mappin–Vaughn, these could have been cached behind support piers and crushed when the structure was razed. As was seen in the distribution of other classes, the area to the west of the house contains considerable refuse, indicating that material was being discarded in that direction. Along the north wall there is a band of high-frequency units inside the perimeter, suggesting that material was being thrown or swept under the house. This same distribution occurs along the south wall of the original structure.

Bone   The distribution of bone by weight is presented in Figure 15.21. An enormous concentration of bone was recovered from the western third of the

area under the log structure. Although analysis of the material is incomplete, it is obvious that a large portion of the assemblage is represented by three species: pig (*Sus scrofa*); chicken (*Gallus gallus*); and turkey (*Meleagris gallopavo*). Upon initial inspection of the distribution of faunal elements, it was speculated that dogs or other animals had dragged the material under the structure. This would have been easy to do, given that the original log house was elevated. This also would have been possible during the period after erection of the frame structure, since there were small holes in the west side of the solid rock perimeter for water lines. Analysis indicates a virtual lack of gnaw marks and other evidence of deleterious taphonomic processes. For the present, we are considering the distribution of bone as a function of disposal. The presence of five units in the upper quintile under the 1840 block suggests that early bone refuse was being discarded to the east side of the original log structure.

Shell   Grams of shell by unit are shown in Figure 15.21. The majority of units containing shell are located around the perimeter of the structure or to the west.

TABLE 15.1. (*continued*)

Mappin/Murphy						
Log structure		1840 block		Perimeter		Total
n	%	n	%	n	%	
95246	26.5	21462	5.9	242066	67.5	358774
7866	30.7	7491	29.2	10304	40.1	25661
40157	64.4	6238	10.0	15991	25.6	62376
579	31.6	26	1.4	1224	66.9	1829
706	24.2	254	8.7	2026	69.5	2915
4431	64.9	181	2.6	2212	32.4	6824
473	25.5	117	6.3	1262	68.1	1852
1535	39.6	237	6.1	2107	54.3	3880
76	21.5	16	4.5	262	74.0	354
3935	53.3	146	1.9	3302	44.7	7383
6598	60.8	1424	13.1	2827	26.0	10849
126	32.8	24	6.2	235	61.0	386

THE ORGANIZATION OF RURAL HOUSEHOLDS: INTERSITE COMPARISON OF SELECTED ARTIFACT CLASSES

Presented here in brief form is a comparison of selected artifact classes from Mappin–Vaughn and Mappin–Murphy. Spanning an occupation period of 1829–1978, these two sites present an opportunity to construct a model of the composition of a frontier household and to observe its change through time. The Mappin–Murphy house site, with its architectural changes over the course of the nineteenth century, yields a very complex cultural history, and any attempts to infer but the simplest behavioral implications are tenuous at best. The Mappin–Vaughn house site, on the other hand, was inhabited for a shorter period (ca. 1860–1905) and presents a more concise cultural history and decreases the chances of confusing temporally distinct deposits.

The data for this discussion are presented in Table 15.1. Each site is divided into subareas based on assessment of house construction stages and, in the case of Mappin–Vaughn, a sealed deposit that dates to approximately 1829–1840 (the units under the 1840 Georgian block), the period of initial use of the original log structure. Listed for each subunit, and then totaled for each house site, are the counts and/or weights for architectural and kitchen-related classes. Intersite comparisons of data are discussed later.

Architectural Classes

Based on in-field assessment and analysis of the distribution of limestone fragments recovered during water-screening, it is inferred that both the Mappin–Vaughn house and the original Mappin log house were constructed on piers. The distribution of cultural material under each structure lends support to this interpretation.

The quantity of brick recovered from Mappin–Vaughn far outweighs that from Mappin–Murphy, in part due to different strategies in removal (i.e., care versus little or no care). Bricks from the east-end fireplace and flue on the original Mappin log structure probably were carefully removed for use in the later central flue in the same structure or in the massive brick fireplaces at either end of the 1840 block. At Mappin–Vaughn, there was no such intent—the chimney simply was razed. Evidence indicates that in 1840, bricks were not being produced locally in any quantity, so they would have represented a semiscarce commodity. By 1915, care in removing intact bricks from a chimney was outweighed by their inexpensiveness and availability.

At both sites machine-cut nails outnumber wire nails. At Mappin–Vaughn, the former compose 58% of the assemblage; at Mappin–Murphy, they compose 61%. At the former site, over 1000 more nails were recovered than at the latter, a reflection of the lesser need for nails in a log than in a frame structure. The closeness in percentage of wire versus machine-cut nails from the two sites may have important implications for dating residential sites from the latter half of the nineteenth century and will be examined in future analyses of other sites in the project area. Obviously, temporal duration and size of structure are important variables to consider, along with construction materials.

Concentrations of fragments of pane glass were found at both sites. Glass from Mappin–Murphy outweighs that recovered from Mappin–Vaughn by over 2400 g, indicative of the discard of more panes. Neither glass assemblage represents the total window glass present during occupation. It is probable that sashes were being salvaged for later use or that a portion of the broken glass was being deposited safely elsewhere.

The amount of plaster–chinking from Mappin–Vaughn exceeds that from Mappin–Murphy by over 40,000 g, indicating that the first house had plastered walls whereas the second did not. The majority of material from the latter site is a lime-based mortar used in the interstices between logs to seal the structure.

Kitchen-Related Classes

The amount of bone from under and around the Mappin–Murphy house is considerably more than that recovered from Mappin–Vaughn, in part a function of the differential preservation characteristics of the two sites. Based on work at other nineteenth-century sites in the area, this pattern holds true—where deposits are protected by standing architecture, faunal preservation is excellent.

Given the incomplete analysis of the material, we can state only that both wild and domestic animals were being consumed at both sites. It is expected that pig remains will far outdistance those of domestic cattle, especially during the early half of the nineteenth century, when cattle would have been valued for their milk.

Mussel shell, on the other hand, is much more prevalent at Mappin–Vaughn than at Mappin–Murphy. Whether this is due to personal preference or to a change in subsistence strategies is unclear. Mussels occur in certain locales along the Salt River and its tributaries and can be harvested easily. In some areas of the Midwest they were collected, and the shells were bored for button blanks. Based on examination of complete mussel specimens from the two sites discussed here, we can say that this was not being done.

The ceramic assemblage from Mappin–Murphy is larger than that at Mappin–Vaughn, reflecting longer occupation at the former site. Disposal patterns at the two sites are similar, the majority of ceramic debris being located just under the perimeter of the house or adjacent to it.

Crockery, on the other hand, is much more common at Mappin–Vaughn than at Mappin–Murphy by a ratio of roughly 2:1. This could be due to several factors, including a lack of personal preference for crockery on the part of the Mappins or differences in disposal patterns or the scarcity of local potters until after the Civil War.[6] Based on our recovery of 16 crockery fragments from beneath the 1840 block at Mappin–Murphy, it is evident that crockery was in the area by that date but may have been difficult to replace.

OVERVIEW OF RURAL HOUSEHOLD ANALYSIS

As indicated previously, analysis of the artifact assemblages of the two sites summarized in this section is incomplete. Just presented was the analysis to date of two of seven excavated historic sites in the project area, showing the techniques and in-

---

[6]At least one potter has been identified in the project area prior to 1840.

ferences used and the rationale behind the techniques. As mentioned in the introduction to the section on household organization, emphasis has not been on identifying specific use areas within sites but on establishing general patterns indicative of past behavior. These patterns include such things as (*a*) household assemblages (i.e., what artifacts are preserved at nineteenth-century sites and in what abundance) and (*b*) refuse disposal—how and where are things discarded and where do they eventually end up?

Future analysis will modify the techniques worked out by South (1977a) for identifying patterns based on ratios of material classes. For instance, the ratio of machine-cut to wire nails from Mappin–Vaughn and Mappin–Murphy centers around 60–40 ± 2%. This trend is testable at other excavated sites to determine if this is due to chance, excavation bias, or if in mid-to-late-nineteenth century sites there is a predictable ratio of nail types. Another area that appears promising is in the ratio of ceramic material to crockery. For the two sites we have discussed there is considerable difference between assemblages. Even more important is the fact that at the later site, Mappin–Vaughn, the frequency of crockery fragments almost equals that of ceramic fragments, in spite of the fact that when broken, ceramic vessels usually will fracture into smaller pieces than will crockery vessels.

SUMMARY

This chapter has presented the preliminary results of a 3-step analysis of historic communities at the communitywide level, the farmstead level, and the household level. Components from the Smith settlement have been used as examples of the types of analyses undertaken. These examples, while being somewhat particularistic by nature, have formed the basis for more extensive work in the future. Patterns in data generated from work in this locale have created models, the implications of which can be tested elsewhere—both in the project area and in other portions of the Midwest. Ideally, these models of human behavior—settlement location, architectural style evolution, refuse disposal, and so on—would have been formulated early enough in the project to aid in the decision-making

process of where to conduct other excavations and intensive mapping. Due to the temporal constraints under which the historic-period segment of the project was working, many of these decisions had to be made earlier than we would have liked.

Data on settlement along the Elk Fork and the Middle Fork indicate that many of the implications of the model of historic settlement that were presented in Chapter 5 hold true. Initial settlement was based on environmental factors, such as tree density and soil fertility, as well as on social factors, such as proximity to kin and friends. Data from the Mt. Prairie settlement support this model as well as indicating that religious affiliation may have been an important factor as well. Settlement decision factors are discussed in more detail in Chapter 17.

Data on subsequent expansion of landholdings suggest that two patterns of land acquisition are present—nucleated and dispersed—each of which implies distinct decisions on the part of landholders. The nucleated pattern implies that a person chose to keep holdings as grouped as possible to decrease the cost and time involved in working widely spaced parcels of land. The dispersed pattern implies a decision to buy land regardless of the distance from the residence. Based on (*a*) the mapping of soil fertility from GLO records and (*b*) the fact that available land often lay adjacent to an entrant's original tract(s) but was passed over when new land was purchased, we believe that these patterns are real rather than imagined.

The sample of farmsteads surveyed intensively suggests that development of a farmstead was a factor of wealth and diversity of economic productivity. Although they have yet to be quantified, data on farmstead patterning indicate that certain elements occur repetitively and in predictable spatial association with other elements. The evolution in size and organization of farmsteads is tied directly to developmental stages of the model of historic adaptation and change. As a shift toward economic specialization and production for a market economy occurs, mechanization and larger landholdings force adoption of more specialized buildings, often forcing spatial rearrangement of the farmstead.

Classification of residential structures created paradigmatic classes, selected dimensions of which were used to construct a typology of houses in the project area. Dates assigned to these structures reflect an evolution from simple one-room cabins to architecturally complex two-story houses. Future analysis will include (*a*) comparison of growth in family size to growth in house size and (*b*) separation of stylistic and functional elements of rural architecture.

Excavation of two family-related structures in the Smith settlement has provided information on house construction as well as patterns of refuse disposal and artifact composition of rural nineteenth-century households. Disposal patterns were noted as being similar at the two sites; the majority of material was recovered just under the house perimeter or out in the yard. Due to the restricted nature of the excavations, it is unknown whether or not there were areas designated as trash dumps that were located some distance from the houses and that might contain greater quantities of material.

Subsistence data indicate that a fairly restricted range of fauna composed the majority of the meat-based diet. The Mappin–Murphy faunal assemblage is by far the better preserved of the two and contains large quantities of pig remains, along with elements of deer, cow, tree squirrel, rabbit, and turkey. Mussels were consumed in small quantities.

In summary, it might be noted that the data set generated from analysis of the sites excavated in the project area is one of the few historic data sets from the southern Prairie Peninsula. It is a rare opportunity when one can obtain an extensive sample of portable artifacts from the residences of persons for whom there exist land entry records, census data, tax records, probate records, and so on. These factors, coupled with the fact that these persons came from different socioeconomic classes (Mason 1982) and that the set of sites spans all periods of historic settlement, make the data set all the more important.

PART VI

Patterns of Settlement

The two chapters in this section examine settlement patterns for the prehistoric and historic periods. Chapter 16 presents data derived from an extensive survey and an intensive set of surface artifact collections to develop a model of changing patterns of settlement during prehistoric times. The site survey was designed to provide a sample of survey units representative of geographic and environmental variation across the entire project area. Termed *probabilistic survey*, it provides a vital complement to *purposive survey*, which focused on areas to be affected directly by the Cannon Reservoir and/or related construction activities. The distributions and environmental contexts of probabilistic sites that yielded datable artifacts are discussed, and inferences are evaluated in light of comparisons made between surface artifact collec-

tions from 20 sites in Putman Bottom. Results bear directly on the models presented in Chapter 5, and several provocative relationships are detected among such factors as environmental change, site locations, population size, and economic intensification in the region.

Chapter 17 examines data derived from the analysis of documentary sources to detect patterns of pioneer settlement in the Cannon Reservoir region. These patterns are analyzed with respect to two major classes of variables: environmental and social. A third set of variables, agricultural specialization, also is examined to determine whether location varies according to kinds of specialized activity. Finally, implications of the 3-stage model of historic settlement are discussed in light of data presented in this chapter and in Chapter 15.

16

Prehistoric Settlement Patterns

ROBERT E. WARREN

Locations of archaeological sites on regional landscapes can provide useful insights into prehistoric interactions between cultures and their regional environments. When sites can be dated or assigned to discrete cultural units, it is possible to reconstruct patterns of settlement and to compare patterns defined for different cultures or time periods in order to detect changes in man–land interactions through time. Changing settlement patterns can then be examined in light of other dynamic factors (e.g., human population density, environmental change, and differing social contexts) to evaluate possible causes of observed change.

In this chapter, selected results of archaeological site survey and surface artifact collections in the Cannon Reservoir region are used to test several aspects of the model of prehistoric adaptations (Chapter 5). The first sections describe the design of the survey and its general results, the procedures used to order sites by cultural period, and changes in site frequencies through time. Geographic distributions and hypothesized environmental contexts of dated sites are examined in the third section, and temporal trends in changing locational

patterns are isolated. In the fourth section, surface artifacts from an intensive "siteless survey" (Dunnell and Dancey n.d.) of a large bottomland locality are used to define dimensions of content variability among sites. Correlates are identified between inferred functional site types and observable surface characteristics of sites, and these are used to classify sites discovered during survey into hypothetical functional categories. Finally, the concluding section integrates the results of site context and site content analyses and traces changing patterns of settlement through time.

SITE SURVEY

The Cannon Project area is a 1149 km² (443 mile²) region that encloses parts of all major environmental zones in the middle Salt River valley. Because it never has been feasible to search the entire region for archaeological sites, sampling procedures were used to select areas for site survey. There have been two approaches to survey sampling, each with different goals and designs (Warren 1979). A *purposive*

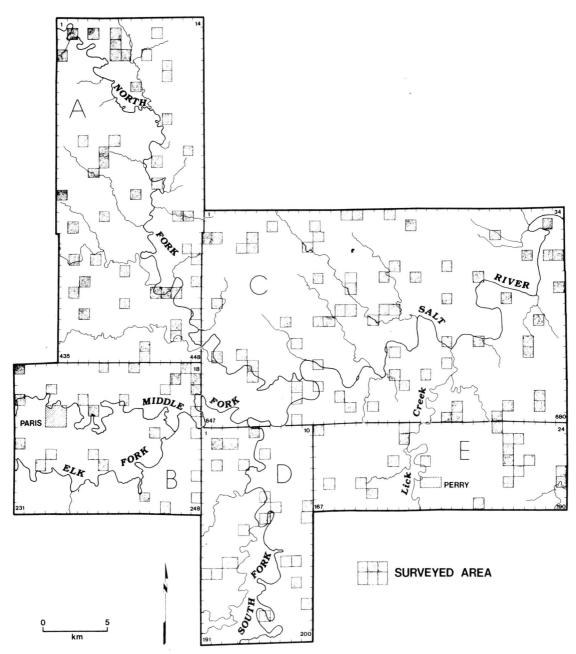

Figure 16.1. Map of the probabilistic survey region, showing quarter-section quadrats represented in the 10% sample. Geographic subareas are labeled A–E. Numerals in subarea corners are quadrat labels. Paris and Perry are modern communities excluded from the survey region (from Warren 1979).

survey, begun in 1959 (Henning 1961), sought to locate and record archaeological sites lying in the paths of reservoir waters and related construction activities. Results of this survey are valuable for analyzing site locations in certain areas and were necessary for ranking candidates for more intensive investigation by their potential research significance. However, results also are strongly biased toward bottomland contexts in the heart of the survey region and are not suitable for evaluating settlement diversity in the region as a whole.

To circumvent these problems, a doubly stratified *probabilistic survey* was designed and implemented in 1977 to control bias in survey area sampling procedures (Warren 1979). It divided the region into five geographic subareas, each of which was sampled independently to ensure dispersion of survey units across the sampling area. It also controlled for land areas falling within different drainage classes (Chapter 3) to increase the likelihood that survey units were proportionately representative of environmental variation in the region. Since a major goal of this chapter is to define and interpret locational variability of sites in the region at large, only results of the probabilistic survey are examined here.

Sampling units of the probabilistic survey consist of legal quarter-section quadrats, most of which are regular and cover .65 km^2 (.25 mile^2) areas (Figure 16.1). With the exclusion of 6 units that fall in modern urban areas, the total sampling frame consists of 1766 quadrats. The first stage of sample stratification segregated the frame into five subsets, each of which comprised a contiguous geographic portion of the region (Subareas A–E). The North Fork and its tributaries are bracketed by Subarea A, the Middle and Elk forks by Subarea B, the Salt River and lower Lick Creek by Subarea C, the South Fork by Subarea D, and the upper reaches of Lick Creek and surrounding uplands by Subarea E. Quadrats in each subarea then were numbered sequentially by row (west to east), then by column (north to south), and a table of random numbers was used to select (without replacement) sample units comprising 10% of quadrats in each subarea (177 total quadrats).

The five subarea samples were then each substratified to ensure proportionate representations of drainage classes. To determine the overall proportion of each drainage class in each subarea, a series of 28,256 points (16 systematically arranged points within each quadrat) was classified by drainage class using appropriate maps (scale: 1:24,000). Drainage class point frequencies within quadrats selected for the 10% sample then were totaled by subarea for comparison with expected values. Quadrats were purposively redrawn if sample proportions deviated more than 5% from expected proportions for any drainage class, an adjustment that was necessary in only one case. Quadrats were redrawn randomly when access to private property was denied (10 cases).

Deviations of sample drainage class proportions from expected values are quite low in the region as a whole (Table 16.1). Mean error is .6% ± .7%. Maximum deviations are minimal (+1.5% in drainage class 4; −1.1% in class 1), and a chi-square test indicates that discrepancies between observed and expected point totals are insignificant at an alpha of .05. Thus, sampling units of the 10%, doubly stratified, semirandom sampling strategy are considered adequately representative of geographic and environmental variation in the region.

Field techniques of the probabilistic survey varied with density of ground cover. When ground surface visibility was greater than 50%, surveyors walked in zigzag patterns through adjacent 20-m-wide corridors in search of archaeological remains. In areas with less surface visibility, a systematic grid network of shovel tests was dug (20-m interval) to locate sites not visible on the surface. Tests were small pits (8000 cm^3) from which soil was excavated and hand sifted to expose artifacts. When necessary, additional tests were used to precisely define site limits. Bias in site detection undoubtedly occurred due to differences in surface visibility. This should not seriously affect interpretations presented here, since degrees of soil exposure tend to correlate with topographic positions in the region and our major concern is with proportional differences in site context occurrences through time, rather than frequencies of sites in different contexts.

A total of 353 sites was discovered by the probabilistic survey. (A *probabilistic site* is defined as any isolable aggregate of five or more surface artifacts

TABLE 16.1.

**Drainage Class Point Frequencies by Subarea in the 10% Probabilistic Survey Sample and a
Comparison of Observed and Expected Drainage Class Totals[a,b]**

	Drainage class					
Subarea	1	2	3	4	5	Total
A	132	199	144	154	91	720
B	53	137	119	67	24	400
C	425	285	151	161	66	1088
D	77	99	63	61	20	320
E	206	59	26	13	0	304
Total	893	779	503	456	201	2832
Percent	31.5	27.5	17.8	16.1	7.1	100.0
Expected total	924.4	777.8	502.1	412.5	215.2	2832.0
Expected percent	32.6	27.5	17.7	14.6	7.6	100.0

[a] Source: Warren (1979).
[b] χ^2 = 6.59, df = 4, p > .10.

having a spatial midpoint that occurs inside a sample quadrat.) Sites are distributed extensively across the region and occur in most environmental zones. However, comparisons of observed subarea totals with frequencies predicted by proportions of the region surveyed in each subarea indicate that there are significant differences in site distribution (χ^2 = 24.3; df = 4; p < .001). Sites are significantly overrepresented in the eastern, central, and southern parts of the sample area (Subareas C, D) and are underrepresented elsewhere (Subareas A, B, E). Sites also vary in density among drainage classes. There is a strong mode in drainage class 4, and densities are progressively lower in classes 5, 3, 2, and 1 (Warren and O'Brien 1981). These trends, both of which also are reflected in contexts of dated probabilistic sites (see following discussions), suggest that prehistoric groups in general focused many of their activities on bottomland forests in the most adequately watered, physiographically diverse, and heavily timbered parts of the region, rather than in areas with less abundant and perhaps less stable aquatic and forest resources.

Projectile points collected from probabilistic sites were used to order sites in time. Unbroken and relatively complete points first were classified,

using a formal system composed of 74 classes and 193 subclasses (Curry and O'Brien 1981). Fifty-five classes and 140 subclasses are represented in probabilistic site collections. Using modes of point subclass frequencies at Pigeon Roost Creek and other dated sites in the Midwest as guides, all subclasses were assigned, where possible, to one of six cultural periods (Early Archaic, Middle Archaic, Late Archaic–Early Woodland, Middle Woodland, Late Woodland, and Mississippian). With the elimination of temporally insensitive forms, there are 45 classes and 117 subclasses of diagnostic points from 75 probabilistic sites.[1]

[1] The 45 classes and 117 subclasses of diagnostic projectile points from probabilistic survey sites are associated with cultural periods as follows: Early Archaic 8.1, 9.0, 12.0, 32.0, 38.1–2; Middle Archaic 18.1, 25.1–5, 25.8–10, 25.12, 25.14–16, 64.0; Late Archaic–Early Woodland 1.1–3, 4.2–3, 5.1–3, 6.1–2, 7.1–2, 13.1, 31.2, 33.2, 36.1–6, 61.0, 68.1–3; Middle Woodland 19.0, 20.1–2, 21.1, 27.2, 30.1–2, 39.1, 40.1–6, 41.1–3, 41.5–10, 41.12, 42.1–4, 43.1–3, 44.1–3, 49.3, 50.2, 58.1–6; Late Woodland 15.1–2, 16.1–3, 28.1–2, 41.4, 45.5, 46.0, 49.5, 67.0, 69.2–3, 70.1–3, 72.1–3, 73.1; Mississippian 70.4, 71.1–3, 72.4–5, 74.1–2. See Curry and O'Brien (1981) for detailed descriptions of classes and subclasses.

Among the 75 probabilistic sites containing temporal indicators are 25 sites with evidence of occupation during more than one cultural period. Counting each period indication as a distinct occupation at each of these multicomponent sites, the sample includes a total of 129 dated probabilistic components. This undoubtedly is a conservative estimate of the actual number of occupations represented, but the cultural framework and sample of dated components are both useful for evaluating general changes in settlement patterns through time.

SITE FREQUENCY VARIATION

In regions that have been surveyed probabilistically, one approach to estimating relative change in human population size is simply to sum for the total number of components represented in each cultural period. Although simple, this approach has a number of potential pitfalls. It must be assumed, for example, that (*a*) there are no differences among periods in the potential surface visibility of components; (*b*) time lengths of cultural periods are constant; (*c*) there is no change through time in the average number of people that occupied each site; (*d*) there are no functional differences among sites, or at least there are no changes through time in proportions of functionally different sites; and (*e*) residential sites were occupied for equal amounts of time each year.

Although none of these potential sources of error can be ignored, the effects of the first assumption appear to have been minor in the Cannon Reservoir region, and the effects of the others can be more or less controlled using independent observations to weight for differential variability. The first assumption, related to rates of geomorphic dynamism, is clearly violated in the region. Excavations document deeply buried components at Pigeon Roost Creek, where surface evidence of occupations predating the Late Archaic period was lacking. However, geomorphic research indicates that Pigeon Roost Creek, and possibly other sites situated at mouths of eastern tributary valleys, occupy unique contexts in which rates of Holocene silt deposition were abnormally high (Huxol 1980; Kochel and

Baker 1982; and Chapter 12). Most other terraces are concave in profile and probably Pleistocene in age (Chapter 3), and their rates of erosion appear to have matched rates of deposition during the Holocene. Moreover, historic cultivation has churned most multicomponent sites that may at one time have been stratified. Thus, the potential for discovering diagnostic artifacts on the surface probably is about equal to the proportions of those artifacts, diagnostic of different periods, that occur below the surface. In uplands, where rates of erosion generally have surpassed rates of deposition during the Holocene (Ruhe 1974), differential surface visibility probably is minimal. In summary, available geomorphic evidence suggests that depositional bias is highly localized in the Cannon Reservoir region and probably is not a major source of error.

The second assumption can be dealt with by transforming site frequencies for each cultural period into estimates of the number of sites occupied per year. The third can be met by controlling for variation of site size, and the remaining two assumptions can be evaluated in light of settlement pattern reconstructions (see subsequent sections of this chapter).

Component totals in the Cannon Project probabilistic sample are as follows: 8 Early Archaic, 18 Middle Archaic, 22 Late Archaic–Early Woodland, 32 Middle Woodland, 37 Late Woodland, and 12 Mississippian components. Standard scores (z-scores) of these frequencies show a linear increase from the Early Archaic to Late Woodland periods, and a sharp decline during the Mississippian period (Figure 16.2). The steady increase during the early and middle parts of the sequence are consistent with the predictions of the prehistoric model (Chapter 5). However, the Mississippian frequency suggests there was a significant decrease in population after about A.D. 1000, a decrease that is clearly anomalous with respect to population trends observed elsewhere in the Midwest for this period. The apparent decrease nevertheless is consistent with inferred settlement pattern changes in the region after A.D. 1000 (Chapter 10).

To calculate the number of dated probabilistic sites occupied per year, component sums were divided by estimated durations of each cultural pe-

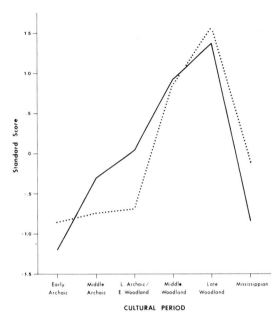

Figure 16.2. Temporal change in weighted and unweighted frequencies of prehistoric sites; site frequencies (—), sites per year (· · · ·).

riod in the region.[2] Results are similar to standardized component frequencies (Figure 16.2). However, they suggest that growth was relatively slower during the Archaic periods and increased rapidly during the Middle and Late Woodland periods. Moreover, the Mississippian decline appears to have been less severe than simple frequencies would suggest; the weighted Mississippian estimate falls between those of the Late Archaic–Early Woodland and Middle Woodland periods.

SITE CONTEXT VARIATION

Dated probabilistic sites are distributed widely in the project area. Environmental contexts also are

[2]Estimated dates and durations of the six major cultural periods in the Cannon Reservoir region are as follows: Early Archaic 9000–6000 B.C. (3000 yr); Middle Archaic 6000–3000 B.C. (3000 yr); Late Archaic–Early Woodland 3000–200 B.C. (2800 yr); Middle Woodland 200 B.C.–A.D. 400 (600 yr); Late Woodland A.D. 400–900 (500 yr); Mississippian A.D. 900–1400 (500 yr).

quite varied, ranging from the level upland prairies to the low flood plain forests of early historic times. In this section, site locations are examined from both perspectives, and changes in distributions and contexts are traced through time.

Geographic Distributions

In Chapter 3 we concluded that environmental variability in the Cannon Reservoir region is expressed along two major dimensions, both of which have independent correlates in geographic space. The first dimension is an upland–lowland gradient of slope position that reflects downslope increases in moisture, forest cover, and biotic diversity, and correlates directly in geographic space with proximity to major perennial streams. The second dimension is an upstream gradient of decreasing topographic relief, decreasing effective moisture, and decreasing densities and widths of mesophytic forests. In very general terms, dimension 2 distinguishes the central and eastern parts of the project area from its northern, western, and southern panhandles.

Despite the geographic independence of these two dimensions, common to both is variation in the abundance and diversity of forest and aquatic resources. Assuming that (*a*) subsistence economies of all prehistoric groups in the region focused on forest and aquatic resources, (*b*) site locations were conditioned by access to important resources, and (*c*) environmental change during the Holocene was expressed along these same two geographic dimensions, one would expect probabilistic sites to be concentrated near waterways in the central and eastern parts of the project area, regardless of their age.

The approximate locations of all 129 dated probabilistic components are plotted by cultural period in Figure 16.3. With the exception of the Early Archaic configuration, which is distinguished by three sites in level upland prairies that are at least 5 km away from major perennial streams, all distributions seem to fit expectations. Sites are most abundant along the Salt River and the lower reaches of its major tributaries, and all sites more than 1–2 km away from major streams are located in the eastern half of the region. These observations are supported by a contingency analysis of site frequencies among subareas (Table 16.2). In contrast to site frequencies predicted for each subarea on the basis of relative land area covered by the probabilistic survey, sites are significantly overrepresented in Subarea C (central and eastern parts of the region) and are underrepresented in Subareas A, B, and E (western and southeastern parts of the region). Sites in Subarea D also are more common than predicted, but this is a rather weak anomaly in light of the fact that most of these sites occur along the lower reaches of South Fork.

In summary, locations of dated probabilistic components tend to aggregate in those parts of the region where forest and aquatic resources were historically most abundant and diverse. This association has two related implications. First, differences in resource availability across the region

were important enough to prehistoric groups to influence relative values of different site locations, and upstream locations generally were less desirable than those downstream. Significantly, the causal direction of this relationship is supported by the predominance, in excavated faunal and floral assemblages in the region, of the remains of forest and aquatic resources (Chapters 10 and 11). The second implication, actually a projection from the first, is that locations downstream from the project area (i.e., toward the Mississippi River) were progressively more productive and desirable to prehistoric groups. If so, this suggests that population characteristics of groups in the project area may have been partially dependent on those of groups to the east. When populations increased along the Mississippi, community fission and expansion of

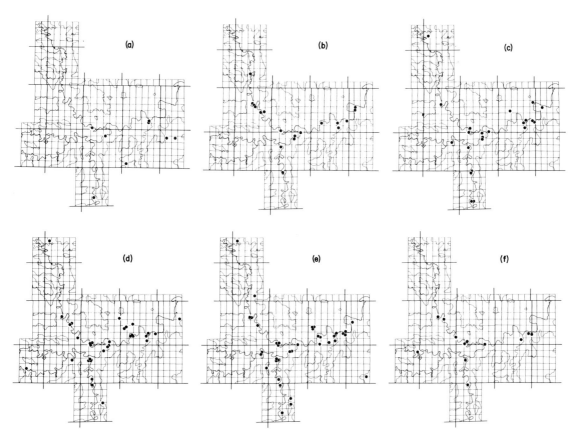

Figure 16.3.   Geographic distributions of probabilistic sites dated to six major cultural periods: (a) Early Archaic; (b) Middle Archaic; (c) Late Archaic–Early Woodland; (d) Middle Woodland; (e) Late Woodland; (f) Mississippian.

TABLE 16.2.

Frequencies of Dated Probabilistic Sites in Five Geographic Subareas and a Comparison of Observed and Expected Subarea Totals[a]

Cultural period	Subarea					Total
	A	B	C	D	E	
Early Archaic	-	-	6	1	1	8
Middle Archaic	6	-	10	2	-	18
Late Archaic/ Early Woodland	2	1	14	5	-	22
Middle Woodland	4	2	20	6	-	32
Late Woodland	5	2	20	9	1	37
Mississippian	2	1	7	2	-	12
Total	19	6	77	25	2	129
Percent	14.7	4.7	59.7	19.4	1.6	100.1
Survey quadrats	45	25	68	20	19	177
Expected total	32.8	18.2	49.5	14.6	13.8	128.9
Expected percent	25.4	14.1	38.4	11.3	10.7	99.9

[a] $\chi^2 = 46.77$, df = 4, $p < .001$

new groups into less desirable contexts may have caused progressive increases in population density up major tributaries of the Mississippi. Conversely, when populations declined along the Mississippi, or exploitable areas were left open between rapidly growing nuclear settlements, it seems reasonable to expect a parallel population decline in the Cannon Reservoir region due to movement of resident groups downstream. This implication is not testable with available data, but upstream–downstream differences in resource availability could have been important conditional factors with respect to decreasing population size in the Cannon Reservoir region during the Mississippian period.

Environmental Contexts

A second perspective on site context variation, complementary to the first, focuses on characteristic positions of sites within regional environments, without regard to broad geographic distributions. Here, we examine continuities and changes in physiographic contexts of dated probabilistic sites and evaluate trends in light of hypothetical re-

sponses of Cannon Reservoir area floral communities to Holocene climatic change.

In Chapter 4, distributions of early historic prairie and timber communities were compared with edaphic traces of earlier community distributions, and it was concluded that climatic change during the Neo-Boreal episode had caused an extensive expansion of timber onto former prairie. The magnitude of this episode, and its effects on Cannon Reservoir area flora, then was used as a baseline from which to project the hypothetical effects of other climatic episodes on the environment during the Holocene. A similar approach is used here to evaluate the possible impact of environmental change on Cannon Project site locations.

To allow simultaneous examination of site contexts and environmental conditions, we use physiographic models to trace the changing characteristics of both. Environmental shifts are projected from a model of early historic distributions of landforms, native vegetation, and the soils formed under different floral communities (Figure 16.4), and climatic trends documented elsewhere in the Midwest. The model, an idealized synthesis of information presented earlier (Table 4.1; Figures 3.3, 4.2), shows (*a*) prairie domination of grassland soils in level uplands and on small, isolated patches of bottomland terraces; (*b*) timber domination of grassland soils along gently sloping margins of upland flats, on crests of narrow upland interstream divides, and on large isolated patches of bottomland terraces; (*c*) timber domination of transitional grassland–forest soils along sloping upland rims and around the headwaters of tributary streams; and (*d*) timber domination of forest soils throughout the remainder of the project area. Using the model as a distributional baseline, we can compare the regional effects of Neo-Boreal climate with

those of previous millennia. Assuming that the postulated magnitudes and directions of climatic trends during other periods are correct (Chapter 4), we can project hypothetical spatial configurations of floral communities for all major episodes of the Holocene. Results are untested in the region, and reconstructed community distributions are speculative, but the general trends shown in the models are consistent with other research (Chapter 4), and the approach is useful for evaluating the possible impact of environmental change on changing patterns of site contexts.

To systematically evaluate site locations, and to trace context changes through time, we compared

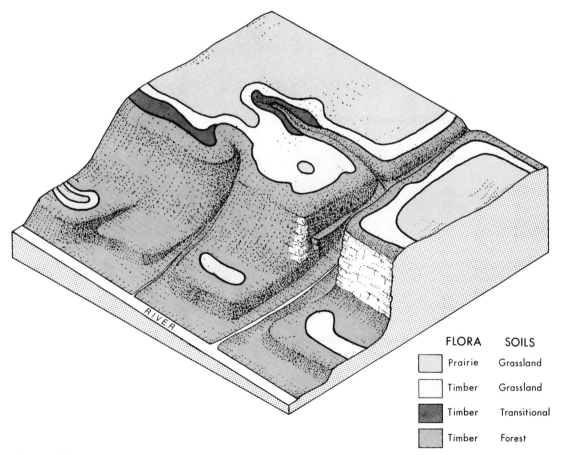

FLORA	SOILS
Prairie	Grassland
Timber	Grassland
Timber	Transitional
Timber	Forest

Figure 16.4. Idealized model of the Cannon region during the late Neo-Boreal climatic episode (Early Historic period), showing general relationships between landforms, native vegetation, and soil distribution.

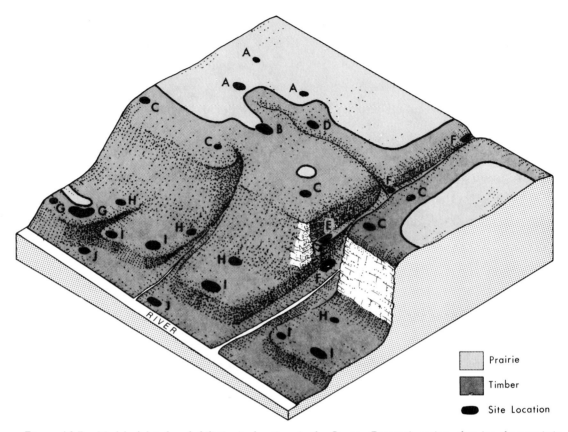

Figure 16.5. Model of dated probabilistic site locations in the Cannon Reservoir region, showing characteristic landforms and native vegetation covers of 10 classes of site contexts (A–J).

the localities of all dated probabilistic sites in terms of their native physiographic, vegetational, and soils characteristics and defined 10 classes of contexts (Figure 16.5). The context classes (A–J), which correlate with progressively lower slope positions, are defined as follows:

A   Level upland prairie, near the GLO prairie–timber ecotone and near a small ephemeral stream (Drainage Class 1);

B   Crest of level upland interstream divide, on or near the GLO ecotone and near a steep-sided ephemeral ravine (Drainage Class 1);

C   Gently sloping margin of level upland forest, directly above a steep declivity to the bottomland of a perennial stream (most Drainage Class 2);

D   Dissected upland forest, near the GLO ecotone and adjacent to a small ephemeral stream (Drainage Class 3);

E   Moderately sloping margin of a high, forested bottomland terrace, above the flood plain of a perennial tributary stream (Drainage Class 3);

F   Gently sloping bottomland forest, at the base of a bluff and near a perennial tributary stream (most Drainage Class 4);

G   Gently sloping margin of a forested, very high bottomland terrace, adjacent to the bank of a major perennial stream (Drainage Class 3 or 4);

H   Gently sloping, high bottomland forest, at the base of a bluff and across a sequence of terraces from the bank of a major perennial stream (most Drainage Class 4);

I Gently sloping margin of a forested, moderately high bottomland terrace, near a major perennial stream (Drainage Class 4); and

J Gently sloping margin of a low flood plain forest, adjacent to the bank of a major perennial stream (Drainage Class 5)

Frequencies of probabilistic components in each context class are presented in Table 16.3. Class totals show a notably high incidence of sites in bottomland contexts (84% are in classes E–J), whereas upland sites are comparatively rare. The three most common contexts, which together contain over 65% of all components, all define locations on high bottomland terraces. This bias is remarkable given the fact that only about 25% of the area surveyed probabilistically was bottomland (Table 16.1), but it is consistent with the proposition that access to both resources and domestic necessities generally favored bottomland settlement in the region (Chapter 5).

Proportions of components, calculated by cultural period and by context class, illustrate several noteworthy trends (Figure 16.6). First, it is evident that the bottomland bias just mentioned is common to all six cultural periods. Although proportions vary, and not all bottomland contexts are represented in all periods, outer margins of high bottomland terraces were occupied consistently (classes G, I), and they never account for less than 35% of components in any period. Second, all cultural periods have unique arrays of context occurrences. Proportional patterns often are similar, particularly for temporally adjacent periods, but no two periods share identical presence–absence patterns among contexts. Finally, with one exception (the Mississippian period) there is a steady rise in the number of contexts in which sites occur. This apparent trend, one of increasing site context diversity, is evaluated after temporal changes in context patterns are described.

Early Archaic

Early Archaic sites occur in only four context classes, but they are widely dispersed both geographically (Figure 16.3) and environmentally (Figure 16.7). A majority are upland sites (62.5%), three of which are uniquely situated near small ephemeral streams in places that historically were covered with prairie grasses (class A). Two are perched on upland bluff edges (C), and three occupy high bottomland terrace margins (G,I).

Projected distributions of contemporary floral communities reflect the initial advance of extensive Holocene grasslands into the Cannon Reservoir region. Forests probably were more extensive during the Early Archaic period than at any later time, and it seems likely that all documented sites were on the

TABLE 16.3.

Frequencies of Dated Probabilistic Sites in 10 Classes of Environmental Contexts

Cultural period	Context class[a]										Total
	A	B	C	D	E	F	G	H	I	J	
Early Archaic	3	–	2	–	–	–	1	–	2	–	8
Middle Archaic	–	–	3	–	1	–	7	1	6	–	18
Late Archaic/ Early Woodland	–	–	2	–	1	1	5	3	10	–	22
Middle Woodland	–	–	2	1	1	5	5	4	11	3	32
Late Woodland	–	3	3	1	1	6	5	5	11	2	37
Mississippian	–	–	1	–	1	–	3	1	4	2	12
Total	3	3	13	2	5	12	26	14	44	7	129

[a]See text for definitions of context classes.

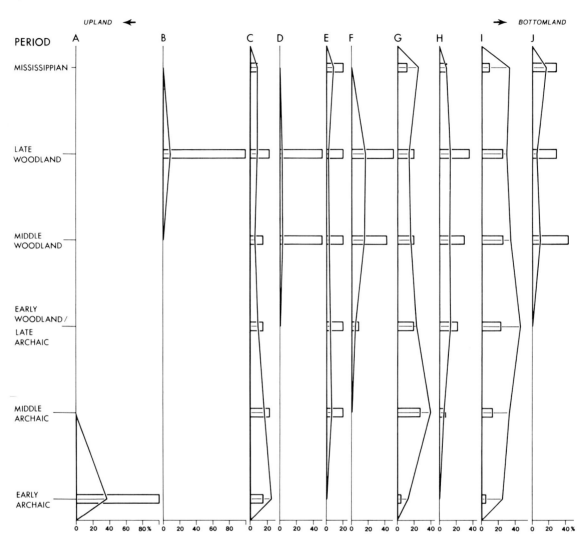

Figure 16.6. Temporal change in proportions of sites within 10 classes of environmental contexts (A–J). Percentage of period indicated by broken line; percentage of class signified by bar.

forest side of the prairie–timber boundary. It is quite possible, however, that sites in class A were near the ecotone, and if it is assumed that these sites represent at least temporary occupations (one, a fairly large Dalton site with a distinct locus of large crude bifaces, is consistent with this proposition), their locations may have been selected so as to maximize access to ecotonal resources. Whatever their specific functions were, the tremendous dis-

persion of Early Archaic sites implies that resources were spaced widely at that time and resource zones were not narrow enough to enable logistical positioning of sites in stable contexts (cf. Chapter 5).

Middle Archaic

Despite several important continuities, site contexts of the Middle Archaic period seem to represent a settlement pattern radically different from that of the Early Archaic (Figure 16.8). There is a sharp reduction in the proportion of upland sites (to 16.7%), due primarily to the disappearance of sites in upland flats (class A). On the other hand, there is a notable increase in the proportion of sites on very high bottomland terraces (G), and bluff-base sites (E,H) occur for the first time. The proportion of sites on margins of lower terraces (I) changes very little. The new focus on lowland contexts probably represents either a major shift in resource orientation or significant shifts in the distributions of resources.

As noted in Chapter 4, environmental reconstructions in other parts of the Prairie Peninsula imply that the Hypsithermal had a profound effect on biota in the Cannon Reservoir region. Prairies

undoubtedly extended beyond their historic limits and probably also invaded many areas currently underlain by forest soils. Valley sides with relatively gentle slopes, which are particularly common along the Salt's major tributaries, may have been transformed into extensive hill prairies and open-canopy woodlands, and many bottomland forests along the Salt River probably gave way to sizable patches of grassland. Forests, although constricted, probably formed galleries along major streams and survived on steeper protected slopes.

Given these changes, it is safe to conclude that Hypsithermal resource distributions were quite different from those encountered by Early Archaic cultures. Zones of forest resources probably were much narrower than at any other time during the

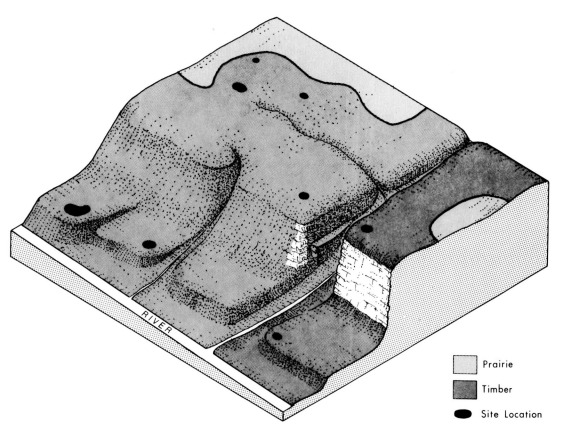

Figure 16.7. Model of Early Archaic period (Pre-Boreal episode) site locations (8/8 plotted), showing hypothetical distributions of contemporary floral communities in the Cannon Reservoir region.

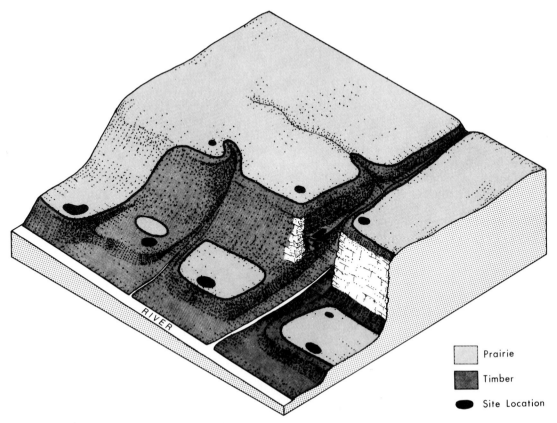

Figure 16.8. Model of Middle Archaic period (Hypsithermal or Atlantic episode) site locations (9/18 plotted), showing hypothetical distributions of contemporary floral communities in the Cannon Reservoir region.

Holocene. The resulting increase in resource accessibility should have obviated the value of many upland locations and could have enabled recurrent occupation of stable bottomland contexts. Observed distributions are consistent, for the most part, with these propositions. Nevertheless, sites are common on upland rims (C), and this anomaly suggests that the degree of settlement mobility was still quite high among Middle Archaic groups. Moreover, it also implies that the Middle Archaic settlement pattern may have been very similar to the Early Archaic pattern. Although the distributions and physiographic contexts of sites changed a great deal, the biotic contexts and functions of sites may have remained the same.

Late Archaic–Early Woodland

Components dated to the Late Archaic–Early Woodland period continue the trend of decreasing proportions of sites in upland contexts (9.1%). All but two components occur in lowlands, and both exceptions are situated on the gently sloping edges of upland flats (C) near major streams (Figure 16.9). Proportions of bottomland sites are similar to those of the Middle Archaic; most are located near major streams on the outer margins of high terraces (G,I). However, several other lowland contexts increase in relative frequency or are represented for the first time. Bluff-base sites in wide valley bottoms (H) replace upland rim components (C) as the third-most common context, and one site is located on the narrow terrace of a perennial tributary stream (F).

The increased proportion of lowland sites in the Late Archaic–Early Woodland period represents a striking contrast to contemporary environmental changes. At the end of the Hypsithermal, effective moisture increased in the Prairie Peninsula, and timber reclaimed many contexts that had previously given way to prairie. The extent of reclamation probably matched closely the modern distributions of forest and grassland soils (Figure 16.4). Forests probably also increased in density, and together these trends should have led to a greater abundance and a broader distribution of forest re-

sources, particularly in upland contexts. Given these environmental changes, the relative decrease in numbers of upland sites during the Late Archaic–Early Woodland period is anomalous from the perspective of changing resource distribution. If the Middle Archaic settlement–subsistence pattern had persisted, there should have been a proportional increase in upland sites, rather than a decline. Thus, observed trends indicate that there was a significant change after the Middle Archaic, either in the kinds of resources exploited or in the settlement strategy used to house and sustain communities. Moreover, contrasts between site contexts of the Early Archaic and Late Archaic–Early Woodland periods suggest that selection for settle-

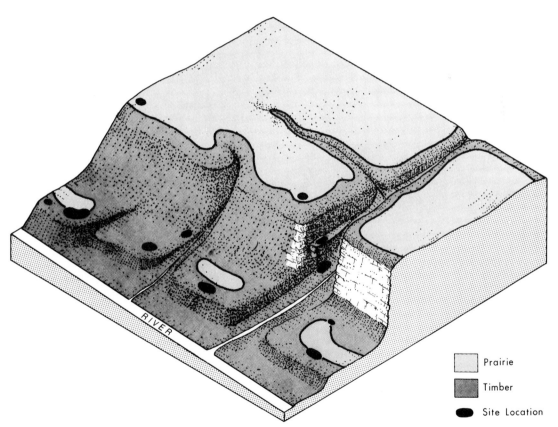

Figure 16.9. Model of Late Archaic–Early Woodland period (Sub-Boreal episode) site locations (11/12 plotted), showing hypothetical distributions of contemporary floral communities in the Cannon Reservoir region.

ment–subsistence pattern change after the Hypsithermal involved cultural factors rather than
environmental ones.

Middle Woodland

There is little change in the relative frequencies
of upland sites after the Late Archaic–Early Woodland period (9.4%), but the proportions of sites in
different lowland contexts change enough to distinguish the Middle Woodland locational pattern
from all others (Figure 16.10). Sites still are most
common on high terrace margins near major
streams (G,I). However, the combined proportions
of these two contexts drop from 68.2% to 50.0% of
the total as bottomland contexts become more diverse. Bluff-base sites (H) occur at the same rate,

but sites on low flood plains of major streams (J) are
documented for the first time, and there is a dramatic increase in the relative frequency of components on terraces of minor tributary streams (F).
Another new context (D), represented by only one
site, is in the dissected upland gallery forest of a
small ephemeral stream.

The Sub-Atlantic climatic episode apparently
was a time of somewhat cooler and more moist
conditions in many parts of the Midwest. However, the magnitudes of change appear to have been
relatively small and may have been reflected only
by a moderate expansion of timber across zones of
transitional grassland–forest soil. Effects on resource distribution in the southern Prairie Peninsula probably also were minor, and it seems un-

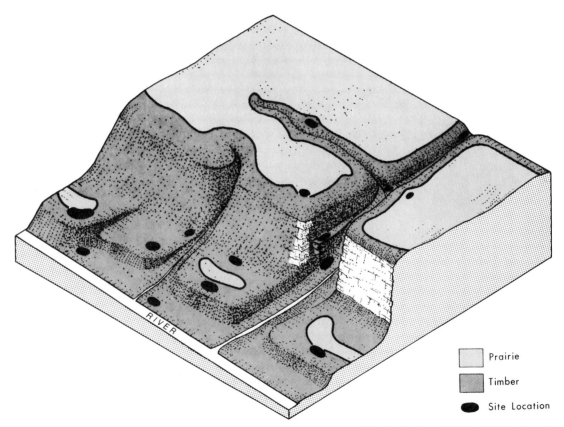

Figure 16.10. Model of Middle Woodland period (Sub-Atlantic episode) site locations (15/32 plotted), showing
hypothetical distributions of contemporary floral communities in the Cannon Reservoir region.

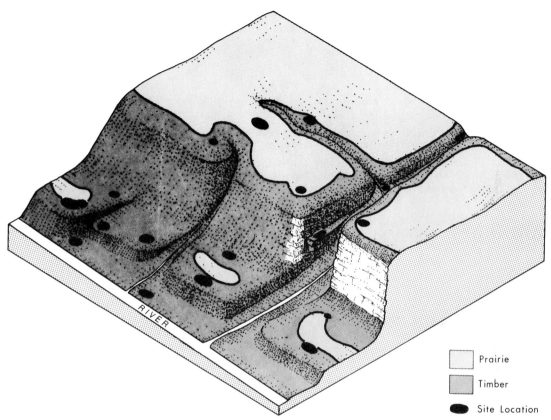

Prairie

Timber

● Site Location

Figure 16.11. Model of Late Woodland period (Scandic, Neo-Atlantic episodes) site locations (18/37 plotted), showing hypothetical distributions of contemporary floral communities in the Cannon Reservoir region.

likely that environmental change had a significant impact on the Middle Woodland settlement pattern in the Cannon Reservoir region. Changes in site context, including a notable expansion up tributary streams and a new focus on flood plains, seem instead to reflect more intensive use of the region. This inference is consistent with the proposed constriction of Middle Woodland resource catchments caused by increasing population densities (Chapter 5) and suggests that cultural factors were responsible for changes in Middle Woodland site locations.

Late Woodland

Similar to the situation in the three previous cultural periods, Late Woodland site locations are significantly biased toward bottomland contexts (Figure 16.11). However, there is a notable increase

in the proportion of upland components (18.9%) to a level that is second in rate of occurrence only to the Early Archaic period. The increase is primarily due to the appearance of three sites on crests of narrow upland interstream divides (B). Proportions of sites in the other two represented upland contexts (C,D) are quite similar to those of the Middle Woodland period. In fact, relative frequencies of components in all other contexts differ very little from previous values, and if not for the unique occurrence of sites in context class B, context patterns of the Middle and Late Woodland periods would be virtually identical.

The Late Woodland period overlaps two climatic episodes, the Scandic and Neo-Atlantic. The former apparently was a time of slightly warmer and drier conditions, and the latter was warm but more

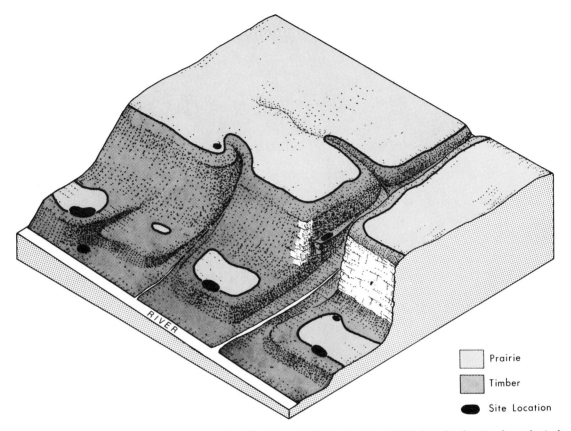

Figure 16.12.   Model of Mississippian period (Pacific episode) site locations (7/12 plotted), showing hypothetical distributions of contemporary floral communities in the Cannon Reservoir region.

moist than the Scandic. On the average, the two episodes probably represent a slight decrease in effective moisture in the southern Prairie Peninsula, which resulted in minor downslope shifts of the prairie–timber ecotone. Effects on resource distributions probably were minimal, and it seems unlikely that environmental change played a determinant role favoring expansion of Late Woodland sites into upland contexts.

Mississippian

Contexts of Mississippian sites represent a reversal of several trends that began during the Middle Woodland period (Figure 16.12). With the exception of flood plain sites (J), which persist during Mississippian times, context proportions are very similar to those of the Late Archaic–Early Woodland period. During the Mississippian, upland components decrease in relative frequency (8.3%), sites disappear along tributary streams (F) and on upland interstream divides (B), and the proportion of sites on margins of high bottomland terraces (G,I) increases for the first time since the Middle Archaic period (i.e., from 43.0% during Late Woodland to 58.3% during Mississippian).

After about A.D. 1100, there was a relatively severe episode of warmth and dryness in the Prairie Peninsula. Conditions did not deteriorate nearly as much as they had during the Hypsithermal, although excavated floral and faunal remains document significant local changes west of the Cannon Reservoir region (Bryson and Baerreis 1968). Effects of the Pacific episode on Cannon Reservoir area biota are unknown, but droughtiness probably caused tree deaths along the prairie–timber border and some expansion of prairie. If resource abundance (or the capacity for resource production) decreased in the area, human economic stress could have increased. Given constant or growing human populations, one might expect these conditions to have caused more intensive use of the region, including a shift toward second-line foods or a greater reliance on food production. Instead, changes in Mississippian site locations seem to reflect less intensive use of the area, as do decreasing numbers of dated probabilistic sites (Figure 16.2). Assuming that the mechanism of this apparent depopulation was emigration, rather than increased human mortality, social and economic conditions outside the region must also have changed to permit extensive human migration (Chapter 4). Thus, environmental factors may have influenced changes in Mississippian settlement patterns in the project area, but explanation of the change will require a much better understanding than we now have of cultural developments in surrounding regions.

Context Diversity

Locations of dated probabilistic sites reflect a number of significant changes in prehistoric use of the Cannon Reservoir region. As noted earlier, a persistent element of these changes apparently is related to increases and decreases in human population density. Site frequencies rise persistently from Early Archaic to Late Woodland times, then drop off during the Mississippian period. At the same time, sites occur in a growing variety of contexts until about A.D. 1000. Assuming that hunter–gatherer population density in an environmentally varied area correlates directly with (a) requisite economic intensification (i.e., the necessary amounts of time and energy invested in serving resource needs of the population; Chapter 5) and, as a result, with (b) the varieties of environmental contexts that must be exploited to house and sustain the population, measurements of site context diversity should correlate with measurements of density.

There are several robust measures of diversity

designed to give results that are independent of sample size. Two of these, equitability (H') and dominance concentration (C), were used earlier to describe trends in tree species diversity among zones of historic prairies and forests (Chapter 3). As applied here, they measure (a) relative similarities among proportions of sites in different contexts (H'), and (b) relative disparities among proportions of sites in different contexts (C). For the sake of clarity, the inverse of dominance concentration ($1/C$) was calculated so that both measures correlate directly with diversity.

Standardized results show very similar trends through time ($r = .97$; Figure 16.13). Equitability (H') increases monotonically, but gradually, among the three Archaic periods, then climbs rapidly toward a mode in the Late Woodland period, and finally drops off during the Mississippian. Except for a reversal during the Archaic periods, dominance concentration ($1/C$) defines a virtually identical pattern. In comparison, both diversity patterns are similar to trends in weighted (wf) and unweighted (uf) frequencies of dated probabilistic sites (Figure 16.2). Equitability correlates highly

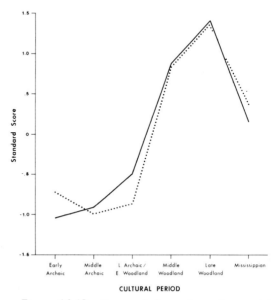

Figure 16.13. Temporal change in environmental diversities of prehistoric site contexts; equitability (—), dominance concentration (. . . .).

with both trends ($r_{H'-wf} = .98$; $r_{H'-uf} = .83$), whereas dominance concentration is very similar to one ($r_{1/C-wf} = .96$) and is fairly similar to the other ($r_{1/C-uf} = .70$). Thus, given the assumptions noted above, results offer independent support for the proposed trends in population density and also imply that changes in site context diversity reflect changing intensities of land use, caused by parallel changes in population density.

SITE CONTENT VARIATION

Results of site context analysis suggest that after the Late Archaic–Early Woodland period, there was a sharp rise in population density and a more extensive use of the region as a whole. Both patterns reach modes during Late Woodland times and drop off thereafter. These trends are consistent with revisions of the model of prehistoric settlement–subsistence change indicated by faunal and floral remains from residential sites (Chapter 10). However, they also suggest there may have been functional differences among sites dated to certain cultural periods, and settlement system roles played by sites in certain contexts may have changed through time. Because locational data alone tell us little about what these different functions and changing roles may have been, and because the sample of dated probabilistic sites may contain a greater range of functional variability than the sample of excavated components, a necessary second step in reconstructing prehistoric settlement patterns is to examine variability among sites in terms of their contents.

Ideally, analysis of site contents would involve a detailed comparison of artifact assemblages from all 129 dated probabilistic components. This is not currently possible. Excavations were carried out at only 10 of the 75 sites, and intensive surface collections were made at only 6 sites. Furthermore, most of this fieldwork also focused on residential occupations, and results do not help us recognize sites with other kinds of functions.

Three sets of data aid in the recognition of site types. The first includes surface artifacts collected from 20 sites in the Putman Bottom locality (Chapter 12). The second includes qualitative observations of site characteristics made by site survey crews in the field. The third includes contexts of the 11 excavated components whose faunal remains are analyzed in Chapter 10. In combination, these data provide a new perspective from which we can better evaluate changing patterns of land use through time.

Putman Bottom

Intensive surface collections in Putman Bottom (Figure 12.5) were used to test one aspect of the settlement pattern model. The proposition is that lowland settings, which contain varied and dispersed natural resources (Chapter 3), are characterized archaeologically by functionally diverse assemblages (Chapter 5). To test this hypothesis, intersite variability in lithic assemblages was analyzed from 20 sites. Technological patterns were isolated and then were evaluated in light of temporal, spatial, and surface magnitude variables in order to derive an empirical hypothesis capable of explaining observed associations. Implications of the empirical hypothesis were then tested, and inferences were compared with deduced expectations to evaluate the validity of the model. Although the objectives of research in Putman Bottom were somewhat tangential to the objectives of this chapter, results of the study are pertinent. The remainder of this section is adapted from parts of the original study (Warren and Miskell 1981).

Methods and Materials

Two systems of artifact classification were applied to Putman materials: size and morphological class (Curry 1979). Both systems are composed of technological partitions. Therefore, neither is suitable for evaluating specific functions of artifacts. However, functional inferences can be derived from morphological attributes, and these hypotheses are testable with other kinds of data (Chapter 9).

The size grade classification is comprised of four arbitrary categories. Artifacts were passed through a graduated series of wire-mesh screens, and identifications were based on the mesh interval that stopped the flow of each artifact (1 inch, ½ inch, ¼ inch, <¼ inch). The morphological classification is composed of 45 technological categories (Miskell and Warren 1979). Thirty-six of these are unformed chipped stone artifact classes, which include nine major morphological groups [COREs; core REJUvenation flakes; core SHATter; PRIMary decortication flakes; SECOndary decortication flakes; tertiary CHUNks; TERTiary flakes; TRIMming flakes; and SHARpening flakes (class symbols are capitalized)]. Each of these nine major groups is subdivided into four categories defined by the presence or absence of (*a*) heat treatment and (*b*) retouch flake scars aligned in a continuous series along the intended working edge of an artifact (combinations include: UN-heat-treated and NOnretouched; UN-heat-treated and REtouched; HEat-treated and NOnretouched; and HEat-treated and REtouched). There also are five formed chipped stone classes (PROJectile POINts; BIFACEs; DRILls and PERForators; FORMed SCRAPers; MISCellaneous FORMed cryptocrystalline), one category for ceramics (CERAMICS), and three categories of ground stone artifacts (UNFOrmed GROUnd stone; MISCellaneous GROUnd stone; FORMed GROUnd stone).

Several complementary analytical techniques were used to identify systematic sources of variance within and among the Putman samples. All focused on artifact size and technological class frequencies and used differing patterns of variables within cases to (*a*) define intersite relationships and (*b*) isolate associated trends among variables. Accordingly, values were standardized by case (i.e., by site) to eliminate magnitude variability, and Q-mode applications were used for all analyses.

Cluster analysis was used to group sites by relative degrees of case similarity. Program TAXON, a sequential agglomerative hierarchical clustering technique (Rohlf *et al.* 1972), generated phenons using the unweighted pair–group method with arithmetic averages (UPGMA). Cophenetic correlation coefficients (artifact class, $r_{coph} = .83$; size grade, $r_{coph} = .80$) signify good fits between original and implied association matrices, suggesting that the samples are suitable for hierarchical arrangement.

Nonmetric multidimensional scaling (NM–MDS) also was used to evaluate intercase relationships. This procedure, first proposed by Shepard

(1962), calculates Cartesian coordinates for cases in reduced dimensionality, where intercase distances are monotonically related to distances among cases in n-dimensional Euclidean space. The TORSCA-9 program of Young (1968) was used to generate coordinates, based on distance matrices obtained from the utility program DSQDSQ (Benfer 1971; Heisler 1975). Stress levels, measures of disparity between original and reduced distance matrices, indicate that acceptable solutions occur in two dimensions for both the artifact class ($s = .09$) and size grade ($s = .01$) data sets.

Trends among variables were evaluated by calculating mean standard scores of variables within each phenon and searching for patterned variation among phenons arranged in Cartesian space by nonmetric multidimensional scaling.

A second line of investigation introduced the dimensions of time, space, and site magnitude in order to isolate covarying external factors that might enhance the interpretive potential of technological patterns. Accordingly, discriminant function analysis (BMD–P7M; Jennrich and Sampson 1977) was used to determine whether an independent set of variables (measures of site context and site magnitude) could form functions capable of discriminating between groups of technologically similar sites (i.e., cluster analysis phenons derived from artifact-class and size-grade data sets).

Surface collections in Putman Bottom yielded 15,969 artifacts. Distributions of these objects indicate that concentrations vary a great deal in size, density, and location (Figure 12.6). For the purpose of comparative analysis, artifact concentrations surrounding the 37 field transit stations (Figure 12.5) were consolidated into 20 cases (sites A–T) on the basis of spatial contiguity of artifacts shown on large scale distribution maps. Samples vary greatly in size ($\bar{X} = 798$; S.D. $= 1747$). Eight sites (C–F, I, K, Q, S) have particularly small samples (57–127 total artifacts), and, because of possible sampling instability, their artifact class patterns should be viewed with caution.

Intersite Relationships

Technological relationships among sites were determined by cluster analysis and nonmetric mul-

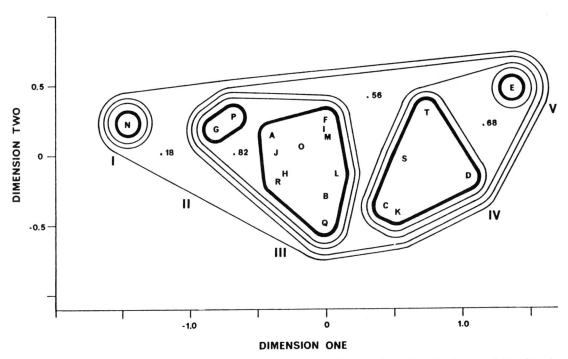

Figure 16.14. Two-dimensional nonmetric multidimensional scaling configuration of intersite relationships in Putman Bottom as defined by size grade patterning (n = 20 sites; stress = .013). Heavy lines denote cluster analysis phenons (I–V); arabic numerals signify correlation linkage levels; letters denote sites (from Warren and Miskell 1981).

tidimensional scaling analysis (NM–MDS) of artifact patterns. Results are presented in two-dimensional plots of cases, in which intercase distances reflect relative degrees of similarity or dissimilarity among sites, and clusters of similar sites (i.e., phenons) are circumscribed by linkage lines.

A configuration of sites defined by size grade patterning is shown in an abbreviated Wroclaw diagram (Figure 16.14). Five phenons (enclosed by heavy lines) are defined at a correlation linkage level of .82. Results of the two multivariate techniques are mutually supportive: (*a*) The two most similar sites, I and M (r = 1.00), are plotted close together in phenon III; (*b*) the two most dissimilar sites, N and E (r = −.71), are plotted farthest apart in phenons I and V; and (*c*) linkage boundaries are regular and enclose progressively distant sets. Of considerable interpretive significance is the essentially unilinear configuration of cases and groups. Although a fairly high stress level (s = .113) was

achieved by a one-dimensional NM–MDS solution for these same data, all phenons can be compressed into a single axis without distorting group integrity. This implies that a continuum of size grade patterns exists on dimension 1, which grades consistently from site N to site E.

Five phenons were defined in a configuration of sites arranged by relative similarities of artifact class patterning (Figure 16.15).[3] Most sites again are strung out along dimension 1, implying that there is one major set of trends among artifact class variables. Furthermore, comparison of case positions in Figures 16.14 and 16.15 indicates that site configurations derived from the size-grade and artifact-class data sets are somewhat similar. Analysis of ordinal relationships between the two data sets,

[3]Two groups, each containing one site (sites C and S) have a relatively low linkage level (.85) but are treated here as a single phenon (phenon III).

based on Spearman rank-order correlations of one-dimensional NM–MDS solutions for each data set, indicates they are in fact significantly correlated beyond the .01 level of probability ($r_s = -.70$, $df =$ 18, $t = 4.2$). Importantly, this implies that the sources of systematic variance explained by the first dimensions of both ordinations are shared; that is,

an empirical relationship exists among size grade and artifact class trends.

The artifact class configuration also shows a distinct second dimension that orders phenons from high to low as follows: IV, III, I, II, V. As a point of caution, it should be noted that sites in phenons scoring highly on dimension 2 (phenons III, IV)

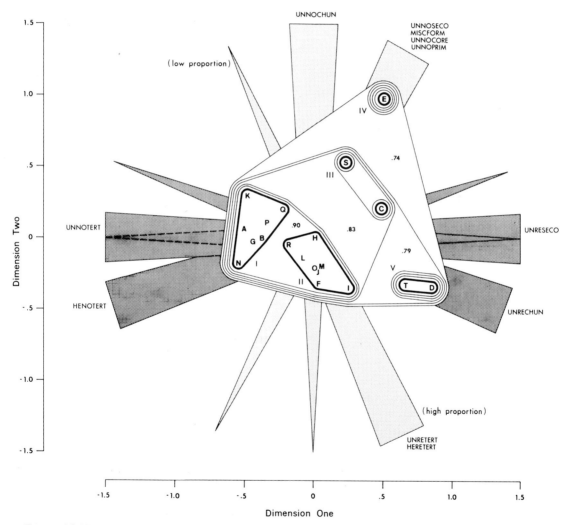

Figure 16.15.   Two-dimensional nonmetric multidimensional scaling configuration of intersite relationships in Putman Bottom as defined by artifact class patterning ($n = 20$ sites; stress = .097). Heavy lines and roman numerals denote cluster analysis phenons; arabic numerals signify correlation linkage levels; letters denote sites; isosceles triangles represent vectors of changing variable scores among phenons (proportions increase toward wide ends).

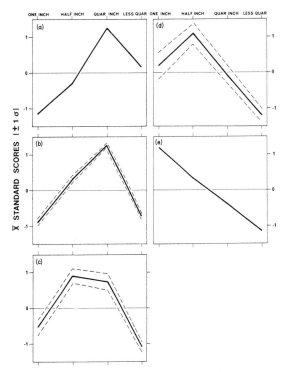

Figure 16.16. Intergroup variation of four size-grade variables on five phenons defined by size-grade patterning (*n* = 20 sites from Putman Bottom). (a) Phenon I (*n* = 1 site); (b) Phenon II (*n* = 2); (c) Phenon III (*n* = 11); (d) Phenon IV (*n* = 5); (e) Phenon V (*n* = 1). (From Warren and Miskell 1981.)

have very small sample sizes, and the interpretive significance of the dimension is debatable.

Artifact Patterning

Analysis of artifact patterning confirms our expectations that trends among variables shift systematically along the major axes of dimensionality defined by NM–MDS. Trends among size grade variables are shown in Figure 16.16, where mean patterns for each of the five size grade phenons are plotted in sequence (i.e., in progression along dimension 1 of the NM–MDS configuration; see Figure 16.14). Directionality of variables is quite obvious among the ordered phenons. They range from predominantly small artifacts in phenon I (¼ inch and < ¼ inch) to predominantly large artifacts in phenon V (1 inch and ½ inch). Intermediate

clusters grade progressively between these two extremes.

Analysis of morphological classes indicates that only 11 of 44 variables show significant or continuous trends among the five artifact class phenons. These variables are represented in Figure 16.15 by narrow isosceles triangles that signify varying mean proportions of artifact classes in different phenons. Each triangle, analogous to a trend-surface vector in two dimensions, is hinged at the centroid (0,0 coordinate) and is oriented so the direction of its long axis, and its expanding width, represents a continuous progressive increase among phenons in the mean standard score of its artifact class. Four artifact classes correlate with dimension 1. Two of these, UNNOTERT and HENOTERT (un-heat-treated and heat-treated, nonretouched tertiary flakes), increase in proportion toward phenon I; the others, UNRESECO (un-heat-treated, retouched, secondary decortication flakes) and UNRECHUN (un-heat-treated, retouched tertiary chunks), increase toward phenon V. On the second dimension, five classes increase toward phenon IV: UNNOCHUN (un-heat-treated, nonretouched tertiary chunks), UNNOSECO (un-heat-treated, nonretouched, secondary decortication flakes), MISCFORM (miscellaneous formed cryptocrystalline) UNNOCORE (un-heat-treated, nonretouched cores), and UNNOPRIM (un-heat-treated, nonretouched, primary decortication flakes). Two others, UNRETERT and HERETERT (un-heat-treated and heat-treated, retouched tertiary flakes), also increase in proportion toward phenon V.

There are several technologically meaningful associations among covarying artifact classes. First, the variables peaking in phenon I represent late, or relatively refined, stages of artifact manufacture. Two additional variables, UNNOTRIM (un-heat-treated, nonretouched trimming flakes) and UNNOSHAR (un-heat-treated, nonretouched sharpening flakes), achieve modes among five of these same sites (A,B,G,N,P) in a corresponding phenon defined by artifact class patterns among sites with large sample sizes (Warren and Miskell 1981). Thus, most sites in phenon I are distinguished by residues of late-stage manufacturing and maintenance activities. Second, all variables peaking in phenon V are retouched artifact classes. They represent varying stages of manufacture, but the persistently high rate of retouch in this direction is suggestive of tool use. Finally, variables peaking in phenon IV include a variety of early- and middle-stage manufacturing residues and a relatively high rate of crude formed artifacts. Although sample sizes in this direction are small and patterns may be affected by sample bias, the coincidence of these five classes is suggestive of the manufacture of heavy-duty tools.

Context and Magnitude

Analysis of technological patterns demonstrates that sites in Putman Bottom can be ordered along sequences of varying artifact size and morphology. The dimensions of time, space, and site magnitude are introduced to determine whether nontechnological variables are associated with these configurations and trends.

Stepwise discriminant function analysis was used to determine if any of a series of context and magnitude variables could discriminate between groups (i.e., phenons) of technologically similar sites (Warren and Miskell 1981). Results of several discriminant analyses indicate that only a few of 35 context–magnitude variables are sufficiently powerful to be entered into the functions. Nevertheless, the identities of these variables are of great interest; they include mean surface artifact density, maximum surface artifact density, and sample size. All are indicators of site magnitude, a dimension that can be expected to associate with varying site functions (Chapter 5).

To evaluate the significance of these implied relationships, rank-orders of site magnitude values were compared with rank-orders of site coordinates (derived from one-dimensional NM–MDS solutions) using the Spearman rank-order correlation coefficient. Results show significant correlations between the three density-related magnitude variables and site sequences generated from the size-grade and size-grade/artifact-class data sets (see Warren and Miskell 1981). The highest correlations are with mean density, whereas a fourth magnitude variable, site size, is virtually uncorrelated with either of the site sequences.

A scattergram of mean surface artifact density on

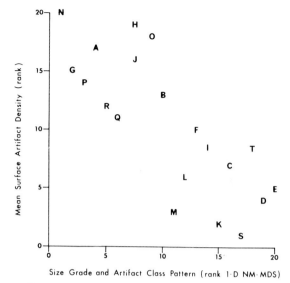

Figure 16.17.   Rank-order scattergram of mean surface artifact density on a one-dimensional nonmetric multidimensional scaling configuration of intersite relationships defined by both size-grade and artifact-class patterning ($n = 20$ sites; stress $= .18$; $r_s = -.79$; $p < .01$) (after Warren and Miskell 1981).

the size-grade/artifact-class sequence illustrates a representative trend (Figure 16.17) and also points out an interesting hiatus on the regression between sites B and F. Inspection of companion plots (not presented here) indicates that gaps occur consistently on regressions of the three density-related variables; most can be described as dumbbell-shaped configurations. Although compositions of the end clusters vary somewhat from plot to plot, the fact that groupings do occur implies that artifact density, in concert with technological factors, is a useful indicator of site type. Furthermore, shapes of the dumbbell regressions suggest that a simple dichotomy of site types is represented in Putman Bottom.

Discussion

Analysis of technological factors and density functions indicates that variability is significant and patterned among sites in the Putman Bottom locality and has a fairly simple structure. Interrelationships among size-grade variables, artifact-class variables, and measures of surface artifact density form a general continuum that ranges from:

1. High-density sites dominated by small artifacts that hypothetically reflect processes of tool manufacture and tool maintenance (nonretouched tertiary flakes, sharpening flakes, and trimming flakes), to:

2. Low-density sites dominated by large artifacts that hypothetically reflect processes of (*a*) tool use (retouched tertiary flakes, retouched chunks, and retouched secondary decortication flakes) and (*b*) manufacture of heavy-duty tools (nonretouched chunks, primary and secondary decortication flakes, cores, and miscellaneous formed artifacts).

Further, site magnitude functions indicate that Putman sites can be sorted into two major groups, each of which is hypothetically associated with a distinct set of systemic functions. These include:

1. *Residential sites* with high artifact densities indicative of intensive and/or recurrent occupation and artifact assemblages that represent light domestic activities; and

2. *Procurement–processing sites* with low artifact densities indicative of infrequent and/or temporary occupation and assemblages that represent resource extraction and/or heavy processing activities.

Several implications of these hypotheses are testable with independent data: (*a*) Both site types should occur *within* cultural periods; (*b*) characteristic locations of the two site types should differ; (*c*) residential sites should contain subsurface evidence of domestic activities; and (*d*) residential sites should contain evidence of recurrent occupation (Warren and Miskell 1981).

Time   If the hypothesized site types represent systemic variation among activities, both types should be represented within specific temporal periods. Artifacts diagnostic of the Late Woodland period are relatively common in the Putman sample, and, assuming that these artifacts are valid indicators of site use in time, they can be used to test the implication. Results indicate Late Woodland compo-

nents occur in all size-grade phenons (5/5), in most artifact-class phenons (4/5), and in both hypothesized site types. Thus, sites occupied during the Late Woodland period were technologically diverse, and this finding is consistent with a systemic explanation of differences among site types.

Space   If the hypothesized site types are differentiated by residential versus extractive activities, locational constraints and site contexts should differ. Residential sites can be expected to have recurrent contextual characteristics reflecting day-to-day domestic requirements, whereas locations of procurement–processing sites should be less structured (assuming they reflect extensive exploitation of dispersed bottomland resources). A map of dichotomized Putman sites (Figure 12.7) suggests that locations generally fit these expectations. Most hypothesized residential sites occur on level to gently sloping surfaces near outer terrace margins, overlooking temporary or permanent water sources. Procurement–processing sites occupy less consistent contexts; many occur between the parallel arrays of residential sites, often on sloping land with less direct access to water sources. Thus, site contexts are consistent with locational implications derived from inferred site functions.

Subsurface Associations   If hypothesized residential sites represent relatively long-term loci of domestic activities, odds favoring the occurrence of subsurface domestic features are greater than among short-term procurement–processing sites. To test this implication, plow zone deposits were removed by heavy machinery from five residential sites (A, G, H, N, O) and two procurement–processing sites (E, I). Features were discovered only at sites N and O, both of which are hypothesized residential sites perched on high terrace margins. Most features appear to represent facilities for storage and/or refuse disposal. Thus, results are consistent with expectations. However, the absence of features at sites A, G, and H is not understood. If the three sites did function as residential sites, they may represent seasonal encampments on lowlying flood plains in which subsurface facilities were not used.

Recurrent Occupation If, as has been suggested, locational contexts of residential sites are conducive to habitation and if locational requirements for residential sites did not vary greatly through time, then cultural–temporal indicators from hypothesized residential sites should demonstrate long-term recurrence of occupations (i.e., multiple components). To test this proposition, sites were dichotomized as multicomponent versus single component, and results were compared with the site type dichotomy. Fisher's Exact Test was used to determine whether observed frequencies (6 residential-multiple; 4 residential-single; 0 procurement-multiple; 10 procurement-single) are too rare to have occurred by chance alone. A value of $p = .005$ was obtained, which is statistically significant at alpha $= .01$. Thus, hypothesized residential sites were used more recurrently through time than chance would allow, a finding that offers indirect (and admittedly weak) support for the hypothesis.

Conclusions

Relationships among sites in the Putman Bottom locality, when viewed from the perspective of technological patterning, are best represented by a one-dimensional configuration of cases. Importantly, proportions of associated technological classes vary systematically along this dimension. Several surface magnitude factors also correlate with the configuration and indicate that sites in the sequence can be segregated into two general groups. Characteristics of these groups suggest that they represent a dichotomy of distinctive sets of functions that are related to patterns of residence versus resource extraction. Four tests of this induced hypothesis offer consistent support.

Although additional research is needed to identify the specific task or tasks represented by procurement–processing sites, descriptions of Australian wood-procurement locations show interesting parallels with sparse lithic scatters in Putman Bottom (Gould 1980; Hayden 1978). The Australian locations have low artifact densities and assemblages dominated by large retouched chopping implements that were manufactured, used, and abandoned near the place of use. Instances of site occupation are brief, and few artifacts are deposited at

any one time. As Binford (1980) points out, however, a series of such events in a bounded locality eventually would build up sparse but detectable scatters of artifacts, including the tools used and the debitage resulting from their on-the-spot manufacture (Gould 1980). Australian wood-procurement locations should not be construed as functional analogues of sites in Putman Bottom, but these observations establish an ethnoarchaeological precedent for recognizing traces of extractive tasks, and they give us provocative insights into the formation processes of procurement–processing sites.

In conclusion, results of intersite analysis indicate that diversity among sites in the Putman locality is directly related to variation in function. Therefore, findings are consistent with the expectation that functional diversity is high among sites in microenvironments that contain varied and dispersed natural resources. Additionally, results also have important implications for understanding site contexts and functions outside Putman Bottom. First, it appears that residential site locations in bottomlands of narrowly banded environments are selected as much by domestic criteria as they are by strategic resource needs. Second, several measures of site magnitude characteristics, especially mean surface artifact density, apparently are relatively sensitive indicators of functional site types. Assuming that the relationship holds elsewhere in the region, estimates of site density can be used as provisional guides to site type identification. Third, the association between functional site types and recurrent occupation in the Putman sample indicates that evidence of multiple components may be a useful indicator of residential occupations.

Probabilistic Sites

Field records of the probabilistic site survey document a variety of site characteristics (Warren 1979). Among these are estimates of relative surface artifact density (low, medium, high), occurrences of diagnostic artifacts (projectile points and pottery), and descriptions of obvious features (e.g., exposed facilities and burial mounds). As suggested previously, two of these characteristics are useful indicators of functional site types in Putman Bottom. Both artifact density and numbers of components correlate directly with "residentialness." Assuming these indicators are applicable elsewhere, they can be used to better evaluate changes in site location and site type in the probabilistic sample.

In applying these correlates to the sample of dated probabilistic components, three categories of sites were defined. Residential sites include all components with (a) no evidence of burial mounds, (b) surface artifact density ratings of medium or high, and/or (c) a collection of diagnostic projectile points whose temporal associations indicate occupation during more than one cultural period. Procurement–processing sites include all those with (a) no evidence of burial mounds, (b) a low surface artifact density rating, and (c) no evidence of occupation during more than one cultural period. All other sites are defined as burial mounds.

The results of the functional classification are presented in Table 16.4. The Early Archaic period has 5 examples of hypothesized residential sites, 2 in context class C and 1 in each of the remaining contexts in which components occur. Hypothesized procurement–processing sites occur only in contexts A ($n = 2$) and I ($n = 1$). All Middle Archaic sites are classified as residential. There are 19 Late Archaic–Early Woodland residential sites, at least 1 in each documented context. Three procure-

ment–processing sites occur, one each in contexts C, H, and I.

Middle Woodland sites include 2 mounds (C, E), 25 residential sites (C-D, F-J), and 5 procurement–processing sites (H-J). There are 3 Late Woodland mounds (2,D; 1,E). Residential sites ($n = 25$) occur in six contexts (B, D, F-I), and procurement–processing sites ($N = 9$) are in six contexts (B-C, F-H, J). Mississippian sites include two mounds (C, E), eight residential sites (G-I), and two hypothesized procurement–processing sites (J). Implications of results are discussed in the following sections.

Excavated Sites

Analysis of 12 vertebrate samples (Chapter 10) suggests that interassemblage faunal variability is attributable to two factors: (a) seasonal effects of warm-season and cool-season occupation in semisedentary settlement patterns (Late Archaic, Early Woodland, Middle Woodland, and late Late Woodland or Mississippian) and (b) local intensification of subsistence practices in a sedentary settlement pattern (Late Woodland). Using the site context classes defined earlier, these 12 components can be used to test certain results of the previous section.

Semisedentary occupations occur in three contexts. All warm-season components (Cooper, LA; Miskell, LA; Hatten Village, MW) are on outer mar-

TABLE 16.4.

Occurrences of Hypothesized Residential Sites, Procurement/Processing Sites, and Burial Mound Sites in 10 Classes of Environmental Contexts

Cultural period	Context class[a]									
	A	B	C	D	E	F	G	H	I	J
Early Archaic	R, P	–	R	–	–	–	R	–	R, P	–
Middle Archaic	–	–	R	–	R	–	R	R	R	–
Late Archaic/Early Archaic	–	–	R, P	–	R	R	R	R, P	R, P	–
Middle Woodland	–	–	R, M	R	M	R	R	R, P	R, P	R, P
Late Woodland	–	R, P	P, M	R	M	R, P	R, P	R, P	R	P
Mississippian	–	–	M	–	M	–	R	R	R	P

[a] Symbol "R" = hypothesized residential site; symbol "P" = hypothesized procurement/processing site; symbol "M" = hypothesized burial mound site.

gins of very high terraces (class G), a context that apparently was heavily used for residential occupation during prehistoric times. Cool-season components occur in classes F (Pigeon Roost Creek, LA–LW), G (Hillside, MW; Cooper, LW), and I (Collins, EW). The Late Archaic sample at Pigeon Roost Creek confirms residential locations of this period along tributary streams (Table 16.4) and suggests that wintering on tributaries may have been common. Nevertheless, cool-season occupations are just as common along major streams, and if there is a trend here, it is the potential for greater variability among contexts of cool-season settlements.

Both Late Woodland occupations are interpreted as sedentary villages that were inhabited all year long. Muskrat Run is located on a small tributary stream (F) and Victor Bridge is on a high terrace at the base of a bluff (H), confirming Late Woodland residence in these two contexts (Table 16.4). Also of interest is the fact that neither is located in the traditionally "most popular" residential contexts (I and G). Furthermore, neither is ideally situated for access to aquatic resources, yet fish and amphibians comprise dominant proportions of both assemblages. Thus, both villages may represent "second-line" residential contexts, perhaps reflecting in locational terms a Late Woodland shift toward "second-line" resources caused by population growth and crowding of village resource catchments.

DISCUSSION AND CONCLUSIONS

Site contexts and available site content information indicate that there were significant changes in prehistoric settlement patterns in the Cannon Reservoir region. Some undoubtedly were influenced by the environmental effects of climatic change, whereas others are attributable to the cultural factors of increasing and decreasing population density.

Early Archaic

During the Early Archaic period, the southern Prairie Peninsula had an essentially modern array of faunal and floral resources. However, forests generally were much more extensive than during the early nineteenth century, and the densities and distributions of many species probably were much different. Open woodlands and prairie–forest transitions should have been uncommon and highly localized in level uplands, probably limiting the development of undergrowth and possibly the populations of browsing species, such as deer. Thus, many resources important during later times may have been widely dispersed and relatively rare. Human populations apparently also were small and of low density, and resource distributions would have favored group mobility. Site contexts and contents in the Cannon Reservoir region are consistent with this proposition, and the relatively wide dispersion of hypothesized residential sites suggests that Early Archaic groups practiced a mobile foraging economy. Furthermore, we can speculate that this economy involved a three-part seasonal round: (*a*) warm-season bottomland encampments (G, I); (*b*) cool-season upland encampments that were scheduled for the collection of autumn mast (C), and (*c*) cool-season upland encampments that were scheduled for the procurement of mast-related vertebrates (A).

Middle Archaic

During the Middle Archaic period, prairies displaced forests in most upland and many bottomland contexts. Prairie–timber transitions were extensive along upland margins and valley bottoms, and many forests (particularly those along the Salt's major tributaries) were probably less dense than forests documented in GLO records. Aquatic resources and some forest species probably also declined in numbers, but it seems likely that populations of edge species remained stable or grew. Deer may have been more abundant than before and may also have been more accessible, due to regional narrowing of environmental zones and local expansions of suitable habitat. Human populations appear to have grown as well, yet site locations show a more constricted distribution along major streams. This is probably due to a continued reliance on forest and forest-edge species, which had aggregated along streams as a result of climatic change. Settlement–subsistence systems are difficult to interpret with available data, but the suggestion that all 18 Middle Archaic components may have functioned as residential encampments implies that groups often moved from place to place to occupy temporary camps in locales with undepleted resources, rather than establish more permanent settlements out of which smaller groups traveled to perform specific tasks. Thus, results are consistent with the proposition that Middle Archaic groups in the Cannon Reservoir region maintained a mobile foraging economy similar in many respects to that of the Early Archaic (Chapter 5). Nevertheless, site contexts were notably different from those of earlier times, and species exploitation patterns may have changed.

Late Archaic–Early Woodland

Despite probable expansion of forests after the Hypsithermal, site locations during the Late Archaic–Early Woodland period were similar to those of the Middle Archaic in their proximity to watercourses. Site contexts continued to diversify, however, despite the further decline in proportions of upland sites. Moreover, we see the first appearance since the Early Archaic of sites that might have functioned as specialized nonresidential procurement–processing locations (16.7% of the total). These occur in uplands and in two different bottomland contexts and are consistent with the interpretation, derived from faunal and floral remains, that a semisedentary settlement system had been adopted in which small task groups were more likely to conduct extractive tasks away from residential camps or villages. Results also are consistent with the proposition that both warm-season and cool-season residential sites were located in bottomland contexts since only 1 of 19 possible residential sites is located in the uplands.

Middle Woodland

Climatic conditions during the Middle Woodland period changed relatively little from the Late Archaic–Early Woodland but probably were somewhat more moist. Thus, changes in settlement

probably were due more to cultural factors than environmental ones. Population densities apparently were much higher, perhaps due to increased growth rates caused by the decreased mobility of Late Archaic–Early Woodland foraging strategies (see Binford and Chasko 1976; Dumond 1975). Growth is reflected in the higher diversity of site contexts and in the expansion of residential sites into valleys of small tributary streams (F) and into other possible "second-line" residential contexts (e.g., D, H, and J). As a result of this apparent crowding, foraging catchments probably diminished in size, and groups were forced to rely more heavily on local resources. This is consistent with the recovery of three possible cultigens at Hatten Village SA 6 (chenopod, knotweed, maygrass) and pepo squash at Pigeon Roost Creek (Chapter 11). Nevertheless, faunal remains from these same sites show no evidence of a shift toward "second-line" vertebrate resources, and seasonal evidence indicates that settlement systems still were semisedentary, with complementary warm-season and cool-season occupations. Thus, population densities in the region, though higher, apparently had not reached a threshold favoring sedentism. Site locations offer little firm support for this interpretation. However, the fact that proportions of hypothesized procurement–processing sites are virtually identical in the Middle Woodland and Late Archaic–Early Woodland samples suggests that similar amounts of nonresidential extractive tasks were necessary during both periods. Also, the predominance of residential sites in valley bottom contexts suggests that criteria for selecting the locations of warm-season and cool-season occupations were similar to those of the previous period.

Late Woodland

Late Woodland physical environments, although somewhat variable, probably were quite similar to the previous period, and it seems unlikely that climatic change had a great impact on Late Woodland cultural adaptations. Population density apparently increased significantly, and this trend may explain the notably different settlement–subsistence system that appeared in the Cannon Reservoir region by about A.D. 700. Residential sites appear to have been occupied all year long for the first time, and "second-line" resources (e.g., fish and amphibians) were relied on more heavily. Moreover, the contexts of residential sites continued to diversify. Excavations at Muskrat Run and Victor Bridge document permanent villages in possible "second-line" residential contexts, and magnitudes of surface artifact distributions suggest that several other villages were established in uplands.

Proportions and distributions of nonresidential sites also changed. Hypothesized procurement–processing sites are more common, accounting for 24.3% of dated sites, and they occur in a variety of upland and bottomland contexts. This increase may be an effect of the establishment of sedentary villages. As residence stabilized, there may have been a greater need for the recruitment of small specialized groups to carry out extractive tasks some distance away from villages since residential groups no longer moved seasonally from localities with depleted resources into others with greater local productivity. Although the specific function, or functions, of procurement–processing sites currently is unknown, the higher proportion and more diverse contexts of these sites during the Late Woodland period might reflect an intensification and more widespread impact of extractive activities.

Documented burial mounds also appear for the first time in the sample of dated probabilistic sites, suggesting that mound burial was most commonly practiced in the region by sedentary Late Woodland groups. Frequencies of site types also suggest that one of the most common uses of upland margins (C) during the period was for mound construction.

Mississippian

Site frequencies indicate that the gradual rise in human population density that followed man's initial occupation of the Cannon Reservoir region was reversed after about A.D. 1000. Consistent with this interpretation is the fact that faunal and floral remains suggest groups returned to a semi-sedentary settlement system analogous to that of the Late Archaic–Middle Woodland periods. Site contexts show a parallel decline in diversity, and the pattern of Mississippian period context proportions is similar to that of the Late Archaic–Early Woodland period. Less common than previously are upland sites and sites along tributary streams, although sites in "first-line" residential contexts (e.g., G) increase relative to proportions of Late Woodland sites. Thus, as population density decreased, there was extensive desertion of village locations that had less than optimal domestic characteristics and inequitable access to desirable resources. With less competition for the most favorable residential locations, occupation of "second-line" places no longer was necessary. Remnant groups once again were free to reside in contexts that had been valued by hunter–gatherers in the region since Early Archaic times. Also of interest is the drop in the proportion of hypothesized procurement–processing sites to 16.7%, perhaps reflecting a lower incidence of activities by specialized task groups due to seasonal abandonment of settlements.

This model of population decline and apparent broadening of the economic base during the Mississippian period provides a stark contrast to contemporary cultural developments along larger rivers in the Midwest (Chapter 4). Communities in many of these areas were quite large and complex, were growing rapidly, and had intensive subsistence economies heavily dependent on maize agriculture.

There are several possible causes of the anomalous reverse trend in the Cannon Reservoir region. First, environmental change associated with the Pacific climatic episode may have contributed. The Prairie Peninsula and northern Great Plains were relatively warm and progressively drier after about A.D. 1000, and it is possible that recurrent droughts in the Cannon Reservoir region caused crop failures among Late Woodland groups that already were stressed by high population density and were beginning to intensify their economies by increasing dependence on maize. Thus, climatic deterioration could have hindered agricultural intensification, forcing groups to move downstream toward soils with more stable moisture contents. This hypothesis cannot be tested with available Cannon Project data, but it is discounted somewhat by the fact that agriculture actually intensified in other more climatically sensitive parts of the Prairie Peninsula where decreases in moisture probably were more severe (Bryson and Baerreis 1968).

A more likely explanation is that emigration from the Cannon Reservoir region was voluntary and groups moved downstream toward the Mississippi River into more economically productive localities that either were vacant or selected for much higher population densities than occurred locally due to important economic changes among resident societies. Often associated with the adop-

tion of full-scale maize agriculture in the Eastern Woodlands were increases in community size and the development of spatially aggregated configurations of settlement. Both are attributable to the higher labor demands of intensive resource production (Smith 1976). Aggregation may have opened up productive niches between communities that could be exploited by immigrants from tributary valleys, or members of larger settlements may have recruited outside groups to help perform labor-intensive tasks. In either event, research is needed outside the Cannon Reservoir region to test these propositions.

17

Historic Settlement Patterns

ROGER D. MASON, ROBERT E. WARREN, AND MICHAEL J. O'BRIEN

The study of frontier settlement has been, until recently, a subject primarily for historians, beginning with Frederick Jackson Turner (1893). Subsequently, most historians of the American frontier either have defended or attacked the Turner thesis that federal land-sale policies promoted the development of a frontier democratic system based on land-owning yeoman farmers. As is examined briefly in this chapter, the situation is now changing, due to the entrance of historical geographers into the field. Our study of early historic period (1818–1850) settlement patterns in the Cannon Reservoir area employs many of the research strategies of human geographers, rather than a more traditional historical approach, to test hypotheses derived from the model of historic period adaptation and change that was outlined in Chapter 5.

We believe the end result of settlement geography is an understanding of settlement *systems;* in this case, frontier systems. Unfortunately, many analyses of settlement geography have been concerned primarily with describing the distribution of facilities (farmsteads, hamlets, towns) through the use of terms such as *random, regular,* or *agglome-*

rated. Research has concentrated on formulating mathematical expressions for these distributions instead of striving for explanations of the processes that create these distributions, especially at the rural level. This reduces settlement geography to "the study of the form of the cultural landscape" (Jordan 1966:27). Instead of process, it deals with "(i) the facilities built in the process of human occupance of the land and (ii) their grouping" (Singh 1975:4).

On the other hand, there has been increasing awareness among some settlement geographers that theory is needed to explain the patterns observed in the geographic record (see Bylund 1960; Conzen 1971; and Hudson 1969). Hudson's work is of particular interest, and it forms the basis of our 3-stage model of historic settlement in the Cannon Reservoir area (Chapter 5). His treatment of niche (theoretical) versus biotope (real) space represents a significant step beyond simple characterization of settlement configuration.

In this study we deal with the patterns of location of pioneer farmsteads with respect to two major classes of dimensions or variables: environmental

and social. A third dimension, agricultural specialization, also is examined to determine if location of
settlement varies directly with different kinds of
specialized activity. These aspects of settlement location are at the heart of the settlement system and
form the nucleus for investigations of other portions of the system, such as the structure of communities as discussed in Chapter 15. Finally, implications of the historic model are discussed and
evaluated in light of the data.

THE DATA BASE

Analysis was carried out using quantitative
rather than qualitative data. The latter, termed *narrative sources* by Curti (1959), tend to be either particularistic (referring only to certain individuals or
events) or normative (generalizing about a group or
region). In neither case is it possible to assess the
range of variation present in the structure of a regional population. However, if quantitative data
pertaining to a regional population are available,
some assessment of variation in farmstead location,
farm size, or family wealth can be made.

Primary data sources used in analysis include
land entry records, land patents, poll books, probate records, and population and agricultural census schedules. Plat books of original land entries,
located in the Recorder's office in each county, contain the name of the original entrant and date of
entry for each 40-acre quarter–quarter section purchased (the minimum unit of land that could be
entered after 1832). Land entry began in the fall of
1818, when land in the project area first was offered
for sale, and continued through 1859, when the last
parcel of publicly owned land was sold. As can be
seen in Figure 8.2, most land purchases occurred
during the period 1828–1836, which coincided with
a period of economic expansion and land speculation (Chapter 8).

Land patents are federal deeds verifying that the
original entrant became owner of the land. A person's county of residence at the time he entered
land also is given on patents. This information
helps to distinguish local residents from absentee
owners and Eastern speculators. At least one patent was found for 1041 of 1548 original entrants.

After residents of the project area were isolated

through analysis of land entry and patent information, we used additional data from census schedules, poll books, and probate records to study the
composition of the population. Microfilm copies of
census schedules for 1830, 1840, and 1850 were
consulted at the Missouri State Historical Society
archives in Columbia. Census schedules list heads
of household by name, provide demographic data,
such as the age and sex of members of each household, and, in 1850, list names of dependents. Information on slave ownership also is available in each
census. Data on the occupations of household
members becomes more detailed in 1850, as does
agricultural production data for individual farms.

Since no census data are available for the period
prior to 1830, the Ralls County poll books for the
1820s were consulted. In addition, we checked
county probate records for the names of residents
who died before the next census was taken. Therefore, *resident land entrants* were defined as all entrants appearing in the 1830, 1840, or 1850 censuses; in the poll books from the 1820s; in probate
records; or having a local county of residence listed
on a patent. Of 1548 original entrants, 1164 were
defined as residents.

Environmental dimensions for correlation with
land entry data were abstracted from soil series
descriptions provided by the Soil Conservation Service (Watson 1979; unpublished SCS data). Soil series descriptions contain information on slope, topographic features, native vegetation at the time of
soil formation (Warren *et al.* 1982), and drainage
rate, variables that may have influenced prospec-
tive purchasers' decisions about what land to buy.
A computer file containing information on the distribution of soil series in the project area was created from soil maps by estimating the number of
sixteenths of a quarter–quarter section (40 acres)
each soil series occupied in each quarter–quarter
section.

ANALYSIS
OF SETTLEMENT LOCATION DATA

In this section we summarize the background of
the typical project area immigrant and consider the
correlation between location of land entry and

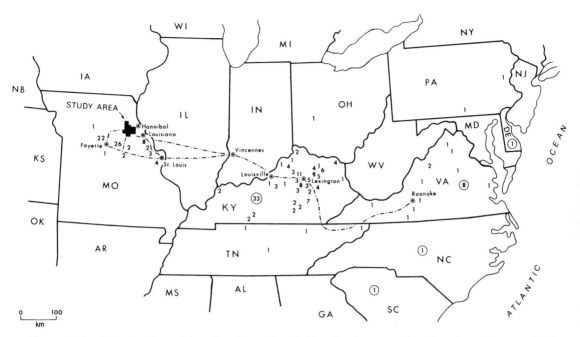

Figure 17.1. Map showing origins of settlers and probable migration routes (–·–·–) to the project area. Circles indicate number of families for which no specific county of origin is known.

three dimensions: environmental, social, and agricultural specialization.

The Regional Population and its Background

River valleys in central and northern Missouri were part of a pre-1860 Upper South cultural and agricultural region (Jordan 1967; Kniffen 1965; Mitchell 1972, 1978; Voss 1969–1970), in part composed of emigrants from Kentucky and Virginia (Figure 17.1). A study of residence location reported in patents and in biographies of early settlers in the project area (National Historical Co. 1884; Owen and Co. 1895) allowed determination of specific counties of origin. Of the 122 families for which a specific county of origin is known (Table 17.1), 63% were from a 34-county area known as the Bluegrass Region of Kentucky (as defined by Davis 1927).

Since emigrants from the Bluegrass Region probably would seek an area with a similar setting, a description of the Bluegrass Region is necessary.

As Brookfield (1969:53) notes, "decision-makers operating in an environment base their decisions on the environment as they perceive it, not as it is." Environmental perception is based on general cultural background and, more specifically, on previous experience with similar environments and available technology.

When the first settlers arrived in Kentucky, they found "a kind of open forest; in which the lawns were tangled with cane, and other luxuriant vegetation, and grass" (Flint 1970, II:208). Francois Michaux, a French botanist who traveled through the Bluegrass Region in 1802, noted that there was little "herbage" between trees, which were far enough apart that "a stag may be seen a hundred or a hundred and fifty fathoms off" (Michaux 1904:231). The parklike nature of the Bluegrass Region was described by Flint (1970, II:174–175) as an area in which trees were "promiscuously arranged for the effect of a pleasure ground," seemingly "having been transplanted to the places which they occupy."

The importance of wood to Upper South agri-

TABLE 17.1.

Origins of Settlers by Number of Families Per County, According to Patent Residences and Published Sources[a]

County	State	Patent	Published	Total
Anderson[b]	Kentucky	1		1
Bath[b]	Kentucky	2	4	6
Boone[b]	Kentucky	1	2	3
Bourbon[b]	Kentucky	4	4	8
Bullett	Kentucky	1		1
Casey[b]	Kentucky		2	2
Clark[b]	Kentucky	1	4	5
Fayette[b]	Kentucky	2	3	5
Franklin[b]	Kentucky	2	1	3
Garrard[b]	Kentucky	1	1	2
Green	Kentucky	1	1	2
Greenup[b]	Kentucky	1	3	4
Harrison[b]	Kentucky	1	2	3
Jessamine[b]	Kentucky		3	3
Lawrence	Kentucky	1		1
Lincoln[b]	Kentucky	5	2	7
Madison[b]	Kentucky	1	3	4
Marion	Kentucky	2		2
Mason[b]	Kentucky	1		1
Mercer[b]	Kentucky	7	1	8
Nelson[b]	Kentucky	2	1	3
Nicholas[b]	Kentucky	1		1
Oldham[b]	Kentucky	1		1
Scott[b]	Kentucky	7	4	11
Shelby[b]	Kentucky	3	2	5
Simpson	Kentucky		2	2
Union	Kentucky	1	1	2
Warren	Kentucky	1	1	2
Washington[b]	Kentucky		3	3
Woodford[b]	Kentucky	1	2	3
Fentress	Tennessee		1	1
Robertson	Tennessee	1		1
Rutherford	Tennessee	1		1
Sullivan	Tennessee	1		1
Augusta	Virginia		2	2
Bedford	Virginia		1	1
Caroline	Virginia		1	1
Franklin	Virginia		1	1
Louisa	Virginia		1	1
Page	Virginia	1		1
Patrick	Virginia	1		1
Rockbridge	Virginia	1		1
Tazewell	Virginia	1		1
Franklin	Pennsylvania	1		1
Northampton	Pennsylvania		1	1
Champaign	Ohio	1		1

[a]Sources: National Historical Company 1884; Holcombe 1884; Owen and Co. 1895.
[b]Counties located in the Bluegrass Region, according to Davis (1927).

culturists should not be underestimated (McManis 1964:90). Farmers made their own houses, furniture, tools, and wagons from wood, especially in frontier areas (Bidwell and Falconer 1925:162). In the early nineteenth century, corn fields were plowed first with a light, wooden, moldboard-plow with an iron tip, and often a wooden harrow was used to complete soil preparation (Bidwell and Falconer 1925:342). Brick or stone houses were rare in the rural Upper South, where a characteristic wooden-house construction style in both log and frame was developed. German log construction techniques and the English "I" frame house style, which diffused through the Upper South, originated in southeastern Pennsylvania (Kniffen 1965: 561). Log houses were built only as temporary structures in the North but were constructed as permanent houses by many in the Upper South, where use of corner-notching techniques produced locked box corners that could be covered with siding (Kniffen and Glassie 1966:56).

Since settlers from the Upper South had a wood-oriented technology and inhabited a forest environment, they judged the quality of soils by kinds and sizes of trees charateristic of an area (Cuming 1904:165; Flint 1970, II:174; Michaux 1904:228). Given this forest-biased perception of the environment, avoidance of prairies for settlement could be predicted. The case of the Kentucky Barrens, a treeless, grass-covered area in south-central Kentucky, confirms this prediction. Michaux (1904:220) encountered only 18 houses in 105 km (65 miles) of road while crossing the Barrens in 1802. The Kentucky legislature, endeavoring to overcome the forest bias, offered 400 acres free to every man who would become an actual settler in the Barrens (Flint 1970, II:175).

Jordan (1964:206) sought to test the hypothesis that southerners from Kentucky and Virginia in the Old Northwest before 1830 avoided prairies because of: (*a*) absence of timber for construction, (*b*) lack of surface water resources, and (*c*) the difficulty of breaking sod. Both Jordan (1964:208) and McManis (1964:38) believe that the major objection to prairies was lack of timber, rather than a belief in the infertility of prairie soils. Jordan (1964:216) concludes, on the basis of narrative sources describing settlement, that mixed vegetation areas (where tim-

ber and prairies interdigitated) were preferred by people of varied origins. There often was an extensive transition zone between forest and prairie, where trees were spaced widely (similar to the Bluegrass tree-spacing described previously) and sod was not as thick as in the centers of large prairies. Thus, cultivation could be carried out without laborious tree-clearing or expensive sod-breaking. Most accounts studied by Jordan (1964:212) state that houses were located in the woods on the edge of the prairie and that crops were grown in the prairie margin.

McManis (1964:70), who used land purchase records as well as narrative sources, studied settlement locations in Illinois and concluded that timbered land sold earlier than prairie and that prairie margins were sold before tracts in the prairie proper. Only timbered areas and prairie margins had been sold by the 1830s, and prairies were used as an adjunct to timbered-area settlement. Houses were located in the timber, and the prairie edge was cultivated and used for pasture (McManis 1964:92). Early records show that most sod-breaking was carried out by northerners (McManis 1964:94).

Correlation of Land Entry with Environmental Dimensions

The project area allows testing of the hypothesis that prairies were avoided and that the prairie–timber boundary was favored for early settlement by Upper South pioneers. In order to test this hypothesis, it is necessary to make several assumptions. First, we assume that the first land entry made by a permanent resident was the location of his house and farmstead. Support for this assumption comes from the fact that of 30 house locations known to date to the initial period of settlement, 27 are located on first purchases (in a few cases a first purchase was from another individual rather than from the federal government). A second assumption is that land with preferred environmental characteristics was entered earlier than other land. A study of environmental characteristics of first entries made by residents between 1818–1859 should provide information about preferred settlement locations.

For an initial understanding of the correlation between environment and settlement location, two

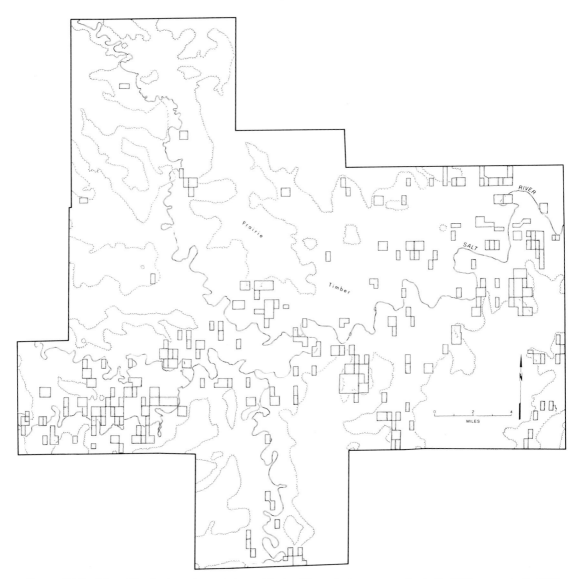

Figure 17.2. Map of first land entries made by residents of the project area appearing in the 1830 census, in the 1820s Ralls County poll books, or who died before 1830.

plots of land entries were made: one for 1830 and one for 1840. The 1830 map (Figure 17.2) shows the location of first land purchases made by 196 individuals who appear in the 1830 census, in the 1820s poll books, or who died before 1830. These entries were plotted on a base map of the project area, which shows rivers and the prairie–timber boundaries mapped by General Land Office surveyors between 1816 and 1822. Inspection of the map shows only one first entry located entirely in the prairie, whereas 36 first entries contain both timber and prairie. In addition, 34 first entries located entirely in timber were close enough to the prairie edge such that a subsequent adjacent purchase of 80 acres would have included prairie. Thus, 71 (36.2%) of 196 settlers owning land by 1830 were in a position to make use of the prairie, whereas 125 (63.8%) were located in timber-only areas.

The 1840 map (Figure 17.3) shows first entries made by residents who first appeared in the 1840 census. The 1840 pattern of first entries of residents in relation to prairie–timber boundaries is a continuation of the trend begun in 1830. Of 583 first entries of persons who appear in the 1840 census, only 17 (2.9%) are located entirely in prairie. There are 161 (27.6%) first entries that include both timber

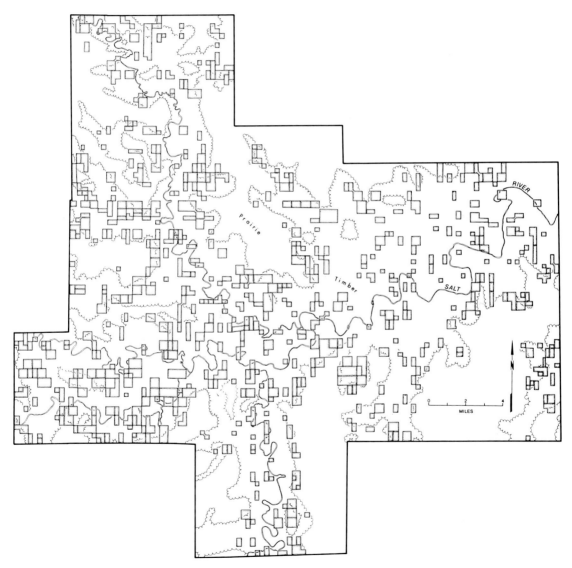

Figure 17.3. Map of first land entries made by residents of the project area listed in the 1840 census.

TABLE 17.2.

Attributes of Environmental Dimensions Used in Multiple Regression Analysis

Dimension		Attribute
Slope (S)	1	0-5% (level or gentle slope)
	2	5-14% (moderate slope)
	3	14-30% (steep slope)
Vegetation (V)	1	Timber-prairie
	2	Timber
	3	Prairie
	4	None (rocky)
Topography (T)	1	Bottomland
	2	Low terraces
	3	High terraces
	4	Slopes and ridgetops
	5	Level upland
Soil drainage (D)	1	Moderately well drained; Moderately well - well drained
	2	Somewhat poorly - moderately well drained; well drained
	3	Very well drained; somewhat poorly drained
	4	Poorly drained
	5	Very poorly drained

and prairie and an additional 101 (17.3%) within a kilometer of prairie, making a total of 279 (47.9%) settlers who probably had access to prairie. The other 304 (52.1%) were located well within timber. Thus, if first entries made by residents are representative of farmstead locations, it is apparent that both prairie edge and timber-only locations were sought by early settlers (Chapter 15).

In order to study land entry decisions in relation to environmental variables in more detail, especially in terms of internal variability within the timber zone, a multiple regression was done. The number of days a tract of land remained unsold was the dependent variable, and a series of environmental dimensions (variables) were used as independents. Four environmental dimensions that vary with soil series and that probably were significant to early-nineteenth-century pioneer agriculturists were used to create 26 environmental classes. A paradigmatic classification was used to order the soil series in terms of attributes of the environmental dimensions. The four dimensions are slope, vegetation, topography, and soil drainage. Table 17.2 lists the attributes of each dimension. Combinations of attributes that actually

occur in the area were used to group the soil series data for Monroe and Shelby counties (Watson 1979) and Ralls County (unpublished SCS data), to create the 26 environmental classes used in the multiple regression (Table 17.3).

Multiple regression analysis was carried out using the Statistical Package for the Social Sciences (SPSS) (Nie *et al.* 1975) multiple regression program.[1] In a preliminary run using all cases, we noted significant differences among the populations of land entries that include: (*a*) first entries by residents, (*b*) subsequent entries by residents, (*c*) entries of Eastern speculators, and (*d*) all others entries. Since significant differences were observed, separate multiple regression analyses were carried out for each population. Only the results of analysis of the first entries of residents will be discussed here. Results for the other populations are discussed in Mason (1981).

Multiple regression analysis produces a multiple regression coefficient (β) for significant dimensions. Magnitudes of beta are not comparable be-

[1]The multiple regression was performed by Duncan Mitchell.

cause of differences in standard error, but the sign of beta for classes found to be significant conveys the necessary information. In this case, a significant negative beta for an environmental class indicates earlier entries of tracts with that dimension, whereas a significant positive beta indicates later entries for that class. Coefficients significant at the .05 level for first entries of residents are shown in Table 17.4.

Environmental classes (EC) associated with earlier first land entries of residents are EC 1, 5, 17, 18, and 25. However, EC 1 (prairie–timber bottoms) and 25 (mined land) each occupies only .1% of the project area (Table 17.3). Thus, although these two classes are statistically significant, their small size contributes very little to the overall pattern. Of more interest are EC 5, 17, and 18, which are level, timbered, high terraces; prairie–timber, moderate slopes; and timbered ridgetops and moderate slopes, respectively. Environmental classes associated with the later first entries are EC 3, 13–15, and 22. Environmental classes 3 (timbered bottoms) and 13 (prairie, high terraces) are rare and occupy only .3% and .4% of the project area, respectively. Environmental classes 14, 15, and 22, however, occupy a significant portion of the project area and represent level, upland prairie (EC 14 and 15) and steep, timbered slopes (EC 22).

Results of the multiple regression analysis of first entries of residents show that moderate slopes and ridge tops in the timber zone, high terraces in the

TABLE 17.3.

Environmental Classes Used in the Multiple Regression Analysis and Percentage of Project Area Each Occupies

Dummy variable	Environmental dimensions				Soil series	Percentage
	S	V	T	D		
1	1	1	1	1	Cedargap	.1
2	1	2	1	1	Fatima, Kickapoo	2.7
3	1	2	1	1	Belknap	.3
4	1	2	2	4	Moniteau	.5
5	1	2	3	4	Auxvasse, Marion	1.8
6	1	2	4	3	Calwoods	1.9
7	1	2	2	5	Piopolis	6.4
8	1	3	1	4	Blackoar, Chequest	.7
9	1	3	1	5	Wabash	.1
10	1	3	2	3	Arbela	.5
11	1	3	3	1	Vigar	.1
12	1	3	3	3	Gifford	1.2
13	1	3	3	4	Chariton	.4
14	1	3	5	3	Mexico, Kilwinning	16.3
15	1	3	5	4	Putnam	12.2
16	2	1	4	1	Gara	.1
17	2	1	4	2	Armstrong	10.2
18	2	2	4	1	Keswick, Gosport, Weller, Winfield	15.1
19	2	2	4	2	Menfro	.1
20	2	2	4	3	Gorin	4.3
21	2	3	4	3	Leonard, Sampsel	10.8
22	3	2	4	2	Goss, Lindley	13.1
23	3	4	4	3	Rockland	.7
24					River, Lake	.1
25					Mine or Quarry	.1
26					No Data	.2

TABLE 17.4.

**Multiple Regression Coefficients Significant at the p = .05 Level
for First Land Entries of Residents[a]**

Dummy Variable	Coefficients	Standard Error
1	−247	102
3	311	101
5	−86	33
13	98	43
14	57	16
15	222	17
17	−64	13
18	−78	13
22	37	17
25	−547	174

[a] R^2 = .14

timber zone, and moderate slopes in the prairie–timber zone were preferred locations for settlement. Level, upland prairie and steep, timbered slopes were avoided. This provides more detailed information about choices made within the timber zone. The hypothesis that the prairie–timber zone was preferred is confirmed, but it was found that two environmental classes within the timber zone also were preferred; these are timbered, moderate slopes and ridge tops and timbered, high terraces.

It is noted that the soil drainage dimension had little effect on time of entry. The same values of the drainage variable are associated with both early and late entries. In future analysis, it would be interesting to rerun the multiple regressions without the drainage dimension. This would reduce the number of environmental classes from 26 to 18.

Although the results of multiple regression analysis produced combinations of attributes of environmental dimensions that were associated significantly with early or late entries of residents, it is important to note that the R^2 value (percentage of variance explained by the multiple regression) is low (i.e., R^2 = .14). Low R^2 values usually mean that variables not included in the analysis are affecting observed patterns. However, before we consider other dimensions, it should be pointed out that use of the amount of time a tract of land remained

unsold as the dependent variable rests on the assumption that land with preferred environmental characteristics was entered earlier than other land. This, in turn, assumes that entrants had knowledge of the environmental characteristics of the tract before purchasing it. Because of correspondence with kin or friends already residing in the area, many entrants probably did have previous knowledge of these characteristics (Chapter 15). However, a significant number of them may have had no more information than the locations of streams and prairie–timber boundaries, both of which were available on plat maps at the federal land office. Thus, after a decision was made to enter a timbered tract, the decision as to which specific tract to enter may have approached randomness for some entrants. Therefore, we can suggest that one reason for low R^2 values is the unknown number of land entry choices made without regard to specific environmental characteristics.

Although other environmental dimensions could have affected land-purchase decisions, it is likely that cultural dimensions also affected locational decisions (Warren et al. 1982). These include proximity to relatives, proximity to people from the same area from which they emigrated, and proximity to people of the same religious affiliation. In other words, land entrants may have located on land with less desirable environmental characteristics in order to be near kin or others with whom they were familiar. Examples of the operation of social variables on settlement location are presented in the next section.

Correlation of Land Entry with Social Dimensions

Further analysis of the distribution of tracts of first entrants (Figures 17.2 and 17.3) indicates that some of these clusters appear to be the result of the operation of social dimensions on settlement location. Since data on social dimensions are limited, no comprehensive quantitative statements about their effects will be made. However, a few examples of the correlation of these dimensions with settlement clustering are presented in the following discussion.[2]

One of the earliest settlement clusters in the project area was located at the head of Griffin Hollow in T55N, R6W. It was begun by three Ely brothers and their brother-in-law, who came from Bath County, Kentucky, in 1819. The Ely settlement (Figure 15.1) was mentioned in the Ralls County road records as early as 1823. A large group of Catholic settlers from Scott County, Kentucky, began settling along the prairie–timber boundary southwest of the Ely settlement, beginning in 1828. This is the only portion of the project area known to have been settled predominantly by members of a single religious denomination. Most of them shared the same religion, came from the same part of Kentucky, and consisted of family groups (fathers and sons settled near each other). These settlers formed an early settlement cluster that extended for about 8 km (measured in a straight line) along the prairie–timber boundary.

In the western part of the project area was another early settlement cluster contemporaneous with the Ely settlement. This was the Smith settlement, located in the northern part of T54N, R9W

and the southernmost row of sections in T55N, R9W (Figure 15.1). The settlement was named for Joseph Smith, who, in 1819, brought a large family from Bath County, Kentucky, that consisted of his sons—Alexander W., Joseph H., John B., and Samuel H.—his daughters—Ann and Mary—and the latter's husband (John Johnson). James Adams' brothers (Ovid and Otho) later entered land nearby, as did the Smith sons after their father died in 1825. A series of intermarriages soon followed. Ann Smith married James C. Fox (the founder of Paris, Missouri) in 1822, and Alexander W. Smith married Susan Fox in 1824. After John Johnson died in 1826, Mary (Smith) Johnson married Otho Adams in 1827. Ovid Adams, John B. Smith, and Samuel H. Smith married daughters of John Yates, who had arrived in 1828 and purchased Joseph Smith's property after the latter's death. The Adams and Yates, at least, appear to have been members of the Church of Christ (now the Disciples of Christ) since Ovid Adams and Nancy Yates were married by a minister of this denomination.

An early settlement cluster, located south of Middle Fork in T54N, R9W (Figure 15.3), was begun by the McGees (John Sr., John Jr., John S., and Robert), James McKamey, and the Simpsons (Robert, John, and Walker). The McGees and McKamey were from Mercer County, Kentucky, and were founding members of the Pleasant Hill Presbyterian Church. The Simpsons also were Presbyterians, but their place of origin in Kentucky is unknown.

The settlement clusters just discussed provide examples of the role of social dimensions (kinship, commonality of origin, and religious affiliation) in determining settlement location (see also Chapter 15). These examples demonstrate that it was a common practice for family groups consisting of brothers and in-laws to emigrate together to form a settlement cluster, with each married adult male establishing his own household and farm near those of other members of the family group. In some cases, their parents also were members of the group. Within a few years, other family groups from the same area of origin or with the same religious affiliation (or both) arrived and settled near the original family group, forming a settlement cluster.

Although settlement in small family groups

---

[2]A portion of the data presented is from a reconstruction of the genealogies of several families in the project area, done by Eugene C. Henning (n.d.). Data from National Historical Company (1884), and Owen and Company (1895) was also employed.

probably was ubiquitous throughout the period of early settlement in all parts of the project area, data on the formation of larger clusters based on commonality of origin and religious affiliation of settlers are limited. It appears that religious affiliation had the greatest effect in promoting the formation of larger settlement clusters among Catholics, who may have been subject to a certain amount of prejudice. The limited data available indicate that Protestants of different denominations settled together, as the proximity of Baptist and Methodist churches in several parts of the project area indicates.

TABLE 17.5.

Descriptive Statistics for the 1850 Agricultural Census of the Project Area (681 Farms)

	N^a	$\%^b$	Mean^c	S.D.^{d}	Max^e
Horses	679	99.7	5.0	2.9	25
Oxen	211	31.0	3.4	1.9	10
Mules and Asses	96	14.1	8.9	15.8	103
Swine	670	98.4	30.6	22.0	175
Cattle	610	89.6	13.9	19.6	200
Sheep	595	87.4	26.0	17.7	170
Wool (lbs)	575	84.4	57.2	39.9	300
Milk Cows	674	99.0	4.5	2.9	30
Butter (lbs)	662	97.2	153.5	102.1	1000
Cheese (lbs)	62	9.1	45.5	40.0	200
Corn (bu)	680	99.9	832.1	608.1	5000
Wheat (bu)	466	68.4	82.2	85.1	700
Rye (bu)	30	4.4	27.3	14.2	60
Oats (bu)	562	82.5	181.3	202.7	1500
Barley (bu)	5	0.7	16.6	10.4	30
Buckwheat (bu)	30	4.4	24.6	27.5	150
Hay (tons)	465	68.3	6.2	6.8	60
Clover Seed (bu)	4	0.6	1.2	0.5	2
Grass Seed (bu)	21	3.1	6.0	8.0	35
Peas and Beans (bu)	24	3.5	17.2	22.0	90
Irish Potatoes (bu)	520	76.4	17.8	14.8	160
Sweet Potatoes (bu)	259	38.0	15.5	14.3	100
Garden products ($)	323	47.4	13.7	18.5	150
Orchard products ($)	315	46.2	25.8	27.8	250
Maple Sugar (lbs)	53	7.8	126.2	142.7	800
Molasses (gal)	41	6.0	10.9	30.6	200
Honey (lbs)	125	18.4	41.6	32.2	200
Tobacco (lbs)	75	11.0	2898.7	3210.6	17,000
Hemp (tons)	14	2.0	1.2	0.6	3
Flax (lbs)	169	24.8	82.6	86.2	500
Flax Seed (bu)	118	17.3	3.6	3.3	22
Hops (lbs)	10	1.5	7.0	6.6	20

[a] N: Number of farms raising or producing the commodity.
[b] %: Percentage of farms raising or producing the commodity.
[c] Mean: Mean number of units of the commodity per producing farms.
[d] S.D.: Standard deviation.
[e] Max.: Maximum units of the commodity in the project area.

Correlation of Land Entry with Agricultural Specialization

In a previous section it was determined that three environmental zones—(*a*) timbered, moderate slopes and ridge tops; (*b*) timbered, high terraces; and (*c*) moderate slopes in the prairie–timber zone—were preferred for farmstead location. In this section it will be shown that different kinds of agriculture were associated with the three zones. Thus, selection of an environmental zone in which to settle may have been determined by the kind of agriculture that a settler intended to practice.

Analysis of the 1850 agricultural census for farmers in the project area (summarized in Table 17.5) showed that an Upper South agricultural complex characterized by mixed farming with a balanced system of crops and livestock emphasizing corn, swine, and cattle (Mitchell 1972, 1978) was present. Study of major producers (probably producers for market) of various agricultural commodities in the project area allowed us to define three kinds of agricultural specialization within the general Upper South complex. *Major producers* were defined as those who produced a commodity in quantities in excess of the mean plus 1 standard deviation, with the exception of tobacco and hemp (Table 17.6). All

TABLE 17.6

Minimum Production Amounts for Various Commodities Necessary for Consideration as a Major Producer

Commodity	Minimum
Mules and asses	5
Swine	53
Cattle	33
Sheep	44
Milk cows	8
Corn (bu)	1441
Wheat (bu)	168
Orchard products ($)	54
Tobacco (lbs)	1
Hemp (tons)	1
Flax (lbs)	169
Flax seed (bu)	7

producers of tobacco and hemp were included since the entire crop probably was produced for market.

The three groups of major producers of agricultural commodities include (*a*) grazing livestock producers who also grew large quantities of grain (presumably as feed for livestock); (*b*) tobacco producers; and (*c*) foraging livestock (swine) and corn producers. Farmers who produced tobacco tended to have tobacco as their only market commodity, whereas grazing livestock producers usually produced several kinds of livestock (cattle, sheep, and mules) plus grain.

Almost all (78 of 87) grazing livestock producers in 1850 for which a location could be determined were located in the prairie–timber transition zone. Their strategy probably was to cultivate the lightly timbered zone and pasture their livestock on the open prairie. The centers of large upland prairies probably remained open range until at least the 1850s, since this zone remained federal public land or was in the hands of absentee Eastern speculators until after 1850. General acceptance of the steel plow in the 1850s (Bidwell and Falconer 1925:285) made cultivation of prairie soils more feasible and led to the end of open range.

Tobacco producers in 1850 were located primarily along streams emptying into North Fork, especially along Crooked Creek. There also was a smaller group of tobacco producers along the Salt River a few miles east of the confluence of the North and South forks. Both areas have relatively large, high terraces, and tobacco producers probably preferred this environmental zone.

The third environmental zone preferred for early settlement was timbered, moderate slopes and ridge tops. The strategy here probably consisted of slash-and-burn agriculture for corn and wheat, plus raising hogs that foraged in the forest. Corn probably was fed to hogs prior to slaughtering.

A rank-ordering by wealth (based on amount of land and slaves owned) of all rural residents of the project area alive in 1850 showed grazing livestock and grain producers were among the wealthiest farmers. Of 92 farmers defined as grazing livestock–grain producers, 44 were among the wealthiest 10% of all rural residents, and 76 of the

92 were among the most wealthy 30%. No grazing livestock–grain producers fell below the sixth decile. Producers of tobacco occur in all wealth ranks, with the majority being in the middle. Although 82.6% of grazing livestock–grain producers were slave owners, only 40% of tobacco producers owned slaves. It appears that instead of a wealthy, slave-owning "small planter" class that, according to Mitchell (1978), was characteristic of the Bluegrass Region of Kentucky and the Upper South in general, there was a wealthy, slave-owning class of stockmen in the project area by 1850. Apparently, slave cowboys were more common than slave tobacco cultivators.

Summary of the Correlations of Land Entry with Dimensions

The pioneer settlement pattern now has been described in terms of both environmental and social dimensions and agricultural specialization. We found that the location of farmsteads depended on the perception of preferred environmental characteristics and the location of other settlers with whom some social affiliation existed. These preferred environmental zones comprised a significant portion of the landscape, providing settlers with a choice of locational strategies through much of the period of initial settlement. In other words, even if settlers restricted their land entries to the preferred zones, they still had to decide on a specific location within the zone or zones. Specific locational choices may have been made on the basis of aesthetic considerations, economic considerations, such as accessibility, or because of social variables, such as kinship, religious affiliation, or commonality of origin.

Social variables probably were most important at the time of initial settlement, when service functions were poorly developed and it was necessary to rely on members of the local group for assistance and specialized skills. Social ties facilitated this cooperation. With the development of towns (Chapter 8), and the appearance of rural nonagricultural specialists (see Mason 1982), these social ties were not as important. Also, as zones with preferred environmental characteristics filled up, settlers probably located wherever good land (as they perceived it) was available and could not afford to be too particular about who their neighbors were.

A third dimension—agricultural specialization—also played a fairly major role in choice of settlement location. Three kinds of agricultural specialization were practiced by 1850: (*a*) grain (primarily corn) and grazing livestock (cattle, milk cows, sheep, and mules) production; (*b*) tobacco production; and (*c*) corn and forest-foraging livestock (swine) production. Grain and grazing livestock production was carried out by wealthy slave owners along the prairie–timber border. Tobacco production was carried out by farmers of moderate means with few or no slaves (although the few producers of large quantities of tobacco did own slaves) on high, timbered terraces. A few of the wealthy livestock producers also grew tobacco if they owned high terraces. The remaining farmers were engaged in corn and hog production on timbered, moderate slopes and produced a surplus of these commodities for sale or exchange whenever possible. It appears to have been the goal of many farmers to produce most of the food items necessary for their own subsistence requirements and then to produce one or more commodities for market.

TESTING THE IMPLICATIONS OF THE MODEL

In this section hypotheses implied by the model of historic adaptation and change are tested using the data presented previously. A temporal framework for the three stages is constructed to guide the discussion.

Temporal Framework

Assignment of temporal boundaries to stages of the historic model is in large measure an arbitrary and compromising task. As noted in Chapter 5, the stages—colonization, spread, and competition—are in reality processes that have occurred throughout the tenure of historic occupation in the region. Nevertheless, land sales data and available population records point to several optimum choices.

The lower end of Stage I, the colonization phase,

begins in 1792. In that year the first well-documented Euro-American settlement was established northeast of the project area by a French salt manufacturer (Holcombe 1884:130–135), who was killed in 1800 by a band of Sac Indians. He was followed by small Anglo-American family groups who settled near the mouth of the Salt River in 1808. Indian hostilities resumed in 1812, and by 1815 the lower Salt Valley had been evacuated (Megown 1878). Settlement in the valley resumed in earnest in 1818, when most of the project area had been surveyed and the threat of interethnic violence had subsided. Thus, a beginning date of 1792 is used here for Stage I, although it is emphasized that permanent occupancy was not established for another 26 years.

The boundary between Stages I and II terminates the colonization phase and introduces the spread phase and is selected here on the basis of population densities and percentage of land purchased. For our purposes, the boundary falls during the decade following 1830. During that period, densities in the Salt River and Jackson townships increased from 1.0/km^2 and .7/km^2, respectively, to 2.5/km^2 and 5.0/km^2, respectively (Table 8.2). Another correlate of the upper end of colonization is town and county formation. Dates in the vicinity of the project area reflect a northwestward trend of the frontier, ranging from 1819 (when New London was founded) and 1821 (when Ralls County was established) in the southeast, to 1831 (when Paris and Florida were founded) in the middle of the project area, to 1836 (when Shelbyville was founded and became the seat of Shelby County) in the northwest (Chapter 8). Together these dates suggest that the frontier or colonization period ended by the mid-1830s, when political boundaries had been established throughout the project area.

Federal land sales data complement these suggestions. Only about 14% of available land had been purchased by 1830, whereas over 85% had been claimed 10 years later (Figure 8.1). Approximately 37% had been purchased by the end of 1834, just prior to two boom years when land sales more than doubled in total area. Given these trends in frontier movement and land purchase, the year 1834 is selected as the optimum terminal data of Stage I.

By definition, Stage III begins when competition becomes more important than spread as a process. Both processes acted for extended periods of time, however, and boundary selection must be relatively arbitrary. Federal land sales data indicate that nearly 100% of available land had been acquired by 1860 (Figure 8.1), implying that transactions since that date had been affected by competition among landowners. Regional population did not peak until about 1900 (Watson 1979), however, suggesting that competition for land was most effective after the turn of the century. Lacking land transaction data bearing directly on this issue, we tentatively select a median estimate of 1880 as the optimum terminus of Stage II.

Hypotheses and Observations

Two characteristics of historic occupation in the Cannon Reservoir region—settlement distributions and vectors of realized niches—are pertinent to testing and supplementing hypotheses derived from the developmental model. The results of our research bear directly on these issues, but it must be stressed that several lines of investigation have not yet been explored fully, and some conclusions are tentative.

Colonization, 1792–1815

Settlement characteristics of the colonization stage (1792–1834) conform generally to expected results but also change through time, underlining the dynamic nature of settlement processes. Settlements of early French saline operators were small, and their locations were constrained by the contexts of salt springs. Most operations were maintained in sequence at a few localities.

These occurrences illustrate several important trends. As predicted by Hudson's (1969) model, settlements of the earliest inhabitants were so few that intraethnic contacts within the region could not have greatly affected settlement behavior. However, adaptive fitness was controlled primarily by extraregional market fluctuations and varying degrees of interethnic hostility, whereas the most important vector of the realized niche was the location and productivity of a small number of salt springs. Thus, the earliest Euro-American settlements in the region can be considered specialized outlying components of the resource catchment of a distant trade center. For these reasons, the locational pattern of early settlement essentially was random with respect to the region as a whole, whereas the contexts of individual settlements were highly focal and predictable. We suggest therefore that our observations are inconsistent with Hudson's (1969) prediction of regular spacing of colonial settlements because of the unidimensionality and small "size" of the earliest realized niche. We conclude that Hudson's expectation of regular spacing among colonial settlements must assume that: (a) social units are self-sufficient; (b) production is not symbiotically tied to (or in fact an extension of) external economies; and (c) primary niche vectors are not highly specialized or restricted to a few randomly distributed points in space.

Colonization, 1818–1827

Settlement behavior during the remainder of Stage I (1818–1834) is of particular interest since it represents a second period of colonization in the Cannon Reservoir region that qualitatively was distant from that of the initial period. Immigrants in this case were nearly all subsistence or surplus agriculturists who largely were independent of extraregional economies and whose exploitive activities were suited to a set of environmental factors that were expressed recurrently in many parts of the middle Salt River valley. Thus, according to our revision of the model, conditions favored a shift toward a regular spacing of settlements. However, we also have suggested that there are tangible benefits to settling near other frontier settlements. We therefore expect a compound pattern containing regularly spaced settlements interspersed with several settlement clusters.

Our observations describing the contexts and spacing of later Stage I settlements are presented here in two sections. Federal land records indicate rates of land purchase increased dramatically after 1827, when the effects of crowding and purchases by absentee speculators could have had confounding effects on patterns of settlement. In order to control for these factors, we first examine the period 1818–1827, when only about 4% of available land had been purchased (Figure 8.1). The period

1828–1834, when up to 37% of available land was entered, is treated in the following section.

Environmental contexts of settlements established between 1818 and 1827 were strikingly different from those of the earliest colonists. General locations of land purchases illustrate several recurrent trends: (a) Most were situated within 2 km of a perennial stream; (b) nearly all were centered within forested areas, although many were very near the prairie–timber ecotone (Figures 3.21 and 17.2); (c) most appear to have centered on upland rims, gently sloping valley sides, and, in some localities, high bottomland terraces. Very few occurred in homogeneous level uplands or low flood plain contexts. In summary, two seemingly discrete sets of niche vectors are represented: (a) forested upper valley sides near ecotonal boundaries and perennial tributary streams and (b) forested rolling hills or bottomland terraces near major rivers (Warren *et al.* 1981).

Significantly, the former association is more common and offers support to a proposition advanced by some settlement geographers (e.g., Hewes 1950; Jordan 1964; Peters 1970). The proposition maintains that forest edge environments attracted frontier settlement because of ready access to fuel, building materials, natural pasture, and sparsely timbered soil that did not require a heavy investment of labor to clear it for agricultural use.

Of equal significance are bottomland settlements, most of which were concentrated in the southwestern portion of the project area around the lower reaches of Middle Fork and Elk Fork (Figure 15.7). Although General Land Office plats depict these areas as forests (Figure 3.16), modern soils distributions indicate that both localities contain extensive components of soils developed under prairie or transitional prairie–timber vegetation (Figure 4.2). Thus, we expect that tree densities were relatively low in many parts of these localities (Figure 3.21) and timber would have been relatively easy to clear. This interpretation is supported in an 1831 letter written by a farmer who had purchased 320 acres of partially improved land between lower Otter Creek and Middle Fork (Powers 1931). He indicates that most farms in the area contained parcels of prairie (his own was about 25% prairie), and he states that the most desirable land for agriculture was "lighter timbered" and easily cleared, yet also commonly had soil that was "very black, loose, and strong, of considerable depth."

Given these observations, we conclude that the two seemingly discrete sets of environmental factors identified previously had several important vectors in common: (*a*) direct access to a perennial stream, (*b*) proximity to lightly timbered rich soils that were easily prepared for cultivation, and (*c*) direct access to forests for fuel and construction materials (Warren *et al.* 1981). Access to prairies also was desirable, but the settlements in the southwestern portion of the project area indicate that direct access was not critical (compare Figures 15.4 and 15.7).

Data concerning locational patterns of early colonial farmsteads indicate that our expectation of a compound pattern is supported. A number of farmsteads are distributed in a regular pattern within the realized niches just described, yet a significant number are aggregated within five distinct loci or settlement clusters (Figure 15.1). The three easternmost clusters were situated near the ecotone in upland contexts, whereas the two westernmost loci were on sparsely timbered bottomlands or gently sloping valley sides. Results of our investigations of two of these loci, the Mt. Prairie settlement and the Smith settlement, were presented in Chapter 15.

Colonization, 1828–1834

Environmental contexts of settlements established during the final segment of Stage I were similar to those of the early 1820s. Most claims were in forests near perennial streams and occupied upland rims near ecotones or sparsely timbered lowlands or interstream divides. On the other hand, few appear to have been located in areas with strong relief, few were situated in upland prairie, and relatively few occurred deep in timber near major streams. Thus, evaluations of niche vectors seem to have changed very little among Euro-American colonists, although the systematic filling of the preferred niche during Stage I forced alternate adaptation during later periods.

Land sales records also indicate that holdings were more continuous by 1834 and most settlement clusters evident during the preceding period (Figure 15.7) seem to have dissipated because of expansion and infilling. However, a zone of very heavy settlement formed a large (ca. 14 × 18 km), fairly distinct ovoid cluster enveloping the middle and lower reaches of Otter Creek, Middle Fork, and Elk Fork in the southwestern portion of the project area. Available data suggest natural as well as cultural factors attracted heavy settlement. This is a well-drained area with a rolling landscape, containing few areas of sharp relief that would inhibit transportation. Its three major streams flow perennially and parallel each other, so that very few localities are more than 2 km from a fluvial water source. Also, the area was timbered sparsely but continuously, making fuel readily available. Although these characteristics clearly were advantageous for settlement, other localities in the project area shared similar advantages, and natural factors alone are therefore probably insufficient to account for the observed density of settlement. Of at least equal importance was the founding in 1831 of Paris as the Monroe County seat. Paris lies in the center of the 1834 settlement cluster; it served farmers with two mills and was linked by major roads leading to Palmyra, New London, and the Boone's Lick communities of Fayette and Franklin (Chapter 8). These inferences suggest that the realized niche of many colonial settlers had expanded by the end of Stage I to include such cultural variables as access to agricultural services, access to manufactured goods, and access to major routes of transportation.[3]

[3]Research carried out after this book was written confirms the effects of cultural variables on patterns of settlement during the late colonization phase. A multivariate analysis of the physical and cultural contexts of first land purchases in the Smith settlement suggests that two distinct models of land value ordered land purchase decisions in the Smith locality (Warren *et al.* 1982; see also Footnote 2 to Chapter 15). Purchases by early frontier immigrants (1819–1825) focused on sparsely timbered or ecotonal forests on bottomland terraces with soils judged by GLO surveyors to be of good quality. In contrast, later purchasers (1826–1859) favored locations near existing roads, towns and previous purchases, ordinarily in forested contexts with perceived good soils. As purchase choices decreased through time due to the removal of desirable parcels from the pool of available federal land, there was a consistent progression away from optimum locations and toward both level upland prairies and low flood plain forests.

Spread, 1835–1880

Information pertaining to Stage II, the spread phase (1835–1880), indicates that some propositions implied by the historic model are supported. Land-sales distributions show that the realized niche expanded in several directions during this period. Densely timbered bottomlands and sloping upland prairies, both of which had been avoided by colonial settlers, were bought up rapidly during the boom sales years of 1835–36 (Figure 17.3). By 1857 most level upland prairies also had been purchased. Expansion into bottomlands probably was a result of several factors, including improved access roads, maximum soil fertility, and access to largely untapped fuel resources. On the other hand, expansion into upland prairies probably was aided by the availability after 1837 of steel plows capable of tilling extensive tracts of prairie sod. A more detailed understanding of settlement processes during Stage II will require intensive analysis of land resales among immigrants, absentee speculators, budding social units, and expansionist landowners.

Competition, 1881–1970

For Stage III, the competition phase (1881–1970), several new sources of data are available. Most important, perhaps, are county atlases, which pinpoint farmstead and road locations and indicate community sizes and layouts. Complementing these sources are modern USGS topographic sheets, which show current locations of these same features. Together, these records and traditional archival sources have tremendous potential for increasing our understanding of settlement dynamics during the late nineteenth and twentieth centuries and should allow objective testing of implications derived from the historic model. For instance, preliminary analysis of modern farmstead locations suggests the proposal of settlement regularity in space is generally correct. However, site densities are clearly biased toward level uplands and upper valley side locations and are relatively uncommon to rare in valley side and bottomland localities (Warren and O'Brien 1981). This indicates that the realized niche of agriculturists shifted toward extensive upland areas, probably

during late Stage II or early Stage III times. Detailed analysis of locational records will be necessary to quantify the extent of this shift and to evaluate the relative significance of causal factors.

CONCLUSIONS

Historic settlement in the southern Prairie Peninsula was conditioned by a complex series of adaptive and developmental processes. Although many of these processes had clear and distinctive effects on settlement distributions, and most varied in relative importance through time, processes with differing effects often acted concurrently in the Cannon Reservoir region, resulting in compound patterns at many points in time. Nevertheless, our results indicate that general trends of settlement behavior can be modeled in a 3-component temporal series. Further, the compound patterning effected by different kinds of interacting settlement processes can in many cases be isolated and hypothetically linked to specific processes. We therefore suggest that continued testing and refinement of implications derived from the model presented here can lead to a better understanding of frontier development in the Midwest.

The model is composed of three temporally discrete stages: Colonization (1792–1834), Spread (1835–1880), and Competition (1881–1970). In contrast to the propositions of Hudson (1969), we conclude that four major sociocultural processes effected configurations of settlement within temporally shifting realized niches. These include (*a*) *independent immigration*—the in-migration of independent family units, which effected a regular spacing of settlements; (*b*) *interdependent immigration*—the in-migration of linked multifamily social units, which effected a clustered spacing of settlements; (*c*) *budding*—the fission and proximal settlement of expanding family units, which effected a clustered spacing of settlements; and (*d*) *competition*—the natural selection of growing farmsteads within an expanded but constraining realized niche, which effected a regular spacing of settlements. Because of our regional perspective, we also emphasize that configurations of settlement within a realized niche cannot be understood unless the characteristics and spatial distributions of those niches are also understood.

During the earliest (1792–1815) of three periods of Colonization in the Cannon Reservoir region, the process of independent immigration was in effect. However, patterns of settlement in the region essentially were random at that time, in accord with the distribution of a realized niche (i.e., salt springs) that was very small and specialized. We therefore suggest that regular spacing among colonial settlements should not be expected unless one can assume that: (a) social units are self-sufficient; (b) production is not symbiotically tied to external economies; and (c) primary niche vectors are not highly specialized or restricted to a few randomly distributed points in space.

These assumptions can be made with respect to the second period (1818–1827) of Colonization in the Cannon Reservoir region. However, a compound pattern of settlement was then evident (with overlying clustered and regular configurations) due to the simultaneous effects of interdependent and independent immigration. As a result, we can detect within the realized niche five discrete settlement loci that were interspersed with a number of independent farmsteads. Niche space had expanded considerably to include two seemingly independent factors: ecotonal upland rims overlooking perennial tributary streams, and forested rolling hills or bottomland terraces near major rivers. Nevertheless, these two factors had several important vectors in common: (a) direct access to a perennial stream; (b) proximity to lightly timbered rich soils that were easily cleared for cultivation; and (c) direct access to forests for fuel and raw materials. Proximity to prairie was sought by those specializing in grazing livestock production.

The third period (1828–1834) of Colonization was one of continued immigration and budding, when infilling within the realized niche approached a point of saturation. Although the preferred environmental contexts of colonial farmsteads appear to have changed little into this period, the inception of relatively dense settlement around incorporated communities indicates several cultural vectors had increased in importance (e.g., access to agricultural services, manufactured goods, and major roads).

Settlement characteristics of the final two stages, Spread and Competition, appear to reflect patterns expressed along a single trajectory of underlying change. The realized niche expanded continuously, due to technological innovations, to incorporate level upland prairies that were previously beyond the range of economic development. The net effect was a relatively dense concentration of farmsteads in uplands and a more regular configuration of rural settlement.

Since 1970 a series of changes have occurred in the region due to construction of the Clarence Cannon Dam and Reservoir. Reclamation has spawned a new process, *displacement,* that is causing the abandonment of many farms lying in the path of reservoir waters. We anticipate that future models of historic settlement in the Cannon Reservoir region will incorporate an additional stage, one characterized by patterns that only now are beginning to emerge.

PART VII

Concluding Remarks

The objective of the Cannon Reservoir Human Ecology Project is to document and explain 10,000 years of cultural adaptations in the Cannon Reservoir region. Our goal in preparing this volume is to summarize our progress toward the attainment of that objective. Although the breadth of our documentation and the depth of our understanding are in some instances more restricted than we would like, we believe that the contents of this volume represent meaningful steps in the right direction. The fact that our results call for several major revisions of the models of adpatation and change is to us an encouraging sign. Furthermore, the prospects for additional research in the region are still excellent. We have acquired a small mountain of materials from the area, only a fraction of which could be discussed here, and there are many data awaiting analysis. Despite the imminent completion of the Clarence Cannon Dam and Reservoir, additional fieldwork also will be possible in important upland contexts for many years to come. Thus, the information presented in this volume is by no means the final word on cultural adaptations in the Cannon Reservoir region. The conclusions we offer in this final chapter provide useful insights into cultural adaptations in the southern Prairie Peninsula, but it may be more realistic to view them as anchor points from which future lines of investigation can be directed.

18

Conclusions

ROBERT E. WARREN AND MICHAEL J. O'BRIEN

The scientific method is a cycle. Ideas about aspects of the universe are conceived, critically evaluated with relevant observations, and accepted or revised based on the outcome of research. In the first two sections of this book, cultural and ecological theories are used to construct models of prehistoric and historic adaptations in the southern Prairie Peninsula. Observations made in the Cannon Reservoir region are presented in the succeeding four sections, and results of each line of investigation are compared with implications of the models. In this final chapter, outcomes are summarized, and we suggest ways in which the models can be revised.

PREHISTORIC ADAPTATIONS

During prehistoric times, occupants of the Cannon Reservoir region responded to a variety of changing environmental and cultural influences. Common to all adaptations was a focus on forests, both for residence and for resource extraction, but patterns of settlement, subsistence, and community organization changed significantly within this context. To evaluate these changes, we return to the 4-stage developmental framework introduced in Chapter 5.

Stage I populations experienced the most profound of Holocene environmental changes. Forests were more extensive during the early part of this sequence than at any later time, but they rapidly contracted during the Hypsithermal and were replaced in many historically forested locales by prairies and open woodlands. Predictably, settlement patterns followed suit. Early Archaic sites, although rare, are distributed more extensively than those of any other prehistoric cultural period. They occur on bottomland terraces, along bluff margins, and well out into historic upland prairies. It is probable that all three contexts were forested at the time, and each context class may represent a seasonal phase of a logistical, foraging settlement system. This implied residential mobility is consistent with expectations, but site content observations currently do not allow critical evaluation of this aspect of the model.

Despite environmental "deterioration" during

the Hypsithermal, frequencies of Middle Archaic sites suggest that populations in the region increased. Nonetheless, site contexts are much less extensive, and it seems evident that continued exploitation of forest resources resulted in a more compact settlement pattern as resource distributions narrowed. Given forest contraction, resources should have been accessible all year long from bottomland contexts, and occupation of other contexts would not have been necessary. Thus, it is somewhat surprising that hypothesized upland residential sites still occur. Again, interpretations are hampered by a lack of pertinent site content information, but if it can be assumed that these upland sites represent encampments for logistical exploitation of seasonal resources, their contexts imply that, consistent with expectations, Middle Archaic groups practiced a mobile foraging economy analogous to that of the previous period.

After the Hypsithermal, environmental conditions in the southern Prairie Peninsula were relatively stable and approximated those of historic times. Although environmental change cannot be disregarded as a possible cause of subsequent culture change, its effects seem to have been overshadowed by demographic and other cultural factors. During Stage II, populations grew steadily, and residential mobility apparently decreased. Faunal and floral remains reflect a two-part seasonal round in which groups moved upstream or downstream into localities with undepleted resources. Contexts of warm-season and cool-season residential sites generally were the same, and, allowing for seasonal differences in resource availability, "first-line" animal foods were emphasized at both. The apparent selective advantage of the semisedentary system was that as groups increased in size, community mobility became more difficult. In a region with relatively narrow environmental zones, most resources were accessible from relatively permanent basecamps, and continuous mobility no longer was efficient. At the same time, intergroup crowding apparently was not yet a problem, and seasonal movement guaranteed access to food and fuel resources. These interpretations generally are consistent with expectations, although indications of a greater emphasis on "second-line" native plant resources do not seem to be

paralleled by any shift toward "second-line" animal foods.

By the end of the Early Woodland period, the model predicts that due to population growth and crowding of resource catchments, Stage II communities in the Cannon Reservoir region were large, sedentary, and increasingly dependent on horticulture and other relatively time- or labor-intensive economic strategies. Consistent with our expectations are the much higher site frequencies and the expansion of residential sites into more diverse contexts. Both reflect increased population density and use of less desirable settlement locations. Also consistent is the appearance of possible native cultigens at Hatten Village. However, the bulk of our observations are not consistent with expectations, and they suggest that a revision of the model is needed. Although population density increased, it apparently did not cross the threshold of local resource intensification that would have necessitated year-round sedentism. Settlements still were relatively small and impermanent, and seasonal indications of faunal and floral remains suggest the continuance of the semisedentary settlement system of Stage II. Choice of residence locations probably was more limited, but suitable contexts apparently were available, and there is no evidence of any shift toward "second-line" animal foods. Significantly, persistence of this semisedentary lifeway indicates that community resource catchments had not constricted to the point that local shortages of "first-line" foods were a problem. Thus, dependence on intergroup economic security networks was unnecessary, and this may explain the absence in the Cannon Reservoir region of the exotic Hopewell trade goods that are commonly found in contemporary villages along the nearby Mississippi and lower Illinois rivers.

From about A.D. 700–900 (i.e., early Stage IV), cultural adaptations in the Cannon Reservoir region resembled those postulated for Stage III. In contrast, the model predicts this was a time of rapid population growth, increased dependence on maize agriculture, and stable residence in large, complex villages. Later in Stage IV, it was expected that communities were distinguished by societywide redistribution networks, incipient forms of social ranking, and a multitiered socioeconomic hierarchy of settlements. Instead, our observations indicate that neither the magnitudes nor even the directions of postulated trends can be supported. Population density apparently did increase during the Late Woodland period to the point that sedentism was necessary. Faunal and floral remains provide evidence of year-round village occupation and increased reliance on "second-line" vertebrate resources. Residential sites occur in a diverse array of contexts, and there is a notable increase in frequencies of hypothesized procurement–processing sites. There also is evidence of increased village size, and large underground storage facilities are more common. Nevertheless, villages are not so large and complex as expected, and although traces of maize cultivation occur, the anticipated quantity of remains is not evident. Moreover, the expected trends of rapid population growth and more intensive food production after A.D. 900 are the reverse of observed trends. Population actually decreased during the Mississippian period, and, with less competition for space and resources, remnant groups apparently reverted to the less demanding semisedentary lifeway of earlier times.

HISTORIC ADAPTATIONS

Adaptations to the southern Prairie Peninsula changed rapidly and constantly during the historic period as perceptions of grasslands and forests shifted, technology advanced to the point where new niches became available, and exploitation of new areas became profitable. Colonization of the Cannon Reservoir region during the late eighteenth century consisted of sporadic, localized settlements of French salt manufacturers and a few trappers and resulted in only temporary settlement of the region. This early settlement was conditioned by the productivity of scattered saline springs, the availability of water transport, interethnic hostility, and, ultimately, by market fluctuations in distant centers of trade.

Permanent colonization began in 1818 with the immigration of subsistence agriculturalists. Upon entering the region, colonists were faced with numerous decisions concerning where to settle. These decisions were made at two levels: (a) the "macro"

level (i.e., in what part of the region to locate) and (b) the "micro" level (i.e., which specific tract should be selected). Three context variables entered into these decisions: environmental, social, and agricultural.

During the colonization phase, these factors effected an overlapping 2-tier settlement pattern. The upper tier, an aggregated settlement structure, consisted of a series of settlement clusters (five are identified) spaced at fairly regular intervals across the region. One has been identified as an exclusively Catholic settlement; two others were based on kin-affinity and common place of origin. The lower tier, a dispersed settlement structure, varied from regular spacing of farmsteads along the ecotone to complex mosaics of landholdings.

Analysis of two such mosaics (Elk Fork and Smith settlements) demonstrates that among early colonists the preferred niche was land located either in low-density timber or along the prairie–timber boundary. Detailed analysis reveals that land-purchase decisions also considered contemporary evaluations of soil fertility. The latter variable appears to have been particularly important during early phases of settlement, as suggested by population in-filling on a northeastern–southwestern diagonal between the Smith and Elk Fork settlements, along a line perceived by GLO surveyors as containing highly productive soil (cf. Warren *et al.* 1982). In summary, the preferred niche of settlers during the 1820s and 1830s was low- to medium-density bottomland forests and ecotonal upland rims, both of which could be cleared rapidly for agriculture and the timber used for building and fuel.

After about 1836, or during stages II (Spread) and III (Competition) of the model, the realized niche expanded continuously and incorporated level upland prairies that previously were uninhabited. By 1840, 48% of landholdings had direct access to prairie, compared to only 36% in 1830. Intensification of livestock production, especially during the 1840s, opened grasslands to grazing, so that by 1850, 90% of all livestock producers owned prairie land. Tobacco also became an important part of the economy during these stages and high, level bottomland terraces fell under more intensive cultivation. Finally, with adoption of the steel plow and the widespread installation of drainage tiles, the realized niche expanded further to include the extensive and rich, but moist and previously impenetrable, flat upland prairies.

Concomitant with expansion of the realized niche came the founding and subsequent development of numerous towns in the region. Two of these, Paris and Florida, grew disproportionately to the others, and both soon were established commercial centers. This resulted in further expansion of the realized niche and undoubtedly contributed to the rapid rise in population density in the western portion of the project area.

The structure of rural communities was analyzed at three levels: (*a*) macrostructure (discussed previously); (*b*) farmstead; and (*c*) rural household. Examination of rural farmsteads led to the formulation of a general model of a planned, self-contained, efficient unit, the size and complexity of which was tied to individual modes of production.

The rural household was examined at several levels, including formal and functional attributes of residential structures, material composition of households, and patterns of refuse disposal. Structural attributes suggest that residences often change form in predictable fashion and that house size is linked directly to family size and wealth. Detailed examination of construction sequences at one house demonstrates evolution from a double-pen log cabin, to a heavy-timber house with attached cabin, to a heavy-timber house with a large frame addition.

The material composition of rural households was examined at two sites, one of which was occupied continuously from about 1830. Analysis suggests that early historic subsistence focused on pig and turkey, with moderate emphasis on small mammals, deer, and mussels. One important feature of post-1850 household assemblages is the high percentage of crockery, possibly a result of a proliferation of local potters. Further analysis of excavated materials, currently underway, will greatly expand our documentation of the temporal and spatial patterning of rural Euro-American artifact complexes and should refine our understanding of the local effects of evolving technological and economic systems in the Midwest.

GRASSLAND, FOREST, AND MAN: THE FUTURE

In this volume we have sketched a rough outline of 10,000 years of cultural adaptations in an environmentally diverse and sensitive region. As it has so many times in the past, the character of the region soon will change. When it does, many traces of man's tenure in the southern Prairie Peninsula will be lost, but this does not mean that research in the Cannon Reservoir region is complete. Ideas presented here can be tested further with materials not yet analyzed in appropriate ways, and a variety of questions have been raised that require the investigation of nearby areas. Thus, we hope that the cycle of science soon will begin anew to improve our understanding of grassland, forest, and man.

References

Ahler, S.A.
1971 Projectile point form and function at Rodgers Shelter, Missouri. *Missouri Archaeological Society, Research Series* No. 8.
1973 Post-Pleistocene depositional change at Rodgers Shelter, Missouri. *Plains Anthropologist* **18**:1–26.
1975a Pattern and variety in Extended Coalescent lithic technology. Ph.D. dissertation, University of Missouri. Ann Arbor: University Microfilms.
1975b Extended Coalescent lithic technology: supporting data. National Park Service, Midwest Archaeological Center, Lincoln, Nebraska.
1979 Functional analysis of nonobsidian chipped stone artifacts: terms, variables, and quantification. In *Lithic use-wear analysis*, edited by B. Hayden. New York: Academic Press. Pp. 301–328.

Ammerman, A. J., and M. W. Feldman
1978 Replicated collection of site surfaces. *American Antiquity* **43**:734–740.

Anderson, D. C., and H. Semken, Jr. (editors)
1980 *The Cherokee excavations: mid-Holocene paleoecology and human adaptation in northwestern Iowa.* New York: Academic Press.

Anderson, D. G.
n.d. Postdepositional modification of the Zebree behavioral record. In Zebree Archeological Project 1977, edited by D. F. Morse and P. A. Morse. *Arkansas Archeological Survey, Research Series,* in press.

Angus, C. A., and M. E. Ruppert
1977 The Miskell site (23MN542). In Cannon Reservoir Human Ecology Project reports (Vol. II), edited by D. R. Henning. *University of Nebraska, Department of Anthropology, Technical Report* No. 77-04, 1–88.

Asch, D. L.
1976 The Middle Woodland population of the lower Illinois Valley: a study in paleodemographic methods. *Northwestern University Archeological Program, Scientific Papers* No. 1.

Asch, D. L., and N. B. Asch
1977 Chenopod as cultigen: a re-evaluation of some prehistoric collections from eastern North America. *Midcontinental Journal of Archaeology* **1**:39–57.
1978 The economic potential of *Iva annua* and its prehistoric importance in the lower Illinois Valley. In The nature and status of ethnobotany, edited by R. I. Ford. *University of Michigan, Museum of Anthropology, Anthropological Papers* No. 67, 300–341.

Asch, D. L., K. B. Farnsworth, and N. B. Asch
1979 Woodland subsistence and settlement in west central Illinois. In *Hopewell archaeology: the Chillicothe Conference,* edited by D. S. Brose and N. Greber. Kent, Ohio: Kent State University Press. Pp. 80–85.

Asch, N. B., R. I. Ford, and D. L. Asch
1972 Paleoethnobotany of the Koster site: the Archaic

horizons. *Illinois State Museum, Reports of Investigations* No. 24.

Asch, N. B., and D. L. Asch
1980 Archaic subsistence in westcentral Illinois. Paper presented at the 21st meeting of the Society for Economic Botany, Bloomington, Indiana.

Auclair, A. N.
1976 Ecological factors in the development of intensive-management ecosystems in the midwestern United States. *Ecology* **57**:431–444.

Auclair, A. N., and G. Cottam
1971 Dynamics of black cherry (*Prunus serotina* Erhr.) in southern Wisconsin oak forests. *Ecological Monographs* **41**:153–177.

Baerreis, D. A., R. A. Bryson, and J. E. Kutzbach
1976 Climate and culture in the western Great Lakes region. *Midcontinental Journal of Archaeology* **1**:39–57.

Bailey, L. W., R. T. Odell, and W. R. Boggess
1964 Properties of selected soils developed near the forest–prairie border in east-central Illinois. *Soil Science Society of America, Proceedings* **28**:257–263.

Baker, C. M.
1975 The Arkansas Eastman Archeological Project. *Arkansas Archeological Survey, Research Report* 6.

Bauxar, J. J.
1978 History of the Illinois area. In *Handbook of North American Indians, Vol. 15, Northeast*, edited by B. G. Trigger. Smithsonian Institution, Washington. Pp. 594–601.

Beilman, A. P., and L. G. Brenner
1951 The changing forest flora of the Ozarks. *Annals of the Missouri Botanical Garden* **38**:283–291.

Bell, R. E.
1958 Guide to the identification of certain American Indian projectile points. *Oklahoma Anthropological Society, Special Bulletin* No. 1.
1960 Guide to the identification of certain American Indian projectile points. *Oklahoma Anthropological Society, Special Bulletin* No. 2.

Benchley, E., M. Gregg, and M. J. Dudzik
1977 Recent investigations at Albany Mounds, Whiteside County, Illinois. *Illinois Archaeology Survey, Circular* 2.

Bender, M. M., D. A. Baerreis, and R. L. Steventon
1981 Further light on carbon isotopes and Hopewell agriculture. *American Antiquity* **46**:346–353.

Benfer, R. A.
1971 *DSQ, a fortran program*. Department of Anthropology, University of Missouri-Columbia.

Benn, D. W.
1978 The Woodland ceramic sequence in the culture

history of northeastern Iowa. *Midcontinental Journal of Archaeology* **3**:215–283.

Bennett, J. W.
1975 Ecosystems analogies in cultural ecology. In *Population, ecology, and social evolution*, edited by S. Polgar. The Hague: Mouton. Pp. 273–304.

Bernabo, J. C.
1981 Quantitative estimates of temperature changes over the last 2700 years in Michigan based on pollen data. *Quaternary Research* **15**:143–159.

Bernabo, J. C., and T. Webb III
1977 Changing patterns in the Holocene pollen record of northeastern North America. *Quaternary Research* **8**:64–96.

Bettis, E. A.
1980 Holocene alluvial fills in the Prairie Peninsula: proposed correlations and implications for archaeology. Paper presented at the 38th Plains Conference, Iowa City.

Bidwell, P. W., and J. I. Falconer
1925 *History of agriculture in the northern United States, 1620–1880*. Washington, D.C.: Carnegie Institution.

Binford, L. R.
1962a Archaeology as anthropology. *American Antiquity* **28**:217–225.
1962b Archaeological investigations in the Carlyle Reservoir, Clinton, County, Illinois. *Southern Illinois University Museum, Archaeological Salvage Report*, No. 17.
1971 Mortuary practices: their study and their potential. In Approaches to the social dimensions of mortuary practices, edited by J. A. Brown. *Society for American Archaeology, Memoir* No. 25, 6–29.
1979 Organization and formation processes: looking at curated technologies. *Journal of Archaeological Research* **35**:255–272.
1980 Willow smoke and dog's tails: hunter–gatherer settlement systems and archaeological site formation. *American Antiquity* **45**:4–20.

Binford, L. R., S. R. Binford, R. Whallon, and M. A. Hardin
1970 Archaeology at Hatchery West, Carlyle, Illinois. *Society for American Archaeology, Memoir* No. 24.

Binford, L. R., and W. J. Chasko, Jr.
1976 Nunamiut demographic history: a provocative case. In *Demographic anthropology: quantitative approaches*, edited by E. B. Zubrow. Albuquerque: University of New Mexico Press. Pp. 63–143.

Binford, L. R., and I. Quimby
1963 Indian sites and chipped stone materials in the northern Lake Michigan area. *Fieldiana Anthropology* **36**(12):277–307.

Bleed, P., and M. Meier
1980   An objective test of the effects of heat treatment of flakeable stone. *American Antiquity* **45**:502–507.

Borchert, J. R.
1950   The climate of the central North American grassland. *Annals of the Association of American Geographers* **40**:1–39.

Boughey, A. S.
1973   *Ecology of populations* (2nd ed.). New York: Macmillan.

Bourdo, E. A., Jr.
1956   A review of the General Land Office survey and of its use in quantitative studies of former forests. *Ecology* **37**:754–768.

Bozell, J. R.
1979   Unmodified vertebrate remains from the Hatten site (23MN272), Monroe County, Missouri: a preliminary report. *University of Nebraska, Department of Anthropology, Technical Report* No. 79-13, 1–43.

1980a Unmodified vertebrate remains from the Cooper site (23MN799), Monroe County, Missouri: a preliminary report. *University of Nebraska, Department of Anthropology, Technical Report* No. 80-21, 1–140.

1980b Unmodified vertebrate remains from site 23MN308, Monroe County, Missouri: a preliminary report. *University of Nebraska, Department of Anthropology, Technical Report* No. 80-18, 1–26.

1981a Unmodified vertebrate remains from the Pigeon Roost Creek site (23MN732), Monroe County, Missouri. *University of Nebraska, Department of Anthropology, Technical Report* No. 81-05.

1981b Middle and Late Woodland vertebrate resource use in northeast Missouri. Unpublished Master's thesis, Department of Anthropology, University of Nebraska-Lincoln.

Brakenridge, G. R.
1981   Late Quaternary floodplain sedimentation along the Pomme de Terre River, southern Missouri. *Quaternary Research* **15**:62–76.

Branson, E. B.
1944   Geology of Missouri. *Missouri University Studies* No. 19.

Braun, D. P.
1977   Middle Woodland–(early) Late Woodland social change in the prehistoric central midwestern United States. Ph.D. dissertation, University of Michigan. Ann Arbor: University Microfilms.

1979   Illinois Hopewell burial practices and social organizations: a reexamination of the Klunk-Gibson mound group. In *Hopewell archaeology: the Chillicothe Conference,* edited by D. S. Brose and N. Greber. Kent, Ohio: Kent State University Press. Pp. 66–79.

1981   A critique of some recent North American mortuary studies. *American Antiquity* **46**:398–416.

Bremer, R. G.
1975   Cannon Reservoir area historical study. *University of Nebraska, Department of Anthropology, Technical Report* No. 75-06.

Brookfield, H. C.
1969   On the environment as perceived. *Progress in Geography* **1**:51–80.

Brose, D. S.
1978   A model of changing subsistence technology in the Late Woodland of northeastern Ohio. In Lithics and subsistence: the analysis of stone tool use in prehistoric economies, edited by D. D. Davis. *Vanderbilt University, Publications in Anthropology* No. 20, 87–115.

Brown, J. A.
1964   The northern extension of the Havana tradition. In Hopewellian studies, edited by J. R. Caldwell and R. L. Hall. *Illinois State Museum, Scientific Papers* No. 12.

Brown, J. A., et al.
n.d.   Preliminary contributions of Koster site research to paleoenvironmental studies of the central Mississippi Valley. Ms. on file, Northwestern University Archaeological Program.

Brugman, R. B.
1980   Postglacial diatom stratigraphy of Kirchner Marsh, Minnesota. *Quaternary Research* **13**:133–146.

Bryson, R. A.
1966   Airmasses, streamlines, and the boreal forest. *Geographical Bulletin* **8**:228–269.

Bryson, R. A., and D. A. Baerreis
1968   Introduction and project summary. In Climatic change and the Mill Creek culture of Iowa (Part I), edited by D. R. Henning. *Journal of the Iowa Archaeological Society* **15**:1–34.

Bryson, R. A., D. A. Baerreis, and W. M. Wendland
1970   The character of late-glacial and post-glacial climatic changes. In *Pleistocene and recent environments of the central Great Plains,* edited by W. Dort, Jr., and J. K. Jones, Jr. Lawrence: University Press of Kansas. Pp. 53–74.

Bryson, R. A., and T. J. Murray
1977   *Climates of hunger: mankind and the world's changing weather.* Madison: University of Wisconsin Press.

Buikstra, J. E.
1976   Hopewell in the lower Illinois Valley: a regional

approach to the study of human biological variability and human behavior. *Northwestern University Archaeological Program, Scientific Papers* No. 2.

1979   Contributions of physical anthropologists to the concept of Hopewell: a historical perspective. In *Hopewell archaeology: the Chillicothe Conference*, edited by D. S. Brose and N. Greber. Kent, Ohio: Kent State University Press. Pp. 220–233.

Burton, J.
1980   Making sense of waste flakes: new methods for investigating the technology and economics behind chipped stone assemblages. *Journal of Archaeological Science* 7:131–148.

Butzer, K. W.
1977   Geomorphology of the lower Illinois Valley as a spatial-temporal context for the Koster Archaic site. *Illinois State Museum, Reports of Investigations* No. 34.

1978   Changing Holocene environments at the Koster site: a geo-archaeological perspective. *American Antiquity* 43:408–413.

Byland, B. E.
1975   A methodological consideration of archaeological site survey in semiarid environments. Master's thesis, Department of Anthropology, Pennsylvania State University.

Bylund, E.
1960   Theoretical considerations regarding the distribution of the settlement in inner north Sweden. *Geografisk Annaler* 42:225–231.

Caldwell, J. R.
1964   Interaction spheres in prehistory. In Hopewellian studies, edited by J. R. Caldwell and R. L. Hall. *Illinois State Museum, Scientific Papers* No. 12, 133–143.

Callender, C.
1978a   Fox. In *Handbook of North American Indians, Vol. 15, Northeast*, edited by B. G. Trigger. Smithsonian Institution, Washington. Pp. 636–647.

1978b   Sauk. In *Handbook of North American Indians, Vol. 15, Northeast*, edited by B. G. Trigger. Smithsonian Institution, Washington. Pp. 648–655.

1978c   Illinois. In *Handbook of North American Indians, Vol. 15, Northeast*, edited by B. G. Trigger. Smithsonian Institution, Washington. Pp. 673–680.

Cambron, J. W., and D. C. Hulse
1965   *Handbook of Alabama archaeology, Part 1: point types*. University of Alabama: Archaeological Research Association of Alabama.

Chang, K. C.
1962   A typology of settlement and community patterns in some circum-polar societies. Arctic Anthropology 1:28–41.

Chapman, C. H.
1959   The Little Osage and Missouri Indian village sites ca. 1727–1777 A.D. *The Missouri Archaeologist* 21(1):1–67.

1962   Preface to archaeological salvage in Joanna Reservoir area, Missouri. In *Archaeological investigations in the Joanna Reservoir area, Missouri*, by C. H. Chapman, D. P. Heldman, and D. R. Henning. Report submitted to National Park Service, Region 2, Omaha. Pp. iii–vi.

1968   The Havana tradition and the Hopewell problem in the lower Missouri River valley. Unpublished manuscript, Department of Anthropology, University of Missouri-Columbia.

1975   *The archaeology of Missouri I*. Columbia: University of Missouri Press.

1980   *The archaeology of Missouri II*. Columbia: University of Missouri Press.

Chomko, S. A., and G. W. Crawford
1978   Plant husbandry in prehistoric eastern North America: new evidence for its development. *American Antiquity* 43:405–408.

Christenson, A. L., W. E. Klippel, and W. Weedman
1975   An archaeological survey of the proposed William L. Springer Lake Greenbelt Project. Ms. on file, Illinois State Museum.

Clarke, D. L.
1972   Models and paradigms in contemporary archaeology. In *Models in archaeology*, edited by D. L. Clarke. London: Methuen. Pp. 1–60.

Cole, A. H.
1927   Cyclical and sectional variations in the sale of public lands, 1816–60. *Review of Economic Statistics* 9:41–53.

Collins, J. M.
1979   Preliminary results of the 1978 mechanical stripping program. In Cannon Reservoir Human Ecology Project: a regional approach to cultural continuity and change, edited by M. J. O'Brien and R. E. Warren. *University of Nebraska, Department of Anthropology, Technical Report* No. 79-14, 177–201.

Collins, J. M., and M. T. Griffin
1979   Mechanical site stripping: technique refinements and case applications. In Cannon Reservoir Human Ecology Project: recent advances in the archaeology of northeast Missouri, edited by M. J. O'Brien and D. E. Lewarch. *University of*

Nebraska, Department of Anthropology, Notebook No. 5, 70–83.

Conzen, M. P.
1971 *Frontier farming in an urban shadow: the influence of Madison's proximity on the agricultural development of Blooming Grove, Wisconsin.* Madison: The State Historical Society of Wisconsin.

Cook, D. C.
1976 Pathologic state and disease process in Illinois Woodland populations: an epidemiologic approach. Unpublished Ph.D. dissertation, Department of Anthropology, University of Chicago.

Cook, T. G.
1976 Koster: an artifact analysis of two Archaic phases in westcentral Illinois. *Northwestern Archaeological Program, Prehistoric Records* No. 1.

Cottam, G.
1949 The phytosociology of an oak woods in southwestern Wisconsin. *Ecology* 30:271–287.

Cottam, G., and J. T. Curtis
1956 The use of distance measures in phytosociological sampling. *Ecology* 37:451–460.

Cowan, C. W.
1978 The prehistoric use and distribution of maygrass in eastern North America: cultural and phytogeographical implications. In The nature and status of ethnobotany, edited by R. I. Ford. *University of Michigan, Museum of Anthropology, Anthropological Papers* No. 67, 263–288.

Cowgill, G. L.
1974 Quantitative studies of urbanization at Teotihuacan. In *Mesoamerican archaeology: new approaches,* edited by N. Hammond. Austin: University of Texas Press. Pp. 363–396.

Crabtree, D. E.
1972 An introduction to flintworking. *Idaho State University Museum, Occasional Papers* No. 28.

Cuming, F.
1904 Sketches of a tour of the western country (1807–1809). In *Early western travels* (Vol. 4), edited by R. G. Thwaites. Cleveland: Clark.

Curry, M.
1979 Cataloging procedures and analytic techniques. In Cannon Reservoir Human Ecology Project: a regional approach to cultural continuity and change, edited by M. J. O'Brien and R. E. Warren. *University of Nebraska, Department of Anthropology, Technical Report* No. 79-14, 203–223.

Curry, M., and M. J. O'Brien
1981 A classification of projectile points from Cannon Reservoir, northeast Missouri. *University of Mis-*

souri, American Archaeology Division, Monograph Series, in preparation.

Curti, M.
1959 *The making of an American community: a case study of democracy in a frontier county.* Palo Alto: Stanford University Press.

Curtis, J. T.
1955 A prairie continuum in Wisconsin. *Ecology* 36:558–566.

1959 *The vegetation of Wisconsin.* Madison: University of Wisconsin Press.

Curtis, J. T., and R. P. McIntosh
1951 An upland forest continuum in the prairie-forest border region of Wisconsin. *Ecology* 32:476–496.

Damon, P. E., C. W. Ferguson, A. Long, and E. I. Wallick
1974 Dendrochronologic calibration of the radiocarbon time scale. *American Antiquity* 39:350–366.

Dancey, W. S.
1973 Prehistoric landuse and settlement patterns in the Priest Rapids area, Washington. Ph.D. dissertation, Department of Anthropology, University of Washington. Ann Arbor: University Microfilms.

1974 The archeological survey: a reorientation. *Man in the Northeast* 8:98–112.

Davis, A. M.
1977 The prairie-deciduous forest ecotone in the upper Middle West. *Annals of the Association of American Geographers* 67:204–213.

Davis, D. D. (editor)
1978 Lithics and subsistence: the analysis of stone tool use in prehistoric economies. *Vanderbilt University, Publications in Anthropology* No. 20.

Davis, D. H.
1927 Geography of the Blue Grass region. *The Kentucky Geological Survey Reports* No. 6-23.

Deevey, E. S., Jr., and R. F. Flint
1957 Postglacial Hypsithermal interval. *Science* 125: 182–184.

Del Bene, T. A., and G. Holley
1979 Microwear: an observation of scale. Paper presented at the 44th annual meeting of the Society for American Archaeology, Vancouver, British Columbia.

Delcourt, H. R., and P. A. Delcourt
1974 Primeval magnolia-holly-beech climax in Louisiana. *Ecology* 55:638–644.

Denny, S. G.
1964 A re-evaluation of Boone focus: a Late Woodland manifestation in central Missouri. Unpublished Master's thesis, Department of Sociology and Anthropology, University of Missouri-Columbia.

Densmore, F.
  1929 Chippewa customs. *Bureau of American Ethnology, Bulletin* 86.
Denton, G. H., and W. Karlen
  1973 Holocene climatic variation—their pattern and possible cause. *Quaternary Research* 3:155–205.
Dibble, H. L., and M. C. Bernard
  1980 A comparative study of basic edge angle measurement techniques. *American Antiquity* 45:857–865.
Dodds, J. S., J. P. McKean, L. O. Stewart, and G. F. Tigges
  1943 *Original instructions governing public surveys of Iowa: a guide to their use in resurveys of public lands.* Ames: Iowa Engineering Society.
Donham, T. K.
  1979a Community spatial organization and its application to economic system analysis. In The Cannon Reservoir Human Ecology Project: recent advances in the archaeology of northeast Missouri, edited by M. J. O'Brien and D. E. Lewarch. *University of Nebraska, Department of Anthropology, Notebook* No. 5, 94–113.
  1979b Description of a Late Woodland mortuary mound. In Cannon Reservoir Human Ecology Project: a regional approach to cultural continuity and change, edited by M. J. O'Brien and R. E. Warren. *University of Nebraska, Department of Anthropology, Technical Report* No. 79-14, 253–290.
  1981 Woodland ceramic styles in the central Salt River valley, northeast Missouri. Unpublished Master's thesis, Department of Anthropology, University of Arkansas-Fayetteville.
Dorsey, D. B.
  1935 The panic of 1819 in Missouri. *Missouri Historical Review* 29:79–91.
Dumond, D. E.
  1965 Population growth and cultural change. *Southwestern Journal of Anthropology* 21:302–325.
Dumond, D. E.
  1975 The limitation of human population: a natural history. *Science* 187:713–721.
Dunnell, R. C.
  1978a Comment on: temporal models in prehistory: an example from eastern North America. *Current Anthropology* 19:732.
  1978b Style and function: a fundamental dichotomy. *American Antiquity* 43:192–202.
  1978c Archaeological potential of anthropological and scientific models of function. In *Archaeological essays in honor of Irving B. Rouse,* edited by R. C. Dunnell and E. S. Hall, Jr. The Hague: Mouton. Pp. 41–73.
  1980a Americanist archaeology: the 1979 contribution. *American Journal of Archaeology* 84:463–478.
  1980b Evolutionary theory and archaeology. In *Advances in archaeological method and theory* (Vol. 3), edited by M. B. Schiffer. New York: Academic Press. Pp. 35–99.
  1981 Americanist archaeology: the 1980 literature. *American Journal of Archaeology,* in press.
Dunnell, R. C., and D. E. Lewarch
  1974 *Archaeological remains in Home Valley Park, Skamania County, Washington.* Report submitted to U.S. Army Corps of Engineers, Portland District.
Dunnell, R. C., and S. K. Campbell
  1977 Aboriginal occupation of Hamilton Island, Washington. *University of Washington, Department of Anthropology, Reports in Archaeology* No. 4.
Dunnell, R. C., and W. S. Dancey
  n.d. Siteless surveys: a regional data collection strategy. In *The design of archaeological research,* edited by L. M. Raab and T. C. Klinger. Chicago: Aldine, in press.
Eichenberger, J. A.
  1944 Investigations of the Marion-Ralls Archaeological Society in Missouri. *The Missouri Archaeologist* 10.
Elkins, S., and E. McKitrick
  1954 A new meaning for Turner's frontier. *Political Science Quarterly* 69:321–353, 565–602.
Emiliani, C.
  1980 Ice sheets and ice melts. *Natural History* 89(11):82–91.
Fehrenbacher, J. B., B. W. Ray, and J. D. Alexander
  1968 Illinois soils and factors in their development. In The Quaternary history of Illinois, edited by R. E. Bergstrom. *University of Illinois, College of Agriculture, Special Publication* No. 14, 165–175.
Flannery, K. V.
  1968 Archaeological systems theory and early Mesoamerica. In *Anthropological archaeology in the Americas,* edited by B. J. Meggers. Washington, D.C.: Anthropological Society of Washington. Pp. 67–87.
  1976 The early Mesoamerican house. In *The early Mesoamerican village,* edited by K. V. Flannery. New York: Academic Press. Pp. 16–24.
Flint, T.
  1970 *A condensed geography and history of the western United States, or the Mississippi Valley.* Gainesville, Florida: Scholar's Facsimiles and Reprints. (Originally published in 1828.)
Forbes, S. A., and R. E. Richardson
  1920 The fishes of Illinois. *Natural History of Illinois*

(Vol. 3), *Ichthyology*. Urbana: Illinois Natural History Survey.

Ford, R. I.
1974 Northeastern archaeology: past and future directions. *Annual Review of Anthropology* **3**:385–413.
1977 Evolutionary ecology and the evolution of human ecosystems: a case study from the midwestern U.S.A. In *Explanation of prehistoric change*, edited by J. N. Hill. Albuquerque: University of New Mexico Press. Pp. 153–184.
1979 Gathering and gardening: trends and consequences of Hopewell subsistence strategies. In *Hopewell archaeology: the Chillicothe Conference*, edited by D. S. Brose and N. Greber. Kent, Ohio: Kent State University Press. Pp. 234–238.

Fowler, M. L.
1959 Summary report of Modoc rock shelter: 1952, 1953, 1955, 1956. *Illinois State Museum, Reports of Investigations* No. 8.
1971 The origin of plant cultivation in the central Mississippi Valley: a hypothesis. In *Prehistoric agriculture*, edited by S. Struever. Garden City, New York: Natural History Press. Pp. 122–128.
1975 A pre-Columbian urban center on the Mississippi. *Scientific American* **233**:9–101.
1978 Cahokia and the American Bottom: settlement archaeology. In *Mississippian settlement patterns*, edited by B. D. Smith. New York: Academic Press. Pp. 455–478.

Frest, T. J., and L. P. Fay
1980 Peoria loess mollusc faunas and Woodfordian biomes of the upper Midwest. *AMQUA Abstracts*. Sixth biennial meeting of the American Quaternary Association, Orono, Maine.

Fried, M. H.
1967 *The evolution of political society: an essay in political anthropology*. New York: Random.

Frison, G. C.
1968 A functional analysis of certain chipped stone tools. *American Antiquity* **33**:149–155.

Fritts, H. C., G. R. Lofgren, and G. A. Gordon
1979 Variations in climate since 1602 as reconstructed from tree rings. *Quaternary Research* **12**:18–46.

Frye, J. C.
1973 Pleistocene succession of the central interior United States. *Quaternary Research* **3**:275–283.

Geier, C. R.
1973 The flake assemblage in archaeological interpretation. *The Missouri Archaeologist* **35**(3).
1975 The Kimberlin site: the ecology of a Late Woodland population. *Missouri Archaeological Society, Research Series* No. 12.

Gilbert, M. L., and J. T. Curtis
1953 Relation of the forest understory to the upland forest in the prairie–forest border region of Wisconsin. *Wisconsin Academy of Science, Transactions* No. 42:183–195.

Gjerde, J.
1979 The effect of community on migration: three Minnesota townships 1885–1905. *Journal of Historical Geography* **5**:403–422.

Goodyear, A. C.
1974 The Brand site: a techno-functional study of a Dalton site in northeast Arkansas. *Arkansas Archeological Survey, Research Series* No. 7.

Gould, R. A.
1980 *Living archaeology*. New York: Cambridge University Press.

Graham, R. W.
1979 Paleoclimates and late Pleistocene faunal provinces in North America. In *Pre-Llano cultures of the Americas: paradoxes and possibilities*, edited by R. L. Humphrey and D. Stanford. Washington, D.C.: Anthropological Society of Washington. Pp. 49–69.

Graham, R. W., C. V. Haynes, D. L. Johnson, and M. Kay
1981 Kimmswick: a Clovis-mastodon association in eastern Missouri. *Science* **213**:1115–1117.

Gramly, R. M.
1980 Raw materials, source areas, and 'curated' tool assemblages. *American Antiquity* **45**:823–833.

Grantham, L.
1977 *Long Branch Lake archaeological resources (Vol. 1): Ecology, the survey, analysis, and recommendations*. Report submitted to the U.S. Army Corps of Engineers, Kansas City District.

Gregory, R.
1965 *Mark Twain's first America: Florida, Missouri, 1835–1840*. Published by the author.

Gribbin, J.
1978 *Climatic change*. Cambridge: Cambridge University Press.

Griffin, D. E.
1977 Timber procurement and village location in the Middle Missouri subarea. In Trends in Middle Missouri prehistory: a *festschrift* honoring the contributions of Donald J. Lehmer, edited by W. R. Wood. *Plains Anthropologist, Memoir* No. 13:177–185.

Griffin, J. B.
1967 Eastern North American archaeology: a summary. *Science* **156**:175–191.
1979 An overview of the Chillicothe Hopewell conference. In *Hopewell archaeology: the Chillicothe Conference*, edited by D. S. Brose and N. Greber.

Kent, Ohio: Kent State University Press. Pp. 266–279.

Haggett, P.
1965   *Locational analysis in human geography.* New York: St. Martin's Press.

Hassan, F. A.
1975   Determination of the size, density, and growth rate of hunting–gathering populations. In *Population, ecology, and social evolution,* edited by S. Polgar. The Hague: Mouton. Pp. 27–52.

Hardesty, D. L.
1975   The niche concept: suggestions for its use in studies of human ecology. *Human Ecology* **3:**71–85.

1980   The use of general ecological principles in archaeology. In *Advances in archaeological method and theory* (Vol. 3), edited by M. B. Schiffer. New York: Academic Press. Pp. 157–187.

Harris, M.
1975   *Culture, man, and nature.* New York: Crowell.

Hayden, B.
1978   Snarks in archaeology: or, interassemblage variability in lithics (a view from the Antipodes). In Lithics and subsistence: the analysis of stone tool use in prehistoric economies, edited by D. D. Davis. *Vanderbilt University, Publications in Anthropology* No. 20, 179–198.

1979   Snap, shatter, and superfractures: use-wear of stone skin scrapers. In *Lithic use-wear analysis,* edited by B. Hayden. New York: Academic Press. Pp. 207–229.

Hayden, B., and J. Kamminga
1979   An introduction to use-wear: the first CLUW. In *Lithic use-wear analysis,* edited by B. Hayden. New York: Academic Press. Pp. 1–13.

Hays, J. D., J. Imbrie, and N. J. Schackleton
1976   Variations in the earth's orbit: pacemaker of the ice ages. *Science* **194:**1121–1132.

Heisler, D. M.
1975   *DSQDSQ, a fortran program.* Department of Anthropology, University of Missouri-Columbia.

Heldman, D. P.
1962   Salvage archaeology in the Joanna Reservoir area, Missouri, 1960. In *Archaeological investigations in the Joanna Reservoir area, Missouri,* by C. H. Chapman, D. P. Heldman, and D. R. Henning. Report submitted to National Park Service, Region 2, Omaha. Pp. 1–86.

Helwig, J. T., and K. A. Council (editors)
1979   *SAS user's guide.* Raleigh: SAS Institute.

Henning, A. E.
1964   Starr Mound. In *Archaeological excavations, Joanna*

Reservoir, Missouri, by D. R. Henning, A. E. Henning, and K. W. Cole. Report submitted to National Park Service, Region 2, Omaha. Pp. 71–93.

Henning, D. R.
1960   The Joanna Reservoir. *Missouri Archaeological Society, Newsletter* No. 133.

1961   Archaeological research in the proposed Joanna Reservoir, Missouri. *The Missouri Archaeologist* **23:**133–177.

1962   The Garrelts site I (23MN221). In *Archaeological investigations in the Joanna Reservoir area, Missouri,* by C. H. Chapman, D. P. Heldman, and D. R. Henning. Report submitted to National Park Service, Region 2, Omaha. Pp. 212–237.

1964   The Davis site. In *Archaeological investigations, Joanna Reservoir, Missouri,* by D. R. Henning, A. E. Henning, and K. W. Cole. Report submitted to National Park Service, Region 2, Omaha. Pp. 24–70.

1970   Development and interrelationships of Oneota culture in the lower Missouri River valley. *The Missouri Archaeologist* **32:**1–180.

Henning, E. C.
n.d.   *Mappin: a Monroe County pioneer family.* Manuscript, Paris Public Library, Paris, Missouri.

Hesse, A.
1971   Tentative interpretation of the surface distribution of remains on the upper fort of Mirgissa (Sudanese Nubia). In *Mathematics in the archaeological and historical sciences,* edited by F. R. Hodson, D. G. Kendall, and P. Tautu. Chicago: Aldine. Pp. 436–444.

Hewes, L.
1950   Some features of early woodland and prairie settlement in a central Iowa county. *Annals of the Association of American Geographers* **40:**40–57.

Hickerson, H.
1970   *The Chippewa and their neighbors: a study in ethnohistory.* New York: Holt, Rinehart and Winston.

Hill, F. C.
1975   Effects of the environment on animal exploitation by Archaic inhabitants of the Koster site. Unpublished Ph.D. dissertation, Department of Biology, University of Louisville.

Hill, J. N.
1977   Individual variability in ceramics and the study of prehistoric social organizations. In *The individual in prehistory,* edited by J. N. Hill and J. Gunn. New York: Academic Press. Pp. 55–108.

Hodder, I. R.
1977   Some new directions in the spatial analysis of

archeological data at the regional scale (macro). In *Spatial archaeology*, edited by D. L. Clarke. London: Academic Press. Pp. 223–351.

Hodder, I. R., and C. Orton
1976 *Spatial analysis in archaeology.* Cambridge: Cambridge University Press.

Hoffman, W. J.
1970 The Menomini Indians. *Bureau of American Ethnology, Annual Report* 14.

Holcombe, R. I.
1884 *History of Marion County, Missouri.* St. Louis: Perkins.

Holley, G. A.
1981 Lithic use-wear: the effects of tillage. Paper presented at the 46th annual meeting of the Society for American Archaeology, San Diego.

Houart, G. L.
1971 Koster, a stratified Archaic site in the Illinois Valley. *Illinois State Museum, Reports of Investigations* No. 22.

House, J. H.
1975 A functional typology for Cache Project surface collections. In The Cache River Archeological Project: an experiment in contract archeology, assembled by M. B. Schiffer and J. H. House. *Arkansas Archeological Survey, Research Series,* No. 8, 55–73.

House, J. H., and M. B. Schiffer
1975 Archeological survey in the Cache River Basin. In The Cache River Archeological Project: an experiment in contract archeology, assembled by M. B. Schiffer and J. H. House. *Arkansas Archeological Survey, Research Series* No. 8, 37–53.

Howell, D. L., and C. L. Kucera
1956 Composition of pre-settlement forests in three counties of Missouri. *Torrey Botanical Club, Bulletin* 83:207–217.

Hudson, J. C.
1969 A location theory for rural settlement. *Annals of the Association of American Geographers* **59**:365–381.

Hunt, W. J., Jr.
1976 The Late Woodland tradition on the Salt River in northeast Missouri. Paper presented at the joint Plains-Midwestern Anthropological Conference, Minneapolis, Minnesota.
1977a Aspects of Salt River Late Woodland development in northeast Missouri. Paper presented at the meeting of the Iowa Academy of Sciences, Des Moines.
1977b The Muskrat Run site (23RA151). In Cannon Reservoir Human Ecology Project reports (Vol.

II), edited by D. R. Henning. *University of Nebraska, Department of Anthropology, Technical Report* No. 77–03, 89–157.
1977c The Victor Bridge site (23MN380). In Cannon Reservoir Human Ecology Project reports (Vol. I), edited by D. R. Henning. *University of Nebraska, Department of Anthropology, Technical Report* No. 77-03, 49–223.

Huxol, D. L.
1980 Quaternary terraces of the Salt River Basin, northeast Missouri. Unpublished Master's thesis, Department of Geology, University of Missouri-Columbia.

Imbrie, J., and K. P. Imbrie
1979 *Ice ages: solving the mystery.* Short Hills, N.J.: Enslow.

Jakle, J. A.
1976 The testing of a house typing system in two Middle Western counties. *University of Illinois, Department of Geography, Occasional Papers* No. 11.

Jelinek, A. J.
1976 Form, function, and style in lithic analysis. In *Cultural change and continuity,* edited by C. Cleland. New York: Academic Press. Pp. 19–33.

Jennrich, R., and P. Sampson
1977 Stepwise discriminant analysis. In *BMDP-77; biomedical computer programs, P-series,* edited by M. B. Brown. Berkeley: University of California Press. Pp. 711–733.

Jochim, M. A.
1976 *Hunter–gatherer subsistence and settlement: a predictive model.* New York: Academic Press.

Johnson, A. E.
1979 Kansas City Hopewell. In *Hopewell archaeology: the Chillicothe Conference,* edited by D. S. Brose and N. Greber. Kent, Ohio: Kent State University Press. Pp. 86–93.

Johnson, G. A.
1977 Aspects of regional analysis in archaeology. *Annual Review of Anthropology* **6**:479–508.

Jones, A. S., and E. G. Patton
1966 Forest, prairie, and soils in the Black Belt of Sumter County, Alabama, in 1832. *Ecology* **47**:75–80.

Jones, G. N.
1963 Flora of Illinois. *American Midland Naturalist, Monograph* No. 7.

Jones, R. C.
1960 A revision of the genus *Iva* L. *University of Kansas, Science Bulletin* **41**:793–876.

Jordan, T. G.
1964 Between the forest and the prairie. *Agricultural History* **38**:205–216.

1966   On the nature of settlement geography. *The Professional Geographer* **18**:26–28.

1967   The imprint of the upper and lower South on mid-nineteenth century Texas. *Annals of the Association of American Geographers* **57**:667–690.

Joyer, J. E., and D. C. Roper
1980   Archaic adaptations in the central Osage River basin: a preliminary assessment. In Archaic prehistory on the prairie–plains border, edited by A. E. Johnson. *University of Kansas, Publications in Anthropology* No. 12, 13–23.

Kay, M., and A. E. Johnson
1977   Havana tradition chronology of central Missouri. *Midcontinental Journal of Archaeology* **2**:195–217.

Kay, M., F. B. King, and C. K. Robinson
1980   Cucurbits from Philips Spring: new evidence and interpretations. *American Antiquity* **45**:806–822.

Keeley, L. H., and M. H. Newcomer
1977   Microwear analysis of experimental flint tools: a test case. *Journal of Archaeological Science* **4**:29–62.

Keeley, L. H.
1980   *Experimental determination of stone tool uses.* Chicago: University of Chicago Press.

King, F. B.
1976   Potential food plants of the western Missouri Ozarks. In *Prehistoric man and his environments: a case study in the Ozark Highland,* edited by W. R. Wood and R. B. McMillan. New York: Academic Press. Pp. 249–260.

1978   Additional cautions on the use of the GLO survey records in vegetational reconstructions in the Midwest. *American Antiquity* **43**:99–103.

1980   Plant remains from Phillips Spring, a multicomponent site in the western Ozark Highland of Missouri. *Plains Anthropologist* **25**:217–227.

King, F. B., and R. W. Graham
1981   Effects of ecological and paleoecological patterns on subsistence and paleoenvironmental reconstructions. *American Antiquity* **46**:128–142.

King, F. B., and D. C. Roper
1976   Floral remains from two Middle to early Late Woodland sites in central Illinois and their implications. *The Wisconsin Archaeologist* **57**:142–151.

King, J. E.
1973   Late Pleistocene palynology and biogeography of the western Missouri Ozarks. *Ecological Monographs* **43**:539–565.

1980   Post-Pleistocene vegetational changes in the midwestern United States. In Archaic prehistory on the prairie-plains border, edited by A. E.

Johnson. *University of Kansas, Publications in Anthropology* No. 12, 3–11.

King, J. E., and W. H. Allen, Jr.
1977   A Holocene vegetation record from the Mississippi River valley, southeastern Missouri. *Quaternary Research* **8**:307–323.

Kirkby, A., and M. J. Kirkby
1976   Geomorphic processes and the surface survey of archaeological sites in semi-arid areas. In *Geoarchaeology,* edited by D. A. Davidson and M. L. Schackley. Boulder, Colorado: Westview Press. Pp. 229–253.

Klepinger, L., and D. R. Henning
1976   The Hatten site: a two-component burial site in northeast Missouri. *Missouri Archaeologist* **37**:92–170.

Klippel, W. E.
1968   Archaeological salvage in the Cannon Reservoir area, Missouri: 1967. Report submitted to National Park Service, Region 2, Omaha.

1969   The Booth site: a Late Archaic campsite. *Missouri Archaeological Society, Research Series* No. 6.

1970   Preliminary observations on heat-treated chert from Late Archaic and Woodland sites along the southern border of the Prairie Peninsula in Missouri. *Missouri Archaeological Society, Newsletter* **239**:1–7.

1971   Graham Cave revisted: a reevaluation of its cultural position during the Archaic period. *Missouri Archaeological Society, Memoir* No. 9.

1972   An Early Woodland period manifestation in the Prairie Peninsula. *Journal of the Iowa Archaeological Society* No. 19.

Klippel, W. E., G. Celmer, and J. R. Purdue
1978   The Holocene naiad record at Rodgers Shelter in the western Ozark Highland of Missouri. *Plains Anthropologist* **23**:257–271.

Klippel, W. E., and J. Maddox
1977   The Early Archaic of Willow Branch. *Midcontinental Journal of Archaeology* **2**:99–130.

Klopfer, P. H.
1969   *Habitats and territories: a study of the use of space by animals.* New York: Basic Books.

Kniffen, F. B.
1965   Folk housing: key to diffusion. *Annals of the Association of American Geographers* **55**:549–577.

Kniffen, F. B., and H. Glassie
1966   Building in wood in the eastern United States: a time–place perspective. *Geographical Review* **56**:40–66.

Knudson, R.
1979   Inference and imposition in lithic analysis. In

Lithic use-wear analysis, edited by B. Hayden. New York: Academic Press. Pp. 269–281.

Kochel, R. C., and V. R. Baker
1982 Paleoflood hydrology. *Science* **215**:353–361.

Kohler, T. A., and S. Schlanger
1980 Surface estimation of site structure and content, Dolores Project. *Contract Abstracts and CRM Archaeology* 1(2):29–32.

Kuchler, A. W.
1964 The potential natural vegetation of the conterminus United States. *American Geographic Society, Special Publications* No. 36.
1972 The oscillations of the mixed prairie in Kansas. *Erdkunde* **26**:120–129.

Kuttruff, L. C.
1972 The Marty Coolidge site, Monroe County, Illinois. *Southern Illinois University, University Museum, Southern Illinois Studies* No. 10.

La Marche, V. C., Jr.
1974 Paleoclimate inferences from long tree-ring records. *Science* **183**:1043–1048.

Lamb, H. H.
1966 *The changing climate.* London: Methuen.

Lane, R. A., and A. J. Sublett
1972 Osteology of social organization: residence pattern. *American Antiquity* **37**:186–201.

Lewarch, D. E.
1979a Controlled surface collection in regional analysis. In The Cannon Reservoir Human Ecology Project: recent advances in the archaeology of northeast Missouri, edited by M. J. O'Brien and D. E. Lewarch. *University of Nebraska, Department of Anthropology, Notebook* 5, 42–51.
1979b Effects of tillage on artifact patterning: a preliminary assessment. In Cannon Reservoir Human Ecology Project: a regional approach to cultural continuity and change, edited by M. J. O'Brien and R. E. Warren. *University of Nebraska, Department of Anthropology, Technical Report* No. 79-14, 101–149.
n.d. A critical appraisal of survey techniques in Mesoamerica. Ms. on file, Department of Anthropology, University of Washington-Seattle.

Lewarch, D. E., and M. J. O'Brien
1981a The expanding role of surface assemblages in archaeological research. In *Advances in archaeological method and theory* (Vol. 4), edited by M. B. Schiffer. New York: Academic Press. Pp. 297–342.
1981b Effect of short term tillage on aggregate provenience surface pattern. In Plowzone archeology: contributions to theory and technique, edited by

M. J. O'Brien and D. E. Lewarch. *Vanderbilt University Publications in Anthropology* No. 27, 7–49.

Lewis, K. E.
1977 Sampling in the archaeological frontier: regional models and component analysis. In *Research strategies in historical archaeology,* edited by S. South. New York: Academic Press. Pp. 151–202.

Limp, W. F., and V. A. Reidhead
1979 An economic evaluation of the potential of fish utilization in riverine environments. *American Antiquity* **44**:70–78.

Lindsey, A. A., W. B. Crankshaw, and S. A. Qadir
1965 Soil relations and distribution map of the vegetation of pre-settlement Indiana. *Botanical Gazette* **126**:155–163.

Logan, W. D.
1976 Woodland complexes in northeastern Iowa. *National Park Service, Publications in Archaeology* No. 15.

Long, A., and B. Rippeteau
1974 Testing contemporaneity and averaging radiocarbon dates. *American Antiquity* **39**:205–215.

Loomis, W. E., and A. L. McComb
1944 Recent advances of forest in Iowa. *Iowa Academy of Science, Proceedings* No. 61, 217–224.

Loy, J. D.
1968 A comparative style analysis of Havana series pottery from two Illinois valley sites. In Hopewell and Woodland site archaeology in Illinois. *Illinois Archaeological Society, Bulletin* No. 6, 129–200.

Lurie, N. O.
1978 Winnebago. In *Handbook of North American Indians, Vol. 15, Northeast,* edited by B. G. Trigger. Smithsonian Institution, Washington, Pp. 690–707.

MacArthur, R. H., and E. R. Pianka
1966 On optimal use of a patchy environment. *American Naturalist* **100**:603–609.

MacNeish, R. S.
1972 The evolution of community patterns in the Tehuaccan Valley of Mexico and speculations about the cultural processes. In *Man, settlement, and urbanism,* edited by P. J. Ucko, R. Tringham, and G. W. Dimbleby. London: Duckworth, Pp. 67–93.

Margalef, R.
1968 *Perspectives in ecological theory.* Chicago, University of Chicago Press.

Mason, R. D.
1979 The use of historical documents in the Cannon Reservoir historical archaeology project. In The Cannon Reservoir Human Ecology Project: re-

cent advances in the archaeology of northeast Missouri, edited by M. J. O'Brien and D. E. Lewark. *University of Nebraska, Department of Anthropology, Notebook* 5, 129–137.

1982 Euro-American pioneer settlement systems in the Salt River region, northeast Missouri. *University of Missouri, American Archaeology Division, Monograph Series,* in press.

McComb, A. L., and F. F. Riecken
1961 Effect of vegetation on soils in the forest-prairie region. In *Recent advances in botany.* Toronto: University of Toronto Press. Pp. 1627–1631.

McCraken, M. H.
1961 *Geologic map of Missouri.* Jefferson City: Missouri Geological Survey.

McManis, D. R.
1964 The initial evaluation and utilization of the Illinois prairies. *University of Chicago, Department of Geography, Research Paper* No. 94.

McMillan, R. B.
1976 The dynamics of cultural and environmental change at Rodgers Shelter, Missouri. In *Prehistoric man and his environments: a case study in the Ozark Highland,* edited by W. R. Wood and R. B. McMillan. New York: Academic Press. Pp. 211–232.

McMillan, R. B., and W. E. Klippel
1981 Environmental changes and hunter-gatherer adaptation in the southern Prairie Peninsula. *Journal of Archaeological Science,* 8:215–245.

Megown, J.
1878 History of Ralls County, Missouri. In *Illustrated historical atlas of Ralls County, Missouri.* Philadelphia: Edwards Bros. of Missouri. Pp. 9–11.

Michaux, F. A.
1904 Travels to the west of the Alleghany Mountains. In *Early western travels* (Vol. 3), edited by R. G. Thwaites. Cleveland: Clark. Pp. 105–306.

Millon, R., B. Drewitt, and G. L. Cowgill
1973 *Urbanization at Teotihuacan, Mexico* (Vol. 1): *The Teotihuacan map.* Austin: University of Texas Press.

Miskell, T.
1979 Analysis of surface data from Cannon Reservoir. In Cannon Reservoir Human Ecology Project: recent advances in the archaeology of northeast Missouri, edited by M. J. O'Brien and D. E. Lewark. *University of Nebraska, Department of Anthropology, Notebook* No. 5, 52–69.

Miskell, T., and R. E. Warren
1979 Preliminary results of intensive surface collections. In Cannon Reservoir Human Ecology

Project: a regional approach to cultural continuity and change, edited by M. J. O'Brien and R. E. Warren. *University of Nebraska, Department of Anthropology, Technical Report* No. 79-14.

Missouri Botanical Garden
1974 *Environmental assessment: Clarence Cannon Dam and Reservoir.* St. Louis.

Mitchell, R. D.
1972 Agricultural regionalization: origins and diffusion in the Upper South before 1860. In *International Geography* (Vol. 2), edited by W. P. Adams and F. M. Helleiner. Toronto: University of Toronto Press. Pp. 740–742.

1978 The formation of early American cultural regions: an interpretation. In *European settlement and development in North America: essays on geographical change in honour and memory of Andrew Hill Clark,* edited by J. R. Gibson. Toronto: University of Toronto Press. Pp. 66–90.

Mohlenbrock, R. H.
1975 *Guide to the vascular flora of Illinois.* Carbondale: Southern Illinois University Press.

Montet-White, A.
1963 Analytical description of the chipped stone industry from the Snyders site, Calhoun County, Illinois. In Miscellaneous studies in typology and classification. *University of Michigan, Museum of Anthropology, Anthropological Papers* No. 19.

1968 The lithic industries of the Illinois Valley in the Early and Middle Woodland period. *University of Michigan, Museum of Anthropology, Anthropological Papers* No. 35.

Morse, D. F.
1963 The Steuben village and mounds, a multi-component late Hopewell site in Illinois. *University of Michigan, Museum of Anthropology, Anthropological Papers* No. 21.

1973 Dalton culture in northeast Arkansas. *Florida Anthropologist* 26:230–238.

Morse, D. H.
1980 *Behavioral mechanisms in ecology.* Cambridge: Harvard University Press.

Mott, M.
1938 The relation of historic Indian tribes to archaeological manifestations in Iowa. *Iowa Journal of History and Politics* 36:227–314.

Nance, J. D.
1979 Fundamental statistical considerations in the study of microwear. In *Lithic use-wear analysis,* edited by B. Hayden. New York: Academic Press. Pp. 351–363.

Naroll, R.
1962 Floor area and settlement population. *American Antiquity* **27**:587–589.

National Historical Company
1884 *History of Monroe and Shelby counties, Missouri.* St. Louis: National Historical Company.

Newcomer, M. H., and L. H. Keeley
1979 Testing a method of microwear analysis with experimental flint tools. In *Lithic use-wear analysis,* edited by B. Hayden. New York: Academic Press. Pp. 195–205.

Nie, N. H., C. H. Hull, J. G. Jenkins, K. Steinbrenner, and D. H. Bent
1975 *Statistical package for the social sciences* (2nd ed.). New York: McGraw-Hill.

O'Brien, M. J.
1977 Cannon Reservoir Human Ecology Project report: research design 1977–1980. *University of Nebraska, Department of Anthropology, Technical Report* 77-01.
1978 More on Mississippian social organization. *Current Anthropology* **19**:176–177.

O'Brien, M. J., and D. E. Lewarch (editors)
1979 Recent approaches to surface data and sampling. *Western Canadian Journal of Anthropology* 8(3).
1981 Plowzone archeology: contributions to theory and technique. *Vanderbilt University, Publications in Anthropology* No. 27.

O'Brien, M. J., D. E. Lewarch, J. E. Saunders, and C. B. Fraser
1980 An analysis of historical structures in the Cannon Reservoir area, northeast Missouri. *University of Nebraska, Department of Anthropology, Technical Report* No. 80-17.

O'Brien, M. J., and R. E. Warren
1979 Background and research design. In Cannon Reservoir Human Ecology Project: a regional approach to cultural continuity and change, edited by M. J. O'Brien and R. E. Warren. *University of Nebraska, Department of Anthropology, Technical Report* No. 79-14, 1–49.
1980 The Cannon Reservoir Human Ecology Project: 10,000 years of archaeology. *Archaeology* 33(2): 58–61.

O'Brien, P. J.
1972 Urbanism, Cahokia, and the Middle Mississippian. *Archaeology* **25**:189–197.

Ockendon, D. J.
1965 A taxonomic study of Psorlea subgenus Pediomelum (Leguminosae). *The Southwestern Naturalist* **10**:81–124.

Odell, G. H.
1979 A new and improved system for the retrieval of functional information from microscopic observations of chipped stone tools. In *Lithic use-wear analysis,* edited by B. Hayden. New York: Academic Press. Pp. 329–344.

Odell, G. H., and F. Odell-Vereecken
1980 Verifying the reliability of lithic use-wear assessments by 'blind tests': the low-power approach. *Journal of Field Archaeology* **7**:87–120.

Odum, E. P.
1959 *Fundamentals of ecology* (2nd ed.). Philadelphia: Saunders.

Osborn, A. J.
1972 The Francis site (23MN255). In *Report of archaeological investigations in the Cannon Reservoir area, northeast Missouri: 1968,* by W. E. Klippel, M. Mandeville, and A. Osborn. Report submitted to National Park Service, Region 2, Omaha.

Osborn, A. J., and C. R. Falk
1977 Ecological diversity and aboriginal hunter–gatherers in northcentral Nebraska. In A resource handbook: 1977 archeological field school, edited by A. J. Osborn and C. R. Falk. *University of Nebraska, Department of Anthropology, Technical Report* No. 77-10.

Owen, C. O., and Company (publishers)
1895 *Portrait and biographical record of Marion, Ralls, and Pike counties, Missouri.* Chicago.

Parmalee, P. W., A. Paloumpis, and N. Wilson
1972 Animals utilized by peoples occupying the Apple Creek site, Illinois. *Illinois State Museum, Reports of Investigations* No. 23.

Parsons, J. R.
1972 Archaeological settlement patterns. *Annual Review of Anthropology* **1**:127–150.

Peebles, C. S.
1971 Moundville and surrounding sites: some structural considerations of mortuary practices. In Approaches to the social dimensions of mortuary practices, edited by J. A. Brown. *Society for American Archaeology, Memoir* 15, 68–91.
1974 Moundville: the organization of a prehistoric community and culture. Unpublished Ph.D. dissertation, University of California, Santa Barbara.

Peebles, C. S., and S. M. Kus
1977 Some archaeological correlates of ranked societies. *American Antiquity* **42**:421–448.

Perino, G.
1968a Guide to the identification of certain American

Indian projectile points. *Oklahoma Anthropological Society, Special Bulletin* No. 3.

1968b The Pete Klunk mound group, Calhoun County, Illinois: the Archaic and Hopewell occupations. In Hopewell and Woodland site archaeology in Illinois. *Illinois Archaeological Survey, Bulletin* No. 6, 9–128.

1971 Guide to the identification of certain American Indian projectile points. *Oklahoma Anthropological Society, Special Bulletin* No. 4.

Peters, B. C.
1970 Pioneer evaluation of the Kalamazoo County landscape. *Michigan Academician* 3:15–25.

Peters, R.
1845 *The statutes at large and treaties of the United States of America* (Vol. 3). Boston: Little Brown.

Pflieger, W. L.
1971 A distributional study of Missouri fishes. *University of Kansas, Museum of Natural History, Publications* No. 20, 225–570.

1975 *The fishes of Missouri.* Jefferson City: Missouri Department of Conservation.

Pianka, E. R.
1974 *Evolutionary ecology.* New York: Harper and Row.

Plog, F. T., and J. N. Hill
1971 Explaining variability in the distribution of sites. In The distribution of population aggregates, edited by G. J. Gumerman. *Prescott College, Anthropological Reports* No. 10, 7–36.

Potzger, J. E., M. E. Potzger, and J. McCormick
1956 The forest primeval of Indiana as recorded in the original U.S. land surveys and an evaluation of previous interpretations of Indiana vegetation. *Butler University Botanical Studies* No. 13:95–111.

Powers, R. D.
1931 Letter to James Powers, Greenup County, Kentucky, 1 January, 1831. *Monroe County Appeal,* 13 August. Monroe City, Missouri.

Purdue, J. R.
1980 Clinal variation of some mammals during the Holocene in Missouri. *Quaternary Research* 13:242–258.

Purdue, J. R., and B. W. Styles
1980 Changes in the mammalian fauna of Illinois and Missouri during the late Pleistocene and Holocene. Paper presented at the 38th annual Plains Conference, Iowa City.

Raab, L. M.
1979 The impact of contract archeology on analysis of surface data: prospects and problems. In Recent approaches to surface data and sampling, edited

by M. J. O'Brien and D. E. Lewarch. *Western Canadian Journal of Anthropology* 8(3), 106–113.

Radin, P.
1970 *The Winnebago tribe.* Lincoln: University of Nebraska Press.

Redman, C. L., and P. J. Watson
1970 Systematic, intensive surface collection. *American Antiquity* 35:279–291.

Redman, C. L.
1973 Multistage fieldwork and analytical techniques. *American Antiquity* 38:61–79.

Reeder, R. L.
1980 The Sohn site: a lowland Nebo Hill complex campsite. In Archaic prehistory on the prairie–plains border, edited by A. E. Johnson, *University of Kansas, Publications in Anthropology* No. 12, 55–66.

Reid, K. C.
1980 The achievement of sedentism in the Kansas City region. In Archaic prehistory on the prairie–plains border, edited by A. E. Johnson. *University of Kansas, Publications in Anthropology* No. 12, 29–42.

Rhoades, R. E.
1978 Archaeological use and abuse of ecological concepts and studies: the ecotone example. *American Antiquity* 43:608–614.

Rick, J. W.
1976 Downslope movement and archaeological intrasite spatial analysis. *American Antiquity* 41:133–144.

Ritchie, W. A.
1971 A typology and nomenclature for New York projectile points. *New York State Museum and Science Service, Bulletin* No. 384.

Rochow, J. J.
1972 A vegetational description of a mid-Missouri forest using gradient analysis techniques. *American Midland Naturalist* 87:377–396.

Rohlf, F. J., J. Kishpaugh, and D. Kirk
1972 *NT-SYS; numerical taxonomy system of multivariate statistical programs.* Stony Brook: State University of New York.

Roper, D. C.
1976 Lateral displacement of artifacts due to plowing. *American Antiquity* 41:372–374.

1977 A key for the identification of central Illinois Woodland ceramics. *Wisconsin Archaeologist* 58:245–255.

Rostlund, E.
1952 Freshwater fish and fishing in native North

America. *University of California, Publications in Geography* No. 9.

Rouse, I.
1972a *Introduction to prehistory.* New York: McGraw-Hill.
1972b Settlement patterns in archaeology. In *Man, settlement, and urbanism,* edited by P. J. Ucko, R. Tringham, and G. W. Dimbleby. London: Duckworth. Pp. 95–107.

Ruhe, R. V.
1974 Holocene environments and soil geomorphology in midwestern United States. *Quaternary Research* **4**:487–495.
1975 *Geomorphology: geomorphic processes and surficial geology.* Boston: Houghton Mifflin.

Ruppert, M. E.
1975 Research orientation, 1975. In Cannon Reservoir Archaeological Project report, December 1, 1974–May 1, 1975, edited by D. R. Henning. *University of Nebraska, Department of Anthropology, Technical Report* No. 75-02, 1–17.
1976 The Flowers site (23RA136A). In Cannon Reservoir Archaeological Project report (Appendix III), edited by D. R. Henning. *University of Nebraska, Department of Anthropology, Technical Report* No. 76-04, 1–127.

Ryel, L. A., L. D. Fay, and R. C. Van Etten
1961 Validity of age determinations in Michigan deer. *Papers of the Michigan Academy of Science, Arts, and Letters* No. 46.

Sanders, W. T.
1956 The Central Mexican symbiotic region: a study in prehistoric settlement patterns. In Prehistoric settlement patterns in the New World, edited by G. R. Willey. *Viking Fund Publications in Anthropology* No. 23, 115–127.
1967 Settlement patterns. In *Handbook of Middle American Indians* (Vol. 6): *Social anthropology,* edited by M. Nash. Austin: University of Texas Press. Pp. 53–86.
1971a Settlement patterns in central Mexico. In *Handbook of Middle American Indians* (Vol. 10): *Archaeology of northern Mesoamerica,* Part I, edited by G. Ekholm and I. Bernal. Austin: University of Texas Press. Pp. 3–44.
1971b Cultural ecology and settlement patterns of the Gulf Coast. In *Handbook of Middle American Indians* (Vol. II): *Archaeology of northern Mesoamerica* (Part II), edited by G. Ekholm and I. Bernal. Austin: University of Texas Press. Pp. 543–557.

Saunders, J. E., and R. D. Mason
1979 Historical archeology and documentary research. In Cannon Reservoir Human Ecology Project: a regional approach to cultural continuity and change, edited by M. J. O'Brien and R. E. Warren. *University of Nebraska, Department of Anthropology, Technical Report* No. 79-14, 319–350.

Schiffer, M. B.
1975 Classifications of chipped-stone tool use. In The Cache River Archeological Project: an experiment in contract archeology, edited by M. B. Schiffer and J. House. *Arkansas Archeological Survey Research Series* No. 8, 249–251.
1976 *Behavioral archaeology.* New York: Academic Press.
1978 Some issues in the philosophy of science and archaeology. Unpublished paper delivered at the State University of New York, Binghamton, November 1978.
1979 Some impacts of cultural resource management on American archaeology. In Archaeological resource management in Australia and Oceania, edited by J. R. McKinlay and K. L. Jones. *New Zealand Historic Places Trust Publications* No. 11, 1–11.

Schiffer, M. B., and J. H. House (assemblers)
1975 The Cache River Archeological Project: an experiment in contract archeology. *Arkansas Archeological Survey, Research Series* No. 8.

Schiffer, M. B., A. P. Sullivan, and T. C. Klinger
1978 The design of archaeological surveys. *World Archaeology* **10**:1–28.

Schneider, F.
1972 An analysis of waste flakes from sites in the upper Knife–Heart region, North Dakota. *Plains Anthropologist* **17**:91–100.

Schoenwetter, J.
1979 Comment on plant husbandry in prehistoric eastern North America. *American Antiquity* **44**:600–601.

Schroeder, W. A.
1968 Spread of settlement in Howard County, Missouri, 1810–1859. *Missouri Historical Review* **63**:1–37.

Schwartz, C. W., and E. R. Schwartz
1981 *The wild mammals of Missouri* (2nd ed.). Columbia: University of Missouri Press.

Service, E.
1962 *Primitive social organization.* New York: Random.

Severinghaus, C. W.
1949 Tooth development and wear as criteria of age in white-tailed deer. *Journal of Wildlife Management* **13**:195–216.

Shackley, M. L.
1976 The Danebury Project: an experiment in site sediment recording. In *Geoarchaeology,* edited by D. A. Davidson and M. L. Shackley. Boulder: Westview Press. Pp. 9–21.

Shay, C. T.
1978 Late prehistoric bison and deer use in the eastern prairie-forest border. In Bison procurement and utilization: a symposium, edited by L. B. Davis and M. Wilson. *Plains Anthropologist, Memoir* No. 14, 194–212.

Sheets, P.
1973 Edge abrasion during biface manufacture. *American Antiquity* **38:**215–218.

1975 Behavioral analysis and the structure of a prehistoric industry. *Current Anthropology* **16:**369–391.

Shelford, V. E.
1963 *The ecology of North America.* Urbana: University of Illinois Press.

Shepard, R. N.
1962 The analysis of proximities: multidimensional scaling with an unknown distance function, I and II. *Psychometrika* **27:**125–140, 219–246.

Simenstad, C. A., J. A. Estes, and K. W. Kenyon
1978 Aleuts, sea otters, and alternate stable-state communities. *Science* **200:**403–411.

Singh, R. L.
1975 Meaning, objectives, and scope of settlement geography. In *Readings in rural settlement geography,* edited by R. L. Singh and R. P. B. Singh. Varanasi: National Geographical Society of India. Pp. 4–17.

Smith, B. D.
1975 Middle Mississippi exploitation of animal populations. *University of Michigan, Museum of Anthropology, Anthropological Papers* No. 57.

1978a (editor)
Mississippian settlement patterns. New York: Academic Press.

1978b Variation in Mississippian settlement patterns. In *Mississippian settlement patterns,* edited by B. D. Smith. New York: Academic Press. Pp. 479–503.

Smith, P. E. L.
1976 *Food production and its consequences.* Menlo Park: Cummings.

Sorenson, C. J., J. C. Knox, J. A. Larson, and R. A. Bryson
1971 Paleosols and the forest border in Keewatin, N.W.T. *Quaternary Research* **1:**468–473.

South, S.
1977a *Method and theory in historical archeology.* New York: Academic Press.

1977b (editor)
Research strategies in historical archeology. New York: Academic Press.

Speth, J. D., and G. A. Johnson
1976 Problems in the use of correlation for the investigation of tool kits and activity areas. In *Cultural change and continuity: essays in honor of James Bennett Griffin,* edited by C. E. Cleland, New York: Academic Press. Pp. 35–57.

Stearns, F. W.
1949 Ninety years change in a northern hardwood forest in Wisconsin. *Ecology* **30:**350–358.

Steyermark, J.
1963 *Flora of Missouri.* Ames: Iowa State University Press.

Stoltman, J. B.
1978 Temporal models in prehistory: an example from eastern North America. *Current Anthropology* **19:**703–746.

1979 Middle Woodland stage communities in southwestern Wisconsin. In *Hopewell archaeology: the Chillicothe Conference,* edited by D. S. Brose and N. Greeber. Kent, Ohio, Kent State Press. Pp. 122–139.

Strahler, A. N.
1957 Quantitative analysis of watershed geomorphology. *American Geophysical Union, Transactions* **38:**913–920.

Strakhov, N. M.
1967 *Principles of lithogenesis* (Vol. 1). London: Methuen.

Struever, S.
1964 The Hopewell interaction sphere in riverine-western Great Lakes culture history. In Hopewellian studies, edited by J. R. Caldwell and R. L. Hall. *Illinois State Museum, Scientific Papers* No. 12, 85–106.

1968 Woodland subsistence-settlement systems in the lower Illinois Valley. In *New perspectives in archeology,* edited by S. R. Binford and L. R. Binford. Chicago: Aldine. Pp. 285–312.

1969 Annual cycle of natural plant food availability in the lower Illinois Valley region. In Early vegetation of the lower Illinois Valley, by A. A. Zawacki and G. Hausfater. *Illinois State Museum, Reports of Investigations* No. 17, 58–62.

1971a Comments on archaeological data requirements and research strategy. *American Antiquity* **36:**9–19.

1971b Problems, methods, and organizations: a disposition in the growth of archaeology. In *Anthropological archaeology in the Americas,* edited by

B. J. Meggers. Washington, D.C.: Anthropological Society of Washington. Pp. 131–151.

Struever, S., and G. L. Houart
1972 An analysis of the Hopewell Interaction Sphere. In Social exchange and interaction, edited by E. N. Wilmsen. *University of Michigan, Museum of Anthropology, Anthropological Papers* No. 46, 47–79.

Struever, S., and K. D. Vickery
1973 The beginnings of cultivation in the Midwest-riverine area of the United States. *American Anthropologist* **75:**1197–1220.

Styles, B. W.
1978 Faunal exploitation and energy expenditure: early Late Woodland subsistence in the lower Illinois Valley. Ph.D. dissertation, Northwestern University. Ann Arbor: University Microfilms.

Suhm, D. A., and E. R. Jelks
1962 Handbook of Texas archaeology: type descriptions. *Texas Archaeological Society, Special Bulletin* No. 1.

Sussman, M. B. (editor)
1959 *Community structure and analysis.* New York: Thomas Crowell.

Swain, A. M.
1978 Environmental changes during the past 2000 years in north-central Wisconsin: analysis of pollen, charcoal, and seeds from varved lake sediments. *Quaternary Research* **10:**55–68.

Swanton, J. R.
1946 The Indians of the southeastern United States. *Bureau of American Ethnology, Bulletin* No. 137.

Synenki, A. T.
1977 Explaining the relationship between surface and subsurface remains: a multivariate approach. Unpublished Master's thesis, Department of Anthropology, Southern Illinois University-Carbondale.

Tainter, J. A.
1977 Woodland social change in west central Illinois. *Midcontinental Journal of Archaeology* **2:**67–98.
1981 Reply to 'A critique of some recent North American mortuary studies.' *American Antiquity* **46:**416–420.

Talmage, V., and O. Chesler
1977 *The importance of small, surface, and disturbed sites as sources of significant archaeological data.* Washington, D.C.: National Park Service, Office of Archaeology and Historic Preservation.

Teter, D. C., and M. J. O'Brien
1979 Test excavations at the Crooked Creek site. In Cannon Reservoir Human Ecology Project: a regional approach to cultural continuity and change, edited by M. J. O'Brien and R. E. Warren. *University of Nebraska, Department of Anthropology, Technical Report* No. 79-14, 291–305.

Teter, D. C., and R. E. Warren
1979 A dated projectile point sequence from the Pigeon Roost Creek site. In Cannon Reservoir Human Ecology Project: a regional approach to cultural continuity and change, edited by M. J. O'Brien and R. E. Warren. *University of Nebraska, Department of Anthropology, Technical Report* No. 79-14, 227–251.

Thomas, D. H.
1973 An empirical test for Steward's model of Great Basin settlement patterns. *American Antiquity* **38:**155–176.
1975 Nonsite sampling in archaeology: up the creek without a site? In *Sampling in archaeology,* edited by J. W. Mueller. Tucson: University of Arizona Press. Pp. 61–81.

Thomas, J. L.
1909 Some historic lines in Missouri. *Missouri Historical Review* **3:**5–33, 210–233.

Tolstoy, P., and S. K. Fish
1975 Surface and subsurface evidence for community size at Coapexco, Mexico. *Journal of Field Archaeology* **2:**97–104.

Tomanek, G. W., and G. K. Hulett
1970 Effects of historical droughts on grassland vegetation in the central Great Plains. In *Pleistocene and recent environments of the central Great Plains,* edited by W. Dort, Jr., and J. K. Jones, Jr. Lawrence: University Press of Kansas. Pp. 203–210.

Transeau, E. N.
1935 The Prairie Peninsula. *Ecology* **16:**423–437.

Trexler, H. A.
1914 Slavery in Missouri. *Johns Hopkins University, Studies in History and Political Science* No. 32–2.

Trigger, B.
1967 Settlement archaeology: its goals and promise. *American Antiquity* **32:**149–160.
1968 The determinants of settlement patterns. In *Settlement archaeology,* edited by K. C. Chang. Palo Alto, California: National Press. Pp. 53–78.

Tringham, R., G. Cooper, G. Odell, B. Voytek, and A. Whitman
1974 Experimentation in the formation of edge damage: a new approach to lithic analysis. *Journal of Field Archaeology* **1:**171–196.

Trubowitz, N. L.
1978 The persistence of settlement pattern in a cultivated field. In Essays in memory of Marian E. White, edited by W. Engelbrecht and D. Grayson. *Franklin Pierce College, Department of An-*

thropology, Occasional Publications in Northeastern Anthropology **5**:41–66.

Turner, F. J.
  1893   The significance of the frontier in American history. *Annual Report of the American Historical Association.* Pp. 199–227.

U.S. Army Corps of Engineers
  1966   *Design memorandum number 4, Clarence Cannon Reservoir.* St. Louis District.
  1975   *Reservoir clearing area no. 1, Clarence Cannon Reservoir.* St. Louis District.

Van Zant, K.
  1979   Late glacial and postglacial pollen and plant macrofossils from Lake West Okoboji, northwestern Iowa. *Quaternary Research* **12**:358–380.

Viles, J.
  1920   Missouri in 1820. *Missouri Historical Review* **15**:36–52.

Violette, E. M.
  1906   Early settlements in Missouri. *Missouri Historical Review* **1**:38–52.

Voss, S. F.
  1969– Town growth in central Missouri, 1815–1860: an
  1970   urban chaparral. *Missouri Historical Review* **64**:64–80, 197–217, 322–350.

Warren, R. E.
  1976   Site survey and survey design. In Cannon Reservoir Archaeological Project report (Appendix II) edited by D. R. Henning. *University of Nebraska, Department of Anthropology, Technical Report* No. 76-03, 1–333.
  1979   Archeological site survey. In Cannon Reservoir Human Ecology Project: a regional approach to cultural continuity and change, edited by M. J. O'Brien and R. E. Warren. *University of Nebraska, Department of Anthropology, Technical Report* No. 79-14, 71–100.

Warren, R. E., C. K. McDaniel, and M. J. O'Brien
  1982   Soils and settlement in the southern Prairie Peninsula. *Contract Abstracts and CRM Archeology,* in press.

Warren, R. E., and T. Miskell
  1981   Intersite variation in a bottomland locality: a case study in the southern Prairie Peninsula. In Plowzone archeology: contributions to theory and technique, edited by M. J. O'Brien and D. E. Lewarch. *Vanderbilt University, Publications in Anthropology* No. 27, 119–158.

Warren, R. E., and M. J. O'Brien
  1981   Regional sample stratification: the drainage class technique. *Plains Anthropologist* **26**:213–227.

Warren, R. E., M. J. O'Brien, and R. D. Mason
  1981   Settlement dynamics in the southern Prairie Peninsula: a regional model of frontier development. In Current directions in midwestern archaeology: selected papers from the Mankato Conference, edited by S. Anfinson. *Minnesota Archaeological Society, Occasional Publications in Minnesota Anthropology* No. 9, 15–34.

Watson, F. C.
  1979   *Soil survey of Knox, Monroe, and Shelby counties, Missouri.* U.S. Department of Agriculture, Soil Conservation Service.

Webb, T., III, and R. A. Bryson
  1972   Late- and postglacial climatic change in the northern Midwest, USA: quantitative estimates derived from fossil pollen spectra by multivariate statistical analysis. *Quaternary Research* **2**:70–115.

Wedel, M. M.
  1959   Oneota sites on the upper Iowa River. *The Missouri Archaeologist* **21**(2–3):1–181.

Wedel, W. R.
  1959   An introduction to Kansas archeology. *Bureau of American Ethnology, Bulletin* 174.

Weide, D. L., and M. L. Weide
  1973   Application of geomorphic data to archaeology: a comment. *American Antiquity* **38**:428–431.

Wendland, W. M.
  1978   Holocene man in North America: the ecological setting and climatic background. *Plains Anthropologist* **23**:273–287.

Wendland, W. M., and R. A. Bryson
  1974   Dating climatic episodes of the Holocene. *Quaternary Research* **4**:9–24.

Wetmore, A.
  1837   *Gazeteer of the State of Missouri.* St. Louis: C. Keemle.

Whallon, R., and S. Kantman
  1969   Early Bronze Age development in the Keban Reservoir, east-central Turkey. *Current Anthropology* **10**:128–133.

White, J. P., and D. H. Thomas
  1972   What mean these stones? Ethno-taxonomic models and archaeological interpretations in the New Guinea Highlands. In *Models in archaeology,* edited by D. L. Clarke. London: Methuen. Pp. 275–308.

Whittaker, R. H.
  1967   Gradient analysis of vegetation. *Biological Reviews* **42**:207–264.
  1972   Evolution and measurement of species diversity. *Taxon* **21**:213–251.

1975 *Communities and ecosystems* (2nd ed.). New York: MacMillan.

Wiens, J. A.
1976 Population response to patchy environments. *Annual Review of Ecology and Systematics* **7**:81–120.

Willey, G. R.
1953 Prehistoric settlement patterns in the Viru Valley, Peru. *Bureau of American Ethnology, Bulletin* No. 155.

Williams, J. R.
1974 The Baytown phases in the Cairo lowland of southeast Missouri. *The Missouri Archaeologist* **36**.

Wilmsen, E.
1970 Lithic analysis and cultural inference: a Paleo-Indian case. *University of Arizona, Anthropological Papers* No. 16.

Wilson, H.
1981 Domesticated *Chenopodium* of the Ozark Bluff Dwellers. *Economic Botany* **35**:233–239.

Winsor, R. A.
1975 Artificial drainage of east central Illinois. Unpublished Ph.D. dissertation, Department of Geography, University of Illinois-Urbana.

Winters, H. D.
1967 An archaeological survey of the Wabash Valley in Illinois. *Illinois State Museum, Reports of Investigations* No. 10.
1969 The Riverton Culture: a second millennium occupation in the central Wabash Valley. *Illinois State Museum, Reports of Investigations* No. 13.

Winter, M. C.
1972 Tierras Largas: a Formative community in the Valley of Oaxaca, Mexico. Unpublished Ph.D. dissertation, Department of Anthropology, University of Arizona.
1974 Residential patterns at Monte Alban, Oaxaca, Mexico. *Science* **186**:981–987.
1976 The archaeological household cluster in the Valley of Oaxaca. In *The early Mesoamerican village*, edited by K. V. Flannery. New York: Academic Press. Pp. 25–31.

Wood, W. R.
1976 Vegetational reconstruction and climatic episodes. *American Antiquity* **41**:206–207.

Wood, W. R., and R. B. McMillan (editors)
1976 *Prehistoric man and his environments: a case study in the Ozark Highland.* New York: Academic Press.

Wray, D. E.
1952 Archaeology of the Illinois Valley: 1950. In *Archaeology of the eastern United States*, edited by J. B. Griffin. Chicago: University of Chicago Press. Pp. 152–164.

Wray, D. E., and R. S. MacNeish
1961 The Hopewellian and Weaver occupations of the Weaver site, Fulton County, Illinois. *Illinois State Museum, Scientific Papers* Vol. 7, No. 2.

Wright, H. E., Jr.
1968 History of the Prairie Peninsula. In The Quaternary of Illinois, edited by R. E. Bergstrom. *University of Illinois, College of Agriculture, Special Publication* No. 14, 78–88.
1971 Late Quaternary vegetational history of North America. In *Late Cenozoic glacial ages*, edited by K. K. Turekian. New Haven: Yale University Press. Pp. 425–464.
1976 The dynamic nature of Holocene vegetation; a problem in paleoclimatology, biogeography, and stratigraphic nomenclature. *Quaternary Research* **6**:581–596.
1981 Vegetation east of the Rocky Mountains 18,000 years ago. *Quaternary Research* **15**:113–125.

Wuenscher, J. E., and A. J. Valiunas
1967 Presettlement forest composition of the River Hills region of Missouri. *American Midland Naturalist* **78**:487–495.

Yarnell, R. A.
1964 Aboriginal relationships between culture and plant life in the upper Great Lakes region. *University of Michigan, Museum of Anthropology, Anthropological Papers* No. 23.
1969 Contents of human paleofeces. In The prehistory of Salts Cave, Kentucky, edited by P. J. Watson. *Illinois State Museum, Reports of Investigations* No. 16.
1972 *Iva annua* var. *Macrocarpa:* extinct American cultigen? *American Anthropologist* **74**:335–341
1976 Early plant husbandry in eastern North America. In *Cultural change and continuity*, edited by C. E. Cleland. New York: Academic Press. Pp. 265–273.
1977 Native plant husbandry north of Mexico. In *Origins of agriculture*, edited by C. Reed. The Hague: Mouton. Pp. 862–875.

Yellen, J. E.
1977 *Archaeological approaches to the present: models for reconstructing the past.* New York: Academic Press.

Young, F. W.
1968 TORSCA-9, a FORTAN IV program for non-metric multidimensional scaling. *Behavioral Science* **13**:343–344.

Zawacki, A. A., and G. Hausfater
1969 Early vegetation of the lower Illinois Valley. *Illinois State Museum, Reports of Investigations* No. 17.

Index

415

STUDIES IN ARCHAEOLOGY

Consulting Editor: Stuart Struever

Department of Anthropology
Northwestern University
Evanston, Illinois